SKYSCRAPERS

HIGHER AND HIGHER

Translation: John HELLON

Copy editing: Frances Faure

Design and production: La Page, Brussels

Amanda de Selys, Anne Gerard, Marc Gierst

I.S.B.N. 2-909 283-20-8

86, rue Castagnary - 75015 Paris - France

Telephone (33.1) 40.43.04.98

Fax (33.1) 40.43.98.75

INSTITUT FRANÇAIS D'ARCHITECTURE

SKYSCRAPERS
HIGHER AND HIGHER

CAROLINE MIEROP

PREFACE

PAUL GOLDBERGER
Architectural Critic and Chief Cultural Correspondent
The New York Times

IN COLLABORATION WITH

GEORGES BINDER

AND WITH THE PARTICIPATION OF THE
COUNCIL ON TALL BUILDINGS AND URBAN HABITAT

NORMA
EDITIONS

This book was produced by the
Department of Archives and History of the Institut français d'architecture.
Support has been provided by:

OVE ARUP & PARTNERS
Consulting Engineers

CAMPENON BERNARD SGE

CEP - Contrôle et Prévention

COTEBA
Management

DUMEZ - GTM

EPAD
Établissement Public pour l'Aménagement
de la Région de La Défense

OTH INGENIERIE
Paris

PERMASTEELISA

SCHINDLER

SOGEA

SCI TOUR SANS FINS

TROUVIN INGENIERIE

WATSON
Watson Steel Limited
Structural Steelwork

Additional support has also been provided by
OTIS
which offered the author a scholarship to travel to the United States and Asia.

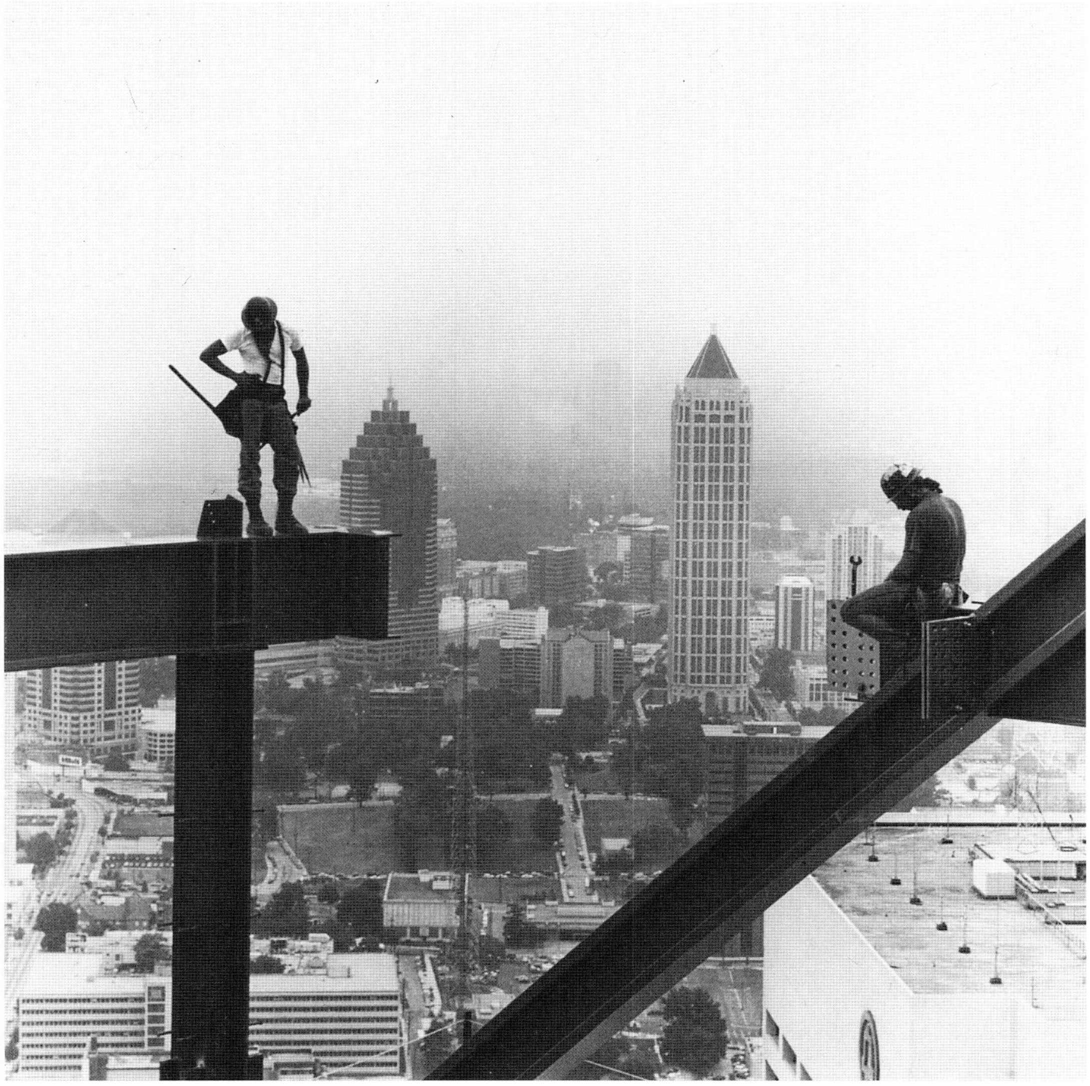

NationsBank Plaza, Atlanta, photograph of the work site. Kevin Roche John Dinkeloo and Associates, 1992.
© Dennis O'Kain.

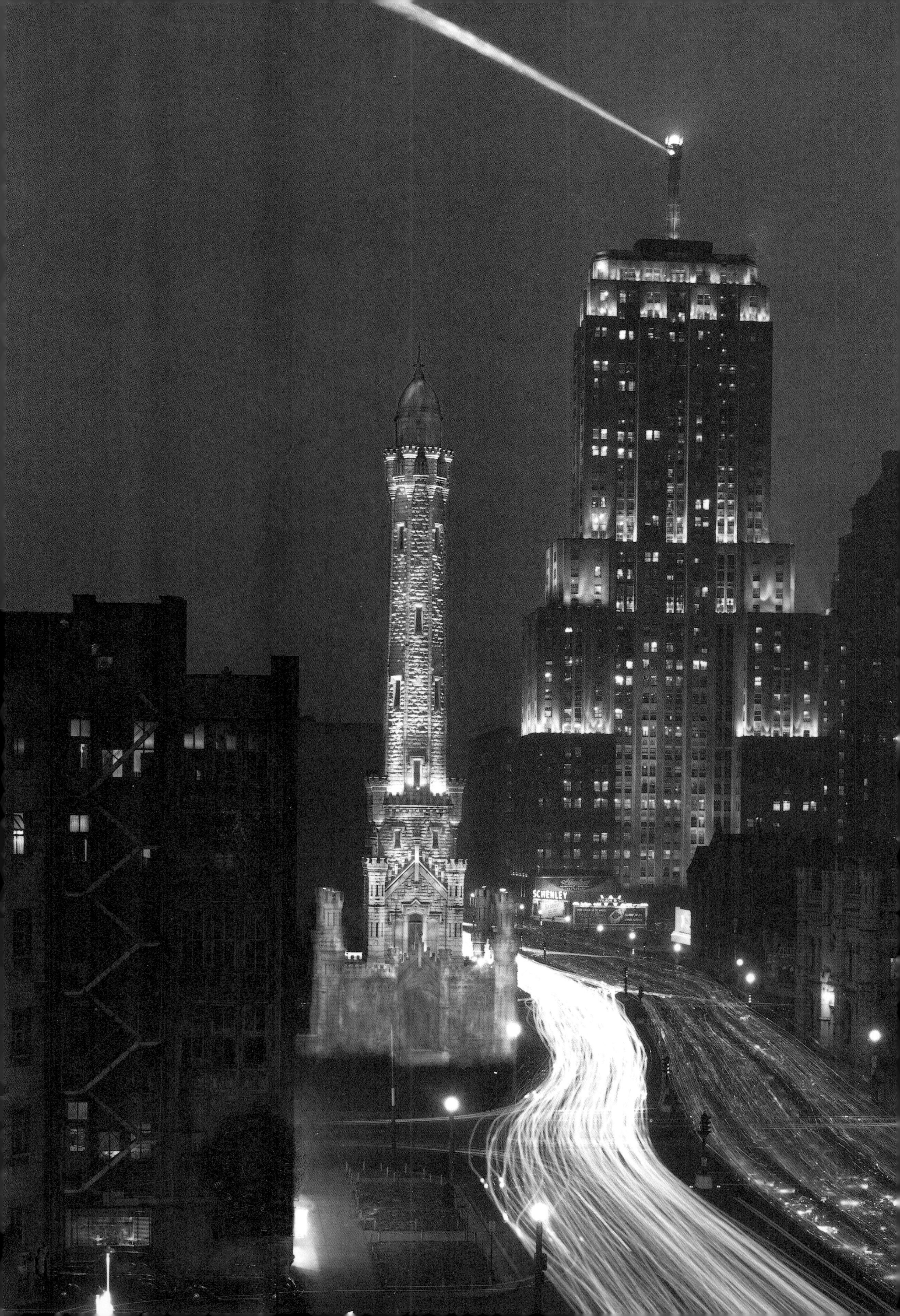
SCHENLEY

CONTENTS

Palmolive Building, Chicago. Holabird & Root, architects, 1929.
In the center, Water Tower, William W. Boyington, architect, 1869.
Chicago Historical Society. Phot. Hedrich-Blessing.

NEWS FROM BABEL

Jean Millier

The origin of this book can be found in the Tour Sans Fins (literally, Tower Without Ends), a project by the architect Jean Nouvel, intended to stand next to J.O. von Spreckelsen's monumental arch as the culmination of the Défense business district in Paris. Unfavorable economic conditions have led to delay in carrying out this audacious and elegant project, a kind of contemporary and extramural counterpart to the Eiffel Tower.

The typology of the skyscraper—the subject of this book—appeals to the imagination rather than to Cartesian logic. For doesn't the idea of a building which reaches the sky go back to the dawn of history? After the Flood, the survivors of the Ark of the Covenant—the nomadic descendants of Noah—who, the Old Testament tells us, spoke a single language, decided to settle in a valley. "Come, let us build a city and a tower whose top may reach unto heaven and make a name for ourselves, lest we be scattered abroad upon the face of the whole earth."[1] (Genesis, XI 4)

Yahweh descended to Earth to check the progress of the city and the tower and, confronted by this invention, unforeseen in his incomparable Creation of the World, reflected bitterly that "henceforward nothing they have a mind to do will be beyond their reach."[2] (Genesis, XI, 6) Not that the Great Architect of the Universe took umbrage at competition from His own creatures whose lives, begun in a garden, had naturally progressed to cities, but He feared that men, taking a legitimate pride in their prodigious urban achievements, would end by forgetting their duty of humility. Fortification towers, watchtowers, temple towers, agreed, but a tower purely to reach the heavens? A city, fine! But a metropolis containing all the inhabitants of the Earth? Thus, since He had promised not to send any more floods, Yahweh confused the speech of this haughty group and dispersed them over the face of the Earth.

Opposite:
Project for a telescopic tower (80 to 100 stories) for the north building of the Metropolitan Life Insurance Company in New York, 1929. Only the base of the tower was executed in 1933. Harvey Wiley Corbett and D. Everett Waid, architects.
Maurice Culot.

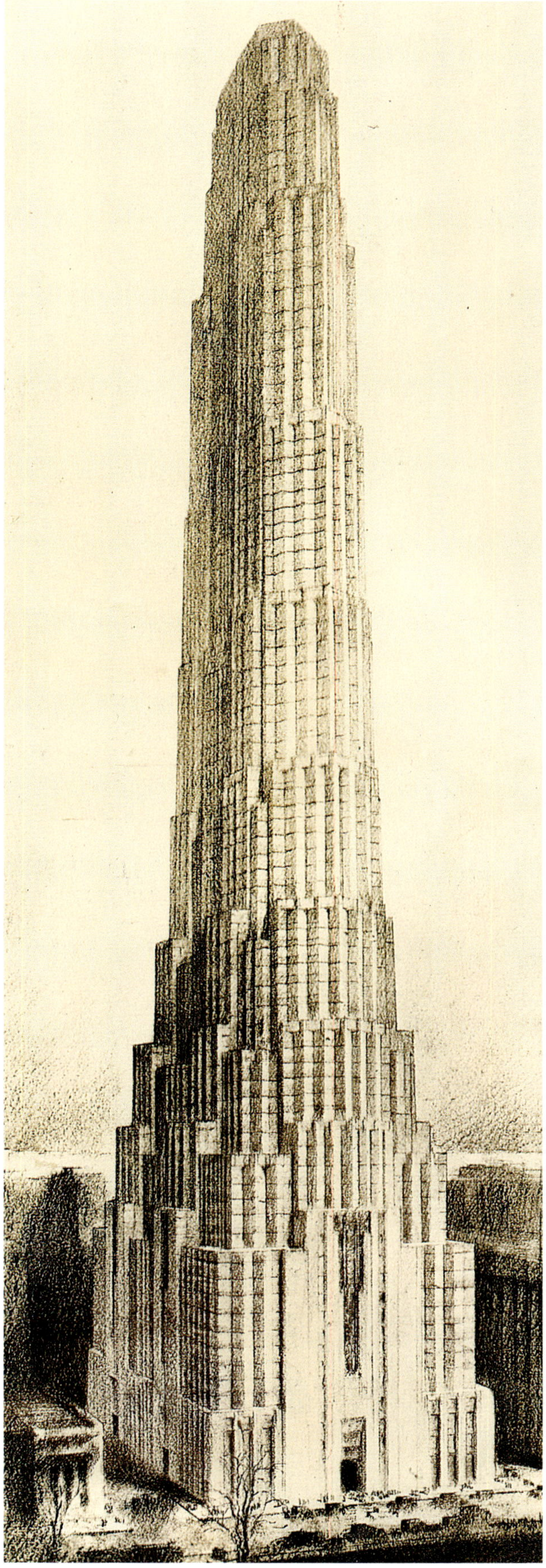

The Bible here uses religious belief to explain a historical fact. In constant expansion, the Babylonian Empire, with its armies of slaves from all the conquered countries used to carry out grandiose projects and glorious monuments, had become impossible to govern. The game of power for its own sake had established relationships of dominator and dominated. Babylon had ceased to be a community and the Empire collapsed at the center, a process which the Bible encapsulates in the image of the city and the tower.

Man's stubbornness was not, however, taken into account, and the fall of Babel proved to be only a highly provisional solution to the question of the megalopolis. The ban on towers—technically difficult to defy—was respected for several millennia right up to the year 1857, when the elevator made its appearance. Today no one imagines God sitting on a throne above the clouds, and the modern skyscraper is perceived as a peaceful challenge that man, freed from the fear of divine wrath, continues to meet so as not to despair of his smallness. It might still be argued from a moral point of view that pollution, overcrowding, and the waste of energy are among the modern weapons the Lord uses as reminders. But this is another matter, for another book.

Not all skyscrapers can claim immortality as works of art—far from it, as Paul Goldberger emphasizes in his introduction. But those which combine intelligent placing, fitness of purpose, technical daring, and architectural beauty are among the most impressive monuments of the twentieth century. It is these skyscrapers that have inspired the concept and the production of this book. It is divided into three parts in an original manner; the first contains the indispensable historical background; the second presents a selection of twenty-one skyscrapers at the planning stage, in construction or completed during the last twenty-five years; the third part compiles an exhaustive and illustrated list of the hundred tallest skyscrapers in the world built until today, for the competitive aspect is not negligible. The race to break the record is an intrinsic part of skyscraper legend, just as it was for the transatlantic liners in the first half of the century.

To build a tower without ends, taller than all the others, has been and remains one of the driving forces behind the construction of skyscrapers. When all is said and done, has not this single ambition often been the deciding factor, beyond economic or civic reasons, if not beyond reason itself?

Right:
Hong Kong in 1990.
In the foreground, the business center Central District with, among others, the Standard Chartered Bank by Palmer and Turner (P&T architects 1990) beside the Hong Kong and Shanghai Bank by the architect Norman Foster (1985); to the right, the Bank of China by Ieoh Ming Pei (1989) and, partly concealed, the twin towers of the Lippo Centre by the American Paul M. Rudolph (1988).
© Paul Warchol, 1990.

1. The New English Bible, Oxford University Press, New York, 1976.
2. Ibid.

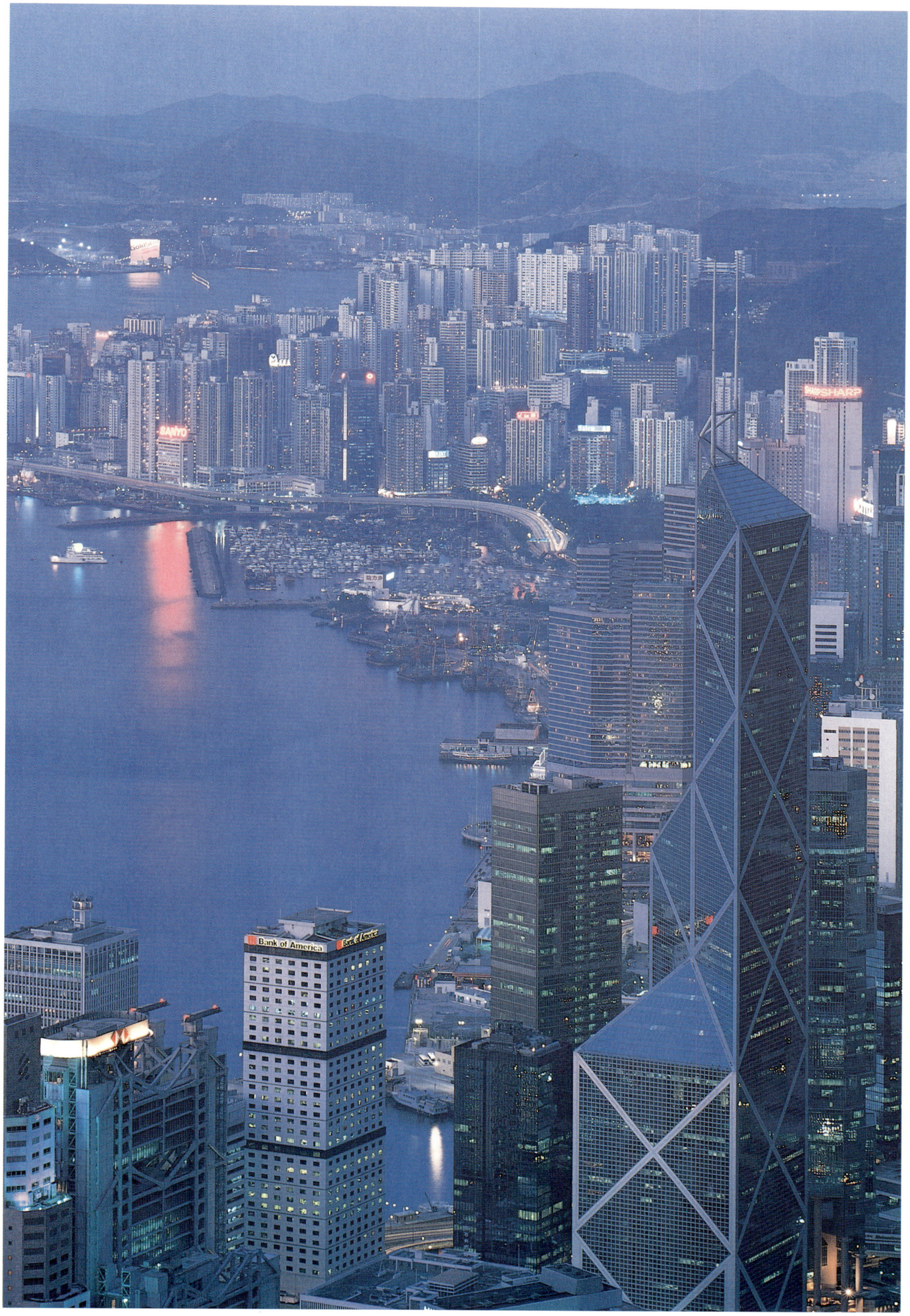

SANYO
SHARP
Bank of America

THE SKYSCRAPER

DESIGN AND URBAN IDENTITY AT THE END OF THE TWENTIETH CENTURY

Paul Goldberger

A generation ago, it was still possible to speak of the skyscraper as an American phenomenon. Of course there were tall buildings elsewhere, but few of them—they seemed always to be somewhat out of place, odd intrusions of the American spirit into other cultures. The real skyscrapers, the important ones, were almost always American—and the real skyscraper cities, like New York, Chicago, and Houston, were absolutely American.

Now, as we approach the end of the century, it is no longer so. America owns the history of the skyscraper, but other countries, other cultures, seem to control more and more of its present and, it seems certain, its future. The sheer quantity of skyscrapers that have been built outside the United States is astonishing; cities that through the 1970's had no very tall buildings at all seem now to have dozens of them, and it is no longer possible to think of the skylines of these cities as representing some kind of intervention of an alien American economic, technological and architectural culture. Skyscrapers are now the culture of Hong Kong, Shanghai, Tokyo, Seoul, Singapore and Bangkok, not to mention of Frankfurt, Paris, Sao Paulo and Sydney. In the latest list of the one hundred tallest buildings in the world prepared by the Council on Tall Buildings and Urban Habitat, 35 of the structures —more than one-third—were not in North America. Skyscrapers are now commonplace in almost every large urban area of the developed world, if not in older historic cores, then on the outskirts, as around Paris, and they have redefined the nature of urbanity in our time.

Is this to the good? Not necessarily. In the rush to adopt what we had once thought of as an American way of building, but which now

Opposite:
One Peachtree Center, Atlanta. John Portman & Associates, 1992. Behind, the two pinnacles of One Ninety One Peachtree Tower (John Burgee Architects with Philip Johnson, 1991).
© Michael Portman.

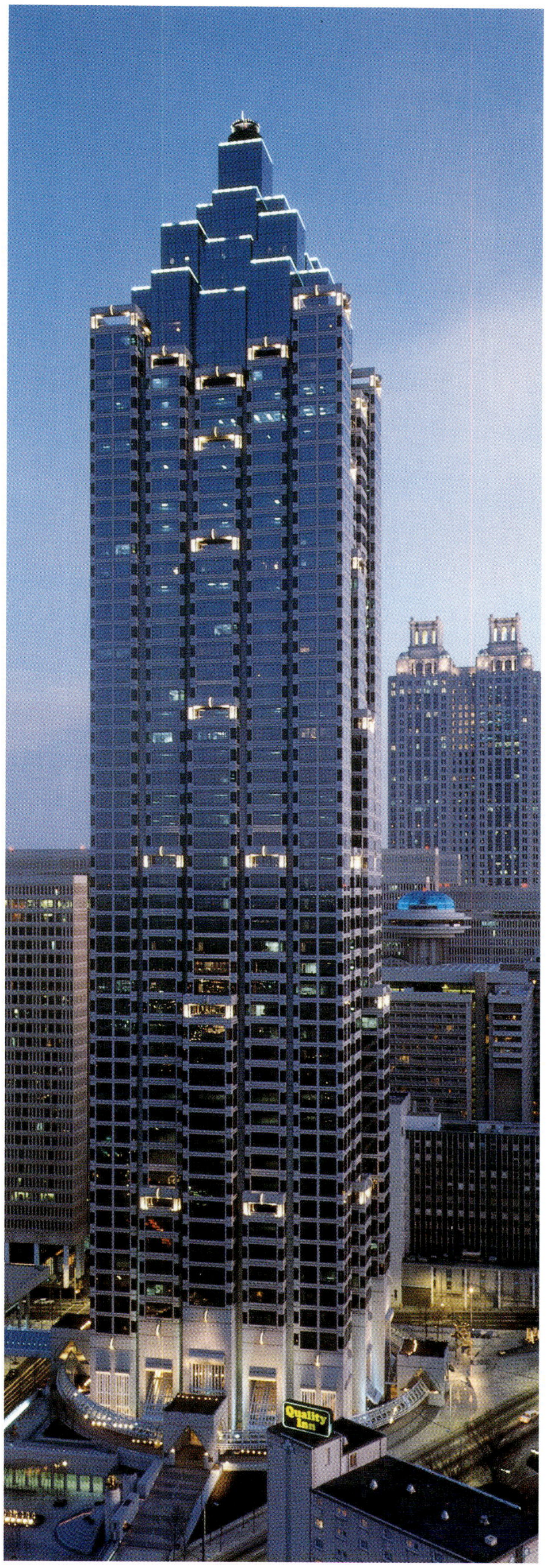

appears to be more appropriately described as a late 20th-century way of building, more than a few cities have sacrificed scale, light, pedestrian amenity and, most difficult of all, the ineffable qualities of their traditional identities. It is a painful fact of our time that buildings seem increasingly to resemble each other no matter where they are built, and that means cities increasingly resemble each other, too. Shanghai was not supposed to look like Dallas, but it does, a little more each day. Frankfurt looks less German than multinational; certain portions of Tokyo's financial district have a look that could be described less as Japanese than as international late-20th-century corporate. The natural settings of Hong Kong and Sydney may still set these cities apart, but much of their architecture feels indistinguishable from what is built everywhere today (though Hong Kong, to be fair, does have two remarkable towers, Norman Foster's Hong Kong and Shanghai Bank, and I.M. Pei's Bank of China—but a photograph that fails to include either of these buildings or the harbor will be difficult indeed to identify as Hong Kong). And if skylines are hard to tell apart, streetscapes are even more difficult; rare is the city in which a photograph of a street or the bases of skyscrapers taken in the last few years could be easily identified.

That the skyscraper has become a force for cultural homogeneity, not to mention of a kind of Western cultural hegemony, is saddening. One had hoped, somehow, perhaps naively, that it would be more; a few years ago it appeared possible that the glorious potential of tall buildings to define the identities of individual cities, to create rather than obscure a sense of place, might be realized in the current generation of skyscrapers. Yet few recent skyscrapers have been able to do this—and of even those few that are distinctive in form, only a handful have seemed genuinely to express qualities about the nature of the place in which they have been built. Cesar Pelli's proposed double tower for Kuala Lumpur—which will be the tallest skyscraper in the world—will be able, surely, to transcend any limitations of its form and become a kind of icon in itself, a structure with such potent symbolic power as to be able to redefine a place in its own image, much as the Eiffel Tower did, and continues to do, for Paris. The towers of Foster and Pei in Hong Kong aspire to do the same, and it is no exaggeration to say that they come fairly close to succeeding.

Yet Pelli's tower at Canary Wharf in London does the opposite: a banal replication of his American work (with less finesse even than many of his superficially similar American towers) the Canary Wharf skyscraper enforces the sense of the tall building as an architectural blot, a structure that obscures the long-lasting and much-cherished special nature of a city and replaces it with an architecture that speaks only a kind of dull international commercial language. Alas, buildings like it—and lesser ones still—are now the most common form of skyscraper all around the world.

It is tempting to say that economics drives such buildings, that the construction of tall buildings today is mainly a matter of money, and that we should expect no more. Far from it; for all that the rampant spread of banal towers has deadened skylines around the world, it is in fact much more than economics alone that has been behind the spread of skyscrapers. They continue to exert a compelling, almost a thrilling, pull: height still represents power, drama, excitement and glamor, both in the North American cities that have had tall buildings for all of this century, and in the Asian and European cities that are still adjusting to the new scale of the skyline.

Dull symbols of cultural homogeneity as many tall buildings may be, the last decade has also shown us how much skyscrapers still retain their sway over architects' imaginations. It is something of a paradox: collectively the current wave of skyscrapers seems banal; individually there is something notable, and on occasion even distinguished, about a great many of them. Even the most mediocre of towers built in the last generation seems to contain within it some degree of esthetic intention, if not always to much result. The boxes that passed for skyscrapers in the first generation after World War II, a way of building that reached its culmination in the large, flat-topped skyscrapers of the 1960's and 1970's, represented an indifference to the design potential of the skyscraper that had been reversed completely by the 1980's. Moreover, the profoundly antiurban quality of most International Style towers, boxes sitting off the street behind deadening plazas, had become increasingly difficult to justify in a period of much greater urbanistic awareness. Indeed, it may not be unreasonable to characterize the whole thrust of the last generation of skyscraper design as a reaction against the International Style, both in terms of the esthetics of the tower and its urbanistic attitude.

Whatever its motivation, and however uneven its results, it is still no exaggeration to say that the recent age of skyscraper proliferation has been a period of near-Baroque glory for the tall building. The cautious beginnings toward more complex expressions that were visible toward the end of the 1970's broke out into full flower in the 1980's. Historicism had a profound effect on skyscraper form, particularly in the United States, where Post-Modernism as a design force, combined with the continued sense that this nation was still the skyscraper's laboratory, led to a determined commitment to emphasize the romantic, rather than the rational, side of skyscraper design. It was a time when skyscrapers began to take as their design themes other skyscrapers: the towers of the 1920's, buildings like John Mead Howells' Panhellenic Hotel in New York and Raymond Hood's American Radiator Building, as well as icons of the such as William Van Alen's Chrysler Building, Shreve, Lamb & Harmon's Empire State Building and Hood and Fouilhoux's Rockefeller

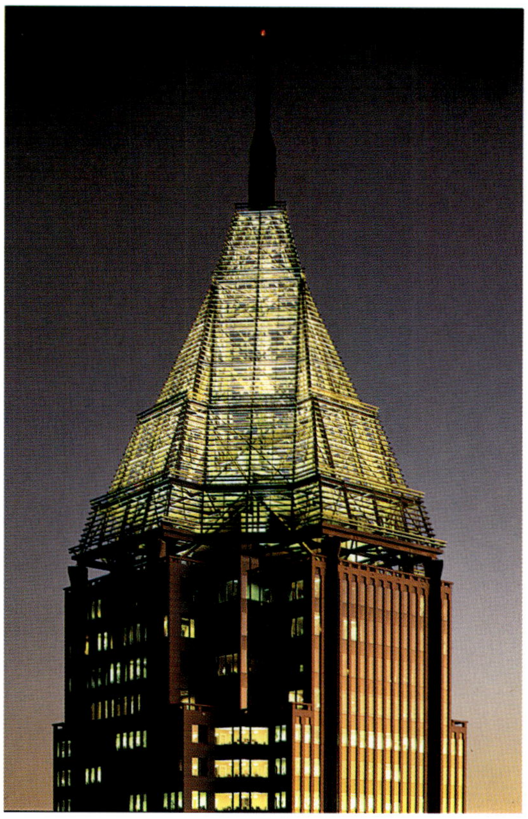

NationsBank Plaza, Atlanta. Kevin Roche John Dinkeloo and Associates, 1992.
Kevin Roche John Dinkeloo and Associates.

Center complex became the inspiration. This historicizing wave yielded numerous buildings of note, including Philip Johnson and John Burgee's Atlantic Center in Atlanta and Transco Tower in Houston; Helmut Jahn's Liberty Place in Philadelphia; Kevin Roche's Morgan Bank in New York; Kohn Pedersen Fox's 311 South Wacker Drive and 900 North Michigan Avenue, both in Chicago; Cesar Pelli's Norwest Center in

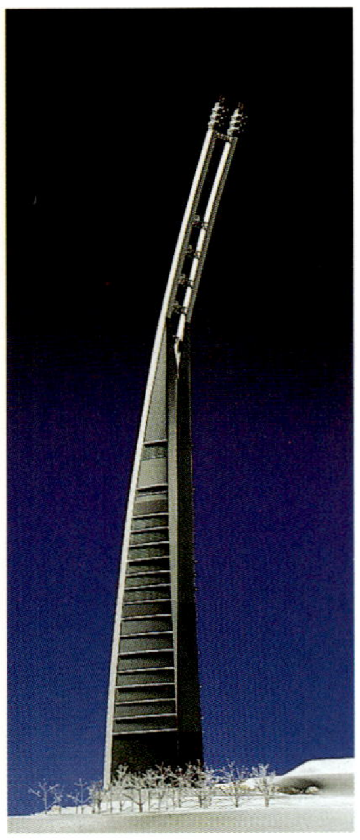

Singapore Tower I, model. Project for a 300-meter high tower (version 1), to be built in Fort Canning Park in Singapore. Crone & Associates, 1992.
Crone & Associates. © Philip Hayson.

Minneapolis and Skidmore, Owings & Merrill's A.T.& T. Corporate Center in Chicago and World Wide Plaza in New York.

In each of these buildings, there is some degree of reference to what is in so many ways the great epoch of skyscraper design, the romantic towers of the period between the two World Wars. This reference could sometimes be almost literal, as in the case of Pelli's evocation of the GE (originally RCA) Building at Rockefeller Center, or Jahn's recasting of the Chrysler Building profile in glass in Philadelphia; or (more commonly) the historicism could be more interpretive, with less commitment to a particular model as to the notion of ornament, texture, a highly articulated top and a base that, unlike most International Style boxes, makes some gestures toward the street.

While this historicizing impulse yielded some superb buildings—I think of Kohn Pedersen Fox's Mellon Bank in Philadelphia, Johnson's Republic Bank in Houston and Pelli's Carnegie Hall Tower in New York in addition to the ones above—historicism seemed to play itself out by the end of the 1980's. The point had been made that International Style rationalism was not able to bring forth viable urban environments or, for that matter, particularly interesting buildings, unless it was in the hands of a master such as Mies van der Rohe or, in his early years, Gordon Bunshaft. The skyscraper had to be rescued from those who would deny its romantic glory, and the historicists performed this rescue mission with vigor and, often enough, with passion and architectural skill. But once the taming of the International Style was complete, the historicists were somewhat at a loss—how to go forward when so much of their effort had been to go backward? It is not surprising that modernism, which never fully disappeared from the esthetic of the late 20th century, began to rear its head again, less in the form of International Style orthodoxy as in a kind of mannered, highly articulated search for visual interest.

And thus we have the latest generation of towers, buildings that view Modernism not as a rational expression of structure so much as an esthetic resource capable of being manipulated as richly as the language of Classicism could be manipulated in the service of historicism. This wave of towers surely includes at its head Foster's Hong Kong and Shanghai Bank, which, while it alludes to a certain rational structure, is in truth a highly exaggerated, almost baroque expression of Modernism's romantic ideals. But it also includes much of the recent work of Kohn Pedersen Fox, Helmut Jahn and Skidmore, Owings & Merrill, all firms that have shifted, gradually or abruptly, away from historicist skyscrapers and toward towers that strive for a richness of modernist expression. It is no accident that many of the architects most active in this latest turn of the esthetics of the skyscraper were historicists in the 1980's, for these new buildings spring from an impulse that is in many ways equally romantic, and is surely equally indifferent to the International Style modernists' haughty insistence that the building's primary responsibility was rational expression of structure. These late modernists, or baroque modernists, view the tower as a complex, highly articulated object, a presence on the skyline as well as on the street, all premises shared by the historicizing wave. The difference is only in the manner of expression, only in the way in which the notions of complexity and tallness and urbanistic presence are manifested. The modernist esthetic, for so long seen as a barrier to richness of expression in the tall building, has now, at long last, become a vehicle for it.

It is not easy to reinvent the skyscraper, and it is not easy to integrate esthetic priorities with engineering developments, which continue to make buildings lighter, more tensile, and more able to take on unusual physical form. There was a period, perhaps a quarter-century ago, when it looked as if the skyscraper had reached a dead end, as if there was nothing more to do; buildings were not going to get much taller, and it seemed as if virtually every esthetic expression had been tried already. Then came the huge boom of the 1980's which proved, if nothing else, how many more variations on traditional themes were possible, and how much potential for richness and discovery still lay within this form. As we move now more firmly into the period of baroque modernist towers, it remains to be seen what masterworks will emerge, or what effect they and their lesser confreres will have on cities, on skylines, and on the skyscraper-glutted culture in general. But it is unquestionably clear now, at the end of the skyscraper century, that the tall building will be as much a part of the 21st century as it was of the 20th.

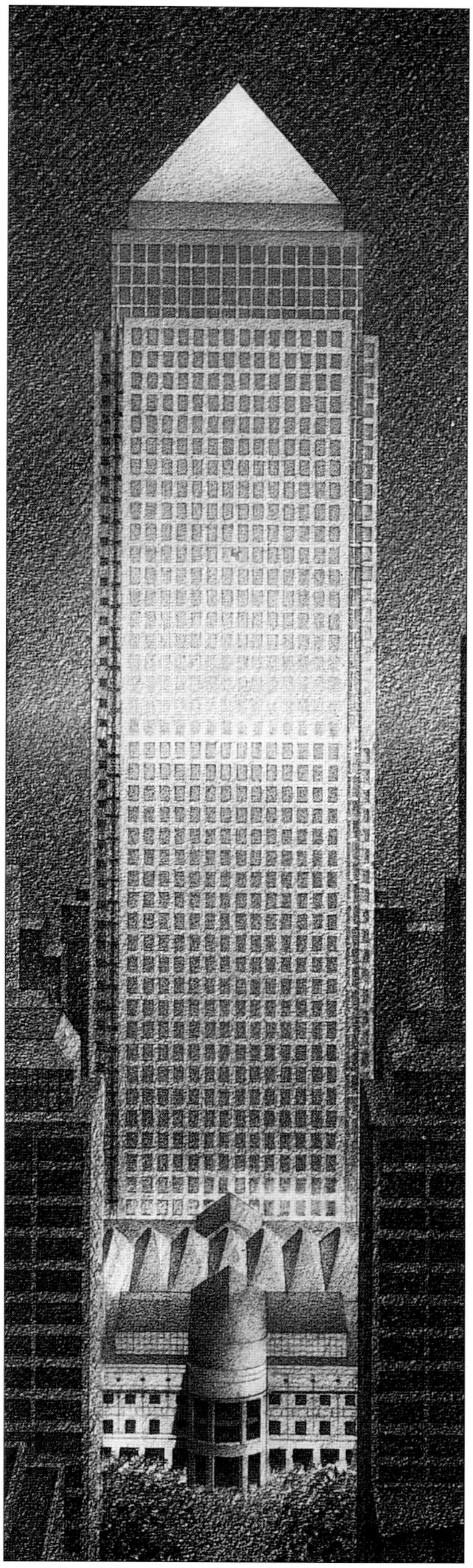

One Canada Square (originally Canary Wharf Tower), London, sketch. Cesar Pelli & Associates.
Drawing by Steve Oles. Cesar Pelli & Associates.

Following pages, from left to right:
Town Hall, Los Angeles. Austin, Parkinson, Martin & Whittlesey, 1928.
Francisco Mujica, History of the Skyscraper, *in Archaeology & Architecture Press, Paris, New York, 1929.*

Trammell Crow Center (originally, LTV Center), Dallas. SOM Houston (Richard Keating), 1984.
DMJM Keating.

Southwest Center, Houston, competition project (unexecuted). SOM Houston (Richard Keating), 1982.
DMJM Keating.

Project for the top of a skyscraper. Jacques Carlu, 1929.
Institut français d'architecture.

Norwest Center, Minneapolis. Cesar Pelli & Associates, 1988.
Drawing by J. Pickard. Cesar Pelli & Associates.

JOURNEY TO THE

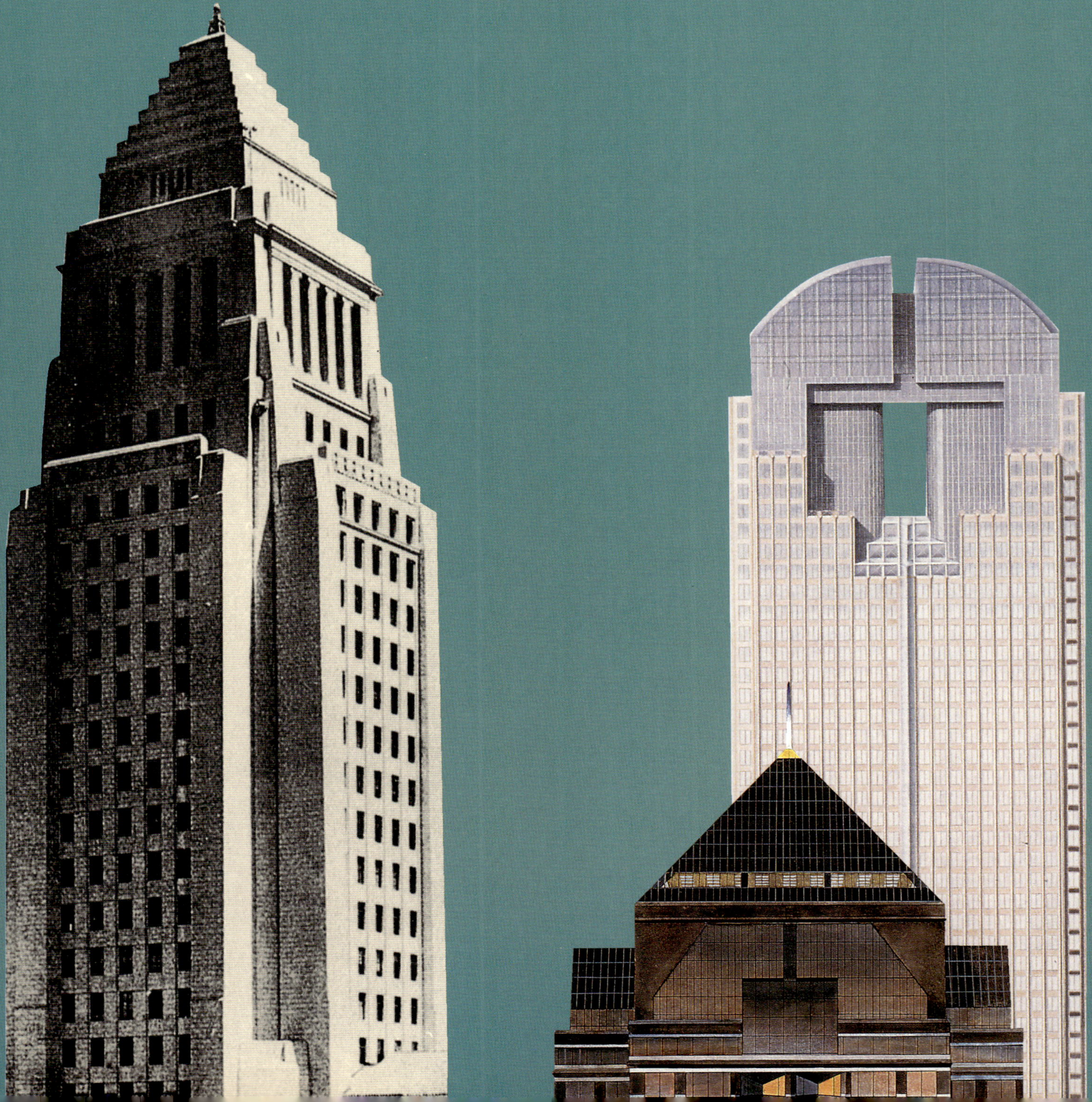

LAND OF GIANTS

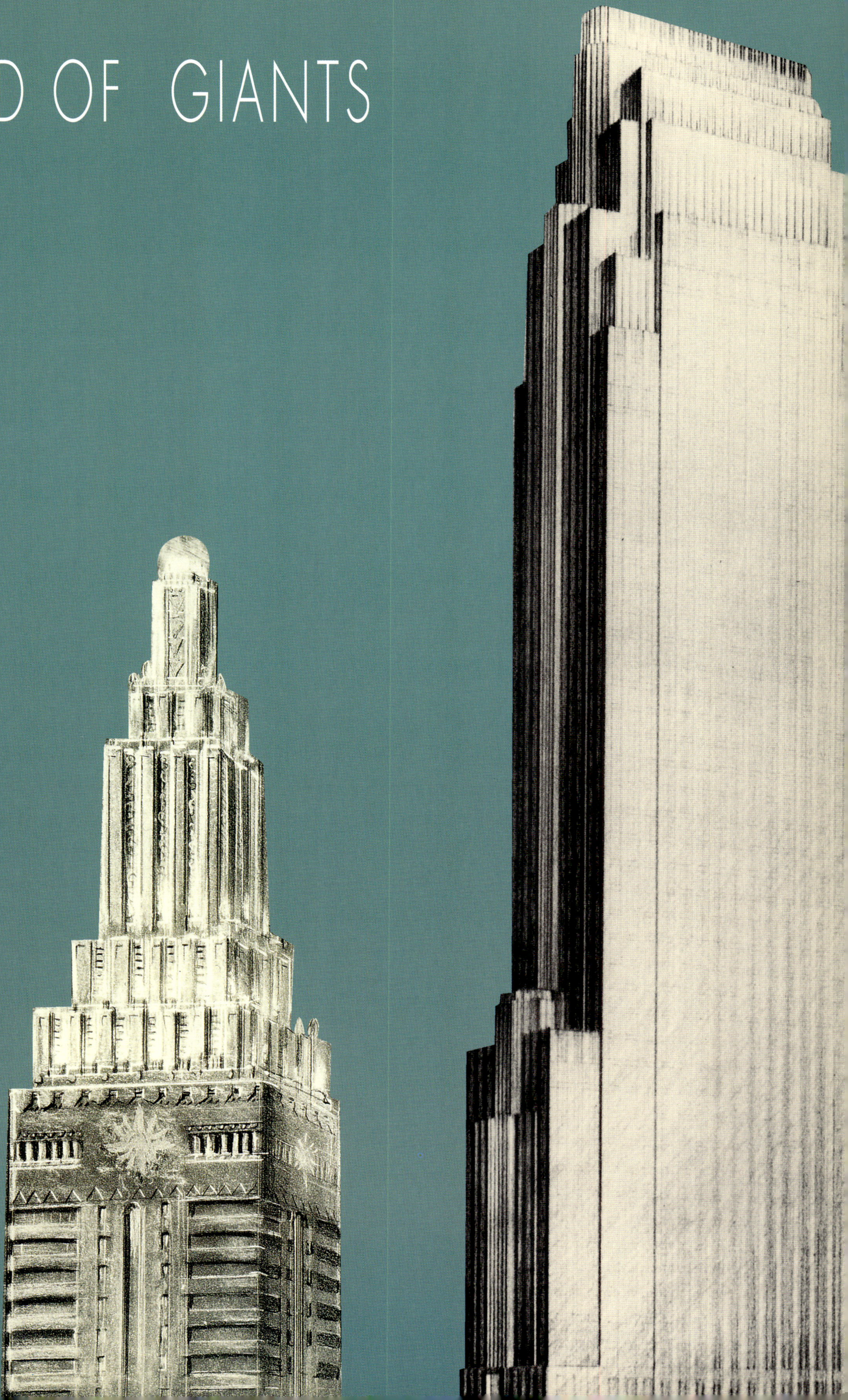

Opposite:
Empire State Building, New York, from an old postcard. Shreve, Lamb & Harmon Associates, architects, 1931.
Roberto M. Behar.

No definition pins down what the word evokes or resolves its mystery. Historians disagree about its origin. Was the first skyscraper the first building with an elevator? Or the first to have a metal frame? Did it see the light of day in Chicago or New York? Who coined the word and when? Does it represent a set of canons? Can it be grouped with campaniles, the towers of Babylon, Inca pyramids? How tall, or how tall in relation to others, does a building have to be to be called a skyscraper?

None of these questions affect the popular archetype. A skyscraper is the Empire State Building, a very tall building that tapers as it rises and punctuates the city skyline with vertical projections as church steeples once did. It is North America, even if today it can be found all over the world. Indissolubly linked to the image of the metropolis, the skyscraper is a symbol of power, intense economic activity, land shortage. It forms part of all the utopias of the century: the vertical city, the self-contained community, the myth of the countryside. The skyscraper is a vertical machine, an ocean liner on dry land, an icon of modernity.

The skyscraper is inviolable. It has not seriously suffered from the waves of protest that have swept from Montreal to Stockholm and Brussels, denouncing the ruthless destruction of cities and traditional ways of life. Europe has condemned its slab-like buildings and tower blocks. America, filled to bursting point with black boxes, plazas, and other avatars of post-war building, has

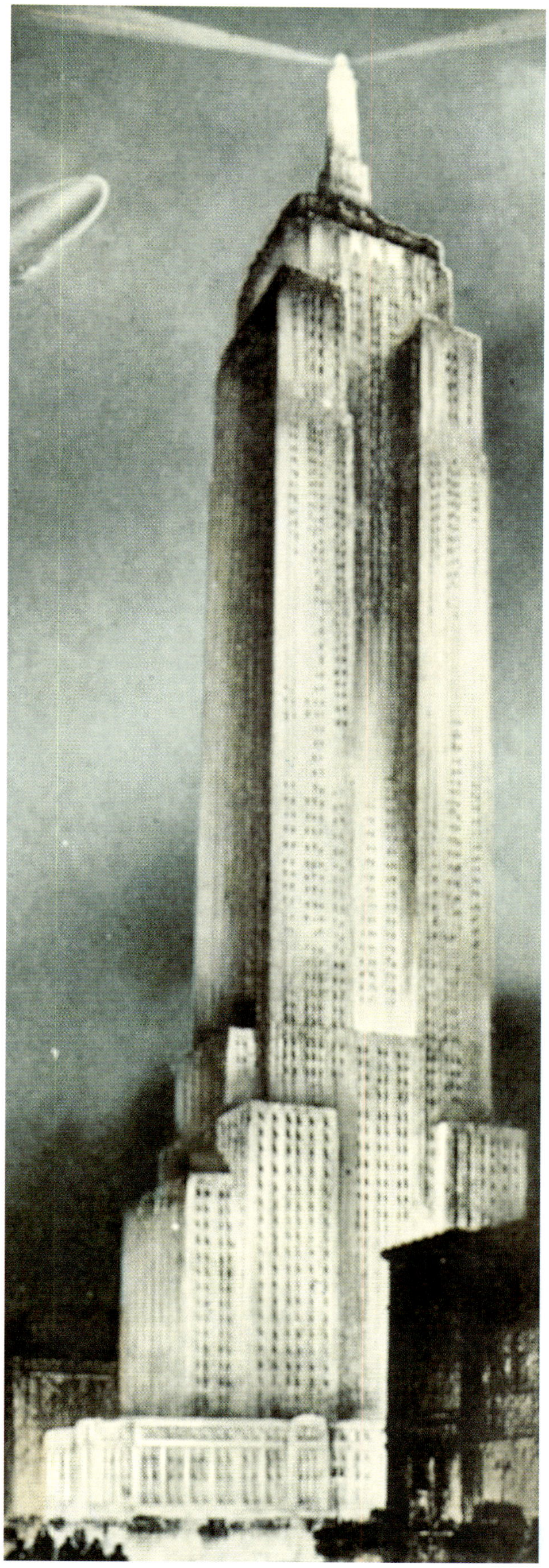

turned back without shame to the exuberant fantasy of its commercial Art Deco architecture.

We thought the skyscraper was dead. But it has emerged unscathed, even re-invigorated from these turbulent times. Constantly assailed, it continues to fascinate. Better yet, the skyscraper, long excluded from the noble domain of art, is back in favor. It is showered with publications and international competitions. The contest to be biggest and best is gathering speed—just like at the beginning of the century. Design, form and materials are in the spotlight.

At this moment a new pause—the most recent skyscraper to be built in the United States was completed in 1992—is encouraging the doubters. But the announcement of its death conceals a re-birth. In far off lands the new skyscraper is rising, ever higher. Like a giant, its stride encompasses the world.

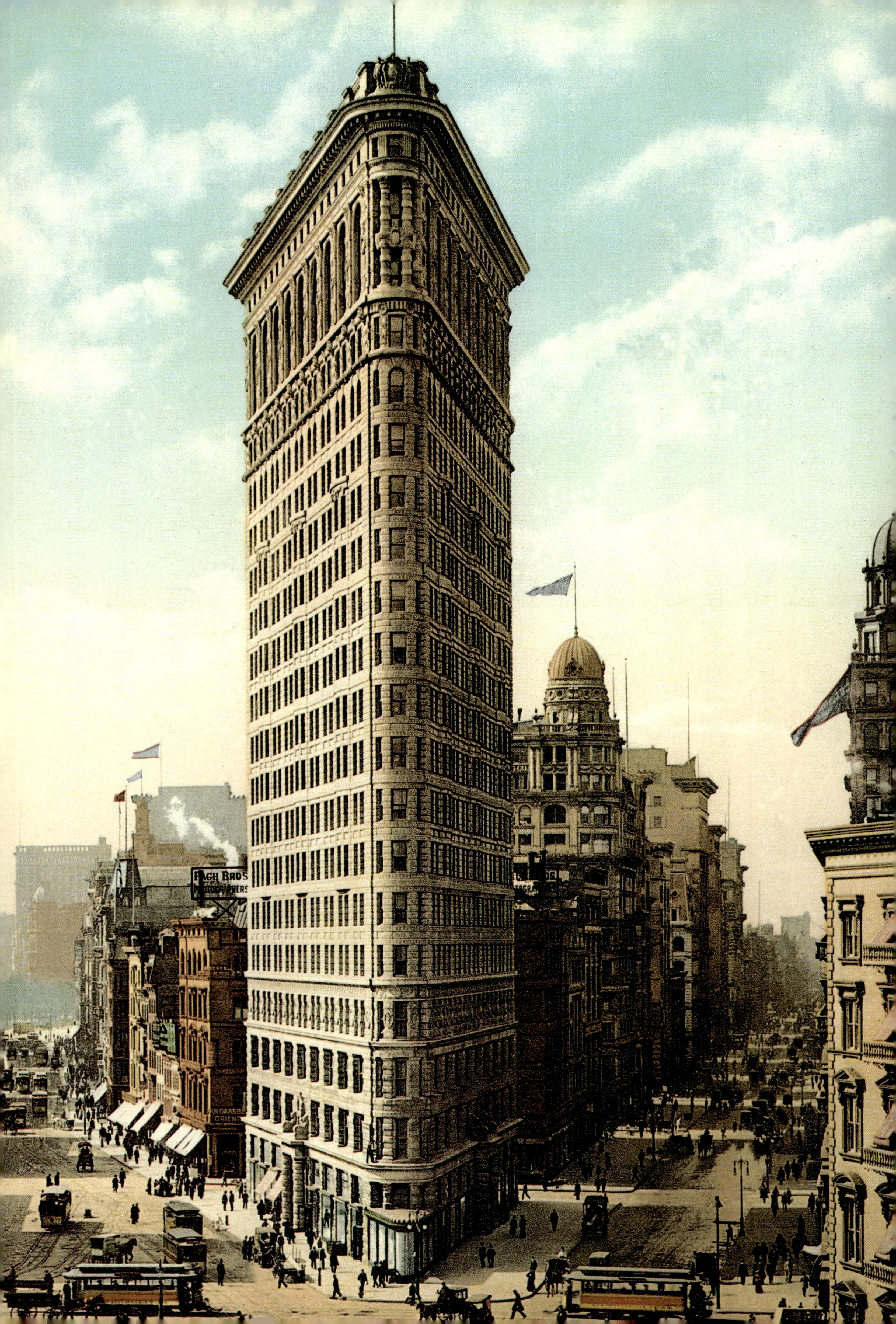
BROS

A PARALLEL HISTORY

"Skyscrapers! There are those that are women and others that are men. Some resemble temples to the Sun, others recall the Aztec pyramid of the Moon .... Without roofs, crowned by terraces, they seem to be waiting for airships, helicopters, men of the future with wings."

Paul Morand, *New York*, 1929.

It is has been determined that the history of the skyscraper begins in Chicago in 1884 with the construction of the Home Insurance Building, designed by William Le Baron Jenney.[1] It was the first commercial building to boast an elevator and to have a metal structure, half cast-iron and half steel, supporting masonry walls. At the time the word skyscraper had nothing to do with architecture. It had marine origins and described a small triangular sail hoisted at the top of a mast and, by extension, anything extraordinarily high.[2] People referred to "tall office buildings," a new kind of project of a scale to match the size of the commercial ambitions of the North American cities at the end of the century. They were to be an ideal testing ground for a generation of some of the most influential architects of modern times, the Chicago School.

The Home Insurance Building[3] is unfortunately no more. But it is surprising to see from photographs just what this ancestor of the skyscraper looked like. An imposing Italianate palazzo, only mildly exaggerated in scale, the building displays a heavy, very horizontal façade in brick and stone, a bossed base, string courses, and an attic balustrade.

The development of the steel skeleton,[4] the constant search for lighter structures, which went hand in hand with their increasing height, quickly liberated architects from this classical handwriting. Glazed bays grew larger at the expense of walls.

Opposite:
Flatiron Building, New York, period photograph. Daniel H. Burnham, architect, 1903.
© Sirot-Angel, Paris.

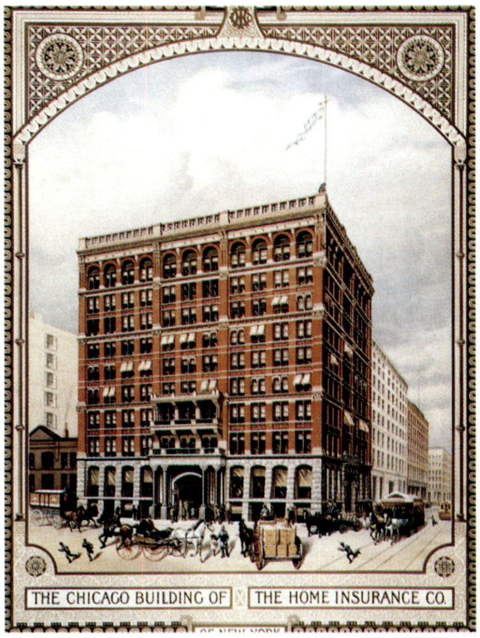

Home Insurance Company Building, Chicago, lithograph, L. Prang & Co (1885-1886). William Le Baron Jenney, architect, 1884-1885.
Deutsches Architekturmuseum, Frankfurt.

Composition was inspired by structure, accentuating the vertical elements with pilasters and bow windows. Ornamentation changed register and contributed to the lightening of façades. The advances of the new school came thicker and faster. With the Tacoma Building by William Holabird and Martin Roche in 1888, the brick façade became no more than a simple screen attached to the structure. The following year the Rand McNally by the same architects was the first building to be entirely constructed in steel. In 1891, the Monadnock Building by Burnham and Root rose sixteen stories high, one of the most impressive of the series and the most unadorned, although built in traditional masonry. Then in 1892 came the Masonic Temple by the same practice. With its 21 stories, its height of almost 100 meters (302 feet) and its public panoramic viewing platform, it was the first building to be dubbed "highest in the world." In 1895 Daniel Burnham and John W. Root designed the very elegant, almost entirely glazed Reliance Building. And in the same year Dankmar Adler and Louis Sullivan provided with the Guaranty Building[5] a true archetype of the modern office building, standing alone, flat roofed, its walls unified over their entire height.

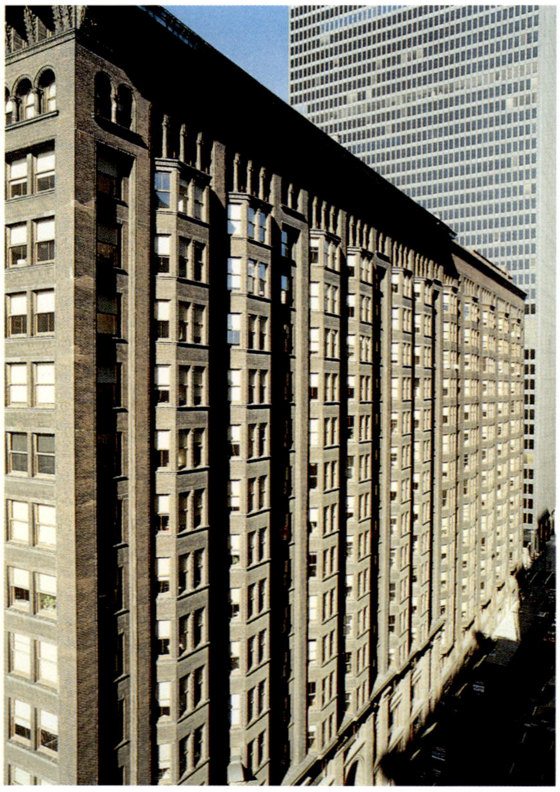

Monadnock Building, Chicago; main façade. Burnham and Root, architects, 1891.
© Benoît Roland.

We owe the metal-framed building to William Le Baron Jenney. It is said of Daniel Burnham that he was the father of tall office buildings, and of Louis Sullivan that he created a new metropolitan image. But the office building with an elevator was invented in New York in 1870[6] and it was Richard Morris Hunt who introduced the type of commercial building surmounted by a tower with his Tribune Building (1873-1875). In 1885 the Statue of Liberty crossed the Atlantic, bringing with her the technology of the engineer Gustave Eiffel. In 1888, Leroy S. Buffington designed the first real office tower, a campanile of 28 stories with a steel frame that he baptized "cloud-scraper." At the time he was considered mad. In 1889, Bradford Gilbert designed the Tower Building in New York, an 11-story structure only 7 meters wide (21 feet 6 inches), resembling a Romanesque tower. In the same year the Eiffel Tower was built. In 1891, the *Boston Daily News* validated the word skyscraper in an article titled "How the Sky-scrapers are Built."[7]

What can be written down in a few lines and covers roughly two decades was actually a revolution, technical certainly, but aesthetic also. But its essential importance lies elsewhere. "The first elevator buildings of Manhattan... were veritable chain reaction bombs, destined to overturn the entire real estate market. The systematic introduction of the elevator equalized rents on every floor of commercial buildings, instantly annulled safe economic investments and, conversely, created new and extraordinary ground rents."[8]

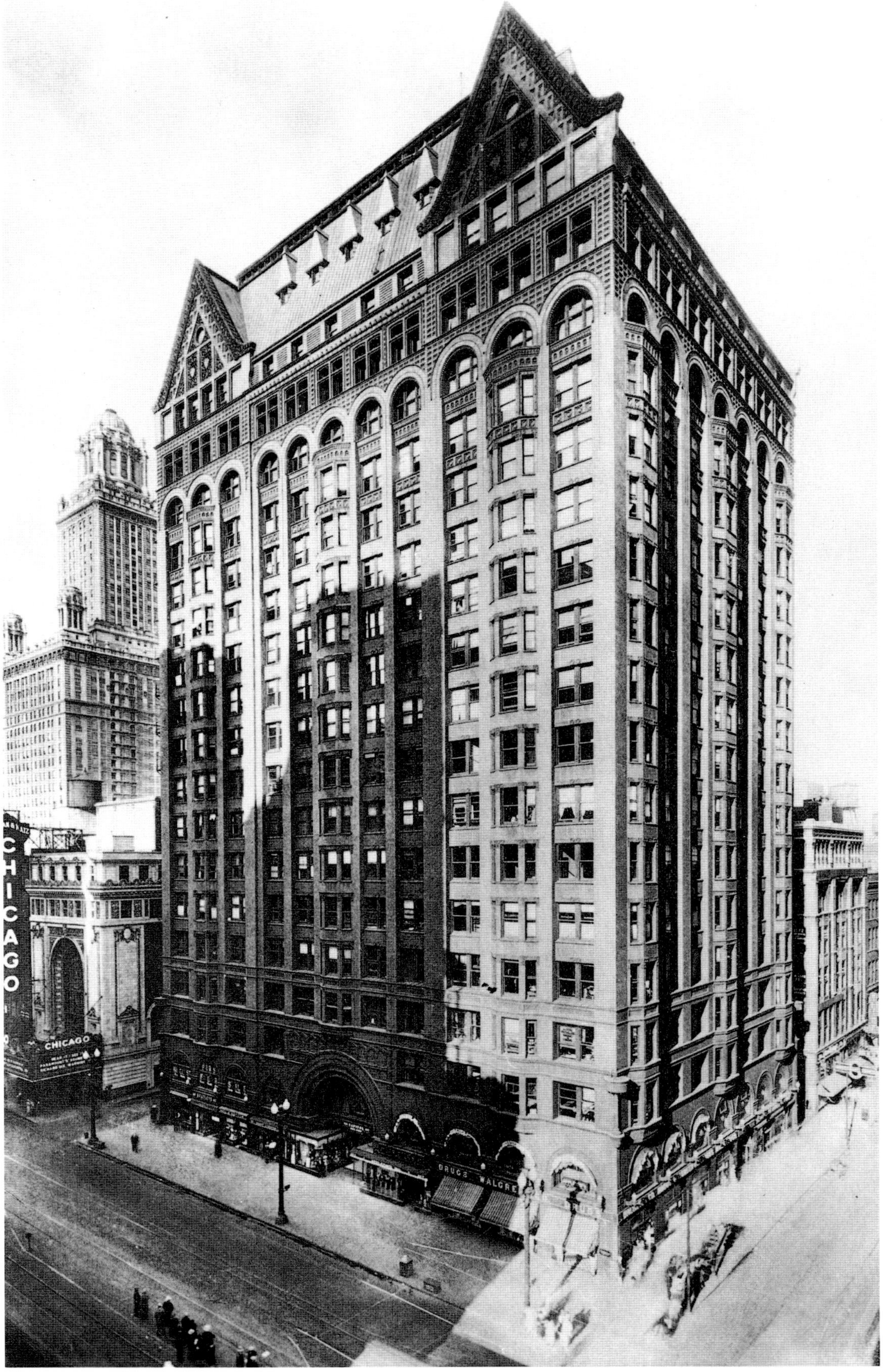

Masonic Temple, Chicago, from an old photograph. Burnham and Root, architects, 1892.

Francisco Mujica, History of the Skyscraper, *Archaeology & Architecture Press, Paris, New York, 1929.*

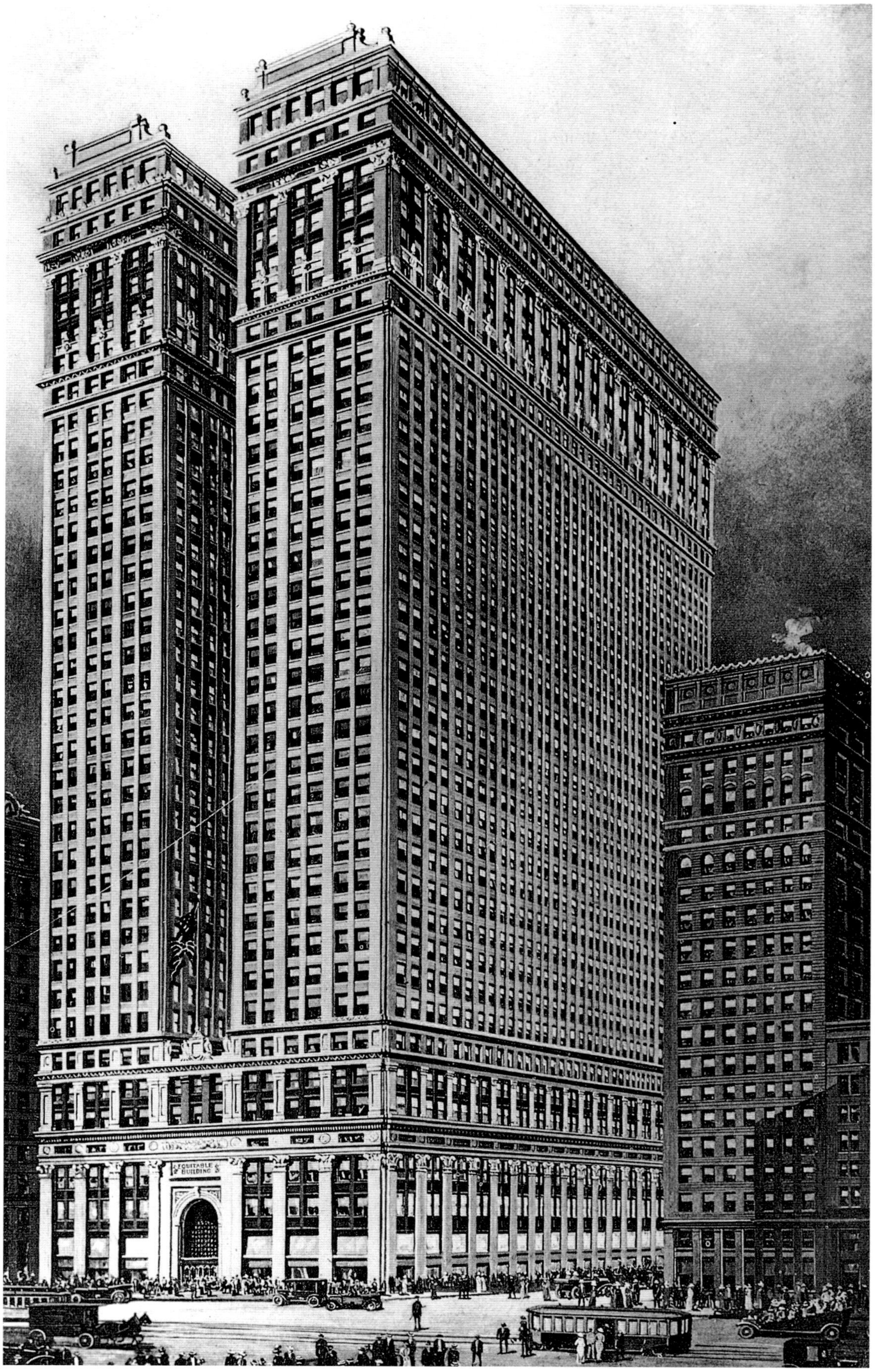

Equitable Building, New York. E.R. Graham, architect, 1915. One of the last buildings of its size built in New York before the building zone regulations adopted in 1916.

King's Views of New York, *Manhattan Postcard Co., New York, 1926.*

The rise of buildings skyward was a gold rush. In New York the last shackles were removed in 1892 with the abolition of a building regulation that made steel frame construction impractical. Before the end of the century Manhattan had overtaken Chicago in the race for the highest.[9] The feverish economic activity, centered around the island's port, concentrated thousands of white collar workers (proximity was an absolute necessity in those days), stimulating an unprecedented explosion of building. But above all, the lots there were small, the land extremely expensive and, until 1916, there was no law to limit the size or the height of constructions. Chicago, on the other hand, suffered the penalty of being first. After the construction of the Masonic Temple, the city council decided in 1893 to limit the height of buildings to some 40 meters (130 feet).[10]

At the end of the century, therefore, all the conditions were in place for the development of a totally original type of urban building: the flourishing of modern industrial capitalism, the means of financing real estate, the organization of work and building sites, technological invention (steel, the elevator, and electricity). It remained to learn how to inhabit these towering neighborhoods, to become accustomed to the new scale of the streets, the new urban landscape. Above all, it was necessary to dare to take the elevator up to the twentieth or even the thirtieth floor (many Europeans still hesitate more than a century later), and agree to work or live there. The history of skyscrapers has always ignored this revolution of mentality that a continent forced on itself in a generation and that is perhaps the most impressive dimension of all. The stir created in Paris by the building of the Eiffel Tower is well known; indeed it's a favorite story with contemporary American architects. But what were the reactions in New York, in Chicago and the other cities soon caught up in the fever of skyscrapers and real estate speculation? The idea prevails that the United States is virgin territory, free of the weight of a long history that leads to conservatism and apathy. This was perhaps the case in Chicago, which a disastrous fire compelled to start again from scratch in 1871.[11] It even appears that this tragic event is not unconnected to the pioneer spirit that characterizes the city and hence, when it comes to architecture, the fertility of avant-garde movements.

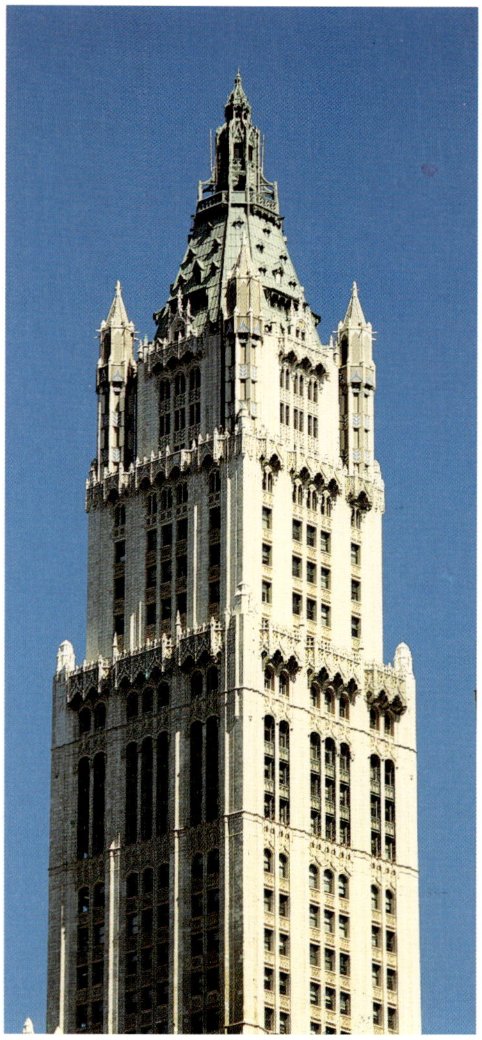

Woolworth Building, New York.
Cass Gilbert, architect, 1913.
© Benoît Roland.

Nevertheless the skyscraper had to make itself accepted. The great upheaval that it raised in the city, a striking symbol of the economic anarchy which gave rise to it, aroused criticism, even counter-attacks. A halt was called in Chicago in 1893. And in New York from the beginning of

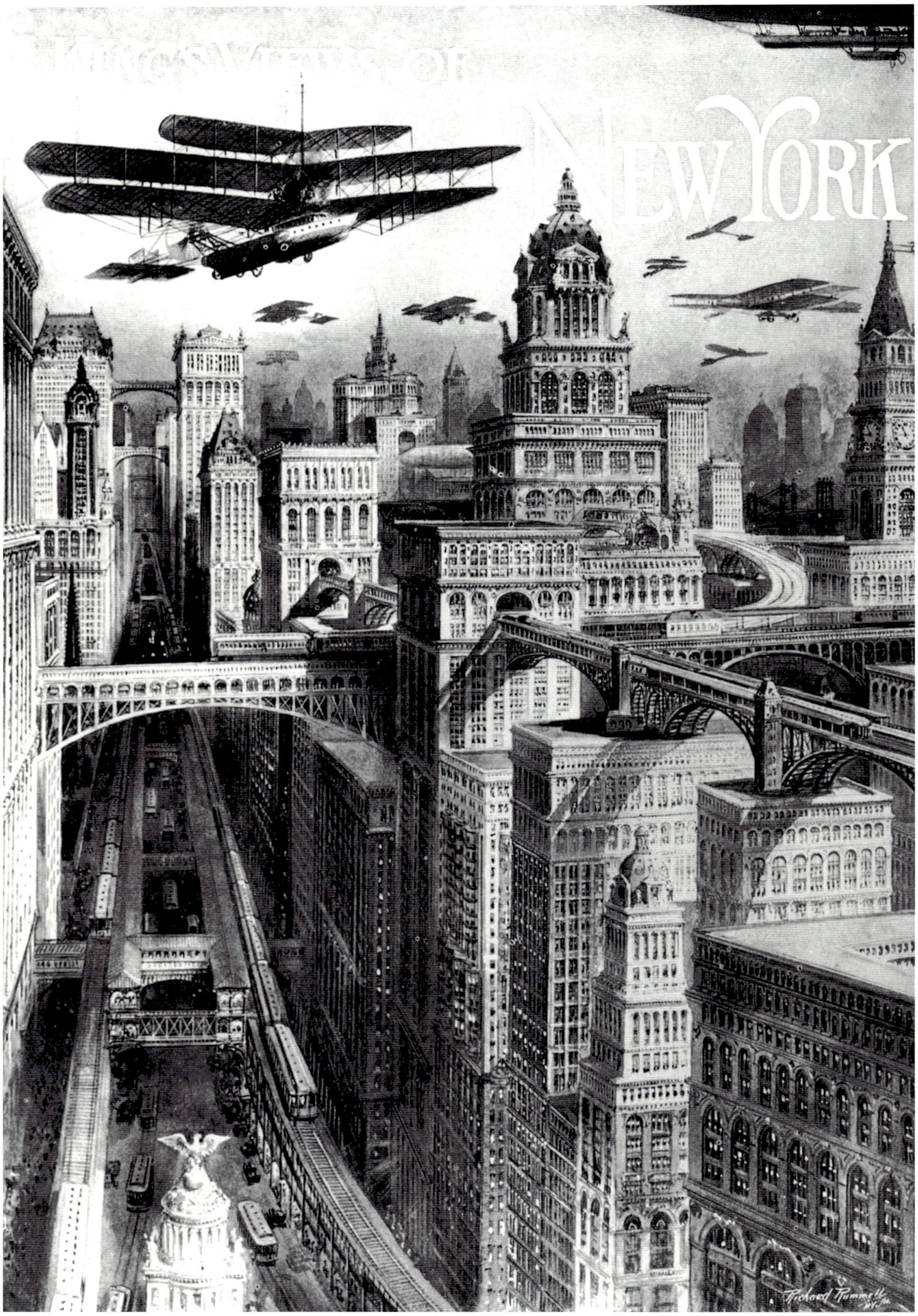

Future New York, a futuristic project by Richard Rummell, 1911. The frontispiece of the King's Views of New York album, Manhattan Postcard Co., New York, 1926 and 1928.

Archives d'architecture moderne, Brussels.

the century, architects, critics, and local politicians rebelled against the transformation of streets into deep and somber canyons.[12]

It was at this moment that an element of propaganda was introduced, explaining the apparent contradiction and total dichotomy between technical function and architectural language which marks the history of the skyscraper from the turn of the century. The propaganda vehicle was the building itself. The gothic envelope of the Woolworth Building—the first true skyscraper built in New York in 1913—has no other object, apart from the happy coincidence of perpendicular gothic with the tower building, than to water down its futuristic image with historical allusion. The allusion was specific, since Frank Woolworth, "king of the penny bazaars," to quote Paul Morand,[13] promoted the building as a cathedral of commerce. Cathedrals, castles, temples and mausoleums took the sky by storm: spires, domes, pyramids, turrets, crenelation rubbed shoulders on the skyline of Lower Manhattan in a carnival fairground only visible in detail from a balloon!

This exercise in seduction reached the sublime with the fashion for Art Deco, a language indisputably popularized by the Paris exhibition of 1925, which achieved its richest and most spectacular expression in the North American skyscraper. Art Deco arrived at just the right moment to imprint traditional Mayan motifs, back in fashion since the 1893 Chicago World's Fair and of which Frank Lloyd Wright's works[14] bear obvious traces, like a standard of American identity on the towers. Art Deco also gave full force to the

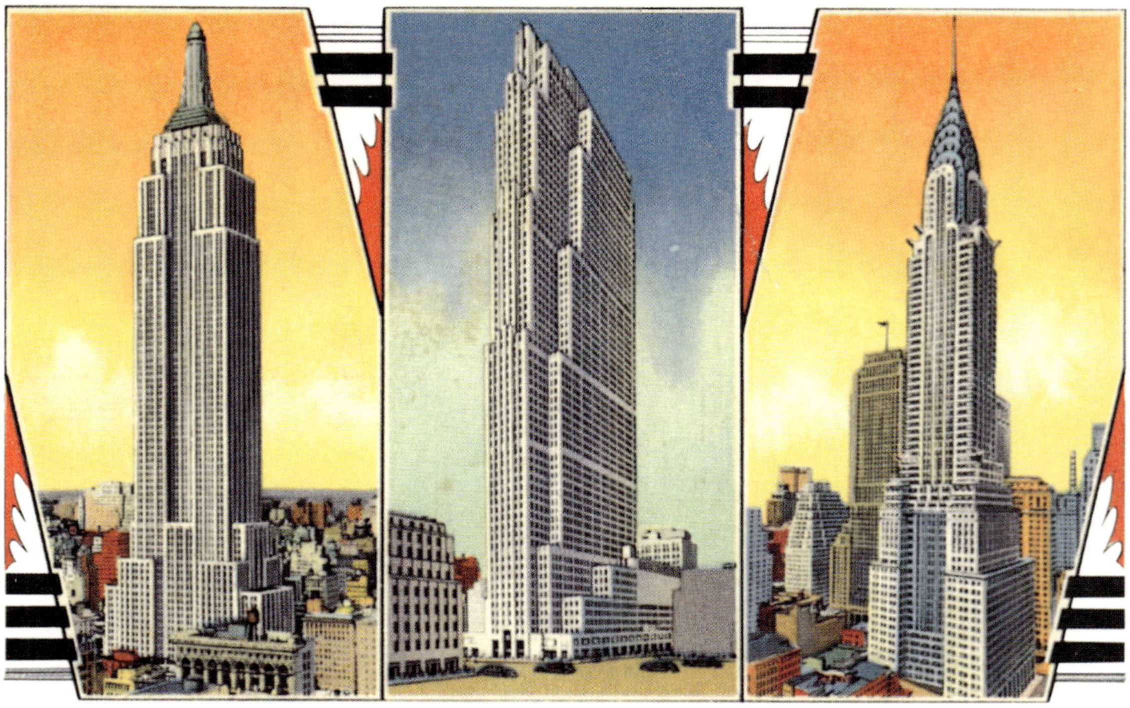

Skyscrapers of New York, from left to right: Empire State Building (1931), Rockefeller Center (1933), Chrysler Building (1930). Postcard circa 1933.
Richard Klein.

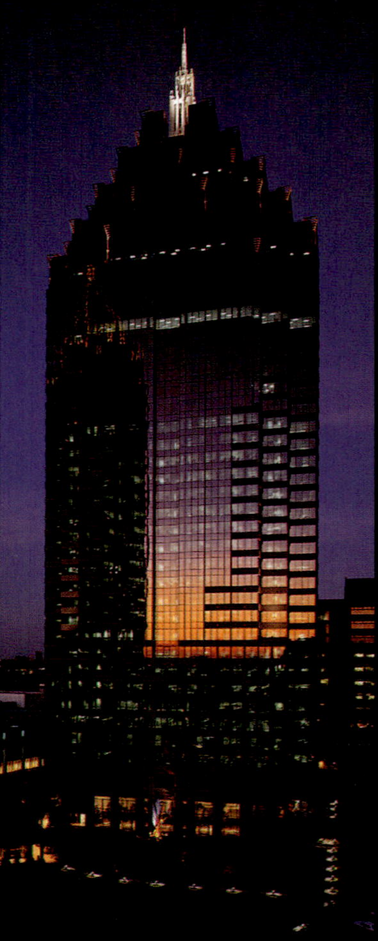

Promenade Two, Atlanta.
Thompson, Ventulett,
Stainback & Associates, architects, 1990.
© Dennis O' Kain.

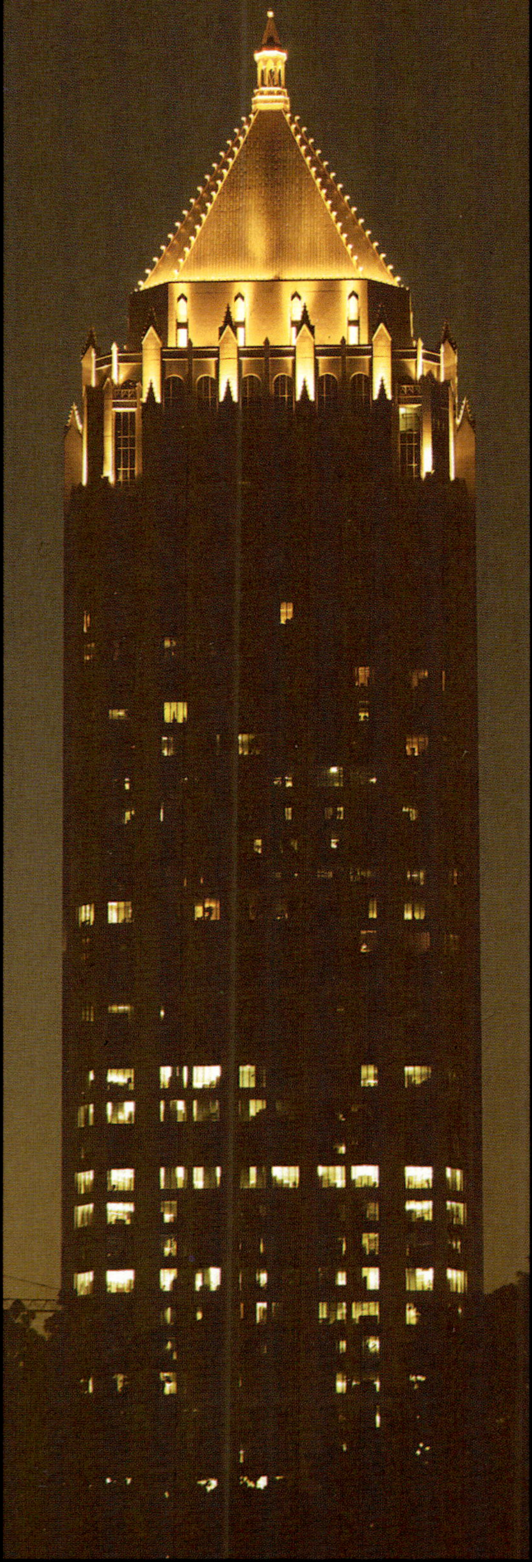

One Atlantic Center, Atlanta.
John Burgee Architects, with Philip Johnson, 1987.
In association with Heery Architects & Engineers.
© Richard Payne.

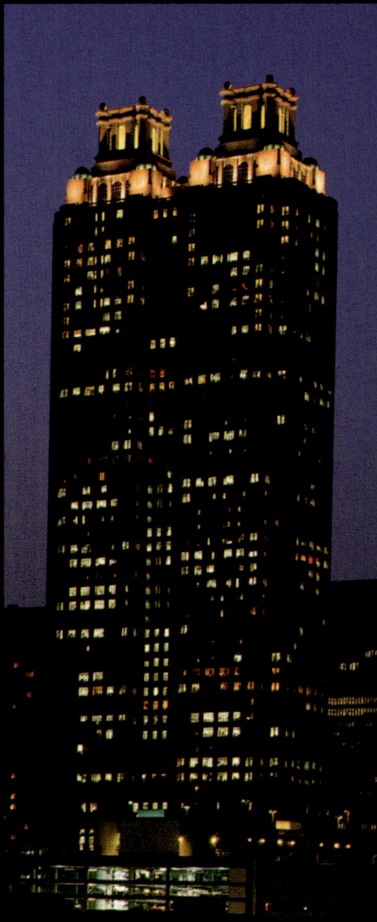

One Ninety One Peachtree Tower, Atlanta.
John Burgee Architects,
with Philip Johnson, 1991.
© Richard Payne.

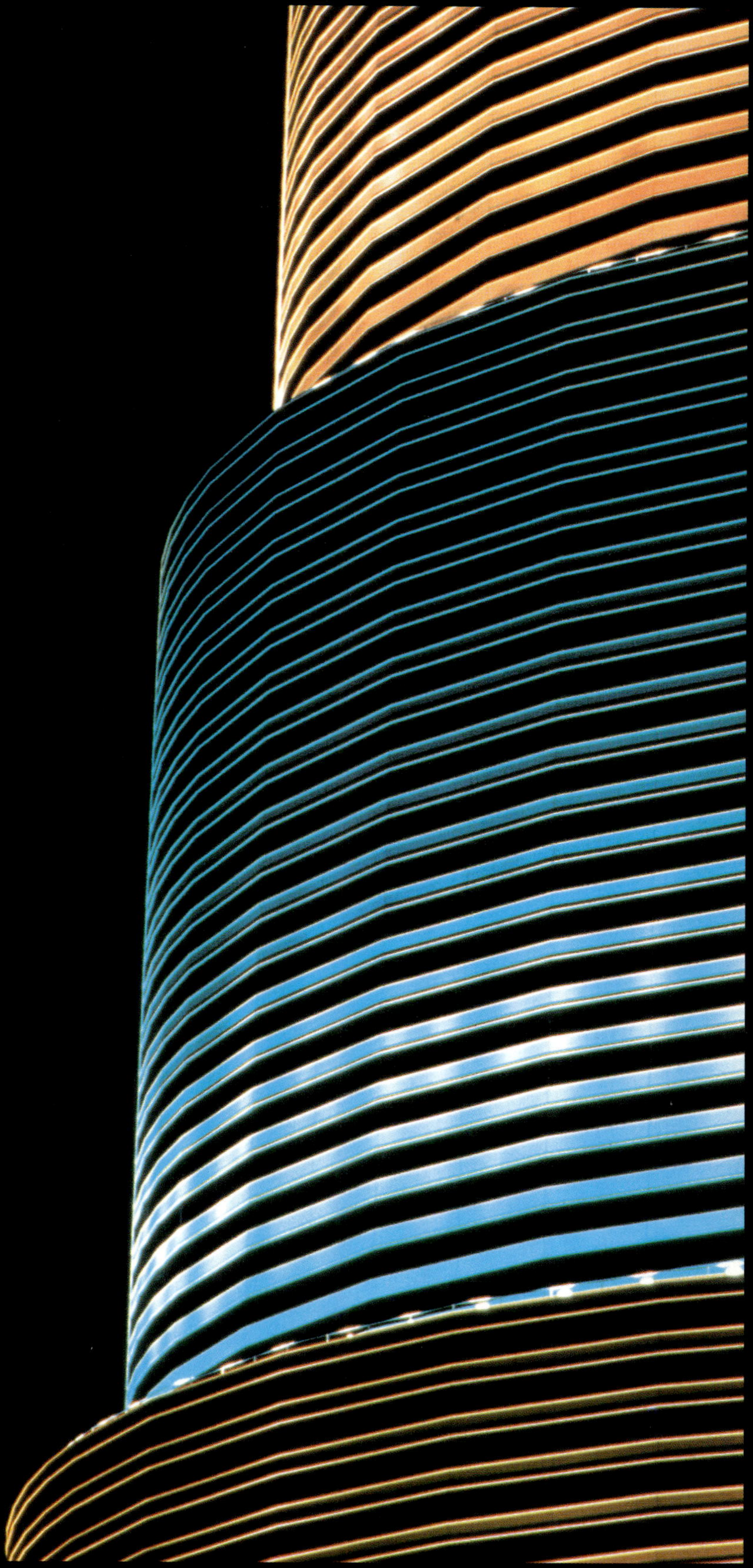

CenTrust Tower
(originally Miami World Trade Center), Miami.
I.M. Pei & Partners, 1987.

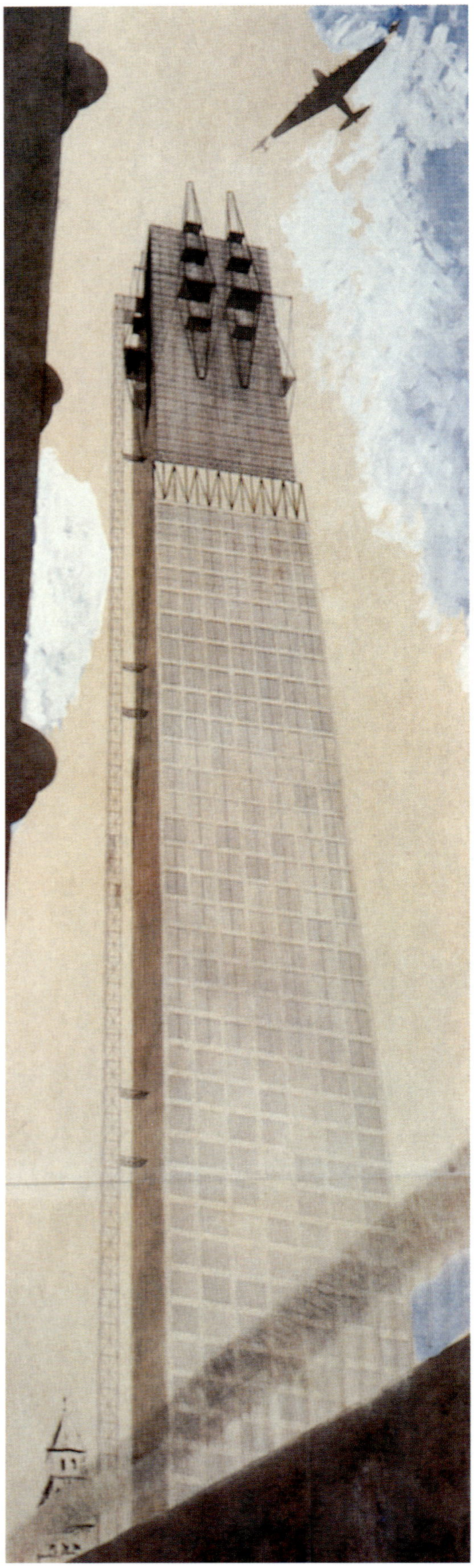

Competition project for the Commissariat for Heavy Industry, Narkomtiazhprom, Moscow, as seen from Red Square. Ivan Leonidov, architect, 1934.
Shchusev State Research Architectural Museum, Moscow.

power of electricity. "Lines disappear; no more walls, no more solids, no more relief; all the skyscrapers, merged and simplified, resemble a huge, square and check-patterned conflagration, fanned by the wind from the high seas."[15]

The skyscraper glows in the night like an advertising sign. The metaphor became literally true in 1932 with the headquarters of the Philadelphia Saving Fund Society designed by the architects William Lescaze and George Howe. A huge sign of the company's initials crowns the skyscraper like an unexpected decorative element. This original device makes no reference to history or any sort of cultural identity but rather to an image of the idea of progress of the kind Russian Constructivism imposed on the world after the October Revolution. The propaganda concept emerges even more clearly. It is undoubtedly the only modernist skyscraper built during this period but

1. William LE BARON JENNEY (1832-1907) was trained both as an architect and an engineer in the United States and Paris. His work, especially structural work, laid the foundations of the Chicago School. Louis SULLIVAN, William HOLABIRD, Martin ROCHE and Daniel H. BURNHAM were all trained in his practice.
2. *Oxford English Dictionary*, Clarendon Press, London, 1971.
3. Originally the building had 10 stories. It was demolished in 1929.
4. A steel skeleton is a framework of beams and columns which support the walls, floor by floor. The structure is covered with masonry insulation.
5. As opposed to the other buildings listed in this paragraph, all in Chicago, the Guaranty Building was built in Buffalo, New York.
6. The Equitable Life Insurance Company office building

its originality has nothing to do with any technical innovation or change in specification. It is a publicity-seeking gambit based on the visual shock of an avant-garde vocabulary.

The hold of the International Style on skyscraper architecture from the fifties, the return in the eighties to historic architectural vocabulary and to natural materials and, today, the ultimate reference to the language of the inter-war avant-garde, paradoxically derive from the same handwriting logic through which the skyscraper brings the symbols and images of the cultural and social consensus into play.

Socialist realism is based on the same themes of taste and popular culture and to it we owe the tallest and biggest buildings of the Soviet Union in the post-war period—buildings of which the scale is comparable to American skyscrapers and which, in contrast, claim to express the heroism of the international proletariat, the greatness of socialism, the immensity of the nation of workers.

Moscow University (1953) and the Palace of Culture and Science of Warsaw (1955), offered by Stalin to Poland, were the highest buildings in Europe until the construction of the MesseTurm in Frankfurt in 1990.[16]

The epic of the skyscraper is a great popular adventure.

Foreign to the movements of the avant-garde, it was long neglected by official history. Pragmatic, often excessive, always out of step with the times, in a time of its own where exception becomes the rule, skyscraper architecture tells a parallel history.

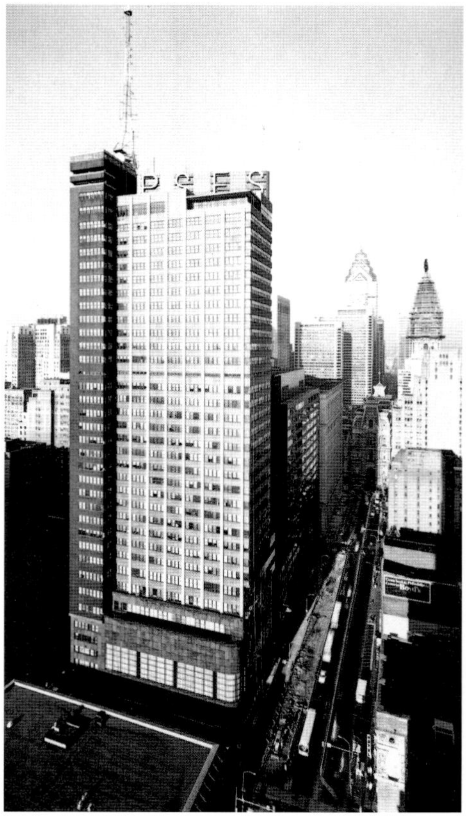

Philadelphia Saving Fund Society (PSFS), Philadelphia, angled view from Market Street. Howe and Lescaze, architects, 1931-1932.
Centre canadien d'architecture (Canadian Center for Architecture), Montreal.
Phot. David Miller, 1987.

was the first "elevator building." It was built in New York in 1870, designed by GILMAN & KENDALL and George B. POST.

7. *The Oxford English Dictionary*, op. cit.

8. Manfredo TAFURI, "La Dialectique de l'absurde", *L'Architecture d'aujourd'hui* No. 178, Paris, 1975.

9. The St. Paul Building by George B. POST beat the height record of the Masonic Temple of Chicago in 1899.

10. Building heights in Chicago were very severely limited until 1923, date of the first zoning ordinance. At the time of the competition for building the headquarters of *The Chicago Tribune* in 1922, only decorative structures could exceed 264 feet (about 80 meters).

11. The great fire of Chicago, which raged in the city for three days on end in 1871, reduced a third of the city to ashes, leaving 100,000 homeless and several hundred dead.

12. In 1908, in an article in the magazine *Architectural Record* entitled "To Curb the Skyscraper," the critic Montgomery SCHUYLER denounced the over-exploitation of ground. He was to be joined in his crusade by the architects George B. POST and Ernest FLAGG.

Winston WEISMAN, "A New View of Skyscraper History," *The Rise of an American Architecture*, Praeger Publishers, New York 1970.

13. Paul MORAND, *New York*, Flammarion, Paris 1929.

14. From 1915 the monumental architecture of Mayan temples directly influenced the work of WRIGHT and, more generally, impregnated American architectural culture in the early part of the century.

15. Paul MORAND, *op. cit.*

16. The MesseTurm in Frankfurt, 257 meters (842 feet) high is the work of architect Helmut JAHN.

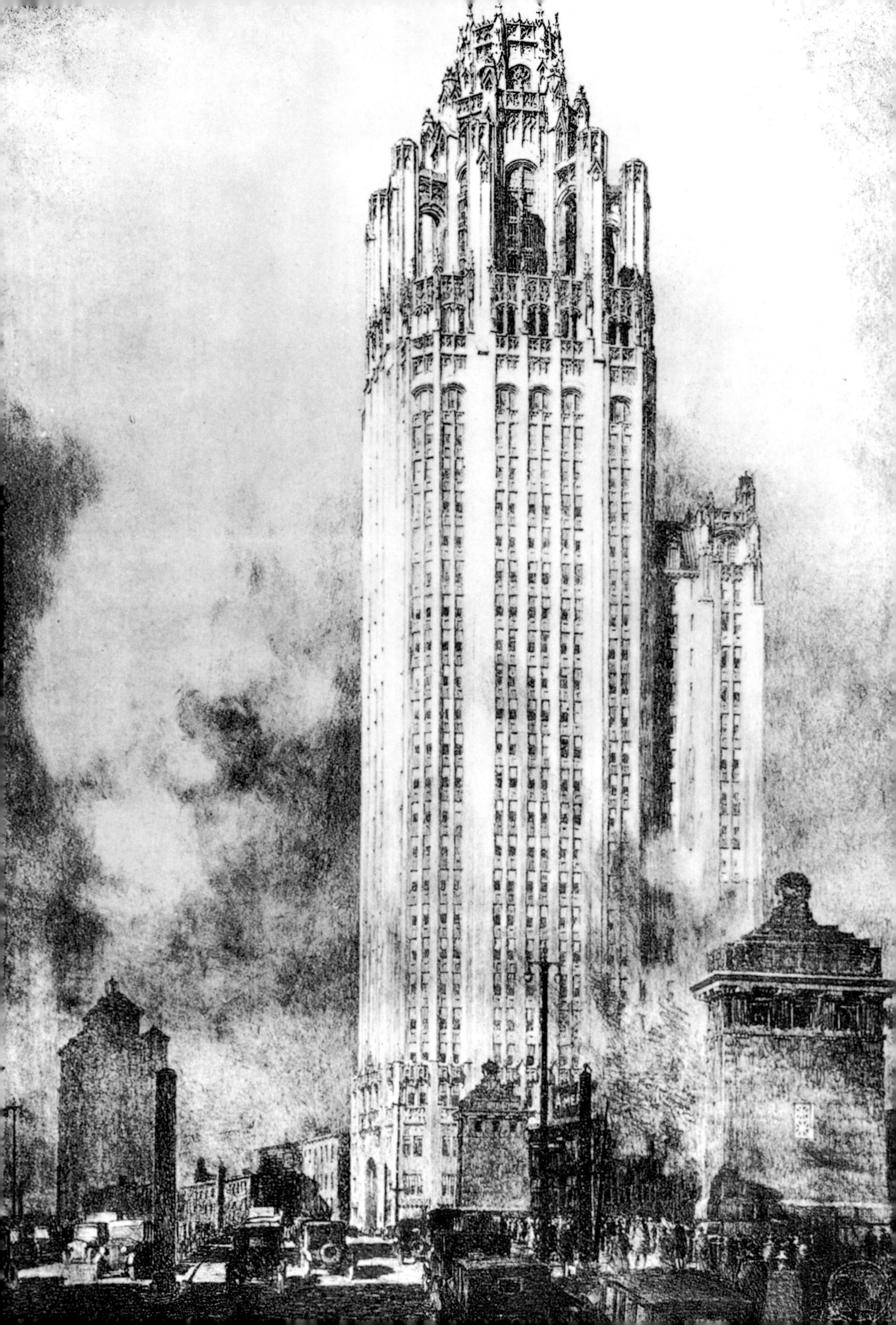

MODERN TIMES

"When we were twenty, around 1925, we heard about the skyscrapers. For us they symbolized America's fabulous prosperity. We discovered them with amazement in the films. They were the architecture of the future, just as the cinema was the art of the future and jazz the music of the future."

Jean-Paul Sartre, *New York*, 1946.

Opposite:
Chicago Tribune Tower. Raymond Hood and John Mead Howells, architects, 1925.
Francisco Mujica, History of the Skyscraper, *Archaeology & Architecture Press, Paris, New York, 1929.*

"The Fourth Stage," volumetric study by Hugh Ferriss on the application of the New York regulations of 1916.
Hugh Ferriss, The Metropolis of Tomorrow, *1929.*

In 1922 the daily, *The Chicago Tribune,* launched an ambitious international competition for the design of its headquarters on the north bank of the river at the edge of the new North Michigan Avenue business district. Neither financial limits nor commercial constraints were part of the specification, just an exhortation "to erect the most beautiful and distinctive office building in the world."[1] Two hundred and sixty-three projects were submitted to the competition jury of which a hundred and forty-five were American, very professional and almost all practical. Of the one hundred and seven foreign projects and the handful of anonymous submissions, a bare twenty were in the spirit of the emerging modernism. The American team of Hood and Howells produced the winning project, a gothic-inspired tower characterized by the use of enormous buttresses, today a protected historic landmark. But, over and above what was actually built, the Chicago Tribune competition was to have a fundamental influence on the history of skyscrapers in Chicago, nationwide and beyond, in Europe, in Latin America and, even at that time, on the shores of the Pacific Ocean in Hong Kong and Shanghai.

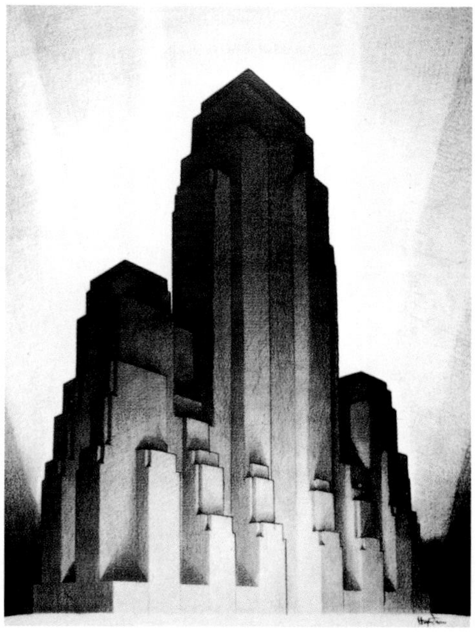

Firstly, the competition was an inventory. Every trend was represented. All at once the architectural debate was thrown open, hastening the evolution of taste and fashions. Indeed,

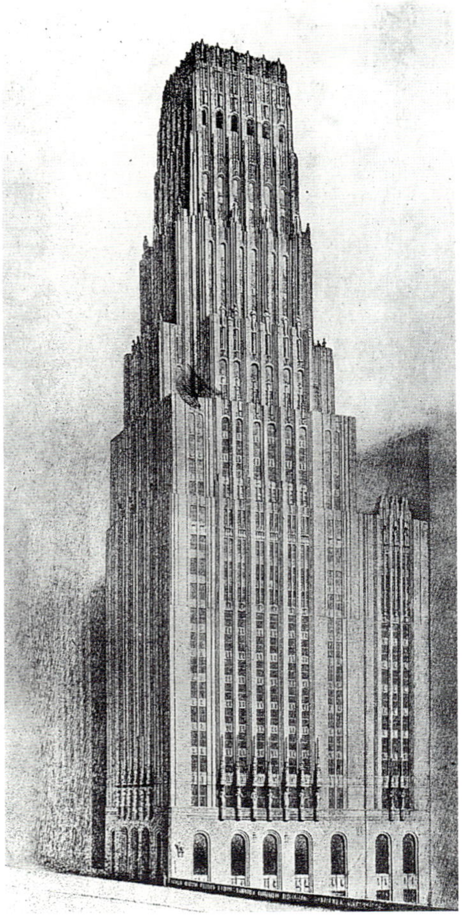

Eliel Saarinen

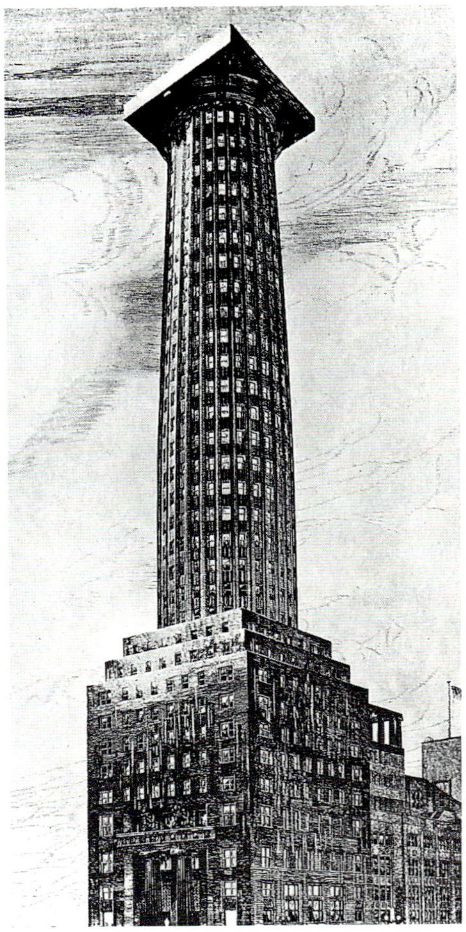

Adolf Loos

1 9 2 2 - T H E C H I C A G O

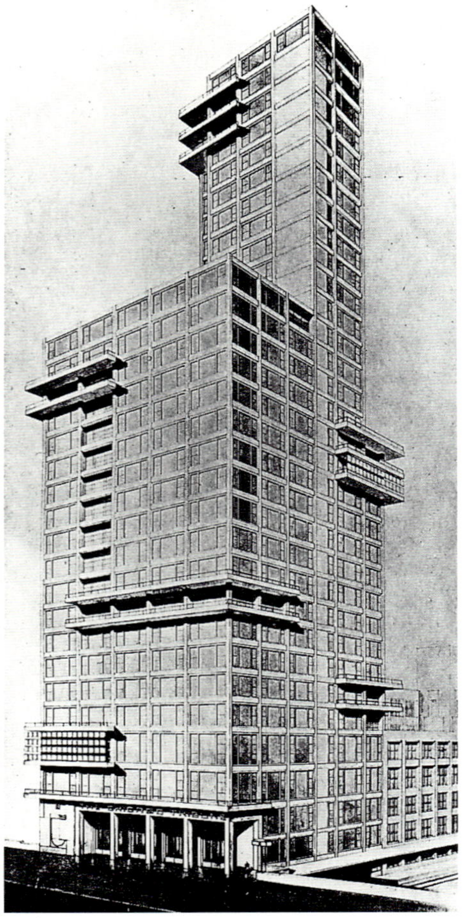

Walter Gropius - Adolf Meyer

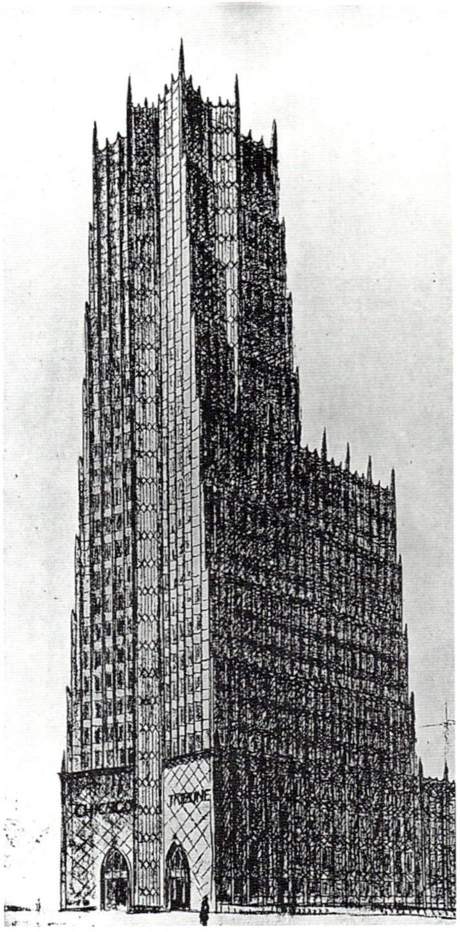

Walter Fischer

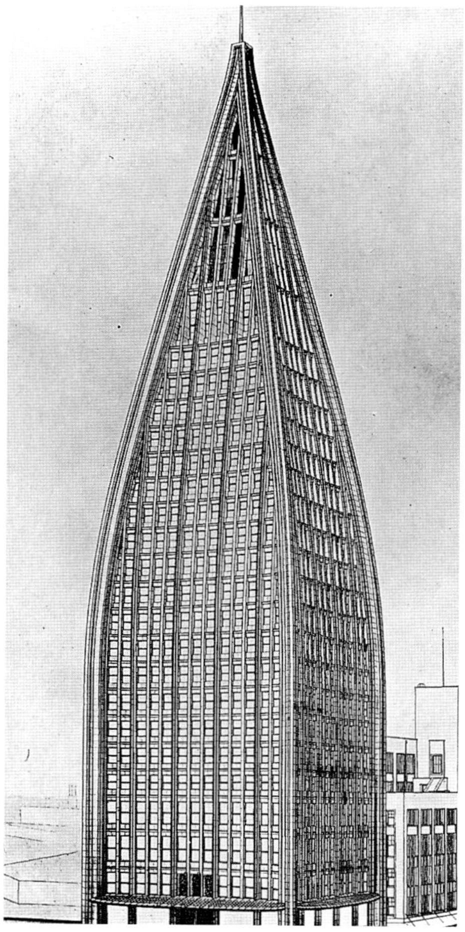

Bruno Taut - Walter Gunther - Kurz Schutz

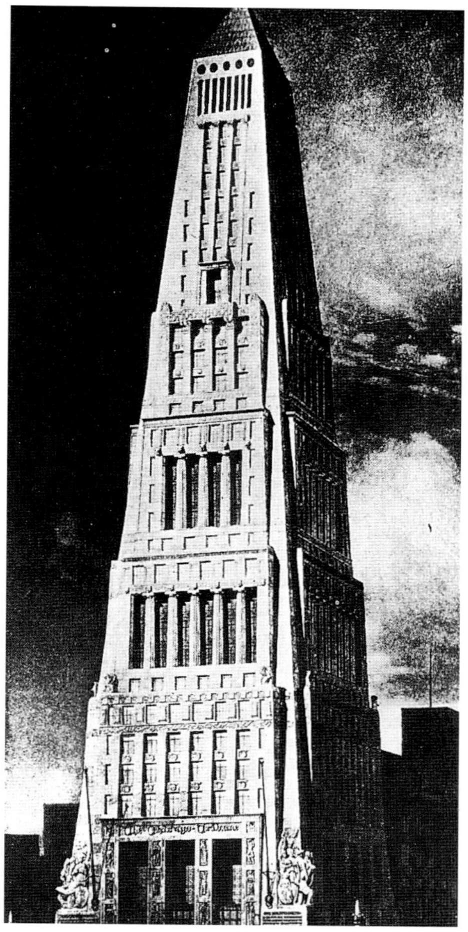

Alfred T. Fellheimer - Steward Wagner

T R I B U N E   C O M P E T I T I O N

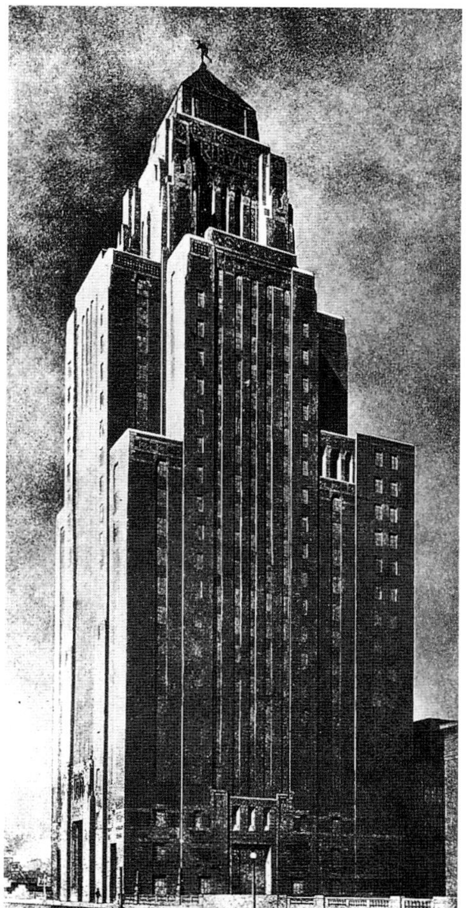

Bertram G. Goodhue

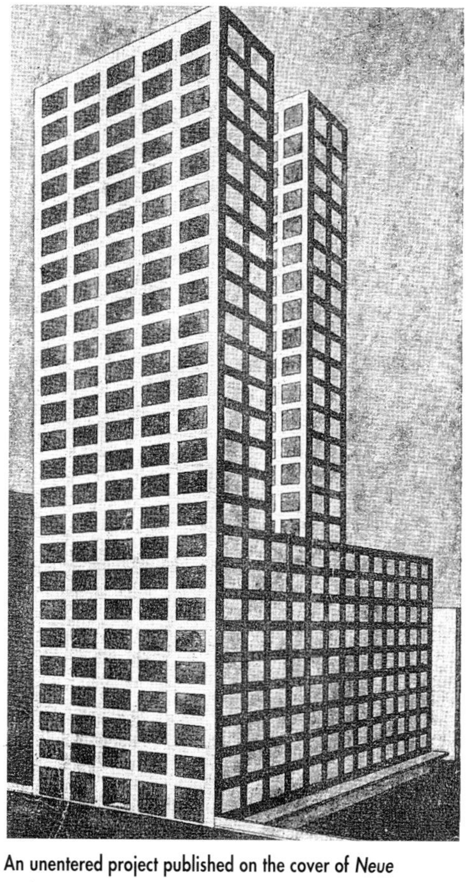

An unentered project published on the cover of *Neue Architektur 1*, "Grosstadtbauten", Aposs, Hanover, 1925.
Archives d'architecture moderne, Brussels.

Ludwig Hilberseimer

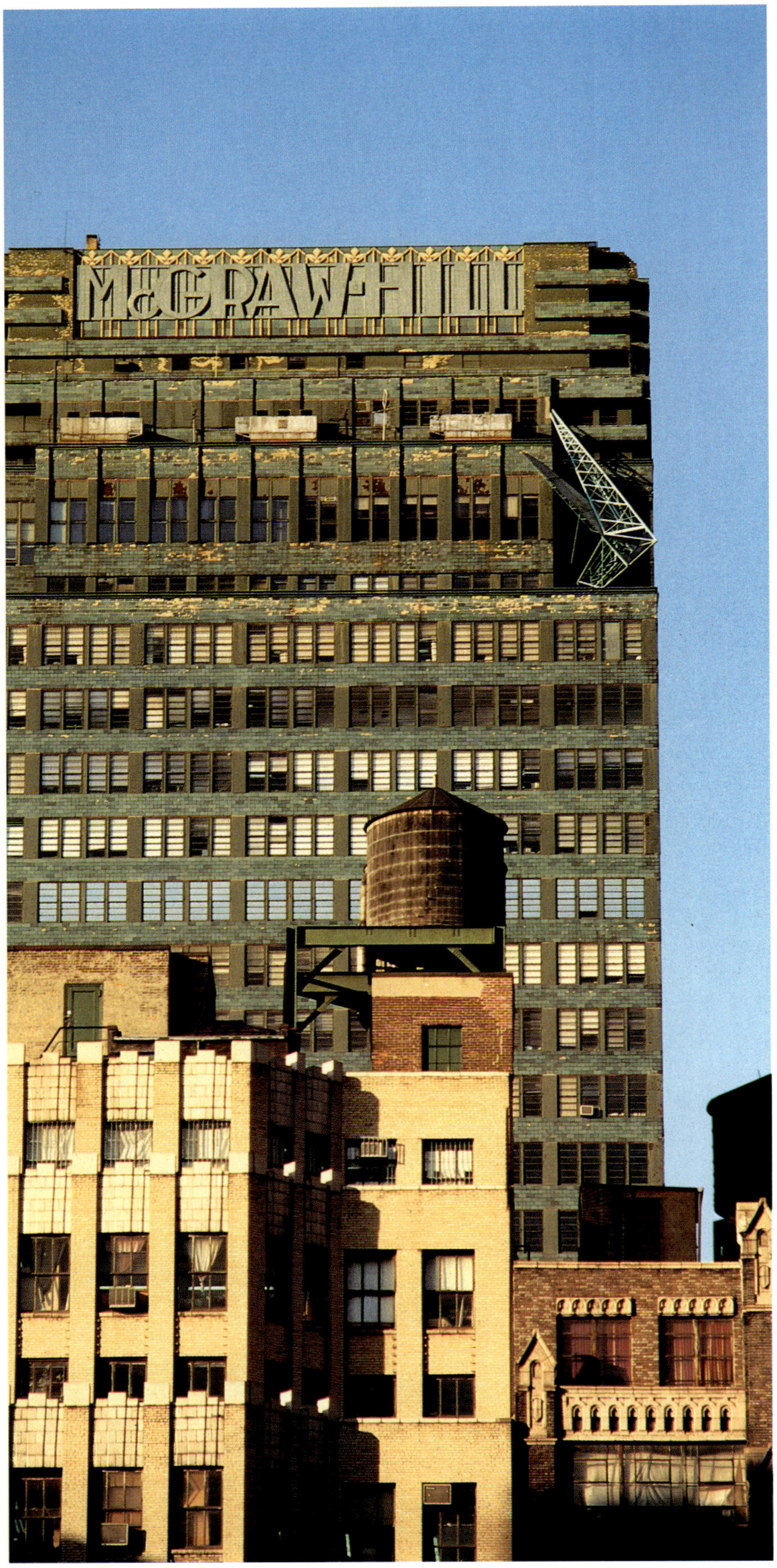

the Chicago Tribune was to be the last of a generation of gothic edifices begun with the Woolworth Building some ten years before.

Paradoxically, it was the winner of the second prize, the favorite of the critics and of Louis Sullivan, that was to enjoy the greater posterity. The project by the Finnish architect, Eliel Saarinen, was to profoundly influence American works of the following decade. It presents a unified composition dominated by an effect of a sculpted mass, tapering, with geometric forms which in addition integrates the regulations in force at the time (the set-back building)[2] with the monumentality of historical styles and the austerity of modern idiom. The Saarinen project, which was to inspire the emblematic images of one Hugh Ferriss, prophesied, to quote Sullivan, "a time to come, and not so far away, when the wretched and the yearning ... shall escape the bondage and the mania of fixed ideas."[3] It prefigures what was to become, a few years later, the archetypal American skyscraper, the American Radiator Building (1924), and the Daily News Building (1930) by the architect Raymond Hood—winner of The Chicago Tribune competition and one of the first to put Saarinen's principles into practice—or, also in New York and among the most famous, the Barclay-Vesey Building (1926) or the Empire State Building (1931), an archetype soon to be replicated in every town on the local scale and usually standing alone, as a symbol of the place's new claim to be called a metropolis.

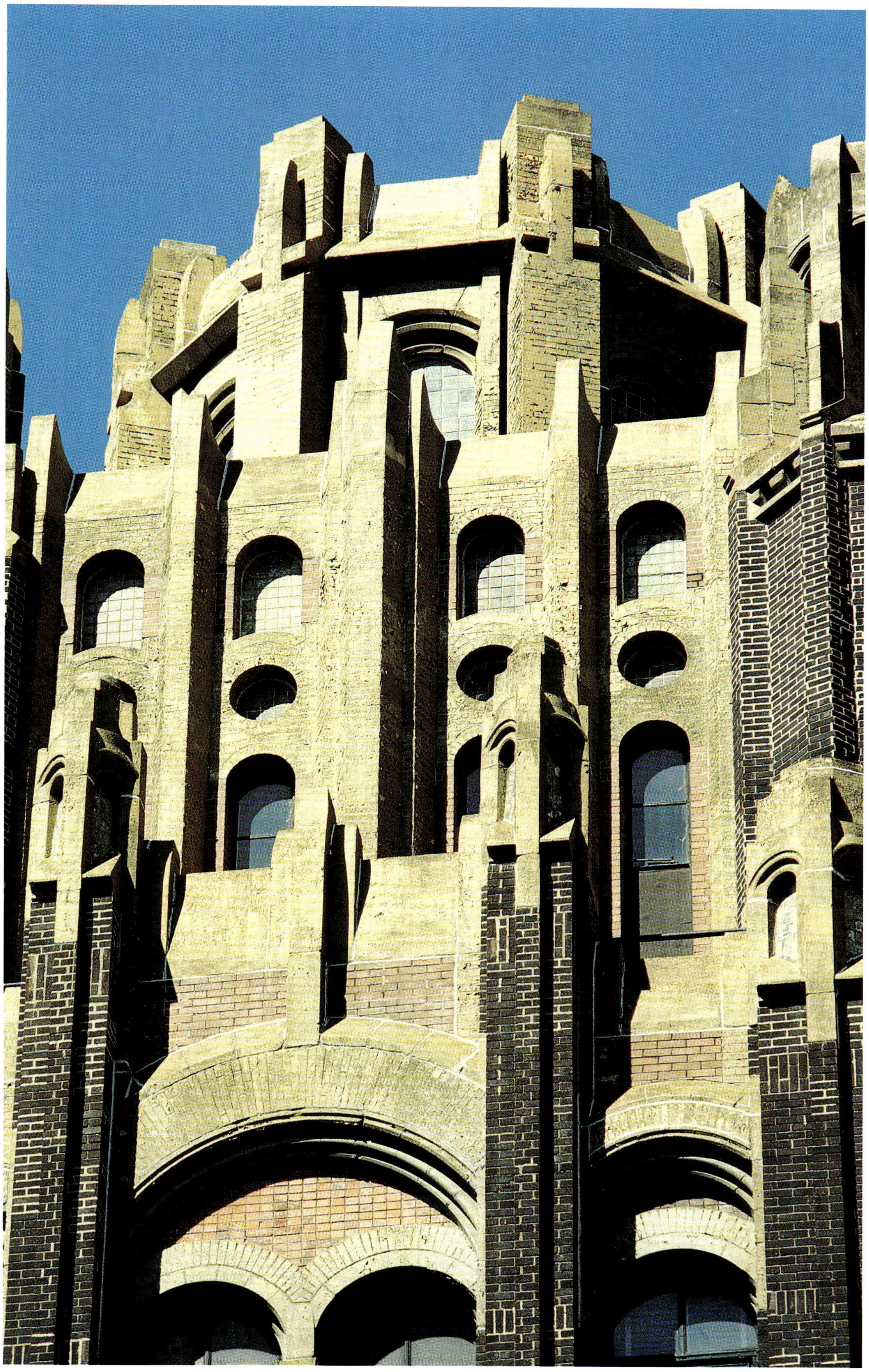

Opposite:
McGraw-Hill Building, New York.
Raymond Hood, architect, 1931.
© Benoît Roland.

American Radiator Building,
New York, detail of the summit.
Raymond Hood, architect, 1924.
© Benoît Roland.

The Chicago Tribune competition also saw the arrival on the scene of a new generation of European architects, from the Bauhaus in Germany and the avant-garde De Stijl movement in the Netherlands. Their skyscraper projects were doubtless technically impractical, (there was talk at the time of superior American know-how), but brought with them radically new cultural aims. This first sowing of the seed imported on the occasion of the competition was to bare fruit ten years later in a big exhibition organized at the Museum of Modern Art in New York by a commissioner whose name was never again to be out of the spotlight, the architect Philip Johnson.[4]
The stage was set for the modernist sequence. In the wings the actors were taking their places—Walter Gropius fled Germany and was installed at Harvard in 1937. In the same year Laslo Moholy-Nagy founded the New Bauhaus in Chicago and Mies van der Rohe, sponsored by Frank Lloyd Wright, accepted the invitation of the Illinois Institute of Technology of which he became director in 1938. But it would be another ten years before the curtain rose, time for the United States to emerge from the economic crisis, and then the Second World War.

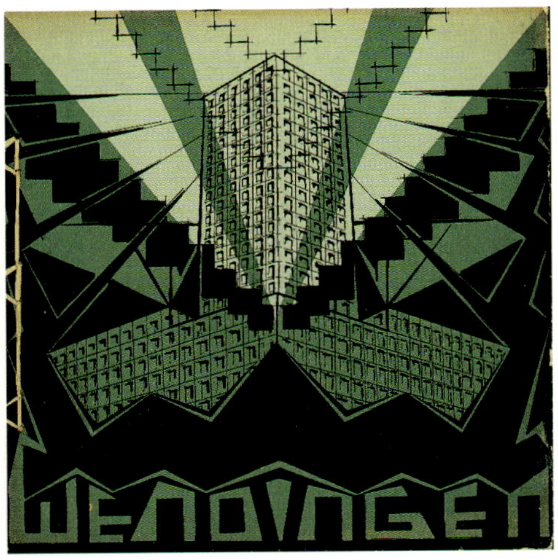

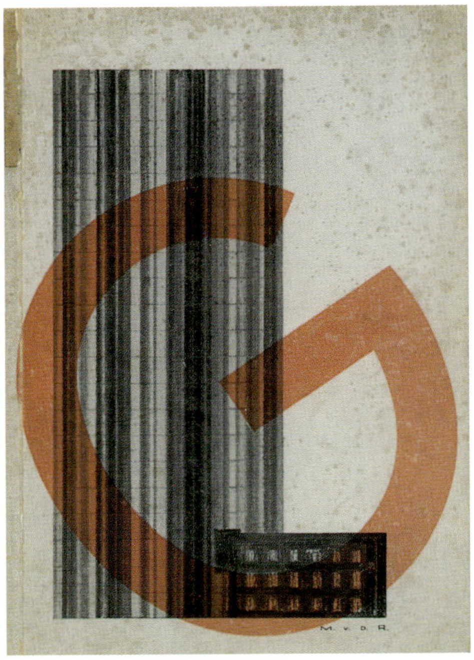

***Wendingen* No. 3, 5th series, 1923. An issue devoted to skyscrapers: "Skyscrapers as Solution of the Housing Problem."**

Mies van der Rohe, project for a glass skyscraper. Published on the cover of the magazine *G, Zeitschrift für elementare Gestaltung*, No. 3, Berlin, June, 1924.
Archives d'architecture moderne, Brussels.

In 1947, Mies van der Rohe undertook his first residential towers for the real estate developer Herbert Greenwald in Chicago: the Promontory Apartments with 21 stories and concrete framework; then in 1948, the Lake Shore Drive Towers, higher, which developed the metallic version.
At the same time in the French town of Amiens construction began of a residential skyscraper 104 meters (340 feet) high, the tallest tower in Europe for more than ten years. The tower was designed by Auguste Perret, apostle of the "new reinforced concrete architecture" and designer of an observation tower in Grenoble built entirely of concrete in 1925.[5] In fact Auguste Perret was commissioned to architecturally plan the new square in front of the railway station as part of the town reconstruction plan drawn up in 1942.[6] He conceived the tower as a belfry, a monumental entry. Perret originally planned the tower to be used for shops and offices. But the 1945 project called for it to contain some fifty housing units. Construction began in 1949, financed by special loans for "experimental construction." Three years later work on the uncompleted building was interrupted. No citizen of Amiens was prepared to live in it!
The concrete carcass lay abandoned for almost eight years. Work eventually restarted in 1959 and the first residents were finally installed in 1960.[7] Argument raged over the Perret tower. Already famous before being built, the foundation

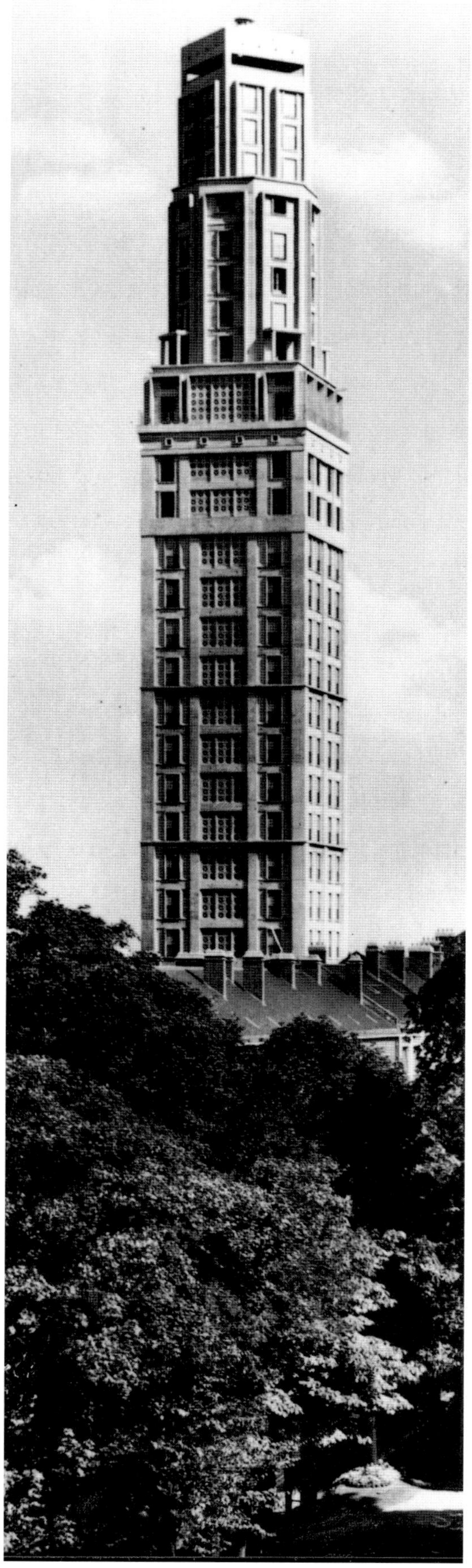

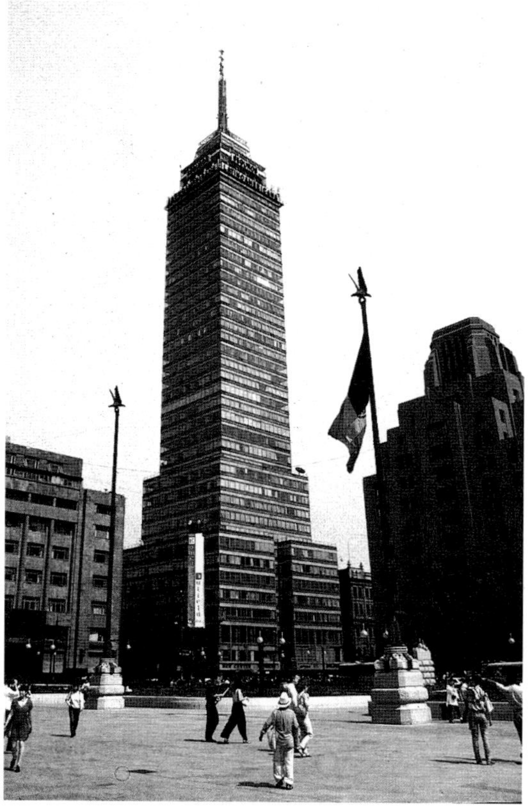

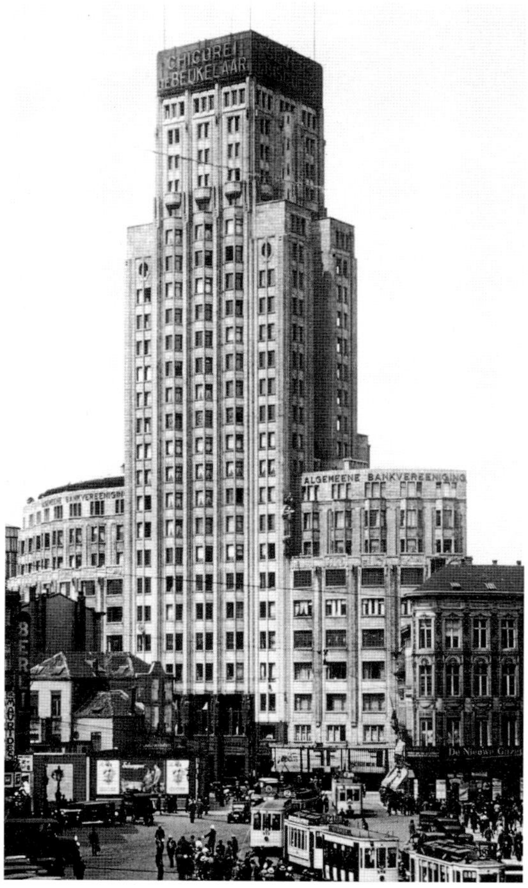

Left:
Tour Perret, Amiens.
Auguste Perret, architect,
1948-1960.
Institut français d'architecture.

Top:
Torre Latinoamericana,
Mexico City.
Ing. Adolfo Zeevaert,
head of project;
Augusto H. Alvarez,
consultant architect.
With a height of 182 meters
(597 feet), it was the tallest
building in Latin America at the
time of its completion in 1952.
© Teseo Lopez Vargas.

Bottom:
Boerentoren
(Torengebouw Algemeene
Bankvereeniging),
Antwerp, photographed
in 1933.
Jan R. Vanhoenacker and
Jos Smolderen, architects;
Emiel Van Averbeke,
consultant, 1927-1932.
With a height of 85 meters
(279 feet), the tallest building
in Europe at the time
of its completion.
Stadsarchief, Antwerp.

stone was laid with great pomp and ceremony in 1950. Abandoned, then completed and now protected as a historical building, it has won its place on the Amiens skyline, only rivaled by the towers of the famous cathedral.
The story was too convoluted to have a sequel. In any case, the object was to build a monument to stand, and remain standing, alone.
The same monumental approach, the same urban symbolism and the same desire to put down roots describes another pioneering tower built in the heart of Milan in 1958. The Torre Velasca, designed by the Studio BBPR[8] with a concrete frame, has 29 stories and contains shops, offices and 72 apartments. In a very different and later version, the Maine-Montparnasse Tower (1973) in the heart of Paris is another illustration of this theory of "picturesque modernism," where a solitary skyscraper is given monumental status.

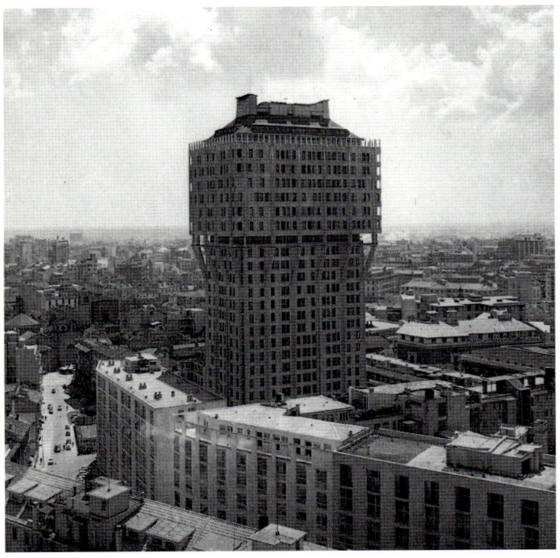

Torre Velasca, Milan.
Studio BBPR, architects, 1958.
© Publifoto, Milan.

There are no symbols or exceptions to the rule in the work of Mies in Chicago. On the contrary, his towers tend towards abstraction, repetition. "I am completely opposed to the idea that a particular building should possess its own character,"[9] he said. Between 1948 and 1969, fourteen Mies-designed towers were built in Chicago, providing the opportunity to perfect a type of architecture that was "simplified, pure, clean, generalized, reasonable, abstract," all qualities that America found difficult to resist.[10] From the beginning of the sixties Mies abandoned residential towers at his practice to devote himself to large office buildings of which the Seagram Building (1958) became the prototype. The history of the Seagram is worth re-telling. It arises from a truly ideal situation; the architect was in effect given carte blanche by the developer Samuel Bronfman, chairman of the Canadian multinational Joseph E. Seagram and Sons, and this included the budget! For example, Mies persuaded his client to buy the extra land needed to make his project compatible with the norms for density permitted on the site. It is, Philip Johnson was to say, the only perfect modernist building ever constructed.[11] Not only did Mies define a new type of urban building, a monolithic tower fronted by a plaza, which was to inspire New York's building code in its new 1961 version,[12] but the materials used—marble, granite, bronze and glass—and the precision of the detailing allowed the building and the open space to be perfectly executed. All Mies' meticulousness is revealed in an attention to detail never achieved since in a building of this size. Neither the tower nor the public space show any sign of age today. The prototype was to carry all before it—except its perfection.

Facing the Seagram Building is another prototype of the modernist tower, Lever House, first major work of Skidmore, Owings & Merrill, undoubtedly the most specialized team in the world in

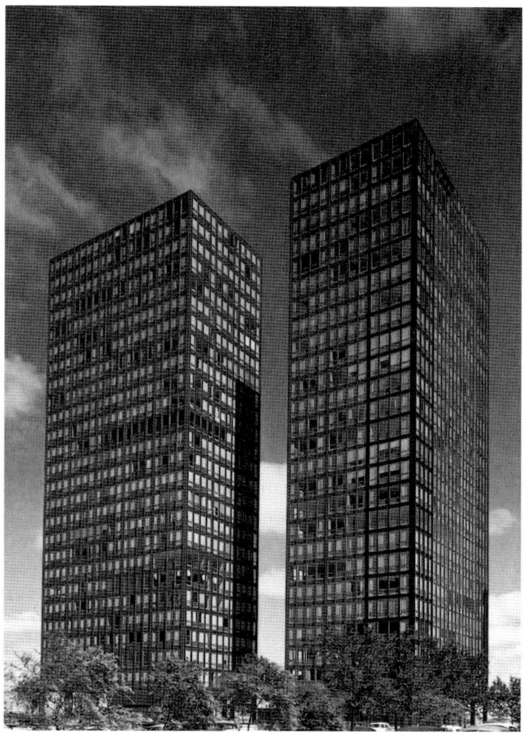

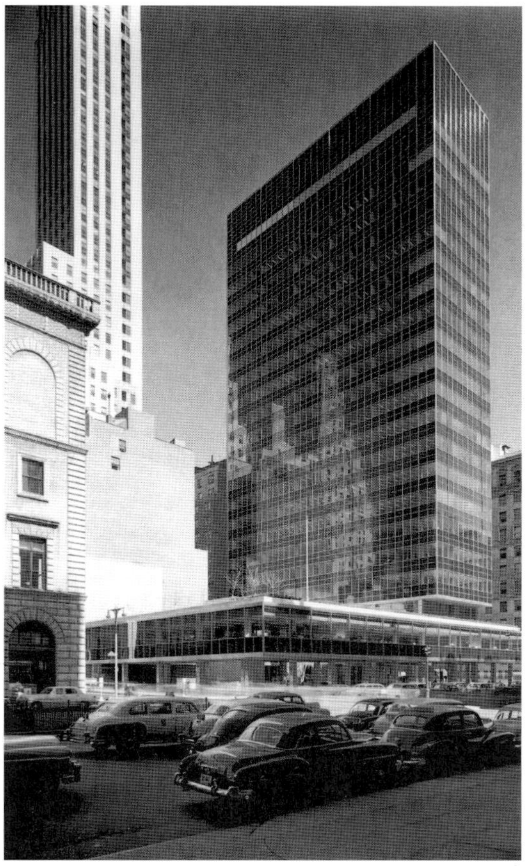

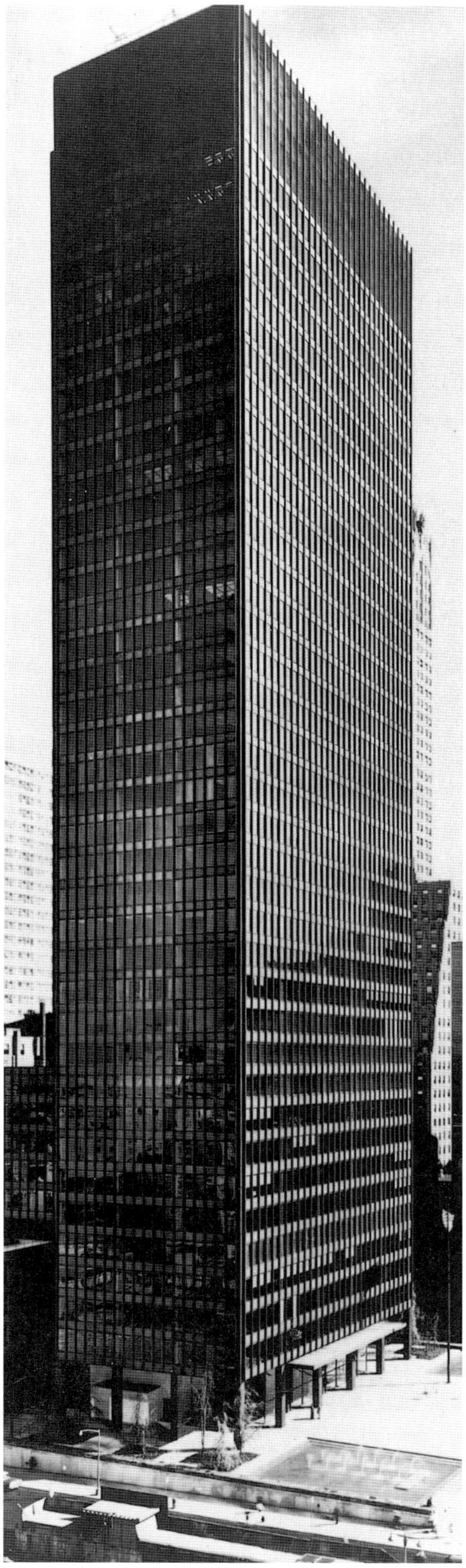

Far left, top:
860-880 Lake Shore Drive, Chicago. Mies van der Rohe, architect, 1951.
Chicago Historical Society. Phot. Hedrich-Blessing.

Bottom:
Lever House, New York. SOM New York, architects, 1952.
© Ezra Stoller, Esto Photographics.

Left:
Seagram Building, New York. Mies van der Rohe, architect, 1958.
Buildings & Data.

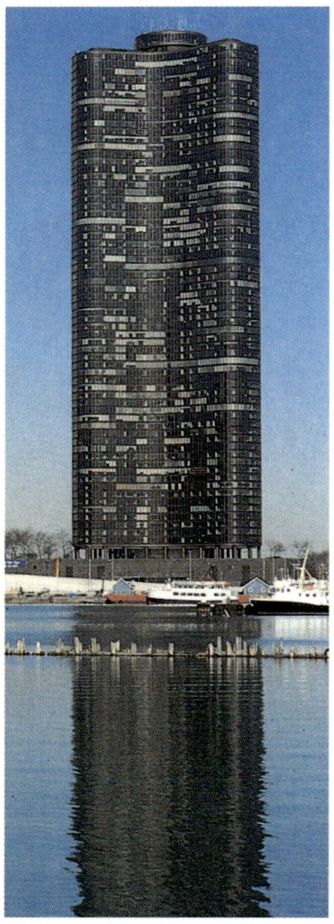

Lake Point Tower, Chicago.
George Schipporeit and John Heinrich, architects, in association with Graham, Anderson, Probst and White, 1968.
© Benoît Roland.

Opposite:
Permanent seat of the United Nations, New York.
On the right the Secretariat Tower; in the center the General Assembly, and in the background the library. International Committee of Architects, Wallace K. Harrison, Chairman, 1952.
Buildings & Data.

skyscraper architecture. That the building antedates the Seagram by a few years does not affect its debt to Mies. Lever House is a true homage to the German master, almost a quotation, in which the memory of the glass skyscraper designed for Berlin, the Barcelona pavilion and the Bauhaus aesthetic are incorporated.[13] Lever House also marks the turning point of commercial architecture in New York after the crisis. As opposed to its predecessors, which were monstrously large and too demanding to manage, the project tends to reduce the importance of the construction in favor of public spaces, lost in terms of rentals but gained for the urban environment. The cloister thus created in the heart of the site is perhaps inspired by the example of the Rockefeller Center and prefigures the famous plaza of the Seagram Building. But in the case of Lever House the public space is unusable and the setting of the tower at right angles to Park Avenue brutally interrupts the alignment of the thoroughfare.

Very few tall buildings during the following decades were to escape the conventions established by these first models. And the replicas rarely attained the quality of the originals. A succession of office towers designed by Mies, then others designed in his manner, were to impose themselves in every city in the world like a totalitarian and often destructive building standard.
In this hackneyed world of boxes and cages, the word skyscraper fell into disuse. The towers were given the bland name of high-rises. In French technical jargon they became the mere acronym IGH.[14]

1. Excerpt from the rules of the competition: "To erect the most beautiful and distinctive office building in the world is the desire of The Tribune...." in *Chicago Tribune Tower Competition & Late Entries,* Rizzoli, New York, 1980.

2. The first regulations (Building Zone Resolution) limiting the height and volume of buildings appeared in New York in 1916. It permitted the height limits to be exceeded in proportion to the setting back from the building line. Many American cities adopted regulations inspired by those of New York, including Chicago in 1923.

3. In an article in the magazine *Architectural Record of 1923,* Louis SULLIVAN severely condemned the choice of HOOD and HOWELLS' "pastiche" project instead of SAARINEN's, which he supported. According to Vincent SCULLY, "The Tribune Competition 1922/1980," in *Chicago Tribune Tower...,* op. cit.

4. The Modern Architecture/International Exhibition, which was a true proclamation of the modern movement, was presented at the Museum of Modern Art in New York in 1932. The expression "International Style" emerges in the publication *The International Style: Architecture Since 1922,* written by Henry-Russell HITCHCOCK, as a complement to the exhibition and its catalogue.

5. *L'Architecture nouvelle du ciment armé* (The New Architecture of Reinforced Concrete) is the title of an unpublished work projected by the brothers Auguste and Gustave PERRET in 1924. The Grenoble Observation Tower was built at the request of the Touring Club de France for the International Exhibition of Hydroelectric Power and Tourism in 1925.

6. The town of Amiens was bombed in 1941. The general plan of reconstruction was by Pierre DUFAU.

7. Construction was completed by the architect François SPOERRY, who acquired the abandoned tower and made major modifications to the original project—division of the floors into two apartments and of part of the tower into offices.

8. The architects of Studio BBPR were Gian Luigi BANFI, Ludovico DI BELGIOJOSO, Enrico PERESSUTTI and Ernesto Nathan ROGERS.

9. Quoted by Peter CARTER, "Mies van der Rohe, an Appreciation on the Occasion of his 75th Birthday", *Architectural Design,* No. 31, March 1961.

10. Vincent SCULLY, *American Architecture and Urbanism,* Henry Holt and Company, New York, 1988 (new revised edition).

11. Philip JOHNSON interviewed by G. BINDER and C. MIEROP, April 20, 1994. JOHNSON was associated with MIES for the Seagram Building project.

12. The New Building Code of 1961 revises downwards the densities authorized by the 1916 legislation. However, it puts into effect a system of incentive zoning which allows the density to be increased in certain commercial neighborhoods in exchange for the provision of public spaces.

13. The Glass Tower project was designed by MIES in 1921 in a competition for the Friedrichstrasse in Berlin. In 1929 MIES designed the German pavilion for the International Exposition in Barcelona. Reference to the pavilion is very explicit in the treatment of Lever House at ground level. Furthermore, MIES was the director of the Bauhaus from 1930 to 1933.

14. French regulations concerning IGH (Immeuble de Grande Hauteur) buildings apply to all buildings of 28 meters (92 feet) and over.

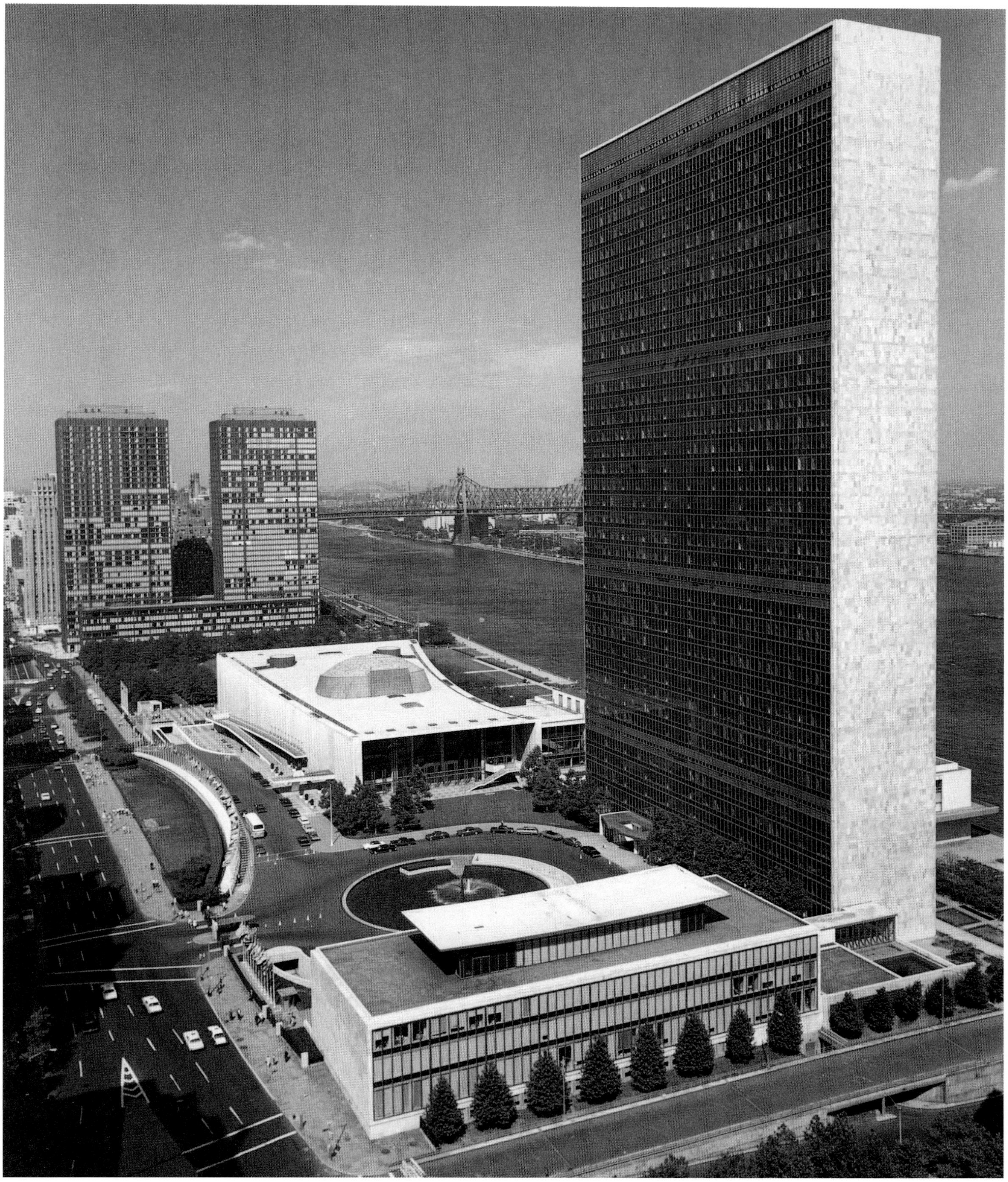

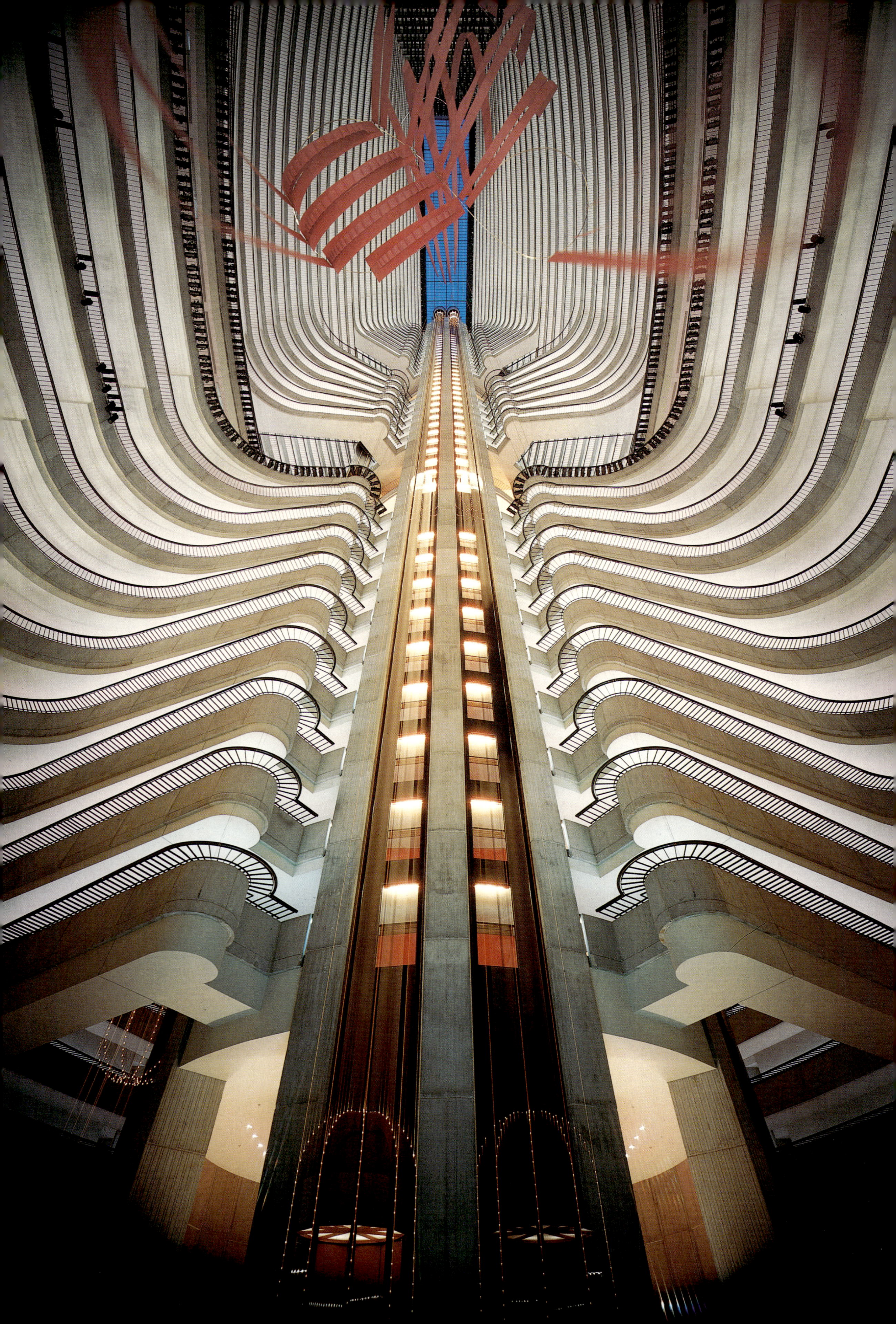

EARTH AND SKY

"One of the new skyscrapers in New York ends in a green and gold pinnacle. It could just as well end in a glass crest, in needles and turrets of crystal! Or in some chimerical kiosk, some frayed sleigh of the Queen of the Clouds, a headdress of music. From the bustling workaday street, the eye that looks upwards always seeks a misty transition towards paradise."

Paul Claudel, *Conversations dans le Loir-et-Cher*, 1928.

Opposite:
Marriott Marquis Hotel, Atlanta, atrium.
John Portman & Associates, architects, 1985.
© Jaime Ardiles-Arce.

In his entry for The Chicago Tribune competition the Austrian architect Adolf Loos provided a parody of the skyscraper. It was an ultimate comment, obviously polemical, on the power of classical forms, which literally applied the analogy with the column. The skyscraper holds up the sky just as once the columns of Egyptian temples with their palm-tree capital supported ceilings "almost unmistakably bearing an allusion to the sky: a blue background sprinkled with stars, the falcon with the disc of the sun, astronomical charts."[1]

This historical metaphor worked efficiently for several decades according to a typology established and codified by the architect Louis Sullivan in the 1880's and consisting of the base, the shaft and the capital—a frieze at entablature level surmounted by a wide projecting cornice. This formula is ideal for a building of about 20 stories. Above this height the typology ceases to work and architects found it necessary to find principles of composition that lent themselves better to the vertical proportion. This led to the appearance of the tower building—the campanile—and then, as a response to rules governing prospect, the setback building, considered since the twenties as the most successfully realized and the most original form of the American skyscraper.

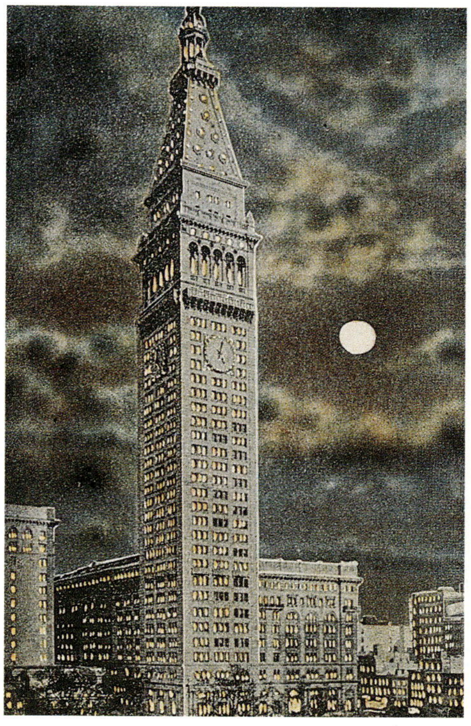

Metropolitan Life Tower, New York, from an old postcard.
Napoleon Le Brun & Sons, architects, 1909.
Institut français d'architecture.

This does not alter the fact that the tripartite formula, with the two focal points at the base and the summit, persists throughout the history of the skyscraper, whichever of the parts the emphasis is placed on, according to period, architect, site or specification.

The base of the skyscraper is the point of contact with the street, the citizen, everyday city life. It negotiates the insertion of the building in the urban tissue, defines its outline and scale as they are perceived in close-up from the surrounding public space. The capital or crown addresses the city as a whole. It is designed to be recognized from afar and, conversely, provides panoramic views over a vast area. In it is concentrated all the symbolic charge of the building as well as its publicity impact. Like the base, it is a special place where the talent "that the architect has as an artist has a real chance"[2] and where special features such as viewing platforms, board rooms, revolving restaurants, "skybars" are added to the workaday specification of the intervening floors. Shops are usually accommodated in the base together with public services and activities in general. In the tower, strictly speaking, are to be found the routine floors, offices, hotel bedrooms or apartments—repetitive, functional, and private; they form the initial shaft of the column. The base of the skyscraper clearly defines its relationship to public space.

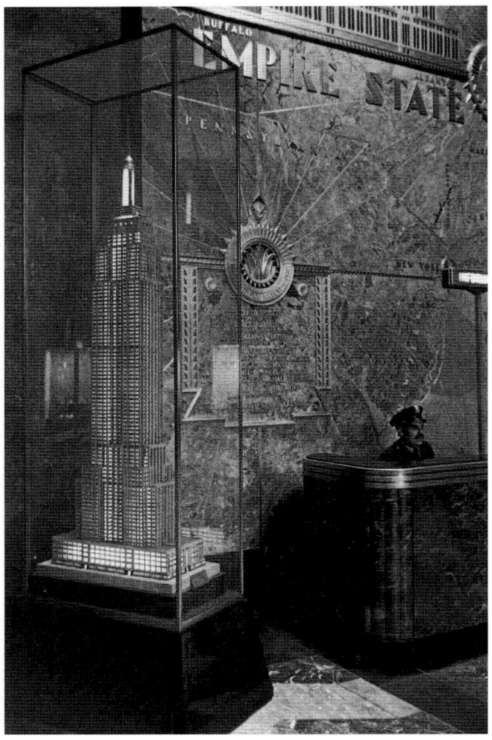

Empire State Building, New York, the lobby. Shreve, Lamb & Harmon Associates, 1931.
© Rapho, Paris.
Phot. Pierre Michaud, 1973.

The comparison between the headquarters of *The Chicago Tribune* (1925) and of the New York *Daily News* (1930), both by the same architects, is very revealing in this regard. In the first, the public area and the spectacular (an observation platform) are situated at the summit of the building. But it is the lobby giving on to the street that is the most theatrical element of the second—a huge globe turns on its axis in a celestial decor of glass and burnished metal.[3]

The reversal, in this case explained by editorial policy, more generally characterizes the status of the entrance during the Art Deco period. Whether it is the Chrysler Building (1930), the Empire State Building (1931), the Field Building in Chicago (1934) or, thirty years earlier, the Rookery Building, re-designed by Frank Lloyd Wright,[4] the lobby becomes a public space in itself and its monumental treatment, in scale and richness of decoration alike, places it in the ranks of genuine public buildings.

It is precisely in giving back this monumental character to the lobby that architects as different as John Portman or Philip Johnson (and his associate John Burgee) were to begin to pave the way in the seventies towards the second generation of "humanist"[5] skyscrapers. The IDS Center in Minneapolis, for example, includes a huge public commercial glass-covered court and is articulated to the street by a peripheral girdle of small shops. In another fashion, architect John Portman was to invent the atrium type hotel

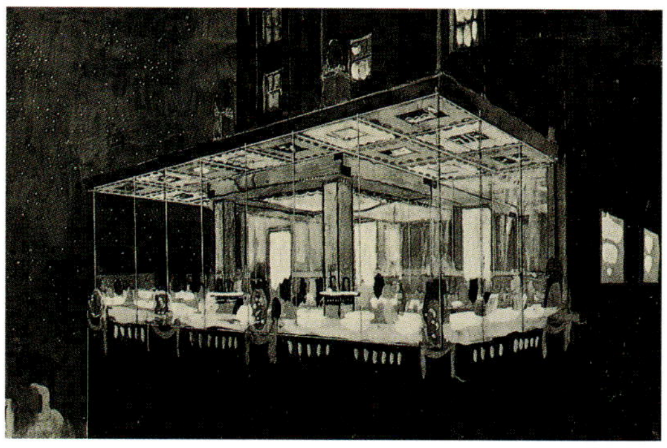

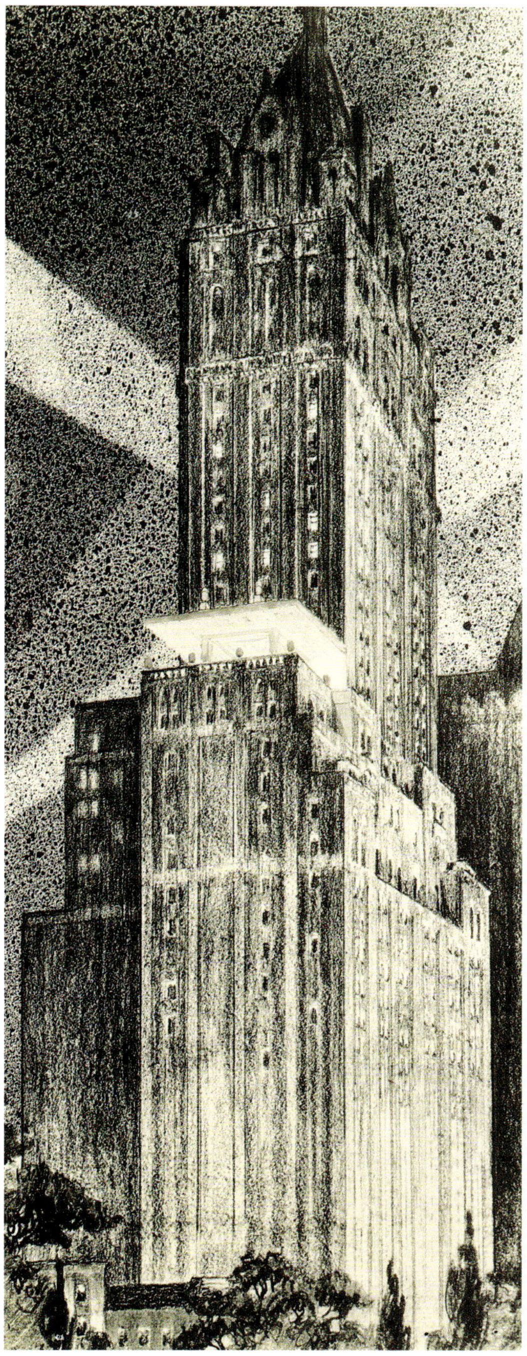

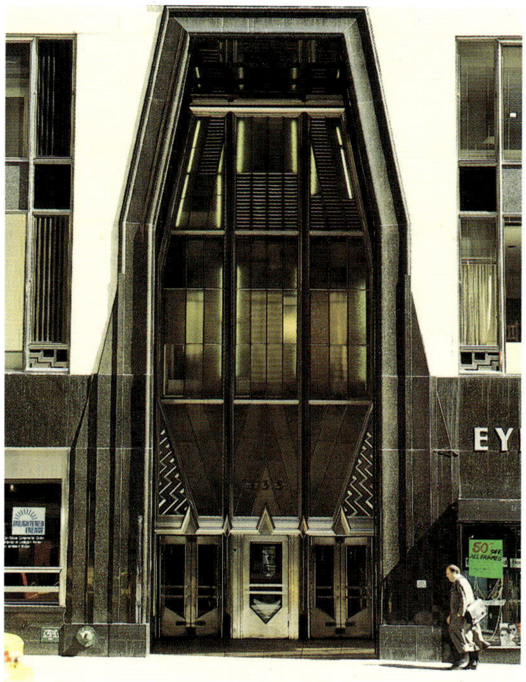

Far left:
Close-up and general view of a restaurant to be built on one of the terraces of the Sherry-Netherland Hotel in New York. Design and drawings by Jacques Carlu, 1929. This hotel, the tallest in the world at the time of its construction, was built facing Central Park in 1926 by Schultze & Weaver, architects, in association with Buchman and Kahn.
Institut français d'architecture.

Left:
Chrysler Building, New York, detail of an entrance. William Van Alen, architect, 1930.
© Benoît Roland.

New York Daily News: the lobby with the huge terrestrial globe. Raymond Hood and John Mead Howells, architects, 1930.
© Benoît Roland.

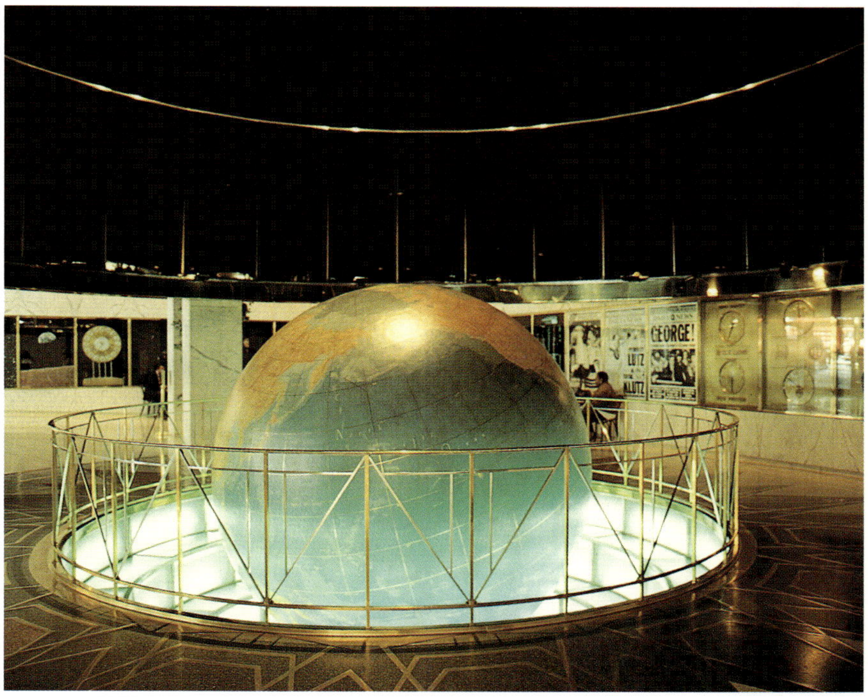

where all the activity of the street is artificially recreated in a world of hanging gardens and piano bars, traversed by a constellation of glass elevators that hang like paper lanterns at a fête—interior town planning, complementing or substituting for exterior public space. Portman was to produce numerous versions of the atrium hotel: in Atlanta (1967, 1975, and 1985), Los Angeles (1977), Singapore (1982 and 1987) and Shanghai (1990), but the formula, very popular from the outset, spread well beyond the architect's personal output.

The public dimension of the base of the skyscraper takes on a special sense in the case of Times Square, and similarly in the Shibuya crossroads in Tokyo, where the façades at ground level become advertising sites, an illuminated wall newspaper—an obvious comparison in a newspaper district named after a great daily.[7] The façades are now obligatorily devoted to advertising up to at least 40 meters (120 feet) high and neon lights occasionally take the entire wall by storm.

Another strategy, inaugurated by the Rockefeller Center and updated a generation later by the Seagram Building, consists of setting back the entrance of the building to the far side of a public plaza. The skyscraper, thus put into perspective, gains in monumentality while retaining its sealed-off, private character. With the World Trade Center the metaphorical threshold becomes the principal element. The two towers form a gate to

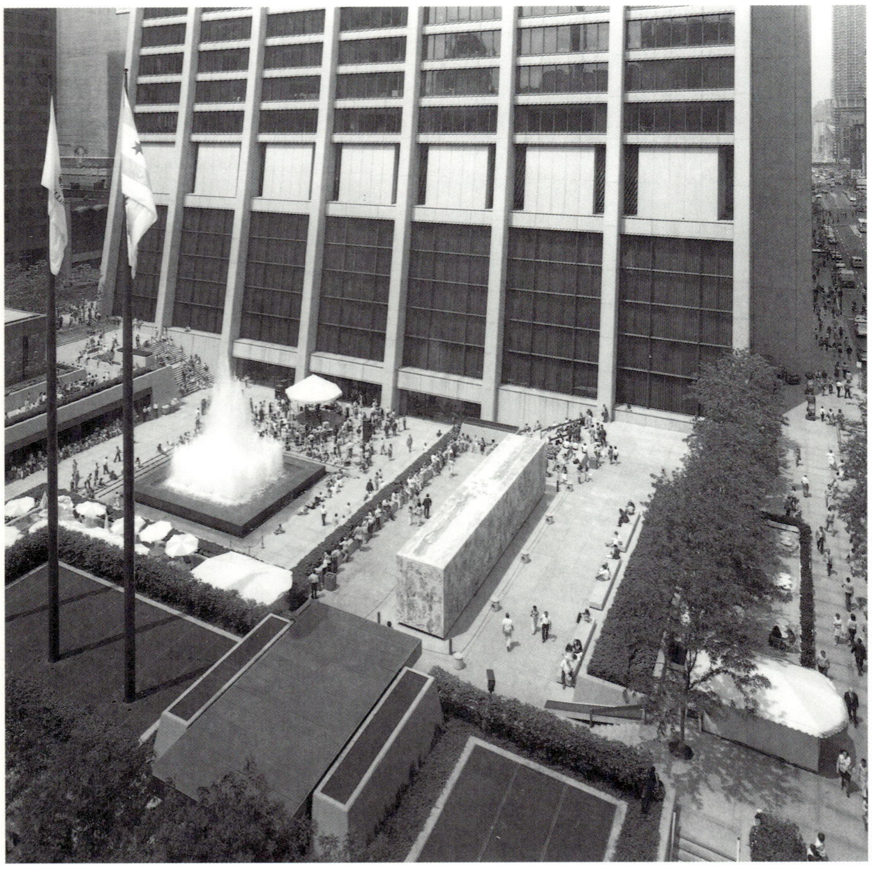

Left:
First National Bank Building, 1969 (now One First National Plaza) and the public plaza on Monroe Street in Chicago, 1972. C.F. Murphy Associates, in association with Perkins & Will.
Chicago Historical Society. Phot. Hedrich-Blessing.

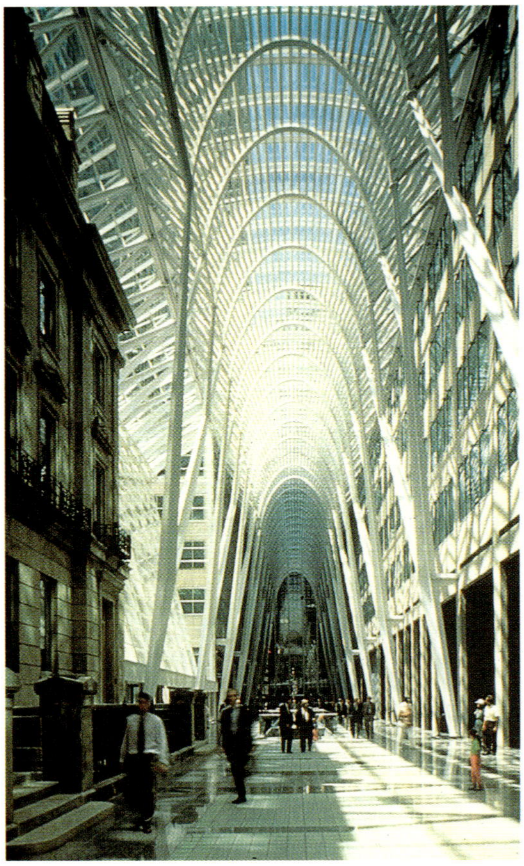

Right:
Galleria, Toronto, covered walkway connecting the Canada Trust and Bay-Wellington Towers (SOM, in association with Bregman + Hamann). Santiago Calatrava, architect, 1992.
© David Burley.

the city, "a doorway as high as infinity, the point where the parallels intersect... it is hardly an accident that this metaphor should be developed in a time of invisible communication."[8]

Another empty space is defined today at the entry to Dallas on the axis of the highway leading to Houston. But here it is a window—an eye of Cyclops which the setting sun lights up at the summit of a glass tower—the Texas Commerce Tower, designed by Richard Keating for SOM in 1987. This hollow motif, already tried out in Miami by the Arquitectonica Group[9] with its square window, spiral staircase, projecting balcony and inevitable palm tree, forms the tympanum in negative of a broad pediment. This macro-capping is a pop-art device acting as a highly recognizable signal as soon as the skyline of the city comes into view in the distance.

A few years earlier an equally enlarged broken pediment had arrived to crown the building designed by Philip Johnson and John Burgee for AT&T in New York,[10] the first post-modern skyscraper to dare to display an old-fashioned top (English Chippendale-style rococo) after several decades of monolithic towers—columns reduced to their shaft without base or capital.

The shock was stunning, the bonds of modernist rigor instantly broken. Helmut Jahn, Kevin Roche, Cesar Pelli, Michael Graves, William Pedersen and the European Ricardo Bofill, who was enthroned by this renaissance, but also each in his own way, Ieoh Ming Pei and SOM—David

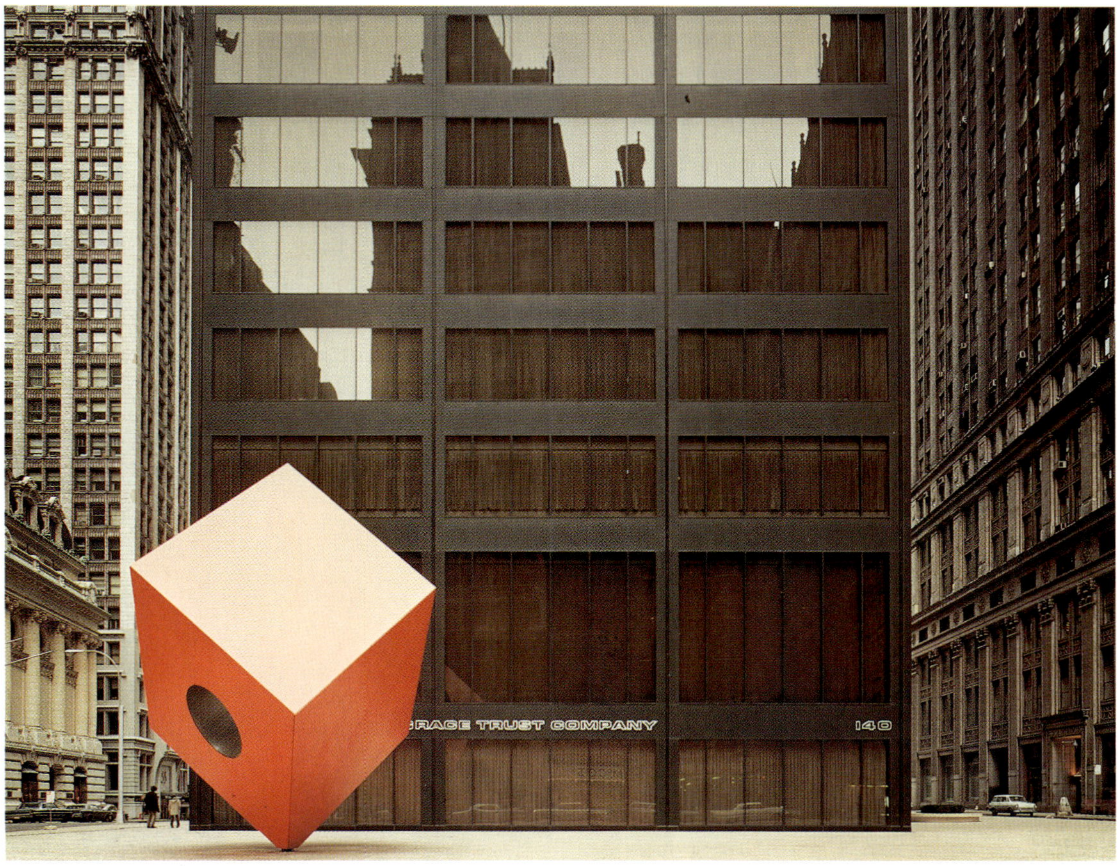

140 Broadway, New York, detail of the esplanade with the red cube sculpture by Isamu Noguchi. SOM New York, architects (Gordon Bunshaft), 1968.
© Ezra Stoller, Esto Photographics.

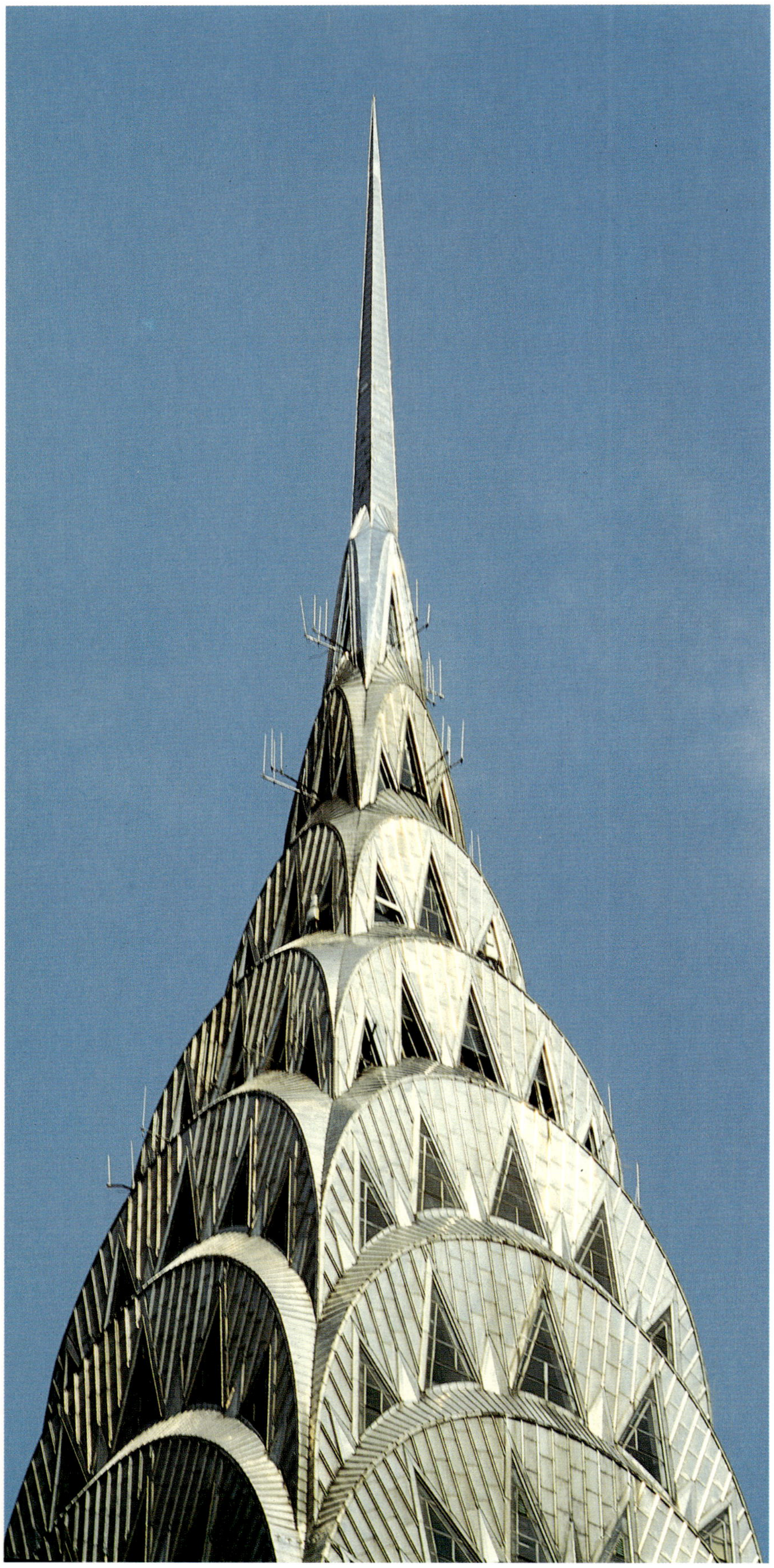

Childs in New York and Adrian Smith in Chicago—rediscovered the lyricism of the tops of the early towers. A skyscraper, said Cass Gilbert at the beginning of the century, is like a piece of music "whose final notes give us the highest pitch of emotion before they are lost in the silence."[11] Some designed projecting attics and cornices, others pinned on pinnacles, plumes or lacy borders on Neo-Gothic lines. Towers, turrets, belvederes, triangular pediments, pyramids, spheres, spirals and crystal formations took possession of the peaks. This crowning theme reached the stage of paroxysm when the whole building began to resemble a summit (the Transamerica Pyramid of San Francisco is an

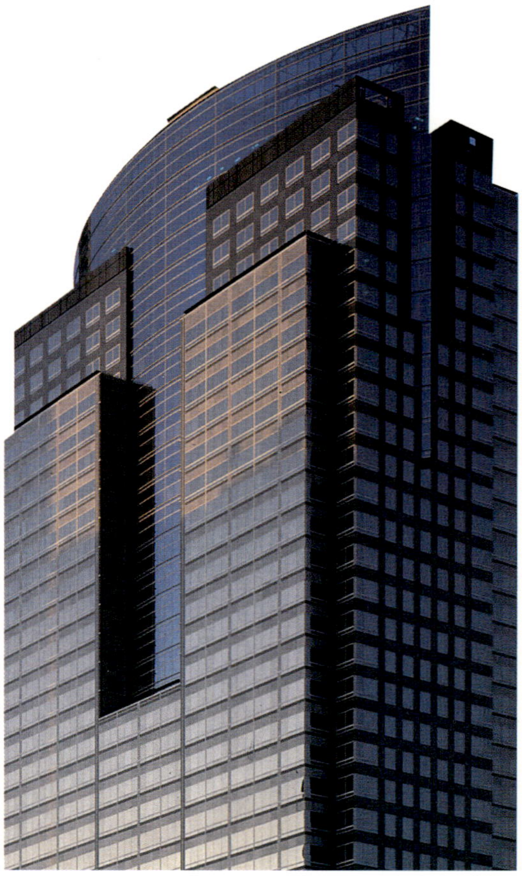

arrow that takes shape from ground level)[12] or when, at the opposite extreme, the summit disappears into the sky, blending with the clouds—a tower without ends as imagined by the French architect Jean Nouvel.[13]

Paradoxically, the summit of a skyscraper is full of technical equipment: elevator mechanisms, air vents, shock-absorbing systems, water tanks—a ship's engine room suspended in the air—to which must be added, when the tower is very tall, a forest of antennae, leaseholders of the roof. Most often the capping is simply to conceal technical functions and equipment. But it can, in an allegory of the machine age, arrange and display this great engine room which elsewhere lies hidden. By night, like the beating heart of a sleeping skyscraper, the illuminated crest of the Gas Company Tower shines out like a torch in the Los Angeles sky.[14] Within the transparent summit of the Tour Sans Fins a huge weight will swing to the rhythm of the high winds like the pendulum of a celestial clock. Elsewhere in the world, visitors wait in line for elevators to carry them to the observation platforms of the World Trade Center (New York), the Sears Tower (Chicago) and the Landmark Tower (Yokohama)—the tallest tower in Japan, planted like a lighthouse at the mouth of the river Ooka.[15] Going up skyscrapers is an undeniable success with the public. Belvederes,

Opposite, left:
Chrysler Building, New York.
William Van Alen, architect, 1930.
© Benoît Roland.
Right:
The Gas Company Tower, Los Angeles.
Richard Keating, architect, for SOM Los Angeles, 1991.
© Joe C. Aker.

Left:
Texas Commerce Tower, Dallas.
SOM Houston, architects (Richard Keating), 1987.
DMJM Keating.
Right:
AT&T Corporate Headquarters, New York.
Johnson / Burgee Architects, 1983.
© Timothy Hursley.

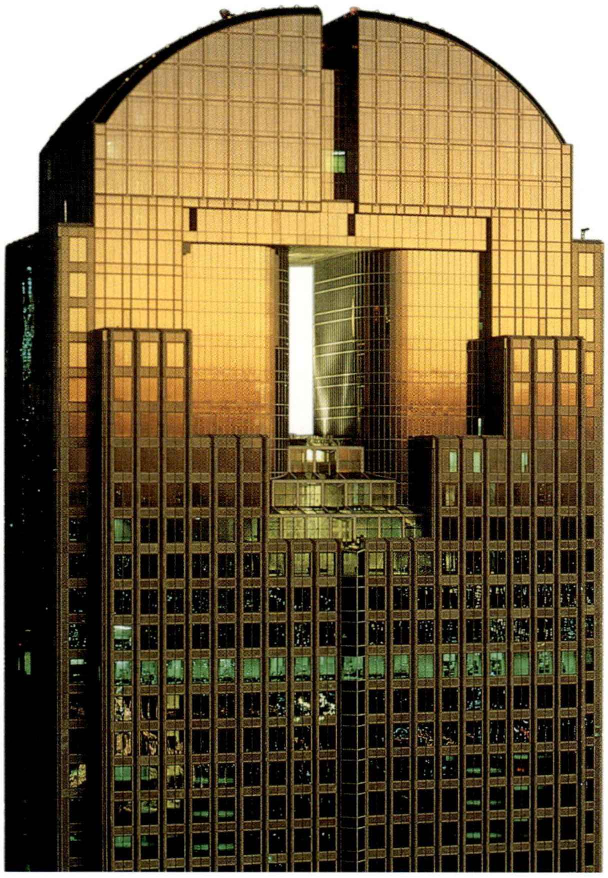

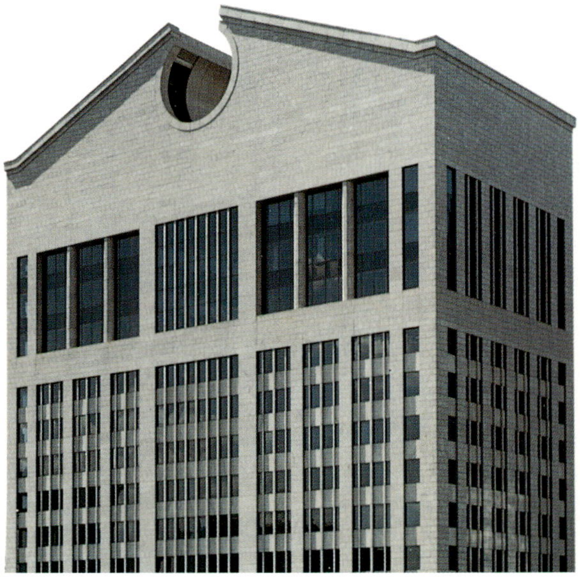

panoramic restaurants (particularly liked by the Chinese), educational exhibitions, "skyshops" have become a highlight of urban tourism.

Where does this seemingly old-fashioned infatuation arise from?
It's true that a city seen from high up is idealized, without noise or smells or danger, but with the readability of a scale model. In fact bird's-eye views were used in abundance during the conquest of the West to promote new towns.[16] You look down to admire, to understand and accordingly to reassure yourself.

Unless it's a higher instinct, pushing mankind towards the celestial heights. "If one of our first fears... is the fear of falling; if the greatest of the human responsibilities—physical and moral—is responsibility for our verticality, how much must the dream that sets us upright, that emphasizes our straightness... that rids us of our weight, that gives us... our sole aerial experience, how much must such a dream be health-giving, comforting, marvelous and moving!"[17]

At the summit of the skyscraper, metaphor becomes reality.

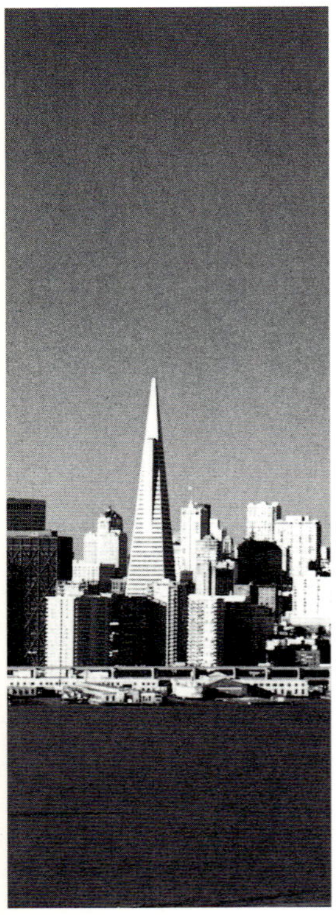

**Transamerica Pyramid,
San Francisco.
William L. Pereira Associates,
architects, 1972.**
Buildings & Data.

1. Joseph RYKWERT, *On Adam's House in Paradise,* The Museum of Modern Art, New York, 1972. The description is retranslated from the French edition : *La Maison d'Adam au paradis,* Seuil, Paris, 1976.
2. Quoted by Diana AGREST in "Le Ciel est la limite", *L'Architecture d'aujourd'hui,* No. 178, Paris, March/April 1975. Published in *English in Oppositions,* No. 11, New York, 1977.
3. The New York Daily News Building was designed by the architects John Mead HOWELLS and Raymond HOOD. The comparison with the headquarters of *The Chicago Tribune* is taken from Katherine SOLOMONSON, "Des Gratte-ciel pour les journaux aux USA", *Enquête sur les sièges de l'info,* Pavillon de l'Arsenal/Hazan, Paris, 1994.
4. The Field Building (now the LaSalle National Bank Building) is the work of the architects GRAHAM, ANDERSON, PROBST & WHITE. The Rookery Building, built by John Wellborn ROOT in 1888, was modernized by Frank Lloyd WRIGHT in 1905. It was restored in 1993.
5. The expression is borrowed, on the subject of the IDS Center, from Paul GOLDBERGER in *The Skyscraper,* Alfred A. Knopf, New York, 1981.
6. JOHNSON / BURGEE Architects, Minneapolis, 1972.
7. The headquarters of *The New York Times* was installed on 42nd Street in 1904 (architect C.L.W. EIDLITZ). The newspaper gave its name to Times Square.
8. Diana AGREST, op. cit.
9. The Atlantis apartment block (Miami 1982) was made world famous by the title sequence of the American TV series *Miami Vice.*
10. JOHNSON / BURGEE Architects, 1983.
11. This quotation of Cass GILBERT, architect of the Woolworth Building in New York (1913), is taken from *History of the Skyscraper* by Francisco MUJICA, Archaeology & Architecture Press, Paris-New York, 1929.
12. Architect William L. PEREIRA (William L. Pereira Associates), 1972.
13. The Tour Sans Fins project (1989) by Jean NOUVEL is intended for La Défense district in Paris.
14. Architect Richard KEATING (SOM Los Angeles), 1991.
15. The Stubbins Associates, Architects, in association with Mitsubishi Estate Company, 1993.
16. These promotional bird's-eye views sometimes deliberately misled potential buyers by giving a completely imaginary picture of the towns they represented. From John W. REPS, *Cities on Stone, Nineteenth Century Lithograph Images of the Urban West,* Amon Carter Museum, Fortworth, 1976.
17. Gaston BACHELARD, "Le Rêve de vol", *L'Air et les Songes,* Librairie José Corti, Paris, 1943.

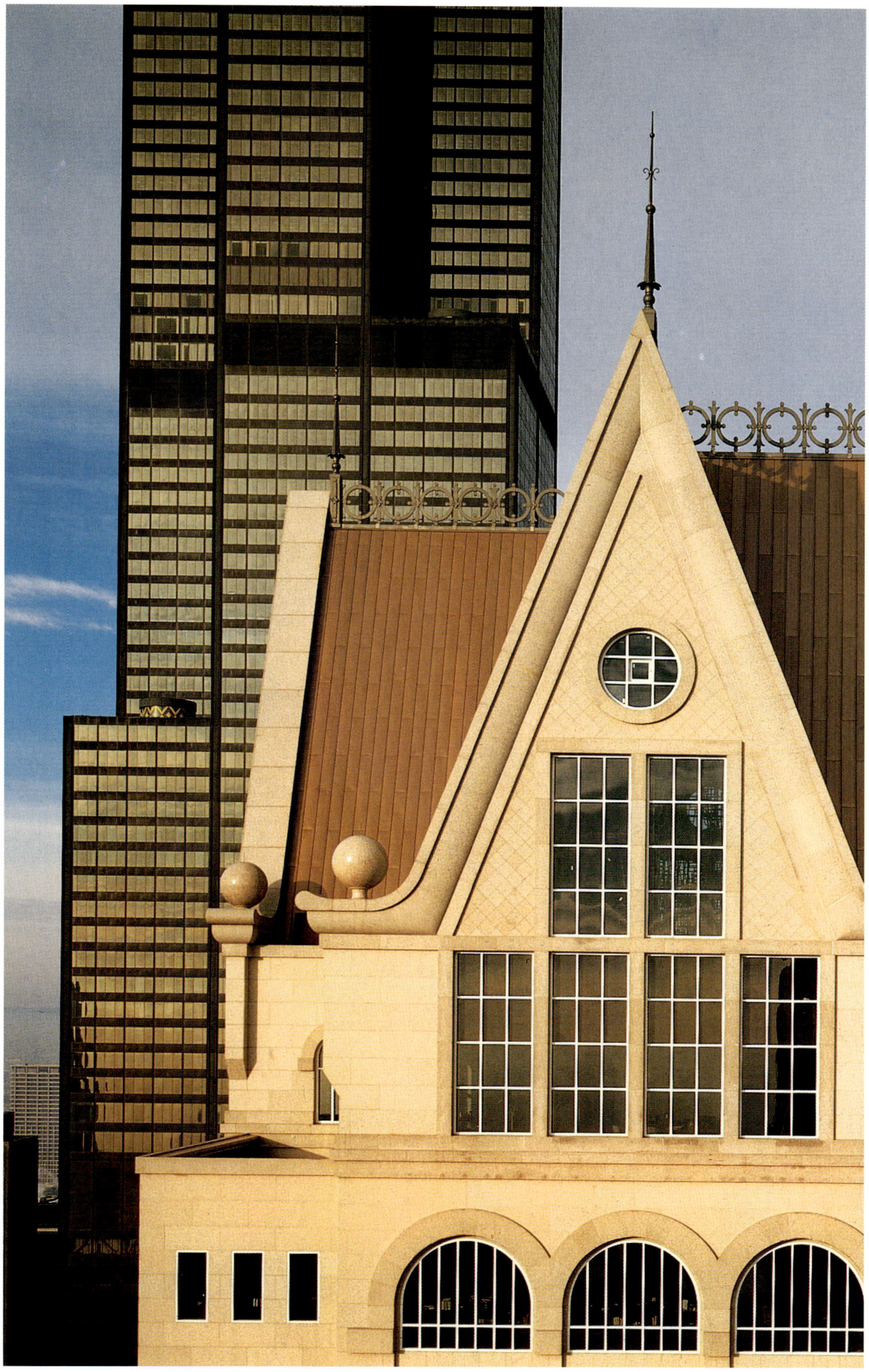

190 South LaSalle, Chicago, detail of the summit. John Burgee Architects with Philip Johnson, 1987. In the background, the Sears Tower (SOM, 1974).
© Nick Merrick, Hedrich-Blessing, 1987.

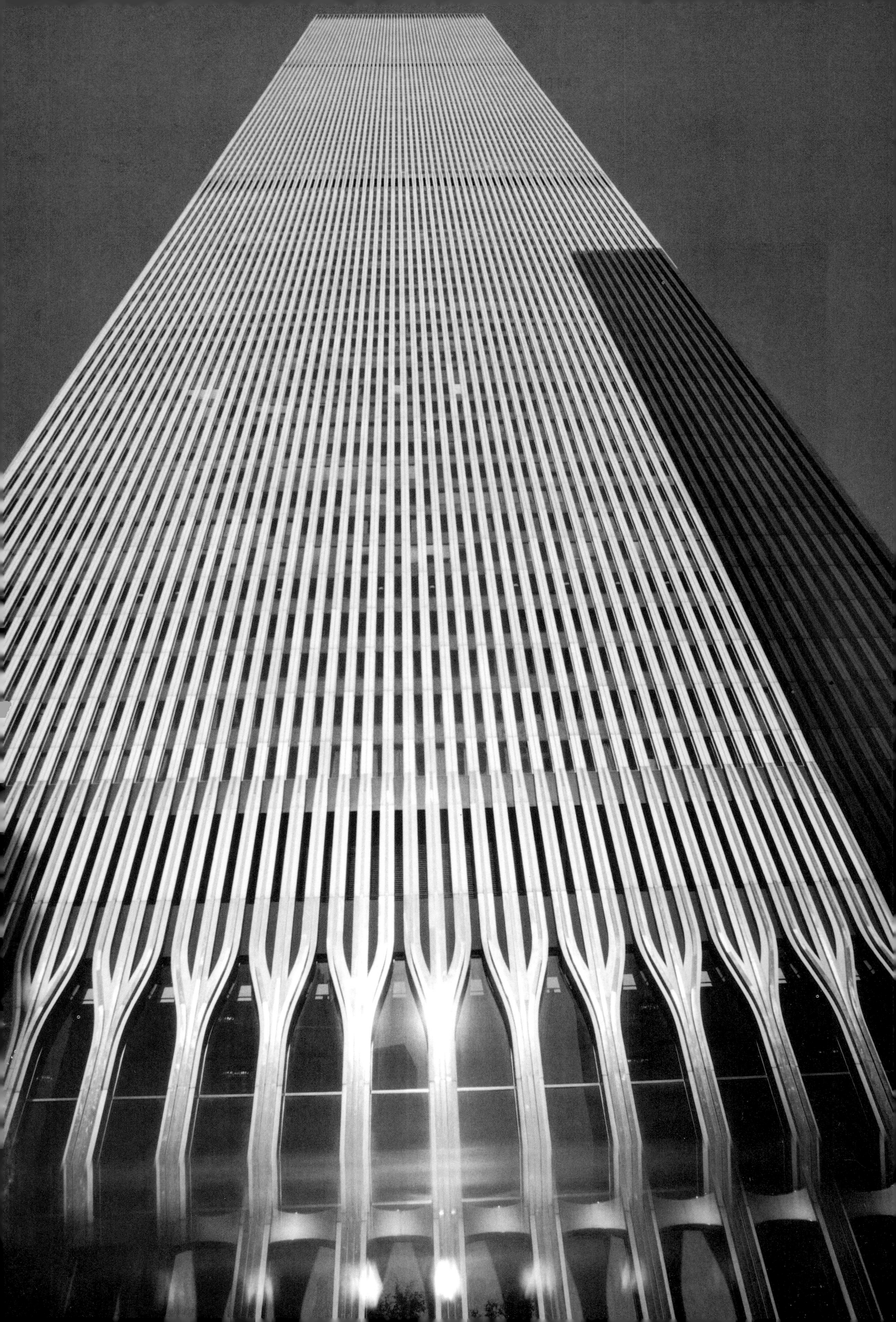

THE HEIGHTS OF TECHNOLOGY

"Some window cleaners start at the bottom of the skyscraper. This gives them time to get used to it; they lose contact with the ground gradually. John prefers to descend, floor by floor. This second method is called the dead leaf technique. According to John it's more human."

Didier Decoin, *John l'enfer*, 1977.

Opposite:
World Trade Center, New York, detail of the exterior "tube" structure. Minoru Yamasaki and Associates, architects, in association with Emery Roth & Sons, 1972.
© Richard Edelman.

The history of the skyscraper is closely linked to technical progress. Load-bearing masonry would never have permitted the construction of inhabited buildings of more than eight to ten stories. The thickness of the walls, in conflict with lighting needs, would also have reduced the available space, seriously compromising the economic viability of the project. Closer to our own time, at the end of the sixties, the development of the principle of tube structure made possible at a stroke the doubling of the number of floors. The obvious impetus given to tall building by the invention of the elevator is also well known.

Nevertheless technology was not the only determining factor. An exclusively technological approach to the history of skyscrapers would constantly run up against contradictions. How to place, for example, the astonishing modernity of the Monadnock Building (Chicago, 1891) when you know that it was built entirely of bricks. How to understand the impact of the New York Headquarters of the AT&T Building (1983), which put Philip Johnson on the cover of Time Magazine, when it brings a vocabulary and materials into play that refer to history. Neither the invention of the telephone or, more recently, the fax machine,

"A City Within a City," cover illustration of the magazine *The Architectural Forum*, January 1932, Part II, "Engineering & Business," Vol. LVI, No. 1.
Archives d'architecture moderne, Brussels.

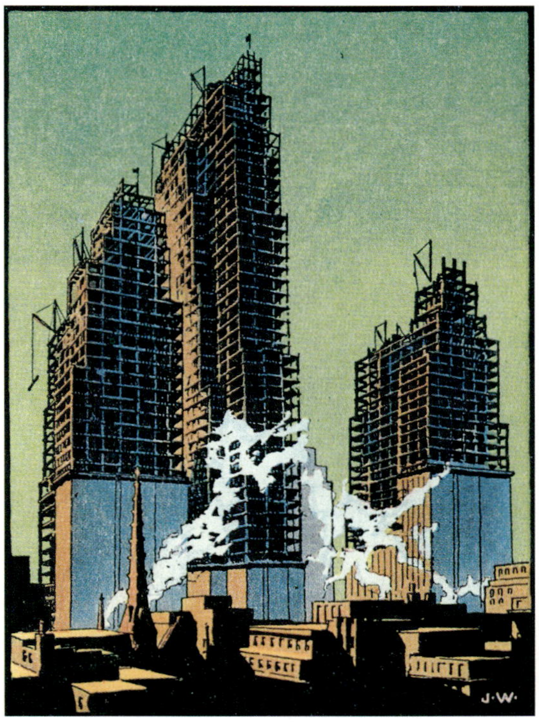

nor the introduction of the fluorescent tube or air-conditioning have significantly affected the design of the skyscraper. At best they have made its use more comfortable and convenient. The American critic Winston Weisman points out, for example, the contradiction that exists between the installation of air-conditioning and the glazed curtain-wall, a question of appearance and the psychological effect on employees. "The first major change brought on by a new material and structural system was in the Price Tower by Frank Lloyd Wright, where reinforced concrete and a core system of cantilevering made possible a more flexible ordering of the floor spaces and an exterior that broke away from the square or rectangular box. But this still leaves fifty years, or half of the skyscraper's history, unaccounted for."[1]

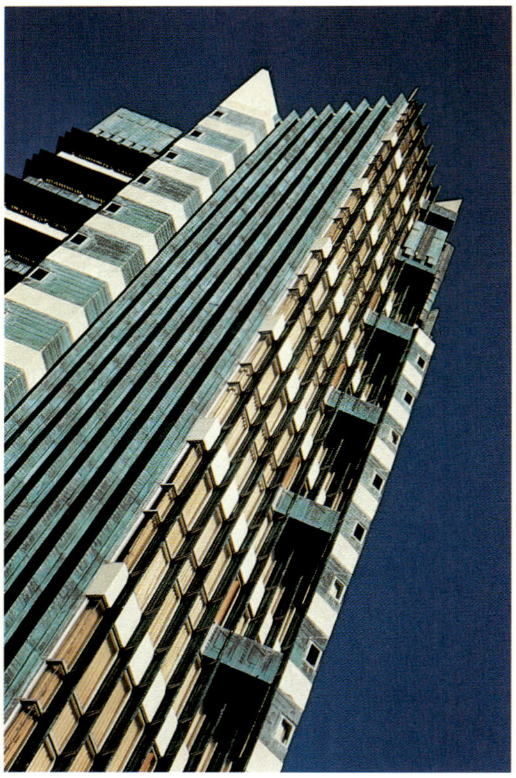

Price Company Tower, Bartlesville, view of the upper floors. Frank Lloyd Wright, architect, 1956.
© J. Spencer Lake.

Tall buildings nevertheless pose a number of problems that architects cannot overcome single-handed. The skyscraper is also the work of engineers. For just as economics, aesthetics, environment, life-styles affect the building sector, so does technology. The increase in scale dramatizes the stakes and multiplies the risks. Because it pushes architecture to its extreme limits, the skyscraper is caricature, large scale model and tour de force rolled into one.

It must be realized, for example, that wind pressure on a building varies geometrically as a function of height. And it is precisely these lateral forces which pose the key problem of the stability of skyscrapers. "If not counteracted by proper design, these forces would cause a tall building to slide on its base, twist on its axis, oscillate uncontrollably, bend excessively or break in two."[2] The height of a skyscraper has always been determined by the capacity of its structure to resist the lateral forces of wind and earthquake; 15 to 20 stories for a steel framework system made rigid by masonry walls; up to 60 stories, 200 meters (650 feet) high for a steel framework system made rigid by a load-bearing core, 30 meters (100 feet) wide; higher still with a bigger core, but this would be to the detriment of the economic viability of the building.
When the structural role is shifted from the core to the outside walls of the building, resistance is increased together, proportionally, with possible height. A tower with a 50-meter wide base (164 feet) can thus rise to 300 meters (984 feet), even 350 meters (1,148 feet). Higher than this, beyond a slenderness ratio of 1:7 (a height 7 times the width of the base) the oscillation of the tower under wind pressure would become uncomfortable while increasing the area would mean too large and somber office floors. This system of load bearing exterior walls or "tube structure"[3] was developed in the early sixties in

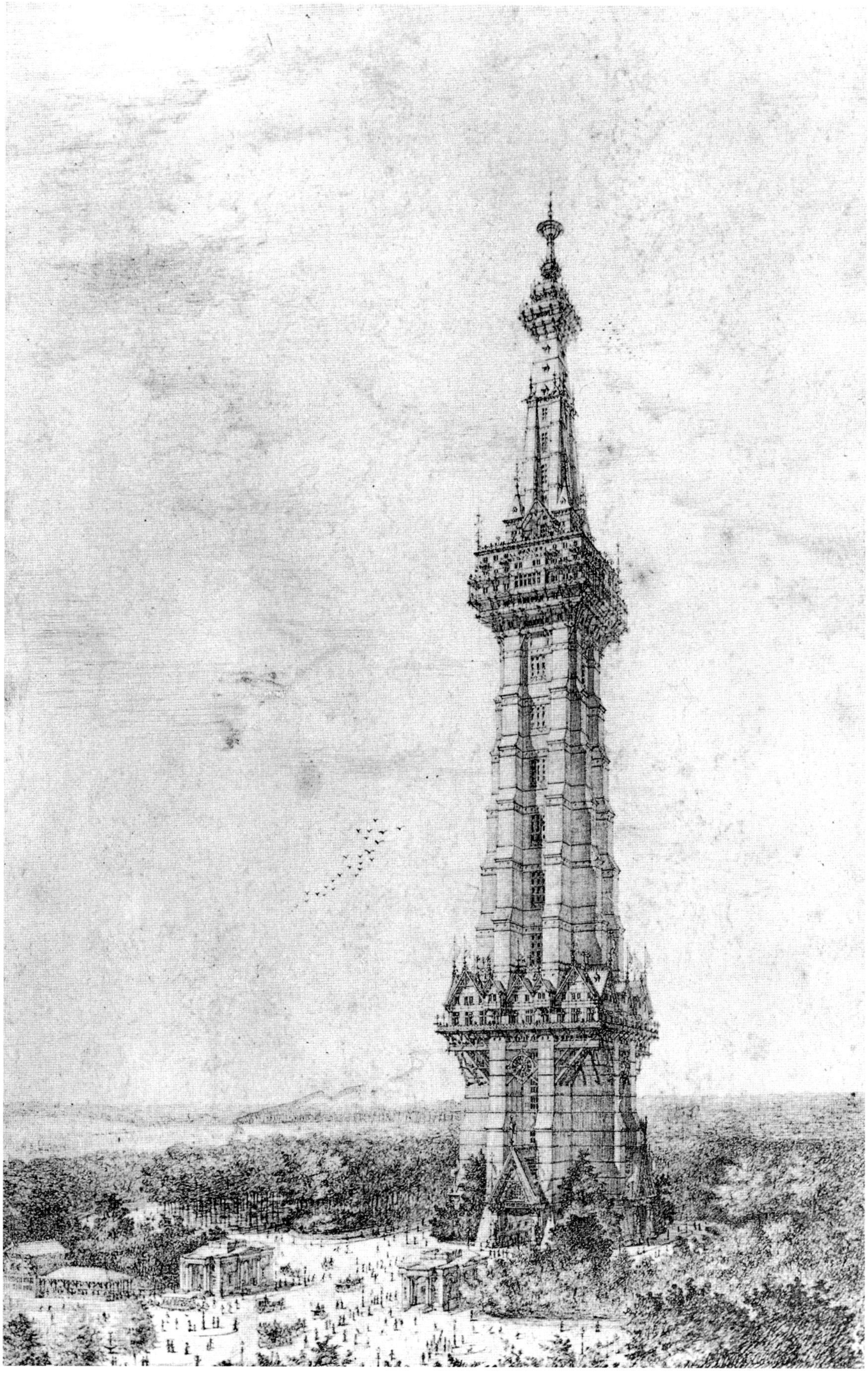

Unexecuted project for a 300 meters (984 feet) high wooden tower to have been built at the entrance to the Bois de la Cambre in Brussels. Léon Govaerts, architect; F. Hennebique and E. Nève, engineers and builders, 1887-1888.
Institut français d'architecture.

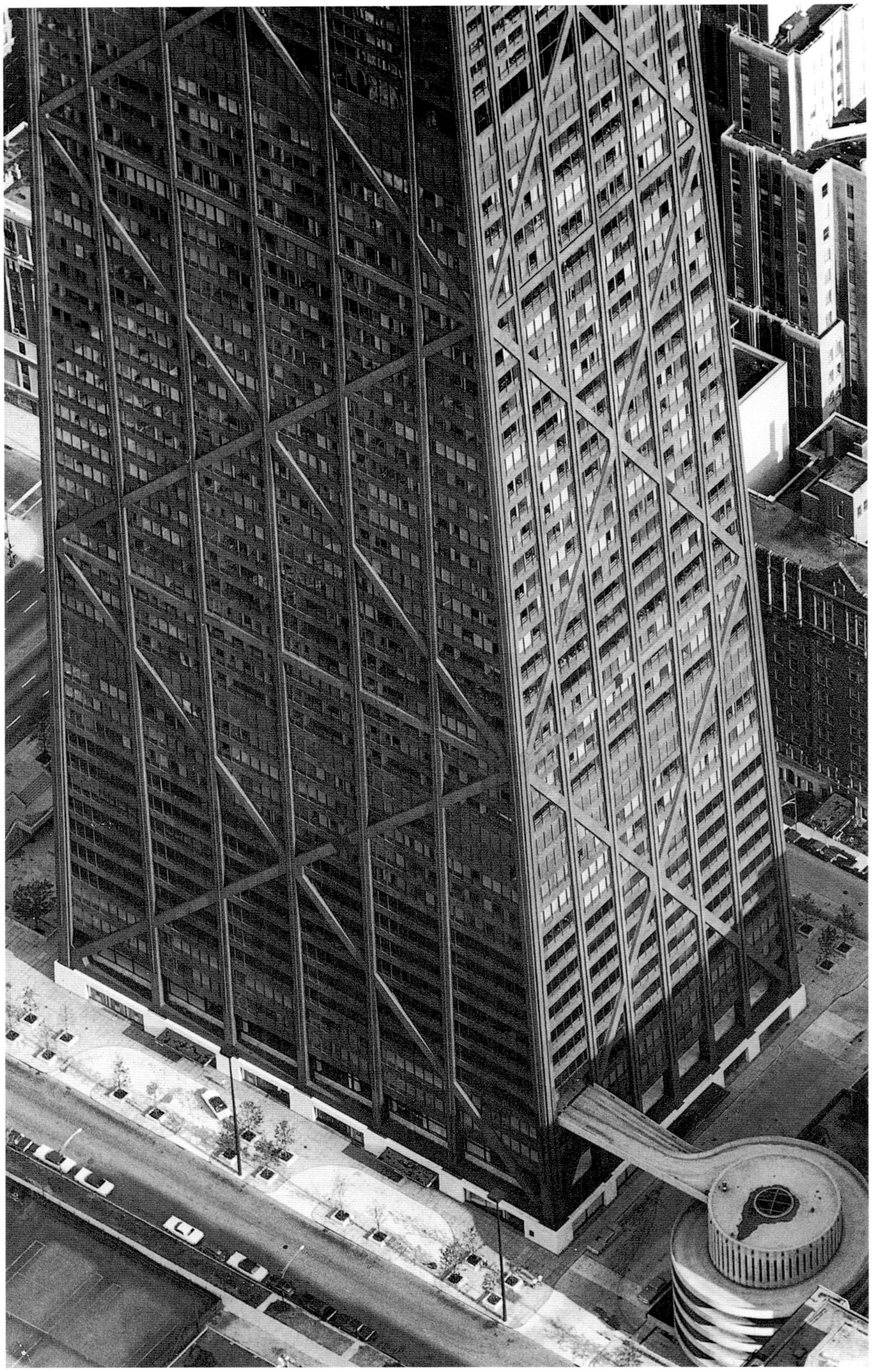

John Hancock Center, Chicago, detail of the exterior "trussed tube" structure. SOM Chicago (Bruce Graham, architect, and Fazlur Khan, engineer), 1969.
© Rapho, Paris. Phot. Georg Gester.

the academic context of the Illinois Institute of Technology (IIT) by the engineers Myron Goldsmith and Fazlur Khan, both of the SOM Chicago office. No spectacular advance has subsequently revolutionized the skyscraper from a structural point of view.

The best-known example of tube structure is the World Trade Center, built in New York in 1972—twin towers 415 meters (1,362 feet) high. The walls of the towers are made up of a rigid lattice of closely spaced columns and beams, defining narrow windows. The multiplication of structural elements on the walls, with the consequent cost of facing, rapidly led to the development of variations in constructions of this size, both more efficient and more economical; the trussed tube of the type used for the John Hancock Center in Chicago or the triangular trusses of Citicorp in New York, the tube-in-tube in which the rigid exterior element is joined by strong beams to a core which is also load bearing, the bundle of tubes—a solution required in buildings over a certain area and used for the Sears Tower in Chicago, or the project by Robert Sobel in Houston for a tower of 500 floors composed of a group of 16 triangular tubes.[4]

As well as steel structures there are those in concrete, more common in Europe. Steel technology is typically Anglo-American and linked to the development in metallurgy whereas concrete has long characterized construction in less industrialized countries. "Concrete is the poor man's material, not iron—a lot of stone and even more labor. By industrializing production it is possible to reduce the workers' level of skill and their number without increasing the cost of the raw material."[5] Only the scarcity of steel which hit America in the early post-war years explains why Mies van der Rohe built his first residential tower with a reinforced concrete frame.[6] The tower is limited to 21 stories but the thickness of the columns required by this technology would have harmfully invaded the interior space if it had exceeded 25 stories. Generally speaking, concrete is particularly well adapted to residential projects, hotels and apartments. The rigidity of the framework can be assured by the positioning of interior walls which also assume the role of partitions—transversal and radial walls in the case of the sixty-story Marina City in Chicago (1964). The narrowness of the spans compared to the width of office floors also permits economical ceiling heights, well adapted to the domestic scale.

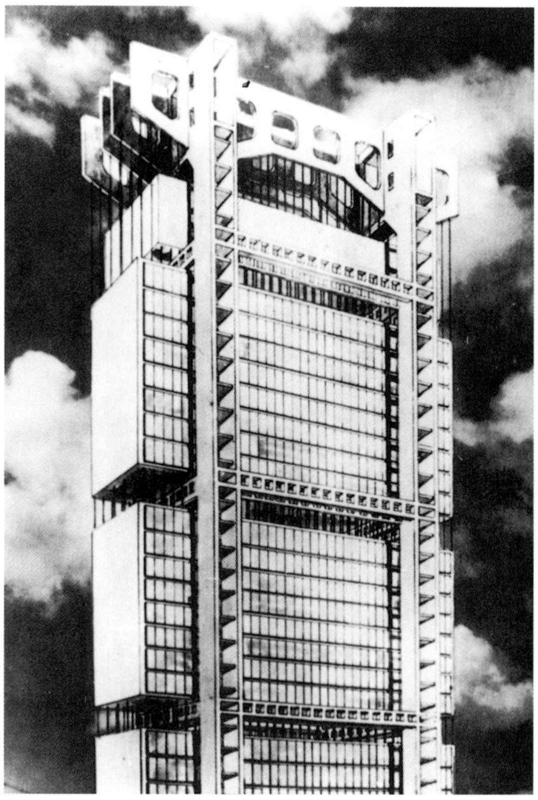

Project for a suspended office building, Buenos Aires, a photomontage. Amancio Williams, architect, 1946. The construction of the tower is made up of two groups of elements: a main structure in reinforced concrete and blocks of metallic floors suspended from it.
Jorge Silvetti, Amancio Williams, Rizzoli / Harvard University, Graduate School of Design, New York, 1987.

The concrete versus steel dichotomy has significantly lessened during the past few years.

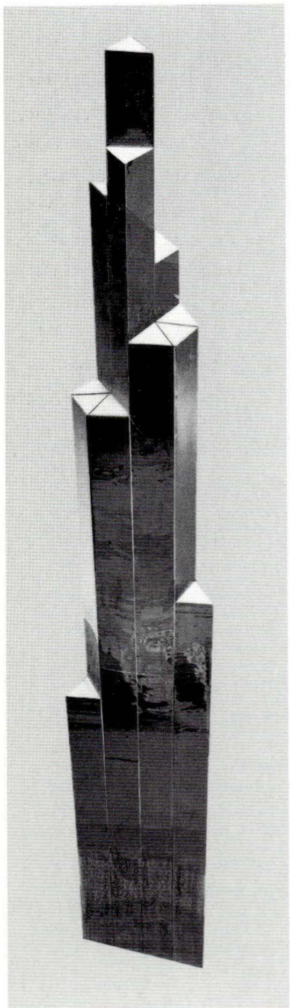

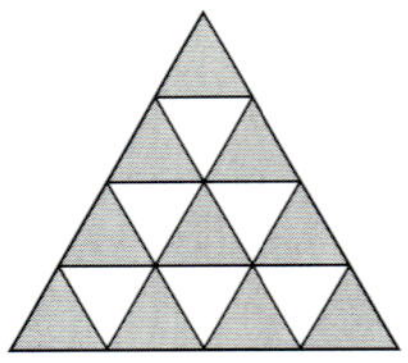

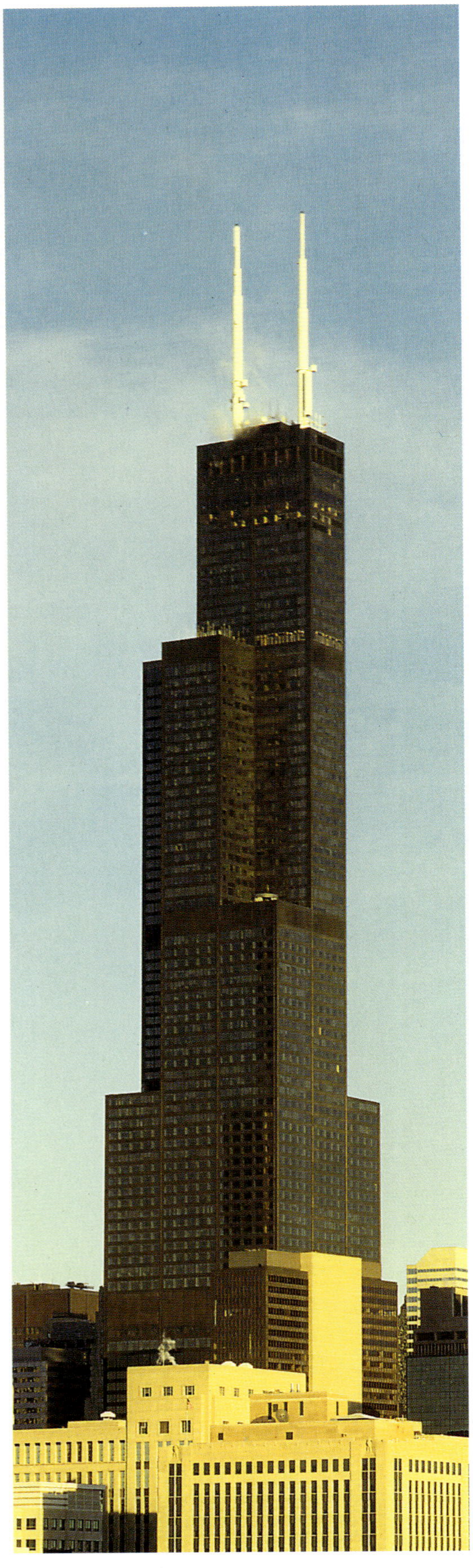

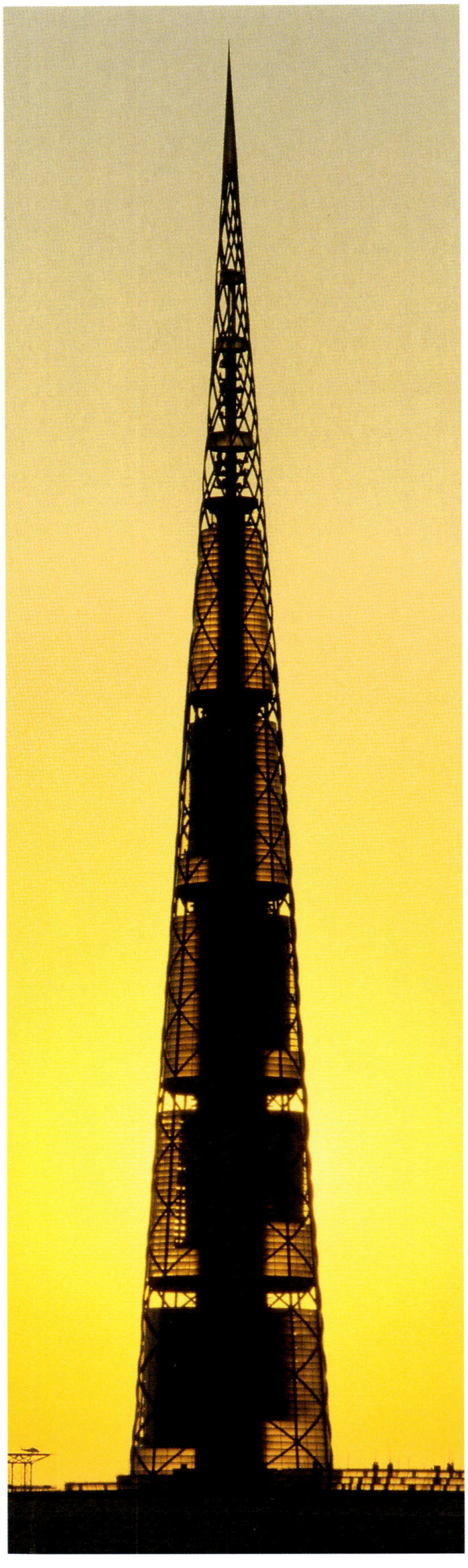

Project for a 500-story tower, Houston. Photograph of the scale model and ground plan. Robert Sobel, architect (Emery Roth & Sons), 1975. The tower is made up of sixteen 60-meter sided triangular tubes, arranged in an equilateral triangle.
Emery Roth & Sons.

Opposite, left:
Sears Tower, Chicago, overall stepped profile. SOM Chicago (Bruce Graham, architect and Fazlur Khan, engineer), 1974. The tower is made up of nine tubes arranged in a square.
© Benoît Roland.

Right:
Millennium Tower, Tokyo, scale model. Sir Norman Foster and Partners, 1989 (unexecuted). The 840 meters (2,756 feet) high tower is wrapped in a helical structure totally integrated with the tapering building form.
Sir Norman Foster and Partners. Phot. Richard Davies.

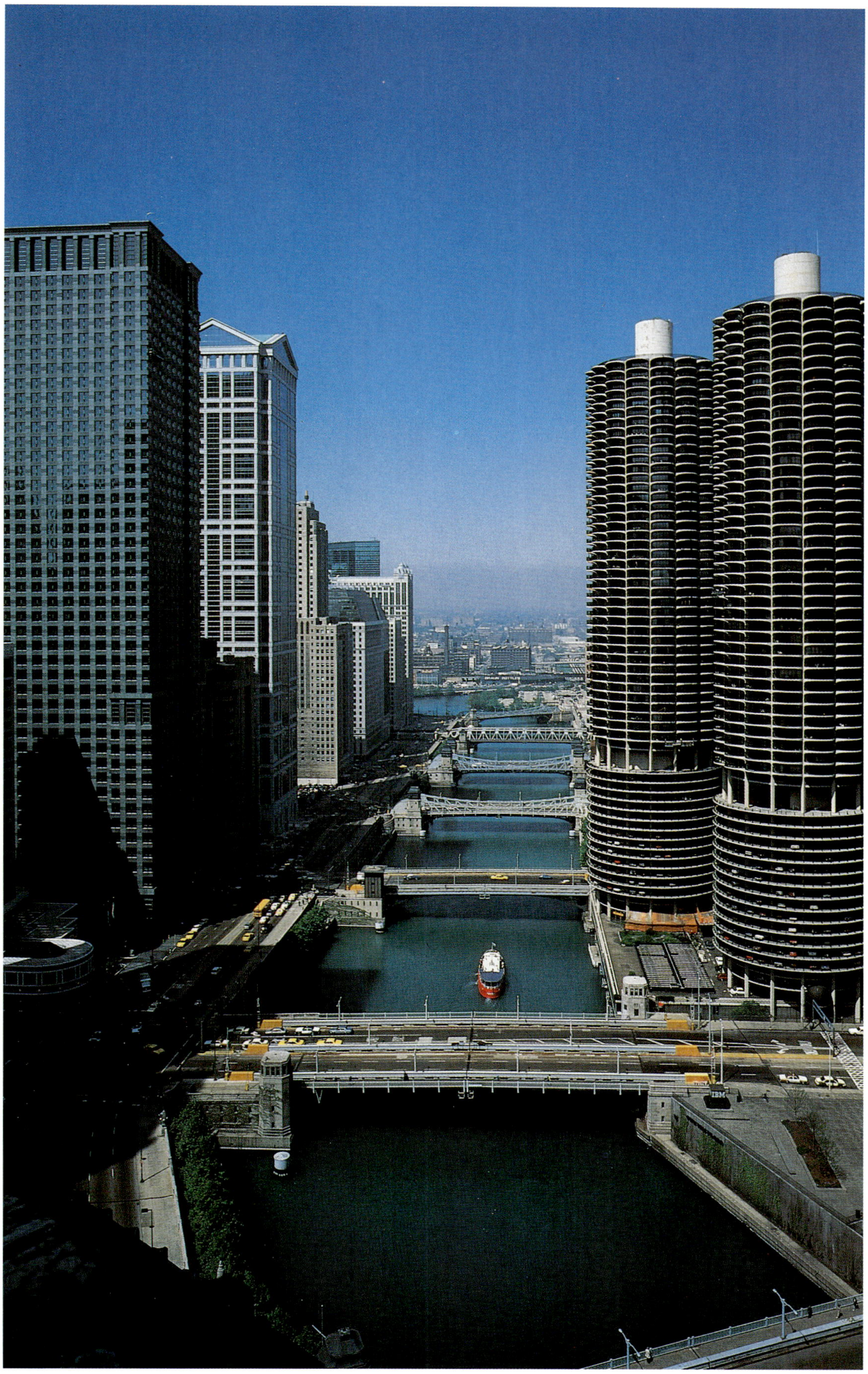

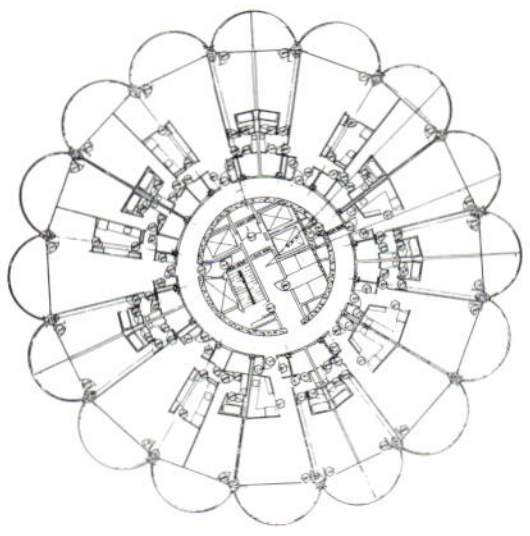

Above:
Marina City, Chicago, typical floor plan of the residential towers. Bertrand Goldberg, architect, 1964. The radiating concrete structure corresponds to the partition walls of the apartments.
Institut français d'architecture.

Left:
General view of the Chicago River. On the left, the Leo Burnett Company Tower (Kevin Roche, 1989) and 77 West Wacker (Ricardo Bofill, 1992); on the right, the two Marina City residential towers (Bertrand Goldberg, 1964).
© John Gronkowski.

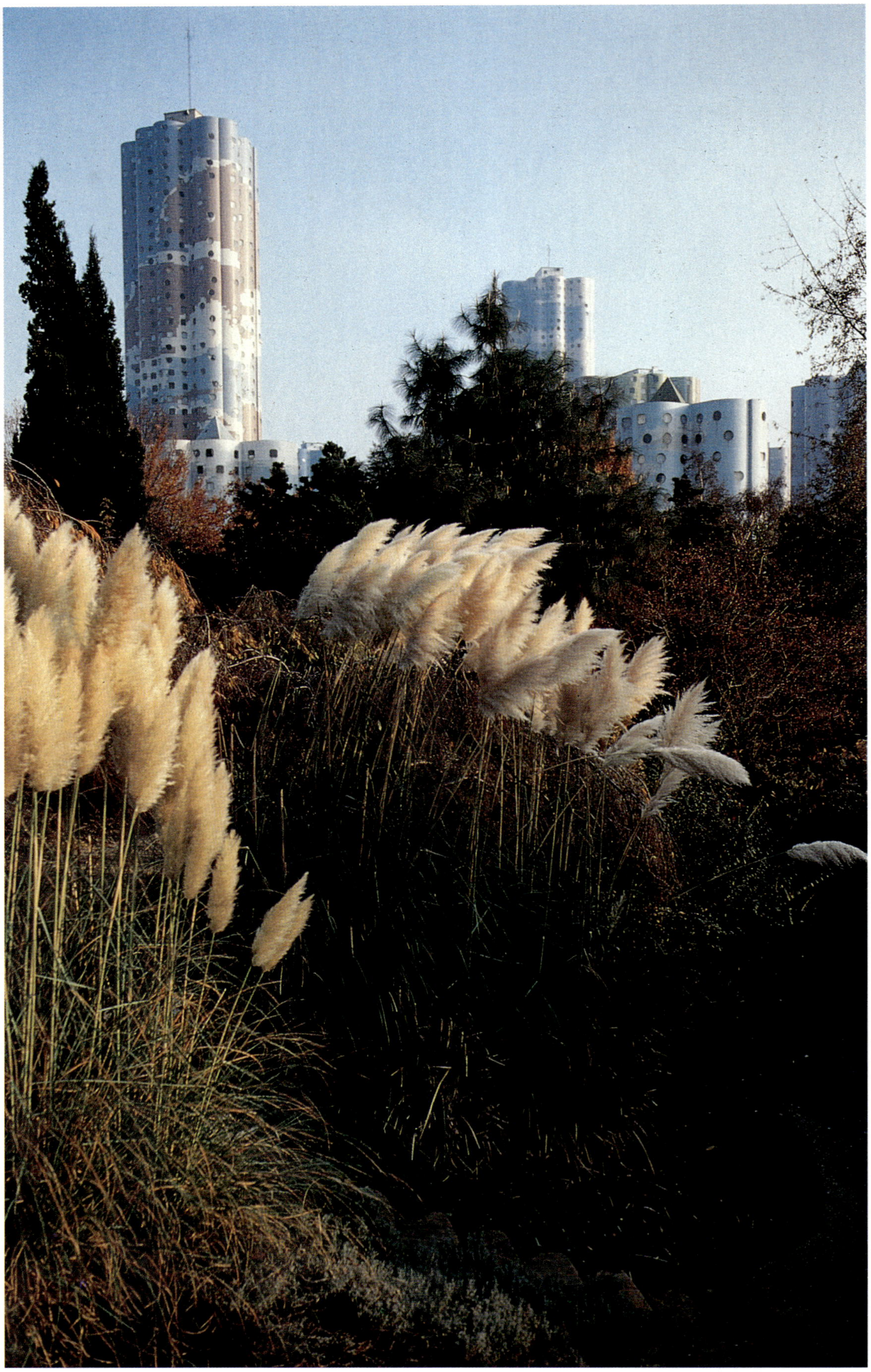

Tours Nuages (Cloud Towers), social housing in La Défense district of Paris. The exterior concrete "tube" structure has a colored vitreous facing. Emile Aillaud, architect, 1977.
EPAD.

Opposite:
Commerzbank, Frankfurt, plan and cross section showing the atrium. Sir Norman Foster and Partners, architects, 1997 (under construction). The triangular arrangement of the three office wings around a central atrium accentuates the slenderness of each part of the tower, 16 meters (52 feet) maximum width for a height of 259 meters (850 feet), and ensures direct natural lighting for each office.
Sir Norman Foster and Partners.

Firstly, concrete now performs competitively with steel. High strength concrete, thanks to chemical additives, can now bear pressure four or five times greater than standard reinforced concrete.[7]

Furthermore, concrete and steel have long been used together to build composite structures in which thinner steel columns are surrounded by concrete. This permits a less cumbersome structure than in the case of a purely concrete column and offers good fire resistance, the fast assembly of steel and the economy of concrete. The mixed concrete and steel structure can take several other forms—load-bearing core in concrete and outside wall framework in steel (as in the case of the Montparnasse Tower in Paris), concrete tube structure on the outside, steel beams and floors on the inside—a solution which would have saved 25 million dollars in Helmut Jahn's project for Southwest Center in Houston.[8]

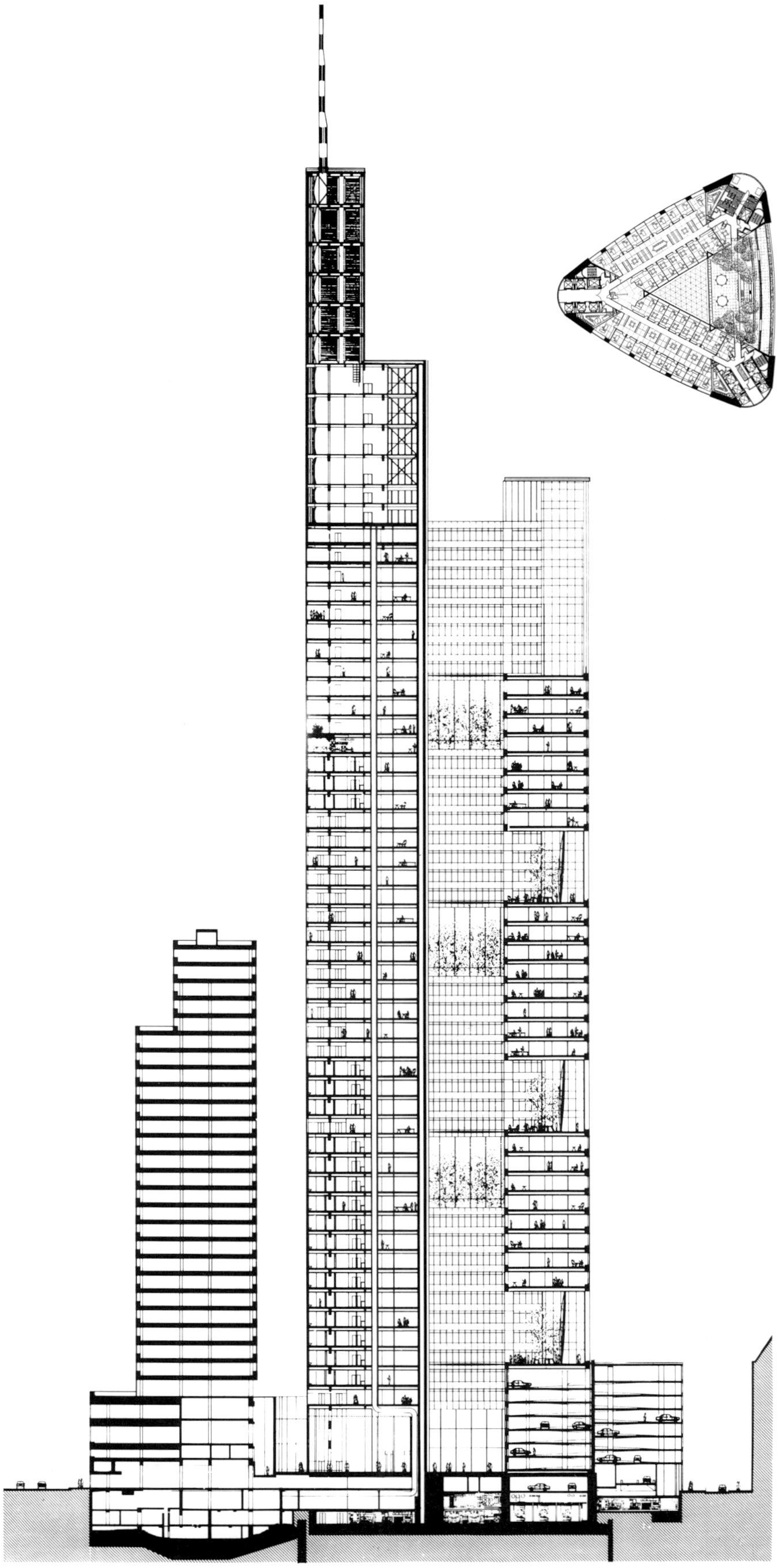

If there is any further progress to be made it lies in the solution to the problem of constructing yet taller and proportionally narrower buildings. An initial solution lies in the architectural arrangement. A group of several towers can be connected by "sky-ways" so that they reinforce each other, the equivalent of increasing the base area of the structure to include all the space between the towers. On a smaller scale, the hollow building arranged round a large atrium offers the same advantages. The Commerzbank under construction in Frankfurt, like the Hong Kong Bank a project by architect Foster and engineers

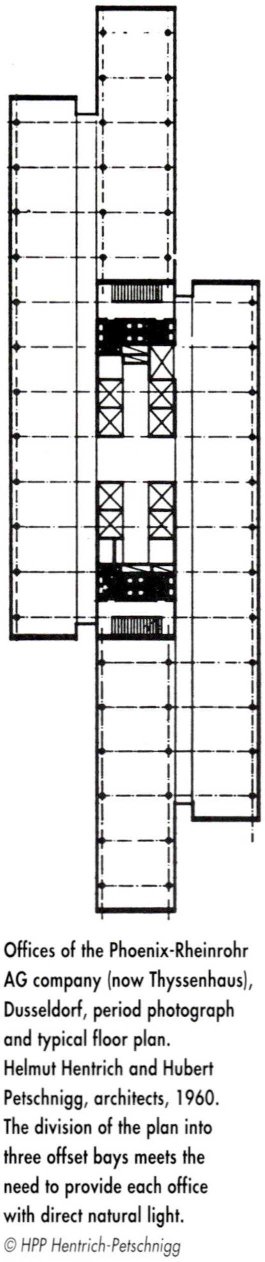

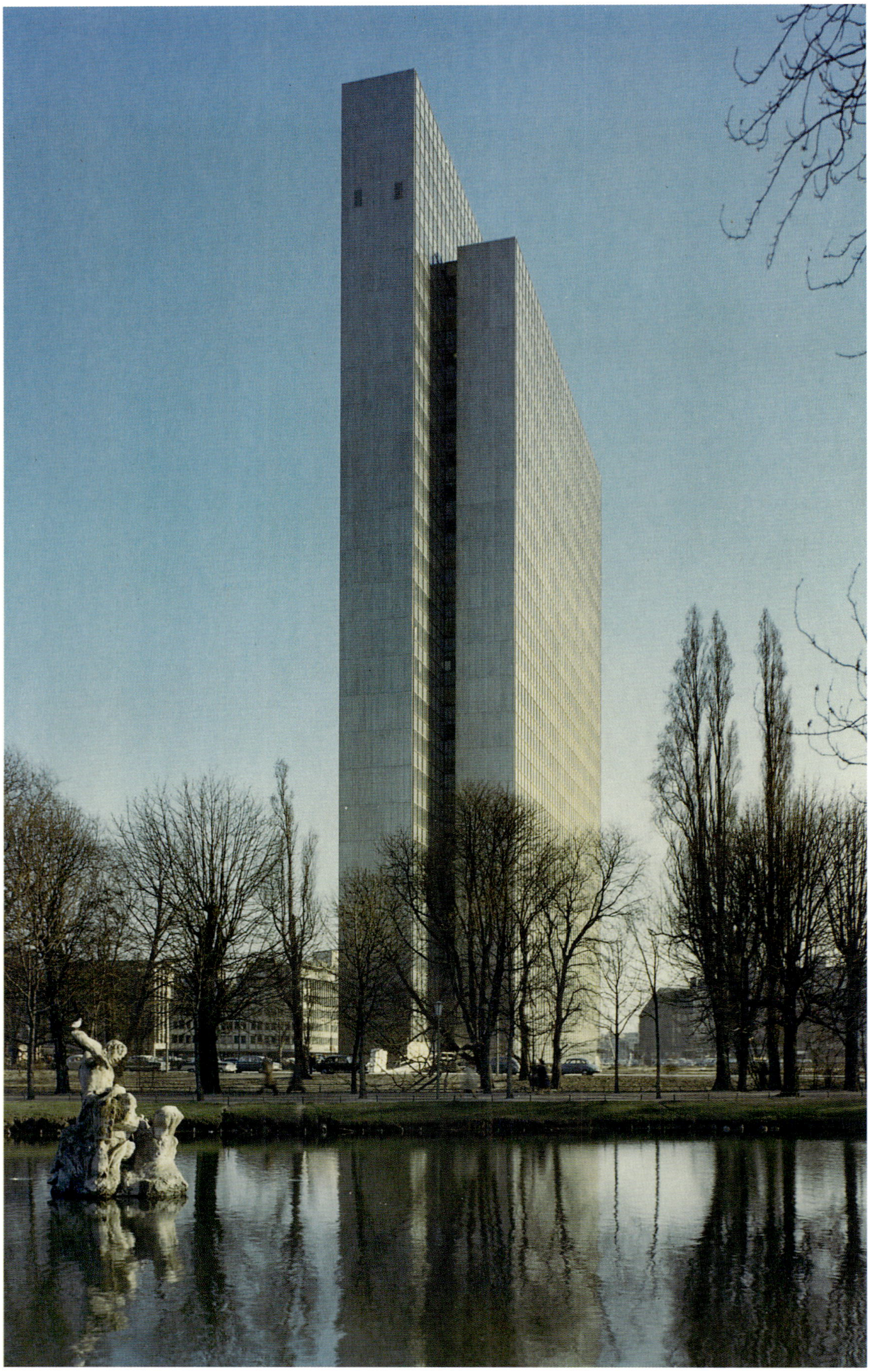

Offices of the Phoenix-Rheinrohr AG company (now Thyssenhaus), Dusseldorf, period photograph and typical floor plan. Helmut Hentrich and Hubert Petschnigg, architects, 1960. The division of the plan into three offset bays meets the need to provide each office with direct natural light.

© HPP Hentrich-Petschnigg & Partner KG.
Phot. Arno Wrubel.

Ove Arup, is 259 meters (850 feet) high, but no section of the building is wider than 16 meters (52 feet). The problem of the slenderness ratio ("aspect ratio") is particularly delicate in Europe, and especially in Germany, where every office worker is legally obliged to be in the immediate vicinity of a window.

Another more technical solution to the problem of the height/width ratio consists of piling huge rigid boxes, each some 10 stories high, one on top of the other. This "superframe" structure not only offers greater wind resistance but, above all, allows greater freedom in interior arrangements. As for the Miglin-Beitler Tower, designed for Chicago in 1989, a rigging technique is explored. Four supercolumns like fins stiffen the tower at the corners, rather in the way that cables hold a mast in position. To sum up, performance has been improved without basic innovation.

The real step forward lies in another direction. It is no longer a matter of increasing the rigidity of the tower, quantitatively strengthening the structure, but of damping the movement. The first damping system was invented by the engineer LeMessurier and placed at the summit of the Citicorp Center in New York in 1977. A concrete mass weighing four tons is released in high winds and moves in countervailing direction to the oscillation of the tower at the same frequency, thus damping the movement. Damping systems of the same type have subsequently been installed at the tops of other buildings to correct excessive accelerations.[10] More recently a pendulum system, a suspended mass that swings in countervailing direction to the tower, has enabled the cost of damping devices to be considerably reduced. The pendulum frees the engineer from the tyranny of the one to seven aspect ratio limit. The height of a tower can now be ten, fourteen times greater than its width. If the system is active, with the movement of the mass preceding that of the tower, the aspect ratio can reach twenty! But the device would have to be totally reliable, for such a tall narrow building would not survive if it failed. Thence the idea of combining an active (motorized) system with a passive one. For tomorrow, more and more efficient dampers can be imagined that would take over resistance to lateral

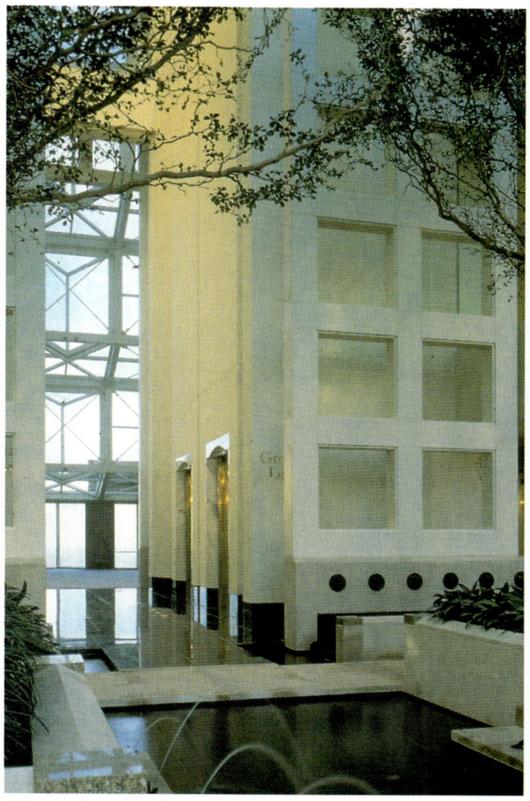

Texas Commerce Tower, Dallas, the winter garden installed in the sky-lobby. SOM Houston, architects (Richard Keating), 1987.
DMJM Keating.

wind pressure all on their own. The load-bearing structure would then only have to bear the force of gravity and could be reduced to its vertical components; the core and the columns. This would be the "ultimate structure" according to engineer Fitzpatrick.[11]

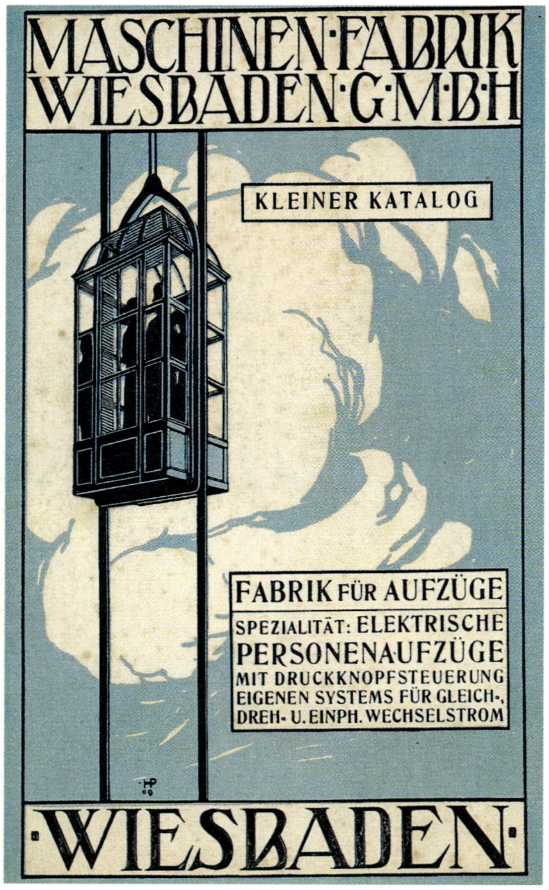

Catalogue cover of the electric elevator factory Maschinen-Fabrik Wiesbaden G.m.b.H., 1909.
Archives d'architecture moderne, Brussels.

Another kind of constraint limiting the height of skyscrapers is the elevators. The higher the building the more people it contains and the more elevators it needs.
Accordingly, the technical core grows larger until it reaches irrational proportions compared to the floor area. The 102-story Empire State Building is served by 74 elevators arranged in 7 batteries. At the lowest level the elevators occupy 30% of the area. Today such a circulation system is considered to be uneconomical above some 60 stories.

Two possibly complementary innovations can reduce this disadvantage in very tall buildings; the double-decker and the sky-lobby.
Double-decker elevators consist of a single unit of two cars, one on top of the other, in the same shaft. By definition, the system halves the number of stops. It is very efficient at busy times—the beginning and end of the working day—but can prove very burdensome with a more varied pattern of use. On average, the capacity of two double-deckers is equivalent to three normal elevators. The system, first put into practice in Chicago in 1968, also assumes two levels of access corresponding to the two cars.[12]

As for the sky-lobby, the principle consists of a variation on the arrangement of elevators in batteries, each serving a group of floors. In this case, each battery begins at the lowest level of the floors it serves. This level is reached by an express elevator directly linked to the ground floor. The sky-lobby, therefore, is the transfer area between an express elevator and a battery of local elevators. Originally utilitarian, the sky-lobby now often provides the pretext for a more spectacular arrangement; a public belvedere, meeting place or employee restaurant. The system is a requirement in the case of mixed-use buildings, where each group of floors—offices, apartments, a hotel—functions as a separate unit.
From a mechanical point of view the elevator has remained at an archaic stage—a motor driven pulley, a cable with the car at one end and a counterweight at the other—generations old and very efficient. Invented by Elisha Graves Otis in 1853, it is also safe. In front of a crowd of spectators and journalists at the Crystal Palace of New York exhibition, he cut the cable of his elevator, which locked in place and did

Opposite:
"Without Attendant Elevators," an Otis advertisement, 1953.
Otis International.

not fall. This rack and pinion safety lock which operates between the guiding rails and the elevator if it moves too fast, is still in use today.

In 1857 the first passenger elevator was installed in New York in the E.V. Haughwout Co. store on Broadway. In 1870 the Equitable Building of New York was the first office building to be equipped with an elevator. Since then the apparatus has undergone numerous improvements and its safety, speed and comfort continue to improve.[13] Steam was replaced by hydraulics and then by electric power. Control buttons appeared early in the century but it was only in the fifties that elevators could be operated without an attendant. Motor speed regulation has reduced jerky starting and stopping, cables are stronger and recent progress in electronics applied to the motor has considerably reduced energy cost. The most spectacular improvements have undoubtedly been made possible by the introduction of computers. The study of the circulation system within towers has become a highly sophisticated discipline: how to achieve the optimal, most economical set-up with the fewest cars in the smallest space? what dimensions to give to the car? what speed? over how many floors? Only computer simulations of traffic can provide the optimal solutions that intervene very early on in the design of a skyscraper. On the operating level, computers decide today which is the best placed elevator to answer a call and, more and more, the installation of artificial intelligence systems allow the

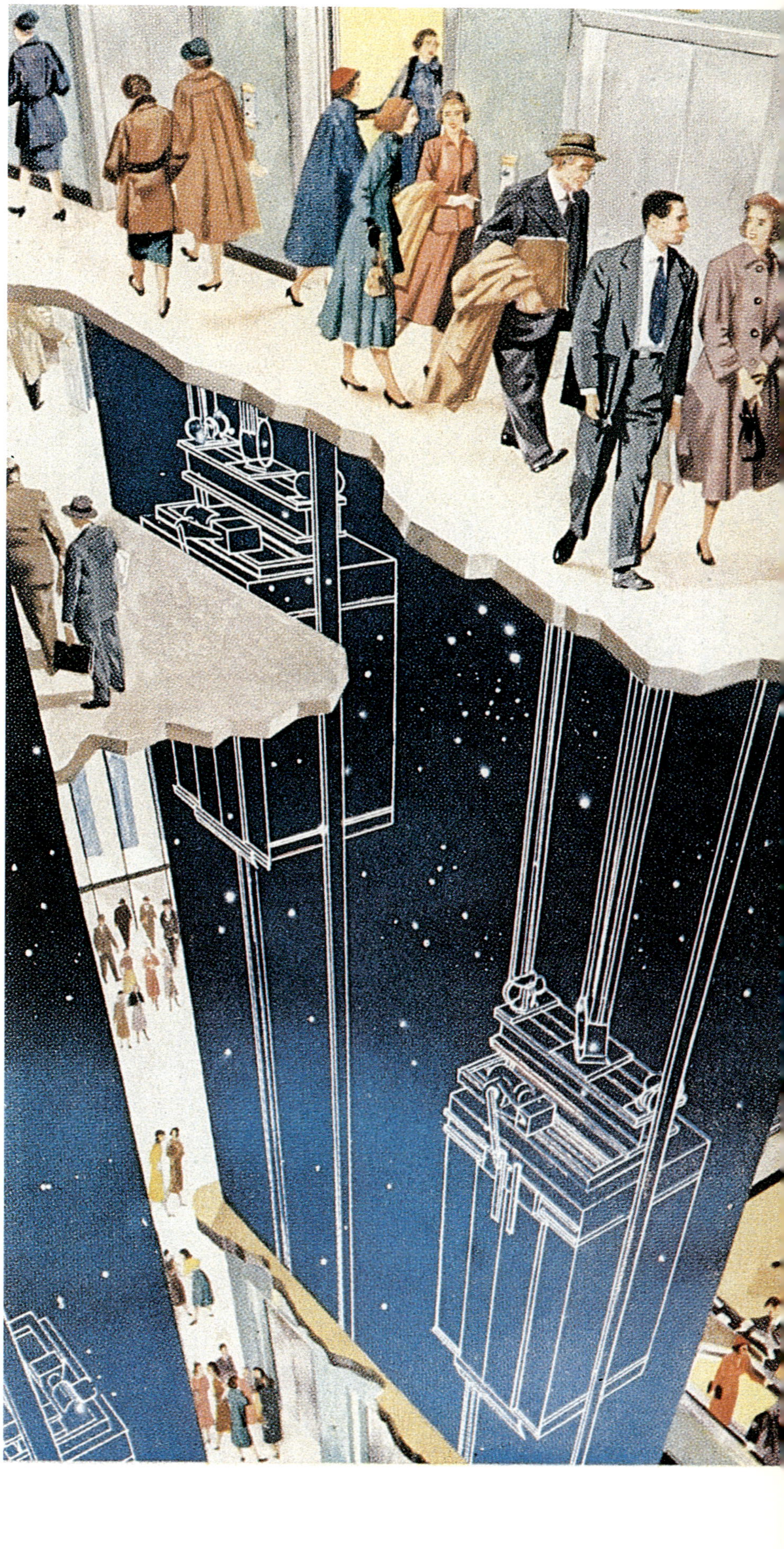

demands of traffic within the building to be anticipated and accordingly to be better and more quickly met.

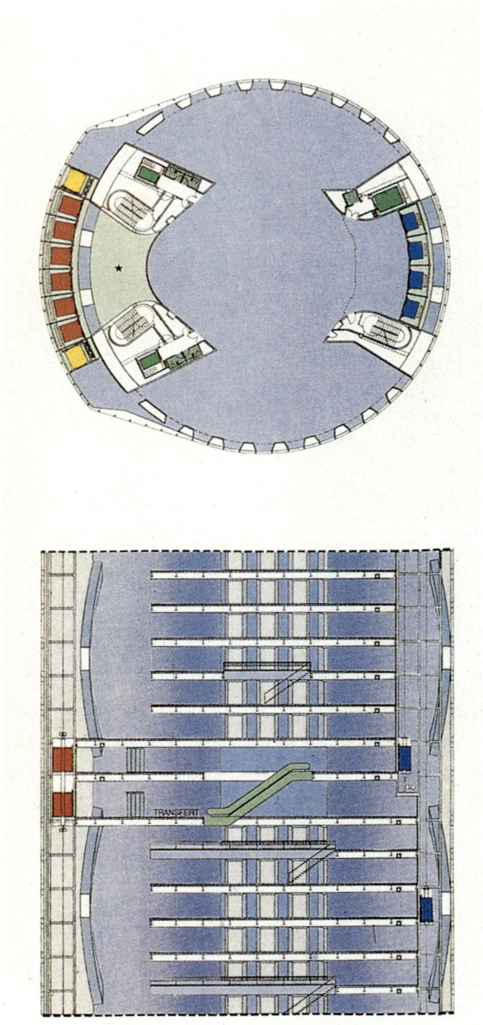

**Tour Sans Fins, La Défense, Paris, typical floor plan and cross section. Jean Nouvel et associés, architects, 1991.
The cross section shows the two-story sky-lobby connected by escalators, corresponding to the two decks of the express elevators (in red); in blue, the batteries of local elevators.**
Architectures Jean Nouvel.

Computer technology is not only applied to elevators. It also monitors energy requirements (lighting, heating, air-conditioning) and the need to activate damping systems. The concept of artificial intelligence, linked to these aspects of technical management, has been wrongly confused with the cabling needed by high performance communication systems, a misapprehension which has given rise to the commercial concept of the "intelligent building." In fact the pre-cabling of an office building only makes sense if the occupier and his real needs are known in advance. Cables, vertical and horizontal ducts, water pipes, water tanks forming part of the fire-fighting system, electronic systems, dampers are all invisible components of the skyscraper machine, components that call for more and more sophisticated techniques and materials. Air-conditioning, related to the comfort of occupants, uses a great deal of space in circulating air. As with the elevators, the division of the air-circulation system into compartments one on top of the other and the creation of technical floors reduces the space taken up.[15] The type of façade and the composition of curtain wall have a direct influence on ventilation, heating and cooling needs and hence on energy costs.[16]

There are also systems for fire fighting—a more acute problem from the psychological point of view. First comes detection, now carried out by highly developed electronic systems. Protection is assured by sprinklers, hydrants for firemen's hoses and a guaranteed electricity supply from a stand-by generator in every tower. Smoke exhaust systems clear smoke from escape routes when evacuation of the building becomes the essential objective. In Los Angeles every skyscraper must allow for helicopter evacuation and cannot, therefore, terminate in anything except a flat roof.

It is also possible to talk of medicine in this technical vein. For skyscrapers can fall sick. Legionnaires' disease was identified in 1976 and is contracted by breathing polluted air circulated by a defective air conditioning system. A veritable psychosis was created by the announcement of the ill effects produced by asbestos or volatile organic compositions such as glues and solvents. Not only are sick buildings now treated but, above all, prevention is the order of the day with initial design planned for health and regular maintenance.

It is true that these technical problems are not restricted to skyscrapers. But very tall buildings

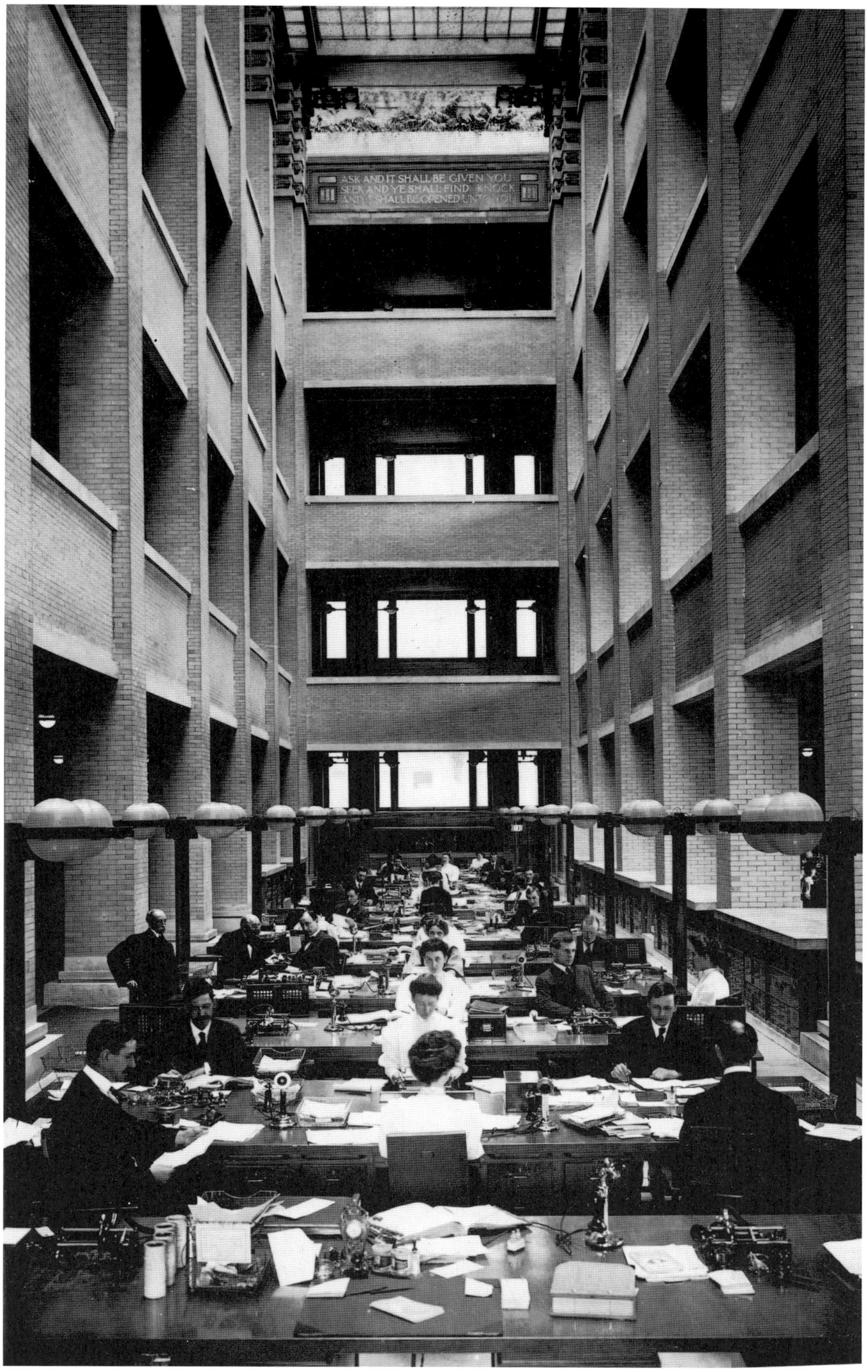

Larkin Company Administration Building, Buffalo. Frank Lloyd Wright, architect, 1903.
Institut français d'architecture.

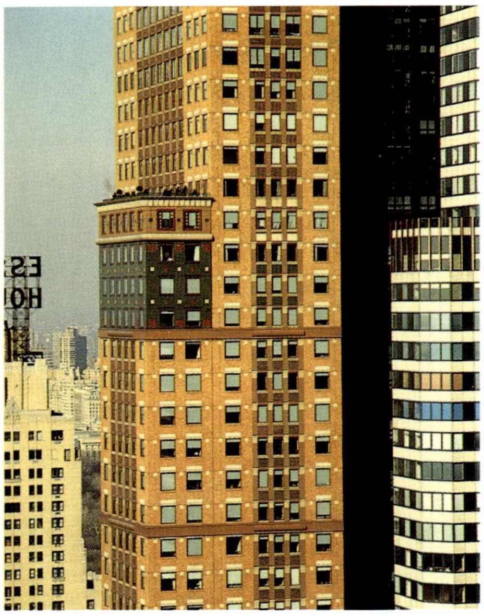

Contemporary curtain walls, New York. On the right, City Spire (Murphy/Jahn, 1989) and its stone facing; in the center, the Carnegie Hall Tower (Cesar Pelli & Associates, 1991) and its facing in colored terracotta.
© Benoît Roland.

exacerbate conditions and necessitate the development of advanced technologies. These technologies are then transferred to projects which present the same kind of conditions in other forms—certain public facilities, for example, where the question of fire is equally acute. Skyscrapers also serve as laboratories for manufacturers of materials in somewhat the same way that space exploration led to new materials and techniques later used in areas as diverse as sport, food and medicine. "A tall building is like a rocket to the moon."[20]

Opposite:
United Nations Secretariat, New York. International Committee of Architects; Wallace K. Harrison, Chairman, 1952.
© Unations, 1952. Institut français d'architecture.

1. Winston WEISMAN, "A New View of Skyscraper History," *The Rise of an American Architecture*, Praeger Publishers, New York, 1970. F.L. Wright's Price Tower was built in Bartlesville, Oklahoma between 1952 and 1956.
2. Jonathan B. TUCKER, "Superskyscrapers," *High Technology*, Vol. 5, No. 1, January 1985.
3. When the exterior walls are made rigid the building behaves like a huge hollow tube. As the interior columns no longer have to resist lateral pressure their position becomes optional and the floor layout more flexible.
4. The tower, imagined in 1975, would cover nine blocks in Houston and be made up of 16 triangular tubes with sides 60 meters (200 feet) wide. The architect, Robert SOBEL, is president of the New York firm Emery Roth & Sons Architects.
5. François LOYER, "L'Europe brutaliste", *Le Grand Atlas de l'architecture mondiale*, Encylopaedia Universalis France, Paris 1988.
6. Promontory Apartments, Chicago, 1947.
7. Reinforced concrete can bear 300 kg/cm² (5,000 psi) at best. High-strength concrete can bear up to 850 kg/cm² (14,000 psi).
8. According to engineer William J. LEMESSURIER, president of LeMessurier Associates / SCI, associated with Helmut JAHN in the Southwest Center project in Houston (1982).
9. The "superframe" principle allows for the construction of vast atriums, as at the headquarters of the NEC company in Tokyo (Nikken Sekkei, 1992).
10. What can be perceived is not the movement of the tower but the acceleration. Above the threshold of tolerance, the occupiers suffer seasickness, elevators malfunction and partitions and curtain walls can be damaged.
11. According to an interview with the English engineer Tony FITZPATRICK, director of Ove Arup & Partners (London), carried out by C. MIEROP, 31 October 1994.
12. The first double-decker elevators were installed in 1968 in the Time-Life Building in Chicago (30 stories). Architects: Harry WEESE & Associates. The principle of double-decker elevators had already been unsuccessfully experimented in New York's Cities Service Building in 1932 (66 stories, CLINTON & RUSSELL, architects).
13. In 1927, 113 accidents were recorded in Manhattan, of which 26 were fatal. The first electric elevators reached a speed of 120 meters (394 feet) a minute. Today they travel at 12 meters (39 feet) a second.
14. The hydraulic elevator came into use in 1872. The system is still widely used in low buildings today. The first electric elevator was installed in 1887.
15. The current trend is for air-conditioning to be decentralized, with a plant on each floor.
16. After several decades of totally sealed outside walls, the merits of windows that open and natural ventilation are being re-discovered.
17. Sprinklers are both a system of detection and protection. They have a seal which breaks when heat reaches about 60°C (140°F) and releases water. They were invented in the twenties in the United States.
18. Smoke exhaust ducts, compulsory in France in all IGH buildings, also take up a great deal of space.
19. The disease first appeared during an American Legion congress, held in Philadelphia in July 1976 in the conference facility of the Bellevue-Stratford Hotel. The building's air-conditioning system pumped outdoor air from in front of a cooling tower emitting clouds of steam containing germs.
20. Vincent DESIMONE, quoted by Jonathan B. TUCKER, op. cit.

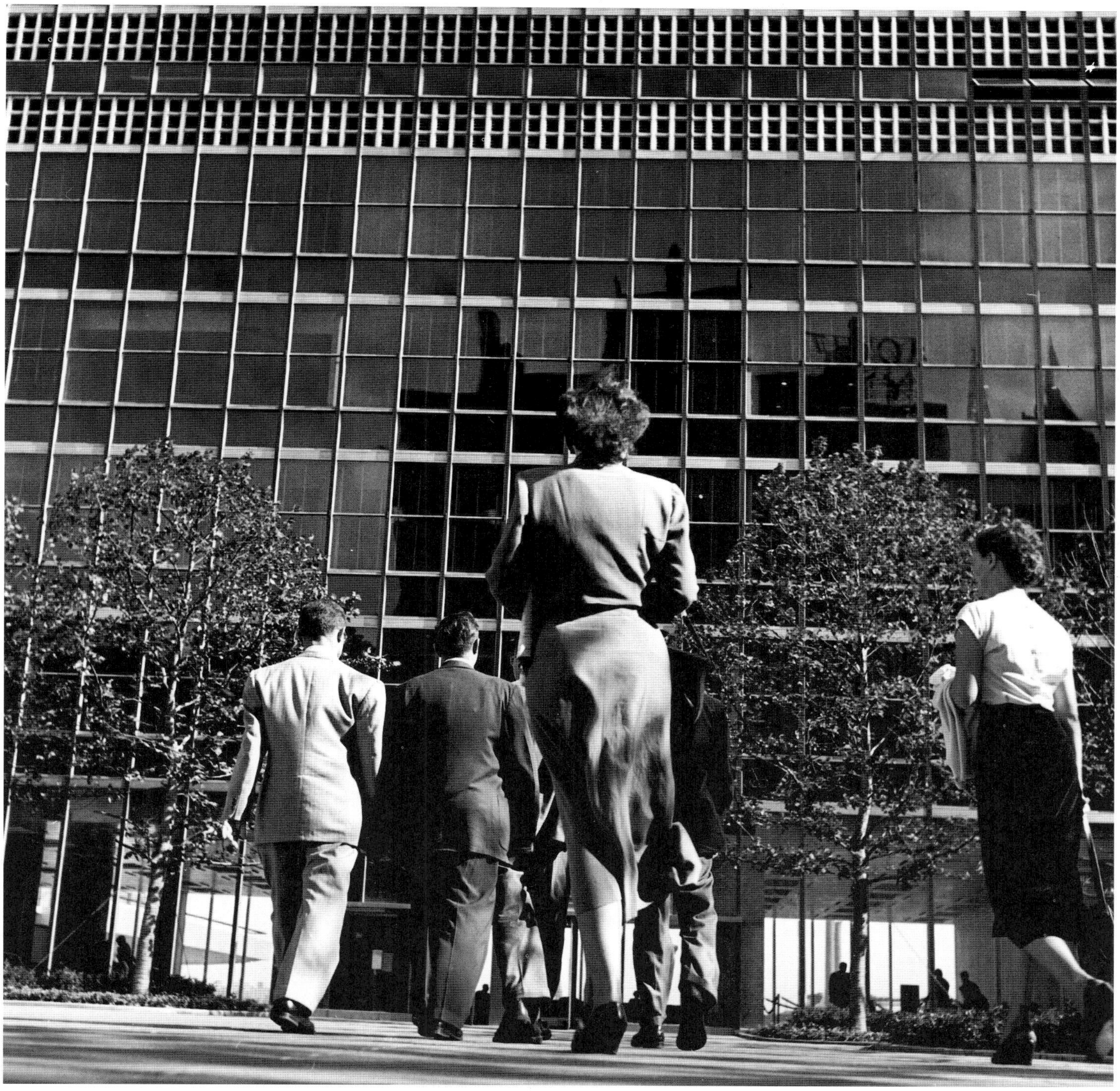

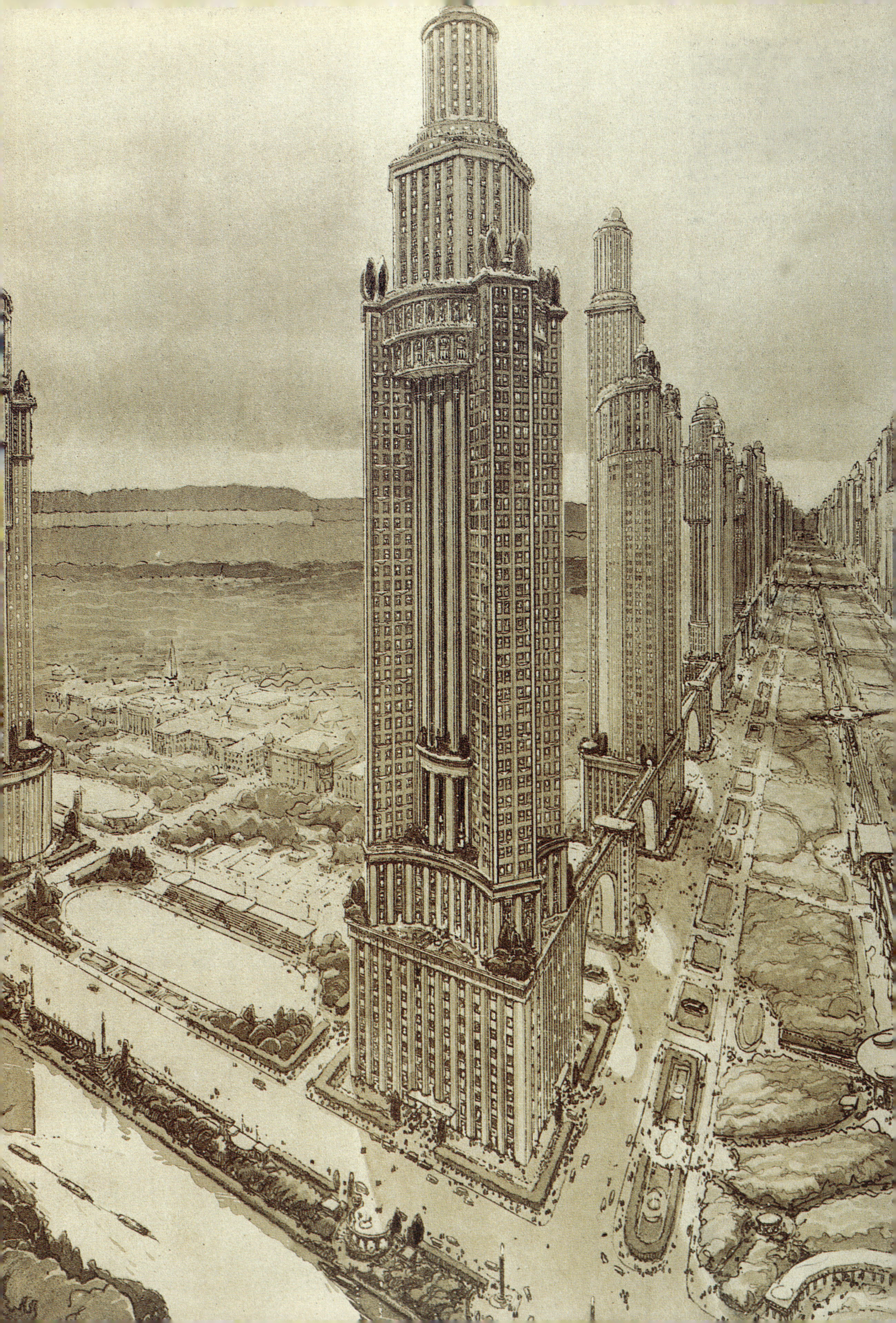

THE VERTICAL CITY

"Just imagine, it stood upright, their city. Absolutely straight. New York is a standing city. Of course we'd already seen cities, us. But at home they lie down don't they, cities, by the sea or a river, they stretch out over the landscape waiting for travelers while this one, the American one, didn't let itself go at all, it stood up stiff there, not bending at all, stiff enough to scare you."

Louis-Ferdinand Céline, *Voyage au bout de la nuit*, 1932.

Opposite:
"L'Avenue des maisons-tours" (The Avenue of House-Towers), a residential tower project for Paris, published in *L'Illustration*, No. 4145, Paris, 1922. Auguste Perret, architect, 1922 (unexecuted).
Perspective drawing by Jacques Lambert. Institut français d'architecture.

The idea of the vertical city exercises a lasting fascination. Rooted at the same time in the romantic imaginary world of science fiction and the most rigorous modernist tradition, a whole century has not withered it. It has willingly adopted all the forms, all the discourse, of the tall building; the stepped buildings by Henri Sauvage (1909), the street of the future by the municipal architect Eugène Hénard (1910), the Elevated Sidewalk City by the American Harvey Wiley Corbett (1913), the drawings of the Città Nuova by the Italian futurist Sant'Elia (1914), the tower houses by the Perret brothers (1920) etc. Neither Jean Nouvel in his Tour sans Fins nor Hiroshi Hara in the Umeda Sky Building escape even today from the metaphor in which the elevators are vertical streets, where the complexity of the services, wealth of the specification, the number of users encapsulates the whole idea of the city contained in a single building, a building that should "lend itself to communication and encourage neighborliness, help to reduce stress...and take part in the life of the city."[1] America has long dreamed of these cities in buildings and has built them. As long ago as 1929, in his *Metropolis of Tomorrow*, Hugh Ferriss imagined an ideal city, punctuated with well-spaced high towers containing "everything that facilitates everyday work and, as well as offices properly speaking, a post office—indispensable—

Peachtree Center, Atlanta, general view of the office buildings. John Portman & Associates, architects, 1961-1992. Peachtree Center is an urban pedestrian area covering 13 blocks.
© Michael Portman.

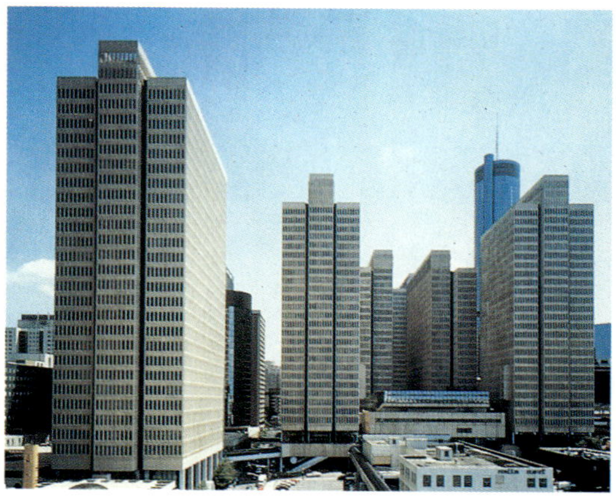

a bank, shops, restaurants, gymnasiums, etc." Of each tower building he said that it was "a city in itself."[2] How not to recognize in Rockefeller Center, built a few years later in New York in spite of the Depression, the realization of Ferriss' dream, applied to an existing city with all the richness and complexity that such a description entails? A group of thirteen towers dominated by the blade-like RCA Building, Rockefeller Center[3] breaks up the urban tissue with a tight network of streets, arcades, plazas and promenades that articulate a project exceptionally rich in public spaces and facilities and in shops. Not only does a group of skyscrapers succeed in creating a genuine piece of city, a real center (midtown Manhattan was hardly exploited by commercial buildings at the time.), but it is the first time that a speculative venture voluntarily under-exploits its rights, reversing the hitherto unchallenged logic of maximization, in favor of an unprecedented cultural and urban environment. In New York's World Trade Center, Philadelphia's Civic Center, and John Portman's Peachtree Center[4] in Atlanta—a thirteen block project in the business center—can undoubtedly be seen the distant descendants of this first prototype, unequaled to this day.

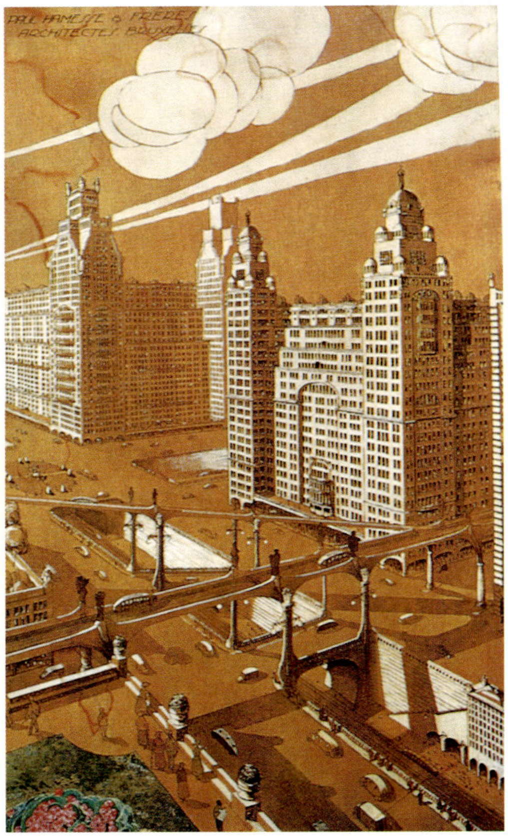

Project for a city of the future. Paul Hamesse, architect, Brussels, 1905.
Archives d'architecture moderne, Bruxelles.

More selectively, the John Hancock Center[5] of Chicago, standing alone on Upper Michigan Avenue, is also a city set upright. People live there in 711 apartments on the 47 highest floors. People work there in 85,000 square meters (915,000 square feet). And there are also shops, a restaurant, a swimming pool, a skating rink and public areas, a plaza (unfortunately underground) and a belvedere. Since its construction in 1969, the tower has acquired a few neighbors which repeat this attempt to achieve an urban mix in more fully realized versions. They include Water Tower Place[7] with its shops, cinemas, offices, a hotel and apartments, Olympia Centre, which contains a department store and, on the other side of the street, 900 North Michigan Avenue.[8]

Put altogether and setting aside the great variation in their shapes, these skyscrapers give a faithful enough representation of the utopias imagined at the beginning of the century to confront the modernization of the great centers of population. The German architect Hilberseimer's "Vertical City," also composed of grouped towers, is organized in superimposed zones. There are four underground levels for the subway system and communication networks, five levels of professional activity—offices today—then fifteen levels of housing on a podium of shops aligned at raised street level, thus considerably reducing daily commuting. The mixed uses of the Chicago skyscrapers tend to do no other than eliminate the inconveniences of tertiary concentration; mainly traffic, pollution and

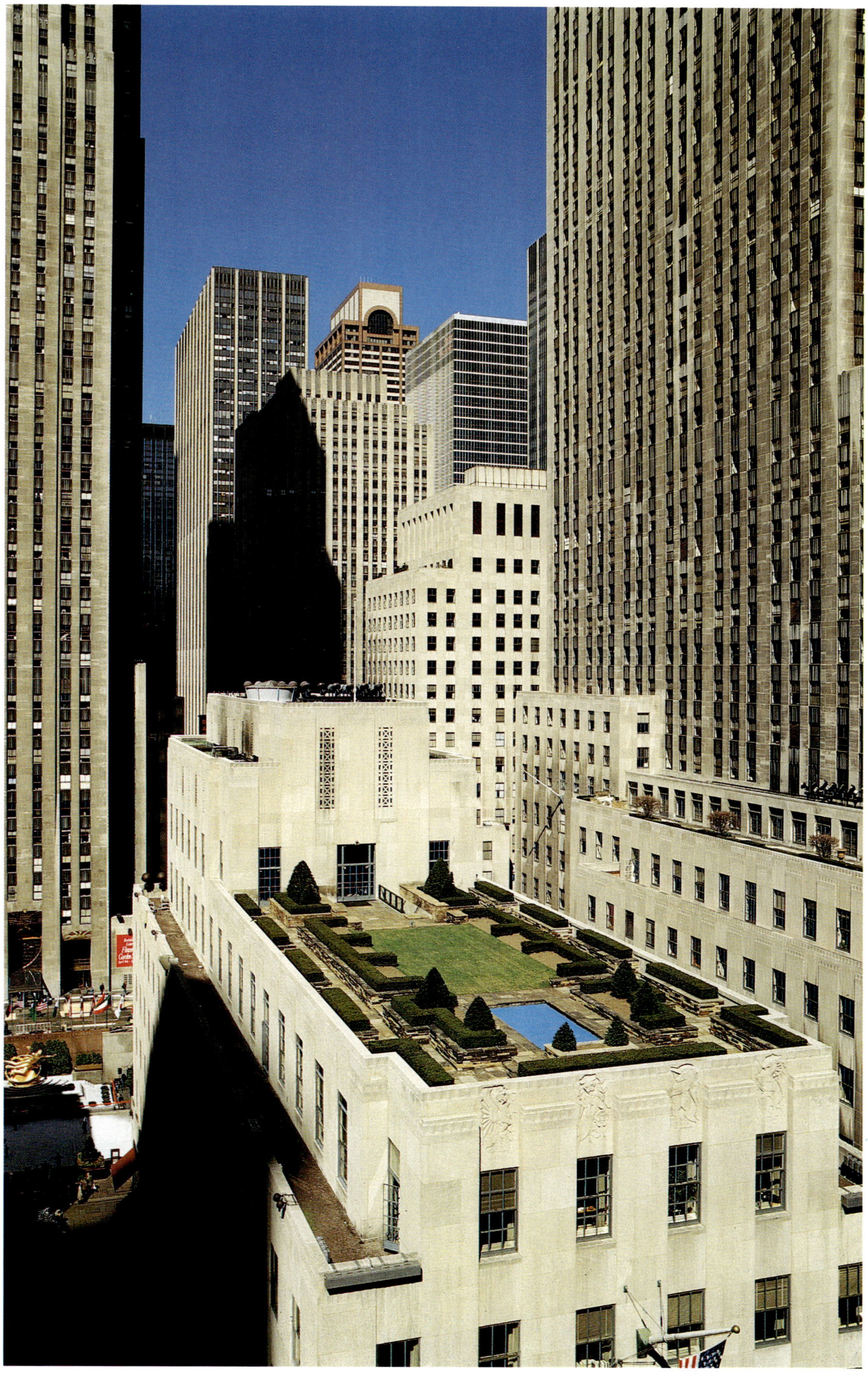

Rockefeller Center, New York, public spaces and hanging gardens. Reinhard and Hofmeister, Corbett, Harrison and MacMurray, Hood, Godley and Fouilhoux, associated architects, and others, 1931-1952.
© Benoît Roland.

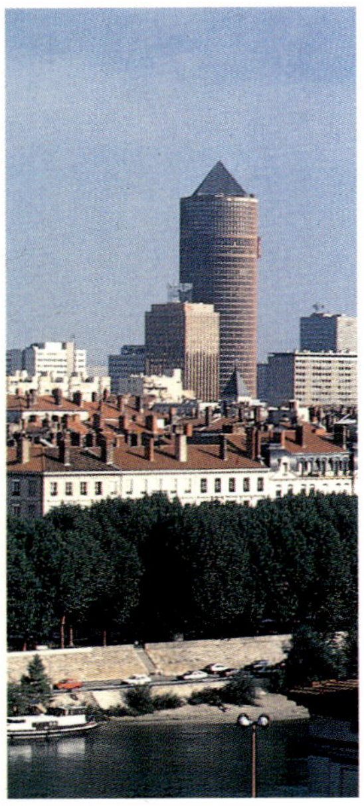

Crédit Lyonnais Tower, Lyons, La Part-Dieu district, view from the river Rhône. Araldo Cossutta, 1977.
SERL.

insecurity. Thus the skyscraper replaces the city, creating a world of its own, perfectly managed and socially homogenous.

To tell the truth the skyscraper and the city have not always been a perfect marriage. If the skyscraper functions as an intrinsically urban symbol—the futurist image of the great metropolis—it has also inspired utopias which are radically hostile to the city; to its appropriate density (of population and of building), to its variety (of people, of transportation, of urban activity) and to its disorder, of which, at the beginning of the century, New York provided an astonishing example. "It's a catastrophe, but a beautiful and dignified catastrophe with which an over-hasty destiny has overwhelmed a people of faith and courage. Let's start again!" declared Le Corbusier.[9]
Paris was not to be another New York. To prevent such a catastrophe Le Corbusier proposed Cartesian logic. The project for a contemporary city which he presented in 1922 and which was to serve as the basis for the famous Plan Voisin proposed for Paris[10] is organized around a business center composed of identical cruciform skyscrapers, arranged several hundred meters apart and symmetrically in relation to two main roads which intersect at the center. All the devices of modern town planning are found in this project—zoning by function, the urban freeway, the artificial ground level, the free-standing skyscraper.
This particular vertical city was to be built. It exists in Paris and in other cities in France, in the rest of Europe and in the United States—Boston, Atlanta, New Haven, etc. The Paris example is, of course, La Défense, a new 750-hectare (1,850 acres) district on an axis with the Champs Elysées. EPAD, the public body for the development of the sector, was established in 1958.[11] It quickly adopted the principle of creating a business district, raised on a pedestrian concourse and made up of a group of towers arranged in staggered formation along either side of the great historical axis. The concourse is girdled by a ring road, defining a "zone without history, undivided into lots."[12] Naturally the project went through several stages of evolution, the first one upwards. The towers, originally limited to 100 meters (330 feet) in height, climbed to almost double in 1969. Then the project was blocked by a severe crisis in the real estate market, to be re-launched in 1978 on a new basis. It was not until the construction of the Great Arch in 1989[13] that the district attained its international dimension and was, finally, adopted by Paris. The principle of the raised concourse is to be found again in Lyons in La Part-Dieu neighborhood.[14] But this project never achieved the scale planned. Just one tower, sculpted like a pencil, emerges in the background of the historical town. So much the better, for this Franco-American tower has succeeded in imposing itself as a landmark, like a second steeple.
Still in France, the Euralille project is recent. The new district maintains the principle of the raised concourse and the alignment of towers, but modified in its relationship to real ground level and

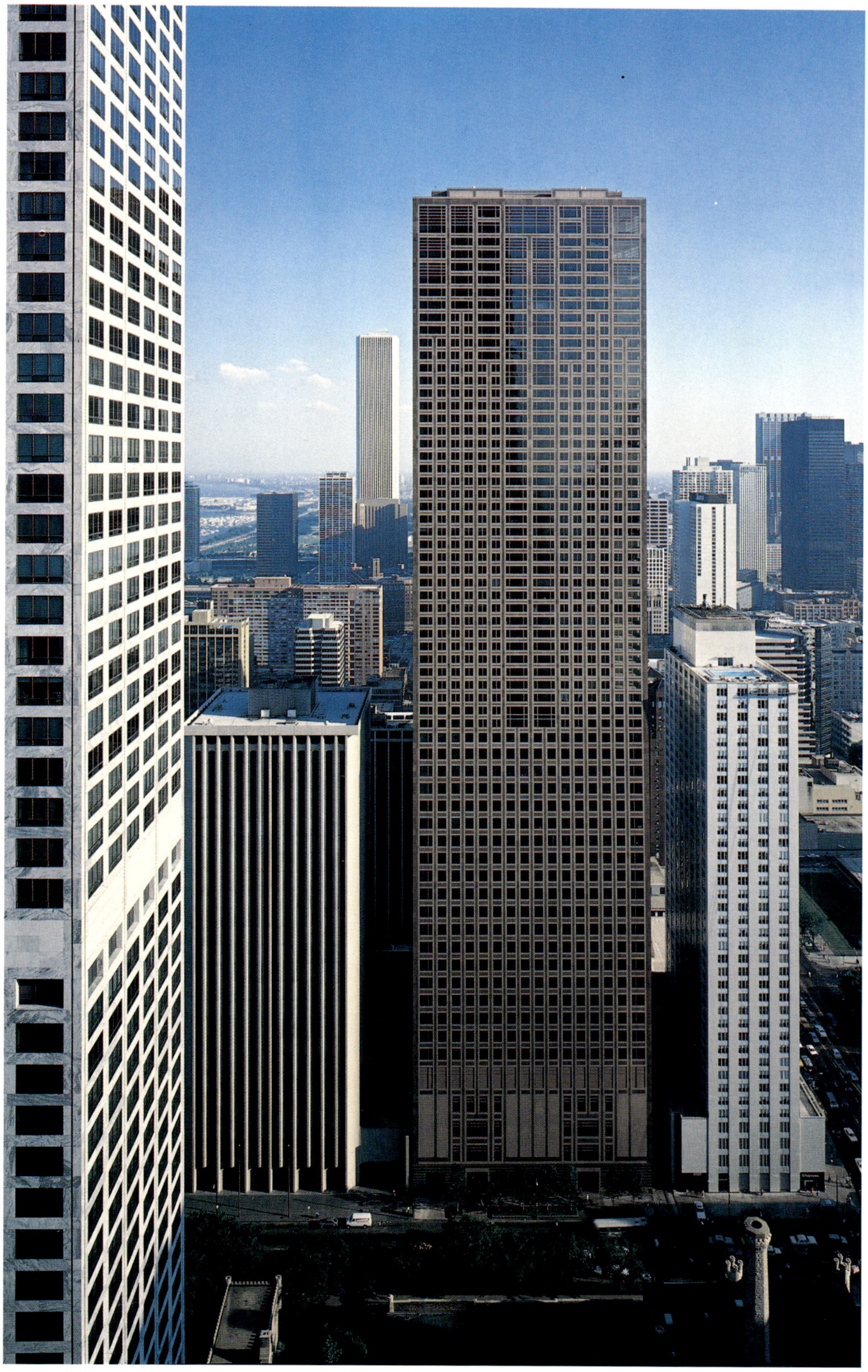

Olympia Centre, Chicago, southern façade towards Superior Street.
SOM Chicago, architects (Adrian Smith), 1986.
The composition of the façade corresponds to the interior arrangement: from the bottom upwards, department store, offices and housing, including a series of duplexes.
© Timothy Hursley.

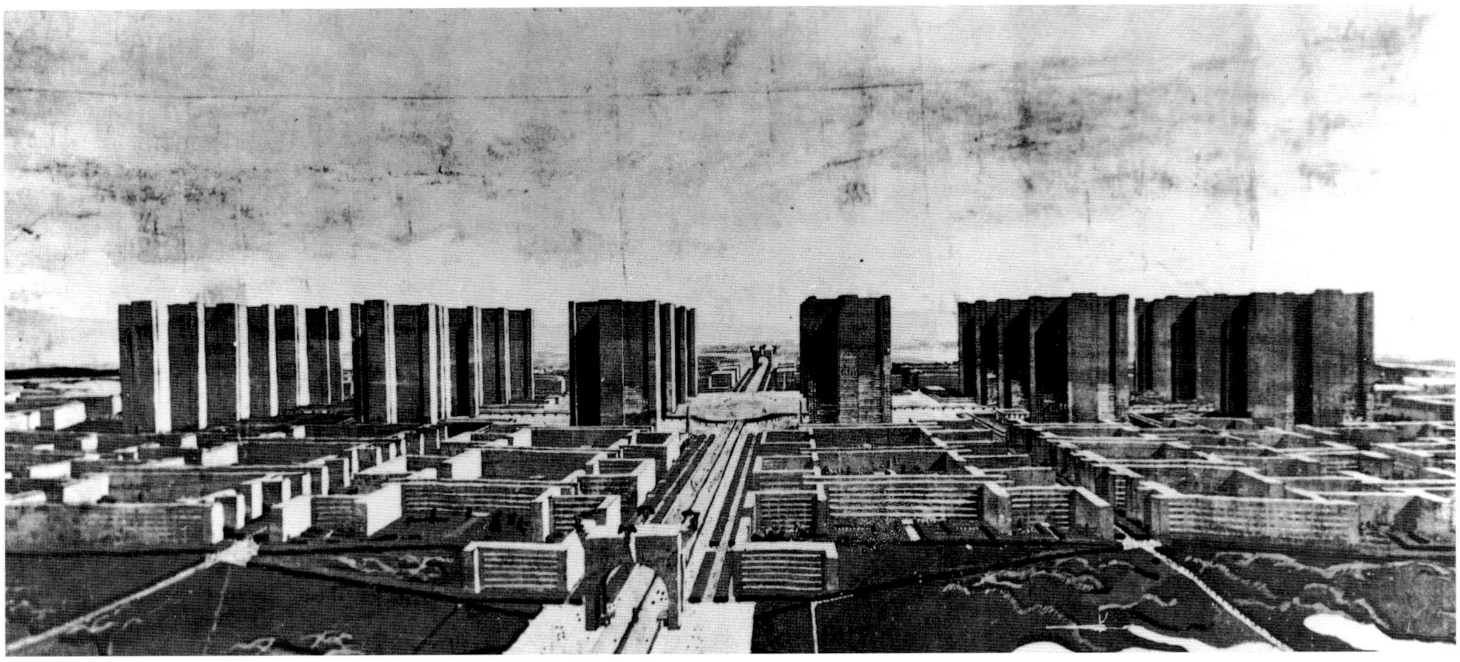

Above:
"Une ville contemporaine de 3 millions d'habitants" (a contemporary city of 3 million inhabitants), general perspective. Le Corbusier, 1922 (unexecuted).
Institut français d'architecture.

Right:
Embarcadero Center, San Francisco, general plan. John Portman & Associates, 1966-1988. Urban pedestrian area covering eight interconnected blocks.
John Portman & Associates.

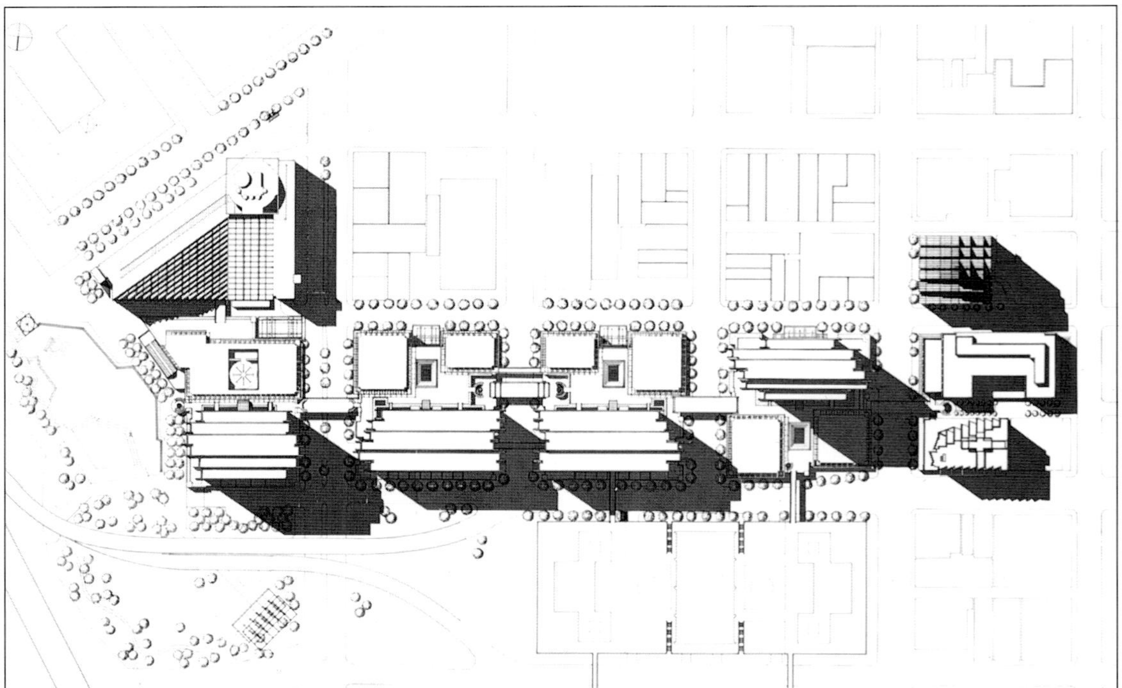

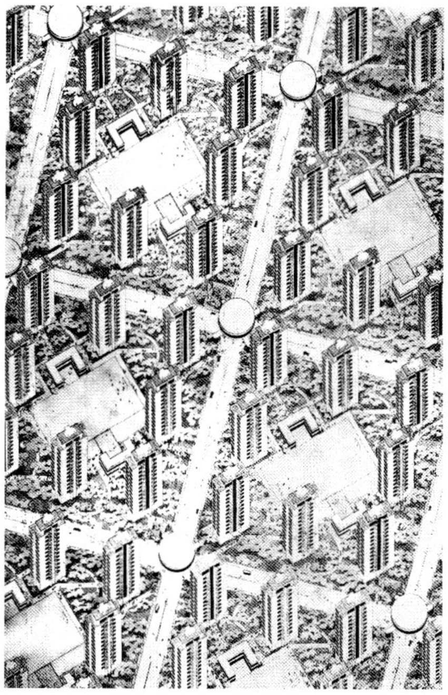

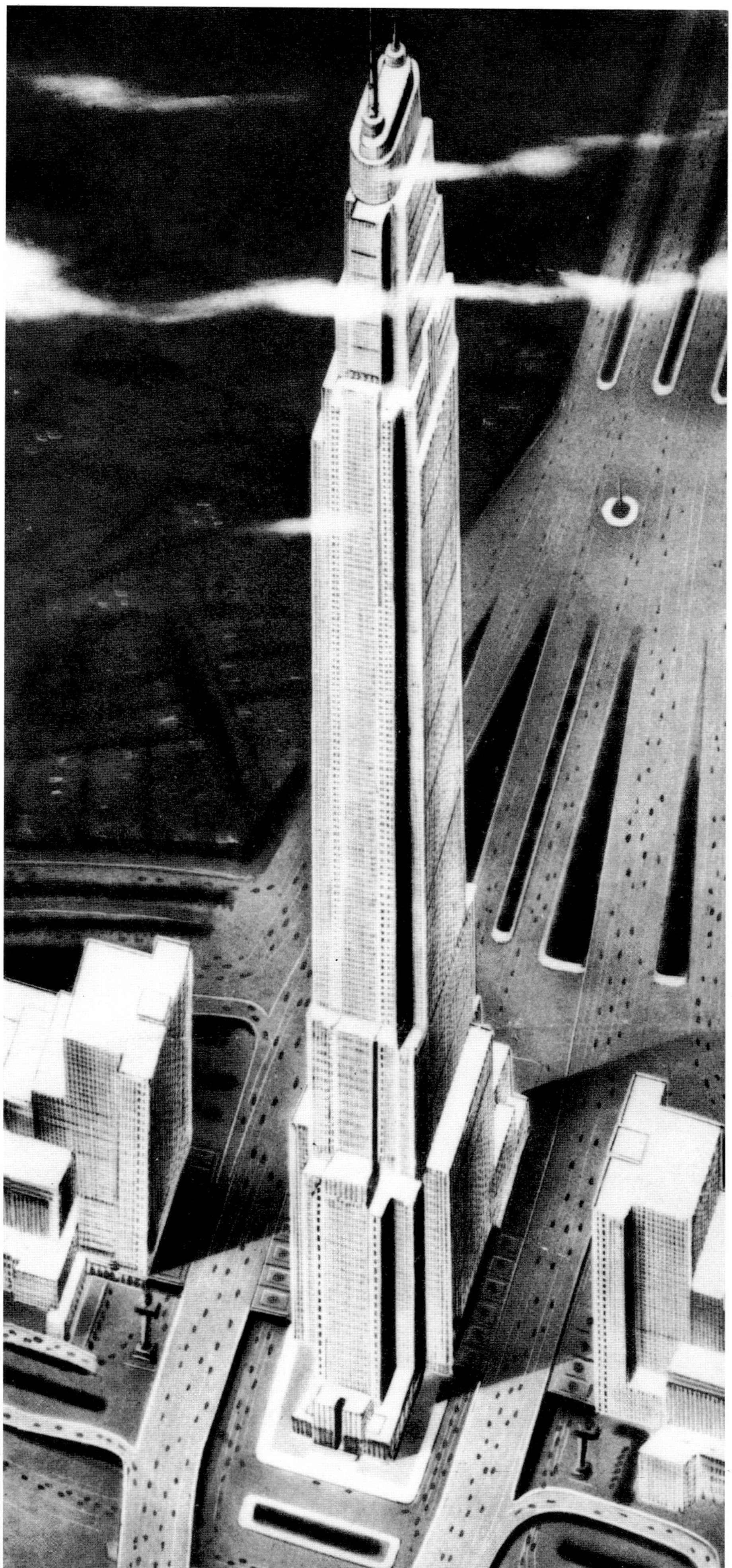

Above:
Theoretical project for a vertical estate of minimal housing developed for the Brussels International Congress of Modern Architecture, 1930.
André Lurçat, architect.
Institut français d'architecture.

Right:
Project for a government building, a 600-meter (1,970 feet) high skyscraper at La Défense, Paris.
Jacques Carlu, architect, ca. 1943-1944 (unexecuted).
Institut français d'architecture.

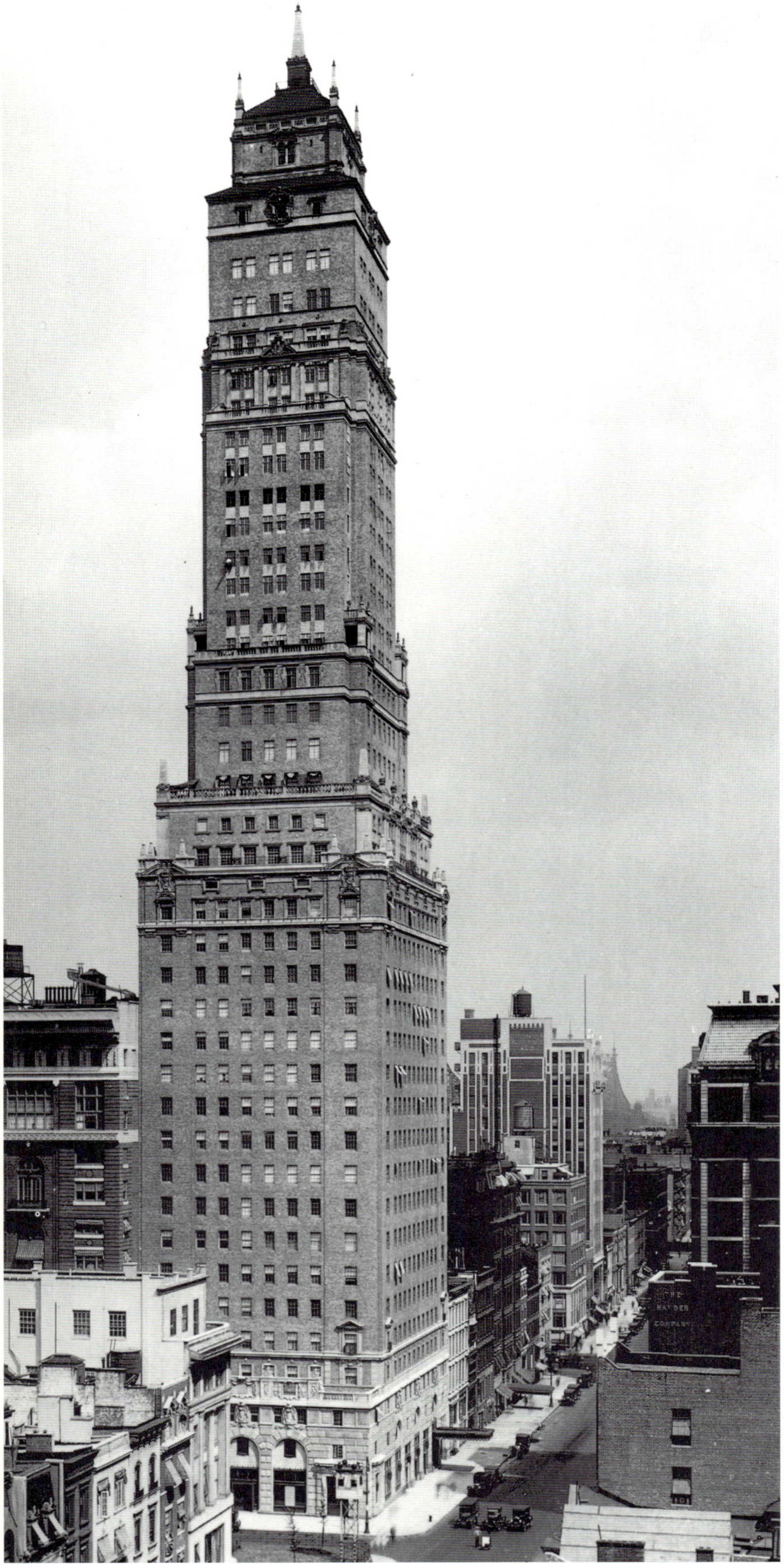

the streets of the city. The project explicitly evokes New York and its skyscrapers. The architect Rem Koolhaas, designer of the master plan, proclaims his "Manhattanism"—the positive value of urban chaos.[15] In Brussels, a city with a gnawing ambition to be a European metropolis, the Quartier Nord—re-christened Quartier Manhattan for the occasion—was completely redesigned in the sixties on the principles of the pedestrian concourse, walkways and towers.[16] The towers were indeed built, but not the walkways. For many years the main entrances to the buildings floated inaccessibly 13 meters (40 feet) above the ground and pedestrians entered them like cars at street level!

Tall buildings are not restricted to business districts. People have lived in apartment buildings with elevators since the 1860s. But until the twenties they did not exceed about 15 floors. These "skyscratchers" were laughable to the architect Emery Roth. To him is owed the Ritz Tower, built in New York in 1926, the first modern residential skyscraper, 41 stories, 165 meters (540 feet) high. The Ritz Tower rapidly became the prototype for a new lifestyle. Half hotel, half apartment block, it was particularly suited to the nomadic world of business and to people who were already deciding to move to the country and to maintain only a *pied-à-terre* in town.
The idea proved worth its weight in gold. "I live on Lexington Avenue, two rooms on the thirtieth floor. I've never lived so high up and I'm all excited!" exclaimed artist Georgia O'Keefe.[17] By

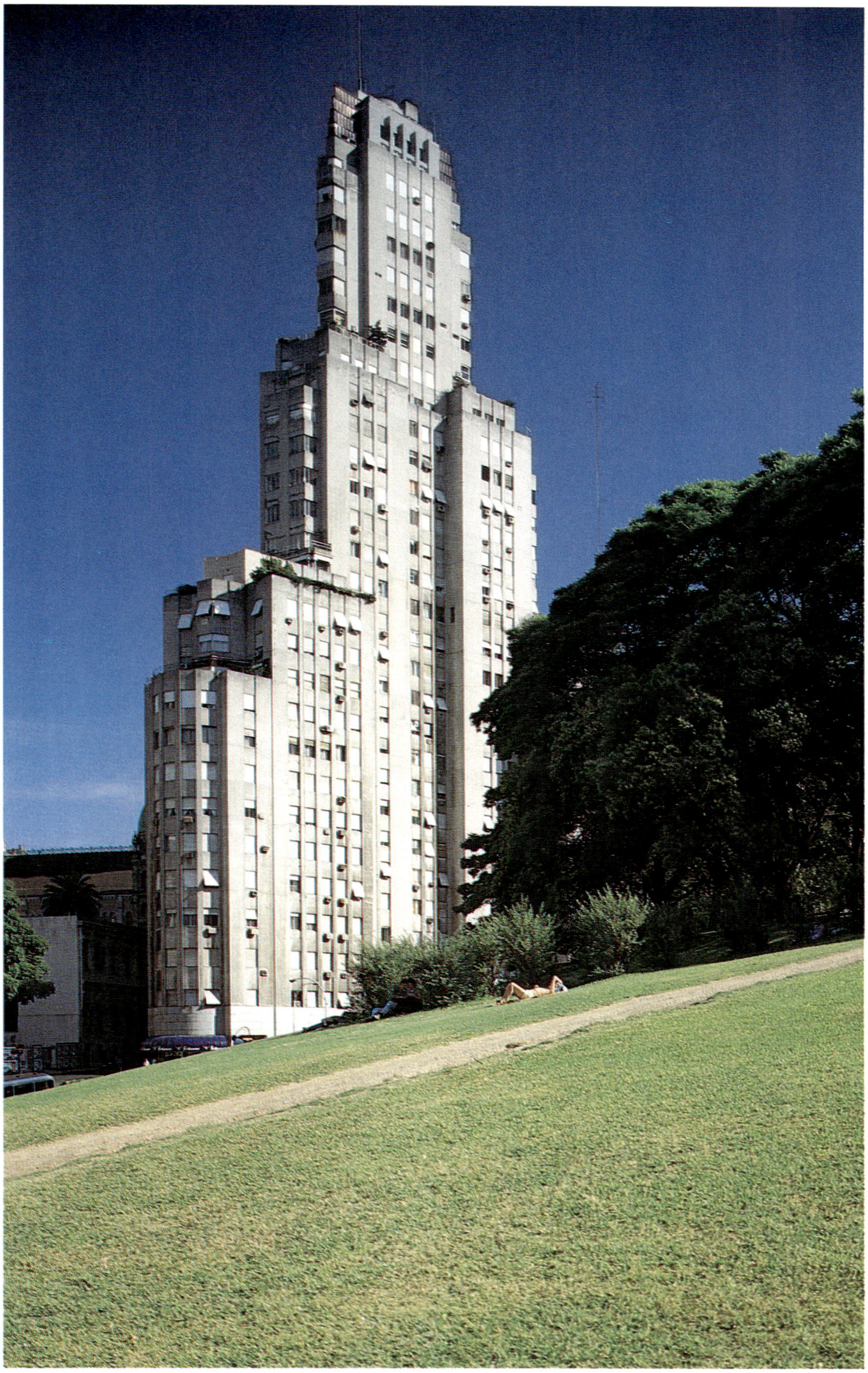

Opposite:
The Ritz Tower in New York, period photograph.
Emery Roth, architect, 1926.
Emery Roth & Sons.

The Kavanagh at Buenos Aires, seen from Plaza San Martìn.
Sanchez, Lagos and de la Torre, architects, 1936.
At the time of its construction this residential skyscraper was the tallest in Latin America and the tallest concrete building in the world.
© Guy Van Beeck.

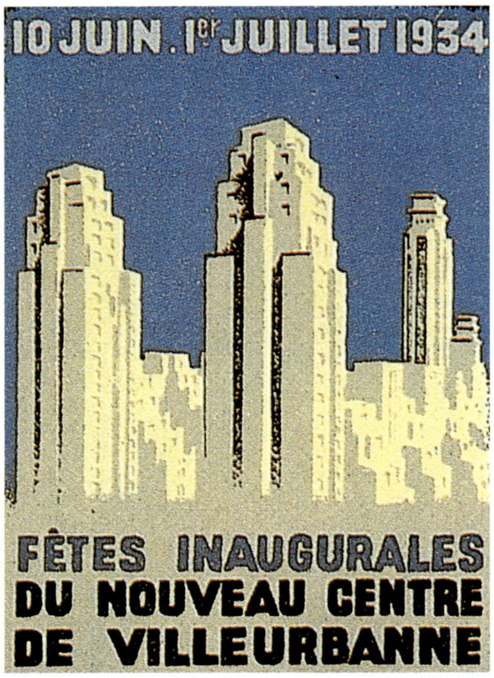

Stamp issued for the festivities to inaugurate the new center of Villeurbanne.
In the foreground, the residential "Gratte-ciel" (M. Leroux, 1934).
Municipalité de Villeurbanne.

the early thirties New York had about 150 skyscrapers of this type. Better yet, the model was exported to other cities and other continents. In 1934, the Park Hotel[18] was built in Shanghai on the same principle of small apartments with hotel service—22 stories high and tower-shaped; it was the tallest building in the Far East.[19] In Buenos Aires the Kavanagh,[20] at 33 stories the highest skyscraper of the period to be built in reinforced concrete, is a residential tower. It can take pride in being the illustration for the "skyscraper" entry in the Larousse dictionary. And from another, more unexpected angle, are not the stepped skyscrapers of the new center of Villeurbanne, built in 1934, also inspired by New York? An image of luxury, even decadence, here represents the ideals of progress and social justice; 1,400 public housing units, built American style on a metal framework are the backbone of a "modern estate... of which the height much exceeds the numerous factories and houses around it."[21]

Euphoria was rapidly to give way to crisis. The post-war period, as is well known, was principally dominated by urban schemes claimed by the decision-makers, developers and town plan-

Opposite:
General view of New York looking towards the Queensboro Bridge.
In the center: the Chrysler Building (William Van Alen, 1930) and, to its right, the residential skyscraper 100 United Nations Plaza (Schuman, Lichtenstein, Claman & Efron, in association with Der Scutt Architect, consultant, 1986) with its pointed terraced summit.
© Benoît Roland.

1. Frédérique DE GRAVELAINE, "La Ville verticale", *La Tour Sans Fins*, published by SCI Tour Sans Fins, Paris, 1992.
2. Hugh FERRISS, *The Metropolis of Tomorrow,* Ives Washburn Publisher, New York, 1929.
3. Rockefeller Center (1931-1940) on 5th Avenue, was designed by the architects REINHARD and HOFMEISTER, CORBETT, HARRISON and McMURRAY, HOOD, GODLEY and FOUILHOUX. The project was continued after the Second World War.
4. The Peachtree Center is made up of a group of towers articulated by a network of collective spaces, facilities and walkways for pedestrians. John PORTMAN carried out a complex of the same type in San Francisco—the Embarcadero Center.
5. SOM Chicago (Bruce GRAHAM).
6. LOEBL SCHLOSSMAN DART and HACKL Architects, 1976.
7. SOM Chicago (Adrian SMITH), 1986.
8. KOHN PEDERSEN FOX Associates, architects, in association with PERKINS & WILL, 1988.
9. LE CORBUSIER, *Quand les cathédrales étaient blanches,* Librairie Plon, Paris, 1937.
10. The Plan Voisin, developed in 1925, proposed the construction of skyscrapers in the center of Paris.
11. The master plan for La Défense was developed between 1958 and 1964. At the time Robert AUZELLE, town planner, and HERBE, CAMELOT, DE MAILLY and ZEHRFUSS were consultants to the EPAD public body.
12. Marie-Christine GANGNEUX, "Tours et détours par La Défense", *L'Architecture d'aujourd'hui*, No. 178, Paris, 1975.
13. La Grande Arche (the Great Arch), which closes the historical axis, is the work of Danish architect Johan Otto VON SPRECKELSEN (in association with Paul ANDREU).
14. The Crédit Lyonnais Tower (1977) was designed by the American architect A. COSSUTTA, initially associated with I.M. PEI. The tower contains 35 levels of offices and, at the summit, a hotel of 7 levels (245 rooms) with a panoramic restaurant. The tower is surmounted by a glass pyramid that lights the hotel atrium; 160 meters (525 feet) high, it easily dominates the other buildings of the business district.
15. The Euralille project, built around the new TGV (high-speed train) station and a 50-hectare (123 acres) business district bordering old Lille, was planned in 1988.
16. The project, that envisaged the construction of 64-high buildings connected at podium level by a set of walkways, was designed by Groupe Structures. Submitted in 1965 and approved in 1967, it necessitated the demolition of 54 hectares (133 acres) of dense urban neighborhood. Construction is still incomplete.

ners to be equally suitable for luxury apartments, office buildings and public housing. It was the day of the suburb, of mass produced housing. And more often than not verticality became synonymous with overcrowding, even poverty.

The problem has been acknowledged. The obsolete towers are beginning to fall. But other towers are rising. Some people live high up, others work there, not only in offices but also in real factories in fully equipped workshops on dozens of strengthened floors with suspended loading bays.[22] Hotels are keeping pace with the rise of office towers, with their degree of luxury seemingly related to their height. Libraries, art galleries, soon museums, hospitals, schools, public gardens... will the entire city emerge above the clouds?

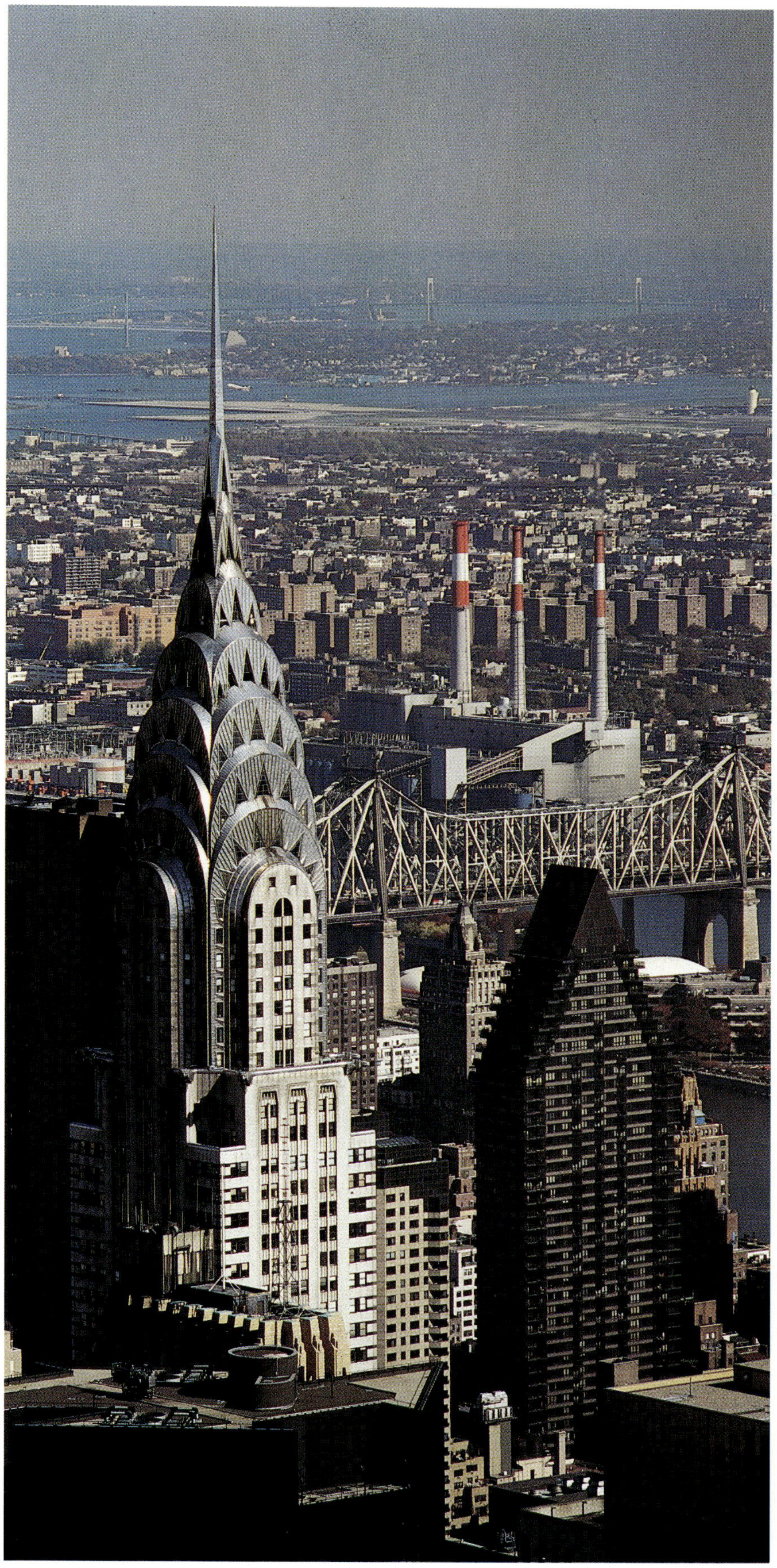

17. Georgia O'KEEFE, New York painter, quoted in *L'Aventure de l'art au XXe siècle*, Chêne-Hachette, Paris 1990 (1929 chapter).

18. The construction of apartment hotels was much more profitable than simple apartments. The hotels were not submitted to any regulations concerning sanitation, ventilation or natural light.

19. The Park Hotel was designed by the architect Ladislaus HUDEC. It contains 205 furnished and unfurnished rooms/apartments.

20. The Kavanagh was built in Buenos Aires in 1936 by architects Gregorio SANCHEZ, Ernesto LAGOS and Luis Maria DE LA TORRE. It was the tallest building in the city. The reference to the Larousse dictionary is given, without further detail, in the magazine *Summa*, No. 251, Buenos Aires, 1988.

21. J.L. MARGERAND, "Une Cité moderne aux portes de Lyon", *La Construction moderne*, 49e année, No. 41, July 8, 1934. The construction of the skyscrapers (architect Morice LEROUX) was part of an overall project that included, as well as housing, a new town hall, a "Palais du Travail" (Palace of Work), shops and a large public square.

22. The Wharf Cable Tower (New Tech Centre), for example, built in 1993 in Hong Kong by Dennis LAU & Ng CHUN MAN, contains 40 stories of warehouses, workshops and offices.

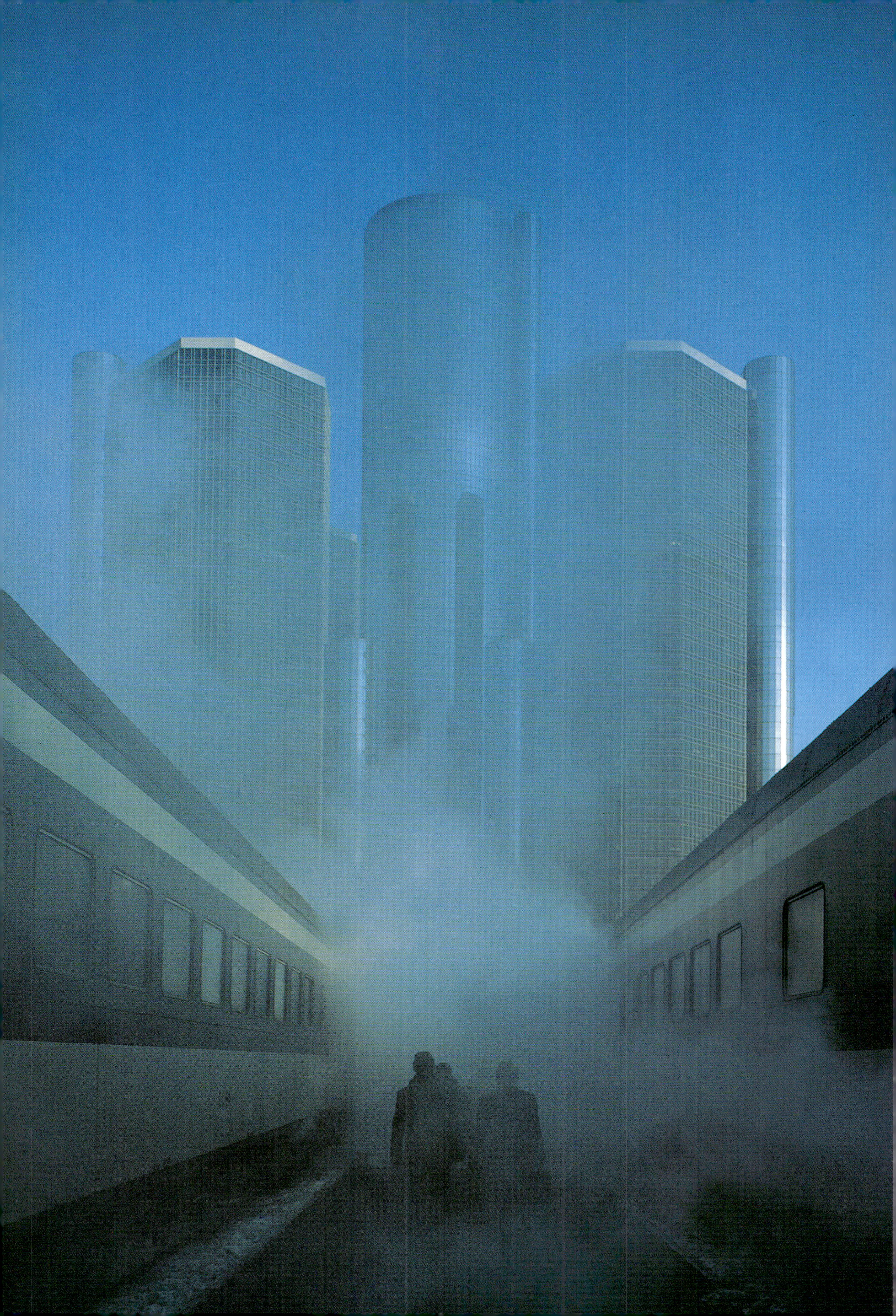

NEW BABYLONS

"There were Babylon and Nineveh; they were built of brick. Athens was gold marble columns. Rome was held up on broad arches of rubble. In Constantinople the minarets flame like great candles round the Golden Horn ... Steel, glass, tile, concrete will be the materials of the skyscrapers. Crammed on the narrow island the million windowed buildings will jut glittering, pyramid on pyramid like the white cloudhead above a thunderstorm."

John Dos Passos, *Manhattan Transfer*, 1928.

Opposite:
Renaissance Center, Detroit. John Portman & Associates, 1977-1981. In the center, the cylindrical tower of the Westin hotel, surrounded by office blocks.
© Timothy Hursley.

The *New York Times* on April 3, 1875, the day it moved its offices, predicted the future of New York in these words: "The commercial metropolis of the New World will soon fulfill Nebuchadnezzar's dream."[1] For Manhattan island genuinely is the fruit of a vision, a shared project, a dream of grandeur. It is often said that the appearance of the skyscraper was linked to the scarcity of land and the pressure of real estate speculation. This is not the complete explanation. If it is true that being near to the seaport presented many advantages, inciting businessmen to congregate on a narrow spit of land—even though transactions had been conducted by telephone since 1879—what about Chicago or, later, Houston, surrounded by endless prairie and plain? And how to explain that these high density areas change location with time, recreating elsewhere the same artificial scarcity of land? The business center of Chicago, for example, shifted north with the construction of The Chicago Tribune Tower, a trend confirmed a few decades later by the construction of the John Hancock Center, still further to the north.

The same phenomenon can be observed in New York with the formation of Midtown Manhattan around Rockefeller Center, although the Empire State

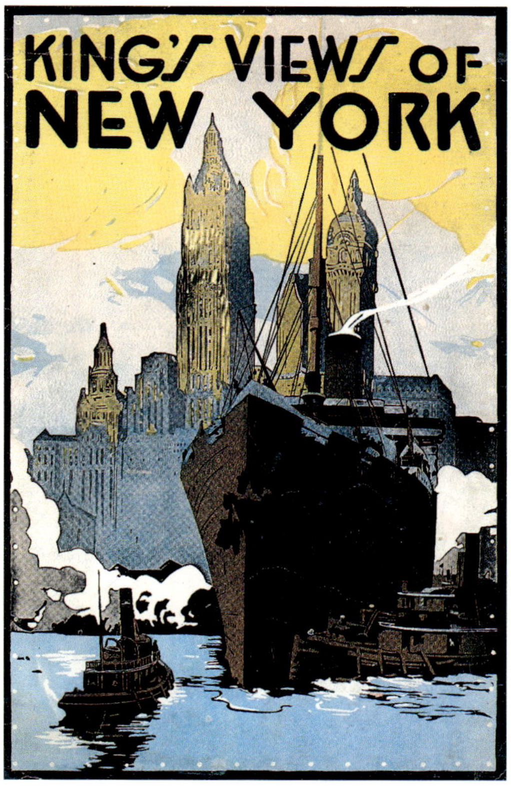

King's Views of New York,
Manhattan Postcard Co, 1926-1928. Cover illustration.
Archives d'architecture moderne, Brussels

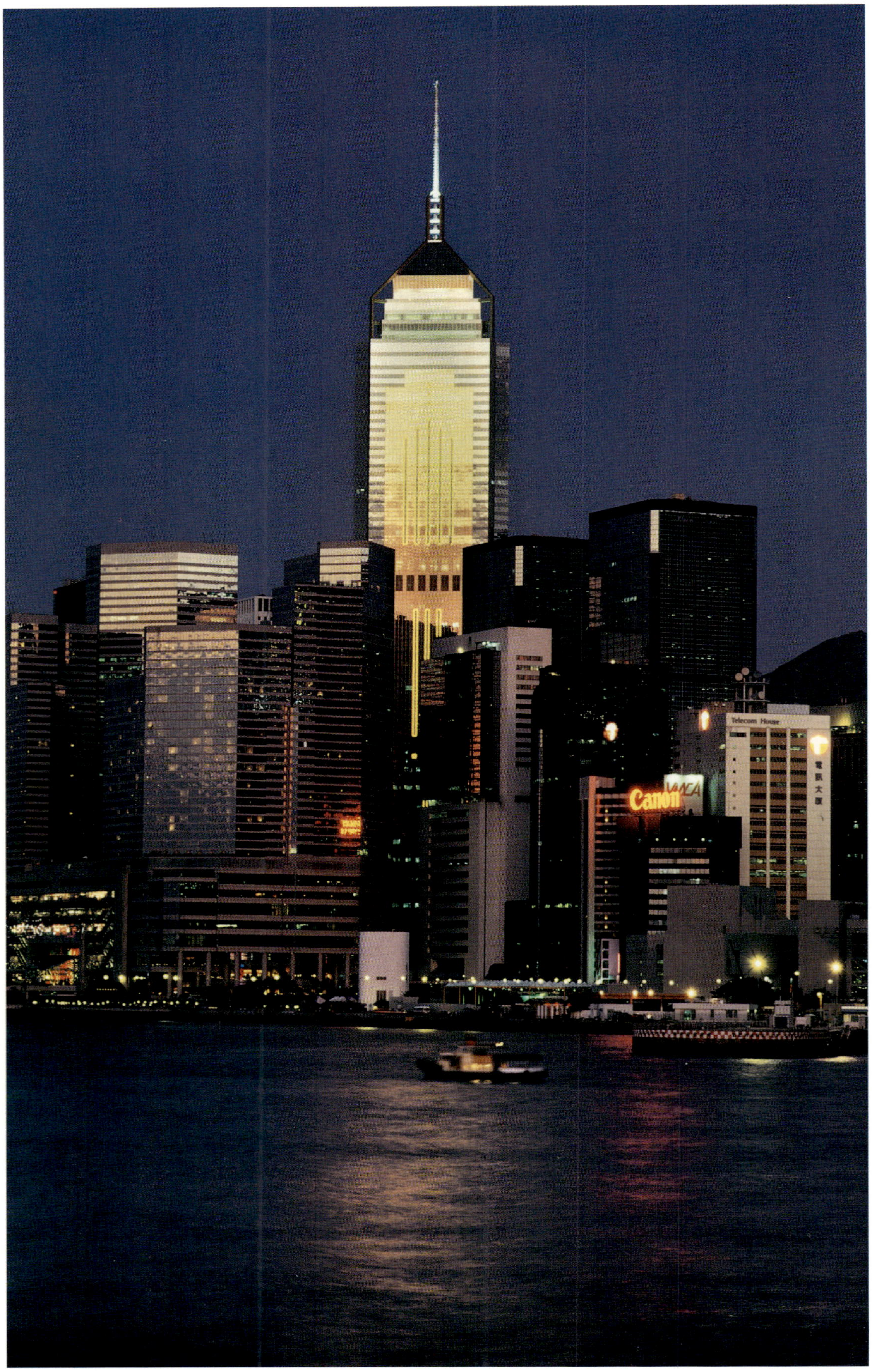

**Central Plaza, Hong Kong, from the bay.
Ng Chun Man & Associates, architects.
The tallest building in Asia at the time of its completion in 1992.**
Dennis Lau & Ng Chun Man.

Building[2] was to continue to stand alone and, for a considerable time, empty.

The American city, as characterized by the skyscraper, was conceived irrationally. Its economics were already recognized as irrational by commissions of inquiry into city center congestion starting in the early twenties.[3]

The phenomenon is cultural. What counts is proximity as a real estate agent naively confessed in Boston in 1881, "to be where everybody else is"[4]—or commercial agoraphobia, as Thomas Van Leeuwen was to say. From the beginning and still today, setting up away from the center represents a major risk. The early failure of the Empire State Building is well-known. And later there is the relative lack of success of the Sears Tower neighborhood, also set apart, but by so little. A very recent instance reconfirms the decisive commercial impact of a highly visible site. It took place in Hong Kong. The developer of Central Plaza, owner of a site distant from Central District during a period of stagnation in the real estate market, decided to counterbalance the disadvantage of an unfavorable location by a powerful concept. He would build the "tallest skyscraper in Asia!" The gamble appears to have paid off.[5]

This story brings two more factors into play, symbolic and psychological, which also explain the creation of skyscraper cities: competition—one of the well- springs of American identity, of free enterprise in general—and the transcendent value of verticality. To be the tallest, an achievement sought after since 1892 and which inspires today's titanic construction of twin towers, 450 meters (1,476 feet) high in Kuala Lumpur, Malaysia, can only be explained in terms of this dual ancestral compulsion.[6]

The New York skyline is thus identified with economic success, a symbol which seems to apply to any city. The number of skyscrapers, their height, their pace of construction are barometers of business prosperity. The history of skyscrapers shows an astonishing parallel with the geographical evolution of capital movement on the map of the world. It would be possible, as an exercise, to suggest an economic interpretation of the list of "the hundred tallest buildings in the world."[7] For the first time in history Malaysia is about to seize first place from the United States—Asia is the rising power! Whereas, until 1973, North America monopolized the list with the exception of two Soviet buildings: the 1953 Moscow University, 239 meters (784 feet) high and the 1955 Palace of Culture and Science in Warsaw, 231 meters (758 feet) high! In 1973 two non-American towers joined the list: the Maine-Montparnasse Tower in Paris and the Carlton Centre in Johannesburg.

Examining the same list, which only takes height into account and does not therefore give a completely accurate account of the real estate activity of a city or region, half the buildings included

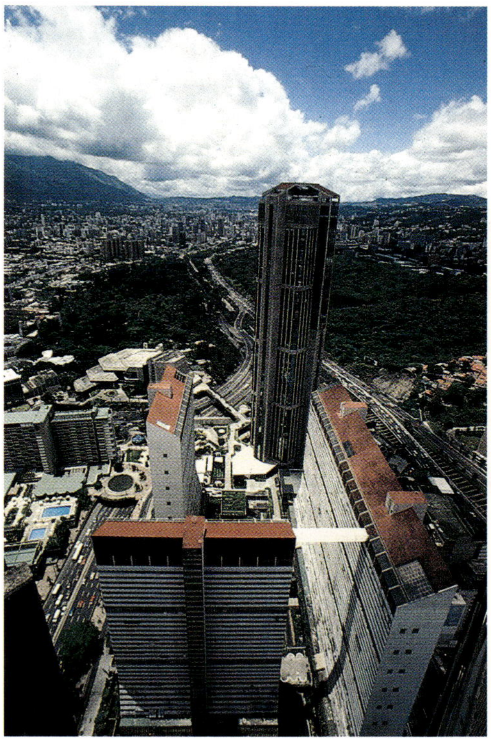

Parque Central, Caracas, general view of the new district. Siso, Shaw y Asociados S.A.M., architects, 1968-1984. In the foreground the residential buildings, 120 meters (394 ft) high. In the background, one of the two office towers, 221 meters (725 feet) high.

© Guillermo De Yavorsky, 1994.

during the last decade have been built in Asia; Malaysia, Hong Kong, the People's Republic of China, Taiwan, North and South Korea, Japan, Singapore and Indonesia, not counting those at the project stage in the "special economic zones" decreed in China since it opened its doors to the market economy. In Beijing alone, for example, the magazine *Far Eastern Review* revealed in summer 1994 that180 projects were underway covering an area of at least 2 million square meters (21 million square feet).[8] The fact is that China today is living through a real estate boom that risks making the urban upheavals of New York and Chicago early in the century pale into insignificance. Not only are skyscrapers appearing in significant numbers, but entire cities are rising at a stroke on what were fields and rice paddies scarcely ten years before. Shenzen, a new city of three million inhabitants on the frontier of Hong Kong's New Territories, is an example. Here foreign businessmen and official delegations rub shoulders in a setting of towers, freeways, luxury hotels and theme parks—last refuge of traditional Chinese arts.

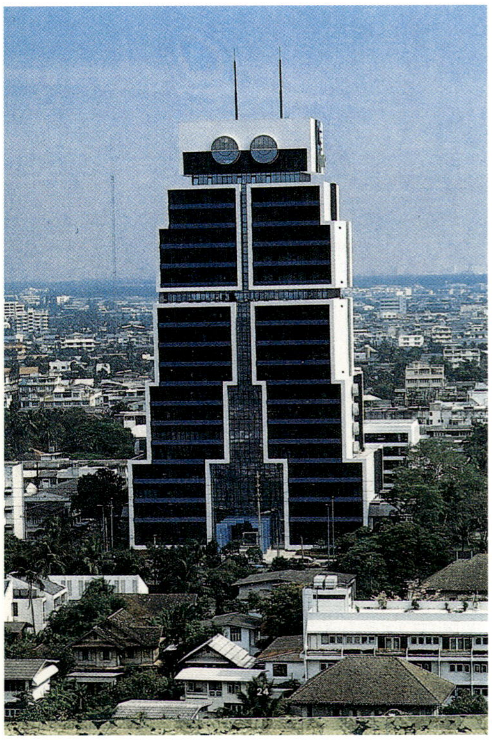

The Robot, headquarters of the Bank of Asia, Bangkok. Sumet Jumsai, architect, 1986.
SJA + 3D.

The cases not only of China but of Malaysia and, even more, Bangkok, Manilla or Jakarta, demonstrate once again that the decision to build tall is not determined by constraints but is definitely a reflection of economic growth or, more accurately, the economic aspiration of a country. It is not the cost of land, lack of space, or even demand that justifies the construction of a tower even higher yet than all the others in the center of Bangkok at a time when no master plan, no large-scale infrastructural project is underway and when the unbearable traffic congestion that renders the city so regrettably famous will not be relieved. Far from it.[9] To a lesser extent the destiny of Kuala Lumpur does not seem much better assured, and its new aspiration to become an international metropolis puts in jeopardy the quality of life the city can still pride itself on.

Other comparisons such as skyscrapers vis-à-vis economy and geography could be pursued such as average rental costs per square meter in a few major capitals with the number and height of commercial buildings. It would not then be surprising that Japan allows itself skyscraper projects of 800 stories—230 meters (750 feet) higher than Mount Fuji! The price per square meter in the center of Tokyo is ten times higher than in Shanghai, five times higher than in Frankfurt or Paris. It goes without saying that such projects will never be carried out. These technological utopias are matters for the research centers belonging to the most powerful construction companies in the country. Ecopolis and other X-Seed 4000 complexes[10] are even less realistic when the topographical and climatic considerations that have considerably

Opposite:
International Maritime Carrier Building, Kuala Lumpur. Tsao & McKown, architects, 1994.
Tsao & McKown.

hampered the spread of tall buildings in Japan are taken into account. The frequency of earthquakes and, more rarely referred to, the abundance and violence of rainstorms with their cost implications for the construction of curtain walls, for example, make skyscraper building particularly expensive and necessitate the prior development of very sophisticated techniques in the domain of stability, among others. The first tall building[11] constructed in Tokyo is situated in the Shinjuku district, the only area of the Japanese capital to have a rock substratum.[12] The city's sole tower district has been developed here, dominated for the past few years by architect Kenzo Tange's new town hall. The nature of the substratum also partly explains the profile of Manhattan; very high at the southern point where the rock outcrops, then lower moving northwards until approaching Central Park where the rock outcrops again and there is another series of skyscrapers.

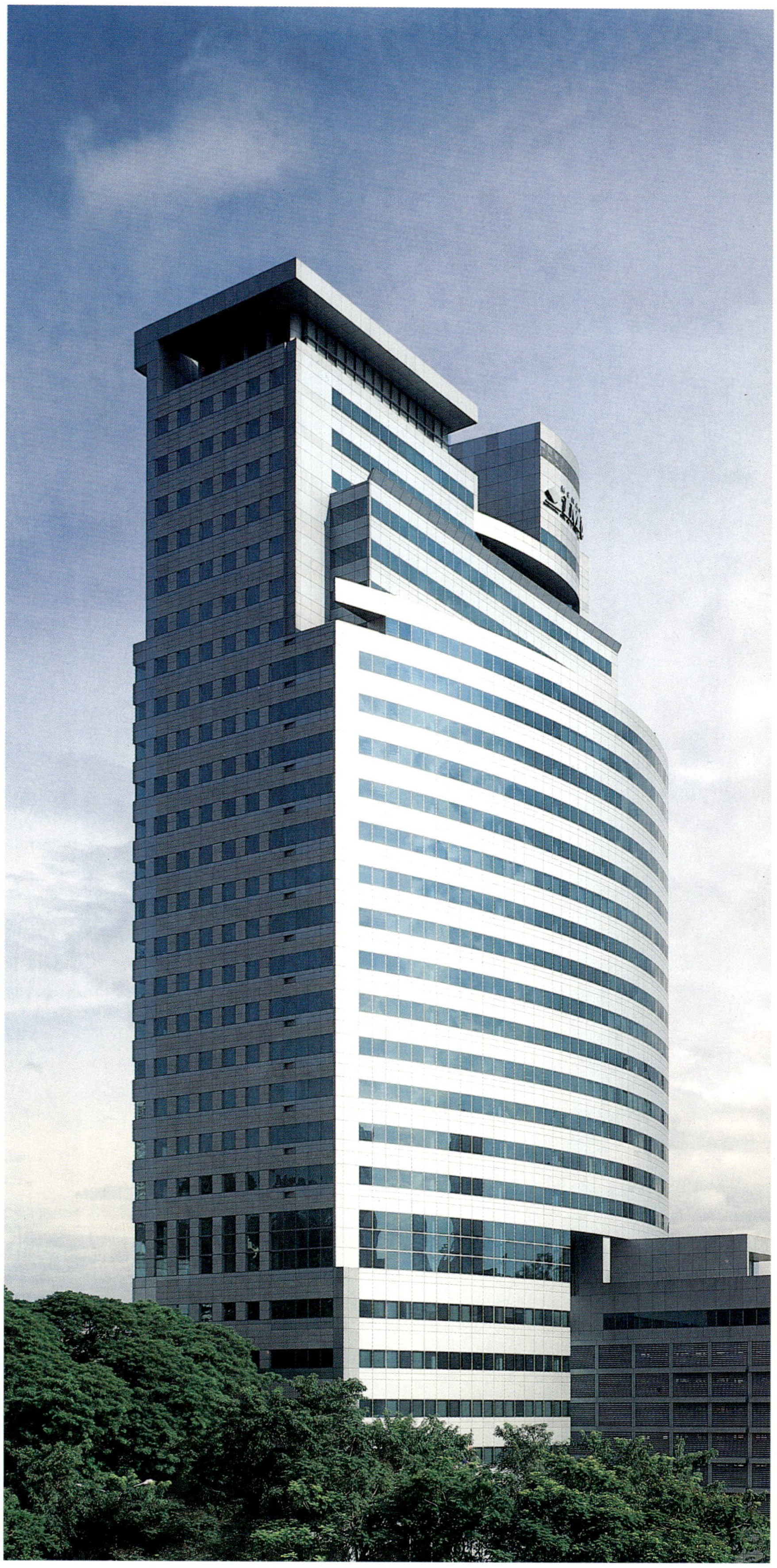

Another brake on the upward climb in Japan is the regulations, generally stricter than in the United States regarding the ratio of floor space to ground area, a constraint that unfortunately provides no qualitative guarantee, as proved by the construction in 1970 of the Hotel Imperial in the center of Tokyo, only seventeen stories high but at the price of demolishing one of the most outstanding buildings designed by Frank Lloyd Wright.[13] The existence of more or less constraining regulations nevertheless makes a difference in the ability of a city to strike the right balance between

Left:
Grollo Tower, Melbourne, 120 stories, more than 500 meters (1,640 feet) high. Harry Seidler & Associates, 1995 (unexecuted).
Harry Seidler & Associates.

Right:
DIB-200, Japan, Super-High-Rise project of 200 stories. Kajima Corporation, architects, ca. 1990 (unexecuted).
Kajima Corporation.

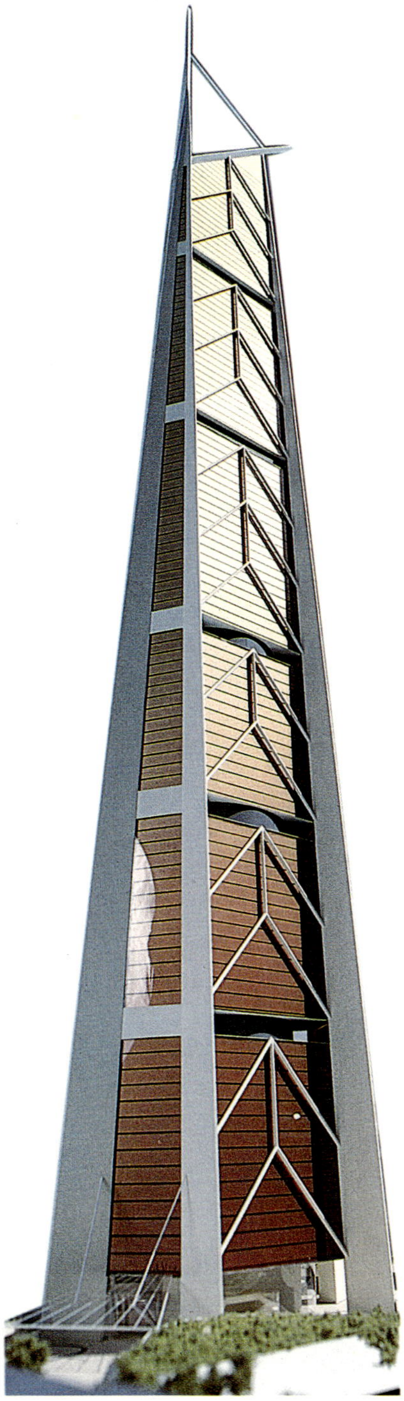

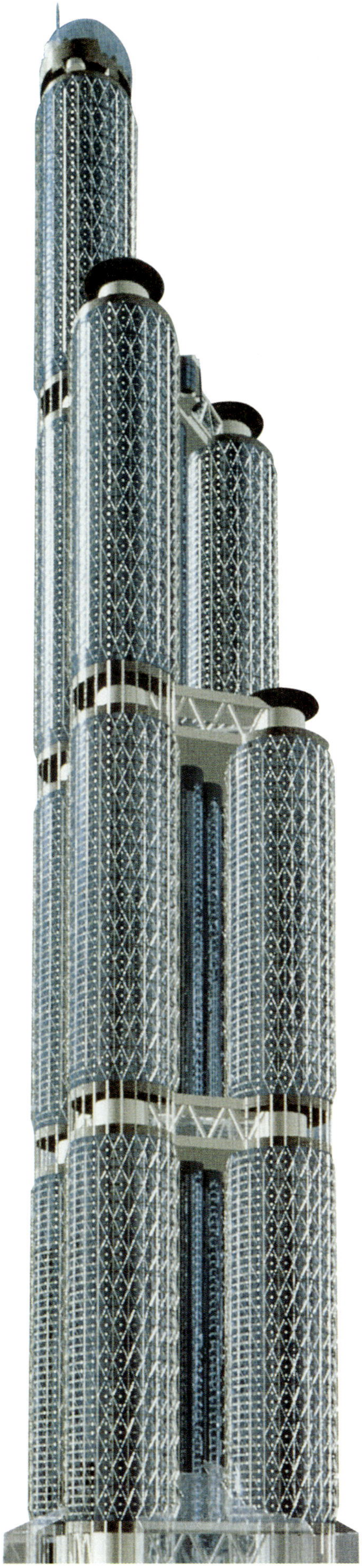

development, identity and quality of life. In this respect, and not forgetting the political price that the good ordering of a city may entail, the case of Singapore is worth dwelling on.

The transformation of Singapore into a center of international business is relatively recent. It virtually coincides with the building of a first skyscraper in 1976, the headquarters of the OCBC bank designed by Ieoh Ming Pei. Singapore is a kind of stepping stone between Australia, India and China but, above all, it owes its expansion to the Vietnam War and the convergent development of the oil industry. Certainly whole sections of the old colonial city have disappeared forever but, from the eighties the government has established a particularly stringent town planning policy controlling the progressive development of various business quarters, preserving heritage, creating large public parks, drastically limiting traffic and, as a corollary, setting up a very efficient public transport system. Singapore now resembles a vast, neo-American garden city studded with very concentrated bunches of skyscrapers where the names of the most illustrious international architects rub shoulders. Works of Ieoh Ming Pei, Helmut Jahn, Kenzo Tange and Kisho Kurokawa are to be found at Raffles Place on the southern bank of the river mouth. On the other bank there are I.M. Pei again, with the tallest hotel in the world[15] and Paul Rudolph. Then, on newly reclaimed land on the bay, there are three hotels by John Portman and projects by Kevin Roche, Philip Johnson and John Burgee. Finally, at Suntec City, Calvin Tsao and Zack McKown, two young New York architects under Pei's patronage, have designed five tower buildings and a congress center.[16] Nevertheless, this idyllic picture does not conceal a city plan for the island which, from new town to new town, systematically eats up virgin countryside and increasingly segregates the urban population.

However this may be, Singapore island, confined to its 618 square kilometers (238 square miles) is condemned to high density architecture. This is also the destiny, pushed to its extreme limits, of Hong Kong.

Hong Kong today is a little more than 100,000 hectares (247,000 acres). In the beginning, the city was built on a island with no more than 7,000 hectares (27 square miles) of dry land which formed all the British possession until the lease of the Kowloon promontory in 1860 and of the New Territories in 1898. The paucity of available land and its dramatic configuration straightway forced the city to develop at the water's edge. The first land to be reclaimed dates from 1851.

In 1956, under pressure from spectacular population growth and the development of manufacturing industry, a new ordinance allowing better use of available land was the starting signal for the city's frenetic development. While the public authorities concentrated their effort on housing and, from 1972, on the creation of new towns, the development of the center was essentially left to private enterprise. This period committed the city to a radical transformation, to its becoming

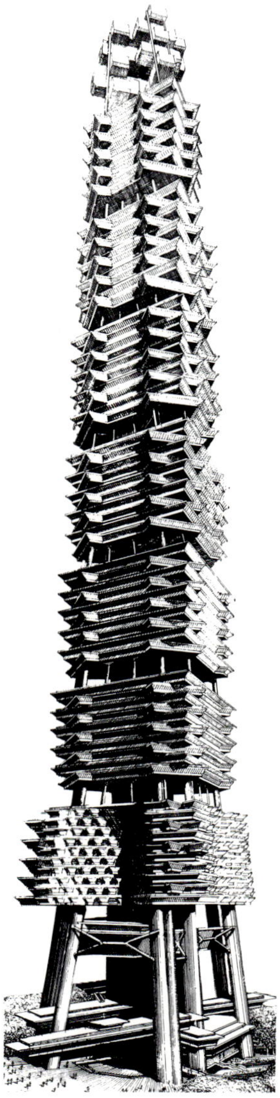

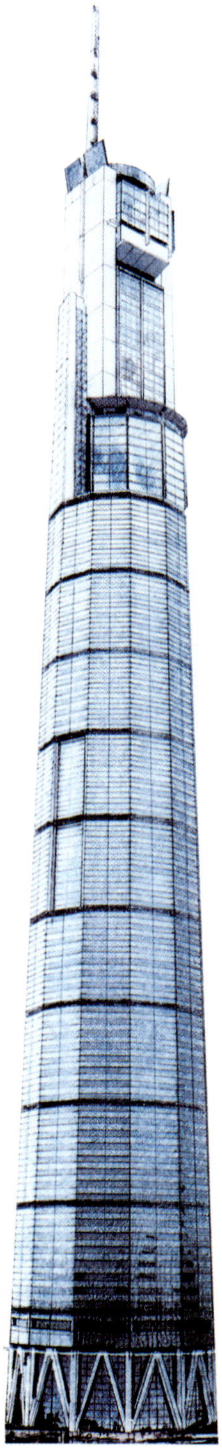

Left:
Sino Land Company Tower, Hong Kong, competition project. Paul M. Rudolph, architect, 1989 (unexecuted).
Paul Rudolph Architects.

Right:
Chongqing, 516 meters (1,693 feet) high. Haines Lundberg Waehler, architects, 1994 (unexecuted).
Haines Lundberg Waehler.

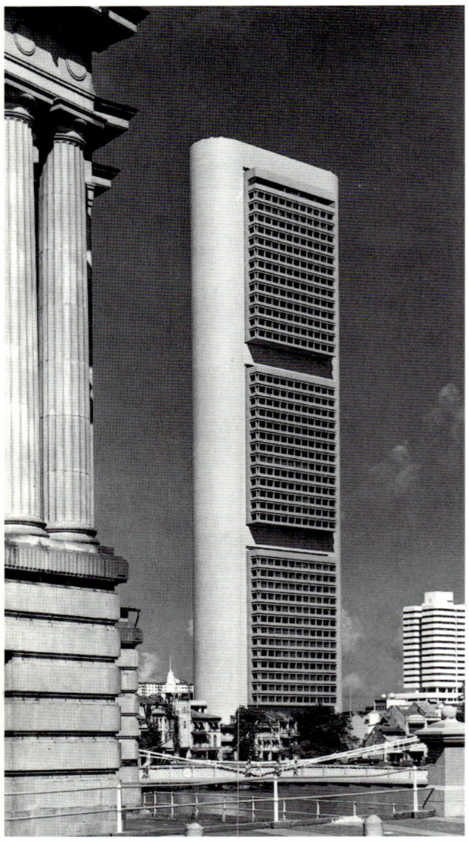

Oversea-Chinese Banking Corporation Centre (OCBC), Singapore.
I.M. Pei & Partners, 1976.
With its 52 stories, the first real skyscraper on the island.
Pei Cobb Freed & Partners.
Phot. Kouo Shang-Wei.

irreversibly vertical, culminating in the formation of a central district where towers upon towers rise in hanging garden steps up the foothills of the Peak. Two essential factors here exacerbate the economic and cultural logic of the over-dense business district: (1) Hong Kong confronts the communist mainland with the arrogance of a free China, an arrogance that the approach of 1997, date of its falling under Chinese aegis, seems to stimulate even more; (2) the narrowness of the strip of land, bound by the sea on one side and a huge rock on the other—the famous Peak of which the skyline is thankfully protected[17]—on which the city endlessly rebuilds itself, accentuates the towers' despairing reach for the sky.

This extreme situation has produced an equally extreme kind of urban development, a veritable laboratory of the city of the twenty-first century, "an enormous monument to the transitory on which an involuntary dignity has been bestowed."[18] Not that Hong Kong has been particularly concerned for the originality or beauty of its architecture. It needed the example of a Foster or a Pei[19] and the development of highly competitive real estate market conditions for quality finally to be granted freedom of the city. The aesthetics derive from the density: an amalgam of hybrid skyscrapers, the swarming mass of pedestrians, the traffic's din, the double-decker trams and double-layered subway network, streets, walkways, escalators and funicular, all collected together on an extraordinary site like a

Opposite:
Citibank Plaza, Hong Kong.
Rocco Design, architects (Rocco Yim), 1993.
Rocco Design.

1. Thomas A.P. VAN LEEUWEN, "Le Gratte-ciel ou le Mythe de la croissance naturelle", *Américanisme et Modernité*, EHESS / Flammarion, Paris, 1993.
2. During the Depression the cost of maintaining a building the size of the Empire State proved disastrous. During the thirties the Empire State Building was ridiculed by the nickname "Empty State Building." Winston WEISMAN, "A New View of Skyscraper History," *The Rise of an American Architecture*, éd. Praeger Publishers, New York, 1970.
3. Manfredo TAFURI, "La Dialectique de l'absurde", *Architecture d'aujourd'hui*, No. 178, March/April 1975.
4. Thomas A.P. VAN LEEUWEN, op. cit.
5. Central Plaza was built in 1992 by the architects Ng CHUN MAN & Associates. It was the tallest building in Asia at the time of its construction, 374 meters (1,227 feet) high. The story is taken from the article "Is Bigger Better?", *Asiaweek*, July 21, 1993.
6. The twin Petronas Towers of Kuala Lumpur are designed by the American architect Cesar PELLI.
7. Since 1972 the list of the 100 tallest buildings in the world has been regularly brought up to date by the Council on Tall Buildings and Urban Habitat, Lehigh University, Bethlehem, Pennsylvania, USA.
8. Kari HUUS, "No Place Like Home," *Far Eastern Economic Review*, July 28, 1994.
9. The Baiyoke Tower II, designed and built by the Thai firm of P lan Architects Co., is due for completion during 1997. It is 320 meters (1,050 feet) high.
10. The X-Seed 4000 complex, designed by Taisei Corporation in 1990, would reach a height of 4 kilometers (2.5 miles). Among the projects for urban utopias developed in Japan at the end of the eighties, DIB- 200 (200 stories) by Kajima Corporation, Aeropolis, 2,001 meters (6,565 feet) high by Hazama Corporation, Sky-City 1000, 1,000 meters (3,281 feet) high by Takenaka Corporation and the Millennium Tower (architect Norman FOSTER) for Obayashi Corporation can be mentioned.
11. Until 1963, because of the frequency of earthquakes the height of buildings in Japan was limited to a maximum of 31 meters (100 feet), 9 to 10 stories. The first skyscraper in Japan, the Kasumigaseki Building (36 stories) was built in Tokyo in 1968 by the YAMASHITA Architects & Engineers.
12. Tokyo is built on an alluvial sub-soil with bedrock 40 meters (130 feet) below ground. In the Shinjuku district it rises to less than 26 meters (85 feet).

back-lit panorama, a wide cinema screen erected in the bay. This dizzying density, sweltering under a tropical sun, generates an energy, a special beauty an "extreme artificiality [that] has acquired the status of something self-evident and inexorable, such as one would associate with a form occurring in nature."[20]

Given that New York embodies better than any other city the myth of the modern metropolis and that not even Chicago or Boston or the cities of Texas and the American West—for all the height and sometimes the beauty of their recent skyscrapers—have been able to create a skyline or urban landscape as memorable or as strong. Given that neither Europe nor any other continent has really counted in the invention of a new urban image, Hong Kong, at the close of the century, has entered into the mythology of the Babylonian cities.

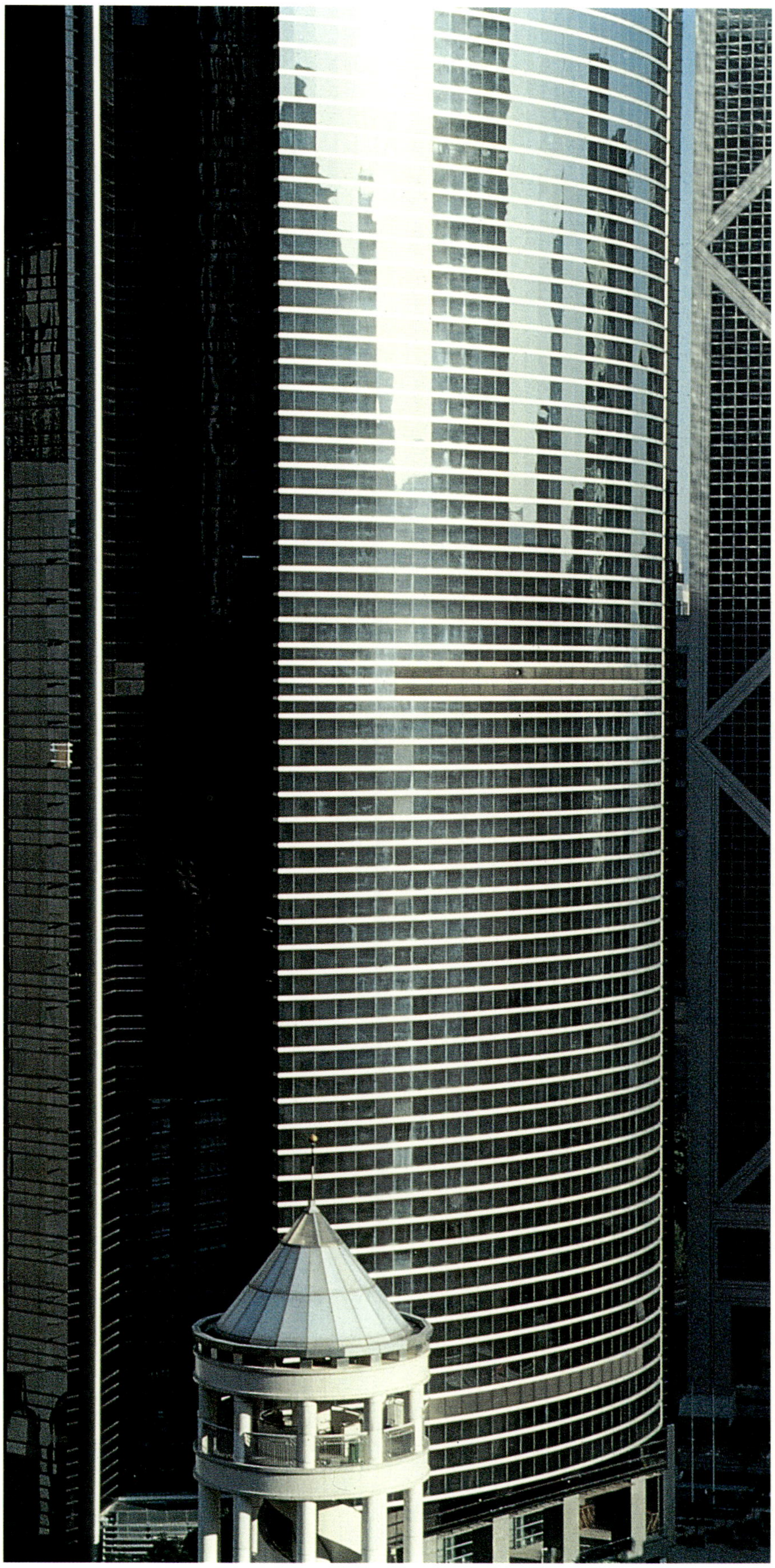

13. The Hotel Imperial (1912-1923), designed by F.L. WRIGHT was demolished in 1968.

14. The Arab oil embargo considerably strengthened the strategic position of Singapore, sole supplier to the American army. Oil exploration and the banking sector were greatly developed during this period.

15. The Westin Stamford Hotel is part of the Raffles City complex completed in 1986. The hotel has 73 stories and 1,250 rooms.

16. The draft project for Suntec City was designed by Ieoh Ming PEI in association with Calvin TSAO and Zack McKOWN.

17. The development strategy defined in 1991 by the Hong Kong government in the "Metroplan" master plan, allows for 20% to 30% of the hilly skyline to remain visible from the opposite side of the harbor.

18. Vittorio Magnano LAMPUGNANI, "The Aesthetics of Density," in *Hong Kong Architecture: Aesthetics of Density*, D.A.M./Prestel, 1993.

19. Norman FOSTER built the headquarters of the Hong Kong and Shanghai Bank in 1985 and I.M. PEI that of the Bank of China in 1989.

20. Vittorio Magnano LAMPUGNANI, op. cit.

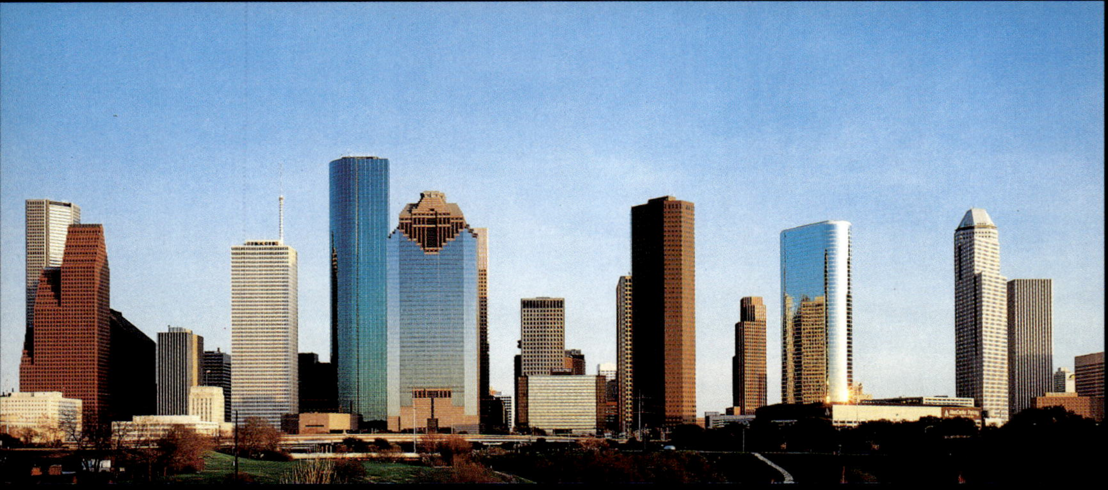

Houston.
© Timothy Hursley.

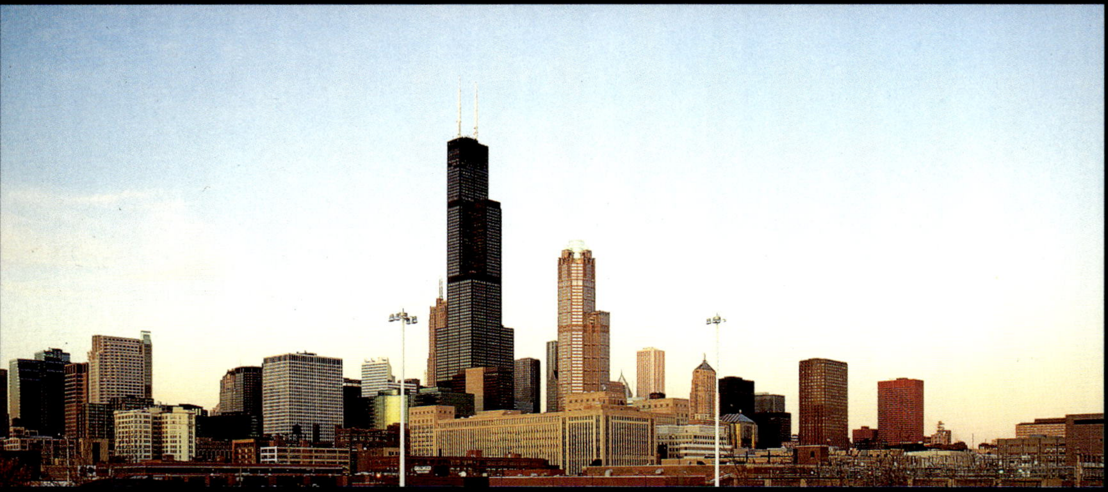

Chicago.
© Benoît Roland.

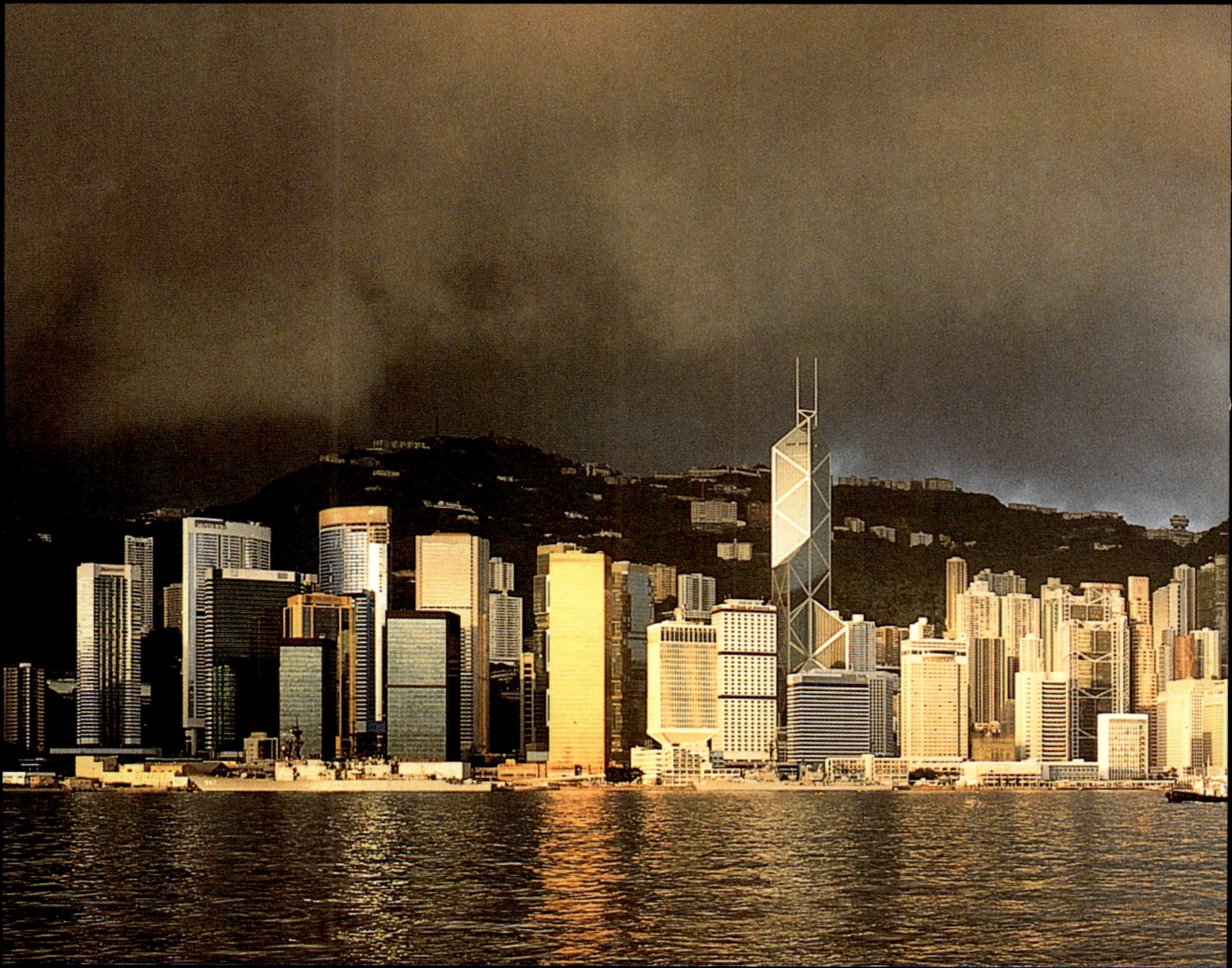

Hong Kong.
© Paul Warchol.

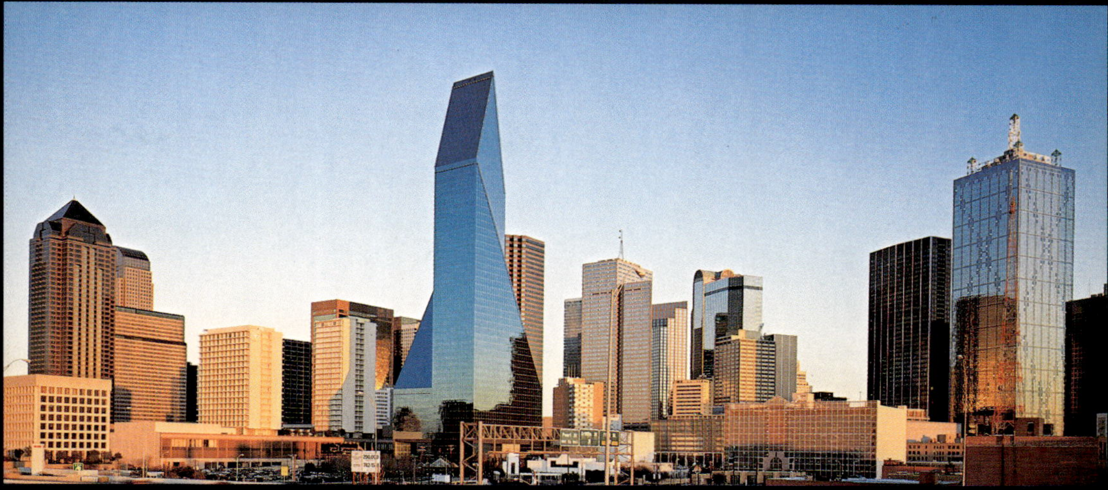

Dallas.
© Timothy Hursley.

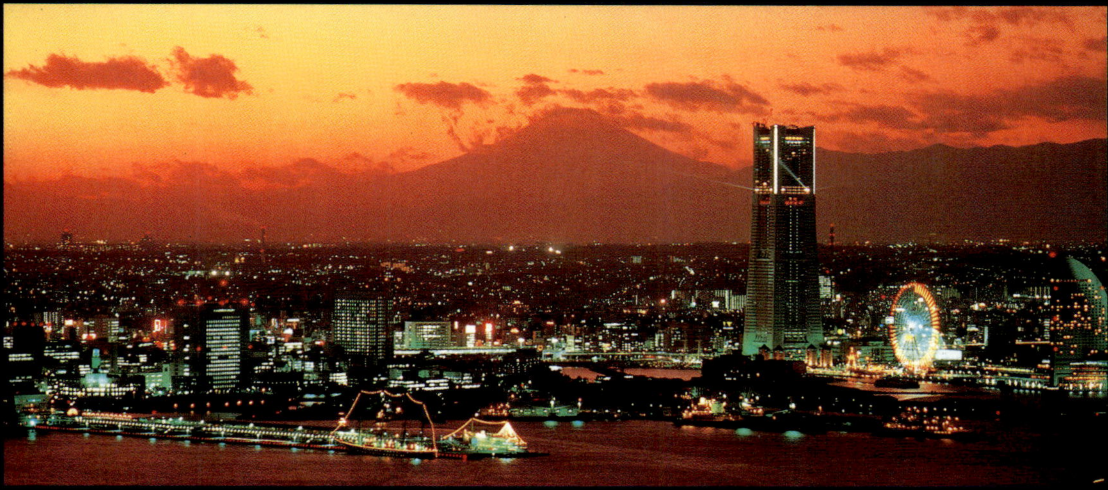

Yokohama.
© Nikko Hotels.

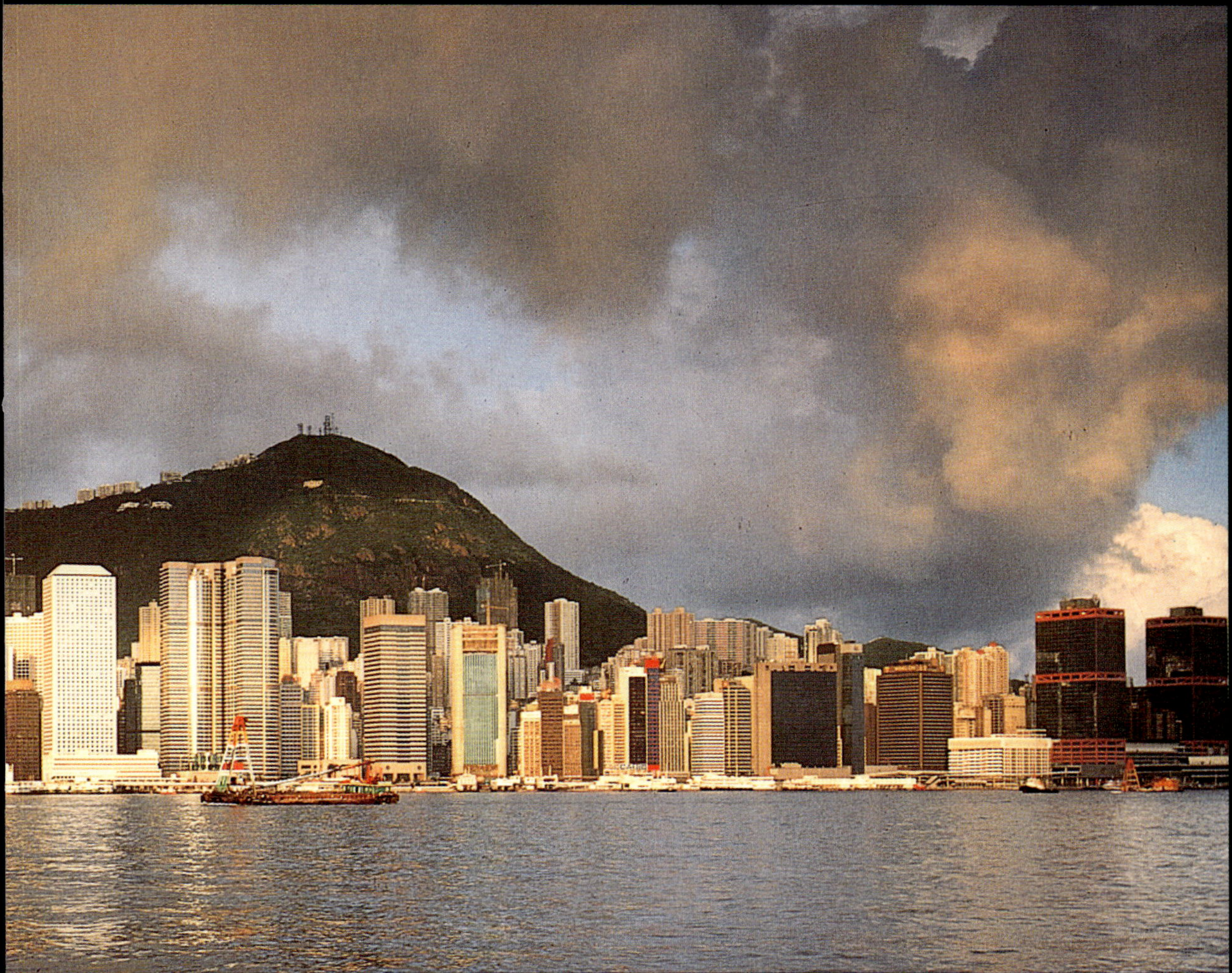

AROUND THE WORLD

Drawing IFA / Valérie Gevers.

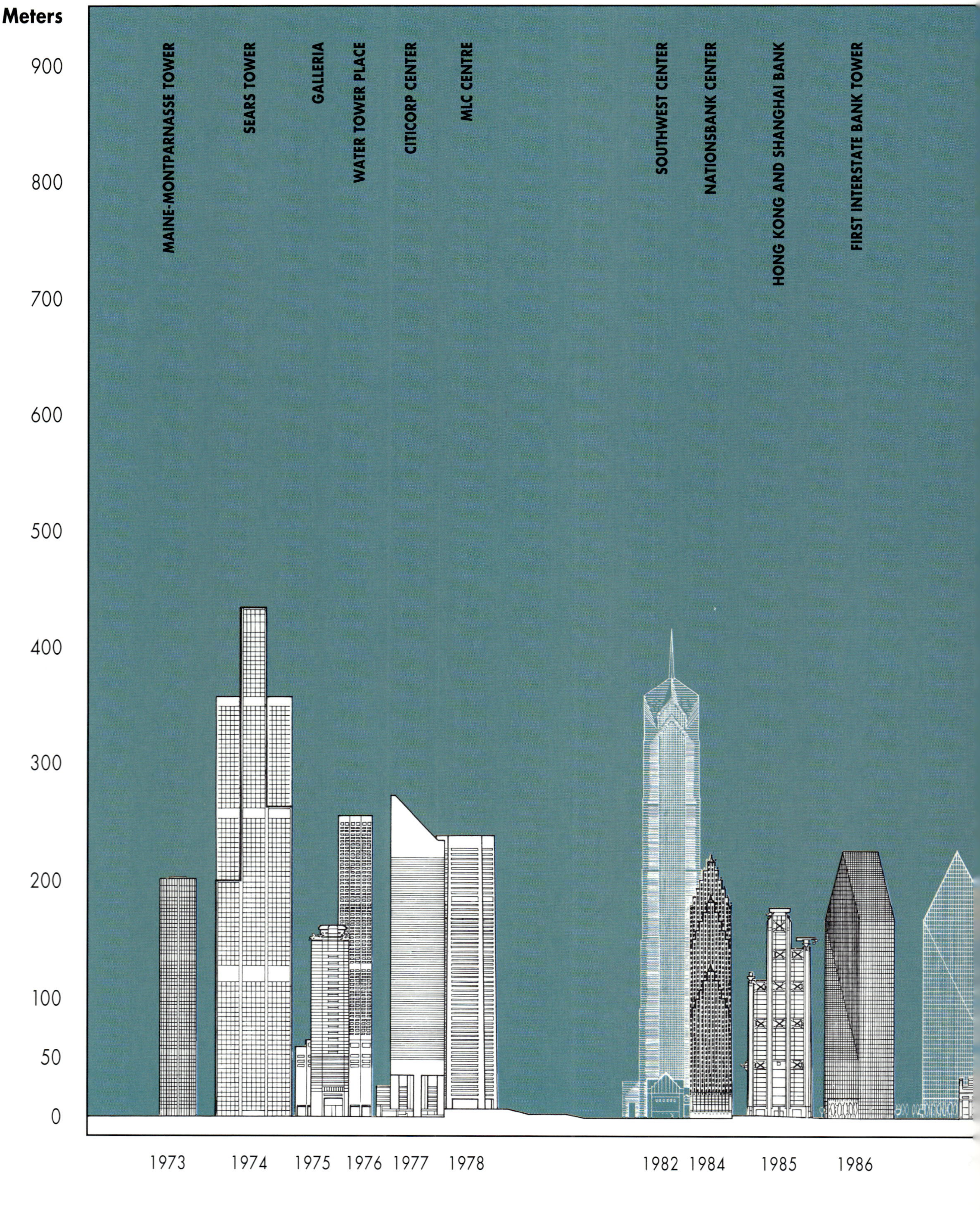

IN TWENTY-ONE PROFILES

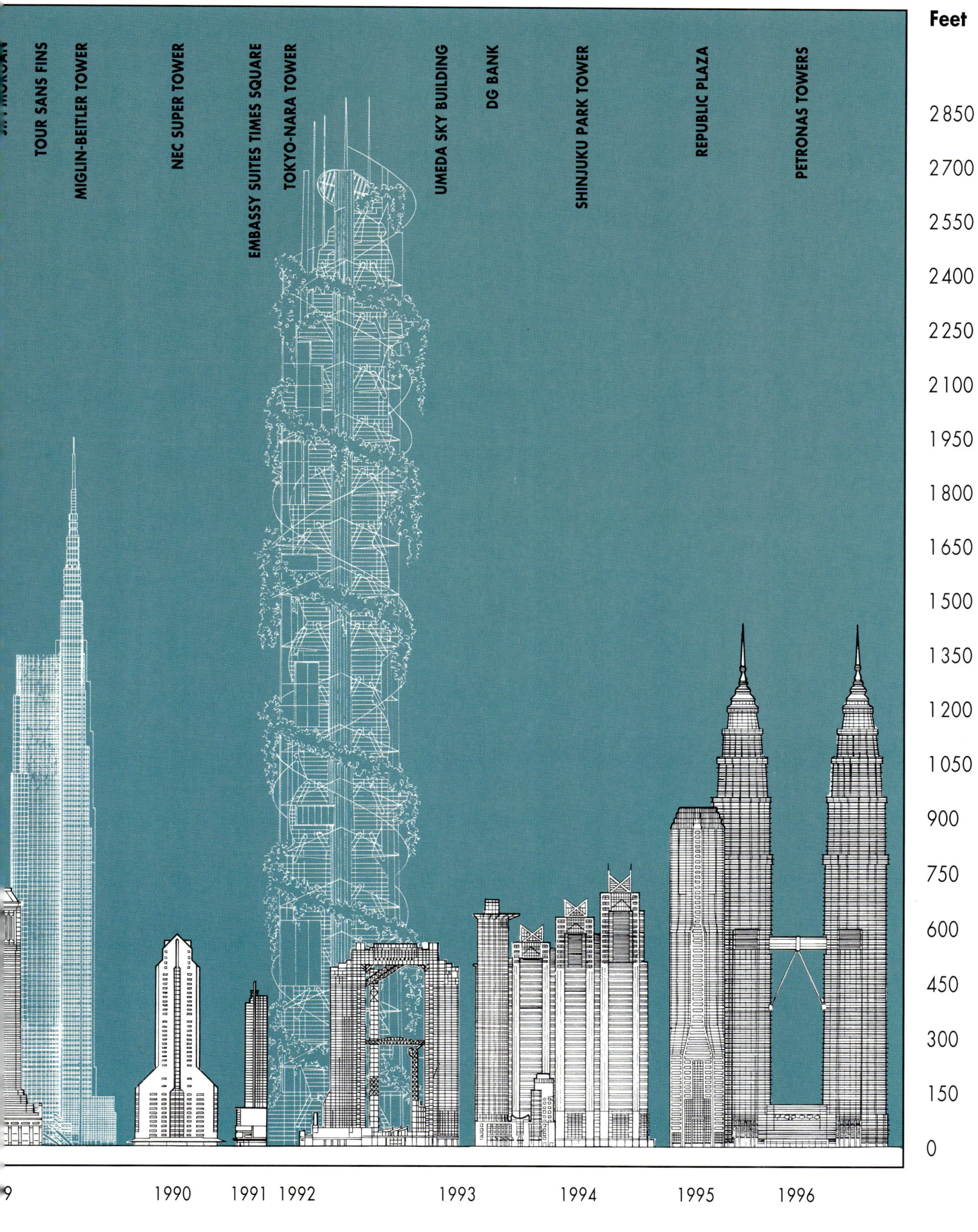

In 1973, for the first time, a very tall tower was built outside North America. And, paradoxically, this black monolith rose in the heart of Paris, complementing the swathes cut through the city by Haussmann and becoming a solitary rival to the Eiffel Tower.

In the same year Manhattan radically changed its aspect, thenceforth dominated by the twin towers of the World Trade Center. But their record height was soon to be surpassed. In 1974, the Sears Tower in Chicago became the highest building in the world. This event gave the place of honor to a city which had always refused to play the second role in an epic of which it had itself written some of the first lines. It also crowned the achievement of a group of engineers and architects, Skidmore, Owings & Merrill, which had imposed its presence in the field of commercial architecture to the point that, since the fifties, it had literally created fashions in skyscraper design. The Sears Tower was a portent of a profound change. Not only was it very tall—its record was to stand for more than twenty years—it was one of the very first deliberately to break with the standardized shape of skyscrapers of the modern period.

Now, in 1995, on the other side of the world, two twin towers, a little taller still and shaped like immense pagodas, are being completed. And, even more surprisingly, they are built in concrete.

Between these twins and the Sears Tower, two decades of new skyscrapers have transformed, sometimes brutally, the landscape of great cities. The torch has been passed from the United States to the other shore of the Pacific Ocean. The architectural vocabulary has enlarged, structures and technologies have been perfected. The hegemony of height has given way to other qualitative criteria: slenderness of proportion, silhouette, landscape....

Opposite:
The Miglin-Beitler Tower on the Chicago skyline, a photomontage. Cesar Pelli & Associates, architects, 1989.
Miglin-Beitler, Inc.

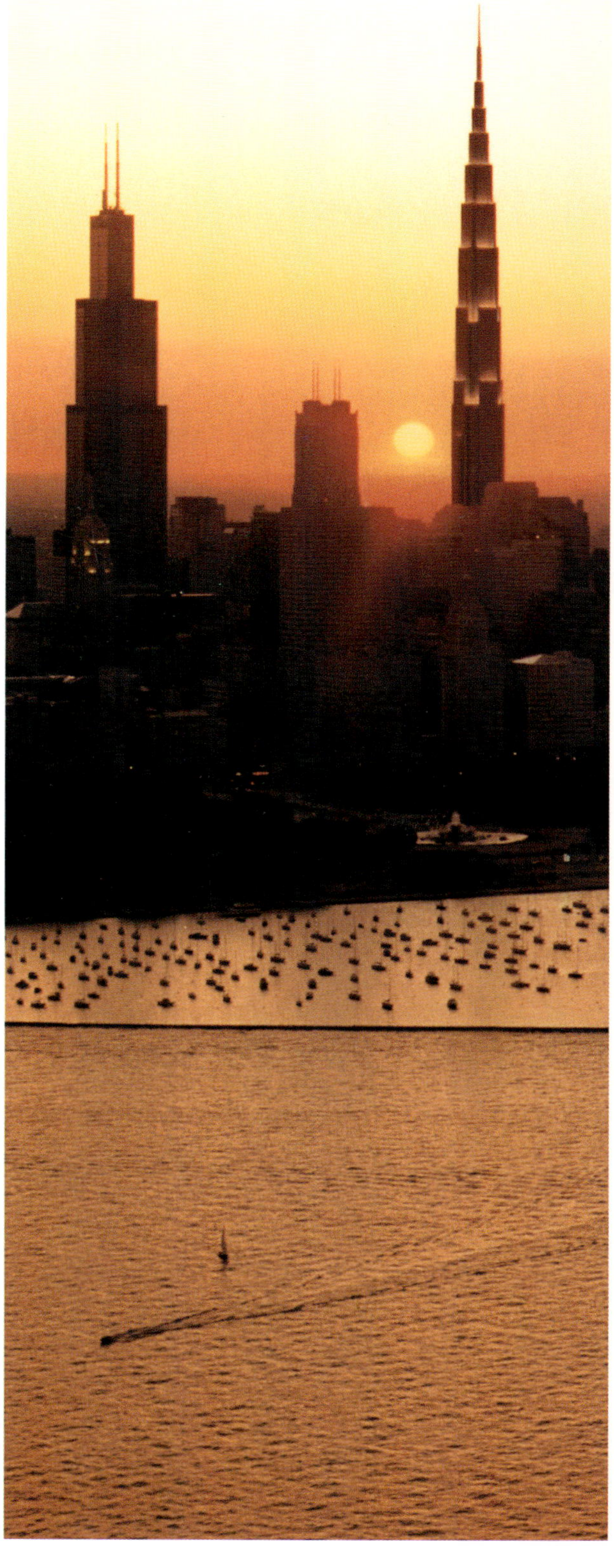

Ecology has come into play and with it awareness of energy cost, the importance of nature, considerations of climate. At the same time the dialogue with the city and its inhabitants has again became a factor. To the acknowledged specialists in high rise construction—the Skidmore Owings & Merrills of America, the Nikken Sekkeis of Japan—a new generation of architectural practices, as well as a few outsiders, have been added. And who should arrive on the scene but prestige architecture's star performers, from Jean Nouvel to Frank Gehry, to join in the race for the sky?

This is the progress to be depicted here in all its diversity by a series of profiles. It describes an imaginary metropolis where twenty-one skyscrapers are ranked in chronological order, each one with a story to tell about architects, engineers and developers; sites, places, cultures and regulations; building programs for offices, housing or hotels; technical prowess, records and, even more, dreams. Twenty-one snapshots of buildings around the world among the thousands which make up the architecture of today.

MAINE-MONTPARNASSE TOWER

Paris - France

Agence d'Aménagement de l'Opération Maine-Montparnasse A. O. M.
E. Beaudouin, U. Cassan, L. de Hoym de Marien, J. Saubot - 1973

"The celebrated vistas of Paris will hardly be threatened by a building planted in a neighborhood where not a single stone deserves preservation. And the sky over Paris is still wide enough for today's generation to be able to inscribe it with the architectural forms of its own time."

A. O. M., 1958.

The setting back of Montparnasse railway station and the building of a huge modern district on the vacated land was already under discussion in 1934. The option was confirmed in 1956 by the development plan for the Paris Region, which gave its blessing at the same time to the creation of the Défense business district to the west of Paris. In the center of the Maine-Montparnasse project, a skyscraper—approved in principle in 1958—would visually terminate the Rue de Rennes, the great thoroughfare cut by Haussmann through the old fabric of the city.

Ten years were to go by before the final project was approved—ten years of hesitation and raging debate which would induce endless revisions to the initial scheme. At the outset the tower was to be 150 meters (490 feet) high. It was successively moved, off-centered, put back in its original position and shortened; in 1971 there was still talk of halving its height! Finally, the height of the tower was raised to over 200 meters (650 feet) under pressure from the Commission supérieure des monuments historiques (a national committee for the preservation of historical monuments), among others. The principle of the podium emerged in 1961, the almond shape of the tower's plan in 1966, a device already applied to the Pirelli Tower in Milan (Gio Ponti, 1956), of which the slender elegance was, it seems, referred to a number of times.

The debate about the height, position and shape of the tower took place at the time in terms of the landscape. The erection of a skyscraper in the center of Paris was to modify profoundly the skyline of the city. It was in this essentially aesthetic context that the repeated interventions of the Commission supérieure des monuments historiques should be understood.

For some, led by André Malraux, who was Minister of Culture at the time, the creation of "new landscapes" was the indispensable concomitant to the establishment of a policy of protection towards old districts. "Paris does not only have places to protect, it

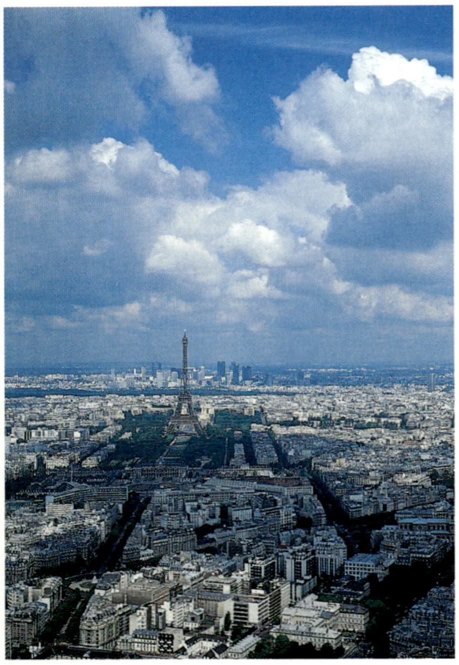

The Eiffel Tower and the Défense business district seen from the top of the Montparnasse Tower.
© Dominique Delaunay, Institut français d'architecture, 1995.

Opposite:
The Montparnasse Tower seen from the Boulevard Edgar-Quinet.
© Dominique Delaunay, Institut français d'architecture, 1994.

Architects: Agence d'Aménagement de l'Opération Maine-Montparnasse (Eugène Beaudouin, Urbain Cassan, Louis de Hoym de Marien, Jean Saubot) — *Consultant architects:* A. Epstein and Sons, Inc. (Chicago) — *Consultant engineers:* Carl A. Morse, Inc. (New York) — *Contractor:* Campenon Bernard — *Developer:* Société d'économie mixte pour l'aménagement du secteur Maine-Montparnasse SEMAMM (semi-public company for the development of the Maine-Montparnasse sector).

Completed in 1973 — 58 stories, 209 meters (686 feet) high — Mixed construction of concrete (sliding shuttering) and steel — Office building 112,000 square meters (1,206,000 square feet of floor space) with public observation deck and restaurant on the 56th floor, and a panoramic terrace forming a 59th floor.

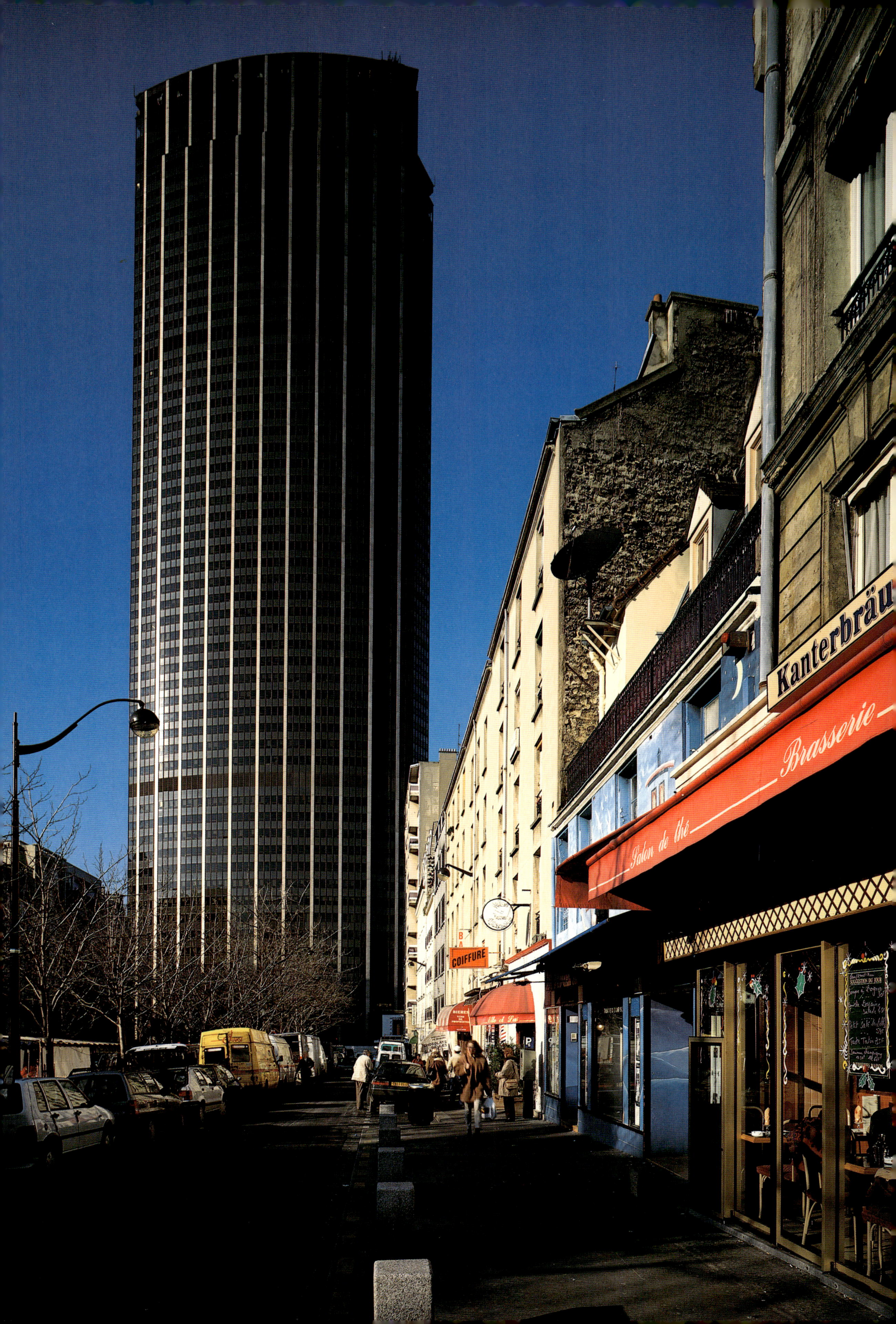
Kanterbräu
Brasserie
Salon de thé
COIFFURE

has places to create," he said when the project was approved. (André Malraux, Conseil général des Bâtiments de France, March 13, 1959.)

For others, alarmed by the arrival of the new neighborhood's first buildings on the Paris horizon—the development is situated on a natural promontory more than 50 meters (160 feet) above the level of the river Seine—the future skyscraper was an outrage to the monumental buildings and grand vistas of Paris. Their hostility would soon focus on the peripheral district of the Défense where the towers, formerly limited to a height of 100 meters (330 feet), were to be allowed, as from 1969, to rise twice as tall.

However, what the debate evaded at the time—heritage, public space—constitutes the essential failure of the project. The old Montparnasse Station was torn down with total disregard, and the barrenness of the façades built in its place truly ruin the neighboring public space.

On the financial side, one of the decisive factors to take the project from the drawing board to the building site was the entry on the scene of a North American property developer, Collins Tuttle and Company, accustomed to dealing with projects of such a scale. It was, in effect, an ambitious proposition. The office tower is the figurehead of a huge complex: a mixture of individual shops and department stores, office buildings placed on the podium, one cube of eleven stories and a slab building of three levels, roof gardens, a sports center with a swimming pool, movie theaters, underground parking, and access to four subway lines, or more than 8 hectares (20 acres) and 300,000 square meters (3.2 million square feet) of floor space on one estate. The strategy adopted by the real estate developer was to divide the

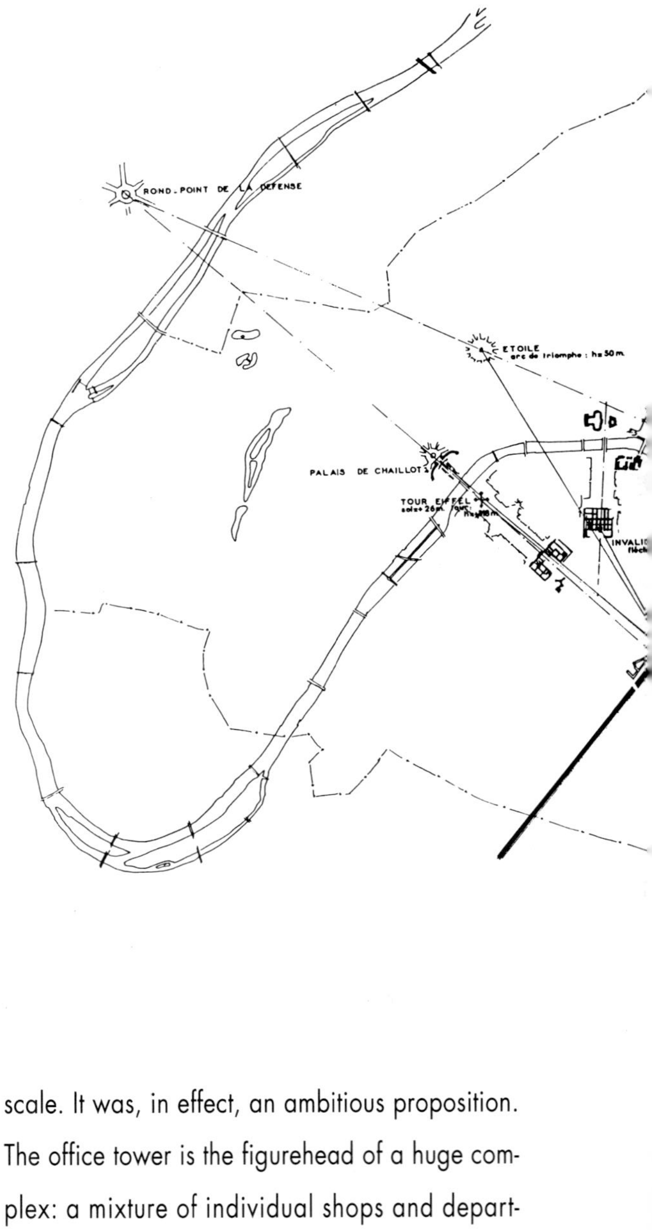

Center:
Parisian points of view.
This 1958 drawing is one among numerous documents showing evidence of the importance given by architects to the idea of landscape and grand vistas.
Institut français d'architecture.

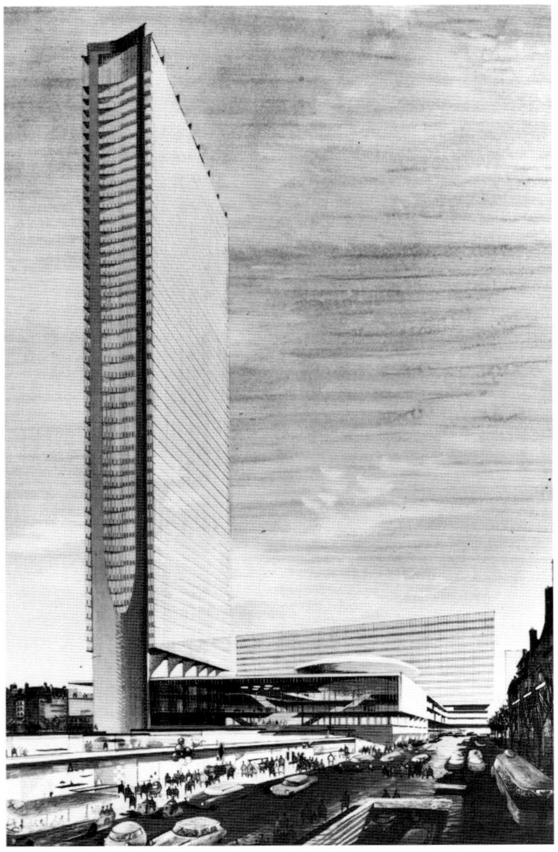

The 1961 project, perspective.
Institut français d'architecture.

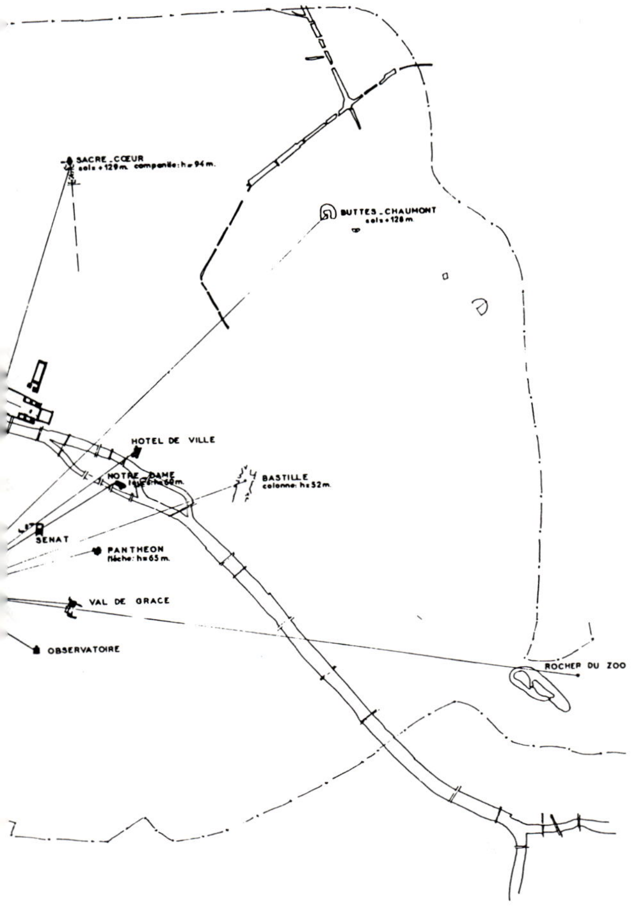

complex into four distinct lots, albeit sharing the same address, thus reducing the tower block to an almost everyday investment—a lot of about 100,000 square meters (1 million square feet). Construction began in 1969, a year which marked a turning point. After the political turmoil of the previous spring, Paris launched itself into a new frenetic era of modernity. It was the year of General de Gaulle's resignation. The Presidency of Georges Pompidou was to see the destruction of Baltard's central market (Les Halles) in 1971 and, in 1977, the construction of Renzo Piano and Richard Rogers' Centre Beaubourg in the heart of Paris. The Montparnasse Tower coincided exactly with the five years in office of this modernizing president. It also gave the French building industry an opportunity to demonstrate its technical mastery. At 209 meters (686 feet) it was the highest tower in Western Europe and remained so until the construction of the MesseTurm in Frankfurt in 1990. It also served as a useful exercise for property developers who put the flexibility of operation of a semi-public economy to the test, particularly regarding environmental regulations.

These were not the only lessons. The building implanted a lasting conviction in the minds of the public and decision makers alike that it should be a unique exercise. In effect, its construction has permitted the measuring of the impact of erecting a building of such a size in an old urban pattern: the density of traffic, for example, the dislocation of public space, the distortion of land value. But more important still, it is because the tower stands alone like a landmark equivalent to the Sacré-Cœur—whose campanile rises 223 meters (732 feet) above the Seine on the opposite side of Paris—or to the Eiffel Tower; it acquires a symbolic value, the monumental status that the architects had planned for it from the beginning.

In another city in another context this bronze skyscraper would doubtless appear almost commonplace apart from its height. In Paris, paradoxically, it acquires a special significance.

Site plan.
Buildings & Data.

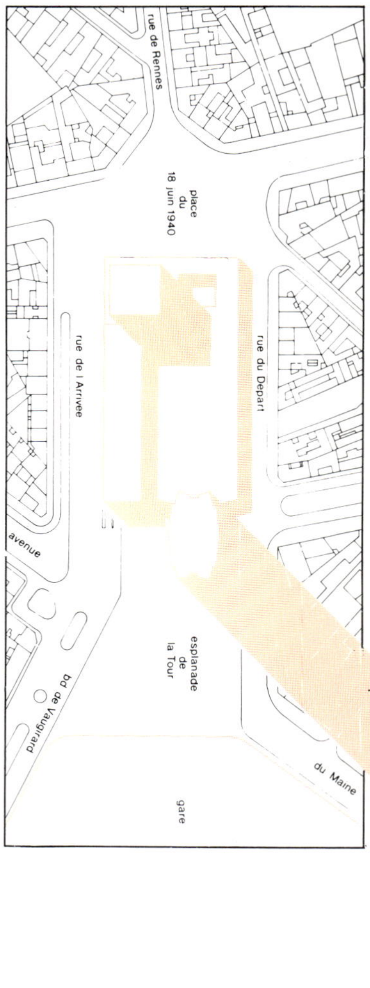

SEARS TOWER

Chicago - United States

Skidmore, Owings & Merrill - 1974

"In the same way as prehistoric animals disappeared when their size became too difficult to carry, the second school of Chicago reached its critical point in two buildings designed by SOM."

Frédéric Edelmann,
150 Ans d'architecture de Chicago, 1833-1983,
Paris Art Center, 1985.

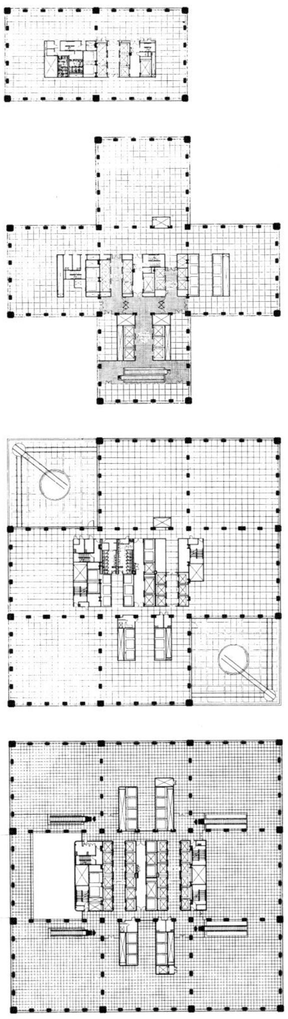

Typical floor plans: from bottom to top, ground floor, 50th, 67th and 91st floors.
SOM Chicago.

The Sears Tower was the tallest in the world for over twenty years. It is the work of a group of architects and engineers which also holds a fair number of records: for longevity (SOM was founded in 1936), range of activity, size of the group, awards, number of skyscrapers built, among them, the tallest inhabited tower, and about fifteen of the hundred tallest skyscrapers listed in the world. The group was founded in Chicago, city of pioneers and city of giants: Sears, 443 meters (1,454 feet); Amoco Building by Edward Durrell Stone, Perkins & Will, 1973, 346 meters (1,136 feet); John Hancock Center by SOM, 1969, 344 meters (1,127 feet); Two Prudential Plaza by Loebl, Schlossman and Hackl, 1990, 298 meters (978 feet); 311 South Wacker Drive by Kohn Pedersen Fox, 1990, 292 meters (959 feet)....

The tower contains almost 40 hectares (98 acres) of office space. When built, it was the largest building in the world after the Pentagon. Out of the 16,500 work stations available, the developer, Sears, Roebuck and Co.—a mail-order and department store chain—only occupies 7,000 situated in the first 49 floors, the widest of the tower. The other stories intended for rental are smaller and better suited to a demand for individual floors for offices. This commercial constraint was the reason for the structure and shape of the tower: 9 cluster tubes square in section rise integrally to a first stage at the 49th-floor level where the tower starts to narrow in successive stages, with the tubes diminishing in number to 7, 5, and finally 2 for the highest floors.

The building gives the effect of having been cut out of a single mass with the play of buttresses, the recognizable structural expression of the architect Graham, and the engineer Khan. Hence the stepped profile which, without departing from the smooth curtain wall formula, opens the way towards typological experiment, the formal tapering, the historical inspiration of the skyscrapers of the following decade. "Graham and Khan have thus broken away from the prosaic milk-carton and cracker-box shapes common to

---

Architects: Skidmore, Owings & Merrill, Chicago (Bruce Graham) — *Structural engineers:* Skidmore, Owings & Merrill, Chicago (Fazlur Khan) — *Mechanical and electrical consultants:* Jaros Baum & Bolles — *Contractor:* Diesel Construction — *Developer:* Sears, Roebuck and Co.

110 stories, 443 meters (1,454 feet) high — 102 elevators — Steel construction — maximum floor area: 4,700 square meters (50,625 square feet); or 9 cluster tubes of 520 square meters (5,625 square feet) — Total area approx 345,000 square meters (3.7 million square feet).

Opposite:
The Sears Tower in the Chicago of the eighties.
© Timothy Hursley.

so many other buildings, whose appearance would not be significantly changed whether they were forty, sixty or eighty stories tall.... Sears Tower clearly and exultantly asserts itself as a giant whose elements assume a lighter character as they rise, in a manner somewhat akin to that of skyscrapers built in the 1920's." (Paul Gapp, *Paul Gapp's Chicago*, published by The Chicago Tribune, 1980.)

It is no less true that the Sears Tower cruelly reveals the limitations of such great height: a gale blows constantly at the foot of the tower and its court is the essence of discomfort—so much so that SOM was commissioned in 1985 to construct a new porch. It was also a matter of enlarging the too small lobby, a porch already replaced during the construction of a second porch designed by other architects as an entrance for tourists. Their derisory scale and obvious mismatch underlined rather than remedied the problems of a dinosaur-scale building trying to live in harmony with a city of human beings. In contrast with the John Hancock Center, built five years previously by SOM, which succeeded in its mission as a catalyst in the development of a new quarter, the Sears Tower has not generated the expected commercial activity. The densification of its neighborhood proceeds very slowly and there are more empty sites than buildings, as if the tallest tower in the world was not enough to resurrect this dead-end locality, lacking in humanity and urban animation.

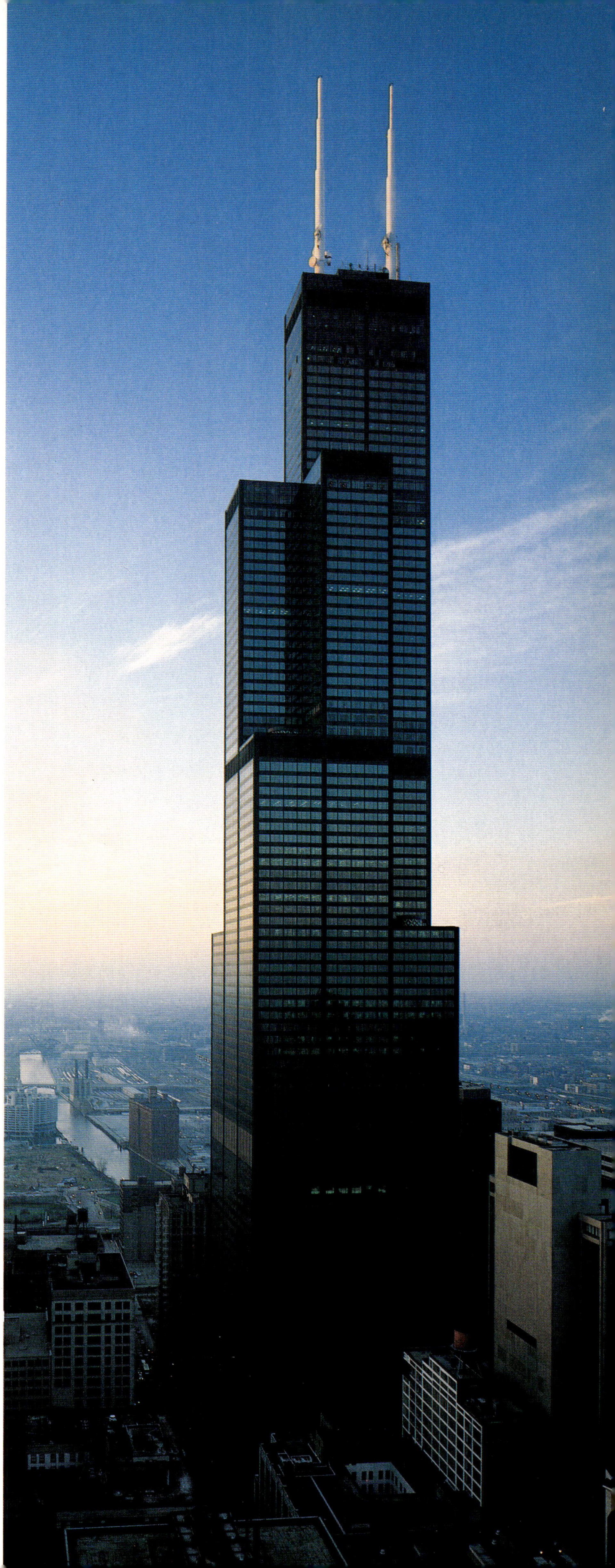

GALLERIA

New York - United States

David Kenneth Specter - 1975

"The advantages which were in fact inherent in such locations—increased privacy, exposure, light and air, as well as use of an outdoor space—were increasingly appreciated; architects began to plan them in advance for use as apartments and, ... at the present moment, the erstwhile janitor's quarters have become the most expensive rentable space in the building."

Hugh Ferriss, *The Metropolis of Tomorrow*, Ives Washburn Publisher, New York, 1929.

Anyone walking in midtown Manhattan near Park Avenue cannot fail to be struck by a capsule in concrete and glass, floating above neighboring skyscrapers, simply tethered to the top of one of them by two slender piles.

This space craft, so incongruous in a business district, is a new kind of apartment, designed for a young multi-millionaire—a vegetarian and a philanthropist—who wished to install his home and his offices in Manhattan, together with the 518 plant varieties that he cultivated and wanted the public also to enjoy. In other words it is a penthouse of about 1,000 square meters (10,000 square feet) on four floors, perched over 160 meters (544 feet) above Fifty-seventh Street, with some 750 square meters (8,100 square feet) of roof garden, a solar heated swimming pool, a space for recycling urban waste and, to crown it all, a windmill to do credit to the image of Don Quixote, with whom its owner likes to identify. Or perhaps it's a reminder of the distant origin of New York, then called New Amsterdam.

This fairy tale, however, did not take place. Money problems, it seems, wrecked the plans of this "farmer of elevators," who never took possession of the premises designed for him. Today the penthouse is a communal recreational space at the disposal of all the occupiers of the tower, an obligatory facility in this area of offices.

The Galleria is, in fact, a residential tower, one of the first to be built on the edge of a dense and purely business district where the City of New York decided in 1973 to encourage a mixed-use urban environment. Thus, for example, the Olympic Tower (SOM, 1974)—an Aristotle Onassis development—was the first on Fifth Avenue to contain both apartments and offices, although in this case nothing about the façade suggests the unusual nature of the project.

The Galleria, on the other hand, takes advantage of the mixed-use function to articulate four different types of building space: the retail and commercial gallery, wider,

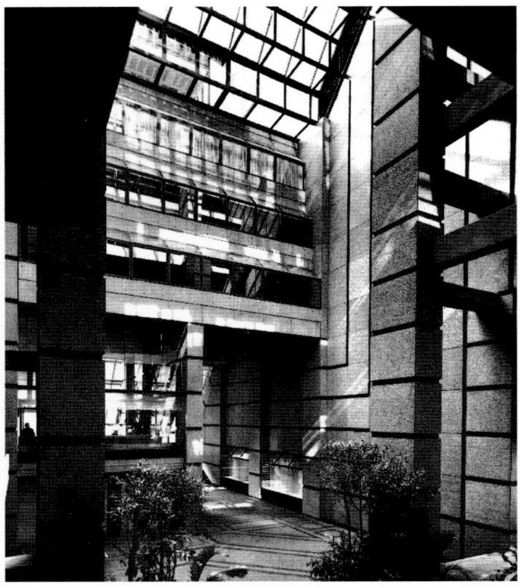

The Atrium.
Norman McGrath, 1975.

Architects: David Kenneth Specter (Gerald L. Jonas) — *Engineers:* Irwin Cantor; Sidney Barbanel, consultants — *Contractor:* HRH Construction Corporation — *Developer:* Madison Equities.

56 stories, 166 meters (544 feet) tall — Concrete construction; the tallest concrete building in New York at the time of its construction — Mixed-use building with housing (250 apartments), offices (11 floors), 3 levels of underground parking, shops, a health center, a swimming pool and a communal center.

Opposite:
General view of the Galleria.
To the left the Ritz Tower (Emery Roth, 1926).
© Norman McGrath, 1975.

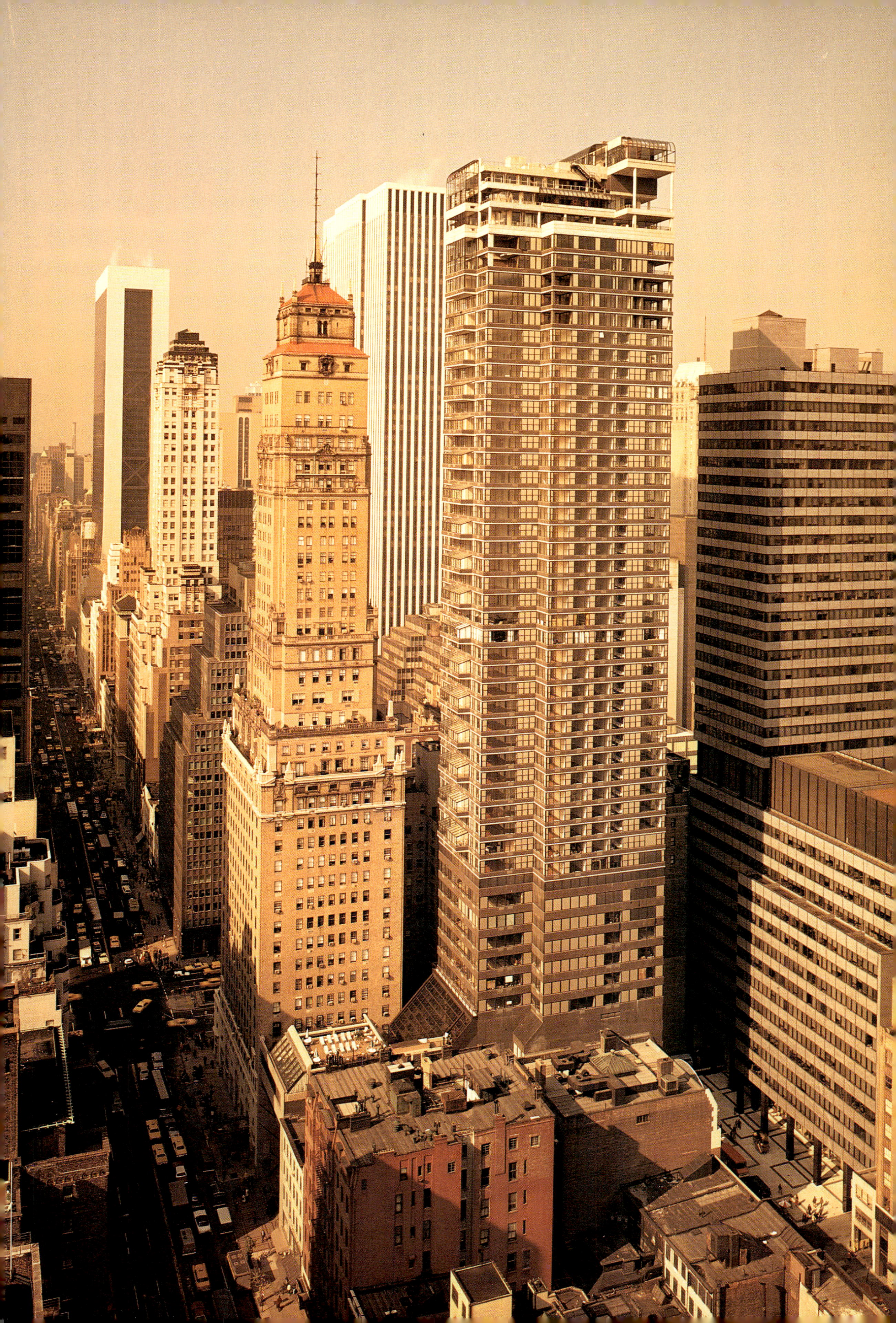

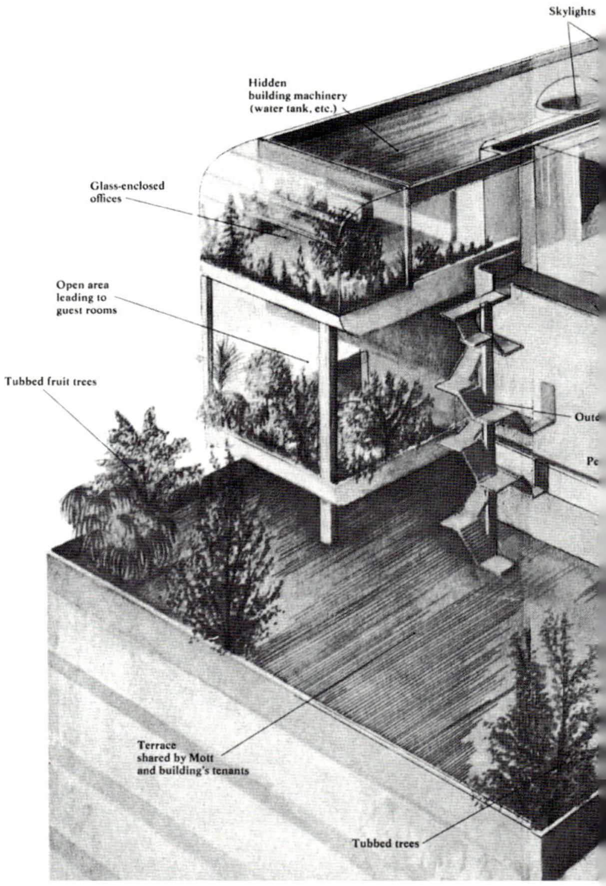

Center:
Penthouse project with roof gardens, 1974.
Drawing: Howard Berelson. David Kenneth Specter & Associates, Architects.

Below:
Housing on the upper floors.
© Benoît Roland, 1995.

with its public areas and large atrium; the office floors, organized in long, uniform, horizontal stripes, the residential tower with its projecting winter gardens, its play of filled and empty spaces and terraces and then, on top, the four-storied penthouse in exposed concrete, now the communal center.

It is certain that this architectural variety, which has nothing in common with kitsch, helped this new skyscraper to integrate into the body of office towers which surround it. For the Galleria has 56 floors, greater than the density normally authorized in the district, a result of the incentives created by the city to promote its program of mixed-use in certain high-density areas. Concessions are made to developers, for example, in exchange for a public walkway or commercial frontage, a theater in the Times Square area or the acceptance of other conditions for the project, often non-profit, which serve the common interest.

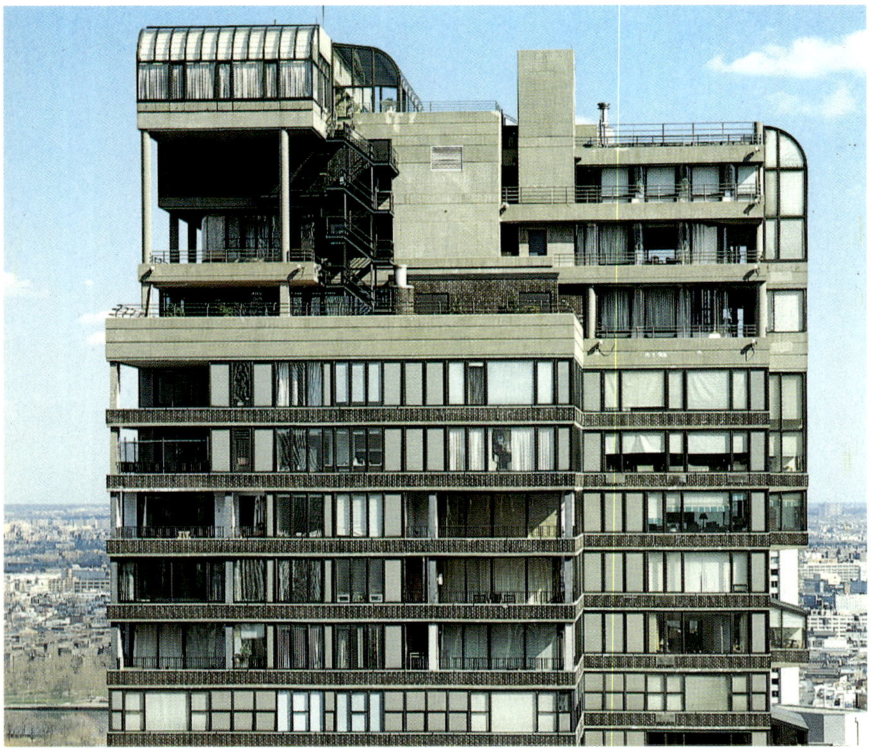

This bonus system was first put into effect in New York in 1961 with the introduction of a new set of building regulations intended to lower the densities permitted by the 1916 ordinance. Inspired by the example of Mies van der Rohe with the Seagram Building, the regulations autho-

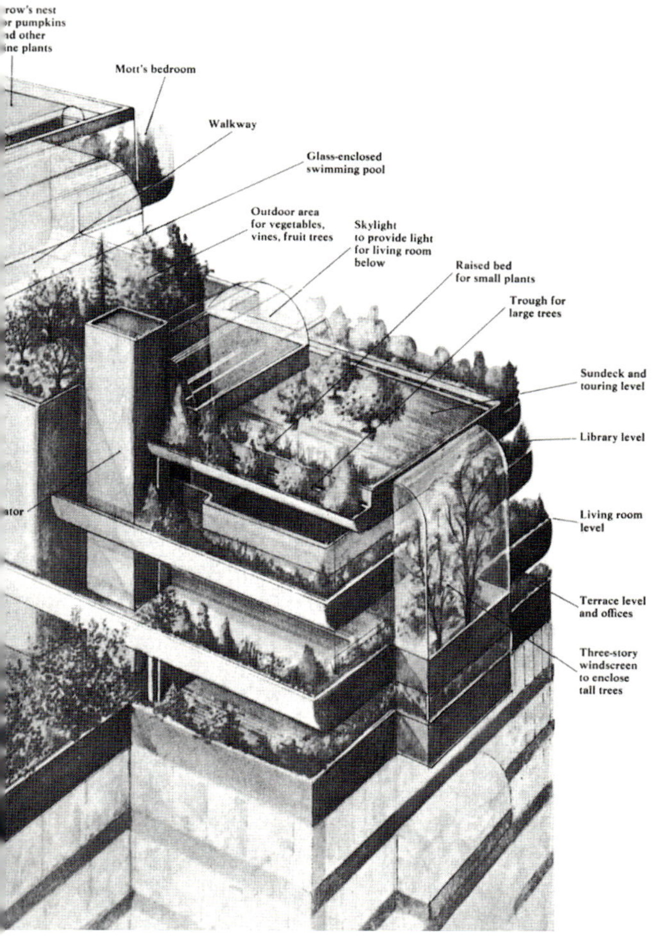

rize 20% extra floor area if the project includes a public plaza—a means of enhancing public spaces in a city where the cost of land precludes any municipal effort. The sad fate reserved for these plazas is well-known, laid out at minimum cost by unscrupulous developers who do everything to discourage passersby from using the space left free. With no trees, no public benches, no fountains, they are little more than private lobbies that happen to be in the open air.

The Galleria has no public plaza, but a shopping gallery traverses it. The fact that it is sparsely occupied, at least at present, demonstrates the limits of a voluntary policy which, at the time, failed to take into account the apparently infallible logic that commercial activity and urban animation have a cumulative effect.

However, the building has fulfilled its role of pioneer, even beyond expectations. "Whether the Galleria will get the heavy sustained use for which it was planned we cannot yet know. But it helps to bring something that more nearly approaches 24-hour-a-day use to this important district, it will make a productive contribution to a city that, just now—and for the immediate future—needs all the help it can get." (*Architectural Record*, Dec. 1975)

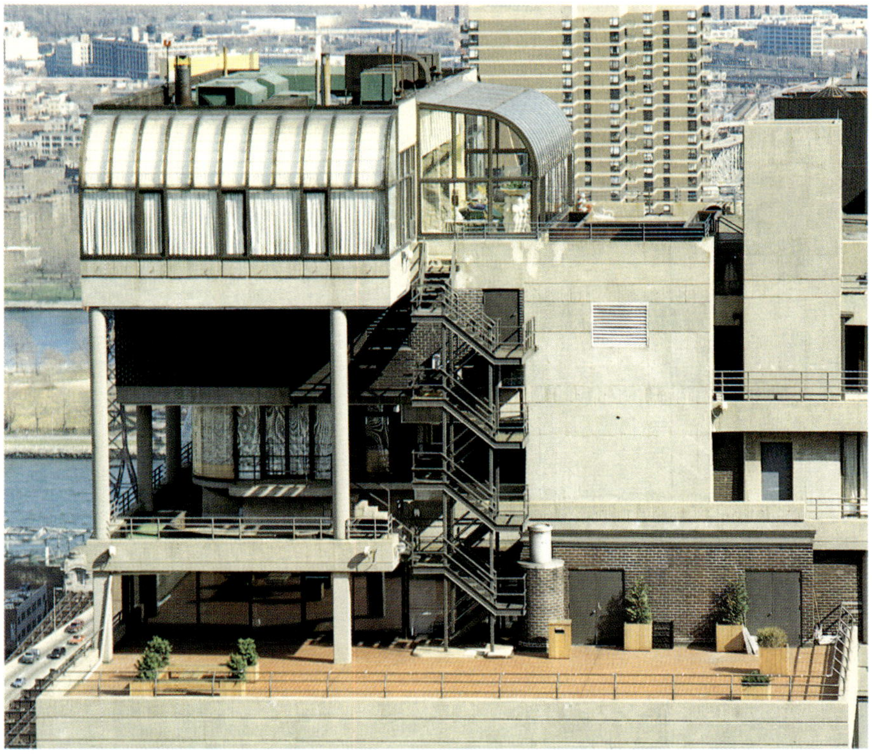

Penthouse, detail.
© Benoît Roland, 1995.

WATER TOWER PLACE

Chicago - United States

Loebl Schlossman Dart and Hackl - 1976

"What we are doing is creating an urban complex of a series of buildings and designing it vertically instead of horizontally."

Donald Hackl, *Engineering News-Record,* July 17, 1975.

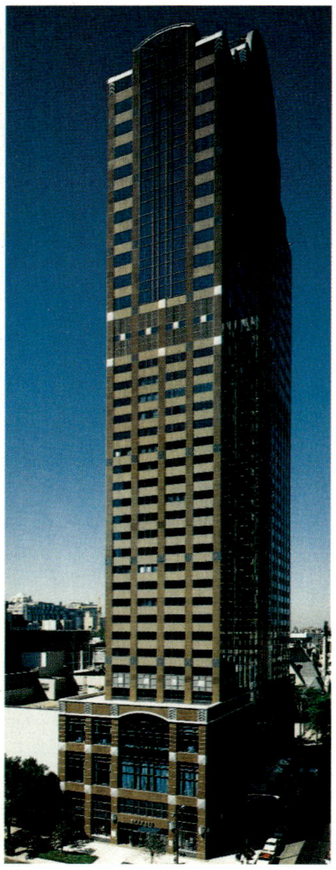

City Place: Michigan Avenue façade.
Loebl Schlossman and Hackl Architects, 1990.
George Lambros Photography.

Water Tower Place is a vertical city. You could live, work, go out in the evening to restaurants and 7 movie theaters, do the shopping in 2 department stores and 133 small shops, take a stroll, participate in sports, even put up your friends in one of the 400 rooms of the Ritz-Carlton hotel without taking a single step out of doors. You could even park your car. But what would be the use of one in such circumstances? This multiplicity of functions and use is not unconnected to the life of the city. Around the building, the urban vitality has nothing in common with the almost schizophrenic binary rhythm of the business center. Here, there is no zoning, no moments when it is deserted, no sense of insecurity. Instead there are spaces, a concentration of energy—and of profits. The concept goes back to the previous decade with the construction of the John Hancock Center (SOM, 1969) on North Michigan Avenue, a pioneering 100-story tower which stacked shops, offices and apartments one above the other. Water Tower Place, the second in the series, pushes the complexity of the program even further. Not only is a hotel added to the offices and apartments, but the shopping area takes on a new dimension, henceforth referred to as the "vertical mall," very effectively related to street level. The building which is visited by 12 million people every year is the catalyst for the development of the surrounding quarter, a quarter so economically successful it has become known as the Magnificent Mile. Other vertical complexes have arrived subsequently, standing shoulder to shoulder with the two original towers and exploring every combination and all the ways of superimposing them. For example, at City Place—a later work of the same architects—offices occupy the best floors at the summit of the tower, further down comes the hotel and below, in a 4-story podium, the shopping center.

Architects: Loebl Schlossman Dart and Hackl, in association with C.F. Murphy Associates — *Consultant architect (commercial space):* Warren Platner Associates — *Structural engineers:* C.F. Murphy Associates (Lou Moro) — *Mechanical and electrical engineers:* TRI Ventures 1 — *Contractor:* Inland Robbins Construction, Inc. — *Developers:* JMB / Urban Investment & Development Company.

74 stories, 262 meters (859 feet) high — Concrete construction; the tallest concrete building in the world at the time of it was built — mixed-use building consisting of 7 commercial levels, 2 office levels, a hotel (15 levels/400 rooms), 260 apartments (40 levels) and four levels of underground parking — Total floor area 278,700 square meters (3 million square feet).

Opposite:
Water Tower Place on the corner of Michigan Avenue and Pearson Street.
To the left, the John Hancock Center (SOM, 1969).
Loebl Schlossman and Hackl, Architects.

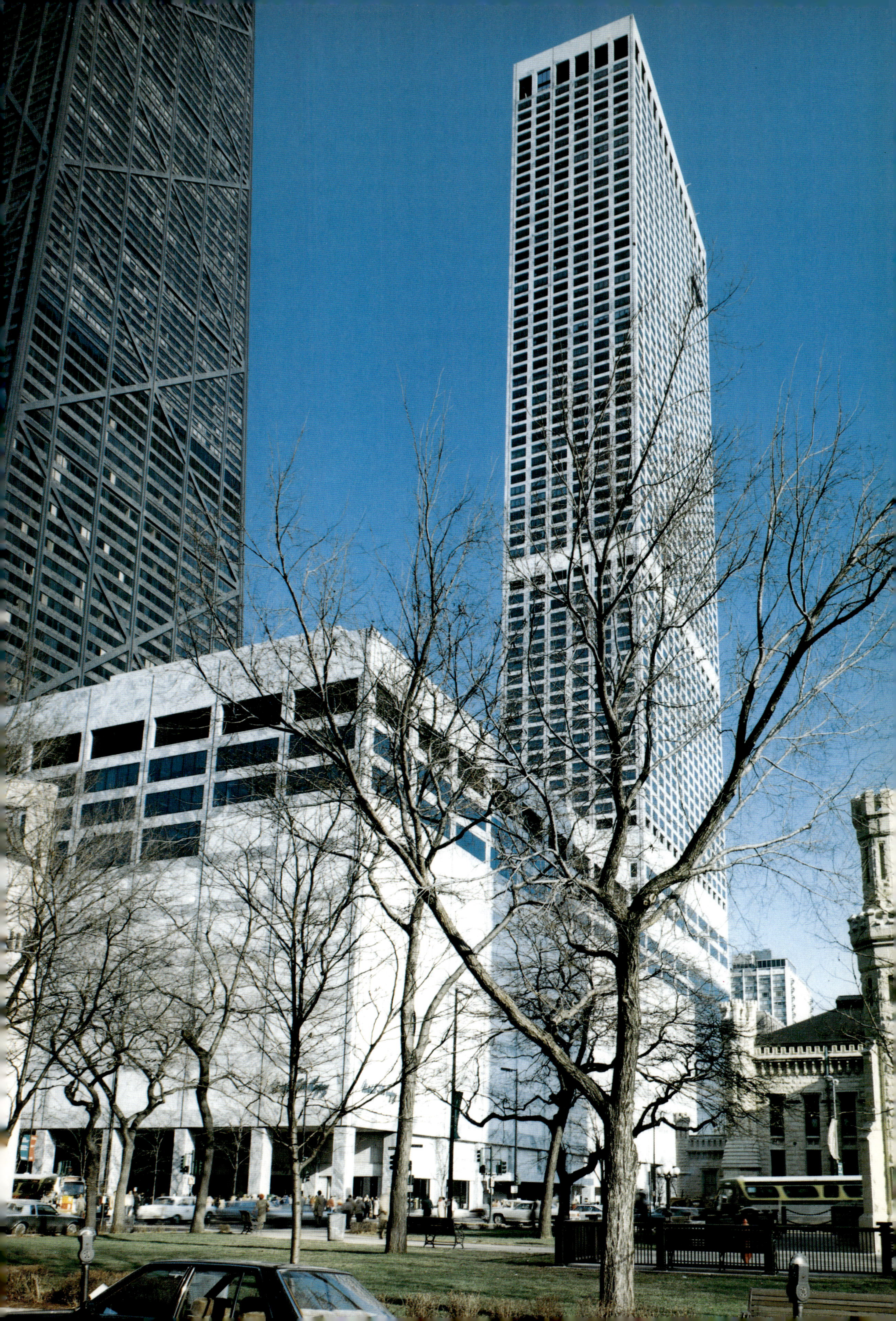

Few cities have seen as large and as successful a development of multi-use skyscrapers. Building regulations usually forbid them. Investors, even architects, regard such bastardized buildings with disfavor; they are more difficult to design, to build and to manage. But Chicago is not a city like any other. As long ago as 1889, the Auditorium Building (Dankmar Adler and Louis Sullivan) contained a theater, a hotel and offices. The community is vertically integrated. "Citizens of Chicago are ready to enjoy the advantages and accept the drawbacks of living high up," said developer J. Paul Beitler. Added to this predisposition is the tolerance of the regulations, unchanged since 1957, which made possible extremely high densities under certain conditions; a FAR (floor space to ground area ratio) of 40, or 140 stories and 600,000 square meters (6.5 million square feet) per city block! Water Tower Place achieves a FAR of 23 and the John Hancock Center next door scores 26.

Such close proximity could not occur without blemishes. With its 74 stories, Water Tower Place risked spoiling the outlook and exposure to the sun of the neighboring tower. The John Hancock company, fortunately owner of a piece of land essential to the developer of Water Tower Place, negotiated the setting back of the new tower as a condition of sale. Things have not always worked out so satisfactorily; for example, 30% of the residents of Marina City

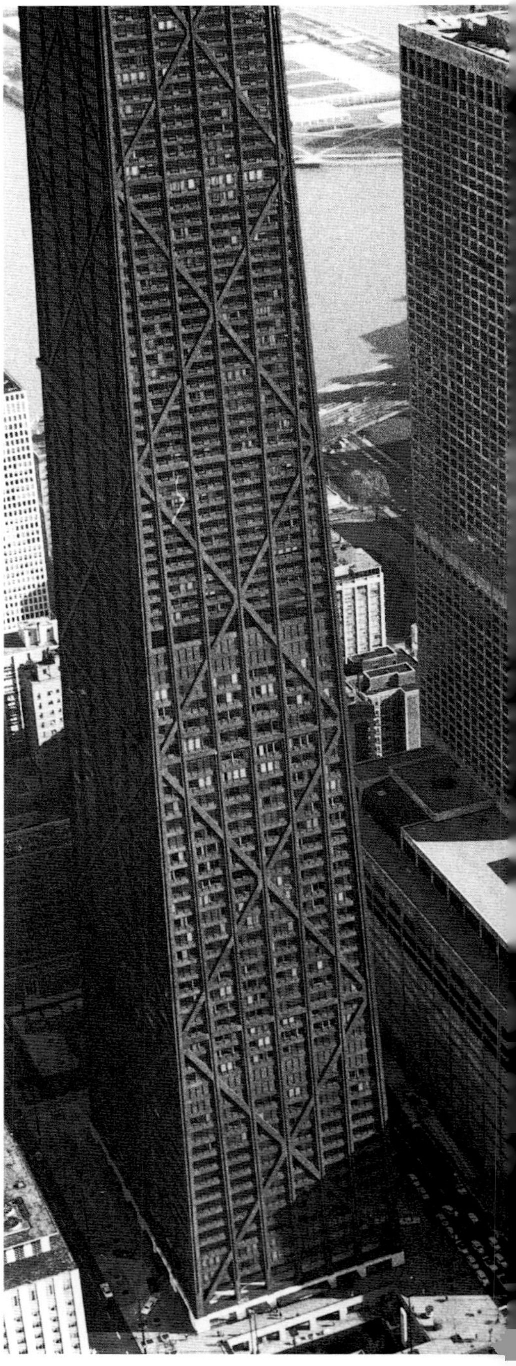

Center:
The John Hancock Center to the left. On the right, offset towards the background, the residential tower of Water Tower Place.
Loebl Schlossman and Hackl, Architects.

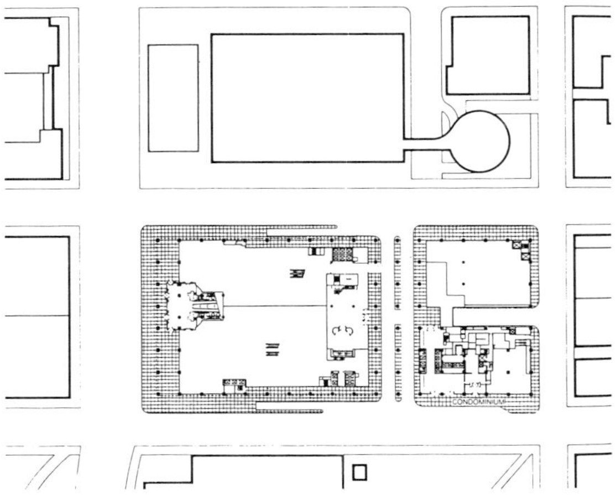

Ground floor plan.
Loebl Schlossman and Hackl, Architects.

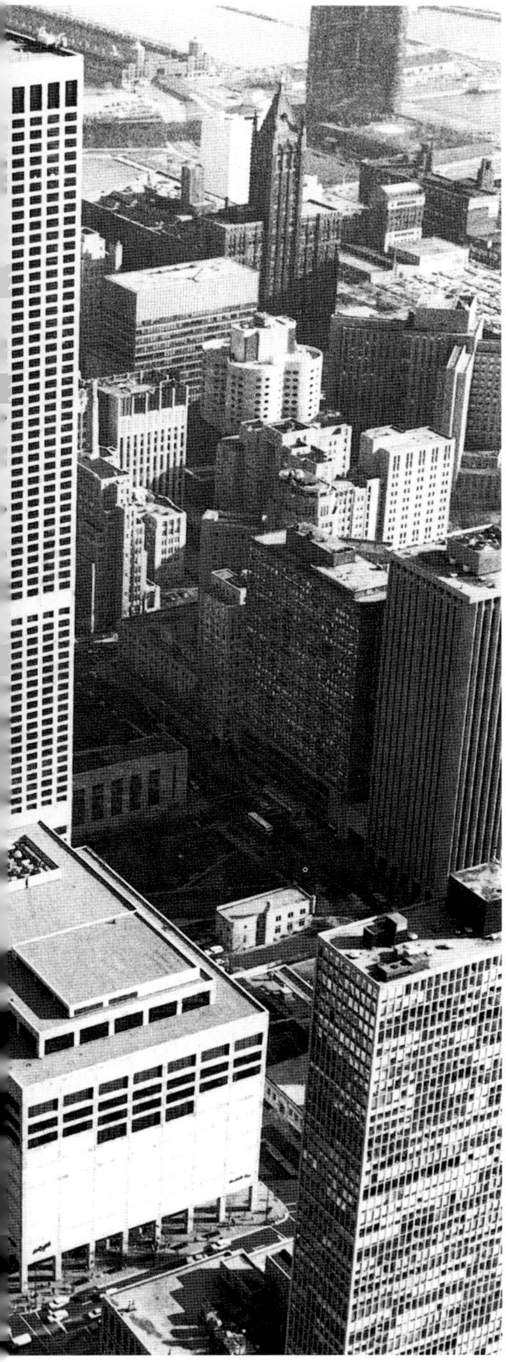

(Bertrand Goldberg, 1964), one of the first mixed-use complexes in the city, no longer enjoy either view or sun since the construction of the taller IBM tower (Mies van der Rohe, 1971) on a neighboring site.

It remains to discuss the architecture once again by comparing Water Tower Place to its prestigious neighbor. The building consists of two distinct elements, a horizontal podium and a tower, which give very clear identities to the commercial block, windowless above ground floor level and open to the street, from the slim residential tower which houses the hotel and apartments. This bipartite arrangement contrasts radically with the monolithic treatment of the John Hancock Center, where only the widening of the volume towards the base provides a variation in the area of the floors. The same principle, in a more supple inclination, can be seen again a few blocks further away in Olympia Centre (SOM, 1986), another tower superimposing offices and housing.

Color provides another contrast with the veined white marble facing of the rectangular, all-concrete Water Tower Place against the black, diagonally braced steel structure. On street level, the hierarchical treatment of the façades of Water Tower Place—colonnade, shop windows, entrances, vehicle access—takes full account of the desire to express context that defines the entire project. But the minor scale of these interruptions is not adequate to break the suburban image given by the blank mass of the commercial podium. Pedestrians fare no better, it's true, at the foot of the John Hancock Center obelisk.

Pushed into the background by its illustrious neighbor bearing the name of another historic tower—the City Water Tower, sole survivor of the great fire of 1871—Water Tower Place plays a tricky supporting role. Accordingly, its performance has been remarked all the more!

CITICORP CENTER

New York - United States

Hugh Stubbins & Associates - 1977

"Architects working on the next generation of New York City skyscrapers should be paying attention to Citicorp, but not merely for its dramatic silhouette or glistening skin."

Architectural Record, No. 6, June 1978.

Citicorp was a new type of skyscraper, without references or any combination of past styles; historicism had not yet reached the commercial stage. It is not a black box like so many office towers built since the sixties. It stands all in white in the heart of midtown Manhattan with its soaring profile, its pointed summit, the binary graphics of its façades, its square plan, its base generously given over to the public, to public space, to city life. Everything puts Citicorp in the avant-garde of the architectural renewal of skyscrapers in the post-modern period.

Citicorp was also at the technical and commercial cutting edge, and from the energy-saving point of view, it was built in the wake of the first oil crisis.

As is often the case with an exceptional work, a whole series of factors converged to make possible the building of this highly distinctive tower. They included the hiring of the architect Hugh Stubbins, the desire and the demands of the developing bank, the conditions imposed by the Lutheran community of Saint Peter, the owners of the site, the influence of the municipal development agency for midtown, without taking into account emerging ecological thinking fostered by the prevailing climate of recession. The opportunity was summarized by the architect in 1970. "With the church as catalyst and the bank as supporter, we can design a new kind of place which all kinds of people will want to enter and become part of," he said (*Architectural Record,* No. 6, June 1978).

In fact the community of Saint Peter had decided on the sale and demolition of its church, standing since 1862 on the corner of Lexington Avenue and 54th Street, on condition that the bank build a new church on the same site, open to the sky and functioning as a genuine cultural center. To this condition was added a second, experimental at the time but later permanently adopted by the City of New York. To compensate for an abnormally high density (a FAR of 18) there would be a combination of

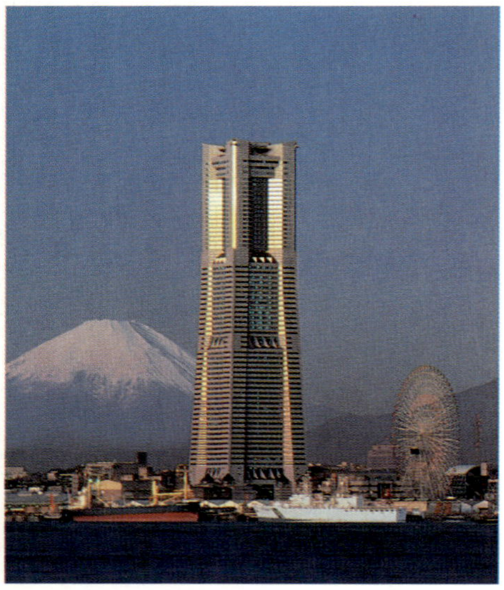

Landmark Tower, Yokohama.
Architect: The Stubbins Associates, 1993.
Nikko Hotels.

Architects: Hugh Stubbins & Associates, Inc., in association with Emery Roth & Sons — *Structural engineers:* LeMessurier Associates / SCI (Stanley Goldstein) and the Office of James Ruderman — *Mechanical and electrical engineers:* Joseph R. Loring and Associates, Inc. — *Landscaping:* Sasaki Associates — *Furniture and decorative elements for the church:* Vignelli Associates — *Contractor:* HRH Construction Corporation — *Developer:* Citicorp, New York.

59 stories, 279 meters (914 feet) high — Steel structure — At the time of construction the largest banking building in the world and the seventh largest building in New York about 160,000 square meters (1,700,000 square feet).

Opposite:
Citicorp Center at the corner of 53rd Street.
© Norman McGrath, 1984.

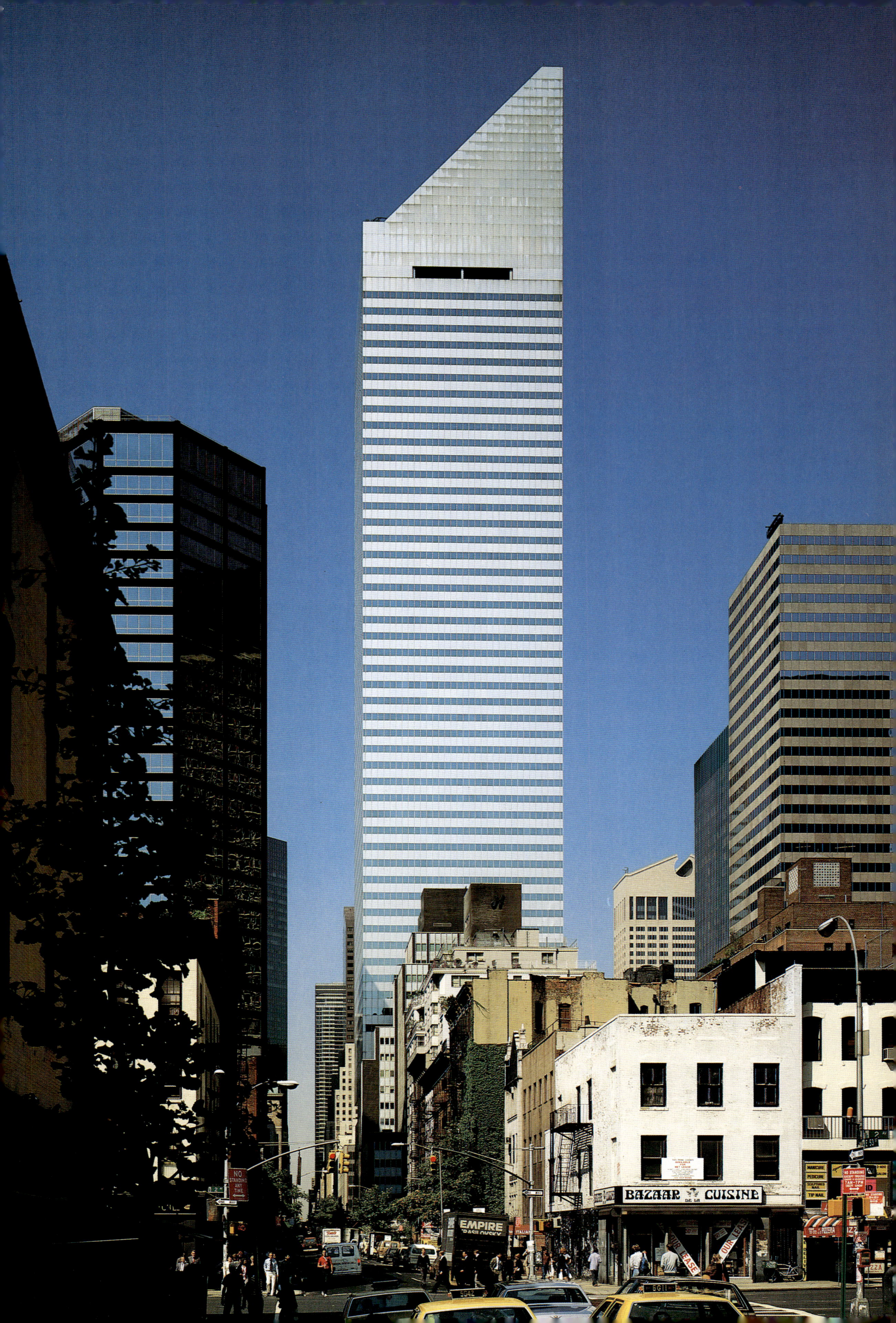
NO STANDING ANY TIME
ONE WAY
EMPIRE
BAZAAR DE LA CUISINE
OUR LEASE
OUR LEASE
MANICURE
PEDICURE
SCULPTURED NAIL
TIP NAIL
NO STANDING EXCEPT TRUCKS 7AM-7PM EXCEPT SUNDAY
6G11

Center, above:
The damping mechanism: axonometric view.
The Stubbins Associates, Architects.

Center, below:
The esplanade at the foot of Citicorp. To the left, Saint Peter's chapel.
© Norman McGrath.

Below, diagrammatic section of the V-shaped buttressing.
The Stubbins Associates, Architects.

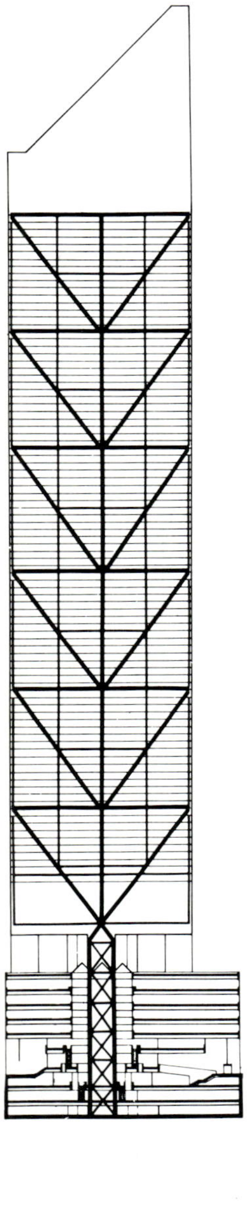

facilities and public spaces in harmony with the street and urban activity. These include a public plaza on two levels with direct access to the subway system, a combined religious space and concert hall (the church is renowned for its jazz concerts), a commercial atrium on 7 levels naturally lit from above and planted with real trees, a public foot way across the block, with the tower proper only occupying 10 square meters (108 square feet) at ground level, the area of the 4 piles which support the building.

It is these four median columns 279 meters (914 feet) high which carry, with the central core, the entire weight of the building. The tower is divided into 6 units of 8 levels, determined by a V-shaped steel buttressing system, deliberately concealed in the façade. This rational and economical structural scheme is complemented by a series of technical innovations. First of all there is the inert mass of 400 tons of concrete resting on an oiled steel plate on the top of the building of which the movement reduces the oscillation of the tower and adds to the well-being of the occupants. This shock-absorbing system, the Tuned Mass Damper, put into practice for the first time during the construction of Citicorp, has since been added to the top of numerous skyscrapers and is today undergoing new developments. Mitsubishi, for example, has researched a complex system involving a hanging mass which has been installed in, among other buildings, Japan's tallest skyscraper, built in Yokohama in 1993... by the architects of Citicorp.

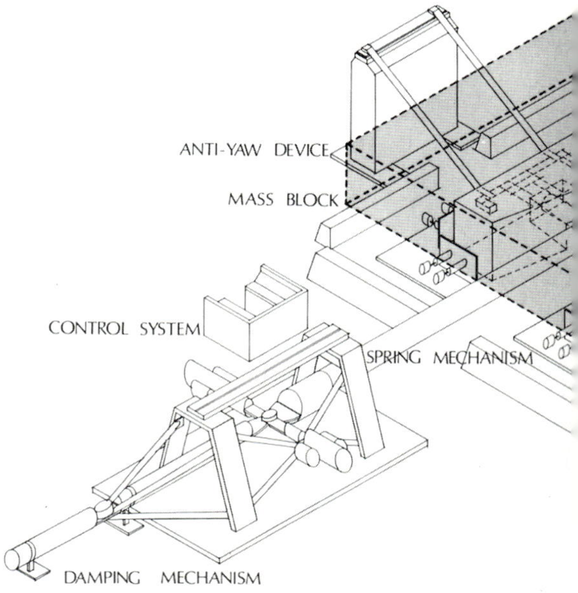

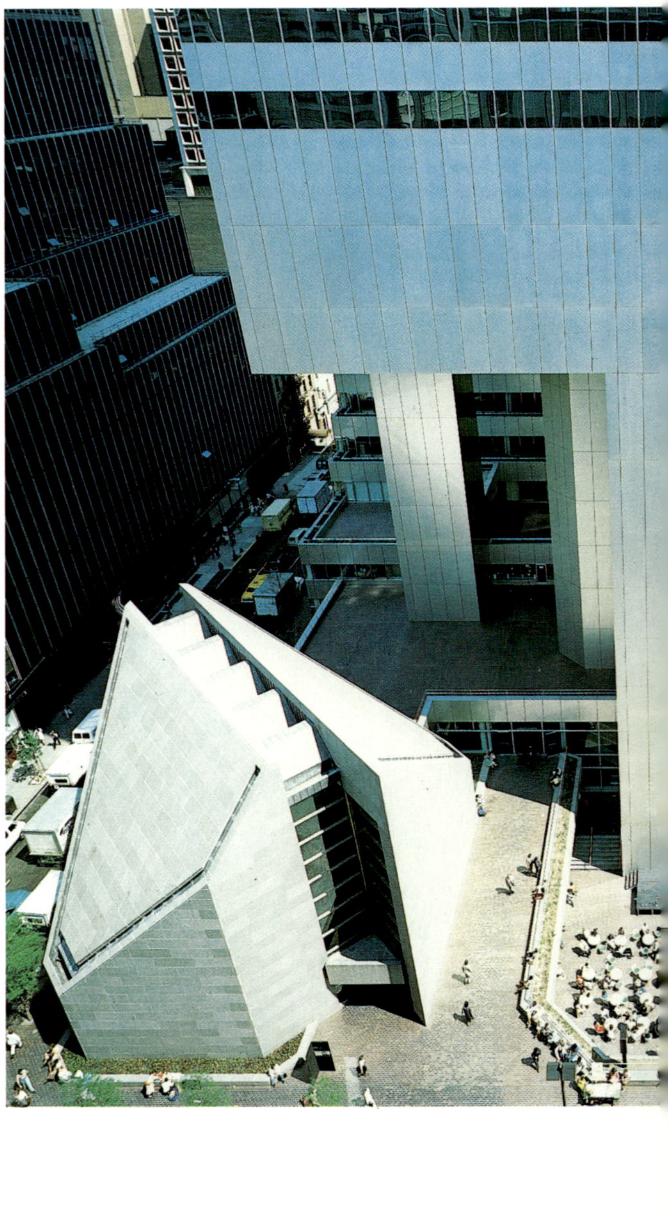

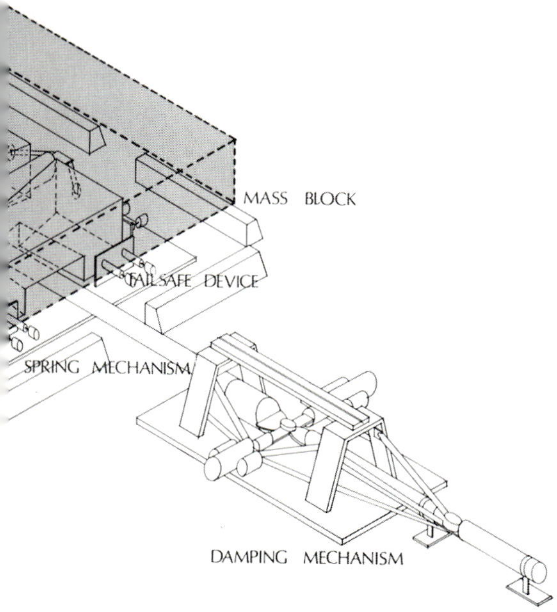

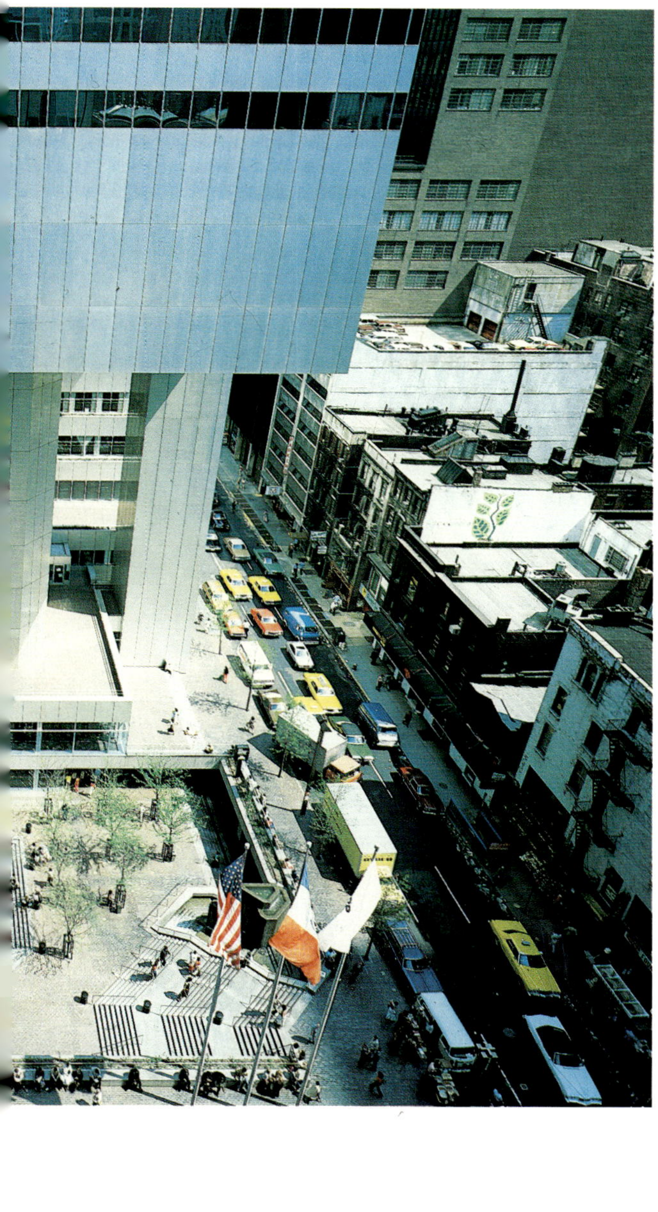

Among the innovations brought into use at Citicorp, the double-decker elevator must also be mentioned. With its entries at two levels, this is the first occasion of its use in New York; there are computer-controlled heating, cooling and lighting systems to save energy.

The natural color aluminum coating of the building, light and shining, was not only an aesthetic choice—New York is a somber, mat city—but also a technical commitment to reducing weight and saving energy. Another, and unexpected, result of the insertion of this huge vertical mirror in the tight grid of streets of the neighborhood was that flowers and trees began to grow in places which had previously been in shadow!

One last technical innovation at Citicorp, albeit fruitless, should be mentioned to which we owe its remarkable profile, so characteristic of today's New York skyline—the corner cut off at 45° from the summit of the tower. Hugh Stubbins' original intention was to build some 100 terraced apartments above the bank but this proposal did not receive local government's seal of approval. The idea then emerged of converting this 5th sloping façade into a huge solar panel, a device which quickly proved to be impractical, at least at that time.

The pointed shape nevertheless survived its apparent lack of function and it is this which, more than anything else, is responsible for the fame of the building—and of the bank. Its picture, promoted by advertising among other means, places Citicorp among the skyscrapers with which New York is now associated.

Perspective drawing of the draft project with terraced apartments at the summit of the tower.
The Stubbins Associates, Architects.

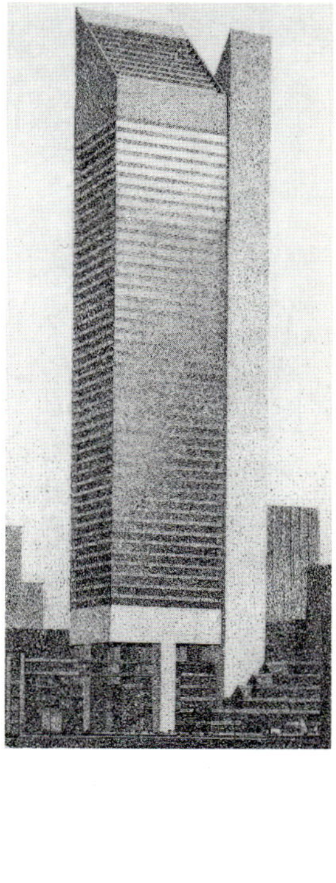

MLC CENTRE

Sydney - Australia

Harry Seidler & Associates - 1978

"Seidler's continuous exploration of the skyscraper is certainly among his principal contributions to architecture. These towers, moreover, provide a convenient means of positioning him in his point of view."

W.H. Jordy, "Introduction," *Harry Seidler, Four Decades of Architecture*, Thames and Hudson, 1992.

The MLC Centre by the Australian Harry Seidler is the exact reflection of his convictions as an architect and of the particular style that he has evolved in contact with his masters, Marcel Breuer and Oscar Niemeyer, his country of adoption—an echo of the Sydney Opera House (Jørn Utzon, 1957-1973) is impossible to ignore—and the Italian engineer Pier Luigi Nervi, designer of the auditorium canopy at UNESCO in Paris (Marcel Breuer and Bernard Zehrfuss, 1954). To Nervi he owes the expressiveness and technical perfection of his structures in concrete.

Seidler proclaims his modernism. There is no question of articulating the tower by a series of steps or of relating it to its urban environment. It rises uncompromisingly vertical and independent in the center of a huge site (the tower occupies only a fifth of the available land), set diagonally in order to avoid a railway tunnel. It is a square tower with the corners cut off, giving it an octagonal shape of which the alternating wide and narrow sides increase the soaring effect.

The form of the tower expresses the structure, a paradigm of the modern movement. Eight peripheral concrete columns are given rigidity by a hyperbolic form at the base which diminishes as it rises. This effect of torsion, reinforced by the gradual tapering of the columns, gives the tower an almost organic plasticity which the architect had hitherto only applied to interior structures, ceilings for example. "When I first discussed the idea of a 250-meter-high concrete tower with Nervi, his advice was to limit the number of exterior columns and let them be heavily loaded. Just as a tree trunk, they should spread outward at their bases for greater stability...," explained Harry Seidler (Kenneth Frampton, "Isostatic Architecture," *Harry Seidler, Four Decades of Architecture*, Thames and Hudson, 1992).

Opposing the verticality of the columns, beams of long pre-fabricated, hollowed-out girders, also functionally logical, form ridges and create a façade of light

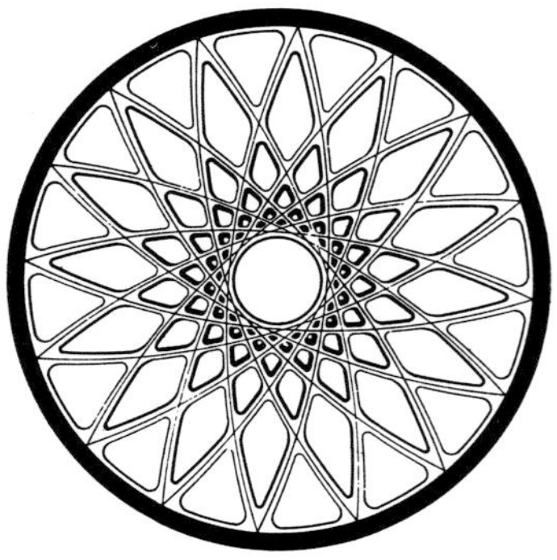

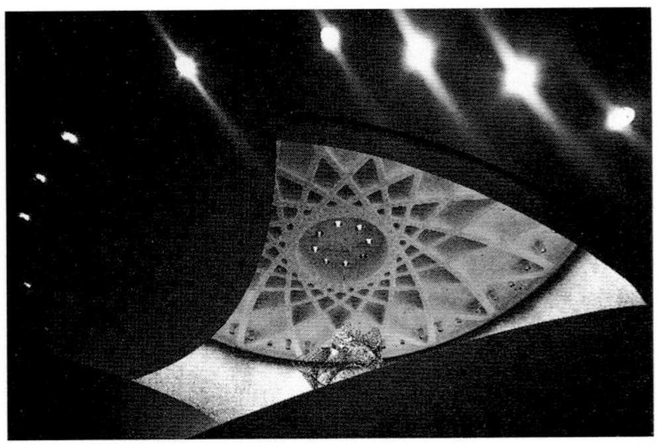

The ribbed ceiling of the theater foyer: plan and photograph.
© Max Dupain.

Opposite:
The MLC Centre in 1979.
Harry Seidler & Associates, Architects.

Architect: Harry Seidler & Associates (Harry Seidler) — *Structural engineers:* Civil & Civic Pty. Mtd, Lehmann & Talty Pty. Ltd, DT Broughton & Associates — *Structural consultants:* Studio Nervi (Milan) — *Mechanical engineers:* Environ Mechanical Services Pty Ltd — *Electrical engineers:* Civil & Civic Pty. Ltd — *Contractor:* Civil & Civic Pty. Ltd — *Developer:* The Mutual Life & Citizens Assurance Co. Ltd.

65 stories, 228 meters (748 feet) high — Concrete structure — 1650 square meters (17,760 square feet) of office building floor area including a commercial and cultural complex with a theater (1,100 seats), private club, cinema, shops, cafés, and restaurants.

and shade. Recessed to the back of the beams, narrow glazed bands protected from the sun and uninterrupted over the width of each wall complete the venetian blind effect of the facing, a metaphor well-suited to the regionalist beliefs of an architect who is also very attentive to the climate of a sub-tropical continent.

The MLC Centre is not only a structural experiment. Seidler seized on the specifics of the commission—the need, among others, to replace the Royal Theater on the site—to create a public environment which extends the commercial web of central Sydney. The tower commands a long open space in front of it that descends in steps towards the north and dispenses two levels of plazas, terraces and shopping galleries. The new theater is also entered from this area. To the sides and rear the tower is backed by a wall of circular bastions, veritable buttresses to protect this "universe in miniature" from garage entrances and traffic, a theme which was to recur in the architect's urban projects.

It is in the fan-shaped pendentives, the corolla-shaped ceilings that the expressionist signature and technical invention of Nervi are to be found. His collaboration with Seidler, begun in the sixties with the construction of Australia Square (Sydney, 1961-1967), was only to end with the death of the engineer in 1979.

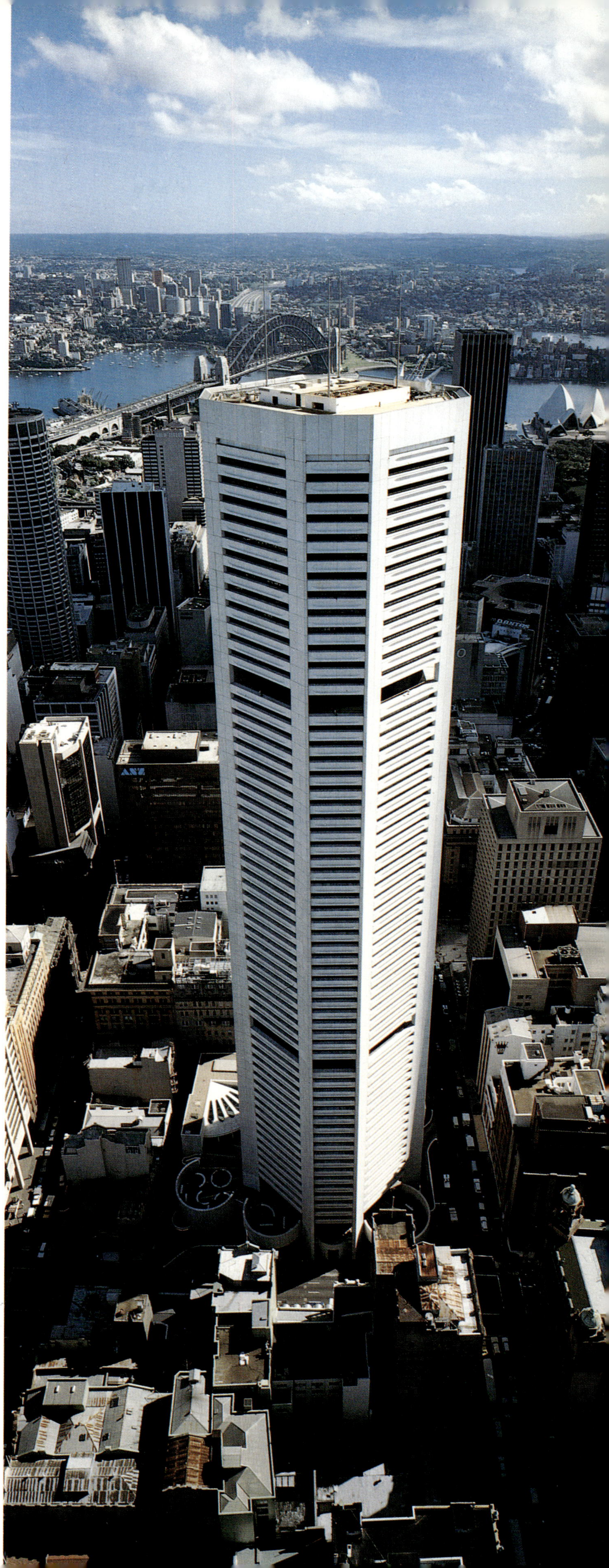

SOUTHWEST CENTER

Houston - United States

Murphy / Jahn - 1982

"If he (the architect) uses convention unconventionally, if he organizes familiar things in an unfamiliar way, he is changing their context, and he can use even the cliché to gain a fresh effect. Familiar things seen in an unfamiliar context become perceptually new as well as old."

Robert Venturi,
Complexity and Contradiction in Architecture,
Museum of Modern Art, New York, 1966.

Architect Helmut Jahn's approach was to transpose a familiar, already old image into a new context. The image was of course that of the traditional American skyscraper of the twenties and thirties. The new context was the sophistication of the project, the multiplicity of technical facilities, the type of structure, the materials available. And in the case of Houston the context included a new city center almost entirely created in the seventies, the decade proceeding the Southwest Center project. Of the project the architect would say that it represented "an attempt to synthesize often contradictory elements in architecture; the pragmatic and the ideal, form and technique, art and social purpose, intellectual rigor and commercial acumen" (*Southwest Center. The Houston Competition*, Rizzoli, 1983). It is exactly this ability to synthesize, this evidence of an approach and of a reference, which has made the Jahn principle successful, first in the United States and then in Europe. Not only did he win the Southwest Center competition against SOM and Kohn Pedersen Fox, but from this project on he established a type of skyscraper that would profoundly mark his own work and American construction of the eighties, typified by historically inspired symbolic forms, separately articulated parts, striking profiles, combined with the handwriting of modernism in the abstraction of design, dematerialization and technological imagery.

This ingenious duality meets both the desire for well-rooted heritage on the part of the investors—a bank in the case of Southwest Center—and the necessary concessions to the ethic of progress, the duty to innovate. It is a highly successful recipe. Southwest Center was never to be built but it nevertheless became the most frequently imitated skyscraper of its period: in New York in 1986 (Park Avenue Tower), in Philadelphia in 1987 (One Liberty Place followed by Two Liberty Place in 1990), in Oakbrook Terrace, Illinois in 1987, in Jacksonville, Florida in 1990, in Chicago in the same year, except that in this case Two Prudential Plaza was designed by other architects (Loebl Schlossman and

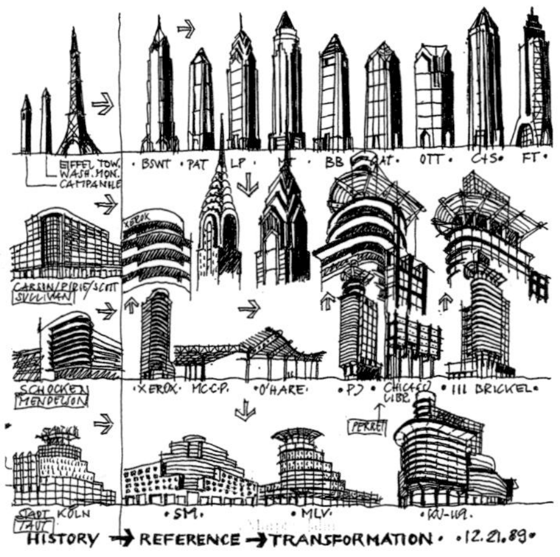

"History > Reference > Transformation. 12.21.89": Sketch by Helmut Jahn.
Murphy / Jahn.

Architects: Murphy / Jahn, Inc. (Helmut Jahn) — *Structural engineers:* LeMessurier Associates — *Developers:* Century Development Corporation and Bank of the Southwest.
82 stories, 427 meters (1,400 feet) — Observation platform on the top floor — Mixed steel and concrete structure: 8 concrete columns connected by two pairs of superdiagonals (nine-story triangular steel frames)—a system christened "the ultimate structure" by its inventor — Floor area about 200,000 square meters (2 million square feet).

Opposite:
Southwest Center in its context, perspective.
Murphy / Jahn.

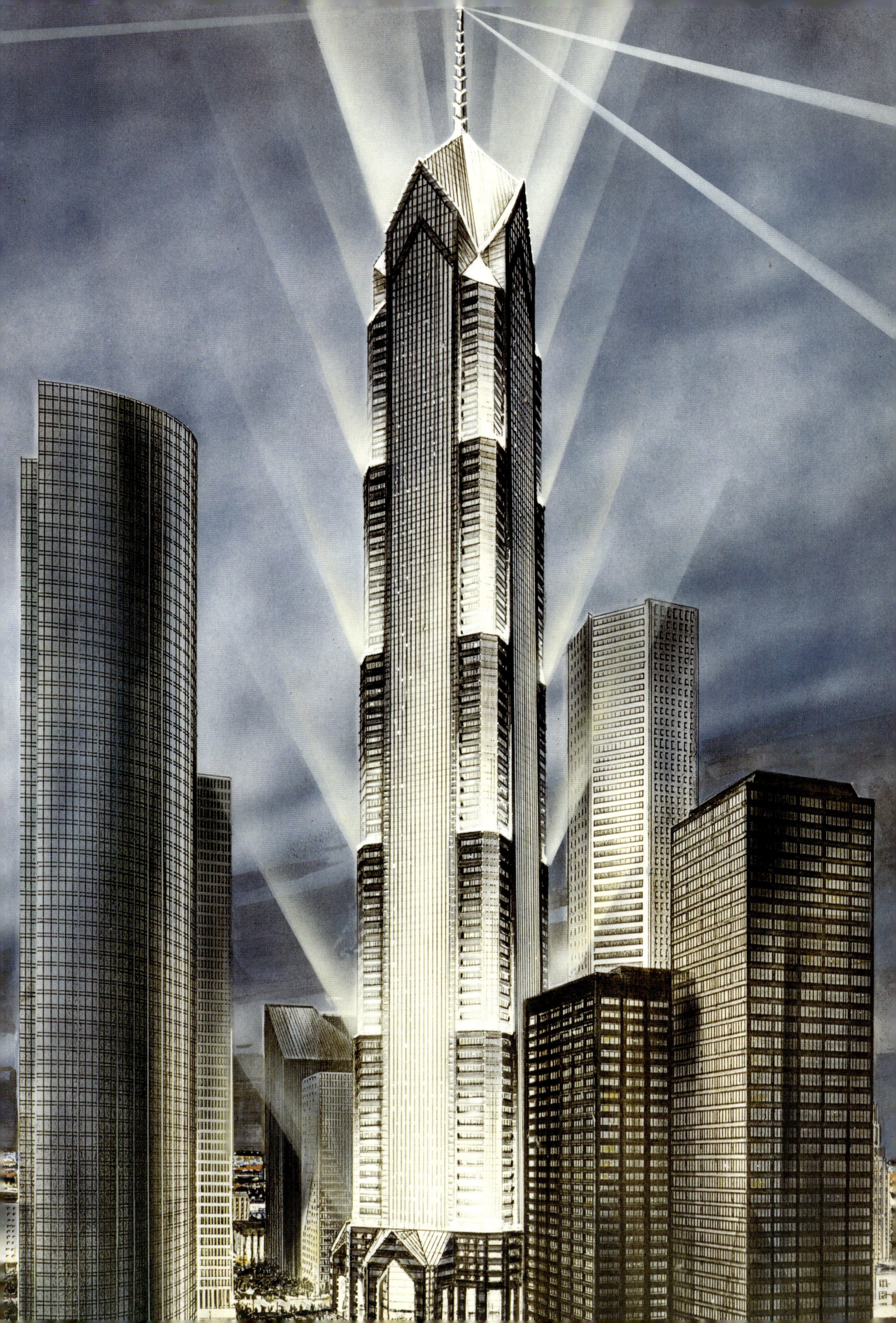

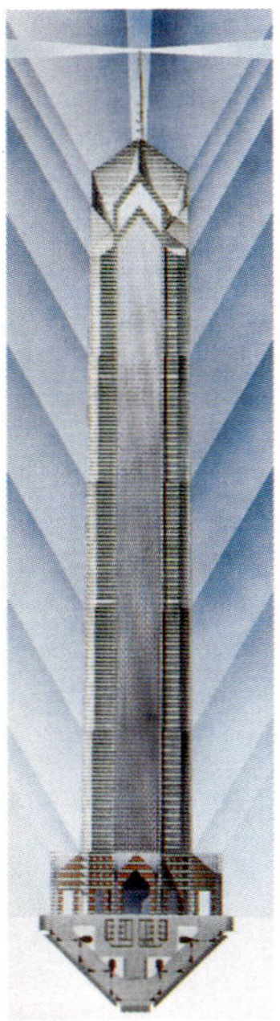

Elevation and part plan of the ground floor.
Murphy/Jahn.

Hackl). Southwest Center can be recognized yet again in San Diego in 1992, not to mention Frankfurt, Los Angeles and other towers in New York built by Jahn in the same vein of romantic modernism of which he became the master.
It could be said, the personal style aside, that the PPG Company's tower in Pittsburgh (Philip Johnson/ John Burgee, 1979-1984), the Transco Tower in Houston (Philip Johnson/John Burgee 1979-1983) and Cesar Pelli's World Financial Center in New York (1980-1988), among others, also belong to this approach. In any case, they are certainly contemporary.
Southwest Center was not Jahn's first attempt at synthesis. There was the minute but much noticed gesture at the summit of the Xerox Centre Building in Chicago (1980) to which Jahn owes his recognition at the firm of C.F. Murphy. Then in 1982 came the extension of the Chicago Board of Trade's Art Deco building (Holabird and Root, 1930) to which Jahn provided the counterpart on a smaller scale, limiting himself to the tracing of a silhouette, almost disembodied as though back-lit. The same approach is illustrated again, this time with exuberance, at the Northwestern Atrium Center in Chicago in 1987 (a project dating from 1979) with a veritable cascade of blue-tinted glass, 37 stories high. Homage is paid to the entrance porch of Louis Sullivan's School of Chicago in a monumen-

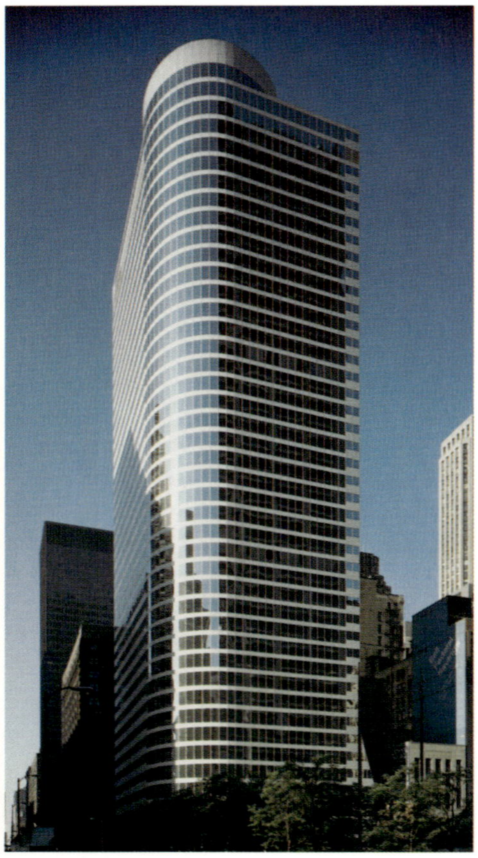

Xerox Centre, Chicago 1980.
Murphy/Jahn.

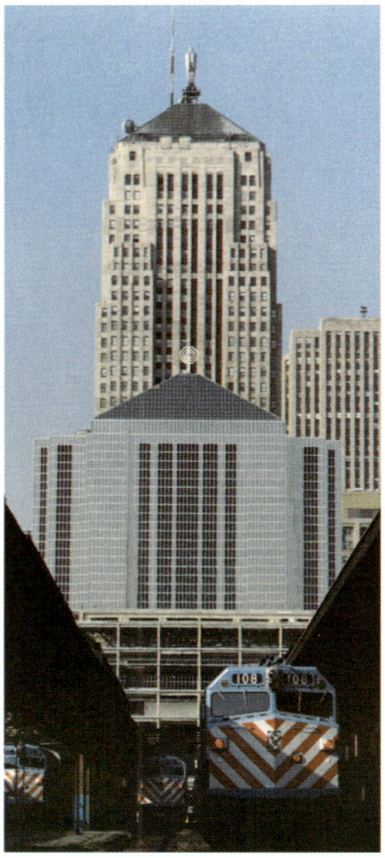

Chicago Board of Trade Addition, 1982.
Murphy/Jahn.

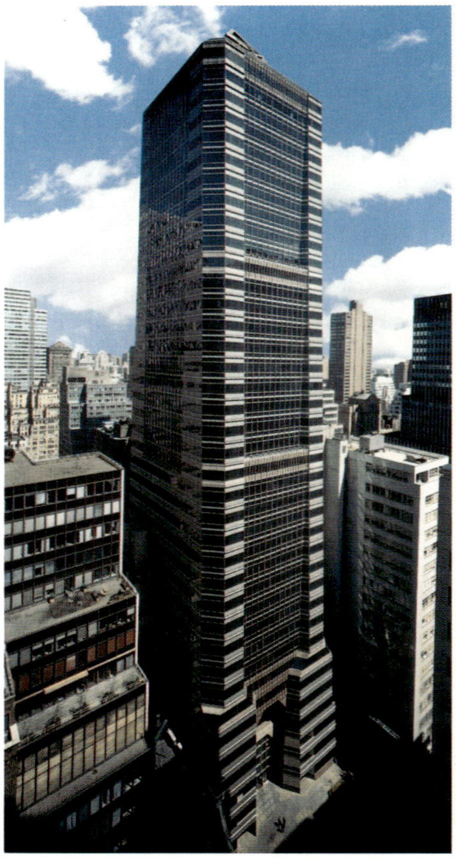

Park Avenue Tower, New York 1986.
Park Tower Group.

tal arch with projections. This spectacular work did not share the fate of Southwest Center, if only due to the particular nature of the project and its site. In fact the building serves as a monumental entry to a rail terminus.

Southwest Center, finally, is a competition project and a winner. It has all the qualities: a clear unified concept supported by very good drawings, the right response to the aims of the developers, a perfect rendering of the sensibility, and cultural ambitions of a period. It is in this respect, without claiming unwarranted parallels, that it can be compared with Eliel Saarinen's project for the The Chicago Tribune competition in 1922. Southwest Center redefined, for a few years at any rate, the new standards of commercial architecture.

Another comparison comes to mind here, with another major competition organized in Louisville Kentucky in 1981, a competition in which Jahn was invited to participate. Michael Graves' winning project, a veritable manifesto of Post-Modernism, was not only built but also became the subject of numerous publications. The project did not, however, launch a new style. Polemical, an unprecedented assembly of references, allusions and sly winks, the Humana Building is a monument, not a model. It remains unique. Southwest Center, on the other hand, launched a new generation of skyscrapers.

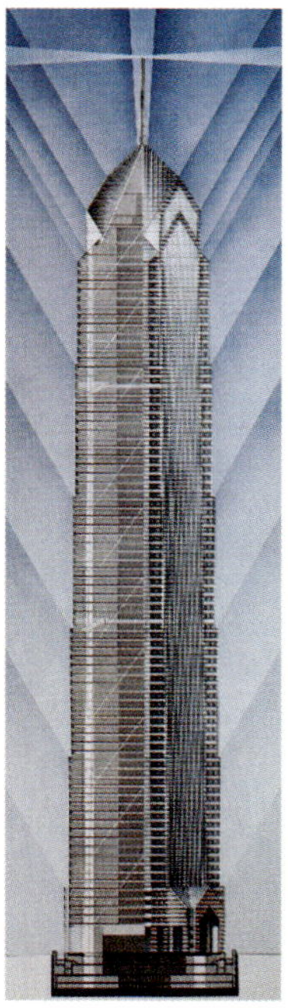

Elevation section.
Murphy/Jahn.

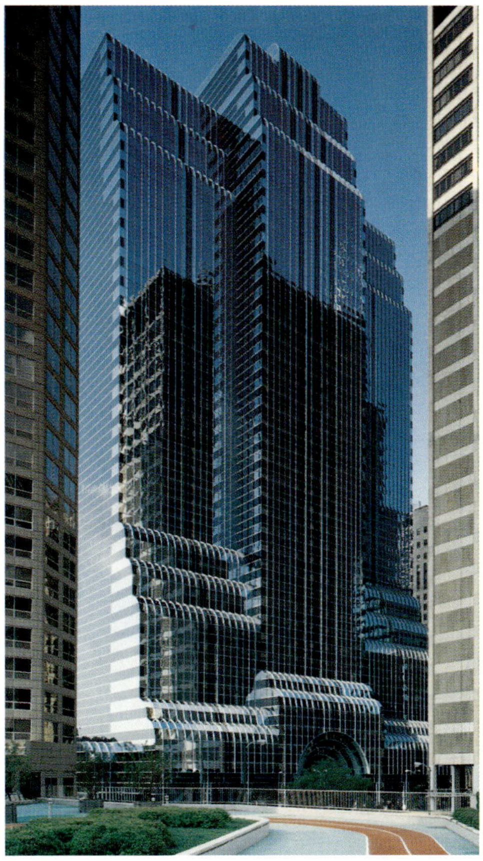

Northwestern Atrium Center, Chicago 1987.
Murphy/Jahn.

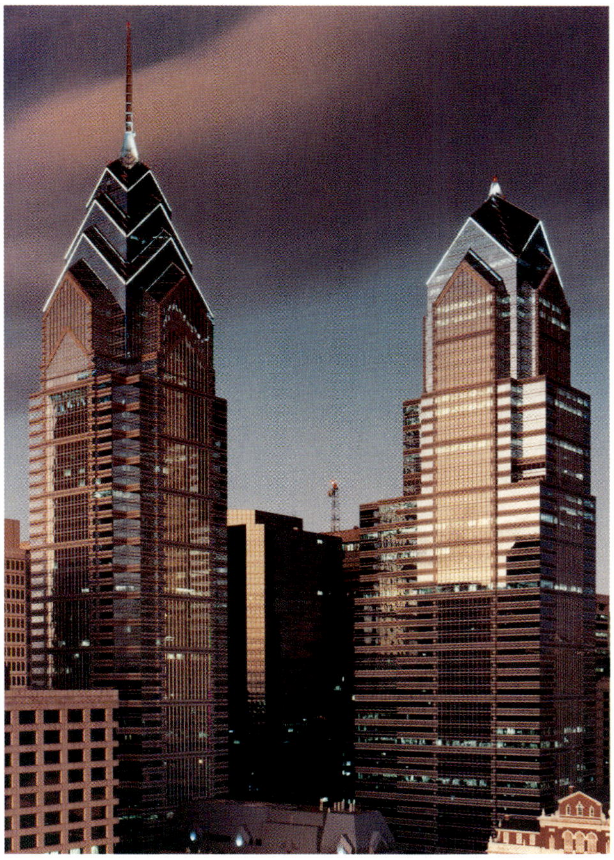

One and Two Liberty Place, Philadelphia, 1987 and 1990.
Murphy/Jahn.

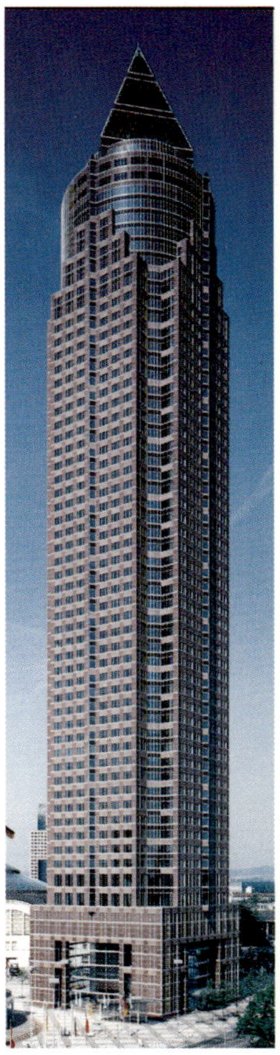

MesseTurm, Frankfurt 1990.
Murphy/Jahn.

NATIONSBANK CENTER

ORIGINALLY REPUBLICBANK CENTER

Houston - United States

Johnson / Burgee Architects - 1984

"Each of these towers has been designed as an architectural one-liner, intended to knock our eyes out for a fleeting instant as we glimpse at it from behind the wheel. Philip Johnson has shown himself to be especially skilled at this kind of thing, particularly in Houston, and he has gained a popular reputation as the foremost living American architect through precisely that talent."

Vincent Scully, *American Architecture and Urbanism*, H. Holt & Co, 1988.

The NationsBank Center is a skyscraper and a city in a building. All the iconography of an old city is resumed in it to make up for the absence of a city around it. The base is clad like a renaissance palace, the gables are stepped and pinnacled like the cathedrals of the north, there are covered arcades as in industrial towns. This eclectic approach is in response to a complex project, a difficult situation. The block is surrounded by open spaces and old, low-rise public buildings. An identity had to be invented.

The project consists of a huge banking hall and its adjoining offices, other offices for rent and, more problematically, the incorporation on the site of an existing building packed with sophisticated equipment that it would have been too expensive to move. Hence the division of the site into quadrants: one for the bank, another for the existing building with a mezzanine extension to the bank, the two remaining parts for the office tower. In the center, a covered arcade with a vault 25 meters (80 feet) above ground level at its highest point serves as the principal axis for circulation and entry. A second axis completes the layout in the form of a cross, punctuated by an old clock.

The building is situated in the business center of downtown Houston. The bank is surrounded by a parking lot, a public garden, a theater, a convention building, and other more or less low-rise buildings ill-matched to the presence of a tower. Above all, the bank is directly opposite another skyscraper built almost 10 years earlier by the same architects.

As far as creating a strong identity is concerned, this is not only the legitimate demand of any developer of a building of such size. In Houston, as in other Texan cities, the architects' ambition is to give a little character to a site almost completely lacking a past. Beyond these considerations and the ability of the architects to respond to them in producing an exceptional work, this skyscraper is even more interesting in that it can be compared with two other skyscrapers built in the same city by the same architects.

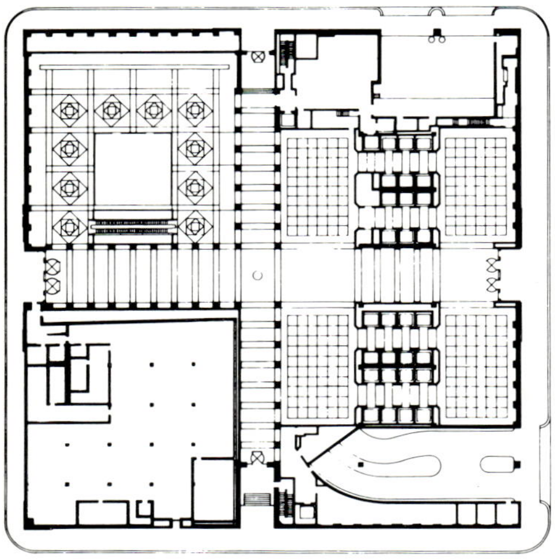

Ground floor plan.
Gerald D. Hines Interests.

Architects: Johnson / Burgee Architects — *Associated architects:* Kendall / Heaton Associates, Inc. — *Structural engineers:* CBM Engineers, Inc. — *Mechanical and electrical engineers:* I.A. Naman + Associates, Inc. — *Developer:* Gerald D. Hines Interests.

56 stories, 238 meters (780 feet) high — Height of the ridge of the banking hall roof: 38 meters (125 feet) — Steel structure — total surface: about 130.000 square meters (1.4 million square feet), office floors ranging in area from 465 to 2,800 square meters (5,000 to 30,000 square feet).

Opposite:
General view of the NationsBank Center on Capital Avenue. To the left, Pennzoil Place by the same architects (1976).
© Richard Payne, 1994.

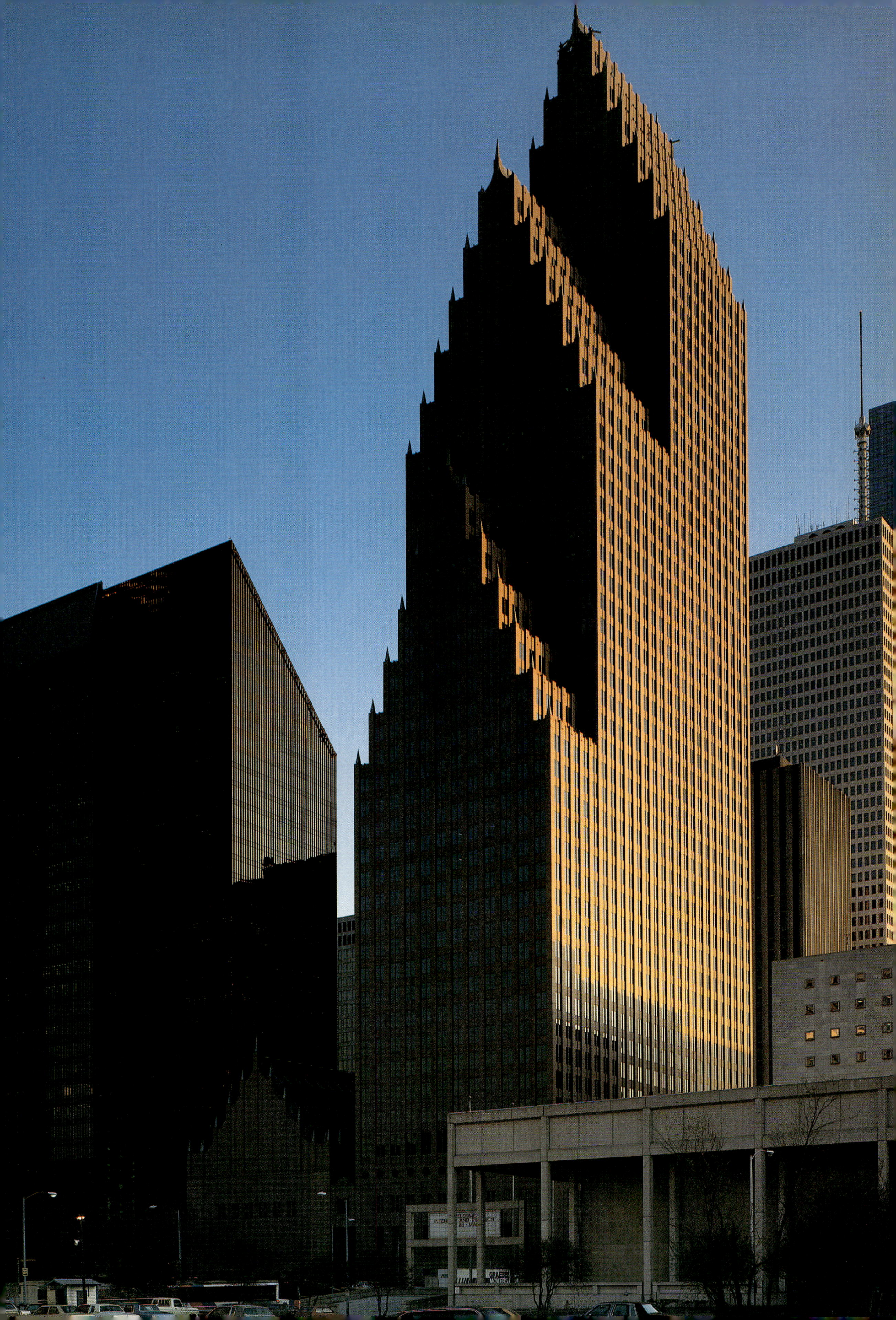

Pennzoil Place was the first to be built, in 1976 on a site adjacent to the bank. An example of pure geometric abstraction, the building consists of two shafts, each a mirror image of the other, rising straight, smooth and black for 36 stories. The two towers are joined at ground level by a large, oblique glass canopy which echoes the pitch at which their summits are sloped. Johnson was to say of this building that it was the most beautiful sculpture ever created by his firm (*Nory Miller, Johnson/Burgee: Architecture*, The Architectural Press, 1980).

How to respond a few years later to the challenge of building another skyscraper next to that one? The architects and the property developer well recall the first sketches which, in opposition to what was finally decided upon, proposed the construction of a sort of second Pennzoil Place. It was proof, if proof were needed, that Johnson and Burgee, champions of the post-modern skyscraper at the time, were little concerned by questions of style, schools of design or labels. The fact that the stepped façade of the tower was dictated by the requirements of the project as well as the area of the office floors, among other things, does not prevent the appreciation of the elegance with

Pennzoil Place, Houston 1976.
© Richard Payne.

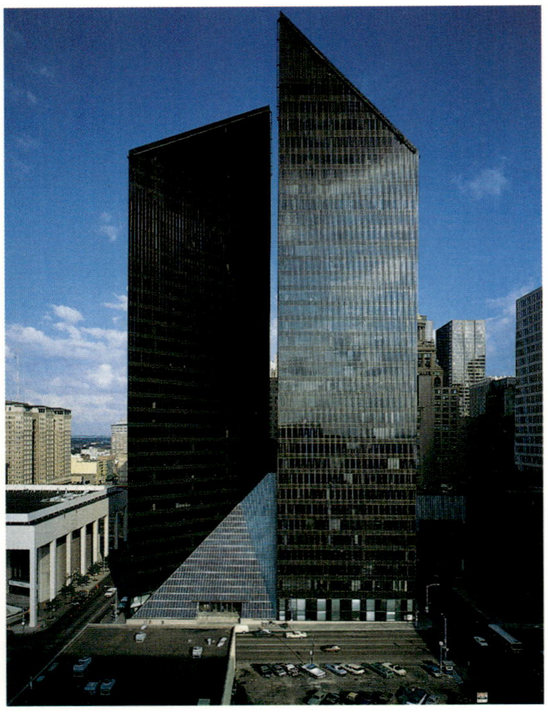

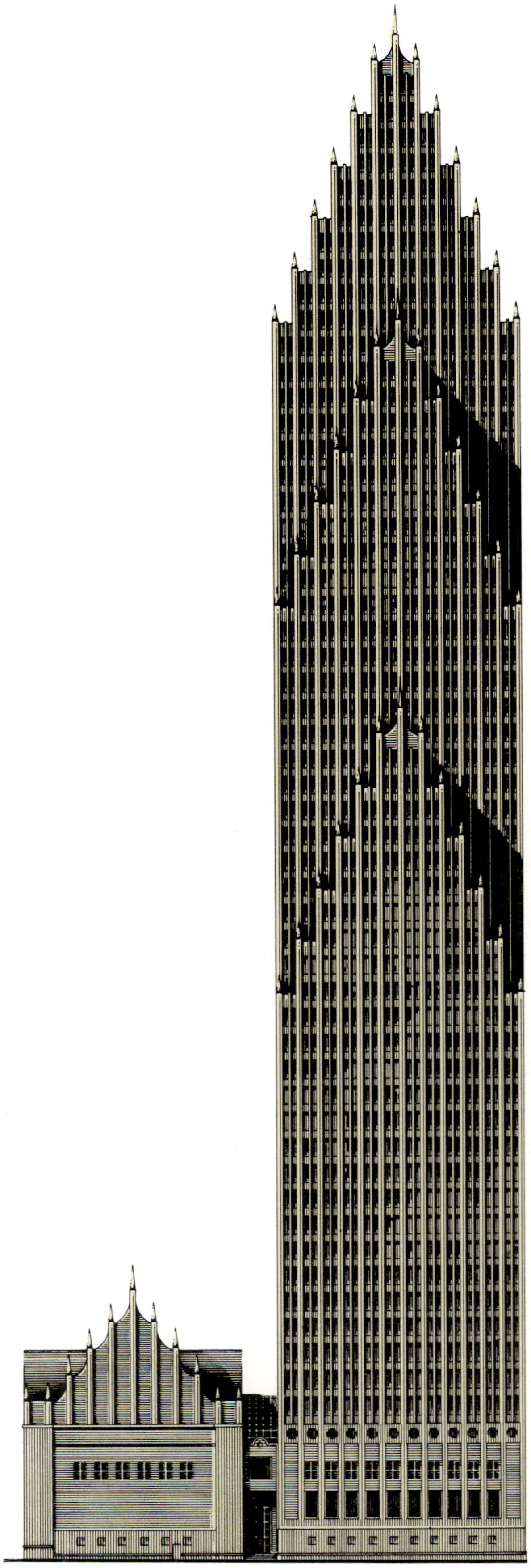

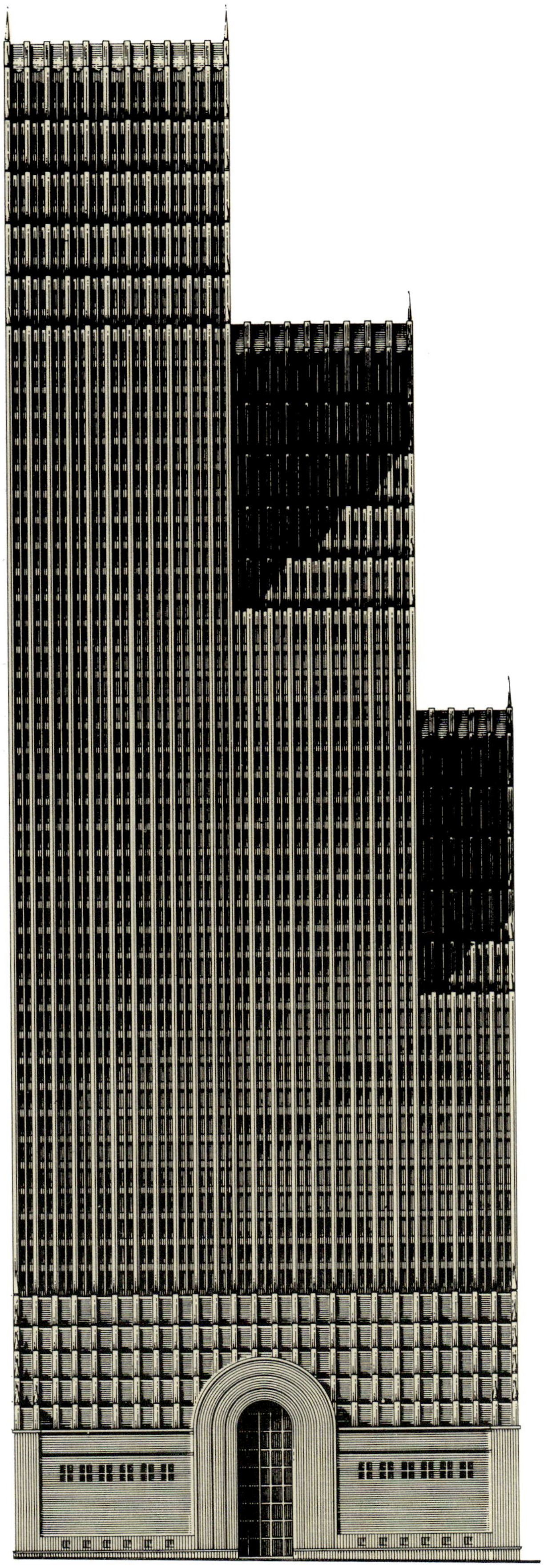

which the silhouette of the NationsBank Center sets off that of the older tower.
Another, equally striking comparison must be made with the Transco tower (1979-1983), conceived in the same year as the NationsBank Center by the same architects and for the same developer, Gerald D. Hines.
Transco is situated in the no-man's-land of a Texan suburb between freeways, hotels, and supermarkets. But it is so tall, so soaring, so recognizable—almost an Empire State Building—that it contains within itself all the imagery of a great American city. The tower benefits, moreover, from being seen from a distance. For neither its long grassed court nor the monumental fountain which closes the perspective succeed in creating the illusion of a context, even suburban. It simply stands there, an object rich and strange.
It is in meeting the need to unify the disparate elements of an area into a real place that the NationsBank Center succeeds so well where Transco fails. Not only does the graduation of the four-gabled masses marry better with the different heights of the neighboring buildings but, even more than this, the building itself forms a complex and hierarchical urban landscape, like one of those town squares in Germany where market halls rub shoulders with the town hall and the cathedral.

Center, from left to right:
North elevation on Capital Avenue.
To the left, the banking hall.
East elevation on Louisiana Street.
Gerald D. Hines Interests.

Below:
Transco Tower, Houston 1983.
© Richard Payne, 1994.

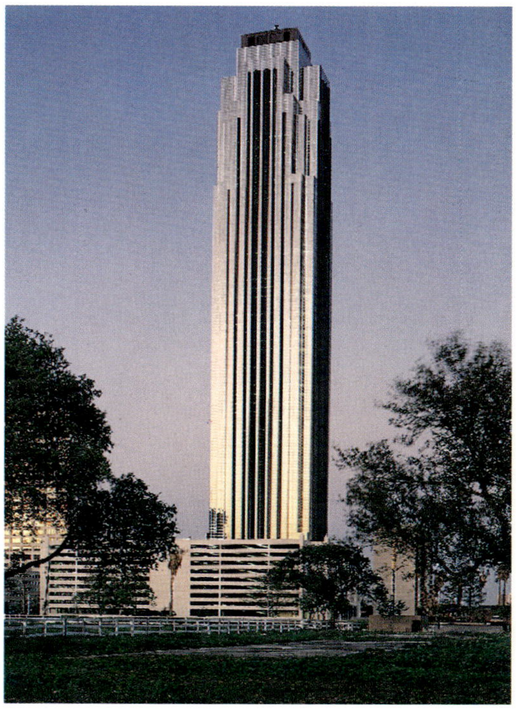

HONG KONG AND SHANGHAI BANK

Hong Kong

Foster Associates - 1985

"The phrase 'made in Hong Kong' has not always implied the very best that money can buy. But buildings of this quality do not just happen anywhere, at any time. They happen because a rare combination of circumstances leads them to happen."

Chris Abel, *The Architectural Review* No. 1070, April 1986.

"Build me the best bank in the world!" When Vandaleur Grayburn, CEO of the Bank of Hong Kong commissionned the firm of Palmer & Turner to build a new headquarters, could he have imagined that, fifty years later, the same order—worded the same way—would give the English architect Norman Foster the opportunity of designing an outstanding skyscraper, after which no very tall building could use excuses of specification or technical constraint to justify its failings or its banality.

The barely profiled stone facing in the Art Deco style of the 1935 bank conceals in reality a building advanced for its time. With its height of 70 meters (230 feet) it was the tallest building between Cairo and San Francisco. Built on a steel framework—the first in Hong Kong—it was equipped with batteries of high-speed elevators, air conditioning and a landing platform for autogiros on the roof. A true symbol of the power and innovating spirit of the bank, the building was to reign for half a century in a prominent position on the colony's bank notes.

Foster, retained by the bank after a competition, began his project in 1979. It was the first time that the firm had built a skyscraper but the conditions of the commission seemed to match this new challenge. The developer-occupier had a tradition of patronage and was more concerned by image than by short-term profitability. There was no mention of any budget limit in the brief. The site too was exceptional. The bank faces the only square in the business district on an axis with the ferry landing stage. It is surrounded by historic monuments and lower buildings. However, since 1990 the Standard Chartered Bank has flanked it with one of its sides.

What Foster has produced is a kind of ultra-sophisticated machine which combines, at the same time, a technological precision worthy of the atomic energy industry and, in contrast, an extremely brutal appearance, almost anecdotal in its superstructures like a giant erector set construction of ladders, triangulated beams and diagonal

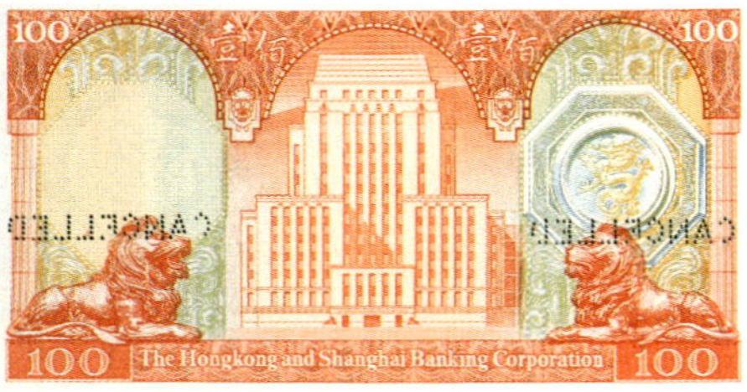

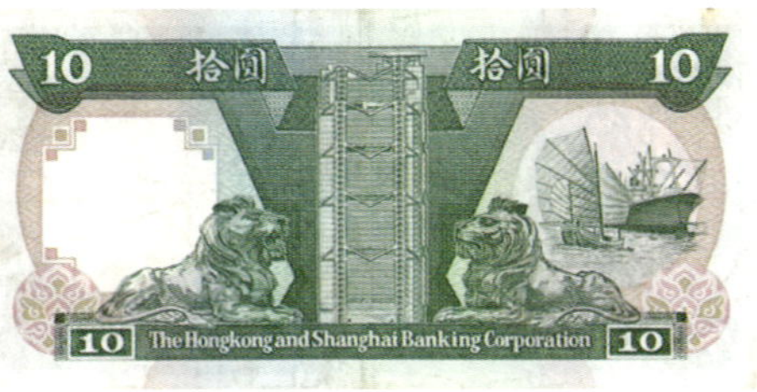

Two Hong Kong dollar notes: 1935 (above) and the new 1985 headquarters.
Hong Kong and Shanghai Bank.

Opposite:
The Hong Kong and Shanghai Bank in the foreground of Victoria Harbour.
© Ian Lambot.

Architects: Foster Associates — *Structural engineers:* Ove Arup & Partners — *mechanical and electrical engineers:* J. Roger Preston & Partners — *Contractors:* John Lok / Wimpey Joint Venture — *Developer:* The Hongkong and Shanghai Banking Corporation.

47 stories, 179 meters (587 feet) high — Steel structure — Office building and banking hall (2,178 square meters, 23,444 square feet) or a total of 98,000 square meters (1,055,000 square feet) — Floor areas: from 976 to 3,215 square meters (10,506 to 34,606 square feet).

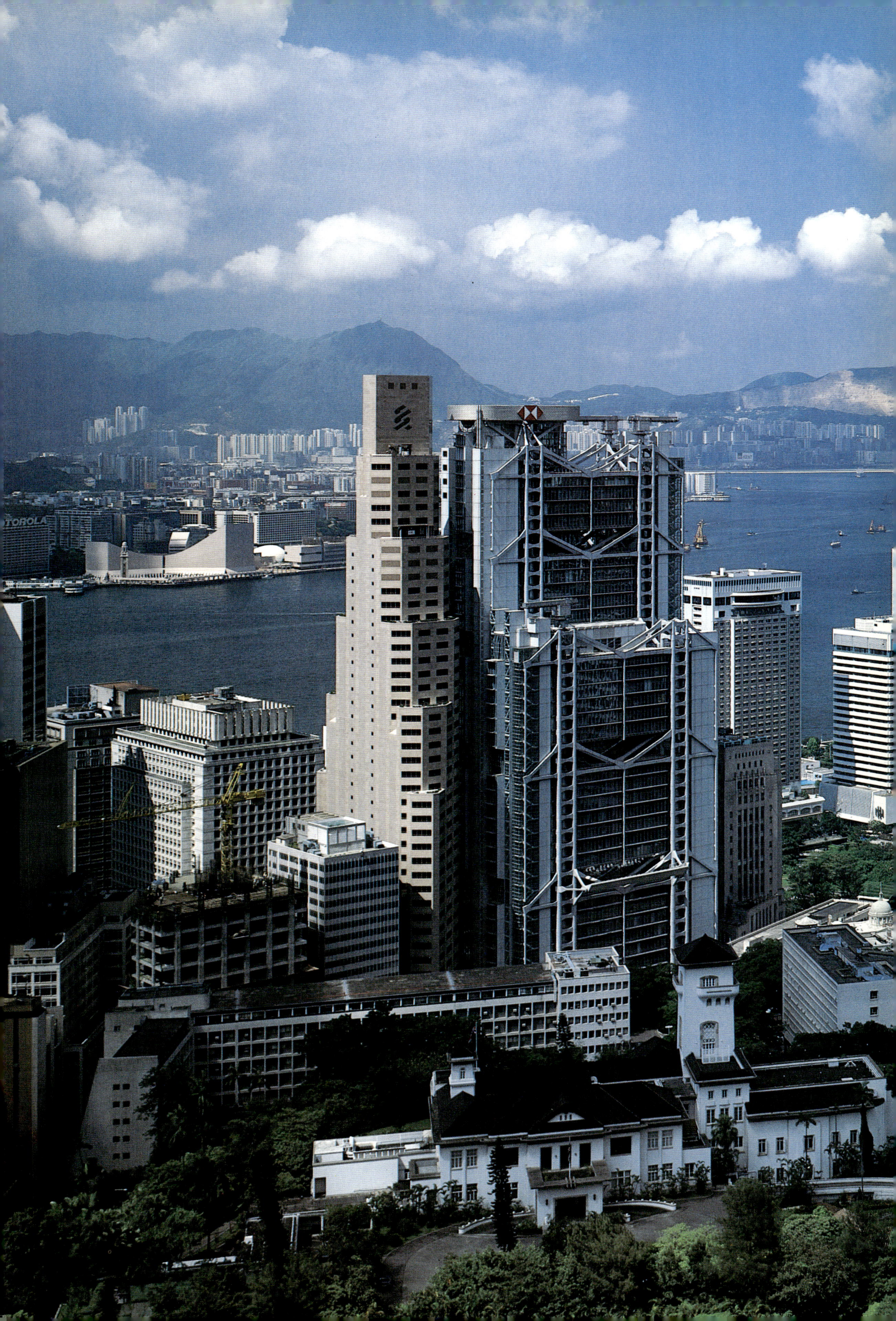

braces. Supporting the building are four pairs of masts linked by impressive Vierendeel beams. Aligned in the form of four parallel porticos, they delimit three clear spans of floor space. Five groups of floors—"villages" in the words of Norman Foster—hang from these porticos. They are of decreasing height, increasing the effect of perspective as with a traditional pagoda.

This visible structure is primarily the corollary of an original interior arrangement which is concerned with public space and the daily working

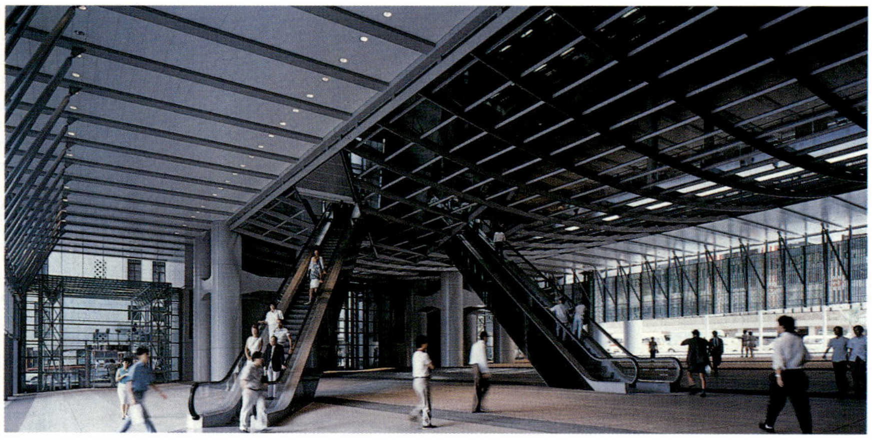

The esplanade at ground level of the bank.
© Ian Lambot.

environment rather than image. The principal of the porticos rids the building of the traditional central core. Instead, a 10-story-high atrium floods the main banking hall and the lowest group of office floors with natural light. And the device also means that at ground level the building is completely empty at its center; the street literally passes underneath the bank and forms an esplanade which follows the natural slope of the ground in a series of steps. A glazed lattice work through which the sun's rays penetrate floats 12 meters (40 feet) above. For the sunlight, reflected by an ingenious arrangement of mirrors, descends through the atrium on to the passersby below, who cast their shadows on the ground. To linger on this esplanade is a memorable experience. In the background are the square and the street, bustling with activity. Buses and trams come and go against the light. In the foreground are the crowd of passersby, the two escalators that penetrate into the bank as though it was a great belly, and the mechanical ballet of the customers going up and down. Looking up, the whole internal activity of the bank comes into view as though in an aquarium. From the inside, leaning over the balustrades, you can view the movement in the street. The whole spirit of the island is concentrated here in these scenes where vitality, action, movement are truly celebrated.

The same theme imbues every floor. In each "village" you move about in the open air in the center of the floor as though you were in a building of only a few stories. Instead of elevator shafts there are escalators.

The portico construction also allows architectural solutions to outside needs, to the constraints imposed by the city. On three of its sides the building is stepped to conform to regulations about overshadowing, which are, of course, a function of the buildings opposite and the width of the streets. On the broad façades the height of the porticos determines the position of the setbacks, whereas at the sides, the groups of floors are set back progressively as though along rails. Nothing would prevent, at least from a technical point of view, the filling up of the empty spaces between each portico with new work spaces

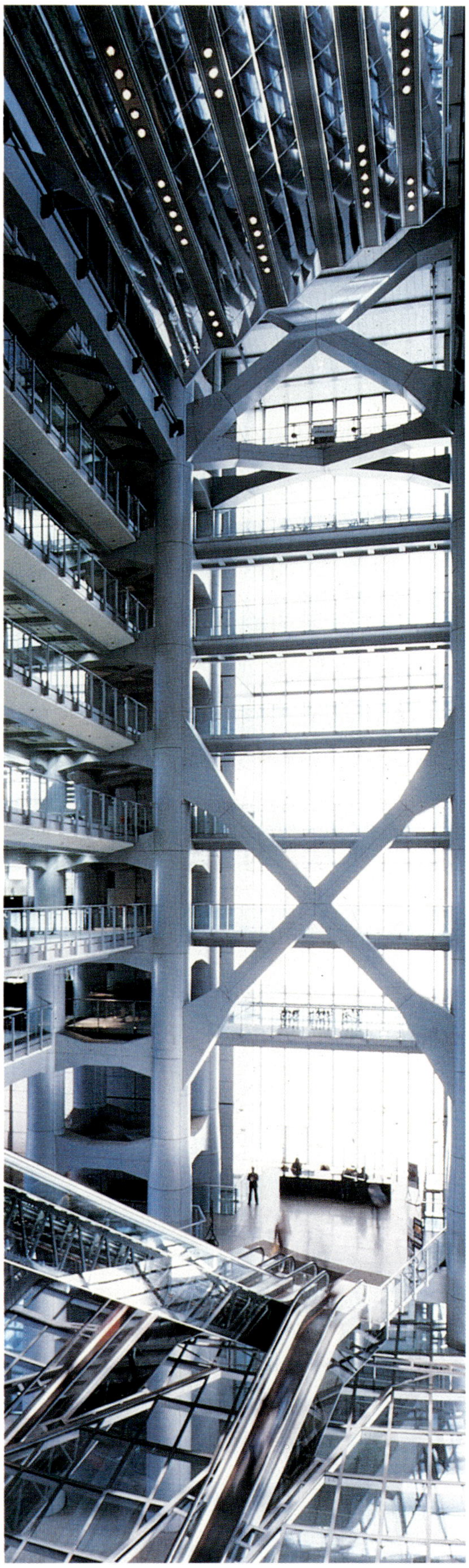

should needs or the regulations change. This potential for enlargement and the adaptability of the interior space in fact meets part of the developer's requirement for absolute flexibility.

Has the Hong Kong and Shanghai Bank had followers? Apparently not.

First, there is the problem of the cost. But it would be unfair to compare a purely speculative project to the building of a headquarters. The bank's density of occupation is lower than in a structure built for rental. Above all, the project included specific demands and a level of interior finish—all the furniture and fittings were specially designed—on which property developers are liable to cut corners. Add to this the experimental nature of the construction from the invention of a welding robot to the use of sea water to supply the cooling system, the technical sophistication in the manufacture of components and their assembly, all of which considerably swelled the budgets for both design and execution.

Cost, however, is not the only factor. An aesthetic commitment to high-tech still disconcerts most clients today. The termination of the Hong Kong lease in 1997 has inclined the island more towards cultural consensus, to tried and trusted formulae. But the shock produced by this very different bank has nevertheless not been in vain. Since it was built, standards of quality have been revised upwards. The appearance of high-level international competition has stimulated local architects and builders. Building is better, finishing is better since the new bank appeared on the scene.

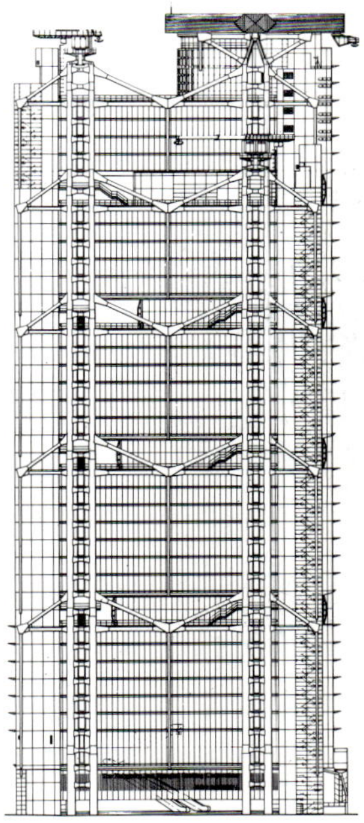

North elevation on Statue Square.
Sir Norman Foster and Partners.

Center:
Interior view of the atrium.
© Ian Lambot.

FIRST INTERSTATE BANK TOWER FOUNTAIN PLACE

ORIGINALLY ALLIED BANK TOWER

Dallas - United States

I.M. Pei & Partners - 1986

"[It is] a glittering, 60-story glass prism; the office tower as laser-cut gem, that never looks the same twice."

David Dillon, "Constantly Changing Minimalist Tower," *Architecture*, December 1986.

Fountain Place is a true paradox: very present from a distance, it dissolves as you approach it.

The metamorphosis is achieved by devices typical of the Ieoh Ming Pei firm, to be found wherever it has left its mark, from Dallas to Paris to Hong Kong, and lies in its significant geometry, abstract form and reflecting mirror glass.

In Dallas the transformation scene takes place at the extreme north of the business district, a characterless assembly of warehouses, shopping areas and open-air car parks, a low-rise environment without towers or historic neighbors; thence the need to create a landmark, an event, an angular sculpture hewn in glass to reflect the clouds crossing the sky, the rays of the setting sun. This glass polyhedron is rigorously geometric in plan and in section, following the diagonal of a double square. It is a 10-sided prism that seems to be in perpetual motion and reminds you of a bird made out of folded paper. Does this image suggest a distant trace of oriental culture in the architect or, more probably, his constructivist perception of architectural form? Pei, it must be remembered, is first and foremost an engineer.

In any event, triangulated façades are already to be observed on the Arco Tower in Dallas (1983) and also, in a way, on the John Hancock Tower in Boston (1976). The Boston building, designed on a lozenge-shaped plan, is wrapped in curtain walling of reflecting glass, prefiguring the technology used 10 years later in Dallas. (A serious fault in its application hindered the building's occupation for several years, giving it a sad notoriety.)

Its geometry also characterizes the tall Bank of China Tower, built in Hong Kong by Ieoh Ming Pei in 1989. But in this case it is the triangulated framework that generates the form. The square base is divided diagonally into 4 quadrants and, as it rises, the volume of the tower is successively reduced to 3, 2, and finally 1 remaining quadrant.

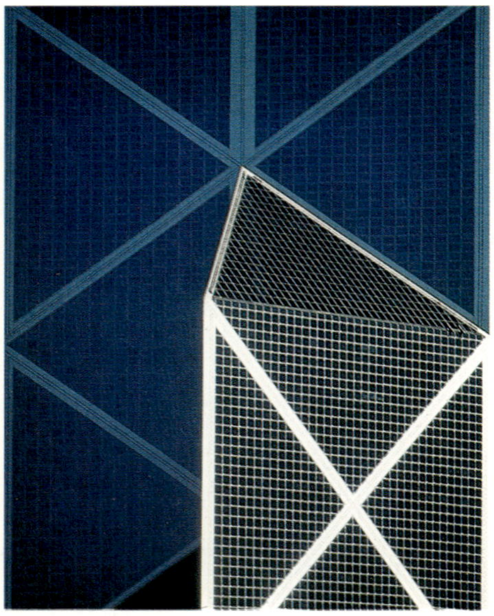

The Bank of China, Hong Kong, detail of the triangulated façade, I.M. Pei & Partners, Architects. 1989.
© John Nye.

Architects: I.M. Pei & Partners (Henry N. Cobb), in association with Architectural Consulting Services, Inc. — *Consultant architects:* Harry Weese & Associates — *Landscape architect:* Kiley Walker (Dan Kiley) — *Structural engineers:* CBM Engineers, Inc. — *Mechanical and electrical engineers:* Cosentini Associates — *Contractor:* HCB Contractors — *Developer:* Criswell Development Company.

60 stories, 219 meters (720 feet) high — Steel structure — Office area: about 106,000 square meters (1,140,234 square feet) — Underground parking for about 900 cars and 9,000 square meters (97,000 square feet) of garden.

Opposite:
First Interstate Bank Tower from the freeway exit.
© Richard Payne, 1994.

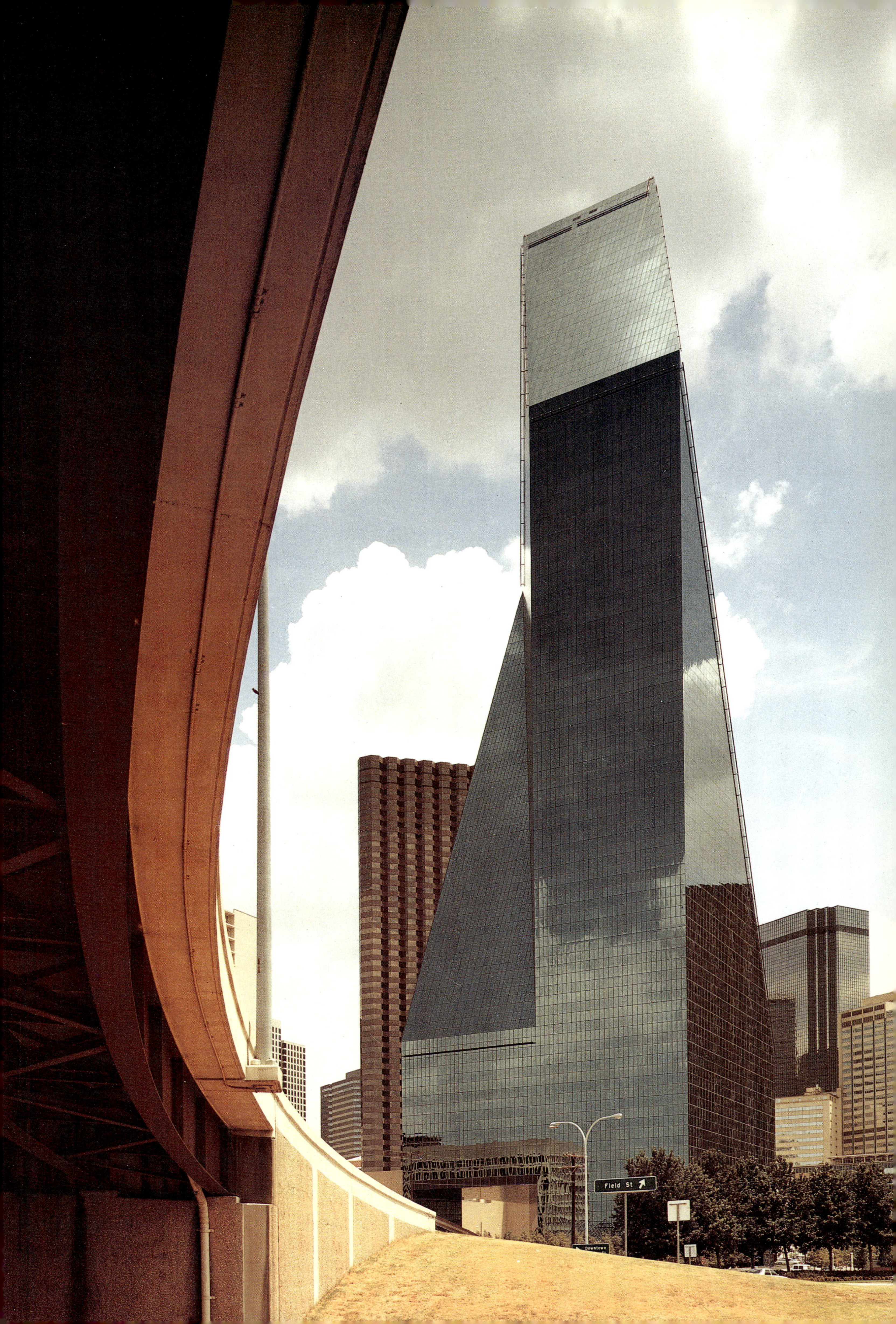
Field St

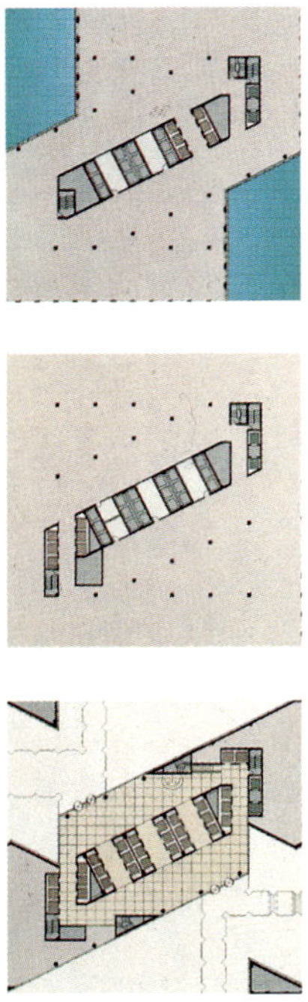

Sample plans: bottom to top, ground, 5th and 21st floors.
Pei Cobb Freed & Partners.

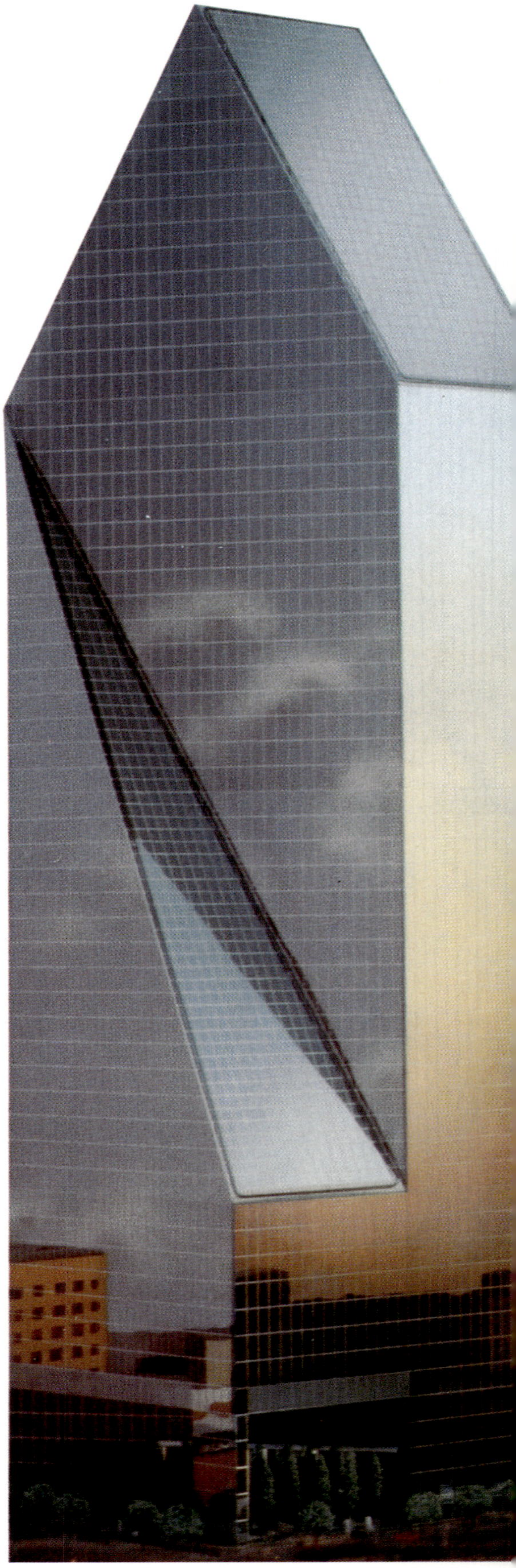

Center:
The initial project for twin towers: photomontage (detail).
Pei Cobb Freed & Partners.

The play of geometry at Fountain Place replaces the "figurative New York strategy" which the firm has always rejected. For the architect it was a question of building a real skyscraper without crowning the building with some hat or other, (according to Henry N. Cobb in an article by David Dillon, "Constantly Changing Minimalist Tower," *Architecture*, December 1986).

The base of the tower is perfectly square, but the square only actually exists from the fifth to the twelfth floor. For at ground level it is half hollowed out, creating two huge porches 20 meters (60 feet) high at either side of the central core. These two open-air lobbies are anterooms to the most spectacular feature of the entire project, the one that gives the building its name. A water garden, created in collaboration with Dan Kiley, the landscape architect, literally invades the base of the tower. Even more than the area actually occu-

Detail of the water garden.
© Wes Thompson.

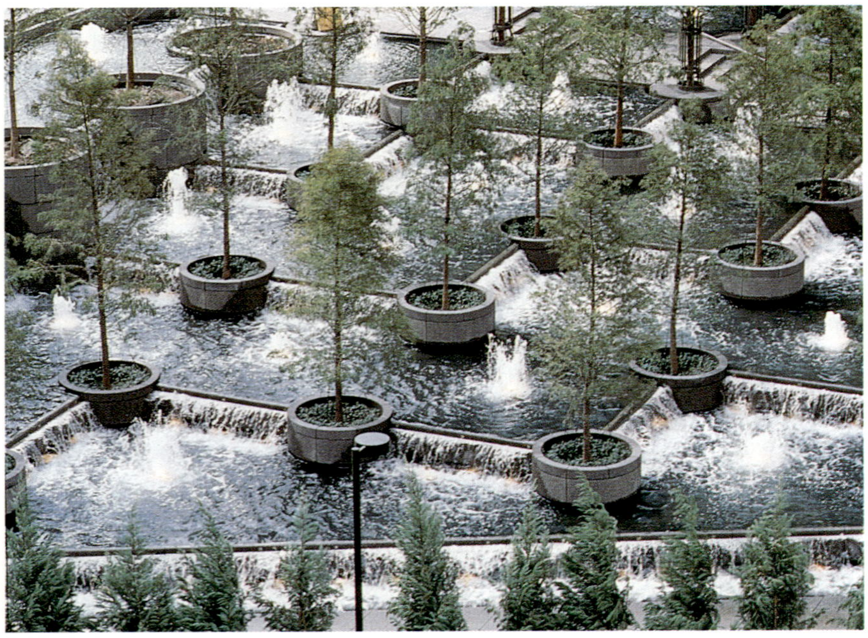

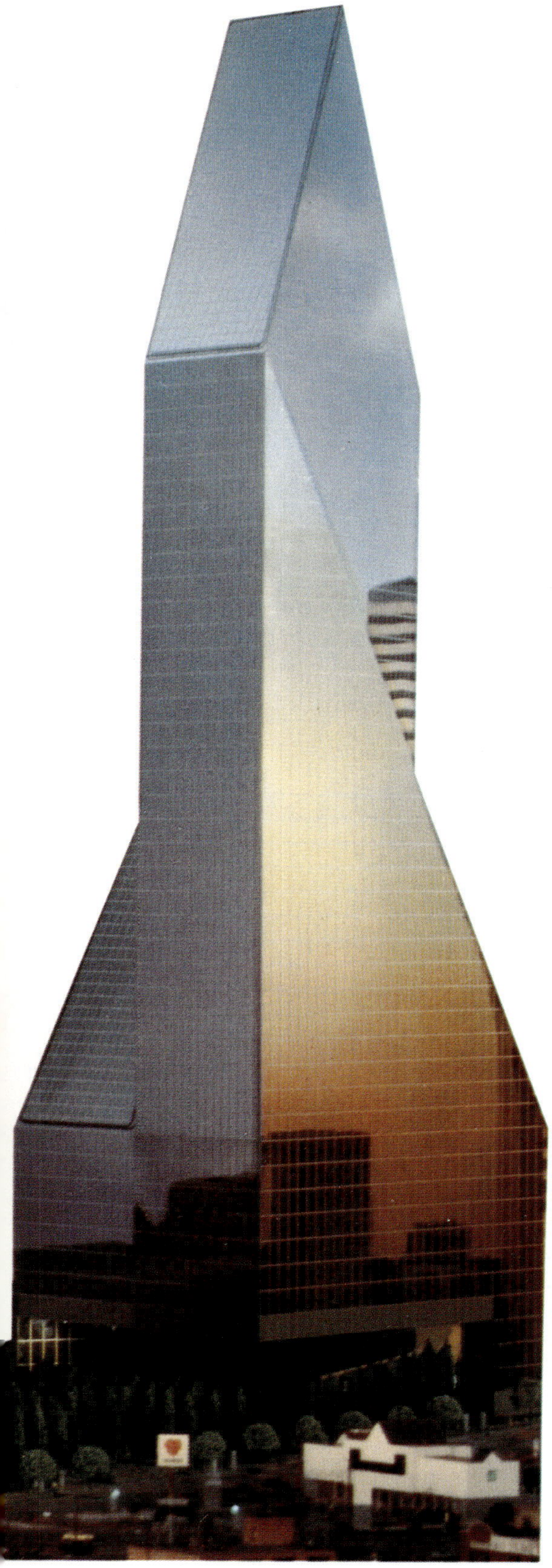

pied by the garden, it is the sound of falling water, the checkerboard pattern of cypress trees—those you actually see, those which are reflected in the glass walls, the fresh feeling of an oasis that dominates the space. Water is everywhere; nature immerses everything at the entrance to the tower and in the garden behind it with its 217 fountains, its park benches, its café terrace. Here architecture is obliterated.

The tower re-imposes itself when seen from a distance. The thing to do, it seems, is to take the nearby freeway, preferably at high speed and at sunset, to see the tower unfold in hues of blues, greens, reds, blacks. And imagine how a second tower, identical to the first and set at ninety degrees to it, would multiply the optical illusions, reflections, colors.

Fountain Place, the most spectacular monument of the Dallas freeways.

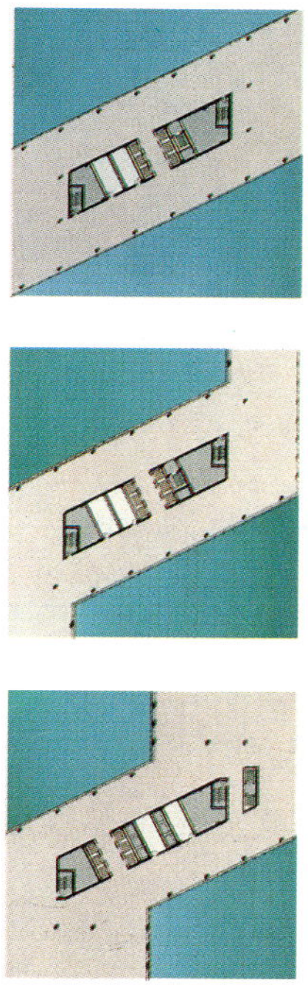

Sample plans: bottom to top, 29th, 37th and 45th floors.
Pei Cobb Freed & Partners.

The open-air entrance lobby.
© Wes Thompson.

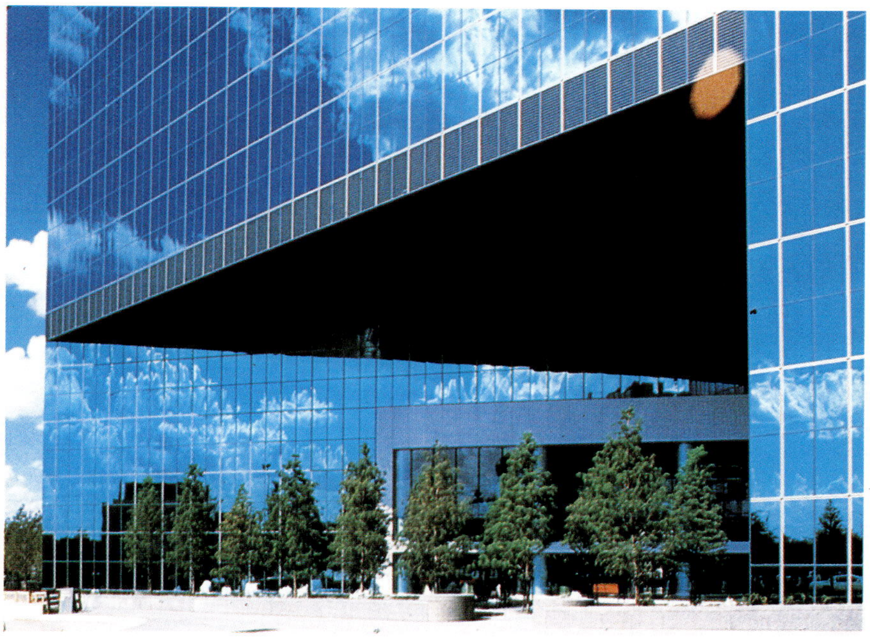

J.P. MORGAN

ORIGINALLY 60 WALL STREET

New York - United States

Kevin Roche John Dinkeloo and Associates - 1989

"This tower of gray granite and reflective glass mimics the form of a classical column, with a base, shaft and capital, but it does so in such a way as to reinvigorate historical form with modern meaning...."

Paul Goldberger, *The New York Times*, March 4, 1990.

In 1841, on Wall Street, The Merchants' Exchange's architect Isaiah Rogers deploys an ionic colonnade along the north side of the famous thoroughfare. Together with the customs building, this is one of the most prestigious monumental constructions of the budding financial district. Half a century later, Charles McKim was commissioned to adapt the building to the needs of a modern bank (National City Bank, 1910). The architect increases the height of the building by four stories and places a Corinthian colonnade above the first one. In 1988, just opposite, a new colonnade in granite takes its place in the alignment of the historic street. Behind the double row of columns, in this unbelievably densely occupied quarter, the biggest winter garden in the city opens out. And it is a public space.

Kevin Roche's entire project for the headquarters of the Morgan company is contained in this brief account: the historical context, with the real estate opportunity to acquire the rights of a neighboring monumental building, the privileges granted in exchange for the project's contribution to improving public space, the theme of columns, inspired by the site and given variations on every scale on the fifty-two stories of the new skyscraper.

The colonnade aligned with the street establishes the new building in perfect continuity with neighboring street-level frontages. Seen from a distance, it is no more than the plinth of a base on which rests a tall, square-based shaft. At the summit, a last row of columns—in reality a set of juxtaposed bow windows—concludes the metaphor.

The column is a form with two historical references. It is both an element in classical architectural composition, a reminder of the first glorious days of Wall Street, and also the epitome of the skyscraper, to the history of which it also belongs. Furthermore, the same form defines another tower built in the same year by the same

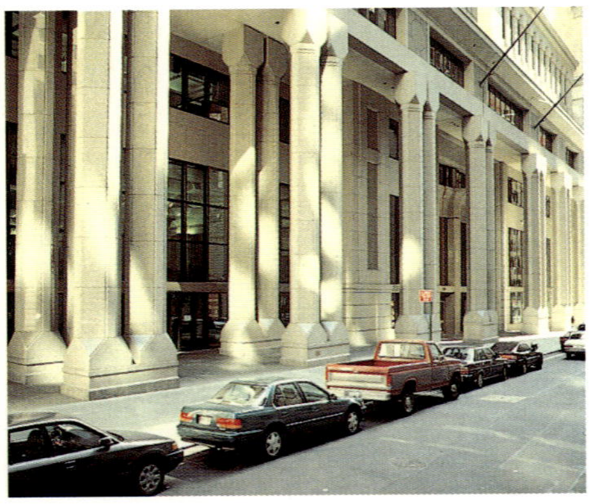

The colonnade of the J.P. Morgan Tower on Wall Street.
© Benoît Roland, 1995.

Opposite:
The J.P. Morgan Tower (center) seen from the East River. In the foreground, the pyramidal silhouette of the 120 Wall Street building.
Kevin Roche John Dinkeloo and Associates.

Architects: Kevin Roche John Dinkeloo and Associates (Kevin Roche) — *Structural engineers:* The Office of Irwin G. Cantor — *Mechanical and electrical engineers:* Syska & Hennessy — *Developer:* Park Tower Group.

50 stories, 227 meters (745 feet) high — Steel structure — Office building floor space of 149,000 square meters (1.6 million square feet) with a public winter garden at ground level; 10 meter (30 feet) high ceiling — 1,200 square meters (13,000 square feet) floor areas: from 2,800 to 4,800 square meters (30,000 to 52,000 square feet).

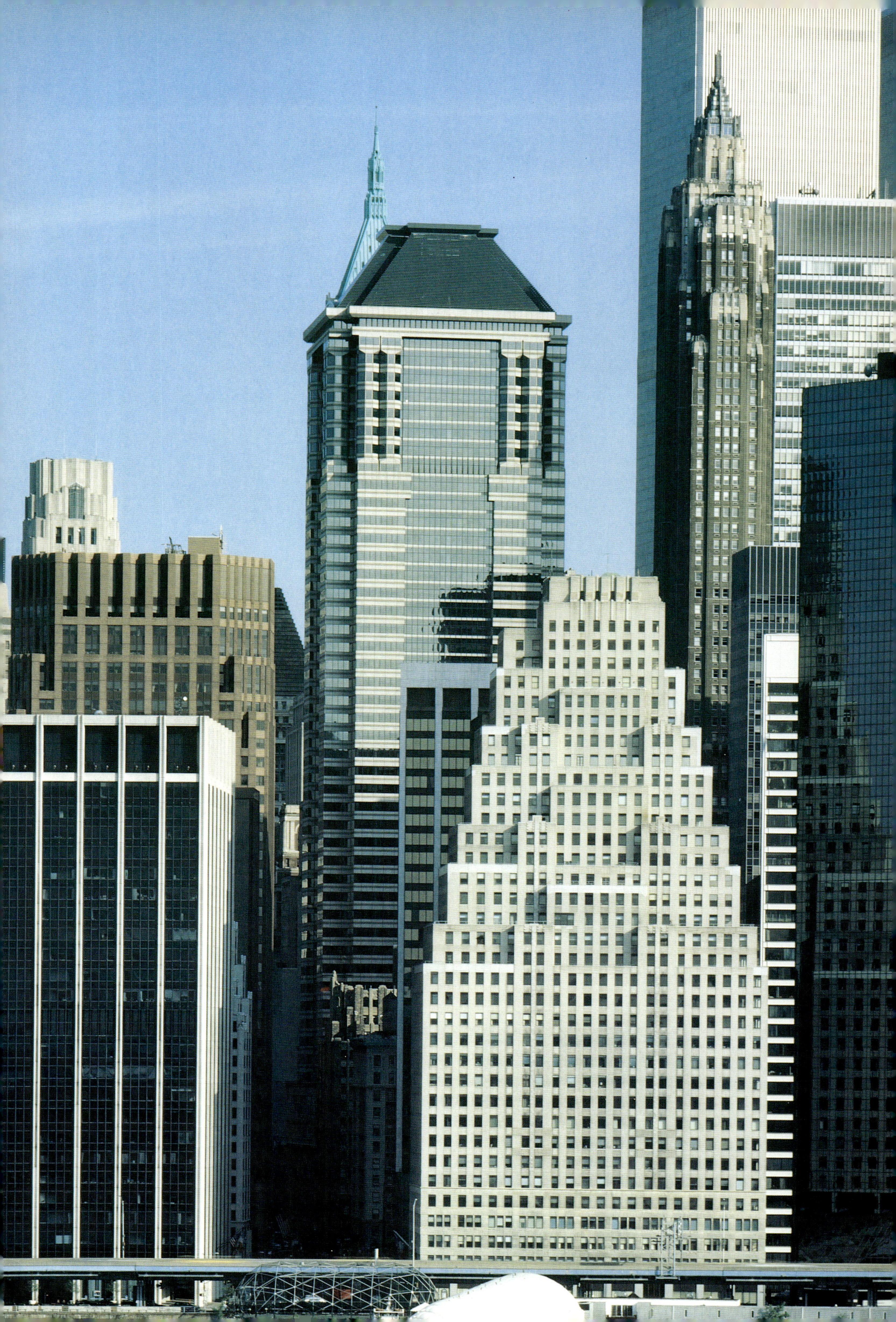

Center:
J.P. Morgan: the public atrium.
Kevin Roche John Dinkeloo and Associates.

Below:
Leo Burnett Company Tower, Chicago 1989.
Kevin Roche John Dinkeloo and Associates.

architect on a bank of the Chicago river—the Leo Burnett Company Tower.

It is characteristic of Kevin Roche to give each of his projects a single, identifiable and clearly referenced form of which the geometry permits every variation of scale. The forms include: the silo (Knights of Columbus, New Haven 1969); the truncated pyramid (College Life Insurance Company, Indianapolis 1971); the pagoda (Ravinia, Atlanta 1986); the ziggurat (750 Seventh Avenue, New York 1990). Another characteristic of the architect is the emphasis given to the entrance; the atrium theme is a leitmotiv in his work. But in the case of the J.P. Morgan it was a matter of arranging on the site for access to the subway system and, taking advantage of this constraint, to create a non-commercial public space. In exchange for this, permission for 10% additional floor space was granted, an opportunity seized by Roche to create a universe of latticework, glass canopies, fountains, and rocks, worthy of an

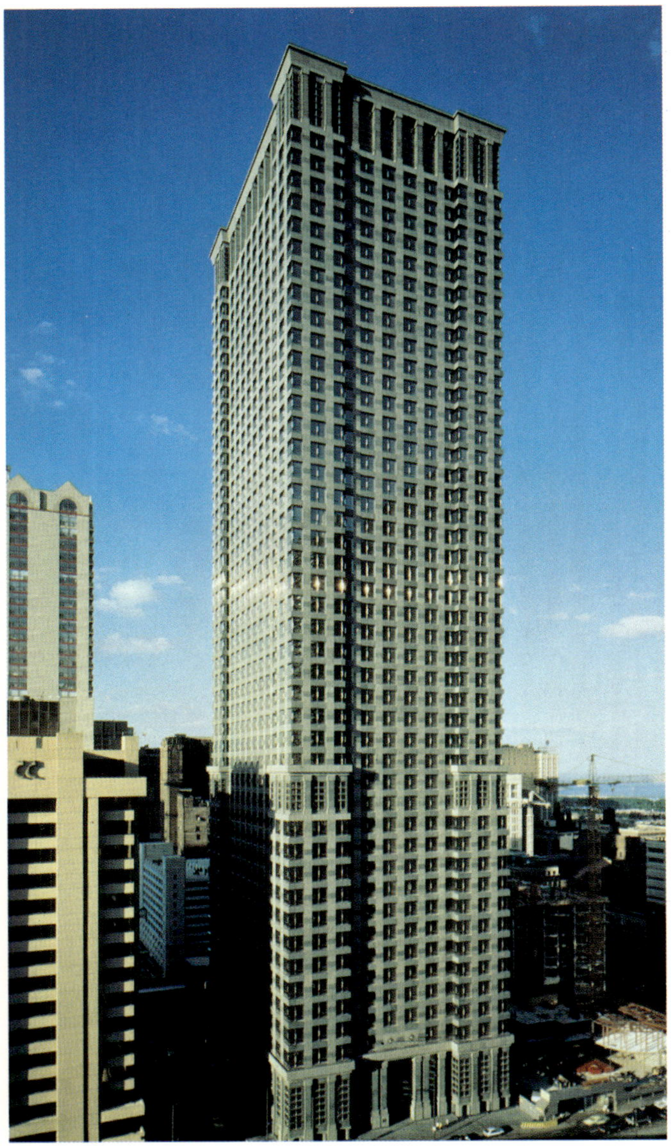

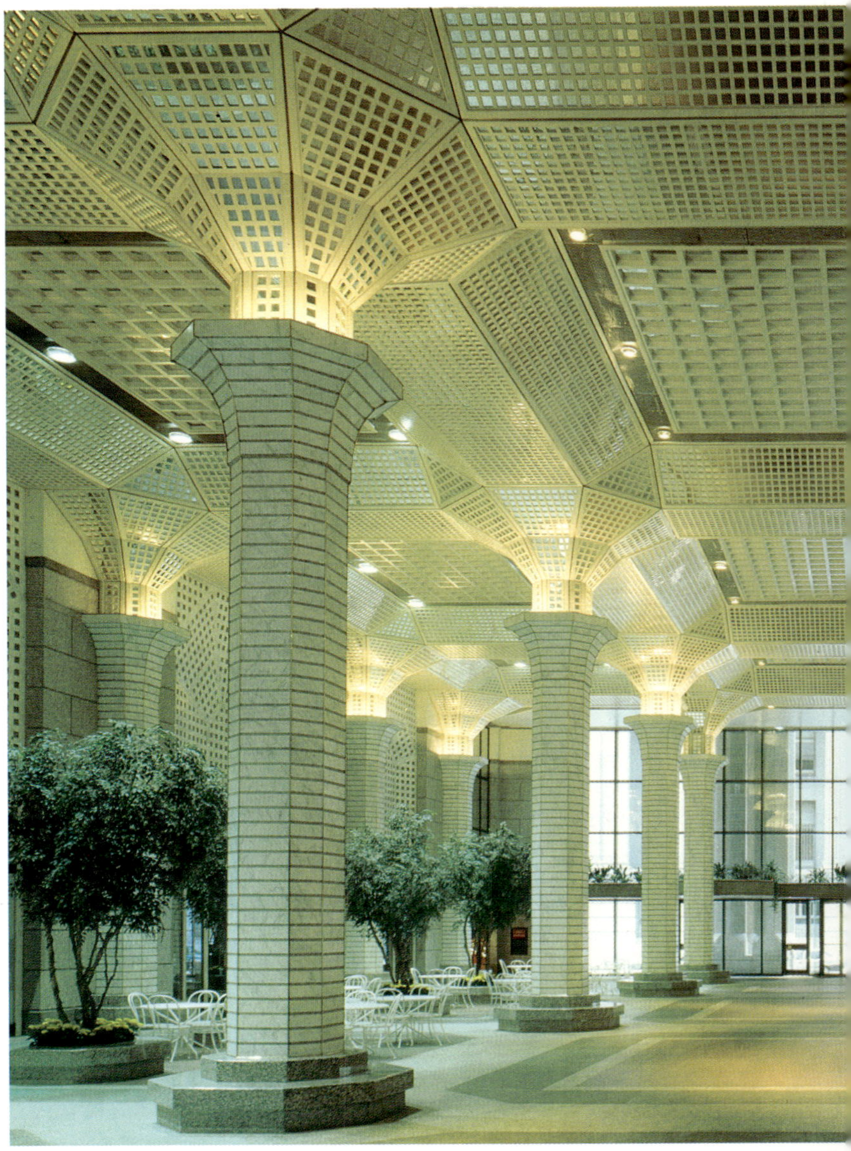

Edwardian pleasure garden in the heart of New York's financial district.

And this was not the only providential real estate factor. The headquarters of the J.P. Morgan Company is one of many examples of air rights negotiated in the historical center in the vicinity of a protected landmark. More than 30,000 square meters (323,000 square feet) were thus transferred from the land area of the old Merchants' Exchange to the site of the new project. And so the skyscraper joined the ranks of the historic tall towers of lower Manhattan; the Bank of Manhattan Building—70 stories, 1930; the Cities Service Building—290 meters (950 feet) high, 1932.

With this building and a few others of around the same time, New York recovered something of that rare imaginative daring which was its glory at the beginning of the century. The reference to history is not limited here to the imitation of its forms. It is a certain way of conceiving the city and a commitment shared by architect and developer alike.

750 Seventh Avenue, New York 1990.
Kevin Roche John Dinkeloo and Associates.

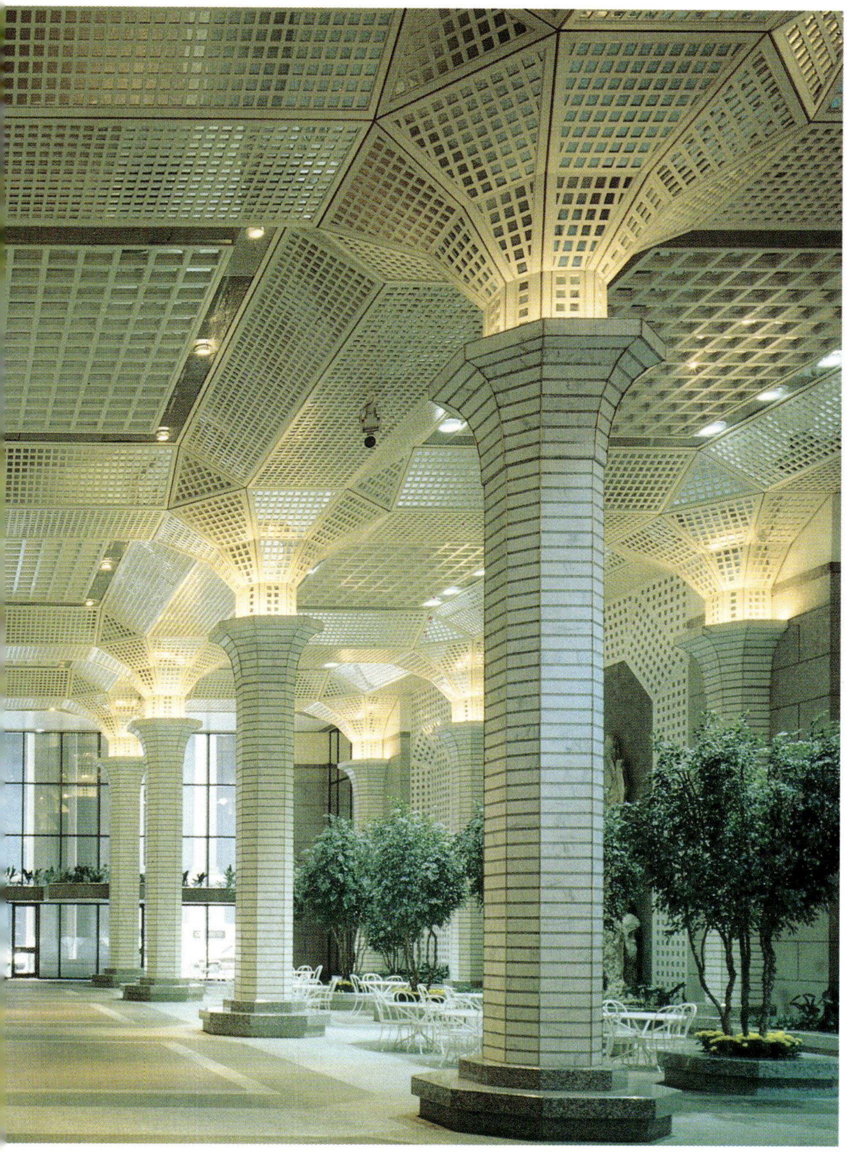

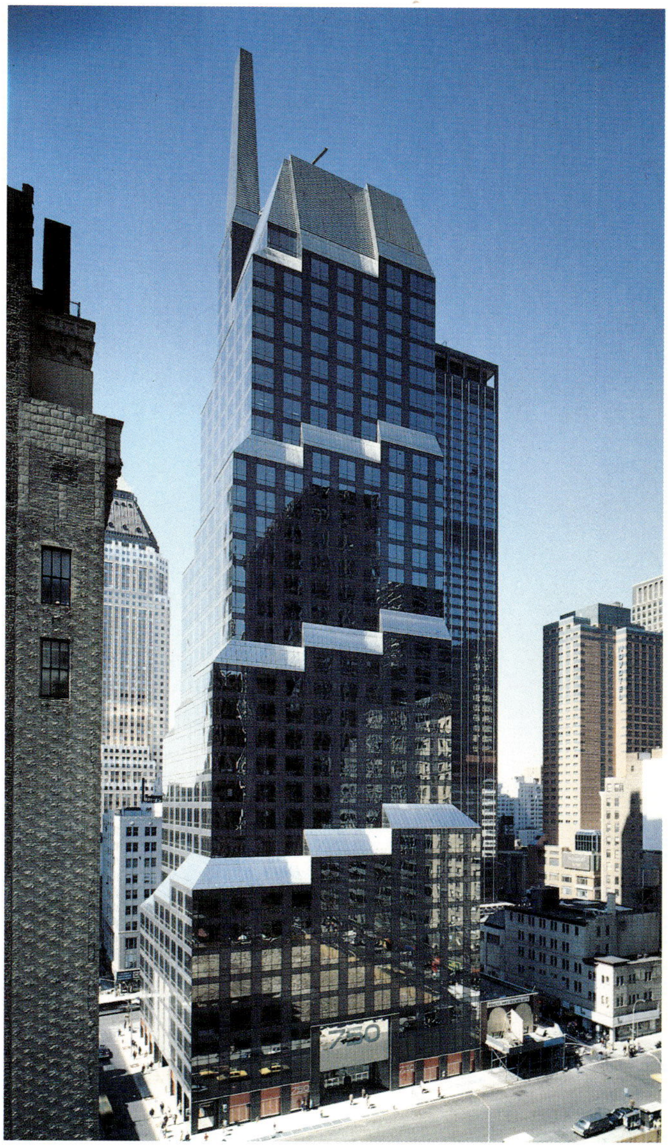

MIGLIN-BEITLER TOWER

Chicago - United States

Cesar Pelli & Associates - 1989

"It was for Chicago, after all, that Frank Lloyd Wright proposed his mile-high building and where the architectural master Daniel Burnham advised his followers 'Make no little plans.'"

Isabel Wilkerson, *The New York Times*, June 4, 1989.

"Make no little plans!" This philosophy of Daniel Burnham (1846-1912), the inventor of the big office building, was all it needed to make Chicago property developer J. Paul Beitler decide to enter the race and take over the torch of the tallest building, valiantly carried by the Sears Tower since 1974. And to win this challenge in the same city, a few steps from the Sears Tower and the famous Loop, the overhead railway of the 1890s that delimits one of the oldest business districts in the modern world!

But being the tallest was not enough for Beitler. He wanted a skyscraper that soared like an arrow. The *Washington Post*, not entirely uncritically, announced "somewhat like a delicate ballet dancer among broad-shouldered football linemen." (Bill Peterson, "Architectural Ballerina Seeks Spot on Chicago's Brawny Skyline," *The Washington Post*, June 1, 1989). The intention was to create a new symbol and to offer small enterprises a unique opportunity of having their offices perched high in the sky like the giants of the world economy.

Cesar Pelli was the architect chosen by Beitler as the ally to make his dream a reality. They were well-acquainted, as the architect was at that time building a 50-story office tower in the heart of the Loop, at the top of which Beitler subsequently installed his offices. Pelli was in fact to design the highest skyscraper in the world but it would be neither the Miglin-Beitler Tower, nor any other tower in Chicago. Yet all was ready for building to commence. The city, well-known for its favorable disposition towards developers (its zoning plan has not been reviewed since 1957), had endorsed the project, which had also been authorized by the Federal Aviation Administration. The technical hazards of the tower's very great height and slenderness (a height more than 8 times its width) had been studied in great depth, especially regarding its possible behavior under

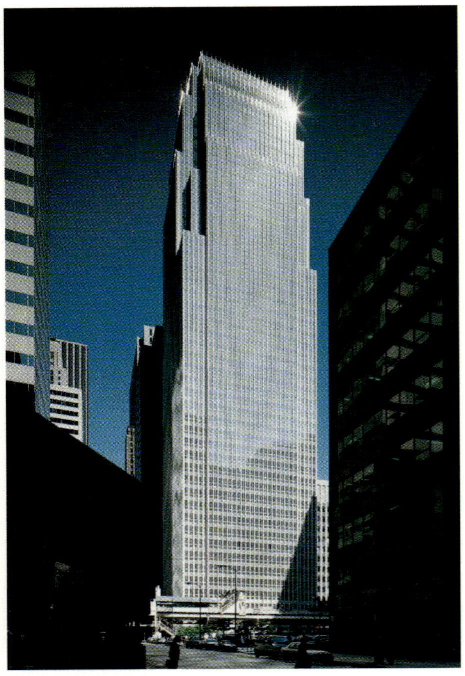

181 West Madison, Chicago.
Architects: Cesar Pelli & Associates, 1990.
© Jon Miller / Hedrich-Blessing.

Opposite:
Scale model of the Miglin-Beitler Tower.
Miglin-Beitler, Inc.
© Kenneth Champlin & Assoc.

Architects: Cesar Pelli & Associates — *Associated architects:* HKS, Inc. — *Structural engineers:* Thornton-Tomasetti P.C. — *Mechanical and electrical consultants:* Environment System Design — *Developer:* Miglin-Beitler, Inc.

125 stories, 609 meters (1,999 feet) high — 360 degree observation platform at the 118th floor — Mixed steel and concrete structure — total floor area 180,000 square meters (1,900,000 square feet) of which 107,000 square meters (1,155,000 square feet) of offices; 12 levels of parking (840 cars), shops and restaurants on 3,500 square meters (38,000 square feet), "Sky-center" conference center 420 square meters (4,500 square feet); cinema, museum, sports club and, at the summit, a communication center — office floor areas: from 605 to 1,700 square meters (6,500 to 18,250 square feet).

wind pressure. A cruciform tube structure enveloped in concrete, which gives the tower its external aspect, also has the dual function of imparting rigidity combined with sway resistance. From a business point of view there was disagreement. On the one hand there were Beitler and those who recognized that a clientele existed to rent non-standard size office floors (as little as four times smaller than the average floor). And this clientele—companies where unqualified staff were diminishing, to be replaced by executives, each demanding an office with a view—was growing. The tower, after all, did not exceed the density permitted on the site and its total floor area was three times less that Sears', ten times less than New York's World Trade Center! On the other hand, there were those who had believed the project to be risky from the outset and whose opinion appeared justified by the economic crisis. The local press reflected worries about the future of the Loop, where the streets were already judged to be somber and inhospitable. Did Chicago need a new skyscraper there?

The project has remained at the scale model stage. It is to be seen today in J. Paul Beitler's office, behind double sliding doors that open like the curtains in a theater. It stands white against a black background, lit by the steadily brightening rays of an artificial moon.

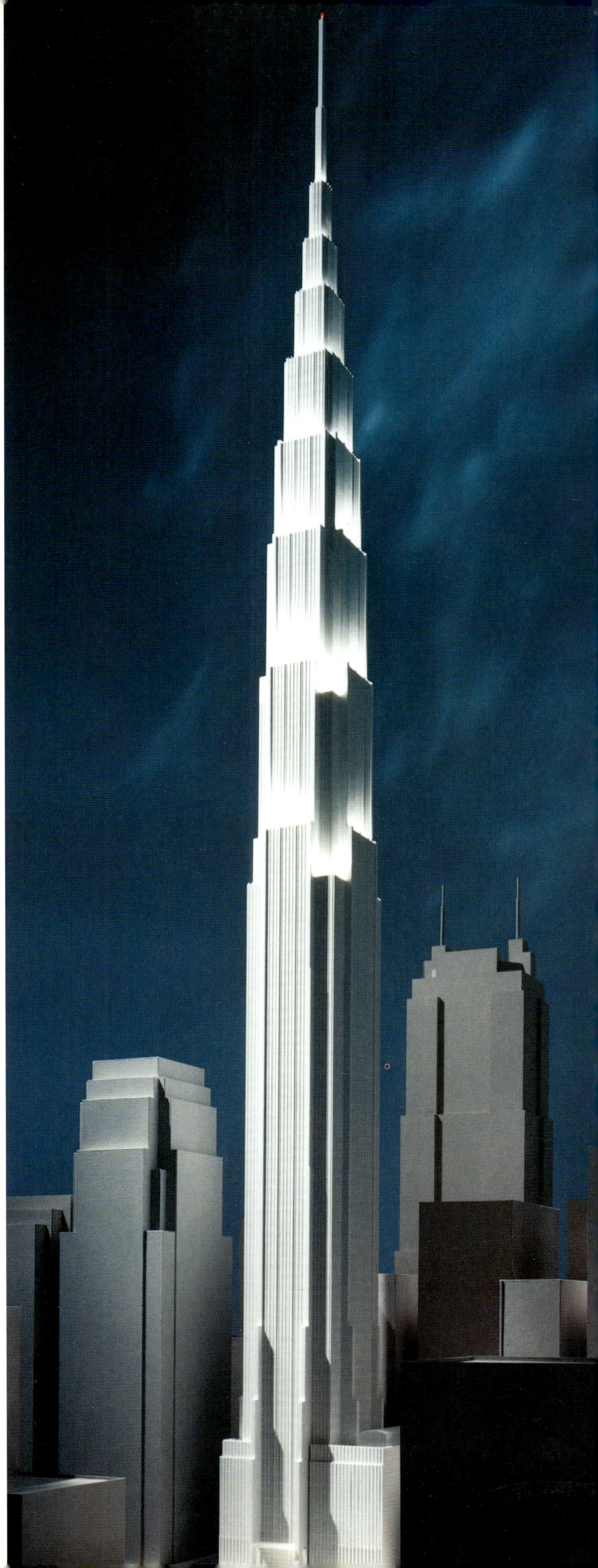

TOUR SANS FINS

Paris La Défense - France

Jean Nouvel et Associés - 1989 / 1994

"With this project there is a real difference, not only decorative.... It could represent a genuine revolution in the history of inhabited towers. It is also the first time that Europe has taken the initiative, that a European architect conceives a new chapter in the history of the skyscraper."

Rem Koolhaas, *l'Architecture d'aujourd'hui*, No. 262, April 1989.

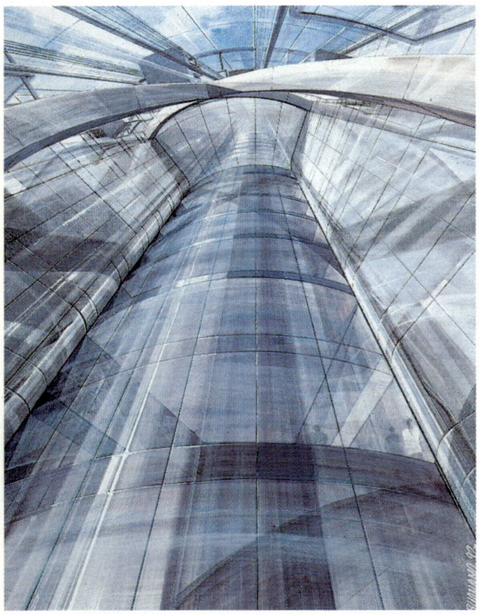

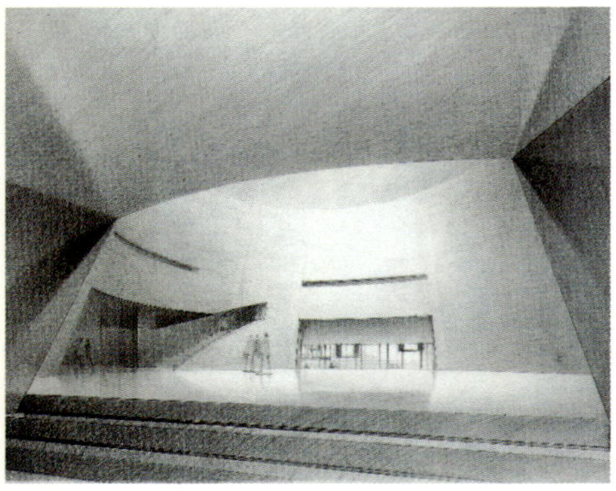

The "urban windows."
Perspective drawing by A. Buonomo, 1992. Architectures Jean Nouvel.

Interior view of the public lobby.
Perspective drawing by Vincent Lafont, 1992. Architectures Jean Nouvel.

Opposite:
La Tour Sans Fins in the Paris landscape, photomontage. In the center, the Great Arch of La Défense.
© Georges Fessy.

In 1989, the Etablissement public d'aménagement de la Défense (a public agency for the development of the Défense district) in conjunction with the Caisse des Dépôts et Consignations, launched a grand competition for the construction of an office tower on the Triangle de la Folie. This is a residual angular site on the perimeter of the Défense district bordered by major traffic intersections; the ring road and railway lines. The competition was won by the architects Jean-Marc Ibos and Jean Nouvel with a project for a very unusual tower.

The tower is open. As opposed to an American skyscraper, the adventure in space does not end as you leave the elevator. Did not Le Corbusier once exclaim, disappointed by his New York experience, "Two hundred meters up you'd think you were in the basement!" (Le Corbusier, *Quand les cathédrales étaient blanches*, Librairie Plon, Paris, 1937.)

There's none of that with the Parisian tower. The design plays on the twin registers of interior and exterior. The tower is reached by a footbridge. From the inside trains can be seen gliding by. To reach an upper level there is an obligatory stop at a transfer floor, an impressive sky-lobby arranged on 2 levels linked by escalators, a completely new principle in Europe. At the summit of the tower, for the enjoyment of the general public, 3 exterior elevators, projecting from the tower, connect with the batteries of express elevators. On the parapet of the belvedere there is no enclosed area within 30 meters (98 feet) and the view stretches over more than 70 kilometers (40 miles).

The tower is circular with a diameter of 43 meters (141 feet). At the center of the floors, deliberately free of any mechanical apparatus, a central thoroughfare or patio connects with atriums glazed with huge windows, "urban windows" in the words of the architect. They are deep openings of at least 12 stories, crossed by express elevators, which directly relate the heart of the tower with the city. This arrangement gives substance to the metaphor of the vertical city with its places for meeting and exchange, its public facilities. It is a city at work, dense and complex, in which thousands of office

Architects: Jean Nouvel et Associés — *Structural engineers:* Ove Arup & Partners (Tony Fitzpatrick) — *Mechanical engineers:* OTH and Trouvin Ingéniérie — *Technical Inspection:* Socotec and CEP — Site Supervision: Coteba Management — *Developer:* Sci Tour Sans Fins.

100 levels, 426 meters (1,397 feet) tall — Panoramic bar on the 88th floor and belvedere on the 92nd floor — Concrete structure and metallic superstructure — Total area: 112,500 square meters (1.2 million square feet).

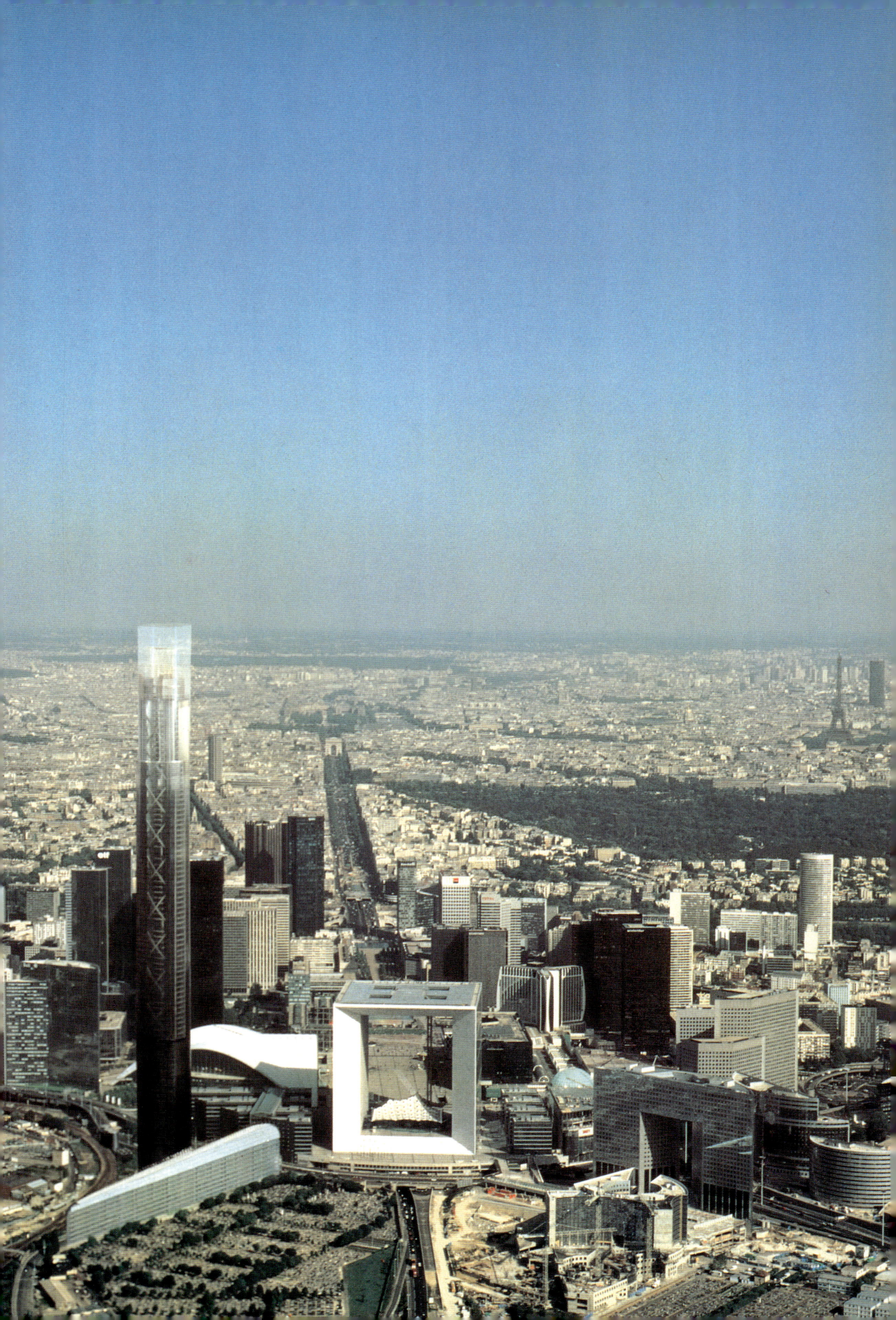

workers, visitors and tourists cross without meeting each other, a city out of science fiction where the coming and going of the elevators can be perceived against a luminous, part transparent, part mirrored background.

It is a tall and slender tower, 426 meters (1,397 feet) tall, a height to width ratio of 10 to 1! This exceptional shape raises the overriding question of the dynamic behavior of the tower in the wind. "Will it vibrate? If the wind is turbulent and blows in gusts, those gusts can buffet the structure and make it vibrate. These oscillations can become perceptible to the public." (Tony Fitzpatrick, Ove Arup & Partners, *L'Architecture d'aujourd'hui*, No. 281, June 1992.) Hence the bringing into play of a damping system conceived on the principal of the pendulum in old clocks. This enormous pendulum will not be hidden. On the contrary, Jean Nouvel wants to use it as a decorative object, to display it and to make it the base of a work of art.

The pierced tube structure of the building is divided into two concrete half cylinders, given rigidity by

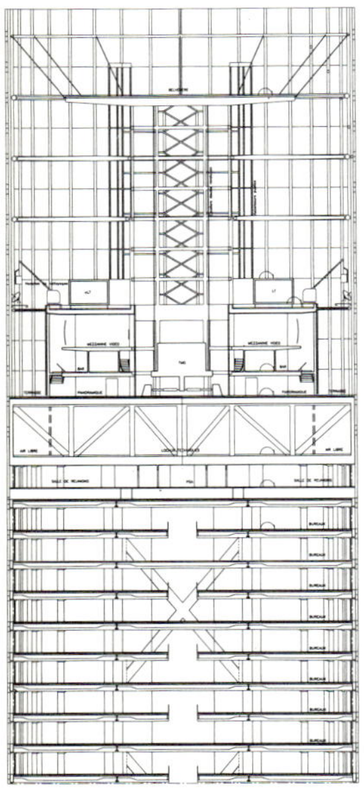

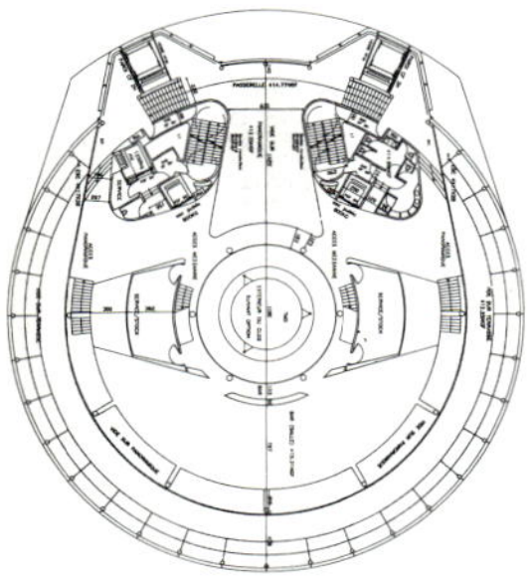

Cross section of the upper floors with the pendulum-like suspended damping mass in the center.
Plan of the damping mass at panoramic bar level.
Architectures Jean Nouvel.

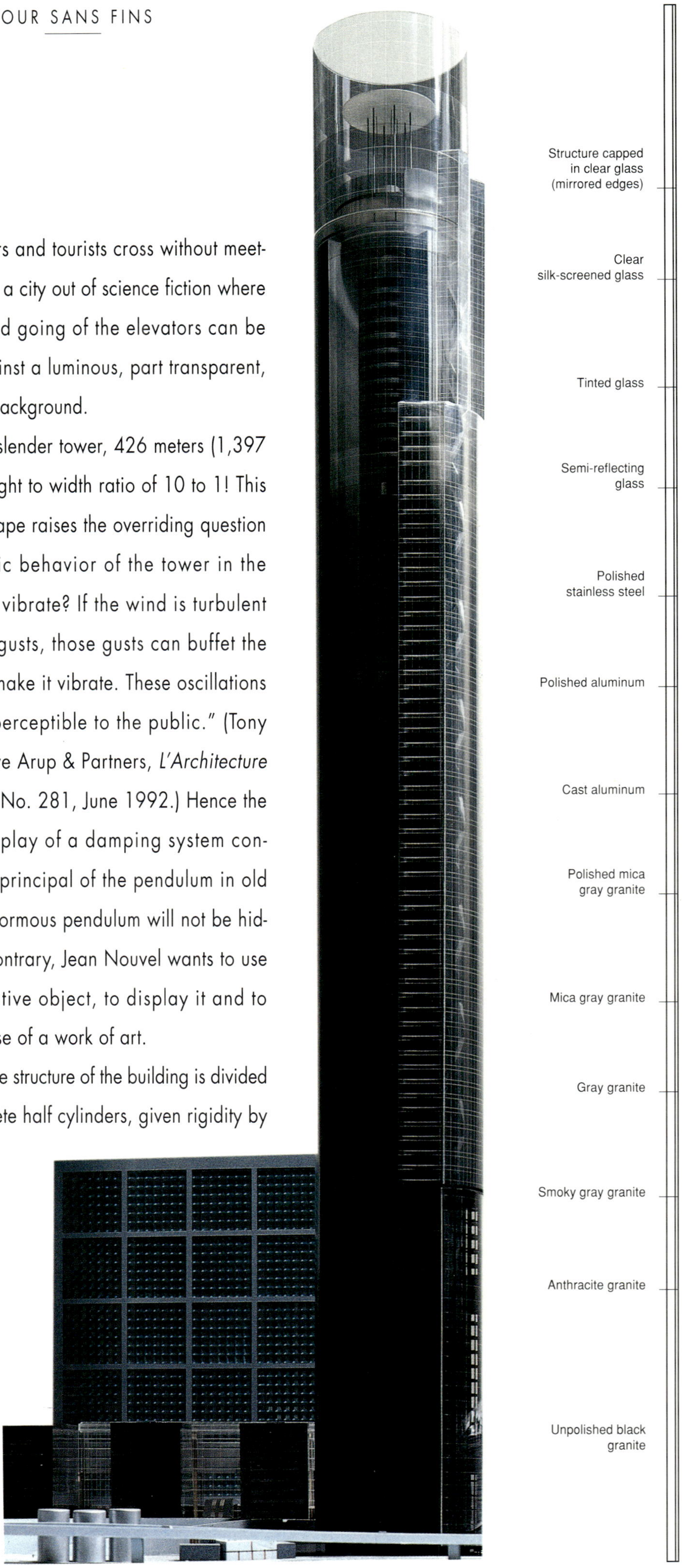

Right:
Photograph of the scale model.
Facing materials.
© Georges Fessy.

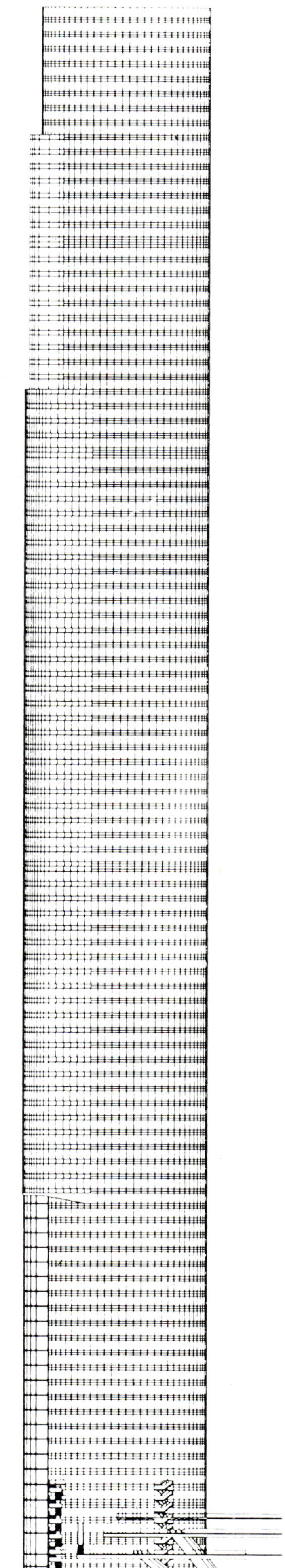

Left:
Southwest elevation.
Architectures Jean Nouvel.

the cross-buttressing of the urban windows. The basements of the bays are contained in the thickness of the beams and the floors, which not only permits the lighting of the floors to be maximized (tubular steel construction usually tends towards opacity), but also makes possible bays glazed from floor to ceiling. One of the architect's favorite themes can be observed here—the dematerialization of the façade, the breaking of bounds.

The tower has no ends. It descends several levels underground like a crater into which escalators plunge, "as though they were cutting a way through the rock." (Jean Nouvel, *L'Architecture d'aujourd'hui*, No. 281, June 1992) From a black granite base, the column grows lighter at it climbs with lighter shades of granite, aluminum, tinted glass, silk screens until, at the top, it becomes transparent, melting into the clouds, disappearing...

The tower seems to pierce earth and sky like the rotational axis of a globe atlas passing through La Défense in Paris. And it is at a tangent with another great symbolic axis joining the Place de la Concorde, the Champs Elysées, the Arc de Triomphe and Otto von Spreckelsen's Great Arch (1989). With the Eiffel Tower, its elder by a century, La Tour Sans Fins also creates a new, technological vista, closed in the background by the Tour Montparnasse.

La Défense lacks an exclamation mark, a landmark, a scale of measurement, "a steeple which designates a neighborhood." (Jean Nouvel, op. cit.)

The project exists. Building it, delayed by the economic crisis, raises a challenge. It would be the ideal event to celebrate the millennium in Paris.

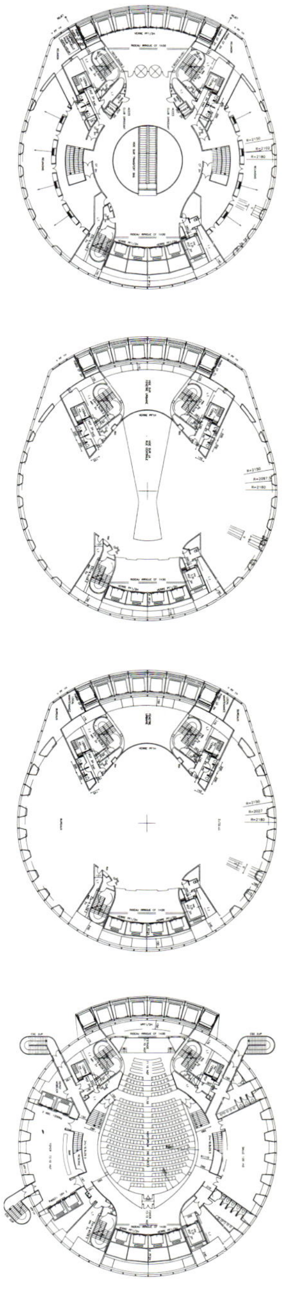

Typical plans: from bottom to top, the conference center (low and high level), a typical office floor, a typical floor with central street/patio, a double-height transfer floor (low and high levels).
Architectures Jean Nouvel.

NEC SUPER TOWER

Tokyo - Japan

Nikken Sekkei - 1990

"One might correctly interpret the atrium as an urban space, or at least as a simulation of urbanity, or perhaps even as an extension or re-creation of the city within the realm of architecture."

Botond Bognar, "An Experiment in Orthodox Architecture with Progressive Aspirations," in *Nikken Sekkei. Building Modern Japan 1900-1990*, Princeton Architectural Press, 1990.

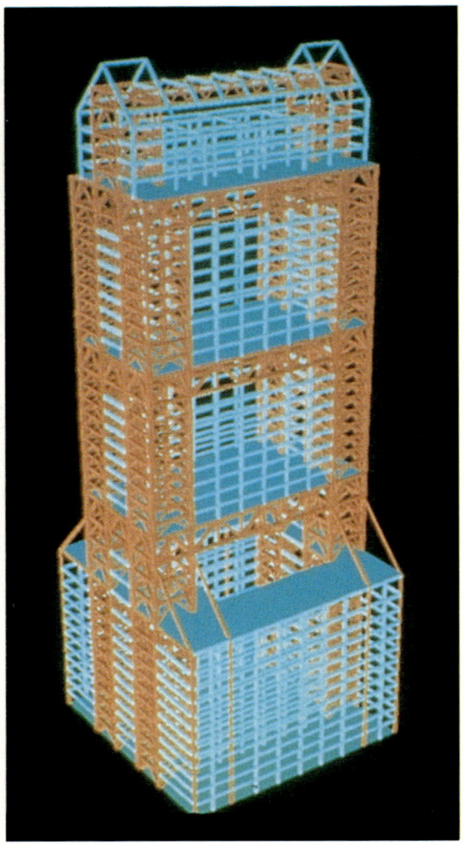

Structural perspective, superframe in red.
Nikken Sekkei.

Opposite:
NEC Super Tower and its urban context.
© The Japan Architect Co.

The headquarters of the NEC company, a telecommunications group, is more than simply a tall building. It is a true skyscraper. It rises more than twenty stories above its neighbors which align at best with the height of its wide base. Its outline in three sections—base, column, and capital—is reminiscent of the first American skyscrapers and narrows as it rises, concluding with a head pointing at the sky. Nevertheless the NEC tower resembles no other skyscraper. Its silhouette looks more like a rocket with a missile clinging to its fins, a Goldorak at the ready, its electronic perfection contrasting with the inextricable chaos of the surrounding neighborhood.

It doubtless seems banal to make a parallel between this technological imagery and the activities of the NEC company. But it is none the less true that this universe of airwaves, satellites and electronic circuitry is exploited by both architect and client to create an environment and an identity that functions both outside, in terms of image, and inside as a unifying concept.

In the case of the NEC tower the technological metaphor can also be applied to the structure, which is very sophisticated. To envisage a building of this size in Japan, bearing in mind the seismological constraints involved, perfectly mastered as they may be, is already an achievement. But the difficulty was doubled in this case by an additional structural constraint: an empty space 40 meters (131 feet) wide and 15 meters (49 feet) high had to be contained between the base and the central shaft of the building. For this reason it is constructed around a steel "superframe"—a kind of megastructure 10 stories high formed of enormous beams and columns which spans the space like a bridge.

The empty space is an air conduit, a means of controlling the turbulence created at the foot of a tower of this size, making possible its insertion into a very densely built

Architects: Nikken Sekkei (Kunihiro Misu, Keiichi Okamoto, Ryo Togashi) — *Structural engineers:* Nikken Sekkei (Hiromi Kihara) — *Mechanical and electrical engineers:* Nikken Sekkei (Katashi Matsunawa, Ryosuke Hashiura) — *Contractors:* Kajima Corporation and Obayashi Corporation — *Developer:* NEC Corporation.

43 stories (+ 1 penthouse), 180 meters (590 feet) high — Superframe type steel structure — office building, total area 145,000 square meters (1,560,780 square feet) including an underground garage of 17,500 square meters (188,370 square feet), an exhibition space of 2,000 square meters (21,000 square feet), a reception room of 2,000 square meters (21,000 square feet), a cafeteria of 4,000 square meters (43,000 square feet) and various facilities designed for management and staff.

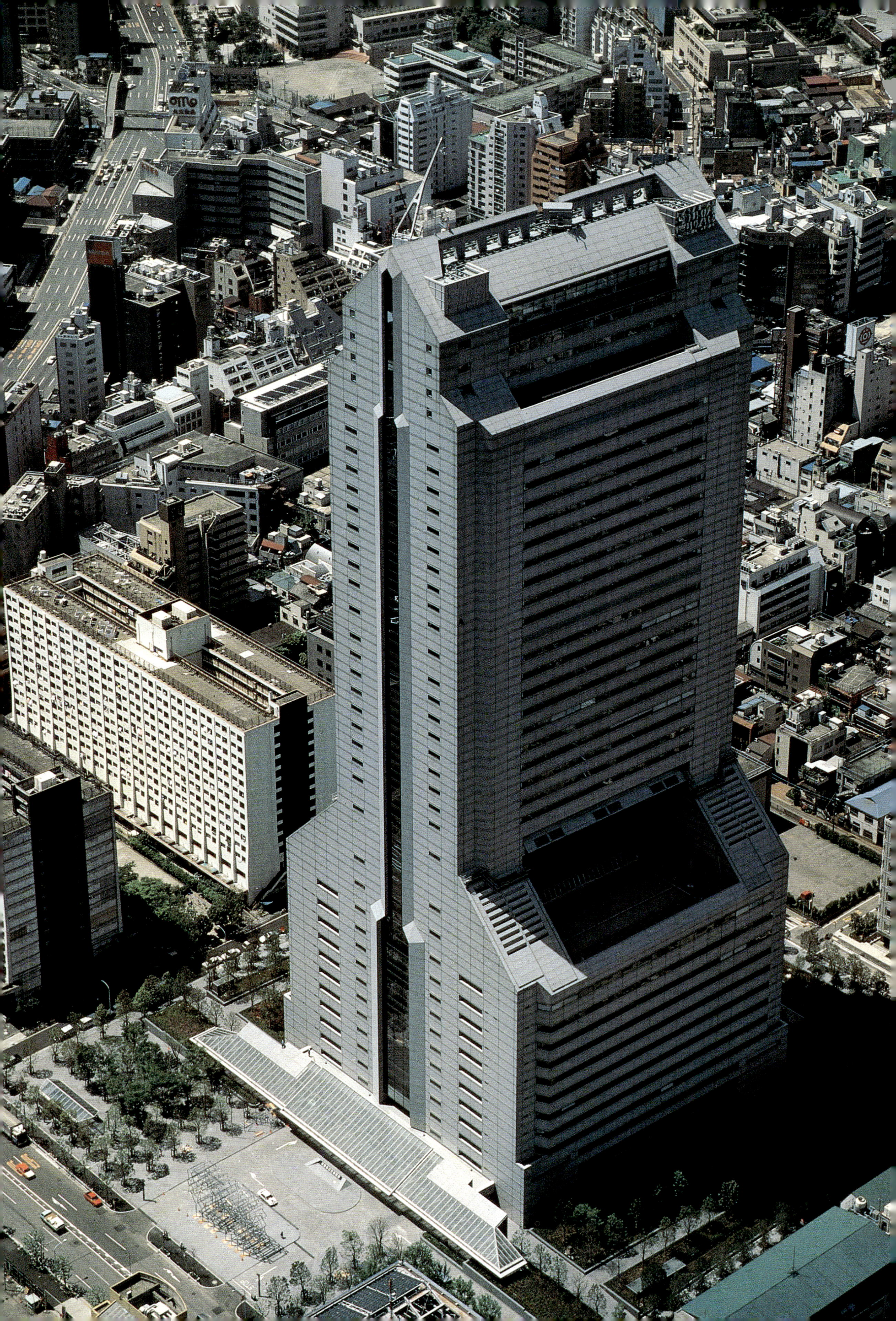

and inhabited neighborhood. But it also fulfills the role of a light well. The atrium around which the 13 lower levels of the tower are arranged are naturally lit through a glass canopy. The atrium has long been one of the Nikken Sekkei practice's favorite themes. Not only is it a convivial area, it also permits natural ventilation instead of air-conditioning, considerably reducing the energy needs of the building. The canopy controls flow of air, completely or partly opening according to weather conditions. It is no spurious gadget, for the Shinjuku NS Building, constructed by the same architects in Tokyo in 1982 on the principle of the large atrium, achieved an energy saving of 40%, compared to a building of similar size entirely dependent on air-conditioning.

The atrium is also the place where the bulk of the details, refinements and *jeux d'esprit* of the architectural handwriting are concentrated. There are marble paving and paneling, overhead walkways, escalators and staircases suspended in space, a witty reference to the flying objects and saucers of the age of capsules.

The creation of an empty space and a huge atrium are but two examples of the numerous devices employed by Nikken Sekkei to achieve their primary objectives of energy conservation and environmental protection. For one of the characteristics of the firm, which is made up of both architects and engineers, is precisely to associate the architectural concept and technological options from the outset. This clearly explains their reputation for performance and their success, particularly with large scale pro-

Center:
Transversal section of the NEC tower and typical plans
Left: plan at open space level.
Right: plans at shaft level and top floors.
Nikken Sekkei.

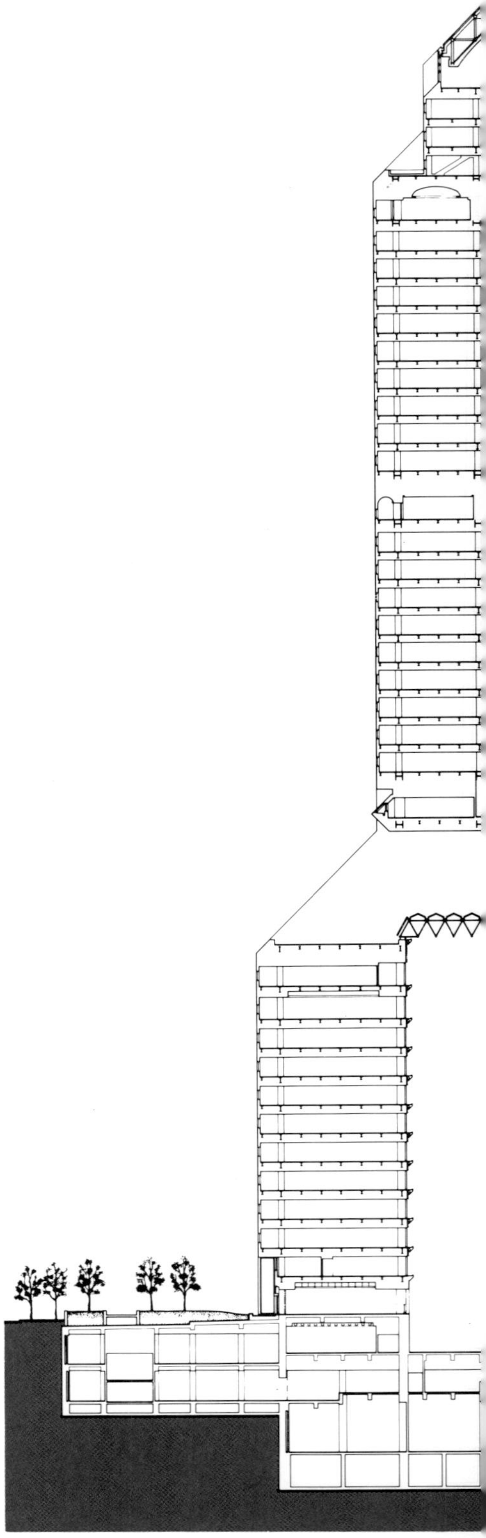

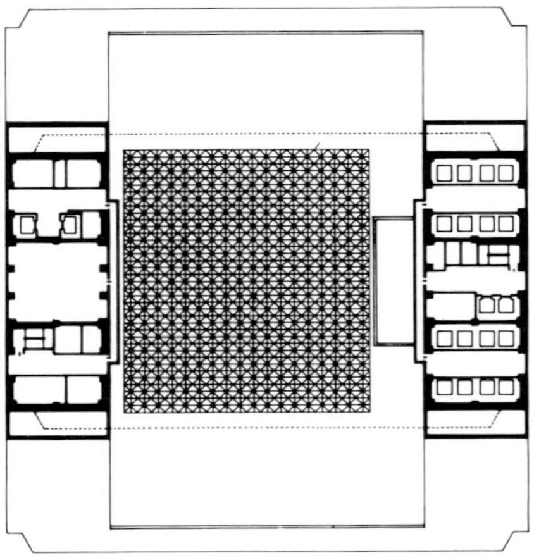

Below:
National Labor Youth Center, Tokyo 1973: the first Nikken Sekkei building with an atrium.
© The Japan Architect Co.

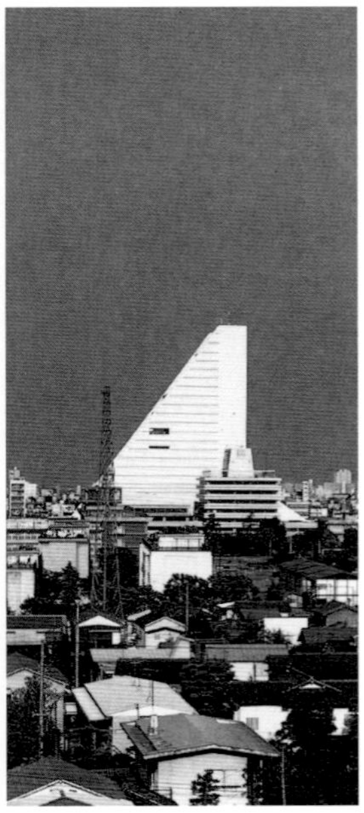

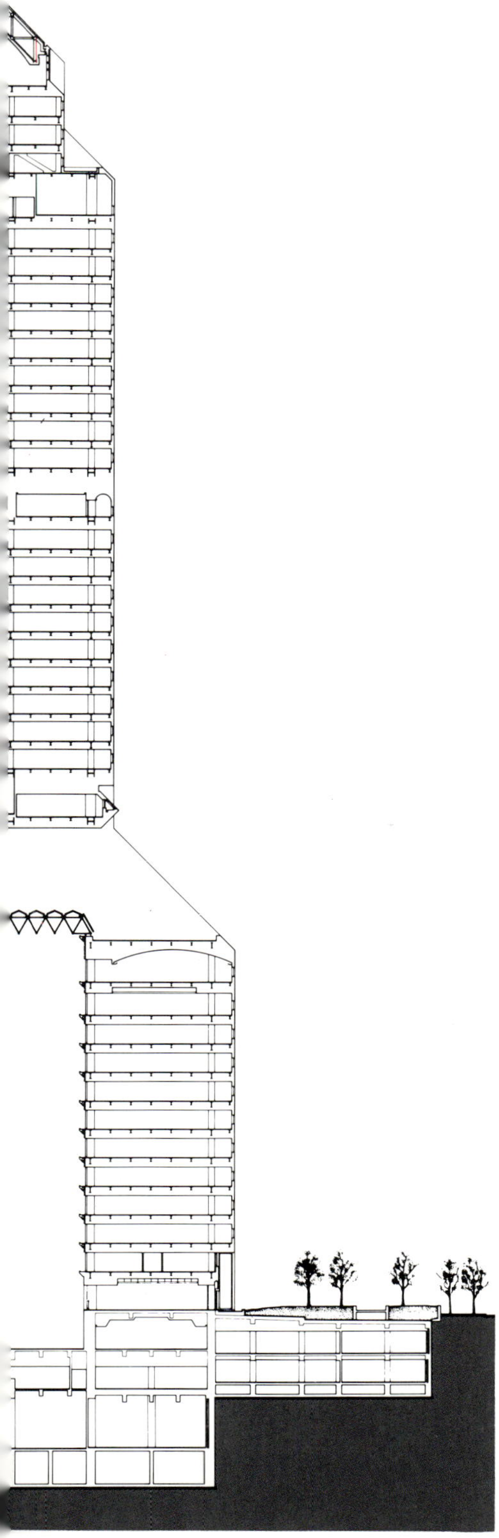

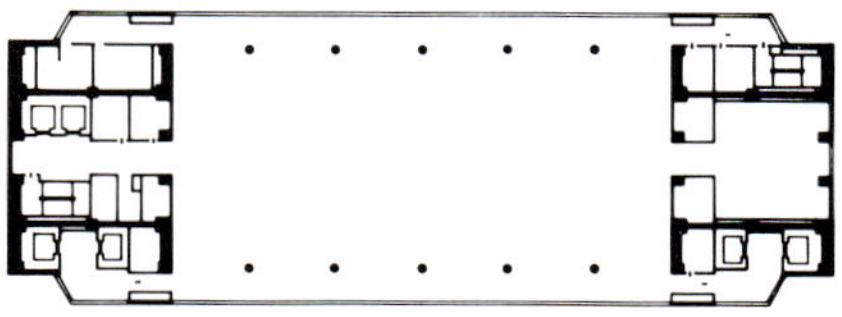

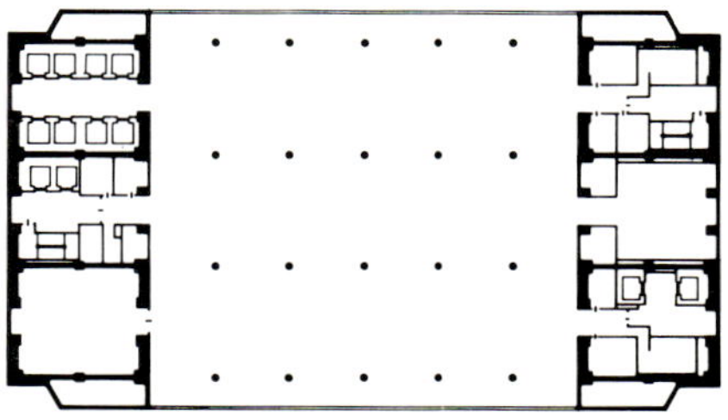

jects. Nikken Sekkei are the designers of about half the tall buildings in Japan.

The parallel with the American practice Skidmore, Owings & Merrill is obvious. Both are very large, specialize in commercial buildings and are present in several cities (Osaka, Tokyo and Singapore in the case of Nikken Sekkei), linking architecture and engineering in highly organized teamwork which relegates individual contributions to the background. Nikken Sekkei, however is run on Japanese lines: staff join the practice after completing their studies and remain there for the length of their career.

Unlike the SOM firm, which bears the name of its founders, Nikken Sekkei is an acronym consisting of the initial characters of the words Japan and architecture with the addition of the word design. And there is a more fundamental difference between the two organizations. It is "...the Japanese penchant for phenomenological weight, for unlike SOM, much of the best work of Nikken Sekkei has been influenced by the paradoxically monumental Japanese feeling for massive construction, having its ultimate origin perhaps not only in the seismic conditions of the country but also in those massive wooden forms to be found in archaic Shinto shrines and in the low dark, superstructural forms of Buddhist temples." (Kenneth Frampton, "Introduction," in *Nikken Sekkei...*, op. cit.)

Shinjuku NS Building, Tokyo: view of the atrium. Arch. Nikken Sekkei, 1982.
© Osamu Murai.

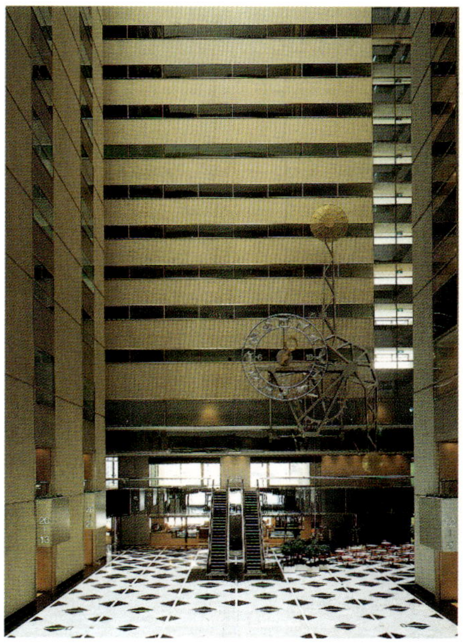

EMBASSY SUITES

TIMES SQUARE

New York - United States

Fox & Fowle Architects - 1991

"The lack of available lots in many an historic downtown is forcing developers and owners to build over landmarks. Such structural gymnastics are practical for expanding and converting outdated but historically significant buildings into new, economically viable facilities."

Marc S. Harriman, "Spanning History," *Architecture*, November 1991.

Building a 460-room hotel on Times Square at Broadway and 47th Street was a real challenge. Not only did the hotel have to be built over the Palace Theater (Kirchhoff and Rose, 1913), a protected historical monument, but it was one of the first to be subjected to planning regulations that provided for the installation of signage 40 meters (130 feet) high at the foot of every building facing Times Square.

Building above a historical monument involves renting and using the air rights above the site. The procedure is common in North American historical centers, especially New York. An additional constraint is sometimes added to the technical problems of this type of superimposition: the continuing functioning of the old building in question. Thus in 1990 the firm of Fox & Fowle built an office building at 1675 Broadway on top of a theater which never closed. In the case of Embassy Suites the project coincided with the restoration and enlargement of the Palace Theater which meant that it was closed. It was also given a new entrance.

The operation grew from a narrow site backing on to the theater. Here the theater and hotel entrances are accommodated as well as, spread over 6 floors, the hotel reception with shops, lounges, restaurant and conference facilities. The tower strictly speaking, reserved for bedrooms, begins on the 8th floor. It surmounts the theater on a bridge of beams and lattice 40 meters (130 feet) wide and three stories high. The load is transferred to the ground by 4 supercolumns arranged 2 by 2 in front of and behind the theater.

This structural and technical base, containing all the public functions of the building, corresponds to the regulation band of illuminated advertising signage. The band is cut by long horizonal striations; the marquee, emphasized with neon, and a series of recesses and skylights which light the windowless areas.

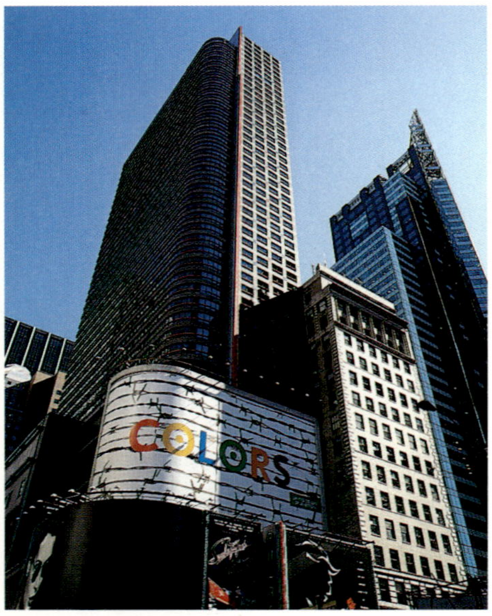

View of the hotel on Times Square. To the right, the Bertelsmann Building (originally One Broadway Place) by SOM, 1991.
© Benoît Roland.

Architects: Fox & Fowle Architects, in association with HSD/Hotel Service Division, for the hotel service concept — *Structural engineers:* DeSimone Chaplin & Dobryn and Associates — *Mechanical and electrical engineers:* Syska & Hennesy — *Exterior signage consultant:* Cosentini Lighting Design — *Theater restoration:* Sol Niego, architect — *Contractor:* HRH Construction Corporation — *Developer:* Silverstein Properties.

44 stories, 143 meters (470 feet) high — Mixed steel and concrete structure — Hotel 460 rooms with public and commercial areas and conference center of about 3,000 square meters (32,000 square feet); theater at ground level; total area 40,000 square meters (430,000 square feet).

Opposite:
Embassy Suites from Times Square.
Fox & Fowle Architects.

At tower level the axis of the composition is inverted. A vertical projection divides the tower into two distinct segments. The higher, vertical and more opaque segment on the right, corresponding to the technical core, is square patterned with window breasts and piers. The left segment is the bedroom wing and is more transparent, with a large, entirely glazed suite on the rounded corner of each floor.
Unfortunately the summit of the tower does not have the importance promised by the initial drawings.
There is no jazz-age superstructure—impossible not to be reminded here of the neighboring McGraw-Hill tower (Raymond Hood, 1931)—, no vanes or neon banner. Nonetheless, the tower does function as a quotation with its mixture of terra-cotta bands, its streamlined corner in the ocean-liner style, the multi-colored materials, not to mention the effect of the electric decoration which does just as much to pay homage to the heroic age of New York Art Deco in its geometric phase.
With this tower, as in the case of a first office tower at 767 Third Avenue (1981) or the Grand Palais building (1992), a 40-story residential skyscraper, Fox & Fowle explore the potential of a tempered regionalism, inclined to modernism, of which the masters were architects like Raymond Hood or William Lescaze.

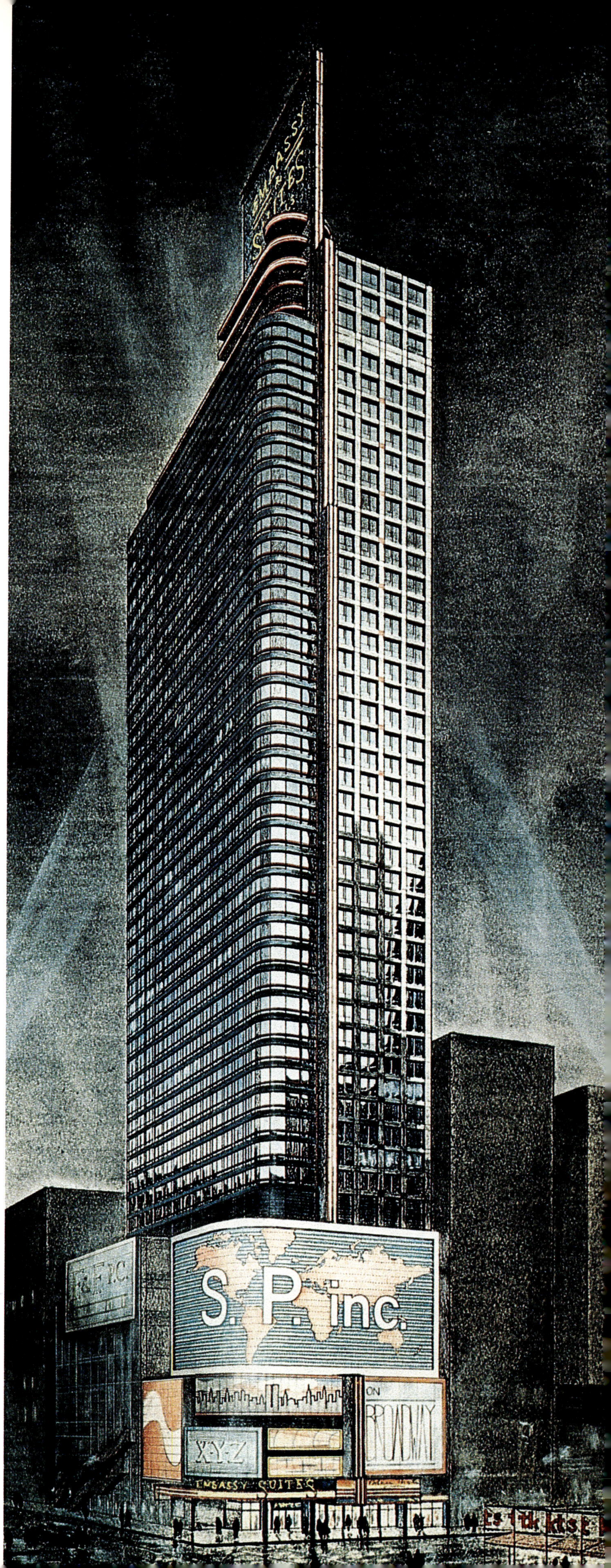

TOKYO-NARA TOWER

Between Tokyo and Nara - Japan

T. R. Hamzah & Yeang - 1992/1994

"While many Western architects, having despaired of previous efforts, now eschew high-rise building altogether, Yeang eagerly embraces the tower type as a necessary and even potentially exciting component of the tropical veranda city, a concept he has pioneered since the mid-eighties."

Chris Abel, "Cool High-Rise," *The Architectural Review*, Sept. 1994.

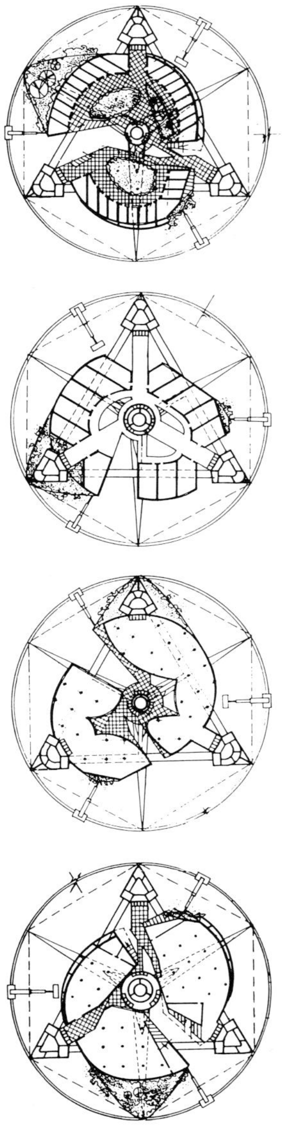

Typical floor plans: bottom to top, offices, community facilities, apartments, and hotel.
T.R. Hamzah & Yeang.

Opposite:
Scale model of the Tokyo-Nara tower.
T.R. Hamzah & Yeang.

When Kisho Kurokawa invited the Malaysian architect Kenneth Yeang to take part in the first Nara Architectural Triennial in 1992, he seized the occasion to do what no developer before him had done. He asked the architect to design a tower incorporating the entire catalogue of bio-climatic attributes that Yeang and his team had developed over some 10 years of building and research on the concept of the tropical skyscraper. The theme of the Triennial—"Symbiosis of History and the Future"—certainly echoed the regional aims of the architect. "Architecture in the age of machinery was devoted to the pursuit of efficiency and universal adaptation. In contrast, architecture in the future will undoubtedly place prime importance on flexibility... and identity with the local environment." (Kisho Kurokawa, "Introductory Message," *Triennial Nara*, 1992, catalogue.)

To these cultural criteria were added the economic justifications of bio-climatic architecture such as energy saving, and those that affect the psychological comfort of the occupiers or ecology: less use of electricity, less waste products, less heat emission; these problems are not restricted to tall buildings, but the urgency of these problems emerges even more obviously in high density urban environments and, most often today, in the hot and humid climates of Southeast Asia.

"Green" architecture, usually restricted to small-scale rural building, here exploits the possibilities offered by technology to create buildings not only economically but also ecologically viable. Putting such an apparently paradoxical project into practice called for the development of a set of tools and principles successively tested by Kenneth Yeang on a series of sample buildings with varying degrees of success. The

Architects: T.R. Hamzah & Yeang (Ken Yeang, with Vincent Le Feuvre, Syahril Nizam Kamaruddin and Roshan Gurung) — *Structural, mechanical and electrical engineers:* Battle McCarthy Consulting Engineers — *Consultant engineers (1994 version):* Vipac — *Developer:* Nara Municipal Office.

210 stories, 880 meters (2,887 feet) high — Mixed structure consisting of a primary structure of main columns (cellular type) and a secondary structure formed with beams in a star configuration with external tie-rods — The tower is divided into 8 groups of 24 stories one on top of the other, independent in terms of resistance as well as energy, water and waste disposal

Mixed-use building with offices, housing, a hotel and community facilities; total floor area: 1.1 million square meters (11.8 million square feet).

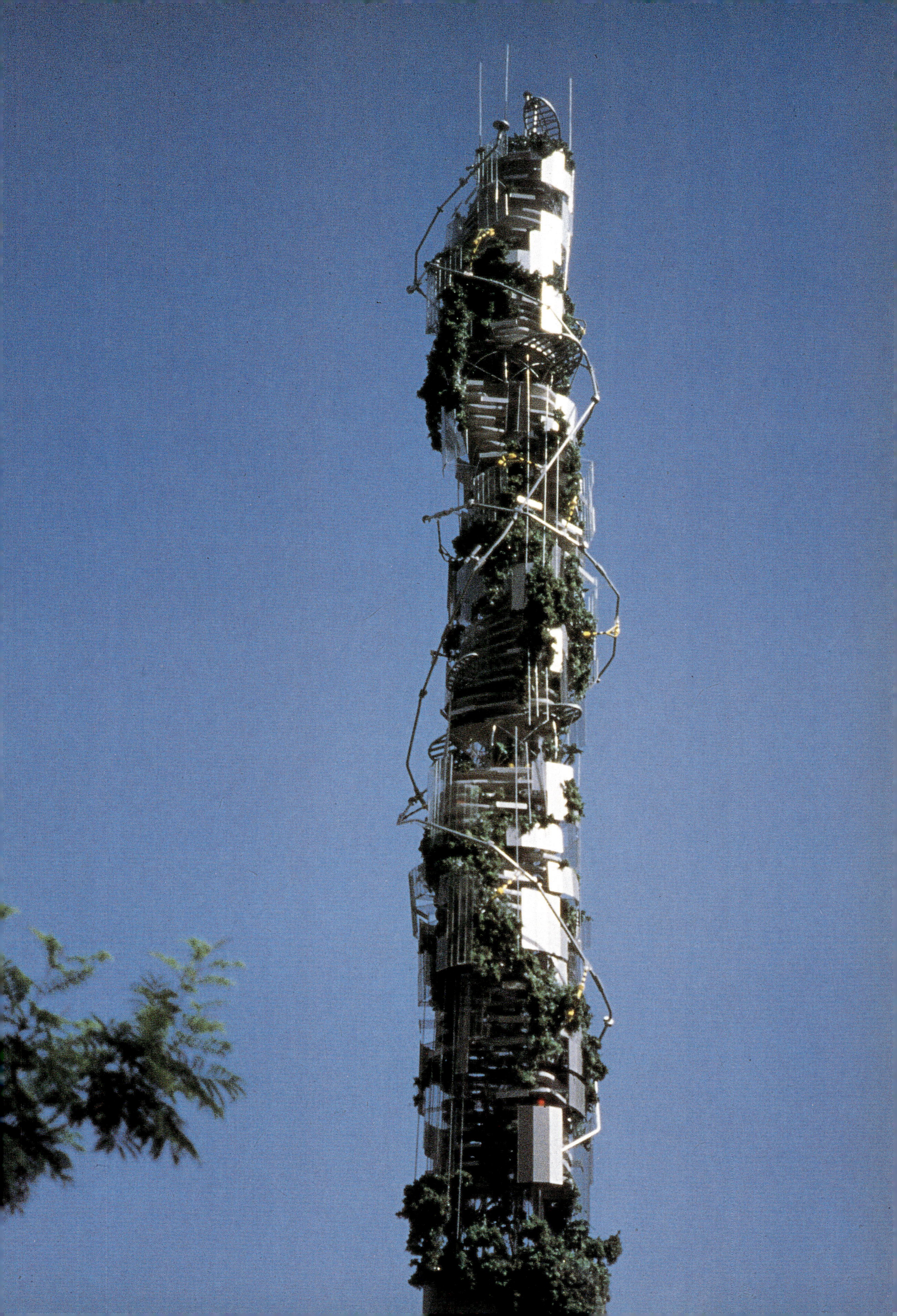

integration of vegetation—"vertical landscaping" in the words of the architect—characterizes the IBM Plaza building (1985) and the Menara Boustead (1986), both built in Kuala Lumpur. The creation of transition spaces, the equivalent of verandas in vernacular tropical architecture, terraces, roof gardens, atriums and skycourts, appears in the Plaza Atrium (1986).

With the Central Plaza tower (1995), also in Kuala Lumpur, the treatment of the façades is determined by their exposure to the sun. The main wall facing west, for example, is shaded by being set back from an impressive outer structure. In some cases exterior wall coverings are adaptable to changes in the season or the weather according to the wishes of the occupants. In the Menara Mesiniaga Tower at Selangor (1992) the hot elevations (east and west) are made up of movable louvers and lattice blinds, combined in this case with other bio-climatic devices. Apart from the difference in scale—the Menara Mesiniaga has only 15 floors—this small Malaysian tower can be considered the first life-size prototype of the ideal project designed by Yeang for Japan, combining the principles of "vertical landscaping," skycourts, the atrium, different materials used for the elevations, rotation of the floor plans so that one above shades one below, plus the principle of using the technical core as a heat barrier.

Two years later the MBf tower in Penang became a more developed, larger scale prototype; 31 stories high, it includes shops, a banking hall and offices as well as 68 luxury apartments arranged around an open air concourse.

Other projects, taller and more complex, are at the design stage: the Ho Chi Minh City tower in

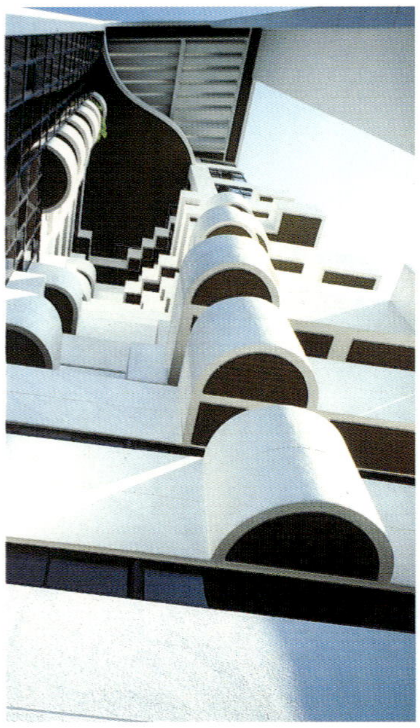
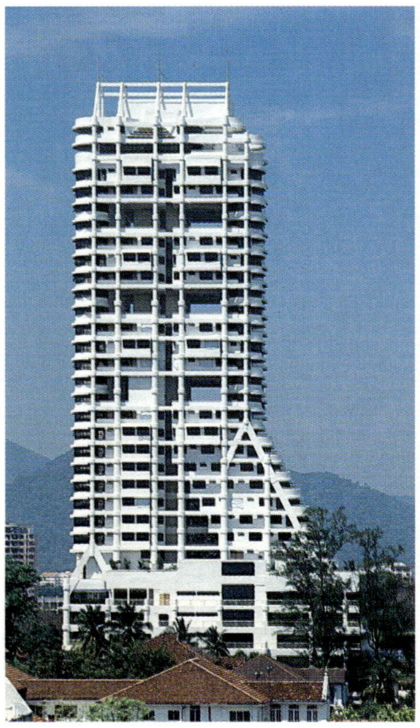
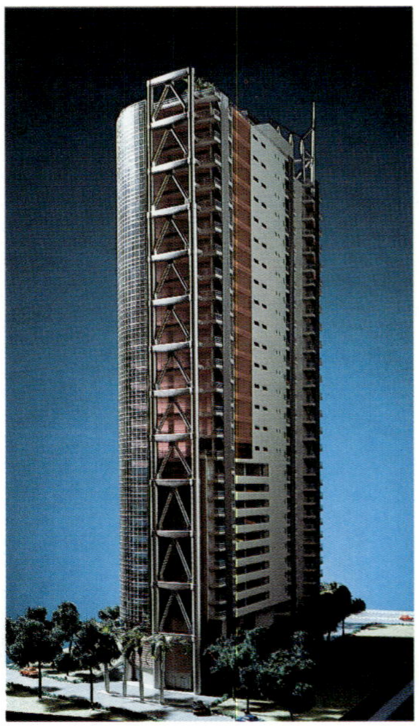

From left to right:

Plaza Atrium,
Kuala Lumpur 1986.
T.R. Hamzah & Yeang.

MBf Tower,
Penang 1994.
T.R. Hamzah & Yeang.

Central Plaza, Kuala Lumpur
1995 (scale model).
T.R. Hamzah & Yeang.

Vietnam, the China Towers complex at Haikou in China consisting of three 35 and 36-story residential towers, and the 37-story Budaya Tower in Kuala Lumpur, currently in construction.

The Tokyo-Nara Tower is on a larger scale. Originally planned to be 84 stories tall, the project is now 880 meters (2,887 feet) tall, almost 10 times its width, with 210 floors of offices, housing and hotel rooms, community facilities and "skycourt oases" articulated by a system of open air atria where elevators, escalators and walkways meet. On the outside, on a spiral rail, "robot arms" facilitate maintenance to the vegetation and cleaning of the façades, giving the image and technology of science fiction to a laboratory project that draws its inspiration from the abundance of tropical vegetation, the hybrid aesthetic of "architecture without architects" and the universe of a Buckminster Fuller or Archigram type technological utopia. It is a project, forecasts Ken Yeang, which opens a new perspective on skyscraper architecture. "The design of energy efficient enclosures has the potential to transform architectural design from being an uncertain, seemingly whimsical craft, into a confident science." (Ken Yeang, "Theory and Practice," *Bio-climatic Skyscrapers*, Artemis, London, 1994.)

But make no mistake. Ecology with Yeang excludes neither fantasy nor artistic ambition. "Bio-climatic factors should not be the only design determinants. There are others such as views, site constraints, etc. Therefore, these aspects and principles should remain as guides for interpretation rather than as dogma for form." (Ken Yeang, op. cit.)

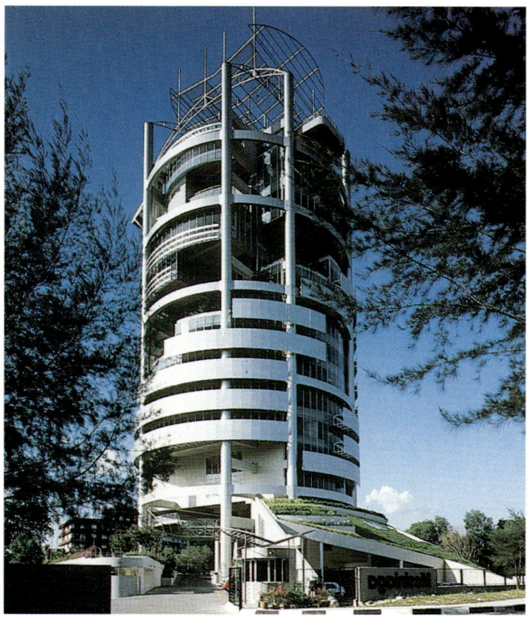

Menara Mesiniaga, Kuala Lumpur 1992.
T.R. Hamzah & Yeang.

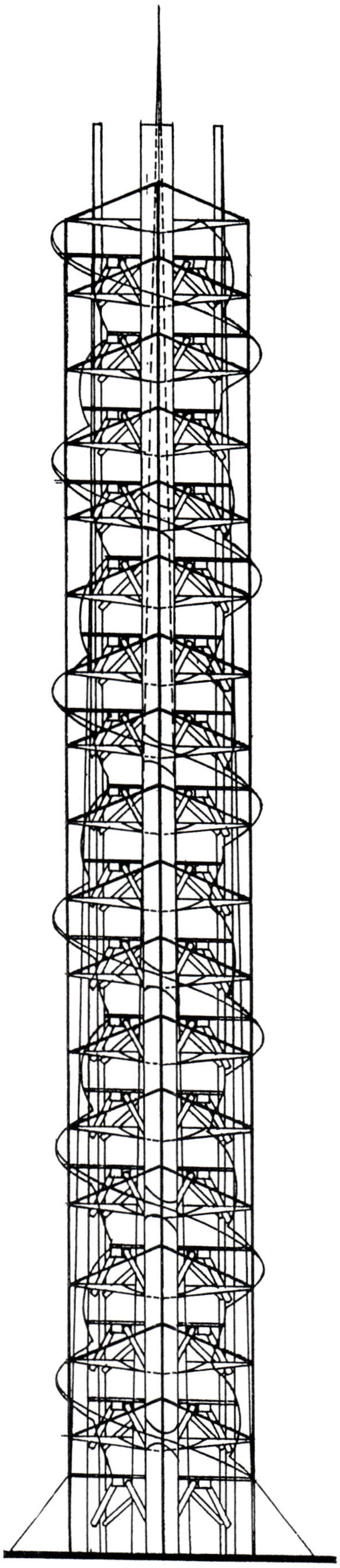

Elevation of the structure.
T.R. Hamzah & Yeang.

DG BANK

Frankfurt - Germany

Kohn Pedersen Fox Associates - 1993

"The DG BANK is no longer a modernist solitaire set within an indifferent spatial context, but is both architecturally and functionally an integral space-defining part of the urban ensemble."

Michael Mönninger, "The Dissolution of the Skyscraper," *DG Bank - Frankfurt am Main*, Oktagon, 1993.

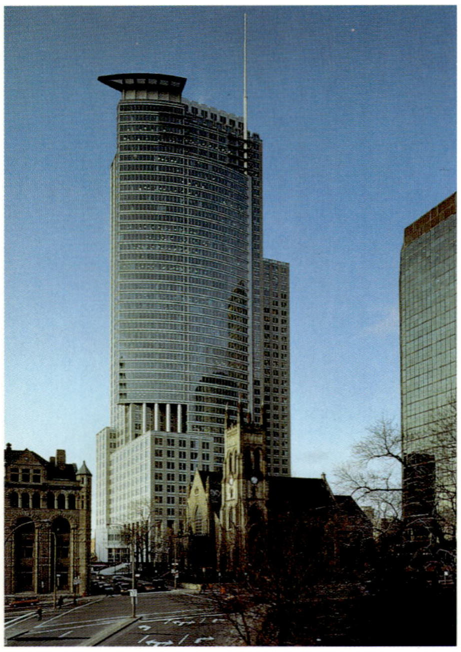

Marathon/IBM Building in Montreal: detail.
Kohn Pedersen Fox Associates, architects, 1992.
© Wayne Fujii, 1992.

Opposite:
The DG Bank seen from the south (detail).
© Norbert Guthier, bff.

Tower blocks do not get a good press in Europe. Generally associated with property speculation, the destruction of heritage, the disintegration of public space and urban tissue, they have usually been pushed towards the nondescript outskirts of cities. Hamburg, Munich, Berlin and other German cities are proud today of having defeated this vertical scourge, leaving to Frankfurt the thankless role of experimental city.

Frankfurt cannot invariably congratulate itself on the success of this special position. But it has gradually realized that a single skyscraper doesn't work on its own, that it has to be grouped with others in an extremely dense and well-articulated Manhattan-type neighborhood in the center of the city—thence the banking district between the railway station and the old town. Furthermore, this group of skyscrapers must be Americanized whether they are symbolic, carry an image, contribute to dramatizing the city skyline, enliven the streets and the life of the pedestrian or add to the character of the quarter. These are the criteria that the new bank has attempted to meet. To put every chance on its side, it obtained the services of the architects Kohn, Pedersen and Fox, one of the New York practices most noticeably involved in the revival of the great American skyscraper tradition.

The headquarters of the DG Bank is the Statue of Liberty. High in the sky floats a wide crown of tapering thorns saluting the old town, the cathedral and the river—an enormous projecting cornice which terminates the powerful ascent of a tower white as a church candle. At night you could mistake it for a ghost with a halo.

At street level, on a suddenly much more modest scale, steps and marquees, entrances and shop windows, cafes, terraces and a winter garden (one of the firm's favorite themes), rub shoulders with the almost chaotic absence of formality of everyday life. Helmut Jahn's Messeturm (1990) had already attempted—and succeeded—in creating

---

Architects: Kohn Pedersen Fox Associates (William Pedersen, Paul King), in association with NHT Nägele Hofmann Tiedemann und Partner — *Structural engineers:* Ingenieursozietät BGS — *Mechanical and electrical engineers:* P & A Pettersson Ahrens and R. R., Reuter-Rührgartner — *Building contractors:* Hochtief AG — *Developer:* DG Immobilien Management GmbH.

50 stories, 208 meters (682 feet) high — Concrete structure ("tube-in-tube" type) — office building of 77,000 square meters (829,000 square feet) including a public banking hall, a transversal winter garden of 900 square meters (9,688 square feet); 27 meters (89 feet) under glass surrounded by shops and 15 housing units of 1,200 square meters (12,917 square feet).

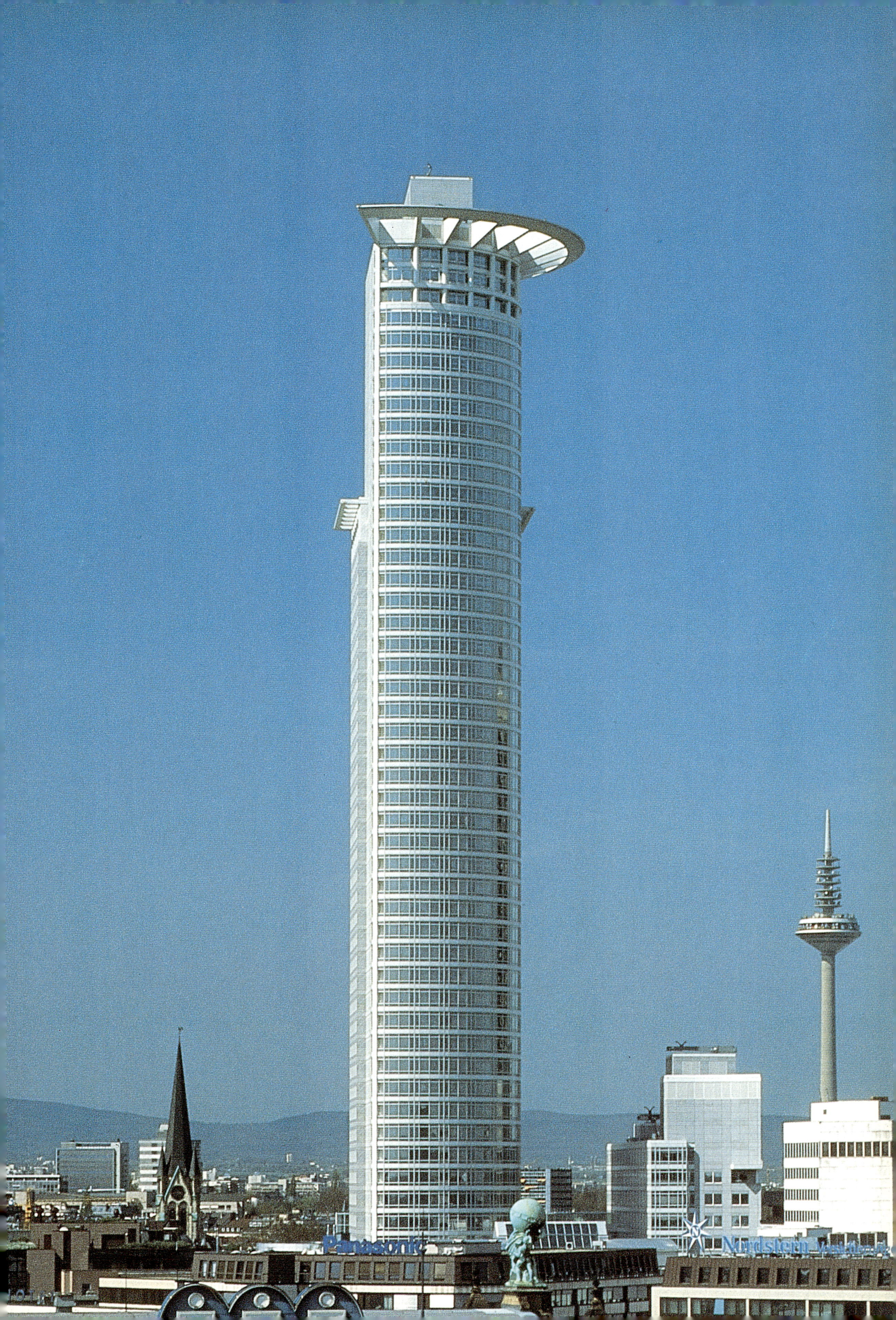
Panasonic
Nordstern

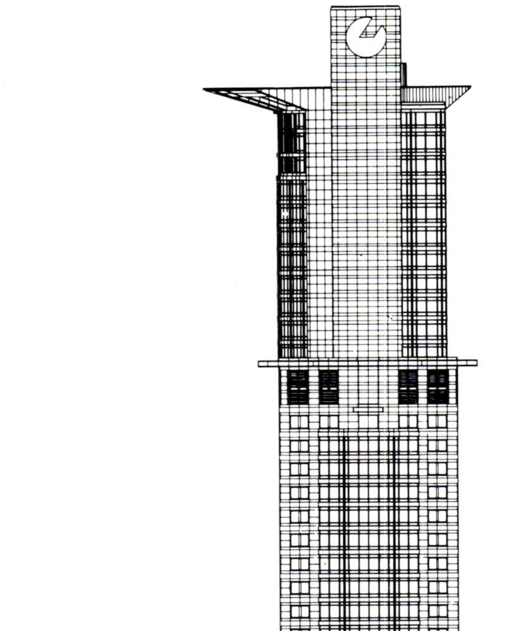

this double interpretation, at both summit and base of the tower, of the archetypal American skyscraper. But in this case, for the first time, the American influence has been carried through in the vertical dimension. The headquarters of the bank are divided between 4 buildings, 2 lower buildings of 28 and 22 meters (92 and 72 feet) which align with the existing cornices on the surrounding streets, and a tower with two different frontages according to the kind of neighborhood each faces. On the residential side it is a square, stone-faced tower of only 150 meters (492 feet), the height of the neighboring towers, among them the previous home of the DG Bank. On the business side a rounded curtain wall rises to a height of over 200 meters (650 feet).

This deliberate disunity—duality, in the words of William Pedersen ("The DG Bank Building in Frankfurt am Main", *DG BANK - Frankfurt am Main*, Oktagon, 1993)—is expressed in a play of dislocations, contrasts and alternations of which the scale remains difficult to decipher. The reconciliation of the neighboring but highly contrasting configurations tends to disjoint the building at the base without effectively integrating it into the urban context, a disjointed context in its own right on the edge of the old and the modern town beside a too wide and too busy avenue. All the urbanization strategies developed by KPF—the plaza, the shops, the inclusion of some fifteen housing units, the covered arcade—are ineffective, convincingly demonstrating the limits of a contextual approach applied to a characterless environment.

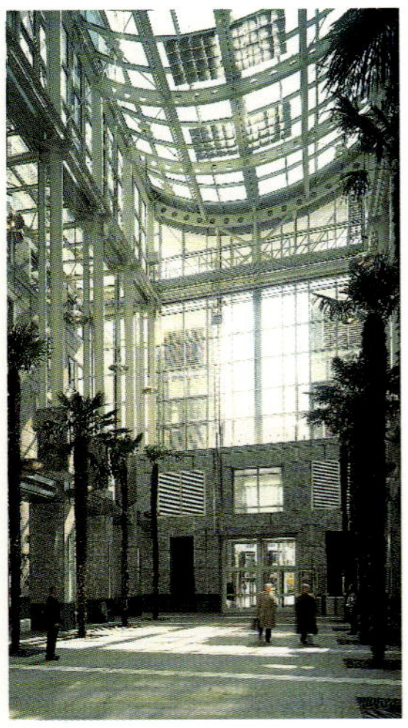

The winter garden.
© Dennis Gilbert, 1993.

Center, top:
Left, north elevation of the bank.
Right, lateral elevation, east.
Kohn Pedersen Fox Associates.

Below:
Plan of the ground level.
Kohn Pedersen Fox Associates.

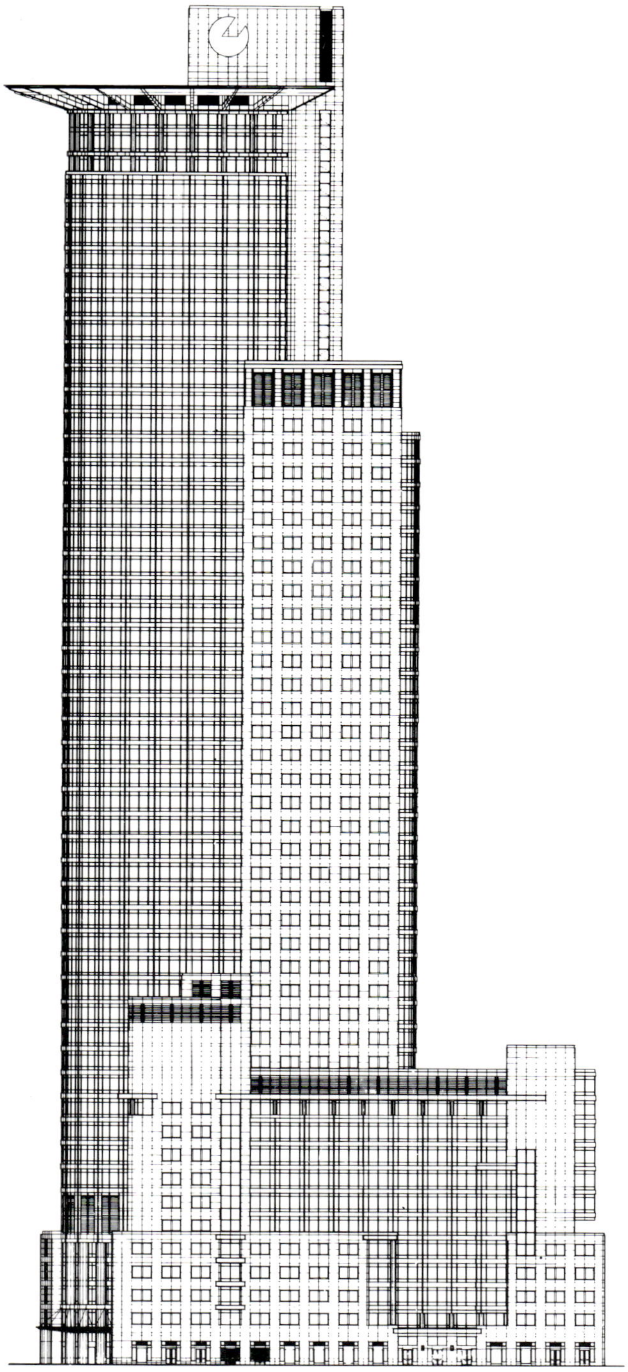

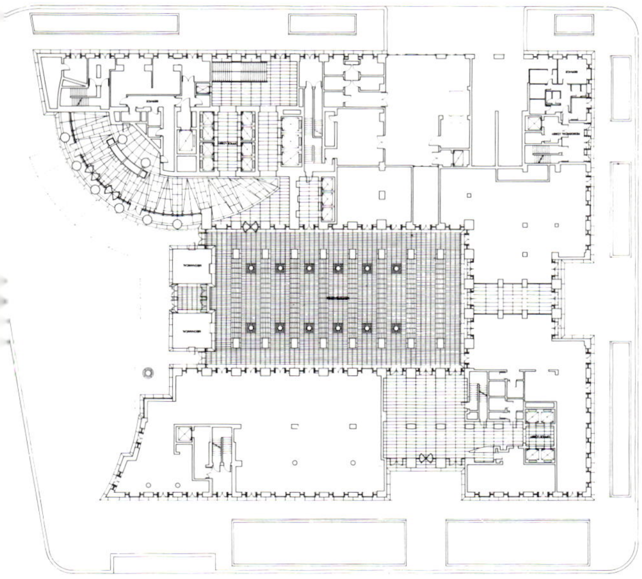

The choice of color, on the other hand, ranging from pale gray to white is one of contrast rejecting both the somber brown of the neighboring tinted glass boxes and the dark red-brick, granite or painted stucco that dominates the landscape of the old town. This standing out as a point of principle is part of the handwriting dear to this New York firm, where classic convention is adapted to a typically modernist vocabulary: glass curtain walling, brushed aluminum facing, canopies like the peaks of caps, broken angles, flat roofs and over-enlarged cornices—no doubt a homage to Louis Sullivan. The new aesthetic orientation of the KPF firm can be recognized here. At the end of a decade rich in "Neo-Classical" skyscrapers in which stone and marble, rules of composition, architectural motives (string courses, colonnades, oriel windows), and decorative elements were piled on, pastiched, sometimes inflated to the point of parody, KPF renounced a grandiloquence which had proved not to function at such a scale. "...We found that the strategies of classical composition had limitations of scale when enlarged. We were not capable of overcoming these limitations when confronted with the realities of construction methods employed in today's tall buildings." (William Pedersen, "The DG Bank Building", *DG BANK-Frankfurt am Main*, Oktagon, 1993.)

It is nonetheless true that this German tower, like the contemporary IBM Tower in Montreal, remains very faithful to the KPF trademark: breaking up of the masses, refinement of detail, technical mastery—the qualities that have propelled the practice into the first rank of commercial architecture.

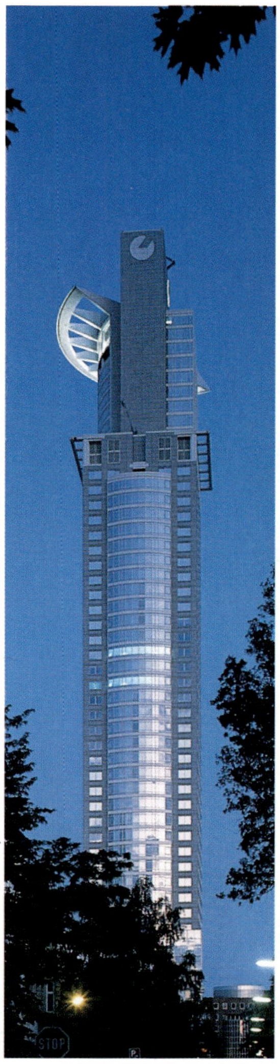

The tower at night.
© Dennis Gilbert, 1993.

UMEDA SKY BUILDING

Osaka - Japan

Hiroshi Hara and Atelier Ø - 1993

"Today's cities are made up of series of isolated buildings among which the skyscrapers form vertical culs-de-sac.... The 'interconnected superskyscraper' is a way of joining together all these individual niches to enrich the public character of the city and create a three dimensional urban tissue."

Hiroshi Hara, "Interconnected Superskyscraper," *GA Document* No. 37, Tokyo, 1993.

With the Umeda Sky Building there's a temptation to see an interpretation in the Japanese manner of the theme of the Great Arch, created at La Défense, Paris, a few years earlier. It is a very tall building in the form of a bridge which acts as a kind of entry to and symbol of a new quarter of the city—the Umeda district north of the railway station—which may well soon become the city center.

The parallel is, however, very superficial. Not only are the two buildings already dissimilar in shape, but their situations in the city and their objectives are completely different. Hara's building is first of all the prototype—reduced in this case to two vertical elements—of a city in the sky in which all the skyscrapers, all the tall buildings, will be inextricably linked by walkways, elevators, escalators, terraces and roof gardens into a three dimensional network of public areas and aerial communication. The architect proposes a veritable space odyssey as a solution to the inevitable necessity for the densification of already built-up areas. A first outline proposal dating from 1988 gives a better picture of this utopia. Their summits in the clouds, 4 towers support an aerial platform—a hanging garden in the words of the architect—with a crater hollowed out in its center down which descends a kind of gigantic ladder. From 4, the towers were reduced to 3 and then 2, the third vertical element finally standing alone as a separate project (a hotel) on a different scale by a different architect (Aoki Corporation). The prototype functions nevertheless. The whole gamut of elements making up the "Mid-air City," the allegory of space travel from the rocket launching tower to the petrified shapes of clouds, are concentrated in the building and endlessly repeated in the mirror images of the glazed curtain walls. With their reflections of different materials—concrete, glass, aluminum—the tower walls also create an illusion in the foreground of a dense imaginary city

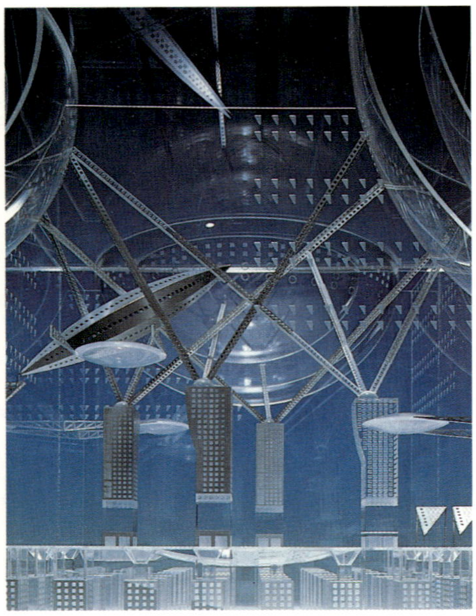

"Toward the Mid-air City," Hiroshi Hara, 1993 (scale model).
© Nobuaki Nakagawa, photographer. Shokokusha Publishing Co, Inc.

Opposite:
Umeda Sky Building at night.
© Nobuaki Nakagawa, photographer. Shokokusha Publishing Co, Inc.

Architects: Hiroshi Hara and Atelier Ø (Hiroshi Yatsuo), in association with Takenaka Corporation — *Structural engineer:* Toshihiko Kimura — *Landscape designer:* Motoo Yoshimura — *Contractor:* Takenaka Corporation — *Developers:* Sekisui House Ltd, in association with Toshiba Co. and Daihashi Co.

40 stories, 173 meters (568 feet) high — Exterior panoramic platform at the top level — Steel structure — office Building including a two-level public belvedere, a restaurant at the center of the two towers, and at the level of the circular sunken garden, a commercial gallery and various public facilities, parking and access to the subway system.

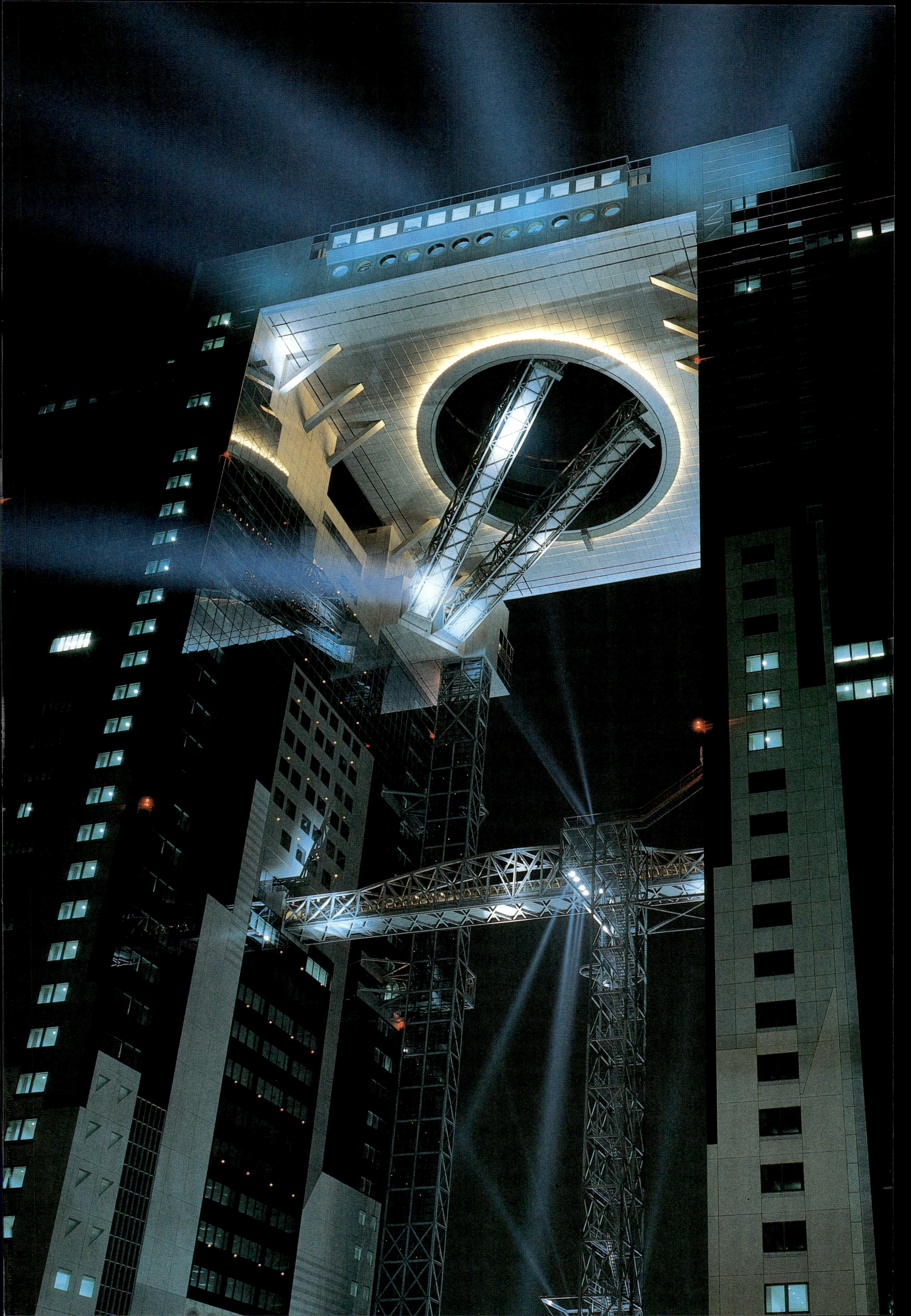

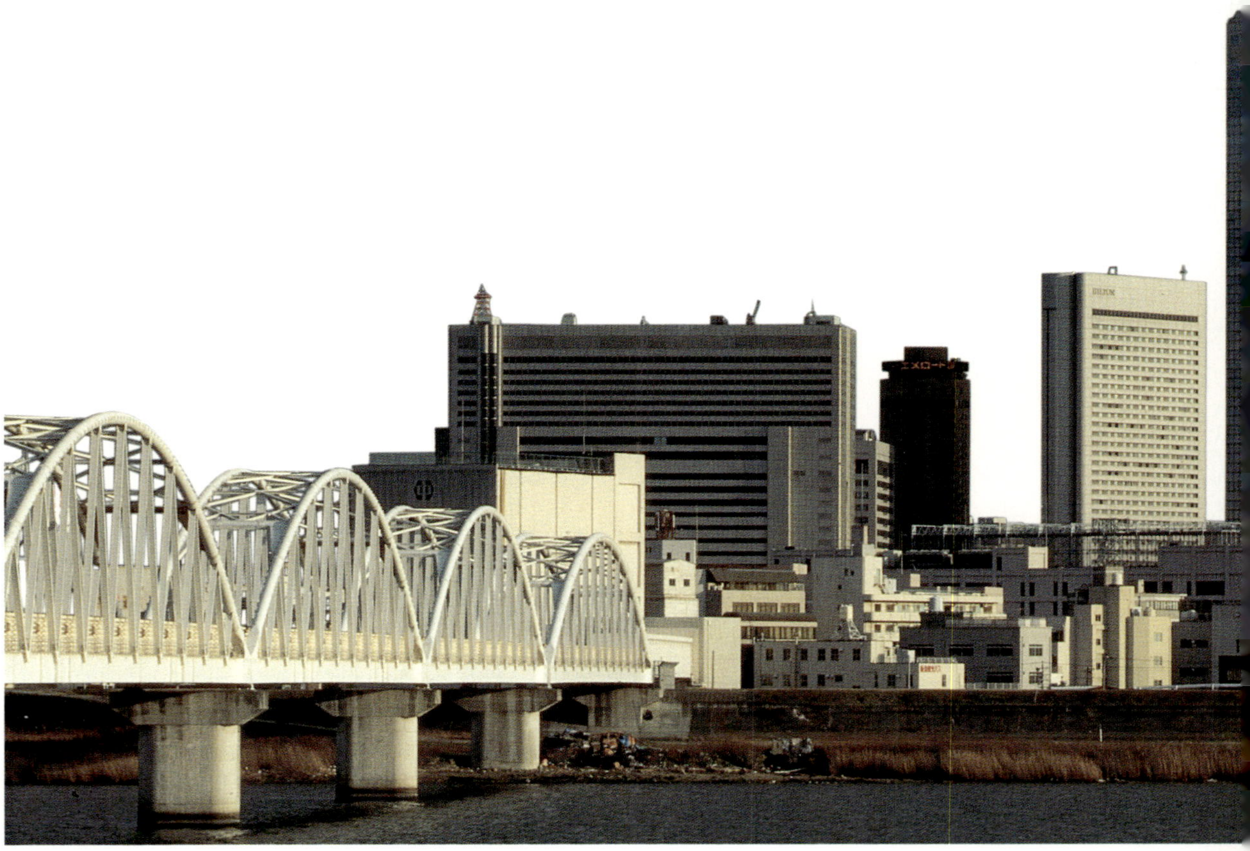

The Umeda Sky Building and the railway station area, seen from the far side of the Shin Yodo River.
© Tomio Ghashi.

blending with the reflections of the real city around them.

This deliberately naive and narrative presentation culminates at the summit of the building where the circular observation walkway grants spectacular views of the city and the river, not to mention the plunging vistas through the central void and an aerial ballet of silhouettes created by the reflection of the comings and goings of visitors mirrored in the sloping glazing that lines the inside of the crater.

And the narrative does not end there. At every turn the building creates its own mythology. There is not a light fitting, an elevator, a part of the visitor's route that does not remind him that the building is a vessel and that his experience is taking place in space. The photomontage that shows the summit of the sky-building emerging from clouds does not only appear on the cover of the owners' promotional brochure. It is to be seen everywhere: on magnets, internal credit cards, notebooks, T-shirts and postcards in the inevitable "sky-shop" that concludes the visit.

Already during the course of construction the raising of the central section between the two towers was organized as a highly-publicized, major public event, to imprint the symbolic image of an ascent skyward in the collective memory. It is true that this apparently banal hoisting and the assembly of all the floating elements required the installation of an extremely sophisticated control system. And anyway, the event had to last for eight hours!

Façade detail.
© Caroline Mierop.

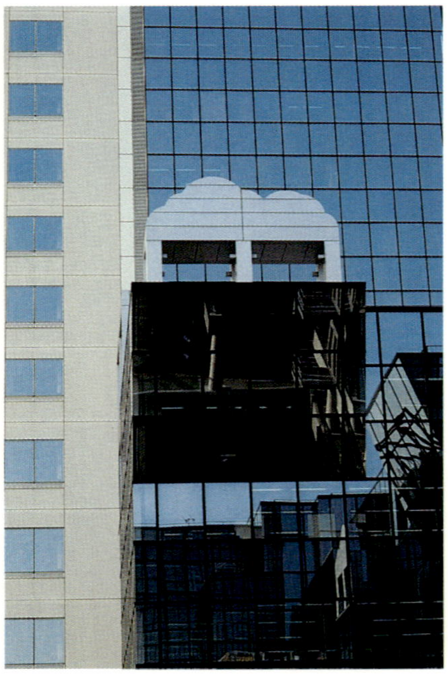

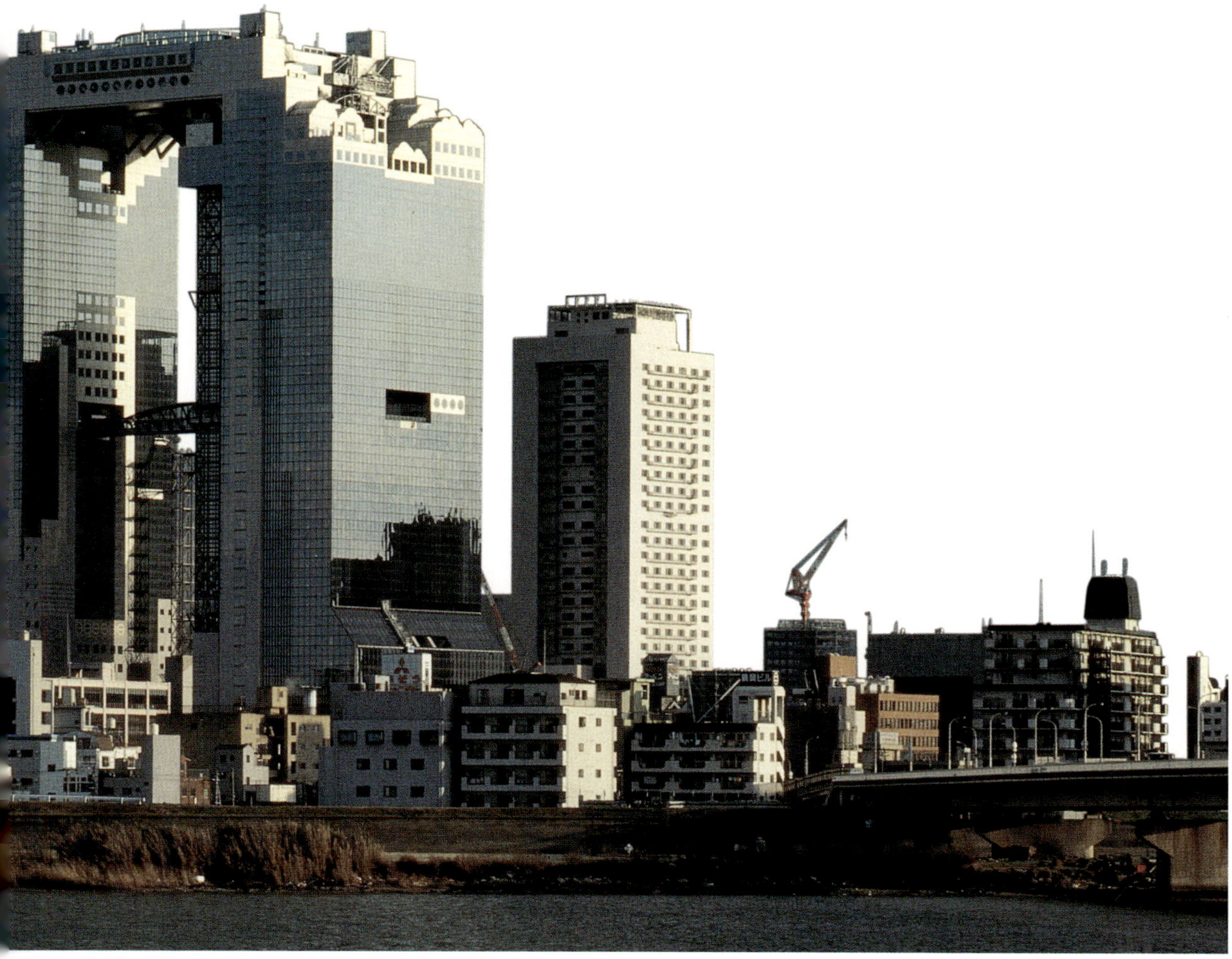

The idea would not have worked if the building was nothing more than a spectacle. The quality of materials, the finish of the detailing as well as the work on the layout and the interior space, the inside/outside connections—doors, windows, terraces—the lobbies, the passages, the signage all assure a pleasing visual effect that breaks with the depressing banality of so much speculative office building. This is where the vital role of the developer comes in, who in this case is also the main occupant. Their determination to make a good job of it, which was not only motivated by a risky not to say unfavorable urban situation, was expressed from the outset by the organization of an architectural competition, then by the choice of a reputedly expensive project and followed through in minute detail from beginning to end by means, among other things, of a specially created internal team. The developer was also responsible for the remarkable use of the public areas, which include an esplanade, gardens, fountains and ornamental lakes, street furniture, sculpture and, inside the building, an art center, restaurants, a shopping gallery entrance to the subway system, and a machine room entirely decorated as a "mechanical zoo."

At night the hanging crater resembles a spacecraft about to land. The myriad spotlights that ring it bathe the gardens in a gentle half-light and dozens of courting couples can be seen embracing on the public benches, enjoying the freshness of the air and the magic of the location.

The center of the crater.
© Caroline Mierop.

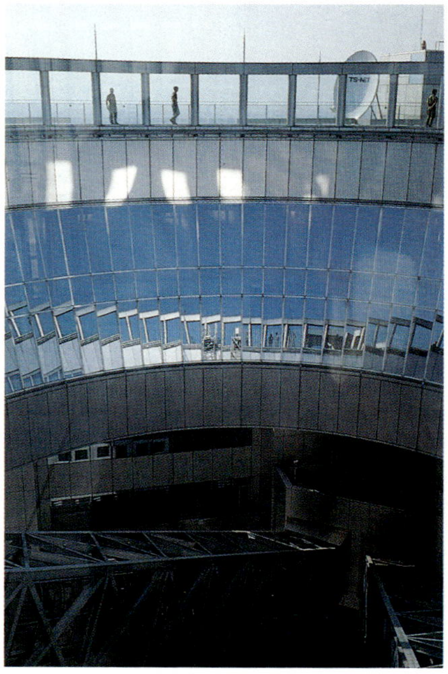

SHINJUKU PARK TOWER

Tokyo - Japan

Kenzo Tange Associates - 1994

"Seated in a small park in front of the Tokyo City Hall, while observing this construction that blocks out the sky with its enormous mass through the branches of a small cherry tree that moves in the light breeze..., the famous words of Le Corbusier came to mind: "It's a catastrophe; it's a magnificent catastrophe."

Paolo Riani, « Il Ciliegio e l'Edificio », *l'Arca*, No. 46, Feb. 1991.

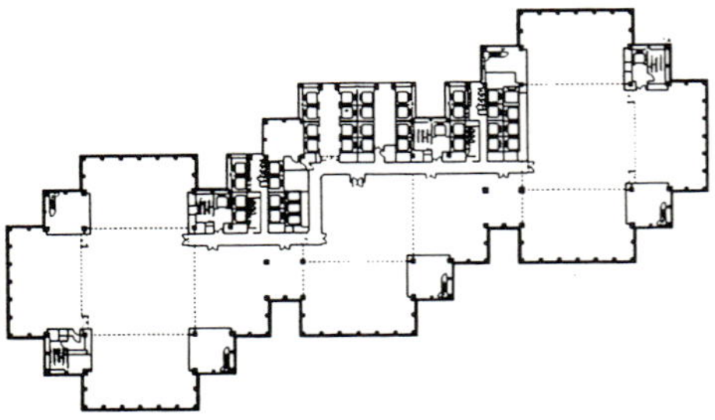

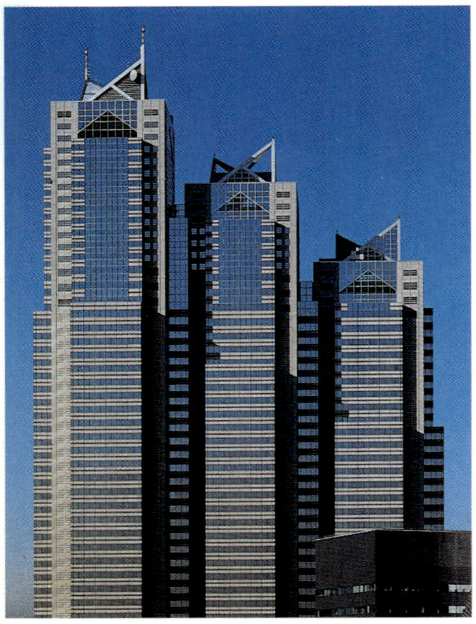

Typical floor plan.
Kenzo Tange Associates.

Detail of the summit of the building.
© Studio Murai.

Opposite:
The silhouette of Shinjuku Park Tower at sunset.
© Studio Murai.

Seen from in front, the Shinjuku Park Tower, named after the nearby Chuo public park in the Shinjuku neighborhood, doesn't look much like a skyscraper. It isn't very tall, at least compared to the two neighboring towers of the new City Hall Complex; nor is it particularly narrow, being less than twice as high as it's broad. Its proportions are closer to an imposing slab building with its 120 meter (394 feet) wide façade. How to visually reduce this mass? How to accentuate the impression of verticality?

The Tange practice's solution hangs on a simple subterfuge, expressed both in the plan and the section, and is to break up the parallelepiped into 3 (apparently) distinct volumes, transforming the slab into three juxtaposed columns.

The device is not new and Kenzo Tange himself put its effectiveness to the test in 1986 in one of Singapore's highest skyscrapers, the 280-meter (920 feet) OUB Centre—the tallest building in Asia at the time of its construction. The breaking up of the rectangular plan into two back-to-back triangles, a device only perceptible at the level of the highest floors, induces an oblique view of the tower, reinforcing the impression of slenderness and accentuating the soaring effect.

A similar optical illusion can be seen in Tokyo at the new Shinjuku City Hall Complex (1991), also by Kenzo Tange where the upper floors are separated into two independent volumes.

In the case of the Shinjuku Park Tower the plan is divided into 3 squares of equal size, offset one from the other to fit the irregular shape of the site. This displacement which helps to break the building up visually also considerably reduces the shadow cast by the tower on the neighboring park. The three square-shaped towers climb in parallel for the first 39 levels with only set back links underlining their verticality. From the 40th floor, first curtain walling, then the termination of the set back links, and finally the succession

Architects: Kenzo Tange Associates — *Structural engineers:* Kobori Research Complex Inc. — *Mechanical and electrical engineers:* Inuzuka Engineering Consultants — *Contractors:* Kajima, Shimizu, Taisei, JV — *Developer:* Tokyo Gas Urban Project.

52 stories, 233 meters (764 feet) at highest point; 209 and 182 meters (686 and 597 feet) for the two other summits — Mixed steel and concrete structure — Mixed-use building: 32,000 square meters (344,000 square feet) shopping and showroom area; 135,000 square meters (1.4 million square feet) offices (30 stories), a 178-room hotel and 4 levels of underground parking — Heating station: 550 square meters (5,920 square feet).

of summits in three ascending steps clearly demonstrate the independence of the three grouped towers. These vertical permutations echo the interior organization of the building. A hotel, in fact, crowns the office building from the fortieth floor. Its lobby, a real winter garden in the sky, occupies the first polyhedron, the swimming pool the second, and the highest contains machinery.

At the foot of the building 6 levels of showrooms and a shopping area are deployed around an impressive, long atrium, housed between the building and the neighborhood heating station which borders the site to the east. This mixture of uses, with the technical and management complexity that it implies, is still unusual in Japan, especially for a building of this size. The Landmark Tower in Yokohama (The Stubbins Associates and Mitsubishi Corporation, 1993) with its commercial atrium, offices and a hotel on the last 15 floors, acted as a pioneer in this regard.

A year later, Kenzo Tange's building inaugurated the formula in Tokyo on the borders of a business center (Shinjuku is the only real skyscraper quarter of the Japanese capital) and of a large city park and a future cultural district planned for development around the new National Theater. It is an integrating element, paradoxically isolated by a network of freeways, which traces the striking silhouette of an immense kite on the city skyline.

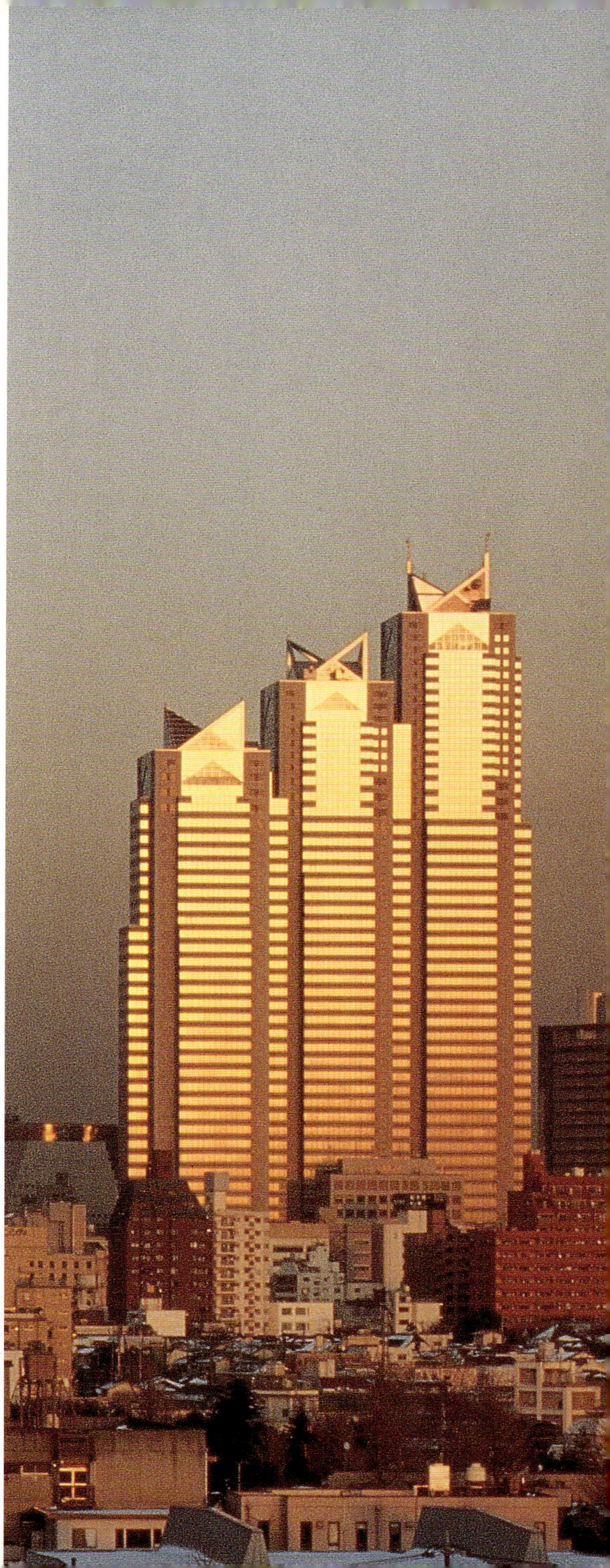

REPUBLIC PLAZA

Singapore

Kisho Kurokawa Architect & Associates - 1995

"Why do children love steam locomotives? Why is a sewing machine a nostalgic thing for us? .... These kinds of machines have transcended their purely mechanical function and serve in addition a symbolic function, and such 'symbolic machines' are an important point of contact between human beings and technology."

Kisho Kurokawa,
"From Metabolism to Symbiosis", *Kisho Kurokawa*, Academy Editions, St. Martin's Press, 1992.

Raffles Place is the center of the business district on the island of Singapore and is developed around a subway station at the mouth of the river. Here are concentrated 3 banks and the 3 tallest towers of the city, culminating at a height of 280 meters (919 feet), the maximum height permitted by the National Aviation Authority. They are the OUB Centre by the Kenzo Tange practice (1986), UOB Plaza (1992) by the same architect but in a more ornamental style, and Republic Plaza just built by Kisho Kurokawa from Japan.

Kisho Kurokawa is not strictly speaking a specialist in commercial architecture. He is mainly known for projects for futuristic cities, exhibition pavilions (Osaka, 1970) and numerous museums, as well as one of the leading theoreticians of contemporary Japanese architecture, an apostle of Metabolism—a strictly Japanese movement born in the sixties in opposition to the claims of Internationalism made by the modern movement in the West. It is in the context of Metabolism (the word is deliberately borrowed from biology) that Kurokawa was to construct his first tall buildings: the Nakagin Tower in Tokyo (1972), a random pile of modular units, the Sony Tower in Osaka (1976) or, in the early eighties, the Wacoal Kojimachi building in Tokyo (1984), a "sentimental machine," half archaic, half futurist, and characteristic of the ambiguity, the ambivalence dear to the architect.

How does this heritage imbue Kurokawa's skyscraper projects a decade later? The high-tech handwriting of the first buildings has long since given way to an architecture of synthesis—Kurokawa talks of androgyny—where past is mixed with present, local culture with universals, traditional craft with advanced technology, art with science, nature with man and the machine in a symbiosis where the dualism of occidental culture is systematically contradicted. The skyscraper project for the Osaka Prefectural Government Offices (1989), for example, well illustrates the symbolic complexity of a

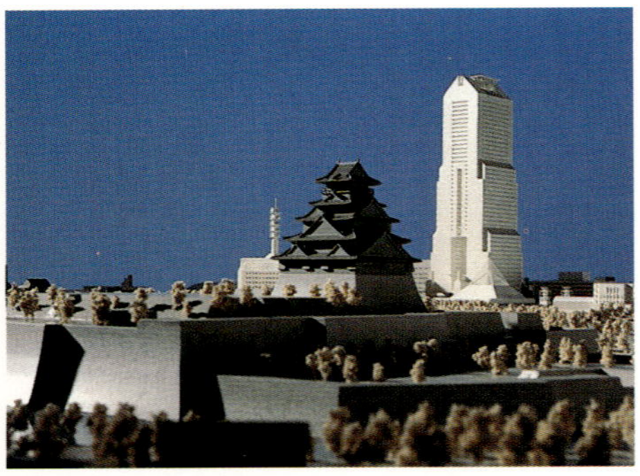

Offices of the Osaka Prefecture, scale model.
Kisho Kurokawa Architect & Associates, 1989.
© Tomio Ohashi.

Architects: Kisho Kurokawa Architect & Associates (Kisho Kurokawa), in association with RSP Architects Planners & Engineers — *Structural engineers:* RSP Architects, Planners & Engineers — *Mechanical and electrical engineers:* Squire Mech Pte Ltd — *Contractors:* Shimizu Corporation — *Developer:* CDL Properties Pte Ltd.

66 stories, 280 meters (919 feet) high — Mixed concrete and steel structure — Office building of 126,237 square meters (1.3 million square feet) with a basement shopping level and 10 parking levels in an adjacent building.

Opposite:
Axonometric drawing of Republic Plaza, 1994.
Kisho Kurokawa Architect & Associates.

shape which at the same time suggests the world of space—the rocket, the missile—and the city's ancient fortified castle. The same ambiguity can be found in Australia at the foot of the Melbourne Central Tower (1991) which, by an inversion of scales, puts the accent on a small historic tower included in the new complex. This intentional marriage of opposites, which also characterizes the Pacific Tower (1992) designed by Kurokawa for La Défense in Paris, explains the multiplicity of meanings inherent in Singapore's Republic Plaza: a lopped stake driven into concrete ground, a lighthouse at the entrance to the port—at night only the glazed summit of the tower is lit—the barrel of a cannon or a rocket ready for firing.

In contrast to Kenzo Tange's principle of breaking up masses, the highly monumental bulk of Kurokawa's tower is counteracted by its progressive reduction. Not only does the tower taper in a succession of sloping faces, it also fades away as the granite facing gradually disappears. Within the outlines of a brutal, almost laconic shape, Kurakawa has produced a complex work of which the sophistication involves neither Mannerism nor ostentatious references. The architect credits this "invisibility" of meaning to tradition and history, in the name of an oriental spirituality which he opposes, once again, to the rationalism of the West.

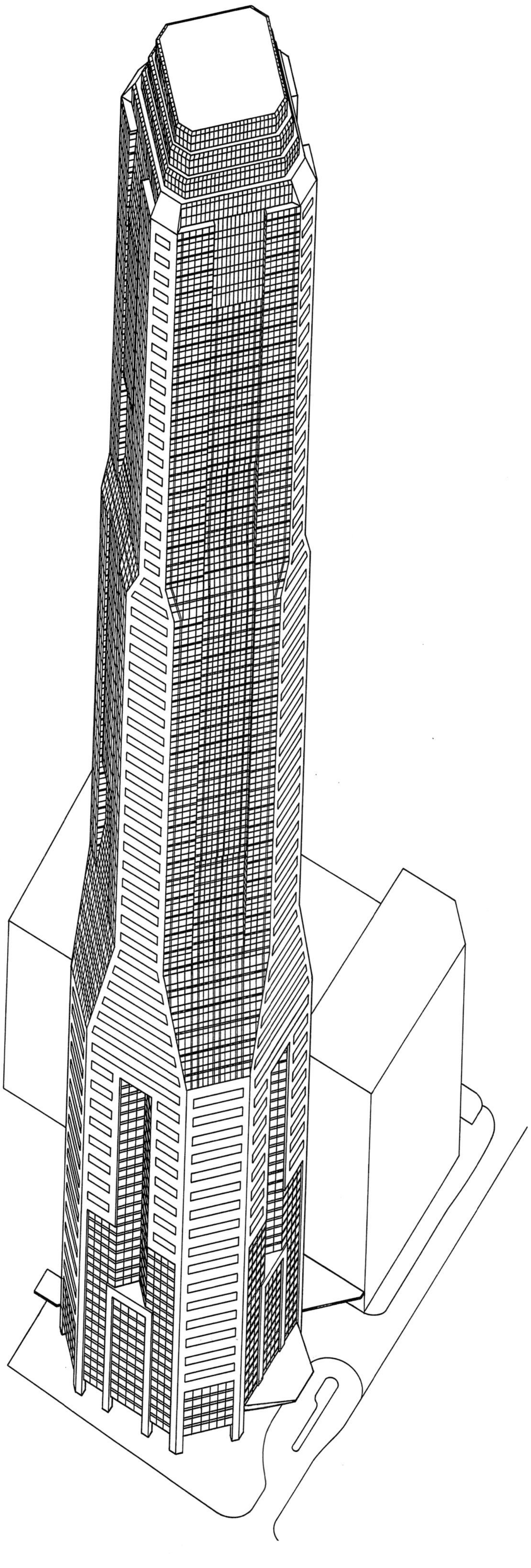

PETRONAS TOWERS

Kuala Lumpur - Malaysia

Cesar Pelli & Associates - 1996

"The Great Pyramid of Cheops, Ulm Cathedral, St. Peter's, the Empire State Building, the Sears Tower; for millennia, the world's tallest buildings have been in the occident."

Jonathan Glancey,
"Booming Far East Reaches for the Sky,"
The Independent, Sunday edition, July 10, 1994.

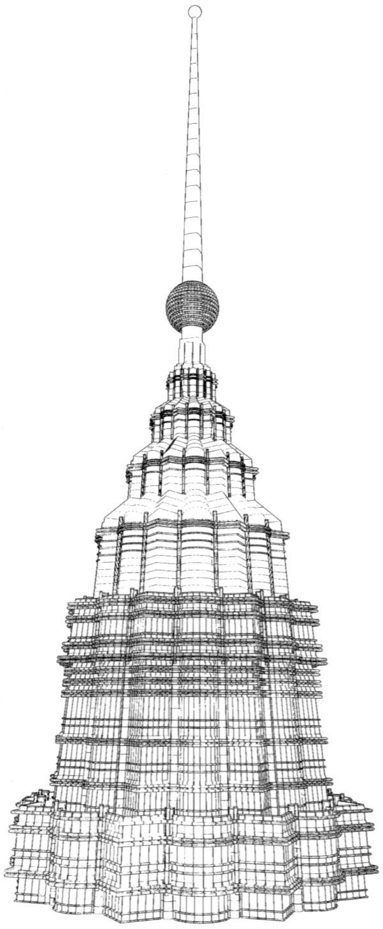

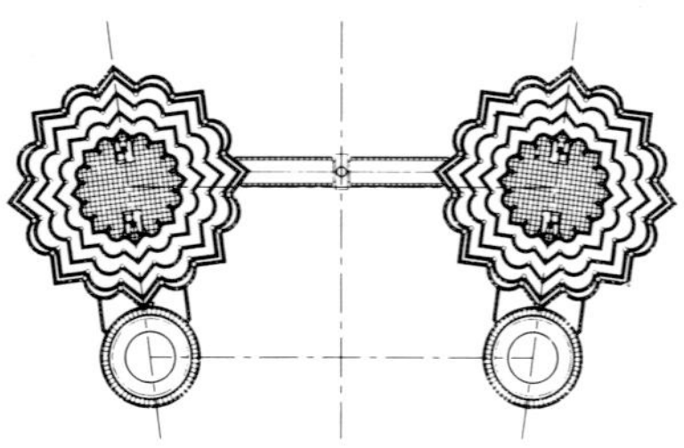

Detail of the summits of the two towers.
Schematic plan of the upper floors.
Cesar Pelli & Associates.

Opposite:
The Petronas Towers, night view, perspective.
Drawing by Lee Dunnette.
Cesar Pelli & Associates

In 1996, after twenty years, the Sears Tower in Chicago will have ceded the title of world's tallest building. And with it the United States loses a symbol of its own invention. Asia is taking up the torch, today Malaysia, tomorrow Chongquing, Hong Kong and Melbourne where skyscrapers are already planned which should break the record claimed by the two Malaysian towers. For they are indeed two twin towers, rising to 450 meters (1,476 feet) like a monumental gate, visible from a distance of 50 kilometers (more than 30 miles). "[This] will put Kuala Lumpur on the map," said one of the architects involved in the project. ("Is Bigger Better?" *Asiaweek*, July 21, 1993.)

The colossal scale of the project is already visibly evident at the building site. There are the dizzying depth of the excavations, the thickness of the concrete cores with a 23 meter (75 feet) sided square at the base, more than 2,000 workers employed at the site, not counting about 20 architects and a team of some 200 managing the site, of which about 30 have already had the experience of Canary Wharf and Euro Disney.

Figures notwithstanding, the project is intrinsically ambitious. The two towers essentially house the offices of Petronas, the national oil company. Each one contains a conference center and a surau, a kind of small mosque. The towers are connected by a bridge at sky-lobby level. At ground level there are a symphony concert hall and commercial center, also designed by Cesar Pelli.

And the project does not end there. The 2 towers are the first phase of a much bigger operation covering 39 hectares (96 acres) on the northeastern periphery of Kuala Lumpur's "Golden Triangle," the capital's business center. A veritable city within a city, the project brings together nearly 2 million square meters (21 million

---

Architects: Cesar Pelli & Associates ; Adamson Associates (Toronto), consultant architects: Kuala Lumpur City Centre Berhad, Architectural Division, Architects of Record — *Structural engineers:* Thornton-Tomasetti Engineers, in association with Ranhill Bersejutu Sdn Bhd — *Mechanical and electrical engineers:* Flack + Kurtz, in association with Tenaga Ewbank Preece Sdn Bhd — *Project management:* Lehrer McGovern Malaysia Sdn Bhd — *Contractors:* MMC Engineering & Construction Co. Ltd and Samsung Engineering & Construction Co. Ltd — *Developer:* Kuala Lumpur City Centre Berhad.

88 stories, 450 meters (1,476 feet) high — High resistance concrete structure — Office buildings of 450,000 square meters (4,844,000 square feet) in total with a commercial center of 150,000 square meters (1,615,000 square feet) on 6 levels and symphony concert hall (850 seats).

square feet) of offices, hotels, shops and recreational facilities arranged around a huge park, the whole complex linked by a ring road and a people-mover loop. The avowed aim of the project is to gradually shift the center of the city towards the site, where a new town hall may also soon by installed.

Questions remain to be raised about a site of this size: the perception of scale, the impact on the city. What effect will the scalloped outlines of Pelli's plan—a geometric motive inspired by Islam—produce when it is repeated on 88 floors? How will these new towers co-exist with their neighbors, those that are planned—Kevin Roche's Ampang is already in construction—and those that are already there, more or less dispersed on the periphery of the site?

The essential question, however, is not one of aesthetics. How can the city cope with the daily commuting of some 60,000 employees expected at the complex? Won't the program of improving service roads, currently under study, clog up the center of the city even more? The opening of the first section of a light railway transit system, with a station serving the site, is scheduled for 1998. Will it be too little, too late?

The dread is that Kuala Lumpur might become a second Bangkok, a city paralyzed by traffic. It would be a high price to pay for holding, for a short time, the record for the world's highest building.

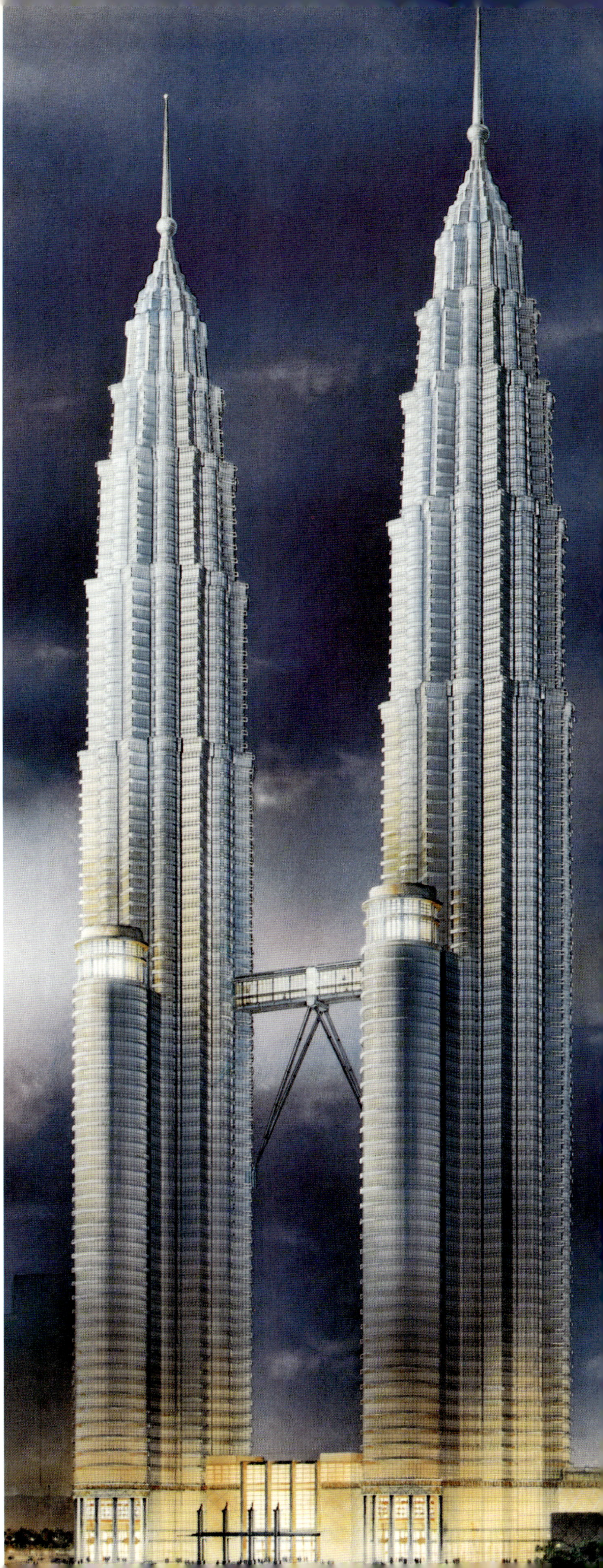

THE RACE

IFA / La Page.

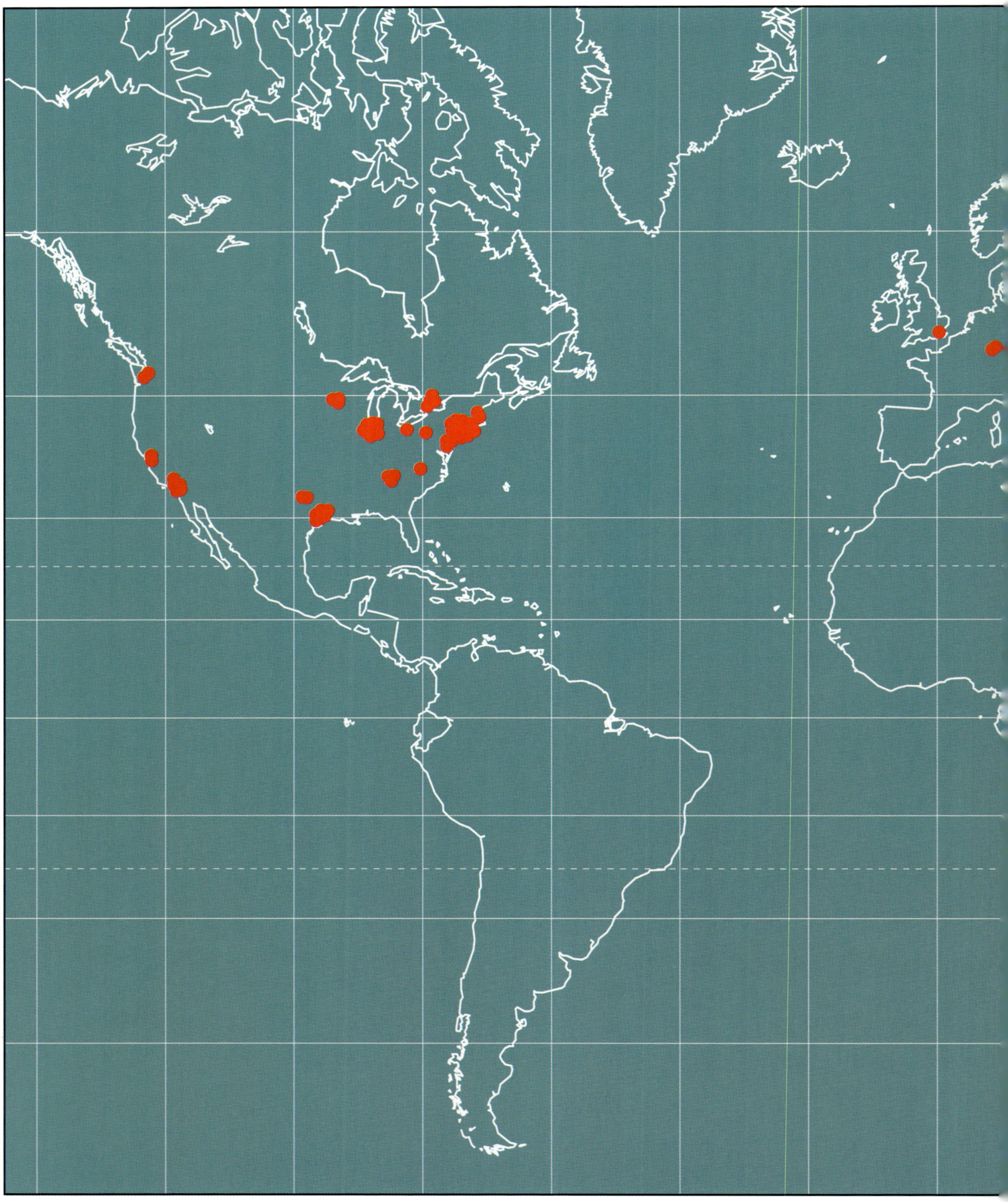

FOR THE RECORD

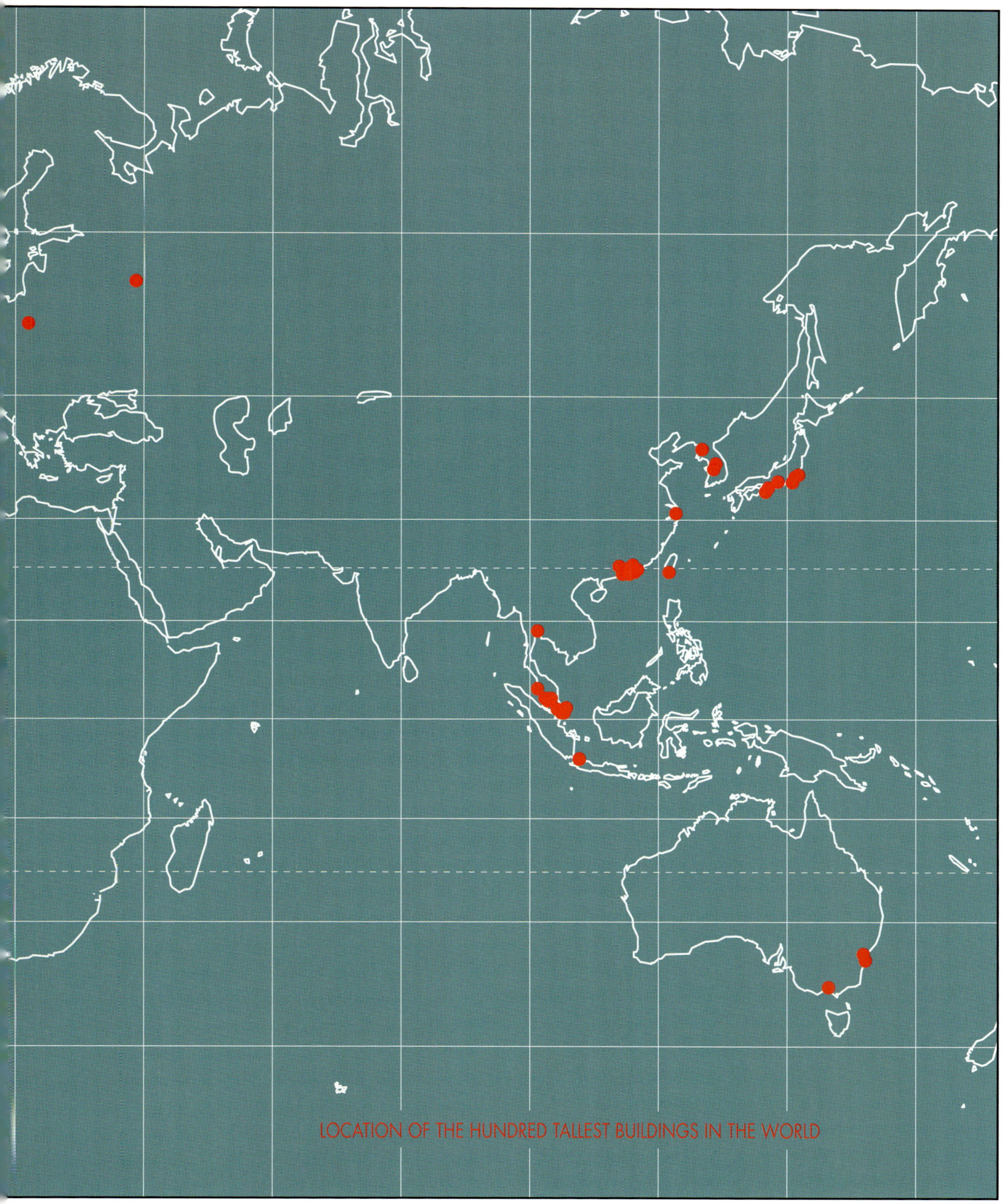

Skyscrapers are defined in superlatives. Since the construction of the Masonic Temple in Chicago in 1892, the first building to boast of being "the tallest in the world," the race to be tallest, or biggest, most beautiful or spectacular has not ceased to fire the imagination of architects and engineers, to whet the appetite of developers, and fuel the competition between great cities.

From the first postcards of New York to the promotional brochures for the most recently constructed Hong Kong skyscrapers, heights are vaunted and compared: the tallest tower on the shores of the Mediterranean, Barcelona 1992; the tallest hotel in the Far East, Shanghai 1934; the tallest in the world, Singapore 1986; the tallest office building in the Southern Hemisphere, Melbourne 1985; the tallest concrete structure, Buenos Aires 1936; the tallest tower in Western Europe, Antwerp 1932, Paris 1973, Frankfurt 1990....

A league table of the 100 tallest buildings in the world is constantly up-dated, as in the field of sport. Monopolized by North American skyscrapers until 1953, when Moscow University, a monument from the Cold War period, was completed, the frontiers of the table then quickly broadened to include South Africa and France from the early seventies, then Canada, Australia, Venezuela and Japan as they crossed the 200-meter barrier.

Opposite:
The Mile High Illinois, project for a one-mile-high tower.
Frank Lloyd Wright, architect, 1956.
The Frank Lloyd Wright Foundation.

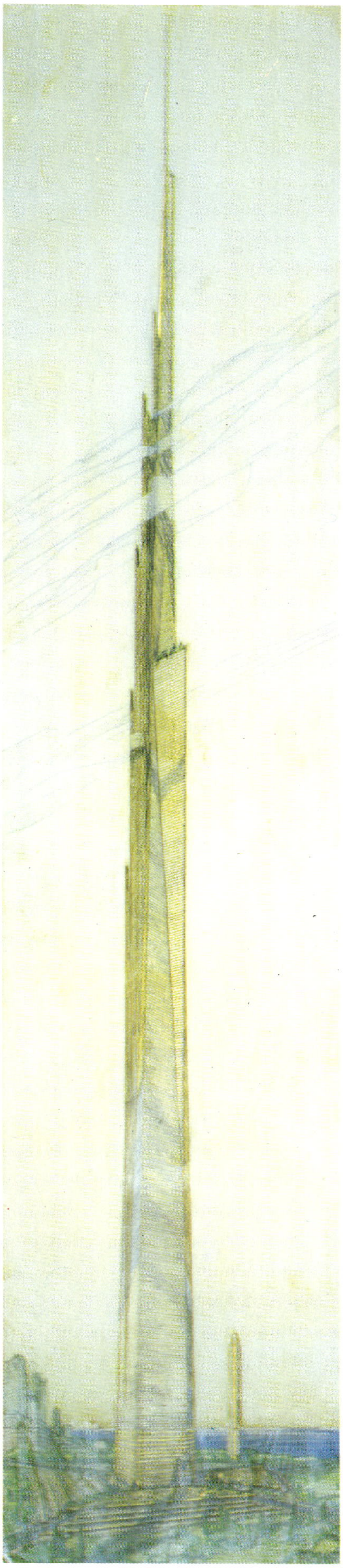

But it took the "Pacific years" for the battle at the summit to shift from the United States to the east: Hong Kong, Singapore, Kuala Lumpur today, Shanghai, Taiwan, and Jakarta tomorrow.

This list of "the hundred tallest buildings in the world" was first drawn up in 1972. It is presented here in an annotated and illustrated version, according to the ranking established by the Council on Tall Buildings and Urban Habitat (Lehigh University, Bethlehem, Pennsylvania, United States) in May 1995. The list includes only skyscrapers already built or under construction and excludes numerous more or less secret, more or less realistic projects which may well very soon reach the starting line of this fiercely contested architectural world championship.

THE HUNDRED TALLEST BUILDINGS IN THE WORLD

Skyscraper		City	Year	Stories	Meters	Feet
1.	Petronas Tower I	Kuala Lumpur	UC 96	88	450	1476
2.	Petronas Tower II	Kuala Lumpur	UC 96	88	450	1476
3.	Sears Tower	Chicago	1974	110	443	1454
4.	Jin Mao Building	Shanghai	UC 98	88	421	1379
5.	One World Trade Center	New York	1972	110	417	1368
6.	Two World Trade Center	New York	1973	110	415	1362
7.	Empire State Building	New York	1931	102	381	1250
8.	Central Plaza	Hong Kong	1992	78	374	1227
9.	Bank of China Tower	Hong Kong	1989	70	369	1209
10.	T & C Tower	Kaohsiung	UC 97	85	348	1140
11.	Amoco Building	Chicago	1973	80	346	1136
12.	John Hancock Center	Chicago	1969	100	344	1127
13.	Shun Hing Square	Shenzhen	UC 96	81	325	1066
14.	Sky Central Plaza	Guangzhou	UC 96	80	322	1056
15.	Baiyoke Tower II	Bangkok	UC 97	90	320	1050
16.	Chrysler Building	New York	1930	77	319	1046
17.	NationsBank Plaza	Atlanta	1992	55	312	1023
18.	First Interstate World Center	Los Angeles	1989	75	310	1018
19.	Texas Commerce Tower	Houston	1982	75	305	1000
20.	Ryugyong Hotel	Pyongyang	UC	105	300	984
21.	Two Prudential Plaza	Chicago	1990	64	298	978
22.	First Interstate Bank Plaza	Houston	1983	71	296	972
23.	Landmark Tower	Yokohama	1993	70	296	971
24.	311 South Wacker Drive	Chicago	1990	65	292	959
25.	Jubilee St./Queen's Road Central	Hong Kong	UC 97	69	292	958
26.	First Canadian Place	Toronto	1975	72	290	952
27.	American International Building	New York	1932	66	290	950
28.	One Liberty Place	Philadelphia	1987	61	287	945
29.	Columbia Seafirst Center	Seattle	1985	76	287	943
30.	40 Wall Street	New York	1930	70	283	927
31.	NationsBank Plaza	Dallas	1985	72	281	921
32.	OUB Centre	Singapore	1986	66	280	919
33.	UOB Plaza	Singapore	1992	66	280	919
34.	Republic Plaza	Singapore	1995	66	280	919
35.	Citicorp Center	New York	1977	59	279	915
36.	Scotia Plaza	Toronto	1989	68	275	902
37.	Transco Tower	Houston	1983	64	275	901
38.	Society Center	Cleveland	1991	57	271	888
39.	AT&T Corporate Center	Chicago	1989	60	270	885
40.	900 North Michigan	Chicago	1988	66	265	871
41.	NationsBank Corporate Center	Charlotte	1992	60	265	871
42.	One Peachtree Center	Atlanta	1992	60	264	867
43.	Canada Trust Tower	Toronto	1990	51	263	863
44.	Water Tower Place	Chicago	1976	74	262	859
45.	First Interstate Tower	Los Angeles	1974	62	262	858
46.	Transamerica Pyramid	San Francisco	1972	48	260	853
47.	G.E. Building (Rockefeller Center)	New York	1933	70	259	850
48.	One First National Plaza	Chicago	1969	60	259	850
49.	Commerzbank	Frankfurt	UC 97	60	259	850
50.	Two Liberty Place	Philadelphia	1990	58	258	848

The list indicates the year the building was completed (building under construction: UC + expected year of completion).
The number of stories includes the ground floor.
The height of the buildings is calculated from the street level of the main entrance to the summit of the building (radio or television antennae, flagpoles not included).

Skyscraper	City	Year	Stories	Meters	Feet
51. MesseTurm	Frankfurt	1990	70	257	842
52. USX Tower	Pittsburgh	1970	64	256	841
53. Gate Tower	Osaka	UC 96	56	254	833
54. Osaka World Trade Center	Osaka	1995	55	252	827
55. One Atlantic Center	Atlanta	1987	50	250	820
56. Wisma 46 Kota BNI	Jakarta	UC 96	46	250	820
57. Korea Life Insurance 63	Seoul	1985	60	249	817
58. CitySpire	New York	1989	72	248	814
59. One Chase Manhattan Plaza	New York	1961	60	248	813
60. MetLife Building (Pan Am)	New York	1963	59	246	808
61. Kompleks Tun Abdul Razak	George Town Penang	1985	65	245	804
62. Malayan Bank	Kuala Lumpur	1988	50	244	799
63. City Hall Complex	Tokyo	1991	48	243	797
64. Rialto Towers	Melbourne	1985	56	242	794
65. Mellon Bank Center	Philadelphia	1990	54	241	792
66. Woolworth Building	New York	1913	57	241	792
67. John Hancock Tower	Boston	1976	60	240	788
68. Bank One Center	Dallas	1987	60	240	787
69. JR Central Towers	Nagoya	UC 99	51	240	787
70. Commerce Court West	Toronto	1973	57	239	784
71. Moscow University	Moscow	1953	26	239	784
72. NationsBank Center	Houston	1984	56	238	780
73. Bank of America Center	San Francisco	1969	52	237	779
74. One Worldwide Plaza	New York	1989	47	237	778
75. One Canada Square	London	1991	50	237	777
76. IDS Center	Minneapolis	1972	57	236	775
77. Norwest Center	Minneapolis	1988	57	236	774
78. First Bank Place	Minneapolis	1992	53	236	774
79. Singapore Treasury Building	Singapore	1986	52	235	771
80. Shinjuku Park Tower	Tokyo	1994	52	233	764
81. Heritage Plaza	Houston	1987	53	232	762
82. Palace of Culture and Science	Warsaw	1955	42	231	758
83. Carnegie Hall Tower	New York	1991	60	231	757
84. Three First National Plaza	Chicago	1981	57	230	753
85. The Equitable Tower	New York	1985	51	229	752
86. One Penn Plaza	New York	1972	57	229	750
87. 1251 Avenue of the Americas	New York	1972	54	229	750
88. Prudential Center	Boston	1964	52	229	750
89. Two California Plaza	Los Angeles	1992	52	229	750
90. The Gas Company Tower	Los Angeles	1991	50	228	749
91. MLC Centre	Sydney	1978	65	228	748
92. Two Pacific Place/Shangri-La Hotel	Hong Kong	1991	56	228	748
93. 1100 Louisiana Building	Houston	1980	55	228	748
94. Korea World Trade Center	Seoul	1988	54	228	748
95. Wing Lok St./Queen's Road Central	Hong Kong	UC 97	54	228	748
96. Governor Phillip Tower	Sydney	1993	54	227	745
97. J. P. Morgan	New York	1989	50	227	745
98. Two Union Square	Seattle	1989	56	226	743
99. 333 So. Hope Building	Los Angeles	1975	55	226	743
100. One Liberty Plaza	New York	1973	54	226	743

PETRONAS TOWER I

1

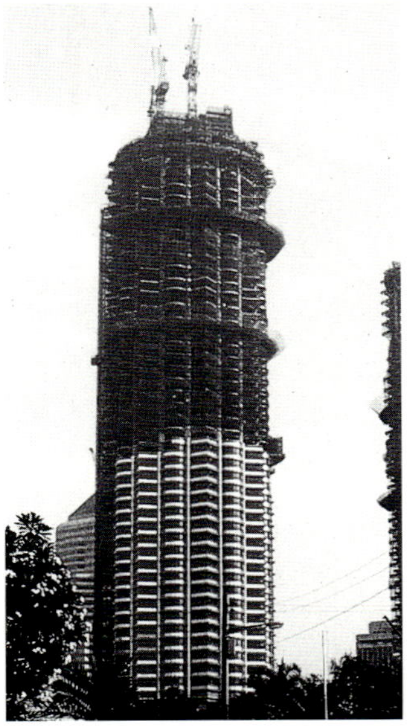

Kuala Lumpur, Malaysia
88 stories
450 meters (1,476 feet)
1996, under construction

Architects: Cesar Pelli & Associates, in association with Kuala Lumpur City Centre – Architectural division.
Structural engineers: Thornton-Tomasetti.
Mechanical and electrical engineers: Flack + Kurtz.
Developer: Kuala Lumpur City Centre (Holdings) Sendirian Berhad.
Mixed steel and concrete structure.
Office tower 435,000 square meters (4.7 million square feet) in the two towers, with shops, concert hall and conference center.

The Petronas twin towers are part of a larger development that includes 4 office towers, several hotels, commercial areas, cultural and recreational facilities arranged around a huge park. They form a kind of monumental gate to this new district situated on the edge of Kuala Lumpur's Golden Triangle and intended to become the true center of the city. The two towers are connected by a walkway at skylobby level.

Cesar Pelli & Associates

PETRONAS TOWER II

2

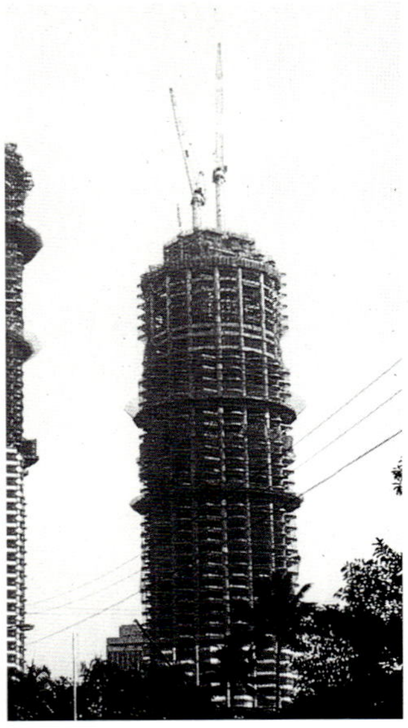

Kuala Lumpur, Malaysia
88 stories
450 meters (1,476 feet)
1996, under construction

Architects: Cesar Pelli & Associates, in association with Kuala Lumpur City Centre – Architectural division.
Structural engineers: Thornton-Tomasetti.
Mechanical and electrical engineers: Flack + Kurtz.
Developer: Kuala Lumpur City Centre (Holdings) Sendirian Berhad.
Mixed steel and concrete structure.
Office tower 435,000 square meters (4.7 million square feet) in the two towers, with shops, concert hall and conference center.

The enormous scale of the project is obvious from looking at the building site: the foundations are 20 meters (65 feet) deep with 1.2 million cubic meters (42.4 million cubic feet) of excavated material; the core has 23-meter square base; the area of each level is 2,600 square meters (28,000 square feet); 1,200 workers work around the clock on the two towers and from 2,100 to 7,000 work on the entire site; about 200 people manage the construction; 20 architects are exclusively attached to the project.

Cesar Pelli & Associates

SEARS TOWER

3

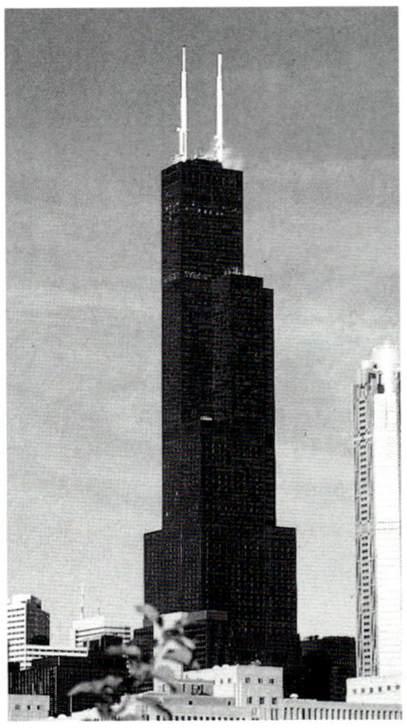

Chicago, United States
110 stories
443 meters (1,454 feet)
1974

Architects: Skidmore, Owings & Merrill, Chicago (Bruce Graham).
Structural engineers: Skidmore, Owings & Merrill, Chicago (Fazlur Khan).
Mechanical and electrical engineers: Jaros Baum & Bolles.
Developer: Sears, Roebuck and Co.
Steel structure.
Office tower, 345,000 square meters (3.7 million square feet), with public observation platform on the 103rd floor.

The tallest building in the world for 22 years and until the completion of the Petronas Towers in Kuala Lumpur in 1996. The two entrance porches were designed by DeStefano + Partners (1993-1994).

© Benoît Roland

JIN MAO BUILDING

4

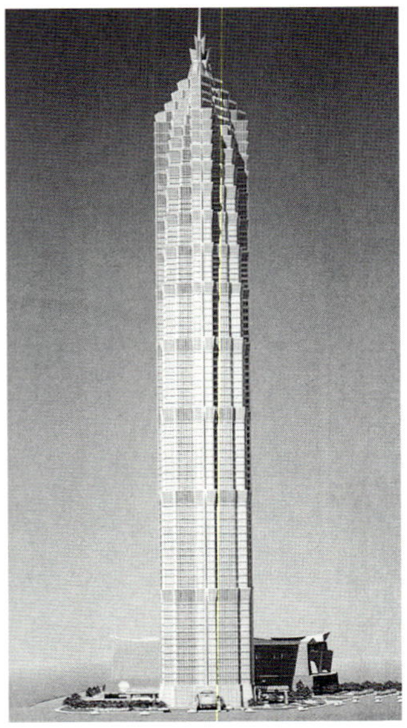

Shanghai, China
(People's Republic), 88 stories
421 meters (1,379 feet)
1998, under construction

Architects: Skidmore, Owings & Merrill, Chicago (Adrian Smith).
Engineers: Skidmore, Owings & Merrill (structure, D. Stanton Korista).
Developer: China Shanghai Foreign Trade Centre Co.
Mixed steel and concrete structure.
Mixed-use building containing offices, 120,000 square meters (1.3 million square feet), a Hyatt hotel (600 rooms) on the upper floors, a public observation platform on the 88th floor, 3 levels of underground garage and a 6-story annex containing a conference and exhibition center, a movie theater and a shopping gallery.

According to its designer, it is a "Sino-Art Deco" building, based on multiples of the figure eight, a lucky number in the Chinese tradition. The tower culminates in a 61-meter (200 feet) high spire. It will be the central point of the new business district of Pudong.

SOM Chicago

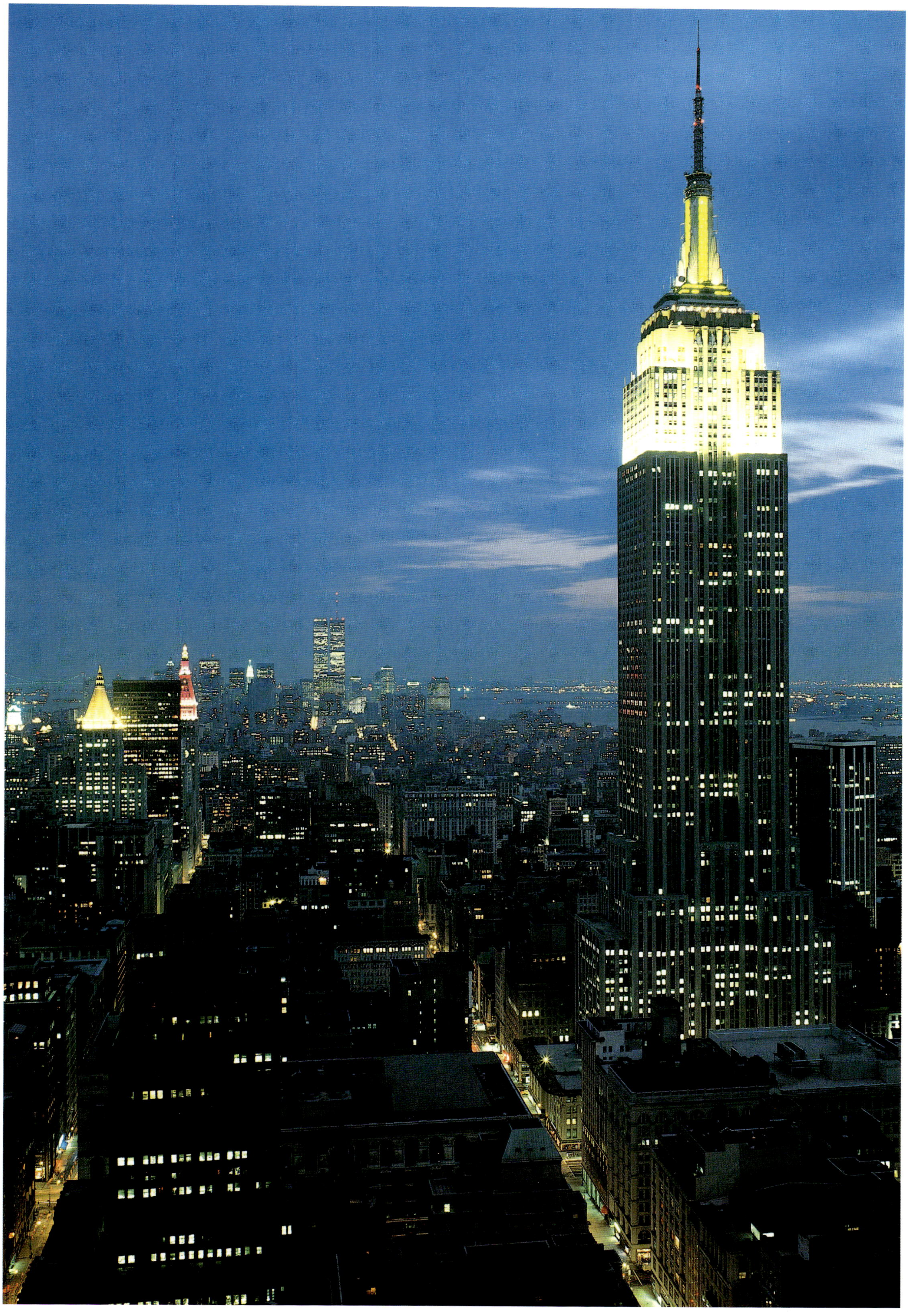

Empire State Building, New York. Shreve, Lamb & Harmon Associates, architects, 1931. At the end of the vista, the twin towers of the World Trade Center (1972-1973).
© Benoît Roland.

ONE WORLD TRADE CENTER

5

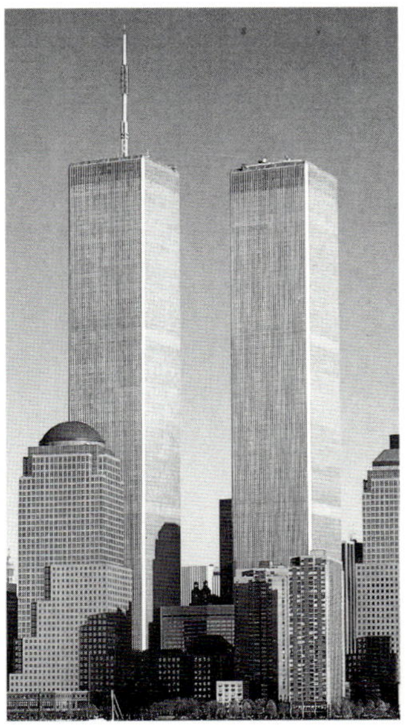

New York, United States
110 stories
417 meters (1,368 feet)
1972

Architects: Minoru Yamasaki and Associates, in association with Emery Roth & Sons, New York.
Structural engineers: Skilling, Helle, Christiansen, Robertson.
Mechanical engineers: Jaros Baum & Bolles.
Developer: The Port Authority of NY & NJ.
Steel structure.
Office tower with the panoramic restaurant Windows on the World on the 107th floor (closed since 1993).

The tallest tower in the world at the time of its construction, six feet taller than its twin. A brutal modernist intrusion on the lower Manhattan skyline, the two towers quickly established themselves as the monumental gate to New York and the United States. The image inspired Philippe Petit, the French tight-rope walker, to make a 45-minute crossing on a 40-meter (130 feet) cable stretched between the two "pillars holding up the sky!"

© Benoît Roland

TWO WORLD TRADE CENTER

6

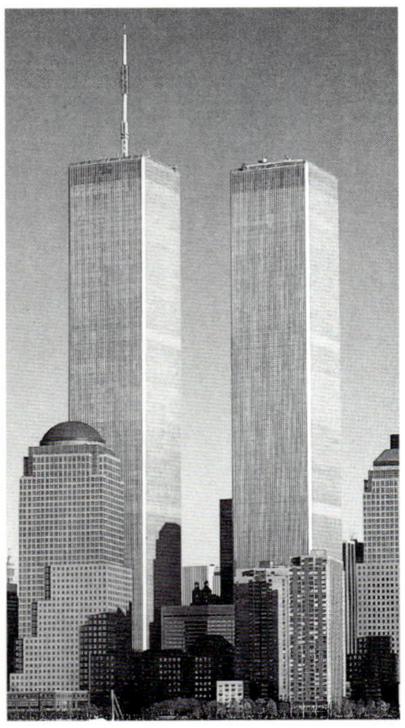

New York, United States
110 stories
415 meters (1,362 feet)
1973

Architects: Minoru Yamasaki and Associates, in association with Emery Roth & Sons, New York.
Structural engineers: Skilling, Helle, Christiansen, Robertson.
Mechanical engineers: Jaros Baum & Bolles.
Developer: The Port Authority of NY & NJ.
Steel structure.
Office tower with public observation gallery on the 107th floor and a panoramic terrace on the 110th floor, accessible by escalators.

On the afternoon of February 26, 1993, a bomb exploded in the underground garage of the World Trade Center killing six people, injuring several hundred, and causing heavy material damage. The structure of the buildings was not affected by the explosion but the security system was destroyed, making the towers non-occupiable for several days—an economic blow to New York City. The towers were repaired and cleaned, and re-occupied on March 18.

© Benoît Roland

EMPIRE STATE BUILDING

7

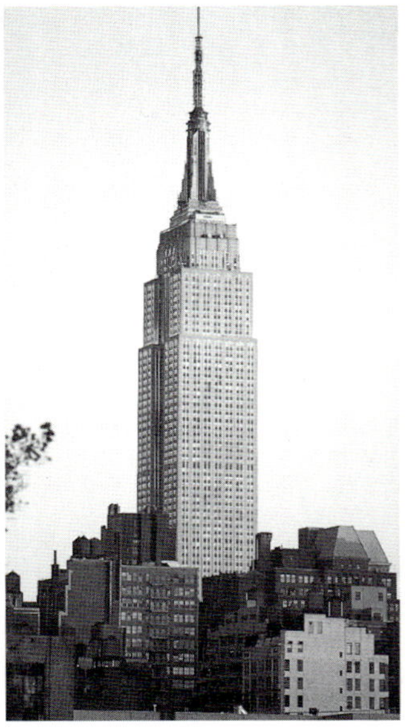

New York, United States
102 stories
381 meters (1,250 feet)
1931

Architects: Shreve, Lamb & Harmon Associates (William F. Lamb).
Structural engineer: H.G. Balcom.
Developer: John Jacob Raskob.
Steel structure.
Office tower, with public observation platforms on the 86th and 102nd floors.

The tallest building in the world for forty-two years, designated a historic landmark in 1981. A true archetype of the American skyscraper and a symbol of New York City, its image has been celebrated by several cult movies from the inter-war years, including King Kong and Tarzan. The tower culminates in a spectacular anchor mast for airships, which proved to be too dangerous, and a television antenna was added later. Since 1977, the summit of the tower has been illuminated at night in the colors of the American flag.

© Benoît Roland

CENTRAL PLAZA

8

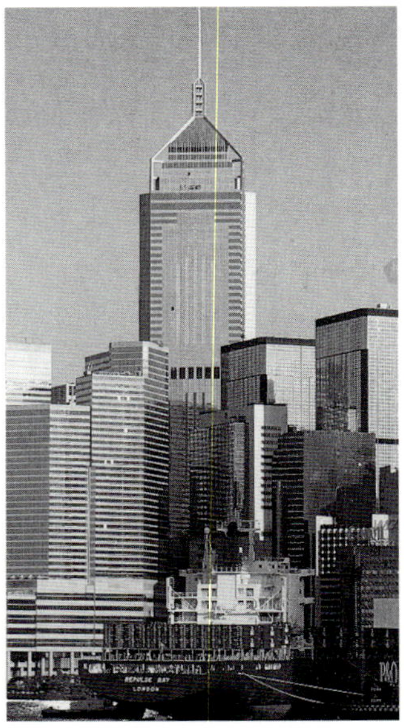

Hong Kong
78 stories
374 meters (1,227 feet)
1992

Architects: Ng Chun Man & Associates, Architects & Engineers.
Structural engineer: Ove Arup & Partners (Hong Kong).
Mechanical engineers: Associated Consulting Engineers.
Developer: Sun Hung Kai Properties, Sino Group, Ryoden Group.
Concrete structure.
Office tower, with skylobby on the 46th floor.

The tallest building in Asia at the time of its construction—a sales argument emphasized by the developer to compensate for its unfavorable location away from the business district.

Dennis Lau & Ng Chun Man

BANK OF CHINA TOWER

9

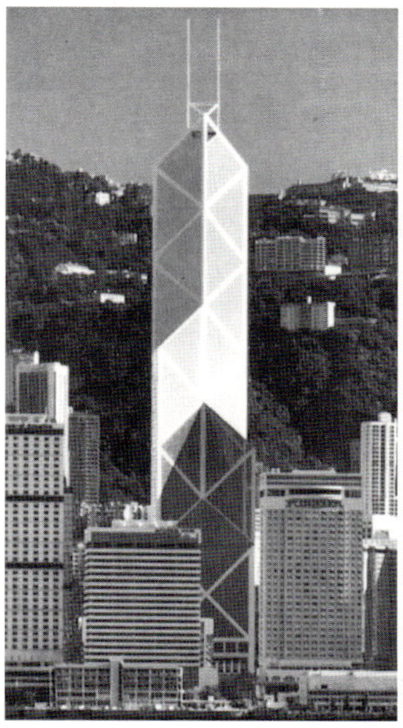

Hong Kong
70 stories
369 meters (1,209 feet)
1989

Architects: I.M. Pei & Partners (Ieoh Ming Pei, in association with Wong / Kung & Lee.
Structural engineers: Robertson, Fowler and Associates (NY); Vallentine, Laurie and Davies (Hong Kong).
Mechanical and electrical engineers: Jaros Baum & Bolles.
Developer: Bank of China.
Mixed steel and concrete structure.
Office tower, 130,000 square meters (1.4 million square feet), with banking hall on three levels.

The tallest tower in Hong Kong at the time of its construction; the Bank of China's riposte to the construction of the new headquarters of the Hong Kong & Shanghai Bank by the English architect Norman Foster.

© John Nye

T & C TOWER

10

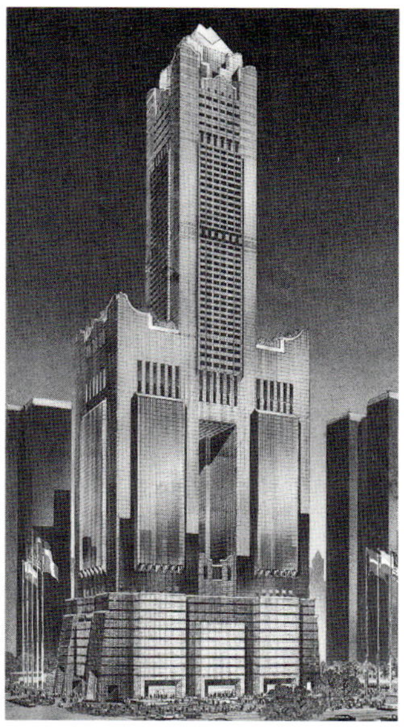

Kaohsiung, Taiwan
85 stories
348 meters (1,140 feet)
1997, under construction

Architects: C.Y. Lee & Partners; HOK Inc., consultants.
Consultant structural engineers: T.Y. Lin Taiwan & Evergreen.
Consultant mechanical engineers: CEC and William Tao Associates.
Developer: Tuntex & Chien Tai.
Steel structure.
Mixed-use building containing shops, offices, a hotel and, from the 72nd to the 85th floors, an ensemble of restaurants, private clubs and a belvedere.

The architects of the tower were also the designers of a first skyscraper, the Grand 50 Tower, 50 stories, 222 meters (730 feet) high, built in Kaohsiung in 1992 in the same spirit of architectural chinoiserie.

C.Y. Lee & Partners

AMOCO BUILDING

(Standard Oil)

11

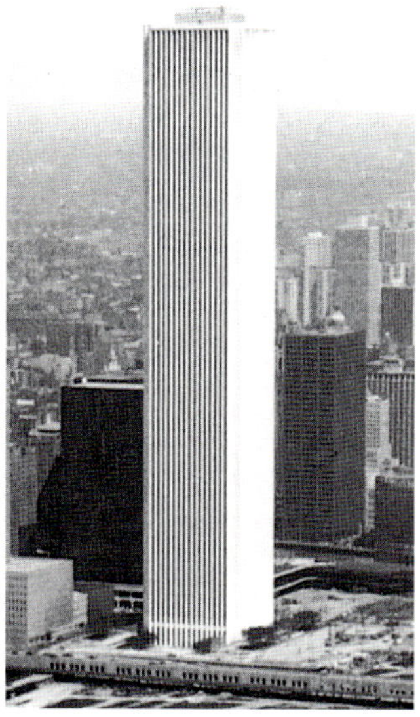

Chicago, United States
80 stories
346 meters (1,136 feet)
1973

Architects: Edward Durell Stone & Associates, with The Perkins & Will Partnership.
Structural engineers: The Perkins & Will Partnership.
Developer: Standard Oil Company of Indiana.
Steel structure.
Office tower, 260,000 square meters (2.8 million square feet), with underground garage (700 spaces), shops at public area level, and restaurant on the 80th floor.

One of the first skyscrapers to be equipped with double-decker elevators. The original white marble facing was replaced by gray granite in 1990.

© Hedrich-Blessing

JOHN HANCOCK CENTER

12

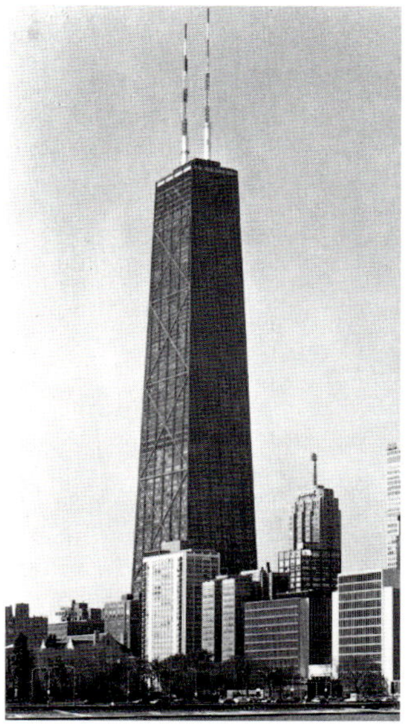

Chicago, United States
100 stories
344 meters (1,127 feet)
1969

Architects: Skidmore, Owings & Merrill, Chicago (Bruce Graham).
Engineers: Skidmore, Owings & Merrill, Chicago (Fazlur Khan).
Developer: John Hancock Mutual Life Insurance Company.
Steel structure.
Mixed-use building, office and residential, 711 apartments on 47 stories, with shops and parking as well as a public observation platform on the 94th floor and a duplex panoramic restaurant on the 95th and 96th floors.

The highest residences in the world.
The base of the building and its public plaza, below the level of the avenue, have recently been remodeled.

Buildings & Data

SHUN HING SQUARE

(Di Wang Commercial Building)

13

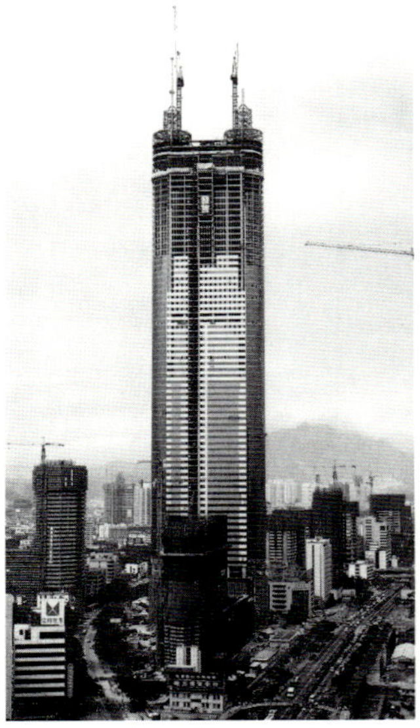

Shenzhen, China (People's Republic), 81 stories
325 meters (1,066 feet)
1996, under construction

Architects: K.Y. Cheung Design Associates, in association with American Design Associates.
Consultant design architects: Y.S. Wang, Shenzhen Architectural Design General Institute.
Structural engineers: Nippon Steel Corporation.
Mechanical and electrical engineers: Associated Consulting Engineers.
Developers: Karbony Investment Ltd.
Steel structure.
Office tower, 138,000 square meters (1,485,000 square feet), with observation platforms on four levels.

The tallest tower in the People's Republic of China, culminating at 384 meters (1,260 feet) at the summit of two masts.
The office tower is part of a larger complex containing 332 luxury apartments, a 22,000 square meters (237,000 square feet) shopping mall, and a car park with 900 spaces, all at about 2 kilometers (1.2 miles) from the Chinese border.

Kumagai Gumi

SKY CENTRAL PLAZA

14

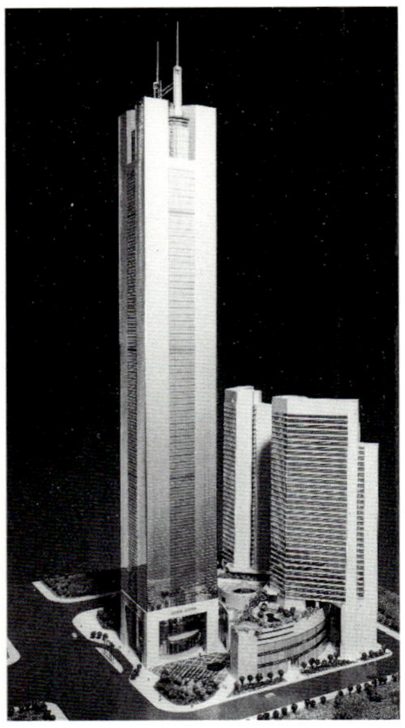

Guangzhou, China (People's Republic), 80 stories
322 meters (1,056 feet)
1996, under construction

Architects: Dennis Lau & Ng Chun Man.
Structural engineers: Maunsell Consultants Asia.
Developer: Kumagai Gumi (Hong Kong).
Concrete structure.
Office tower.

The building culminates at 391 meters (1,283 feet) at the summit of two masts. The complex also includes two residential towers, each of 38 stories, joined by a semi-circular commercial podium on four levels.

Dennis Lau & Ng Chun Man

BAIYOKE TOWER II

15

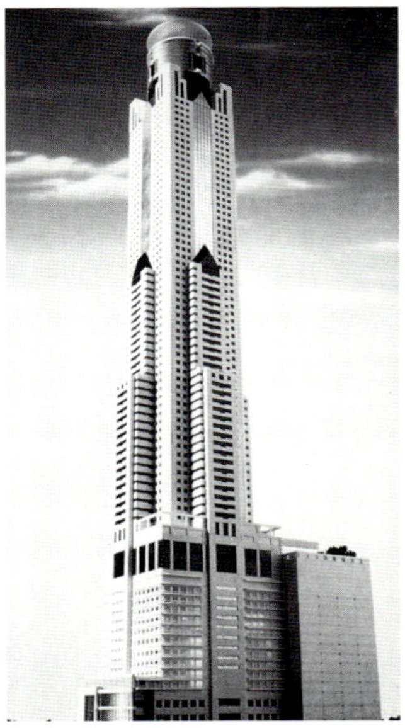

Bangkok, Thaïland
90 stories
320 meters (1,050 feet)
1997, under construction

Architects: Plan Architects Co, in association with Humanist Co. and Plan Associates Co.
Structural engineers: Arun Chaiseri Consulting Engineers Co.
Mechanical engineers: W. and Associates Consultant Co.
Developer: Land Development Co.
Concrete structure.
Mixed-use building containing a 700-room hotel, shops on 16,700 square meters (180,000 square feet), and 890 parking spaces.

The Baiyoke I Tower, 42 stories, 150 meters (495 feet) high, was completed in 1987. The two towers are situated in one of the densest and congested districts of the city.

Plan Architects Co

CHRYSLER BUILDING

16

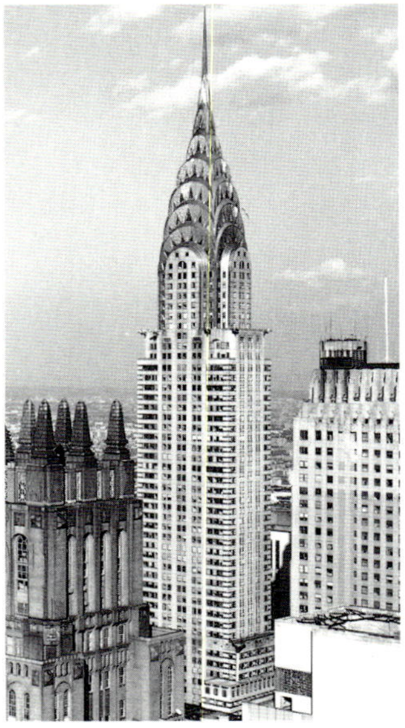

New York, United States
77 stories
319 meters (1,046 feet)
1930

Architect: William Van Alen.
Developer: Walter P. Chrysler.
Steel structure.
Office tower.

In 1930 the Chrysler Building dethroned the Eiffel Tower as the world's tallest building. Four months later it was itself unseated by the Empire State Building. Masterpiece of New York Art Deco and crowned by a spectacular fish-scale summit, the Chrysler Building fulfilled the double function of advertising image for the automobile corporation and symbol of Manhattan. It was designated a historic landmark in 1978.

© Benoît Roland

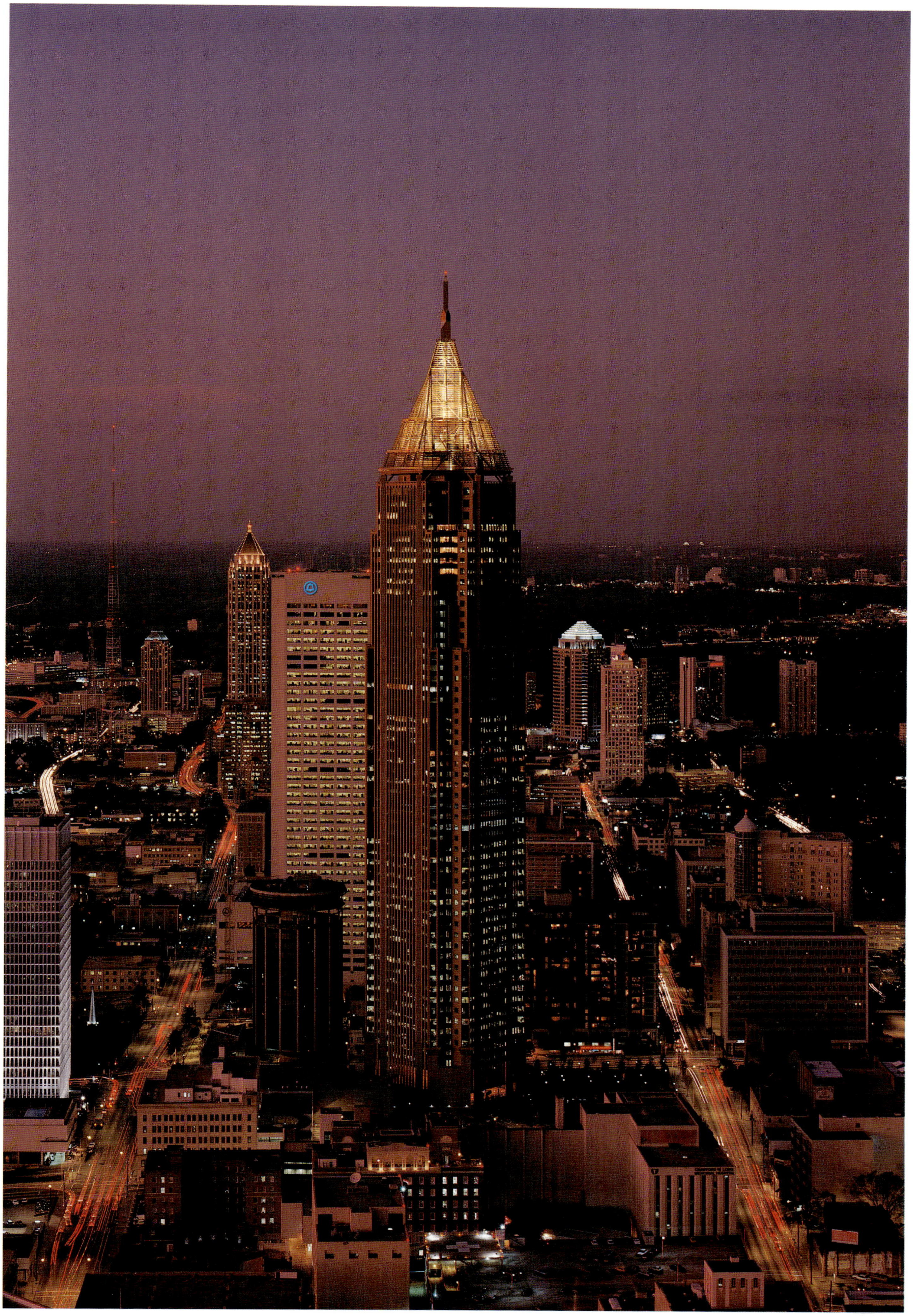

NationsBank Plaza, Atlanta. Kevin Roche John Dinkeloo and Associates, architects, 1992. In the background to the left, One Atlantic Center with its pavilion roof (1987).
© Dennis O'Kain.

NATIONSBANK PLAZA
(C&S Plaza)

17

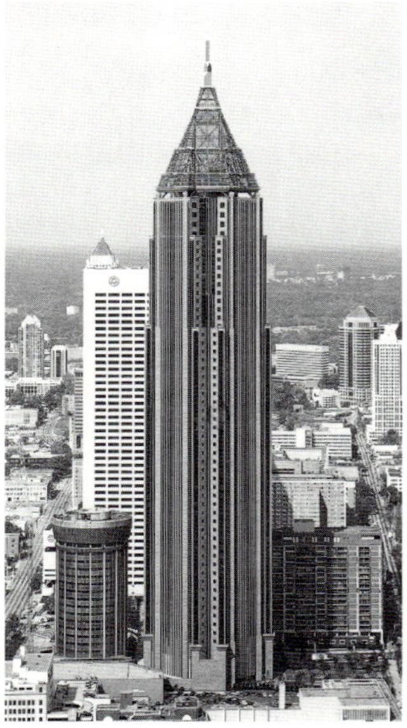

Atlanta, United States
55 stories
312 meters (1,023 feet)
1992

Architects: Kevin Roche John Dinkeloo and Associates.
Structural engineers: CBM Engineers Inc. (Joe Colaco).
Mechanical and electrical engineers: Newcomb & Boyd.
Developer: Cousins Properties Incorporated.
Mixed steel and concrete structure.
Office tower containing 5 underground parking levels and, in a lateral annex of 3 levels, the banking hall, a conference center, sports club, and shops.

Surrounded by a huge park, isolated in a low-rise environment halfway between Peachtree Center and the new urban center of upper midtown, the tower constitutes a major punctuation mark in the city skyline, an effect further emphasized by its being set at a 45° angle to the alignment of the adjacent streets.

Kevin Roche John Dinkeloo and Associates

FIRST INTERSTATE WORLD CENTER (Library Tower)

18

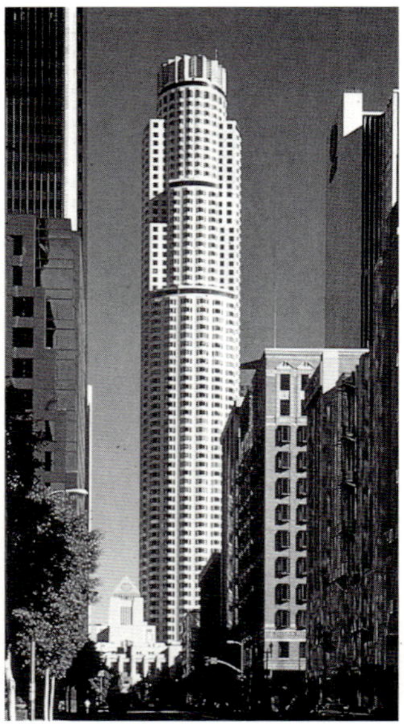

Los Angeles, United States
75 stories
310 meters (1,018 feet)
1989

Architects: Pei Cobb Freed & Partners (Henry Cobb and Harold Fredenburgh); Ellerbe Becket & Associates, architects of record.
Structural engineers: CBM Engineers Inc.
Mechanical engineers: James A. Knowles and Associates.
Electrical engineers: Levine / Seegal Associates.
Developer: Maguire Thomas Partners.
Mixed steel and concrete structure.
Office tower, 120,000 square meters (1,292,000 square feet).

The tower uses the air rights belonging to the site of the Los Angeles municipal library opposite, a historic monument designed by Bertram Goodhue in 1926. This transfer of rights financed the restoration of the library, its extension and the conservation of the garden that surrounds it. The treatment of the ground floor of the tower also creates a pedestrian link between the old center of the city and the new raised district of Bunker Hill (landscape architect: Lawrence Halprin & Associates).

© Jane Lidz

TEXAS COMMERCE TOWER

19

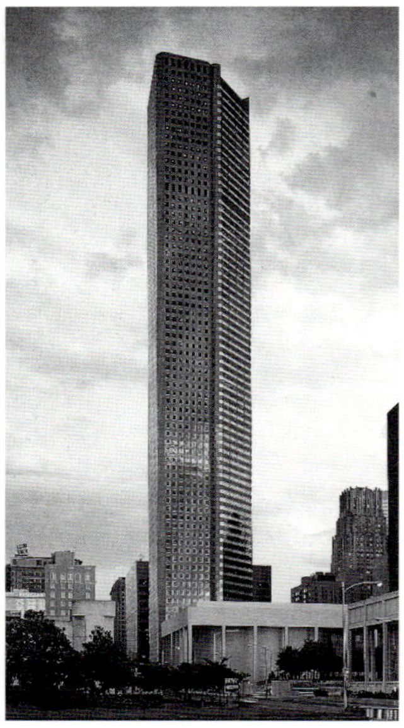

Houston, United States
75 stories
305 meters (1,000 feet)
1982

Architects: I.M. Pei & Partners (Ieoh Ming Pei), in association with 3D / International.
Structural engineers: CBM Engineers Inc. (Joe Colaco).
Mechanical and electrical engineers: I.A. Naman + Associates, Inc.
Developer: Gerald D. Hines Interests, in association with The Texas Commerce Bank.
Mixed steel and concrete structure.
Office tower with a sky-lobby accessible to the public on the 60th floor.

The tallest building in Houston. At the project's outset The Texas Commerce Bank's objective was to project a powerful image.

© Richard Payne

RYUGYONG HOTEL

20

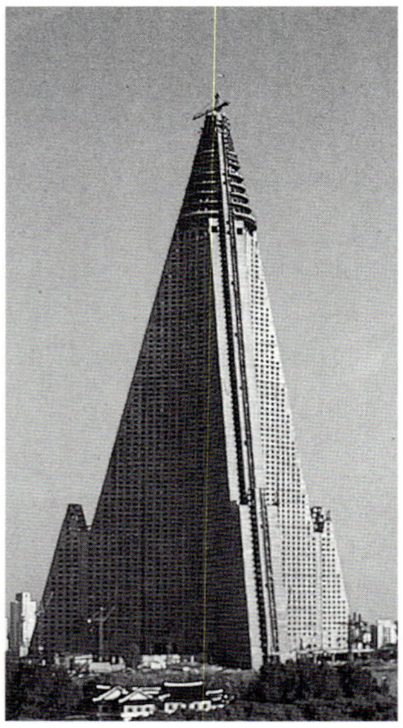

Pyongyang, North Korea
105 stories
300 meters (984 feet)
Under construction

Architects: Baikdoosan Architects & Engineers (H.C. Choi et I.L. Choi).
Engineers: Baikdoosan Architects & Engineers (J.M. Park).
Developer: Government of North Korea.
Concrete structure.
Hotel.

Hotel building work interrupted with no completion date announced. The fabric has been finished since 1991.
The project was designed by the municipal office of public architecture.

© Melvyn Calderon / J.B.Pictures

TWO PRUDENTIAL PLAZA

21

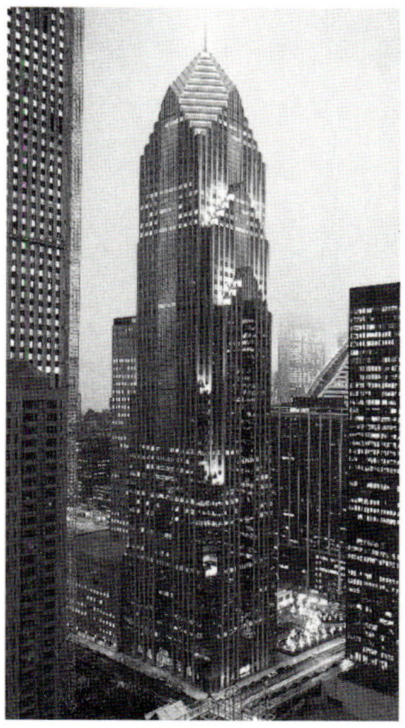

Chicago, United States
64 stories
298 meters (978 feet)
1990

Architects: Loebl Schlossman and Hackl, Architects.
Structural engineers: CBM Engineers Inc.
Mechanical and electrical engineers: Environmental Systems Design Inc.
Developer: The Prudential Property Company.
Concrete structure.
Office tower, 110,000 square meters (1.184 million square feet).

The construction of the tower forms part of a larger operation including the restoration of an existing tower dating from 1955 (41 stories), the creation of a public plaza and a new underground garage.

© Steinkamp / Ballogg Chicago

FIRST INTERSTATE BANK PLAZA

(Allied Bank Plaza)

22

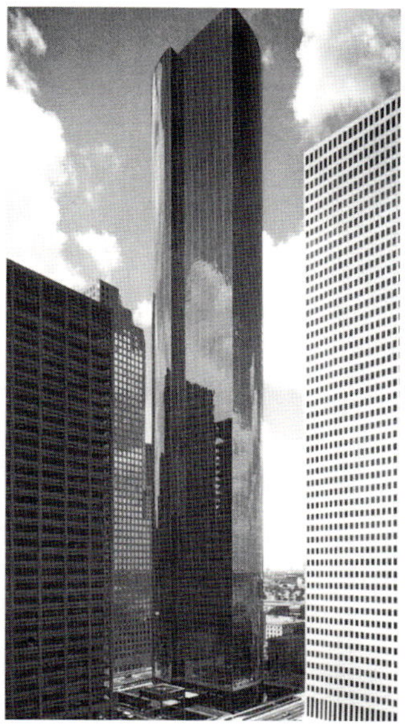

Houston, United States
71 stories
296 meters (972 feet)
1983

Architects: Skidmore, Owings & Merrill (Edward C. Bassett, San Francisco, and Richard Keating, Houston), in association with Lloyd Jones Brewer & Associates.
Structural engineers: Skidmore, Owings & Merrill.
Developer: Century Development Corporation.
Steel structure.
Office tower, 170,000 square meters (1.8 million square feet).

The only skyscraper in Houston that gives as much importance to access from street level as underground access at the pedestrian tunnel network level. The entrances are linked by a 2-level outdoor public space.

© Nick Merrick / Hedrich-Blessing

LANDMARK TOWER

23

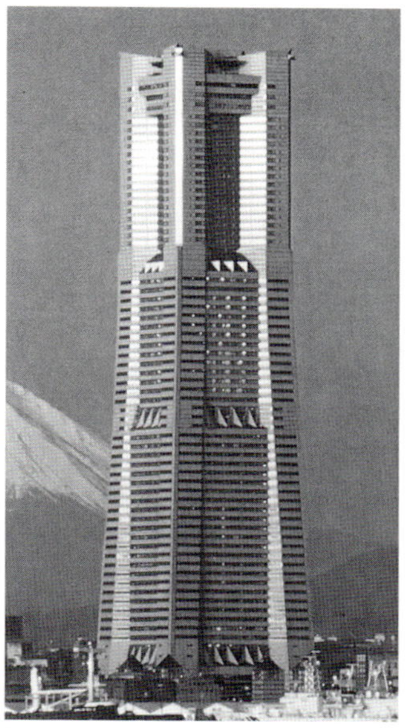

Yokohama, Japan
70 stories
296 meters (971 feet)
1993

Architects: The Stubbins Associates (Design consultants), in association with Mitsubishi Estate Architectural & Engineering Office.
Structural engineers: Mitsubishi Estate Architectural & Engineering Office, in association with LeMessurier Associates, consultants.
Mechanical engineers: Syska & Hennessy.
Developer: Mitsubishi Estate Company, Ltd.
Steel structure.
Mixed-use building containing a vast commercial atrium, 52 floors of offices and a 600-room Nikko hotel on the 15 upper floors.

The tallest building in Japan, set like a lighthouse on the mouth of the Ooka River.
Panoramic restaurants and observation platform at the summit.

Nikko Hotels

311 SOUTH WACKER DRIVE

24

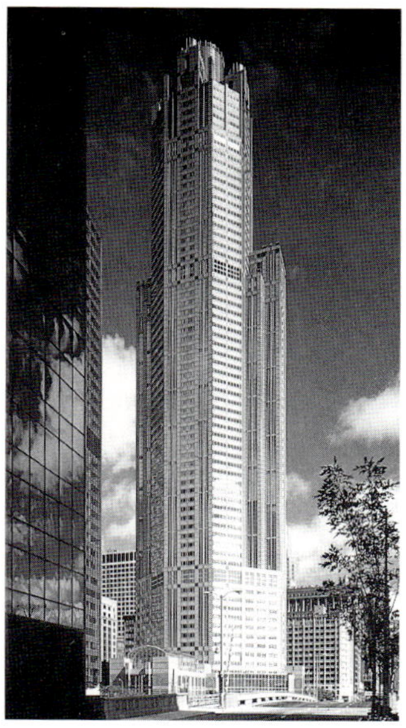

Chicago, United States
65 stories
292 meters (959 feet)
1990

Architects: Kohn Pedersen Fox Associates (William Pedersen, Richard del Monte), in association with HKS, Inc.
Structural engineers: Brockette & Associates ; Chris P. Stefanos Associates.
Mechanical engineers: Brady, Loheman & Pendelton, Inc.
Developers: Lincoln Property Company, in association with Teachers Insurance and Annuity Association.
Concrete structure.
Office tower.

At the foot of the tower are a public space (awaiting two more towers of the same height initially planned), a covered walkway, and a huge winter garden accessible to the public.

© George Lambros

JUBILEE STREET / QUEEN'S ROAD CENTRAL

25

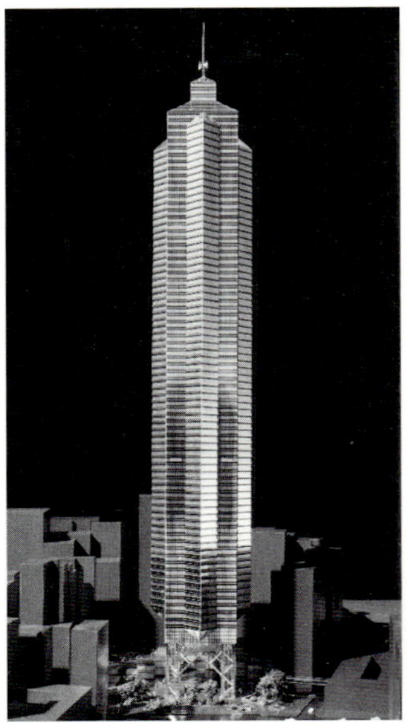

Hong Kong
69 stories
292 meters (958 feet)
1997, under construction

Architects: Dennis Lau & Ng Chun Man, Architects & Engineers.
Engineers: Maunsell Consultants Asia.
Developer: Land Development Corporation.
Steel structure.
Office tower and shops.

The more central of the two developments carried out in the business center by the same developer (see No. 95).

Dennis Lau & Ng Chun Man

FIRST CANADIAN PLACE (First Bank Tower)

26

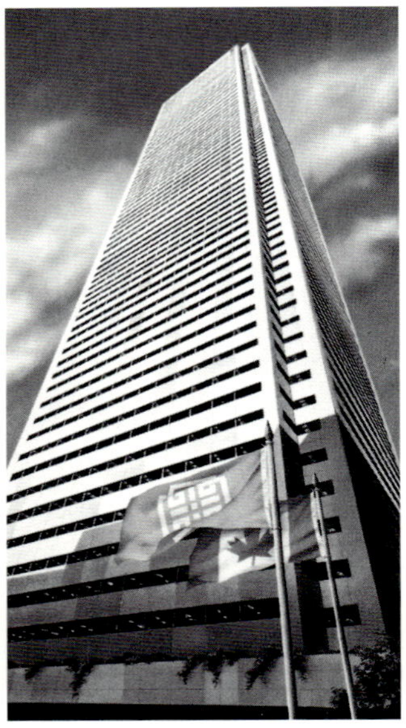

Toronto, Canada
72 stories
290 meters (952 feet)
1975

Architects: Edward Durell Stone & Associates, with Bregman + Hamann.
Structural engineers: M.S. Yolles Associates.
Mechanical engineers: G. Granek & Associates; Andrew Hidi & Associates.
Electrical engineers: Jack Chisvin & Associates; E A. Rae & Associates.
Developer: Olympia & York Developments Ltd.
Steel structure.
Office tower.

The tallest building in Canada and one of the first to be fitted with double-decker elevators.

Buildings & Data

AMERICAN INTERNATIONAL BUILDING (Cities Service Building)

27

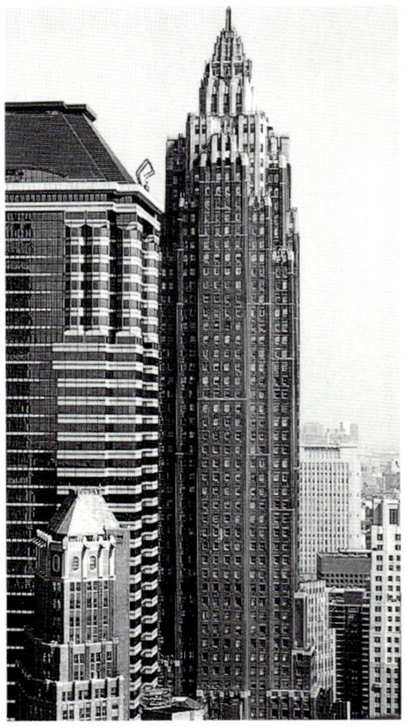

New York, United States
66 stories
290 meters (950 feet)
1932

Architect: Clinton & Russell.
Developer: Cities Service.
Steel structure.
Office tower.

The tower is crowned by a 10-meter (33 feet) luminous cube, "a new style roof, sensational in its originality!" stated the advertising of the time.
Originally it was equipped with the first double-decker elevators which, extremely unpopular and no doubt inefficient in this pioneering version, were quickly done away with. The Art Deco solarium on the 66th floor, however, still exists today.
For a long time the building was called 60 Wall Street, although it is not situated there. Linked by a walkway at 6th-floor level to a building on Wall Street, it took advantage of the prestige of this address.

© Benoît Roland

ONE LIBERTY PLACE

28

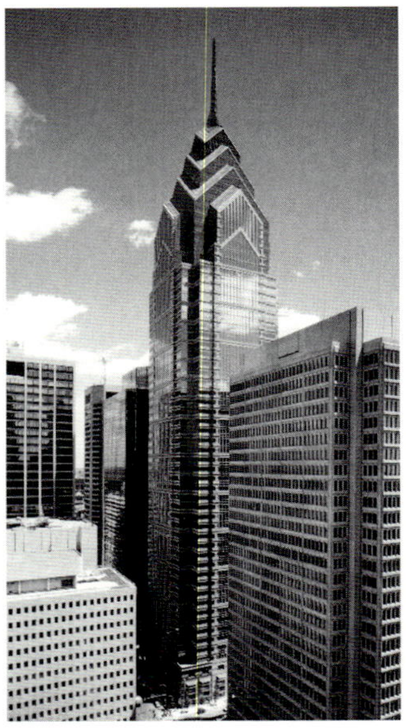

Philadelphia, United States
61 stories
287 meters (945 feet)
1987

Architects: Murphy / Jahn (Helmut Jahn).
Structural engineers: Lev Zetlin Associates, Inc.
Mechanical and electrical engineers: Flack + Kurtz.
Developer: The Rouse Associates.
Steel structure.
Office tower, 125,000 square meters (1.3 million square feet).

The building is part of a complex containing Two Liberty Place, a second office tower—also designed by Murphy / Jahn (see No. 50)—and a hotel.

Murphy / Jahn

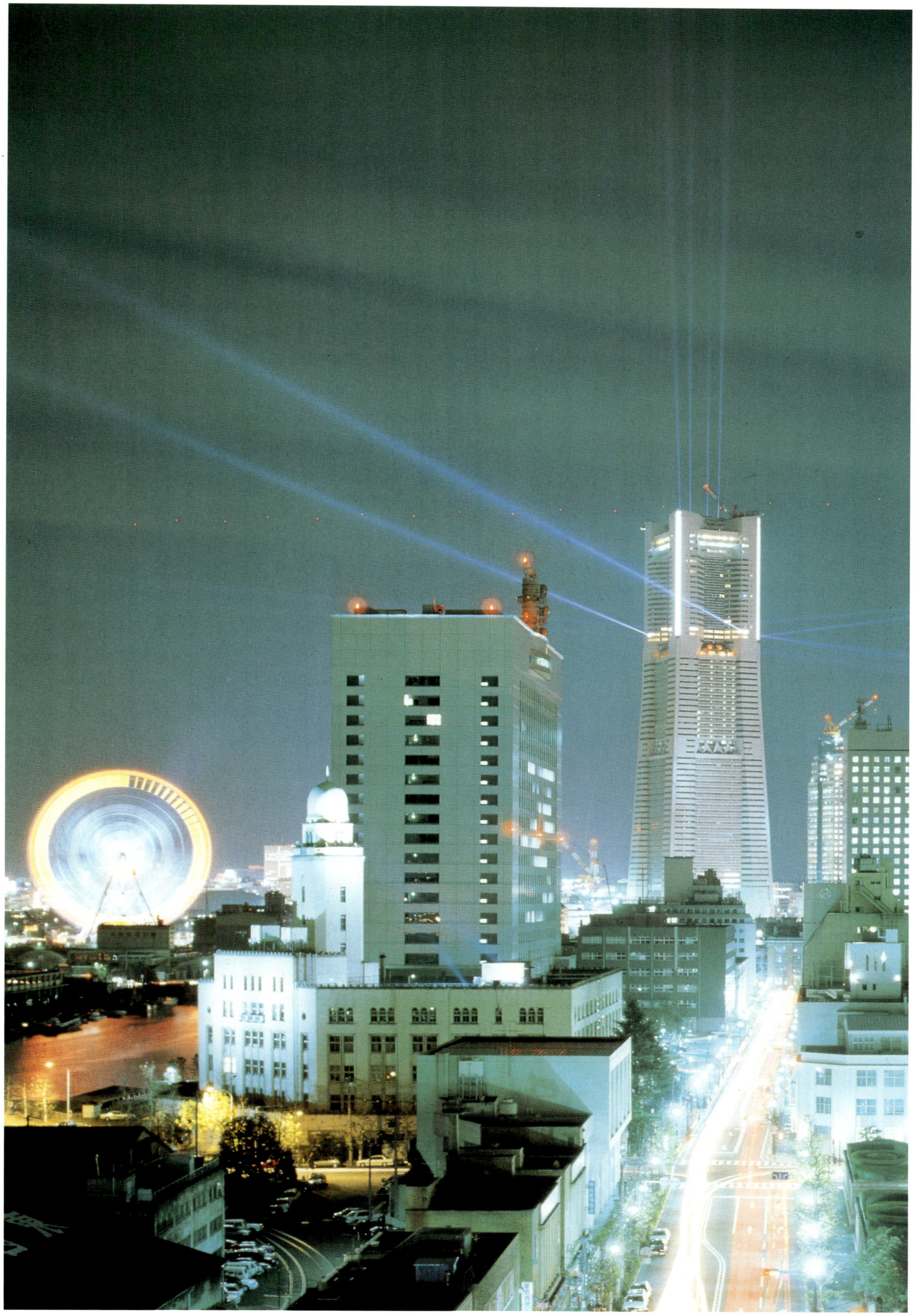

Landmark Tower, Yokohama. The Stubbins Associates, architects, 1993, in association with Mitsubishi Estate Architectural & Engineering Office.
Nikko Hotels.

COLUMBIA SEAFIRST CENTER

(Columbia Center)

29

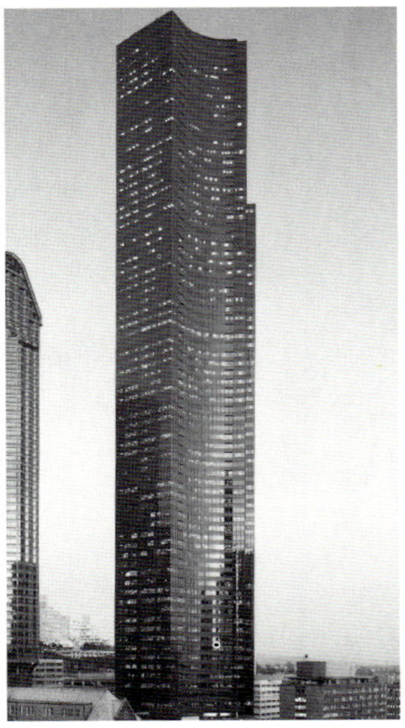

Seattle, United States
76 stories
287 meters (943 feet)
1985

Architects: Chester Lindsey Architects.
Structural engineers: Skiling Ward Rogers Barkshire, Inc.
Developer: Martin Selig.
Mixed steel and concrete structure.
Office tower, 130,000 square meters (1.4 million square feet), with 10,500 square meters (113,000 square feet) of shop space on 4 levels, including public area, and a 6-level underground garage.

The original shape of this tower, of which the ground plan is the trademark, is generated by three segments of a ring, backing on to each other in the form of a triangle and each rising to a different height—42, 60, and 76 stories respectively.
Shops and restaurants occupy 5,000 square meters (54,000 square feet) on the lower levels of the building.

© John Sutton

40 WALL STREET

(Bank of Manhattan Trust Building)

30

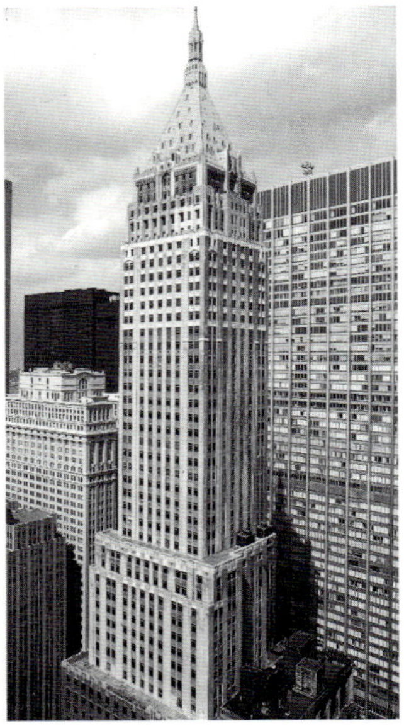

New York, United States
70 stories
283 meters (927 feet)
1930

Architects: H. Craig Severance, in association with Yasuo Matsui; Shreve & Lamb, consultant architects.
Steel structure.
Office tower.

During its construction the tower was in direct competition for the height record with the Chrysler Building, also under construction. Its construction was extremely fast—less than a year, including the demolition of the existing buildings on the site.

© Benoît Roland

NATIONSBANK PLAZA

(InterFirst Plaza at Dallas Main Center)

31

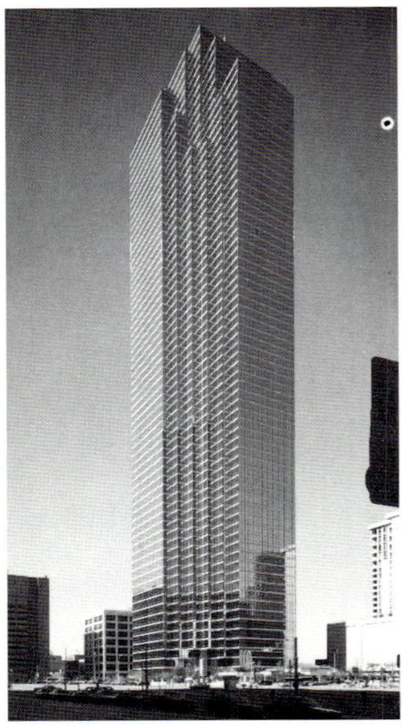

Dallas, United States
72 stories
281 meters (921 feet)
1985

Architects: JPJ Architects (Jarvis Putty Jarvis).
Structural engineers: LeMessurier Associates, in association with Brockette.
Mechanical and electrical engineers: Purdy McGuire, Inc.
Developers: Bramalea Texas, in association with Prudential Realty Group.
Mixed steel and concrete structure.
Office tower, 177,000 square meters (1.9 million square feet), with shopping gallery.

The project originally planned for a hotel (phase 2) and a second tower identical to the first (phase 3).

© R. Greg Hursley

OUB CENTRE

32

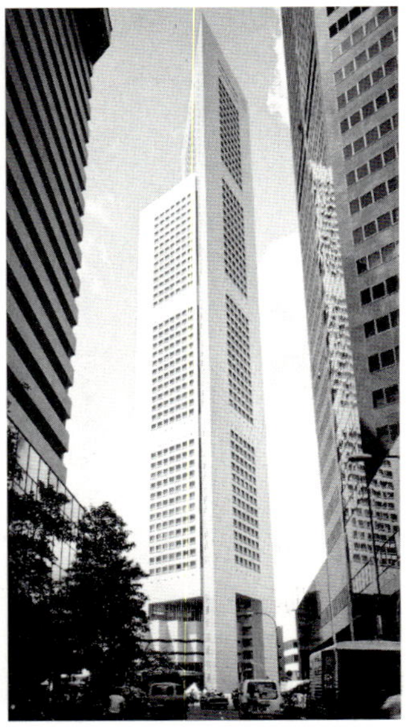

Singapore
66 stories
280 meters (919 feet)
1986

Architects: Kenzo Tange Associates, in association with SAA Partnership.
Structural and mechanical engineers: Bylander Meinhardt Partnership.
Developer: OUB Centre Limited.
Steel structure.
Office tower, 101,784 square meters (1.1 million square feet), with a shopping center on six levels connected to a subway station.

First of the three tallest skyscrapers in Singapore (see Nos. 33 and 34), the OUB Centre is characterized by a tapering effect accentuated by an architectural device dear to the architect artificially dividing the tower into two distinct volumes.

Kenzo Tange Associates

UOB PLAZA

33

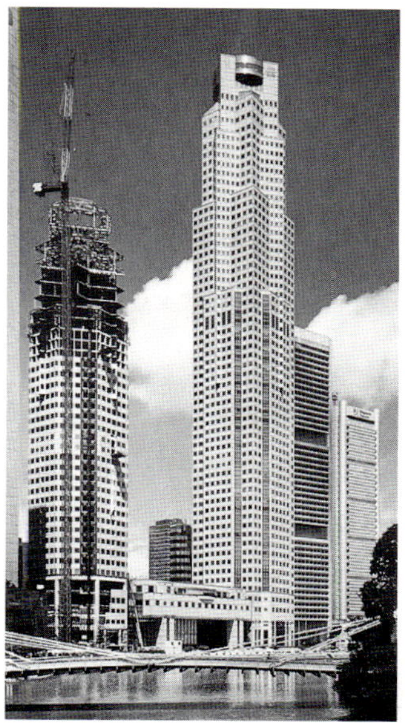

Singapore
66 stories
280 meters (919 feet)
1992

Architects: Kenzo Tange Associates, in association with Architects 61.
Structural engineers: Ove Arup & Partners.
Mechanical engineers: J. Roger Preston & Partners.
Developer: United Overseas Bank Ltd.
Steel structure.
Office tower, 96,700 square meters (1 million square feet).

The tower forms part of the UOB Plaza complex, which includes a second tower of 38 stories (renovation and extension of an existing tower) and a lower linking building which contains the banking hall.
Situated in the city's business center, it is next door to the OUB Tower, built six years earlier by the same architect.

Architects 61

REPUBLIC PLAZA

34

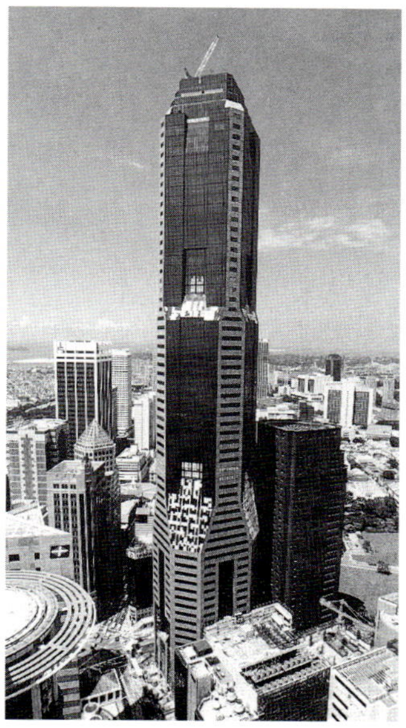

Singapore
66 stories
280 meters (919 feet)
1995

Architects: Kisho Kurokawa Architect & Associates, in association with RSP Architects Planners & Engineers.
Structural engineers: RSP Architects Planners & Engineers.
Mechanical and electrical engineers: Squire Mech Pte Ltd.
Developer: City Developments Limited (CDL).
Mixed steel and concrete structure.
Office tower, 126,237 square meters (1.36 million square feet), with a basement shopping level.

The tower, like the two previous ones, culminates at 280 meters (919 feet), the maximum height authorized by Singapore national aviation.
It is linked at ground floor and mezzanine levels to a 10-story garage.

Kisho Kurokawa Architect & Associates

CITICORP CENTER

35

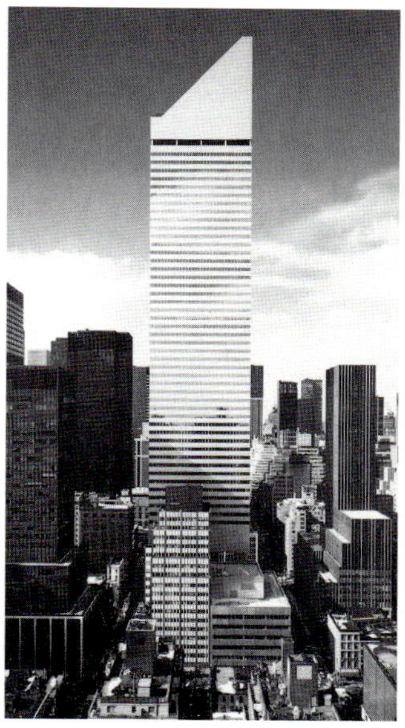

New York, United States
59 stories
279 meters (915 feet)
1977

Architects: Hugh Stubbins and Associates; Emery Roth & Sons, associated architects.
Structural engineers: LeMessurier Associates / SCI and The Office of James Ruderman.
Mechanical and electrical engineers: Joseph R. Loring and Associates.
Developer: Citicorp.
Steel structure.
Office tower with commercial atrium, subway access, and chapel.

The first building to be equipped at the outset with an MTD (Mass Tuned Damper) to reduce lateral oscillation due to wind pressure.

© Norman McGrath

SCOTIA PLAZA

36

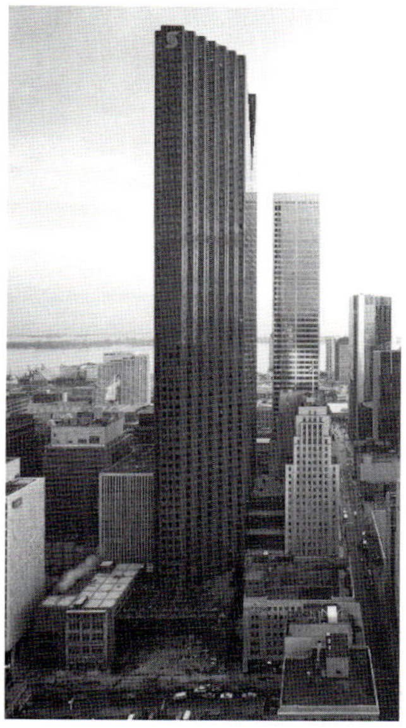

Toronto, Canada
68 stories
275 meters (902 feet)
1989

Architects: The Webb Zerafa Menkès Housden Partnership.
Structural engineers: Quinn Dressel & Associates.
Mechanical engineers: The Mitchell Partnership.
Developer: Campeau Corporation.
Mixed steel and concrete structure.
Office tower, 150,000 square meters (1.6 million square feet).

At the north and south entrances two large glazed canopies artificially re-establish the alignment of the tower with the street. The main banking hall is lit from above by an 11-story atrium and a set of light wells which also light the pedestrian area of the basement.

The Webb Zerafa Menkès Housden Partnership

TRANSCO TOWER

37

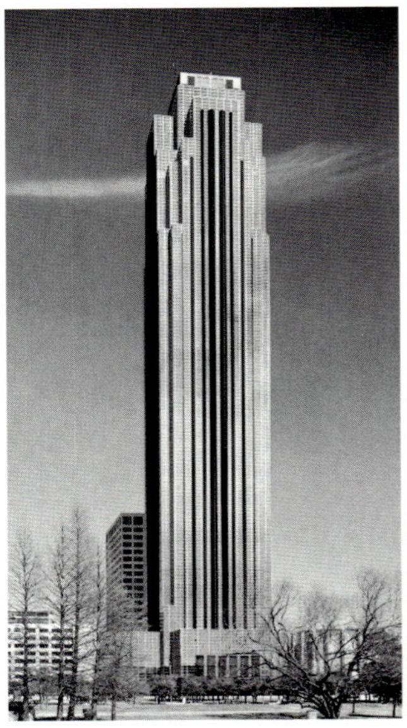

Houston, United States
64 stories
275 meters (901 feet)
1983

Architects: Johnson / Burgee Architects, in association with Morris-Aubry.
Structural engineers: CBM Engineers Inc.
Mechanical engineers: I. A. Naman + Associates.
Developer: Gerald D. Hines Interests.
Steel structure.
Office tower, 150,000 square meters (1.6 million square feet).

A long rectangular garden lies at the foot of the tower with a monumental fountain 20 meters (60 feet) high closing the vista (1985). The rotating searchlight at the summit of the tower repeats the lighting system installed at the top of the Palmolive Building in Chicago (architects Holabird and Root, 1929).

© Richard Payne

SOCIETY CENTER

38

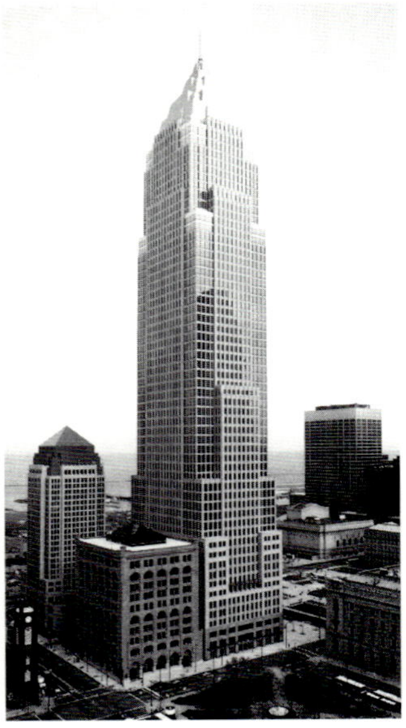

Cleveland, United States
57 stories
271 meters (888 feet)
1991

Architect: Cesar Pelli & Associates, with Kendall / Heaton Associates.
Mechanical and electrical engineers: Flack + Kurtz, Chicago.
Developers: Richard E. Jacobs and David H. Jacobs.
Mixed steel and concrete structure.
Office tower, 127,000 square meters (1.37 million square feet).

The project includes the rehabilitation of the Society for Savings Bank Building (architects Burnham and Root, 1889) and the construction of a 403-room hotel.

© Mort Tucker Photography

AT&T CORPORATE CENTER

39

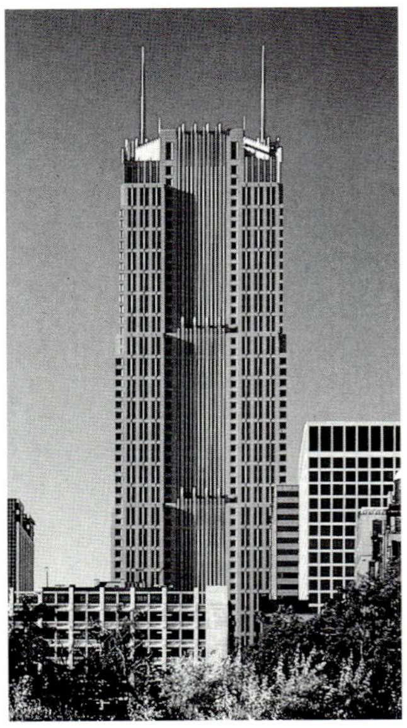

Chicago, United States
60 stories
270 meters (885 feet)
1989

Architects: Skidmore, Owings & Merrill, Chicago (Adrian Smith).
Engineers: Skidmore, Owings & Merrill, Chicago (Stan Korista, Chris Brown).
Developer: Stein & Company.
Mixed steel and concrete structure.
Office tower, 158,000 square meters (1.7 million square feet).

In 1992 the tower was complemented by a second, lower structure of 35 stories as planned in the original project.

© Nick Merrick / Hedrich-Blessing

900 NORTH MICHIGAN

40

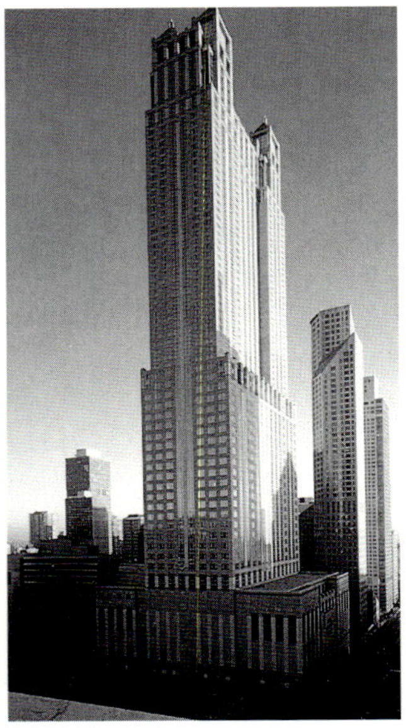

Chicago, United States
66 stories
265 meters (871 feet)
1988

Architects: Kohn Pedersen Fox Associates, with Perkins & Will.
Structural engineers: Alfred Benesch & Company.
Mechanical engineers: Environmental Systems Design, Inc.
Developer: Urban Investment & Development Company (JMB Realty Corporation).
Mixed steel and concrete structure.
Mixed-use building including 125 residential units (from the 48th to 66th floor), a Four Seasons Hotel (from the 30th to 46th floor), 20 floors of offices and a commercial atrium of 8 floors forming the base of the tower.

The building culminates with four corner pavilions which act as four "lanterns" easily recognizable on the Chicago skyline by night.

© Hedrich-Blessing

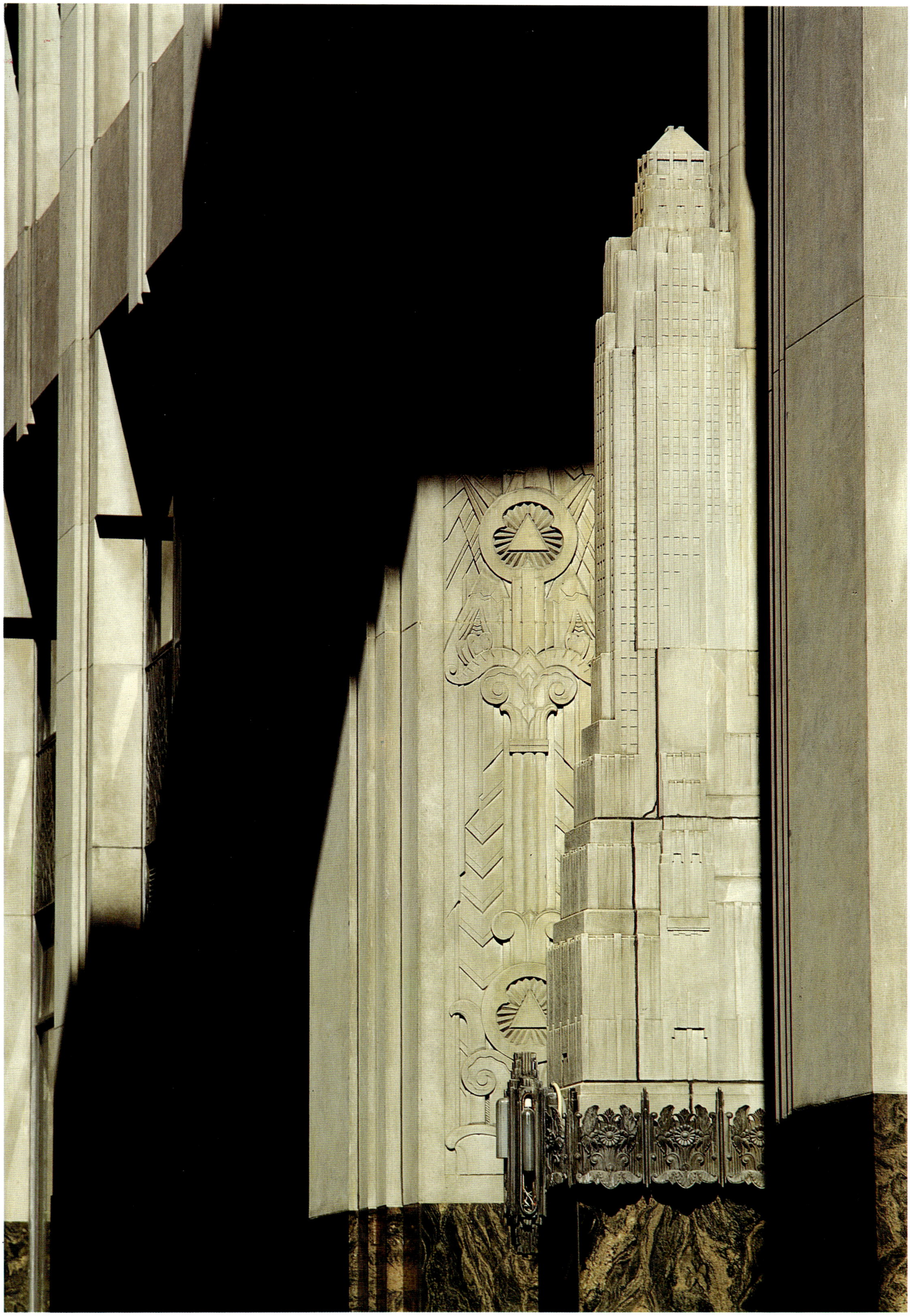

American International Building, New York, detail of the entrance. Clinton & Russell, architects, 1932.
© Benoît Roland.

NATIONSBANK CORPORATE CENTER

41

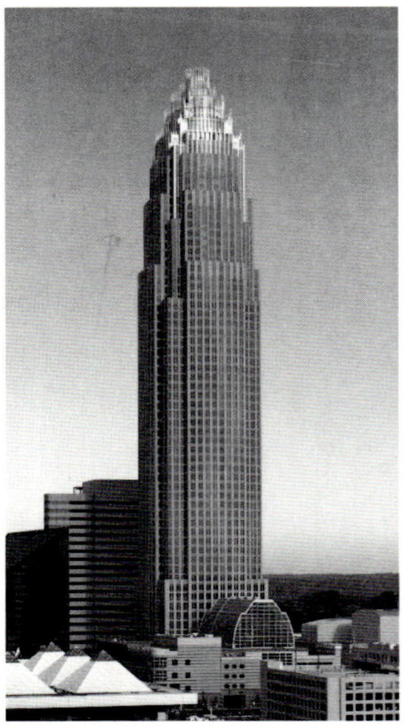

Charlotte, United States
60 stories
265 meters (871 feet)
1992

Architects: Cesar Pelli & Associates, in association with HKS, Inc.
Structural engineers: Walter P. Moore & Associates.
Mechanical engineers: B. L. & P. Engineers, Inc.
Developers: Lincoln Property Company, NationsBank Corporation and Charter Properties.
Concrete structure.
Office tower, 130,000 square meters (1.4 million square feet).

The project includes the installation of two public plazas and a huge public lobby lined by shops.

© Timothy Hursley

ONE PEACHTREE CENTER

42

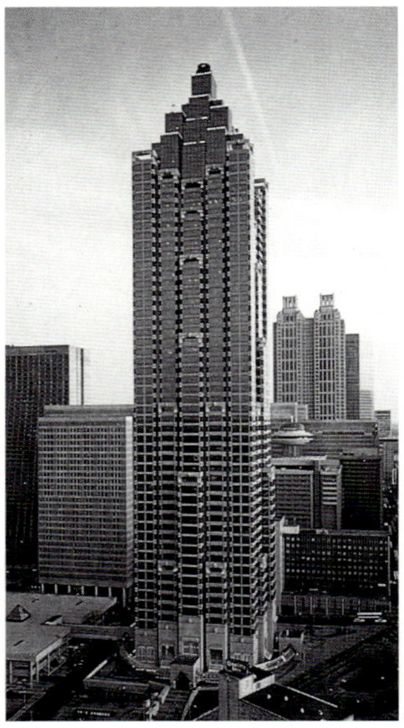

Atlanta, United States
60 stories
264 meters (867 feet)
1992

Architects: John Portman & Associates.
Structural engineers: John Portman & Associates.
Civil engineers: W. L. Jorden & Company, Inc.
Mechanical engineers: Newcomb & Boyd.
Developer: Portman Properties.
Concrete structure.
Office tower, 108,000 square meters (1.16 million square feet).

The ground floor of the building contains a huge public contemporary art gallery, extended out of doors by an open-air exhibition area.

© Michael Portman

CANADA TRUST TOWER

43

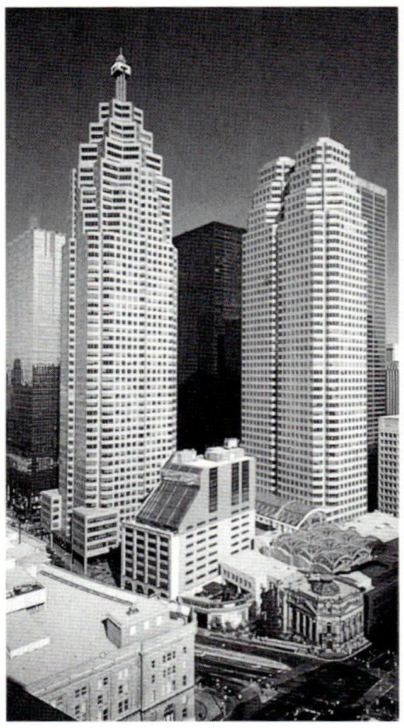

Toronto, Canada
51 stories
263 meters (863 feet)
1990

Architects: Skidmore, Owings & Merrill, in association with Bregman + Hamann.
Structural engineers: Yolles Partnership.
Mechanical engineers: The Mitchell Partnership.
Developer: Brookfield Developments Ltd.
Mixed steel and concrete structure.
Office tower, 104,000 square meters (1.1 million square feet).

The Canada Trust Tower is part of an ensemble including a second, lower tower, the Bay-Wellington Tower, 47 stories, and a covered arcade designed by the Catalan architect Santiago Calatrava.

© Robert Burley

WATER TOWER PLACE

44

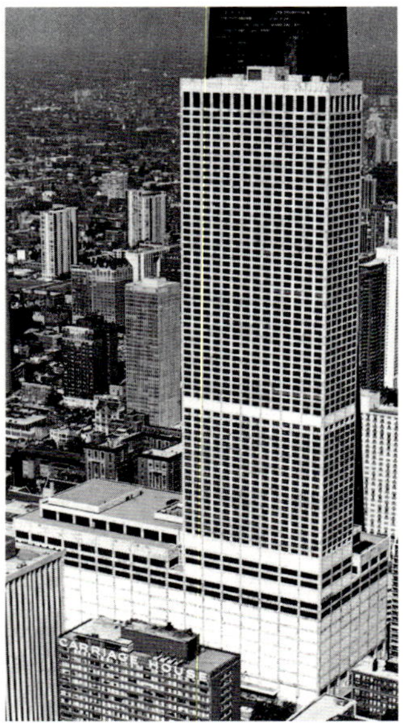

Chicago, United States
74 stories
262 meters (859 feet)
1976

Architects: Loebl Schlossman Dart and Hackl, in association with C.F. Murphy Associates.
Consultant architects (shopping area): Warren Platner Associates Architects.
Structural engineers: C. F. Murphy Associates.
Mechanical and electrical engineers: TRI Ventures 1.
Developer: JMB / Urban Investment and Development Company.
Concrete structure.
Mixed-use building containing 260 luxury apartments, the 400-room Ritz-Carlton Hotel, 21,000 square meters (226,000 square feet) of offices, as well as a commercial atrium, and a seven-screen movie theater.

The world's tallest concrete building at the time of its construction, the offsetting of the tower to the extreme eastern edge of the block was negotiated in order to retain the views and exposure to the sun of the apartments in the neighboring John Hancock Center (see No. 12).

© Tom Cramer

FIRST INTERSTATE TOWER

(United California Bank Building)

45

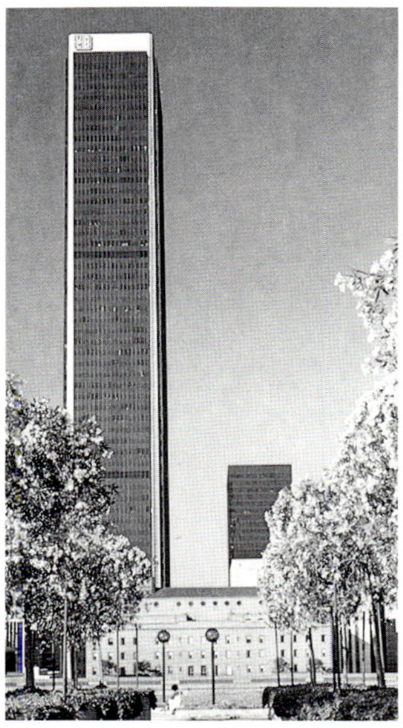

Los Angeles, United States
62 stories
262 meters (858 feet)
1974

Architects: Charles Luckman Associates.
Structural engineers: Erkel, Greenfield Associates, Inc.
Mechanical engineers: Levine and McCann.
Electrical engineers: Michael Garris & Associates.
Developer: United California Bank Realty Corporation and The Equitable Life Assurance Society of the United States.
Steel structure.
Office tower.

The tallest building in Los Angeles for 15 years. Office towers did not appear in the business center of the city until the sixties, after the abolition (in 1957) of a law limiting construction to 13 stories.

© Boyd Connell

TRANSAMERICA PYRAMID

46

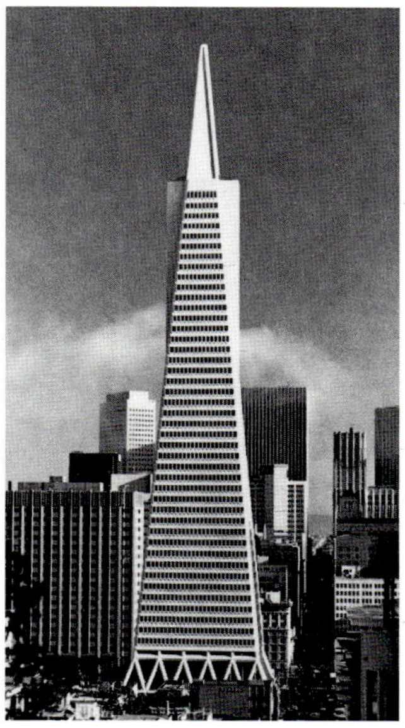

San Francisco, United States
48 stories
260 meters (853 feet)
1972

Architects: William L. Pereira Associates.
Structural engineers: Chin and Hensolt.
Mechanical and electrical engineers: Simonson & Simonson.
Developer: Transamerica Corporation.
Steel structure.
Office tower, 49 000 square meters (527,000 square feet), with a public observation platform on the 27th floor.

Transamerica Pyramid is one of the first skyscrapers, together with the IDS Center in Minneapolis (see No. 76), to have proposed a formal alternative to the box-like buildings of the International Style.

Buildings & Data

G. E. BUILDING

(RCA Building, Rockefeller Center)

47

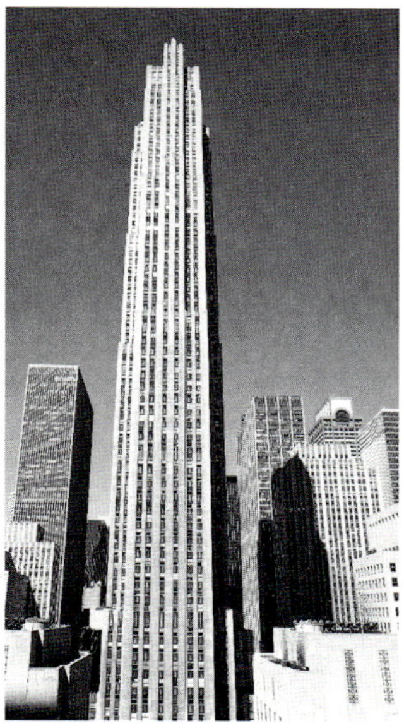

New York, United States
70 stories
259 meters (850 feet)
1933

Architects: Associated Architects (Reinhard and Hofmeister; Corbett, Harrison and MacMurray; Raymond Hood, Godley and Fouilhoux).
Developer: John D. Rockefeller Jr.
Steel structure.
Office tower with public observation platform on the 70th floor and restaurants on the 65th floor.

The RCA Building (now General Electric) is situated in the middle of the complex of some 20 buildings which form Rockefeller Center. The lobby is decorated with murals by José Maria Sert which partly cover murals by Diego Rivera, considered too political at the time, and by Frank Brangwyn. The RCA Building was designated a historic landmark in 1985.

© Benoît Roland

ONE FIRST NATIONAL PLAZA

(First National Bank Building)

48

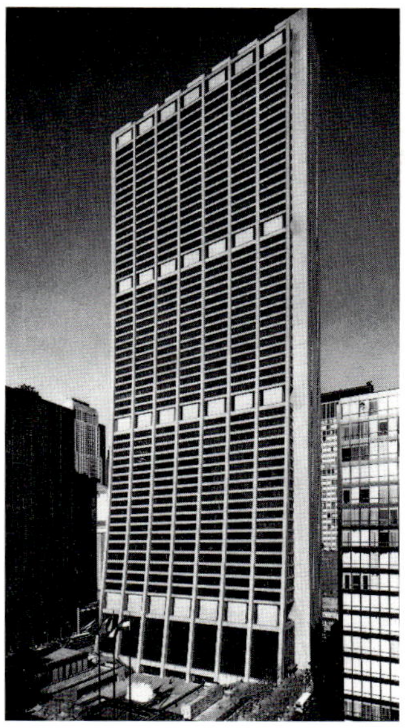

Chicago, United States
60 stories
259 meters (850 feet)
1969

Architects: C. F. Murphy Associates and Perkins & Will.
Engineers: C. F. Murphy Associates and Perkins & Will.
Developer: The First National Bank of Chicago.
Steel structure.
Office tower, 203,600 square meters (2.2 million square feet), with banking hall on the ground floor and mezzanine.

The tower widens at the base following a slightly curved profile. A huge south-facing public plaza planted with trees lies at its foot and gives access to the subway system (mosaic by Marc Chagall).

Buildings & Data

COMMERZBANK

49

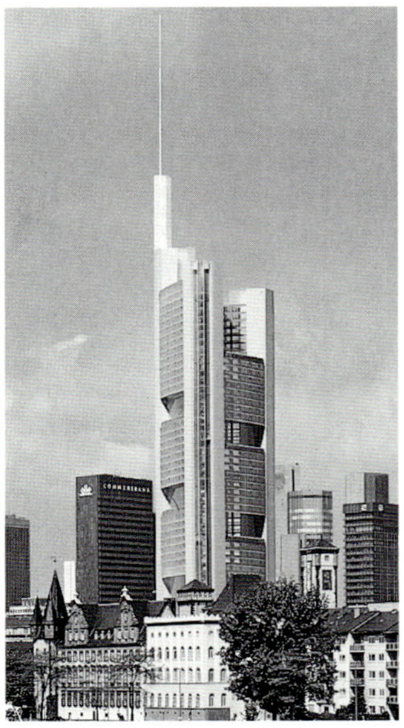

Frankfurt, Germany
60 stories
259 meters (850 feet)
1997, under construction

Architects: Sir Norman Foster and Partners.
Structural engineers, traffic and fire protection: Ove Arup and Partners, in association with Krebs and Keifer.
Mechanical engineers: J. Roger Preston, in association with P & A Pettersson Ahrens.
Electrical engineers: Schad and Hölzel.
Developer: Commerzbank.
Mixed steel and concrete structure.
Office tower.

The tower is made up of three wings arranged in a triangle around a central atrium. On each floor two of the wings contain offices and the third an open air hanging garden. The natural ventilation of the offices and atrium thus achieved contributes to reducing energy costs in the tower.
The tower is part of a larger project including housing, shops, public spaces, and the renovation of an existing high-rise.

Sir Norman Foster and Partners

TWO LIBERTY PLACE

50

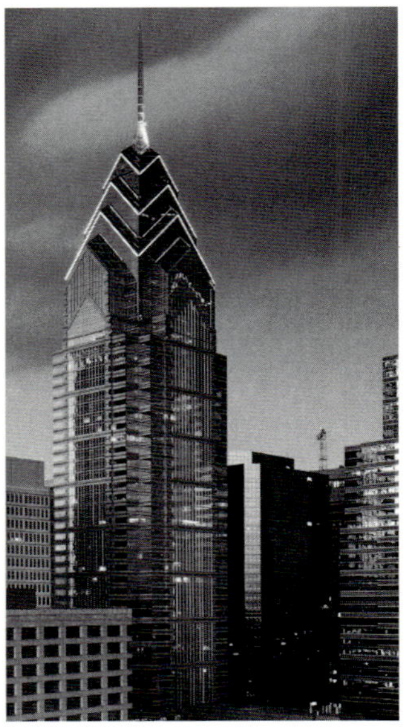

Philadelphia, United States
58 stories
258 meters (848 feet)
1990

Architects: Murphy / Jahn, in association with the Zeidler Roberts Partnership.
Structural engineers: Quinn Dressel.
Mechanical and electrical engineers: The ECE group.
Developer: The Rouse Associates.
Steel structure.
Office tower.

The tower is part of a complex that includes a first office tower, One Liberty Place (see No. 28), also designed by Murphy / Jahn, and a hotel.

Murphy/Jahn

MESSETURM

51

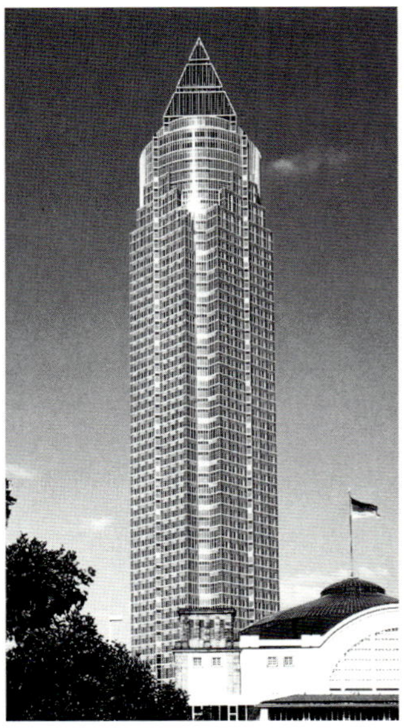

Frankfurt, Germany
70 stories
257 meters (842 feet)
1990

Architects: Murphy / Jahn (Helmut Jahn).
Structural engineer: Dr. Fritz Nötzold.
Mechanical and electrical engineers: Brendel Ingenieure.
Developer: Tishman Speyer Properties.
Concrete structure.
Office tower.

The tallest building in Europe. The tower is part of a complex integrating several low-rise buildings, including a large exhibition hall.

Murphy / Jahn

USX TOWER

(United States Steel Building)

52

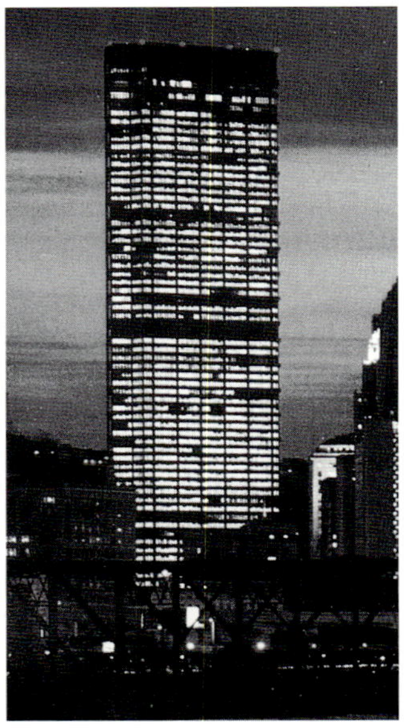

Pittsburgh, United States
64 stories
256 meters (841 feet)
1970

Architects: Harrison & Abramovitz & Abbe.
Structural engineers: Skilling, Helle, Christiansen, Robertson.
Mechanical engineers: Jaros Baum & Bolles.
Developer: United States Steel Corporation.
Steel structure.
Office tower, 270,000 square meters (2.9 million square feet).

One of the largest buildings in the world built on a triangular plan.

The Galbreath Company

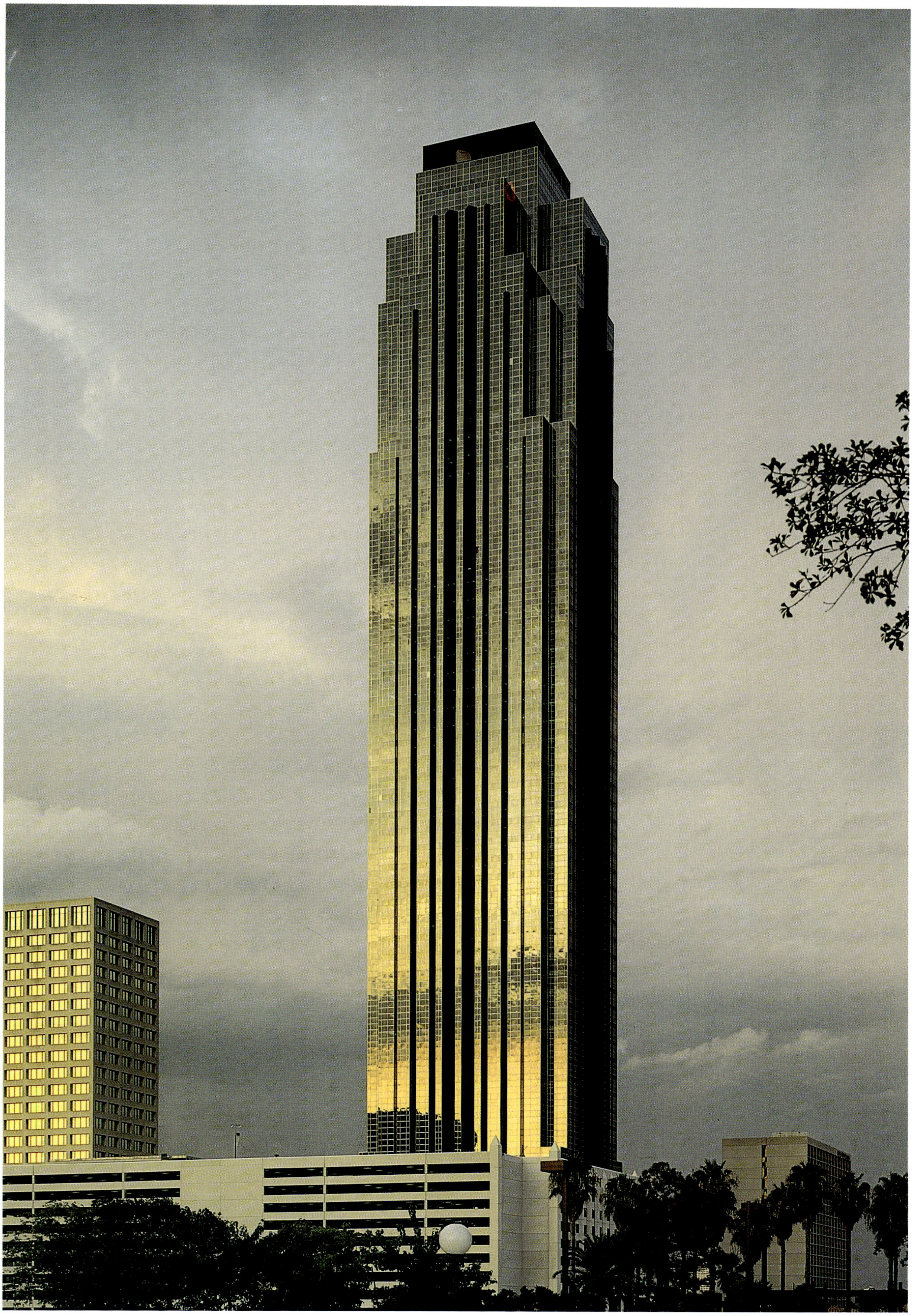

Transco Tower, Houston. Johnson / Burgee, architects, 1983. In association with Morris-Aubry.
© Richard Payne.

GATE TOWER

53

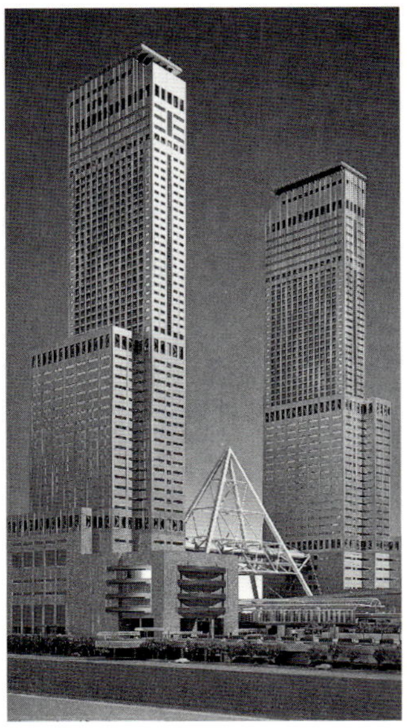

Osaka, Japan
56 stories
254 meters (833 feet)
1996, under construction

Architects: Nikken Sekkei, in association with Yasui Architects and Engineers, Inc.
Structural engineers: Nikken Sekkei.
Mechanical and electrical engineers: Yasui Architects and Engineers, Inc.
Developer: Rinku Gate Tower Building Co., Ltd.
Steel structure.
Office tower.

The initial project includes a second tower, identical to the first. Its construction has been delayed for economic difficulties.

Nikken Sekkei

OSAKA WORLD TRADE CENTER

54

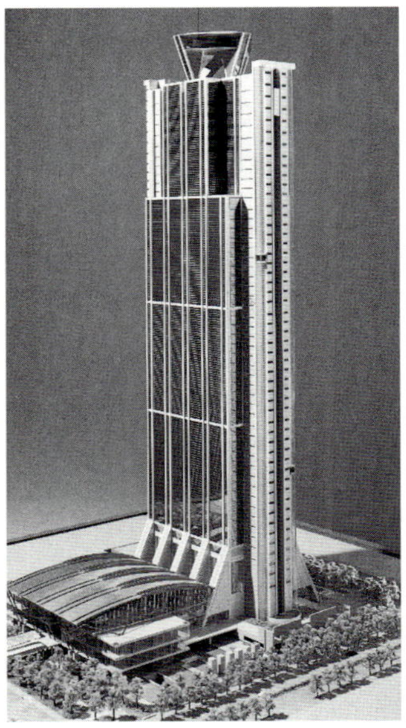

Osaka, Japan
55 stories
252 meters (827 feet)
1995

Architects: Nikken Sekkei.
Engineers: Nikken Sekkei.
Developer: Osaka World Trade Center Building Co.
Steel structure with composite steel / concrete elements.
Office tower, 150,000 square meters (1.6 million square feet), with commercial atrium.
All-Weather Park, 3,000 square meters (32,000 square feet) arranged on three levels and observation platform on the 55th floor; underground garage (800 spaces).

The World Trade Center Tower is the central point of Cosmosquare, a new business park created on a promontory in the Osaka bay (south port). It is surmounted by an inverted pyramid-shaped superstructure supporting the observation platform, reached by a long escalator.

Nikken Sekkei

ONE ATLANTIC CENTER

55

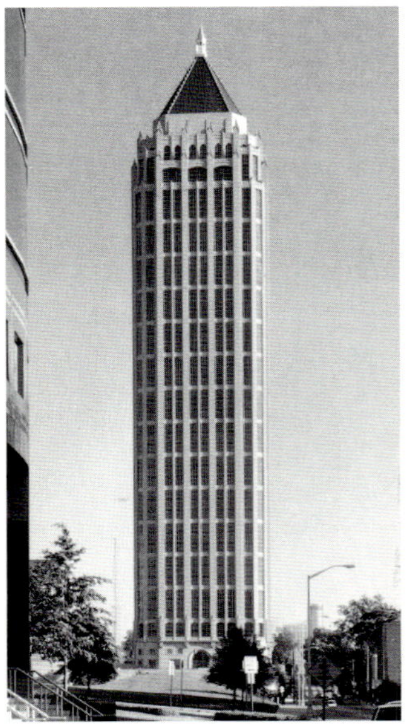

Atlanta, United States
50 stories
250 meters (820 feet)
1987

Architects: John Burgee Architects with Philip Johnson, in association with Heery Architects & Engineers, Inc.
Structural engineers: Datum / Moore Partnership.
Mechanical engineers: Blum Consulting.
Developer: Cadillac Fairview Urban Development, Inc. and IBM Corporation.
Mixed steel and concrete structure.
Office tower, 102,000 square meters (1.1 million square feet).

The pyramidal crown of the tower, inspired by the belfry of Trinity Church in Boston (H.H. Richardson architect, 1877), has made the building particularly popular with the general public and expert critical opinion alike. The block adjacent to the tower is occupied by an L-shaped garage with a restaurant and shops on the ground floor, defining a grassed public space.

© Richard Payne

WISMA 46 KOTA BNI

56

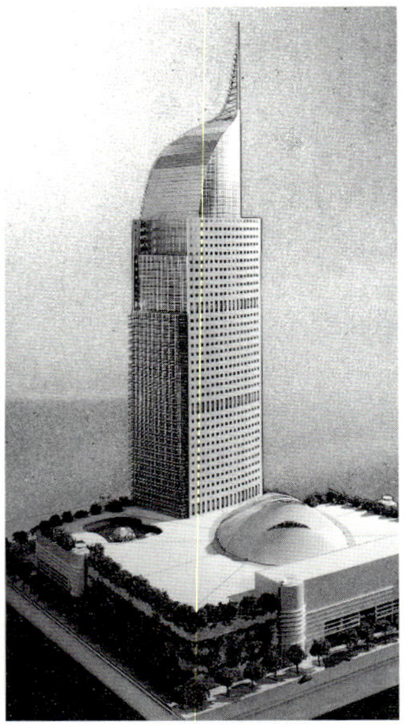

Jakarta, Indonesia
46 stories
250 meters (820 feet)
1996, under construction

Architects: Zeidler Roberts Partnership; in association with DP Architects (architects of record).
Structural engineers: T.Y. Lin South-East Asia Pte.
Mechanical and electrical consultants: Ewbank Preece Engineers Pte.
Developer: Satya Djaya Raya Group.
Mixed steel and concrete structure.
Office tower, 140,000 square meters (1.5 million square feet), including a shopping gallery.

The tower is part of a complex situated in the center of the city and also including the headquarters of the Negara Indonesia Bank, a luxury hotel (716 rooms), and other projected residential and commercial buildings. The architects of the tower are also the authors of the master plan of the complex.

Zeidler Roberts Partnership

KOREA LIFE INSURANCE 63

(DLI-63 Building)

57

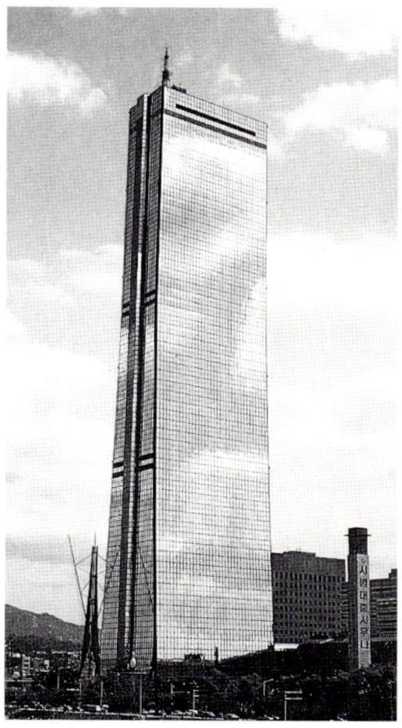

Daesaeng Corporation

Seoul, South Korea
60 stories
249 meters (817 feet)
1985

Architects: C. M. Park (Korea) in association with Skidmore, Owings & Merrill.
Engineers: C. M. Park.
Developer: Dai Han Life Insurance.
Steel structure.
Office tower, 166,000 square meters (1.8 million square feet).

The 7 highest floors of the tower are reserved for an ensemble of restaurants, bars and private clubs, surmounted by an observation platform on the 60th floor. Other services intended for the public occupy the 3 basement levels. A conference center annex stands at the foot of the tower.

CITYSPIRE

58

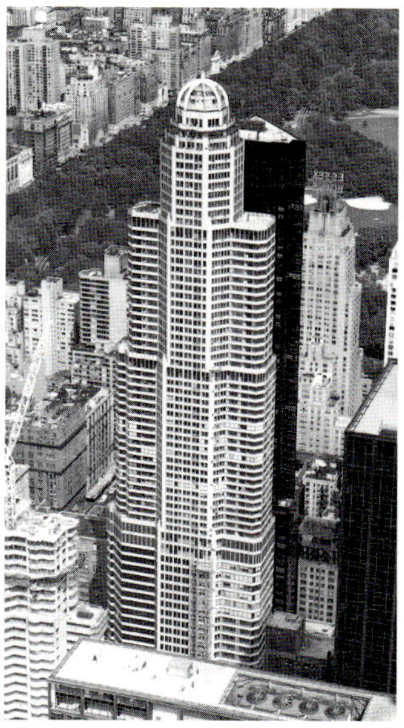

Murphy / Jahn

New York, United States
72 stories
248 meters (814 feet)
1989

Architects: Murphy / Jahn (Helmut Jahn).
Structural engineers: Robert Rosenwasser Associates, consultants.
Mechanical and electrical engineers: Cosentini Associates, consultants.
Developer: Eichner Properties.
Concrete structure.
Mixed-use office, 30,000 square meters (323,000 square feet) and residential (353 apartments) building.

The highest apartments in New York. The skyscraper uses the air rights of the neighboring City Center Theater, designated a historic landmark (Harry P. Knowles architect, 1924).

ONE CHASE MANHATTAN PLAZA

59

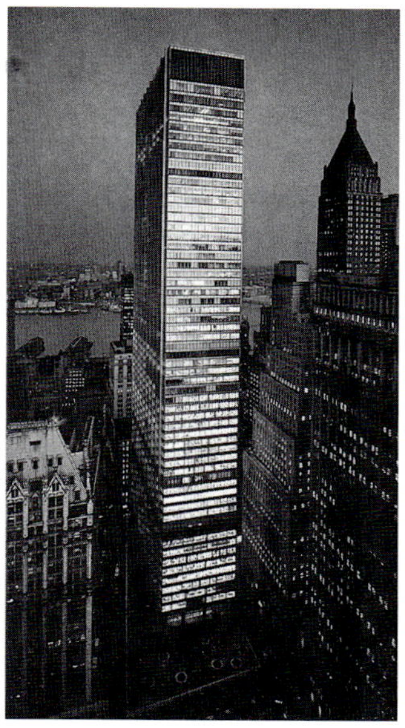

© Ezra Stoller

New York, United States
60 stories
248 meters (813 feet)
1961

Architects: Skidmore, Owings & Merrill, New York (Gordon Bunshaft).
Engineers: Skidmore, Owings & Merrill, in association with Jaros Baum & Bolles (mechanical) and Weiskopf & Pickworth (structural).
Developer: Chase Manhattan Bank.
Steel structure.
Office tower, 200,000 square meters (2.15 million square feet) containing a banking hall, restaurants, shops and technical services in the basement.

The tower occupies two blocks of lower Manhattan. It is the first building in New York (and doubtless in the United States) to have the name of the plaza created at ground level as its address.

METLIFE BUILDING

(Pan Am Building)

60

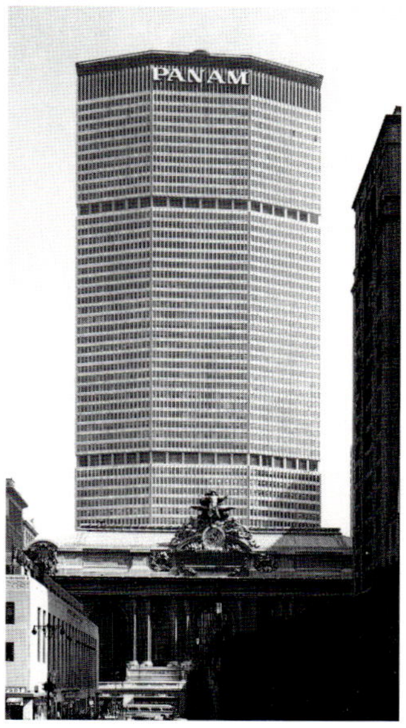

Emery Roth & Sons

New York, United States
59 stories
246 meters (808 feet)
1963

Architects: Emery Roth & Sons, Pietro Belluschi and Walter Gropius.
Structural engineers: The Office of James Ruderman.
Mechanical and electrical engineers: Jaros Baum & Bolles.
Developer: Erwin Wolfson.
Steel structure.
Office tower.

The largest building in the world in terms of area—223,000 square meters (2.4 million square feet)—at the time of its construction. On top of the tower a heliport used to provide a direct connection with New York's JFK airport. Situated on the axis of Park Avenue between Grand Central Station and the elegant Helmsley Building (1929), it raised a good deal of protest at the time of its construction.

KOMPLEKS TUN ABDUL RAZAK (KOMTAR)

61

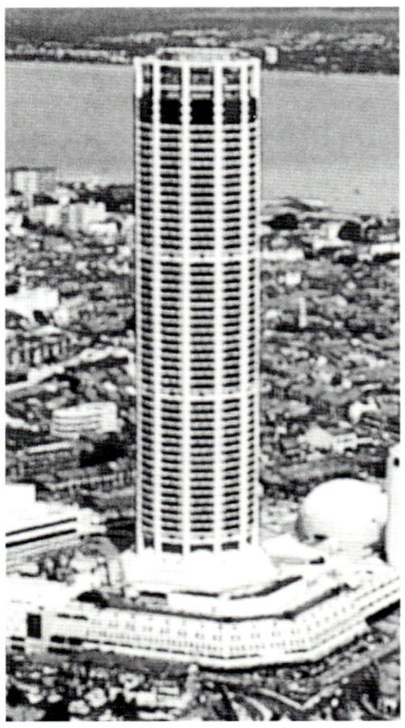

George Town Penang, Malaysia
65 stories
245 meters (804 feet)
1985

Architects: Architects Team 3 International Sdn. / Jurubena Bertiga International Sdn.
Structural engineers: Ove Arup & Partners.
Developer: Penang Development Corporation.
Concrete structure.
Office tower.

A sizeable intervention in the little colonial and touristic George Town.

MALAYAN BANK

62

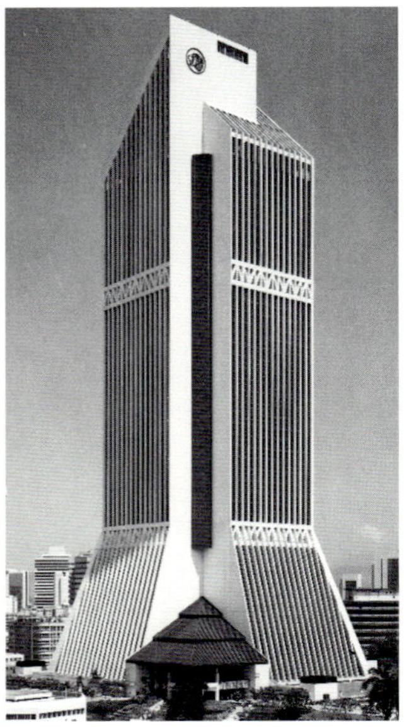

Kuala Lumpur, Malaysia
50 stories
244 meters (799 feet)
1988

Architects: Hijjas Kasturi Associates.
Structural engineers: Jurutera Konsultant.
Developer: Malayan Banking Berhad.
Concrete structure.
Office tower, 170,000 square meters (1.8 million square feet).

The tower, entirely composed on the theme of the square and the diagonal, attempts to create a regional identity by evoking the slopes and roofs of traditional Malaysian architecture.

TOKYO CITY HALL COMPLEX

63

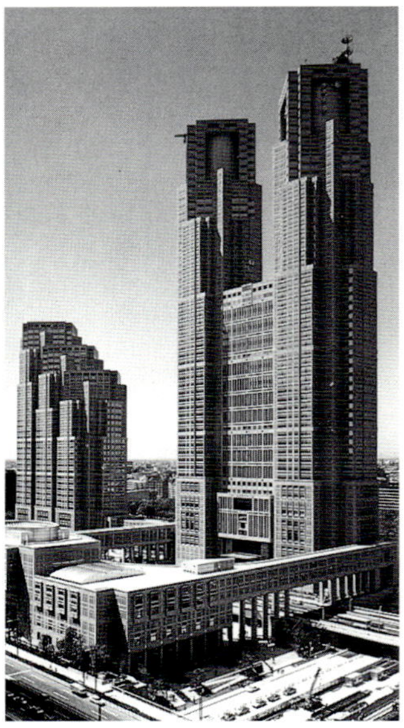

Tokyo, Japan
48 stories
243 meters (797 feet)
1991

Architects: Kenzo Tange Associates.
Structural engineers: Mutoh Associates.
Mechanical engineers: Inuzuka Engineering Consultants.
Developer: City of Tokyo.
Steel structure.
Office tower, 195,000 square meters (2 million square feet), with public observation platform on the 45th floor.

The skyscraper is divided into two square towers from the 33rd floor up. It is part of an administrative complex that includes a second tower of 34 stories. A semi-circular plaza at a lower level than the street connects the main tower to the council chamber, thus creating a unified landscape at pedestrian level. The City Hall Complex dominates the Shinjuku district, the only skyscraper area of the Japanese capital.

RIALTO TOWERS

64

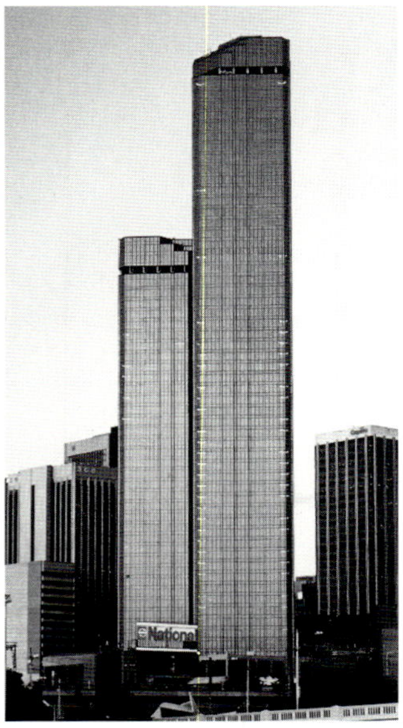

Melbourne, Australia
56 stories
242 meters (794 feet)
1985

Architects: Gerard de Preu & Partners, in association with Perrott Lyon Mathieson Pty.
Consultant architects: Dino Burattini & Associates.
Structural engineers (tower): W. L. Meinhardt and Partners.
Mechanical and electrical engineers: Lincolne Scott Australia.
Developer: St. Martins Properties & Grollo Australia.
Concrete structure.
Office tower.

The tallest building in the Southern Hemisphere at the time of its construction and the second tallest in the world built in high-strength concrete. The building includes a second, lower tower of 43 stories and is part of a complex containing a hotel and a small theater installed in two old buildings.

Hijjas Kasturi Associates

Kenzo Tange Associates

Perrott Lyon Mathieson

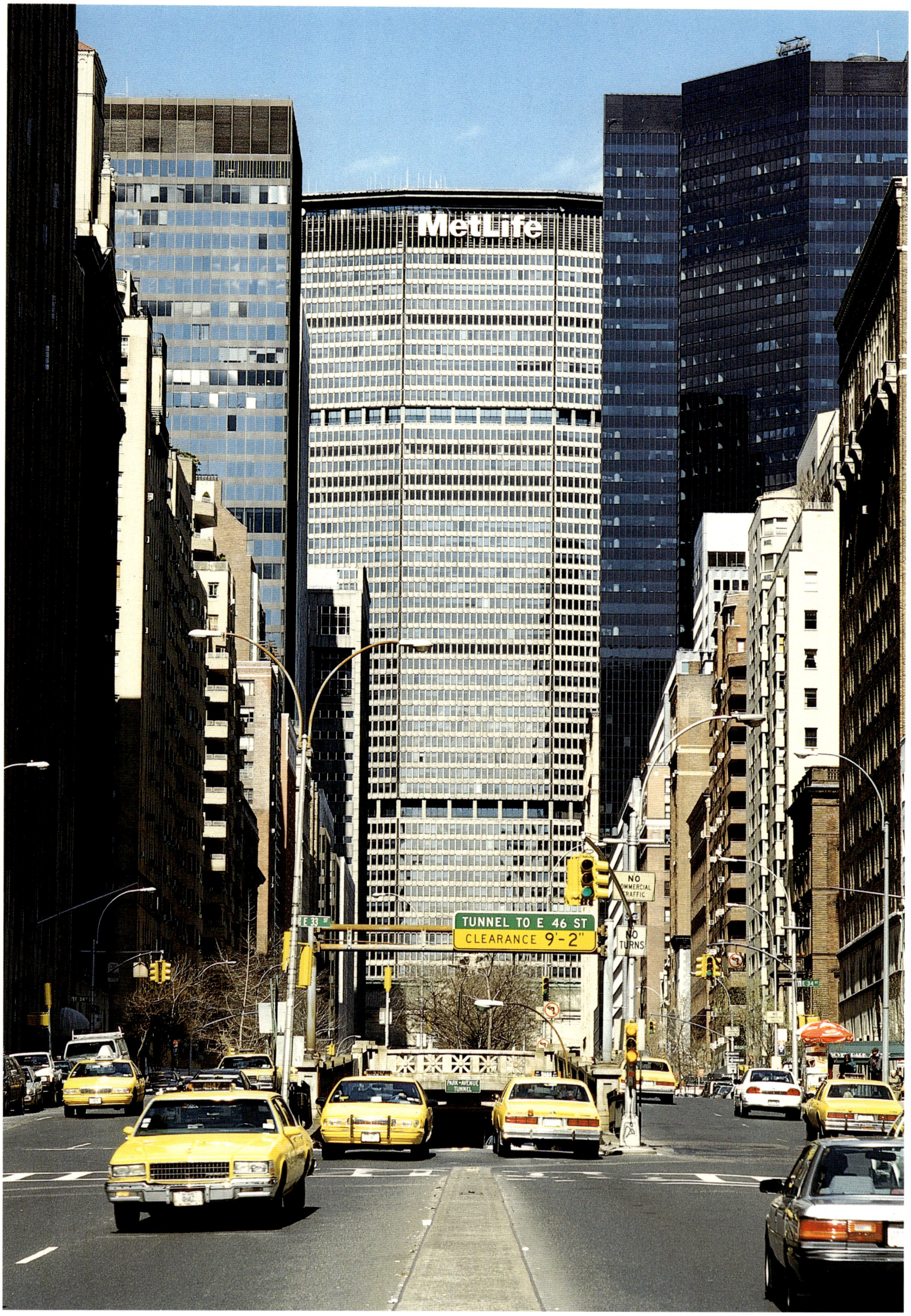

MetLife Building (originally Pan Am Building), New York. Emery Roth & Sons, Pietro Belluschi and Walter Gropius, 1963.

© Benoît Roland.

MELLON BANK CENTER

65

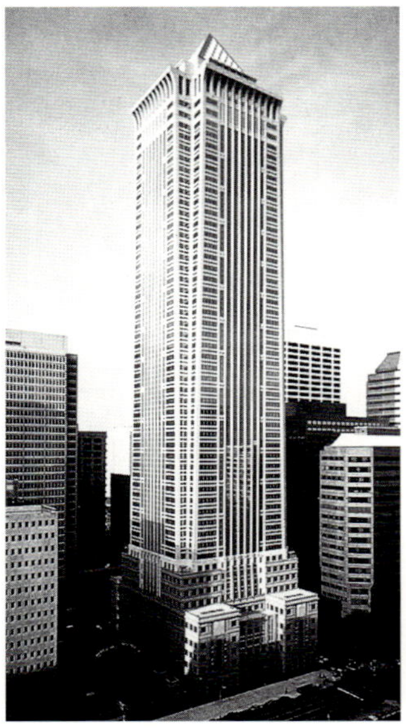

Philadelphia, United States
54 stories
241 meters (792 feet)
1990

Architects: Kohn Pedersen Fox Associates.
Structural engineers: The Office of Irwin G. Cantor (Jeff Smilow).
Mechanical and electrical engineers: Flack + Kurtz (Norman Kurtz).
Developer: Equitable Real Estate and Richard I. Rubin & Co, Inc.
Steel structure.
Office tower, 110,000 square meters (1.2 million square feet).

A true campanile, characterized by wide projecting cornices and a pierced pyramidal summit, the building is one of a first generation of skyscrapers in Philadelphia allowed to exceed 491 feet (about 150 meters), the height of the statue of William Penn on top of the City Hall. (See also Nos. 28 and 50.)

© Peter Olson

WOOLWORTH BUILDING

66

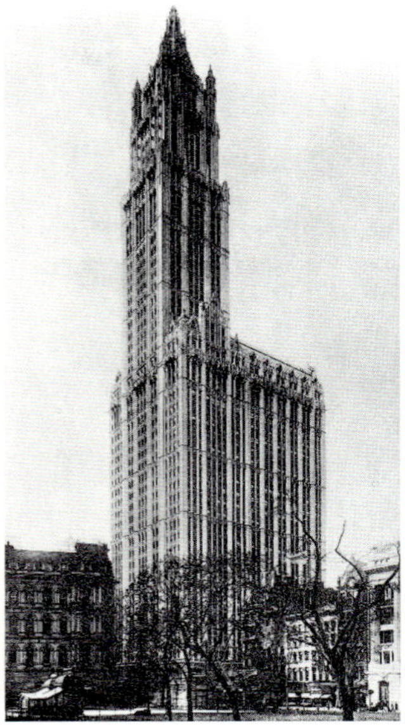

New York, United States
57 stories
241 meters (792 feet)
1913

Architect: Cass Gilbert.
Structural engineer: Gunvald Aus.
Developer: Frank W. Woolworth.
Steel structure.
Office tower, 120,000 square meters (1.3 million square feet).

Christened "cathedral of commerce," the Woolworth Building was to remain the tallest in the world until 1930. The Irving Bank was the first tenant. Completely restored between 1977 and 1981, it was designated a historic landmark in 1983.

Da Capo Press

JOHN HANCOCK TOWER

67

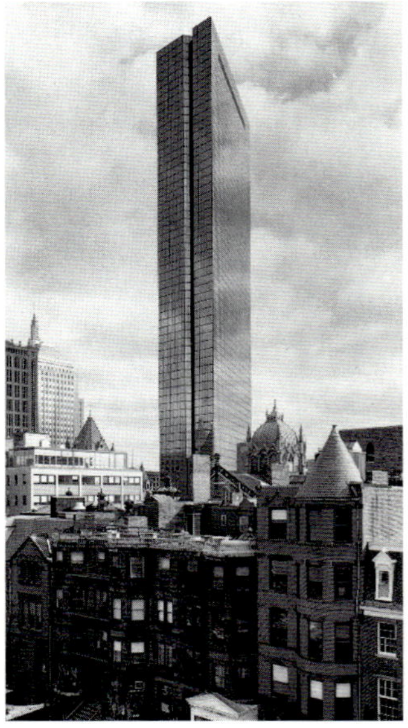

Boston, United States
60 stories
240 meters (788 feet)
1976

Architects: I.M. Pei & Partners (Henry N. Cobb).
Structural engineers: The Office of James Ruderman.
Mechanical and electrical engineers: Cosentini Associates.
Developer: John Hancock Mutual Life Insurance Company.
Steel structure.
Office tower.

A fault in the installation of the curtain wall that caused many glazed panels to fall off seriously compromised the occupation of the tower for several years, also putting the firm of I.M. Pei & Partners into difficulty.

© Timothy Hursley

BANK ONE CENTER

(Momentum Place)

68

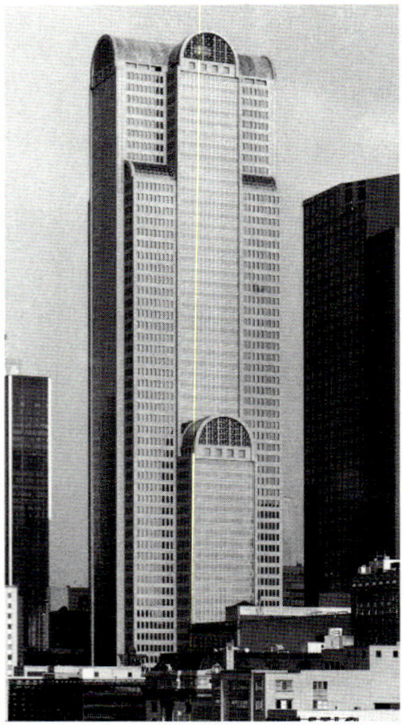

Dallas, United States
60 stories
240 meters (787 feet)
1987

Architects: John Burgee Architects with Philip Johnson, in association with HKS, Inc.
Structural engineers: Datum / Moore Partnership.
Mechanical engineers: Cosentini Associates and Steve Dunn & Partners.
Developer: Cadillac Fairview Urban Development.
Mixed steel and concrete structure.
Office tower, 140,000 square meters (1.5 million square feet).

Typical of the skyscrapers designed by Philip Johnson and John Burgee during this period, the entrance of the tower is emphasized by the luxury of materials, the enlarged scale of the bays and areas of circulation; a granite arch culminating at 20 meters (60 feet), a long walkway paved in marble suspended 5 meters (15 feet) above ground level, a banking hall on 6 levels lit from above.

© Richard Payne

JR CENTRAL TOWERS

69

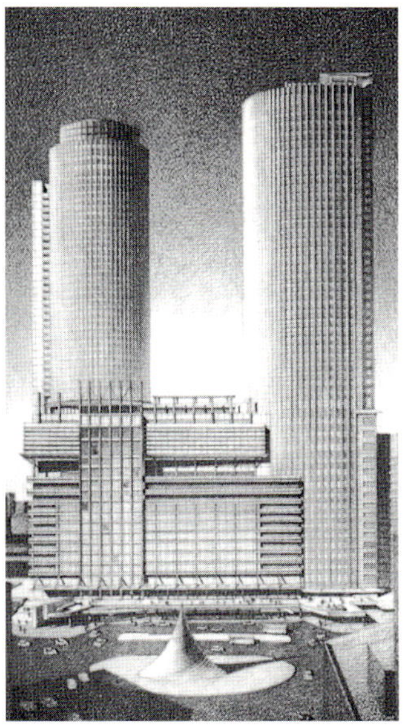

Nagoya, Japan
51 stories
240 meters (787 feet)
1999, under construction

Architect: Seizo Sakata (Sakakura Architectural Institute); Kohn Pedersen Fox Associates, consultant architects.
Engineers: Taisei Corporation.
Developer: Central Japan Railway Company, JR Central Building, Ltd.
Steel structure.
Office tower, 90,000 square meters (969,000 square feet), including a station, shops, cultural, recreational facilities, and garage space at the base.

The complex—410,000 square meters (4.413 million square feet) in all—includes, in addition to the office tower, a second, slightly lower tower containing an 800-room hotel (53 floors) rising to about 230 meters (755 feet). The two towers are linked by a podium of 20 stories containing a department store and cultural and recreational facilities, among other things. Express elevators connect the ground floor of the complex to "sky-street" on the 15th floor, destined to be the true center of the complex.

Kohn Pedersen Fox

COMMERCE COURT WEST

70

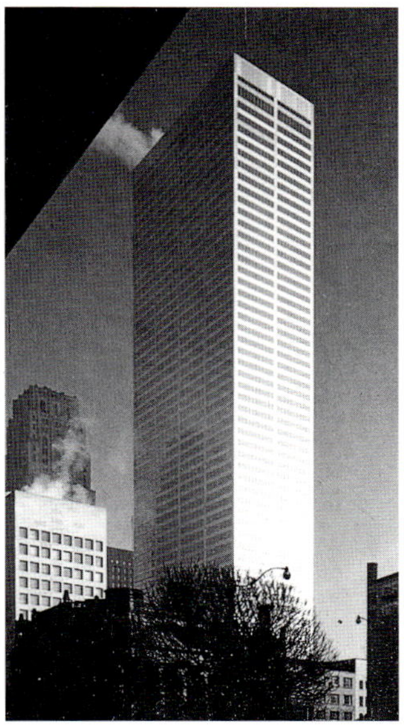

Toronto, Canada
57 stories
239 meters (784 feet)
1973

Architects: Page & Steele; I.M. Pei & Partners, consultants.
Structural engineers: C. D. Carruthers & Wallace Consultants, in association with Weiskopf & Pickworth.
Mechanical engineers: G. Granek & Associates.
Electrical engineers: Jack Chisvin & Associates.
Developer: Canadian Imperial Bank of Commerce.
Mixed steel and concrete structure.
Office tower, 138,000 square meters (1.5 million square feet).

The first building in the world to be equipped with Otis double-decker elevators. The tower is part of a group of four buildings surrounding a public space dominated by a monumental fountain.

© Balthazar Korab

MOSCOW UNIVERSITY

71

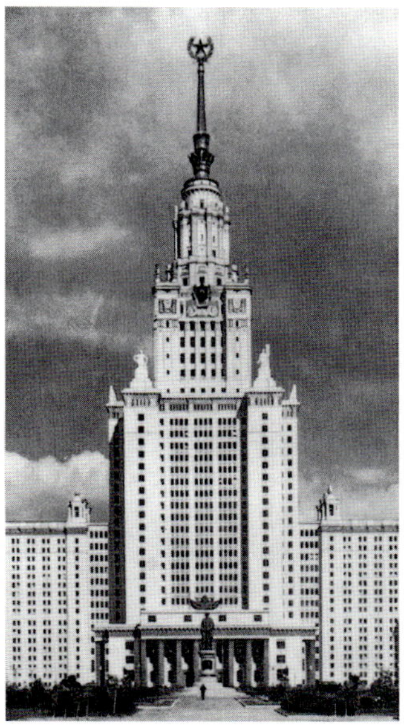

Moscow, Russia
26 stories
239 meters (784 feet)
1953

Architects: L. Roudnev, P. Abrossimov, A. Khariakov and S. Tchernitchev.

The tallest of eight "buildings of great height" (the word skyscraper was deliberately rejected at the time as not conforming with Soviet reality) begun in Moscow in 1949. The university occupies a dominant position on Mount Lenin, the seven others accentuating the concentric radial design of the city's plan of expansion.

Institut français d'architecture

NATIONSBANK CENTER

(RepublicBank Center)

72

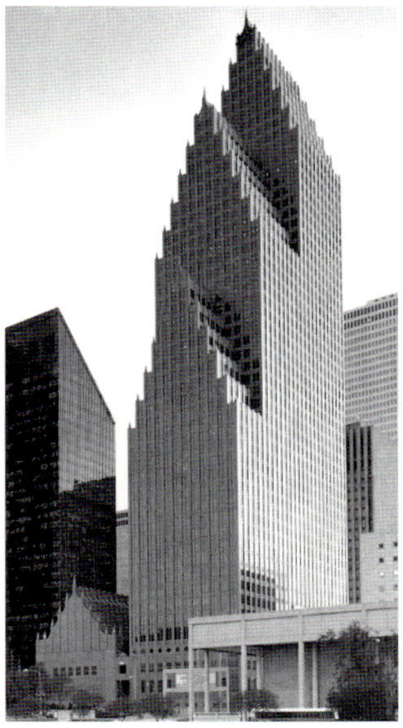

Houston, United States
56 stories
238 meters (780 feet)
1984

Architects: Johnson / Burgee Architects, in association with Kendall / Heaton Associates.
Structural engineers: CBM Engineers, Inc.
Mechanical engineers: I.A. Naman + Associates
Developer: Gerald D. Hines Interests.
Steel structure.
Office tower, 130,000 square meters (1.4 million square feet), also including a huge banking hall.

The construction encompasses a two story technical building already on the site, determining the ground plan in the form of a cross. It directly faces Pennzoil Place, another skyscraper designed by the same architects a few years earlier for the same developer and completed in 1976.

© Richard Payne

BANK OF AMERICA CENTER

73

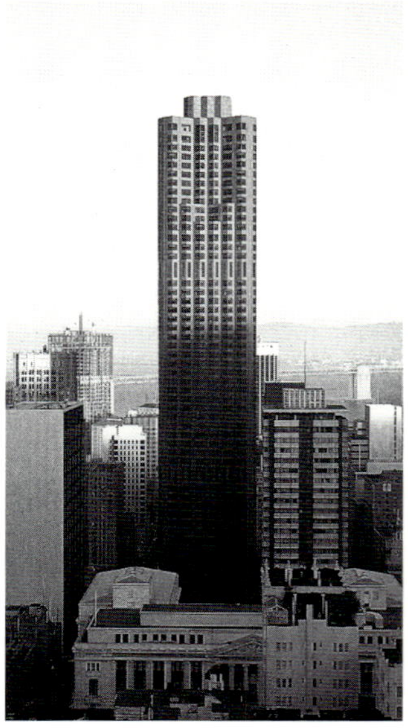

San Francisco, United States
52 stories
237 meters (779 feet)
1969

Architects: Skidmore, Owings & Merrill (San Francisco), in association with Wurster Bernardi & Emmons, and Pietro Belluschi (consultant architect).
Structural engineers: H.J. Brunnier & Associates.
Developer: Bank of America NT & SA.
Steel structure.
Office tower, 140,000 square meters (1.5 million square feet).

As opposed to most skyscrapers of this period and for reasons linked to the highly unusual context of old San Francisco, a very assertive granite cladding was preferred to the smooth, glazed curtain-wall formula. The tower is part of a complex which also includes a 3-story glass pavilion and a shopping center and small auditorium in the basement.

© Ezra Stoller

ONE WORLDWIDE PLAZA

74

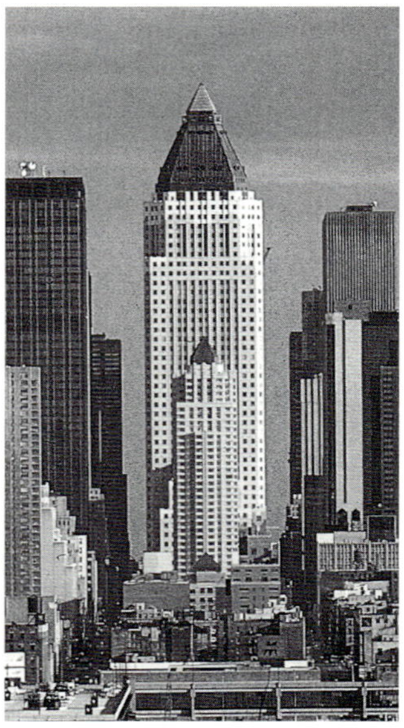

New York, United States
47 stories
237 meters (778 feet)
1989

Architects: Skidmore, Owings & Merrill, New York (David Childs).
Structural engineers: Skidmore, Owings & Merrill (Robert Halvorson and Gary Steficek).
Mechanical engineers: Cosentini Associates.
Developers: New York Communications Center Association (Zeckendorf Company, KG Land New York Corporation, Arthur G. Cohen, Frank Stanton, Victor Elmaleh).
Steel structure.
Office tower, 138,000 square meters (1.5 million square feet).

The tower is part of a larger project intended to promote the development of the West Side of midtown Manhattan and including, as well as offices, a residential tower (38 stories), low-rise housing on the edge of the site, a sports center with swimming pool, cinemas, shops and a central public plaza.

© Jeff Goldberg / Esto Photographics

ONE CANADA SQUARE

(Canary Wharf Tower)

75

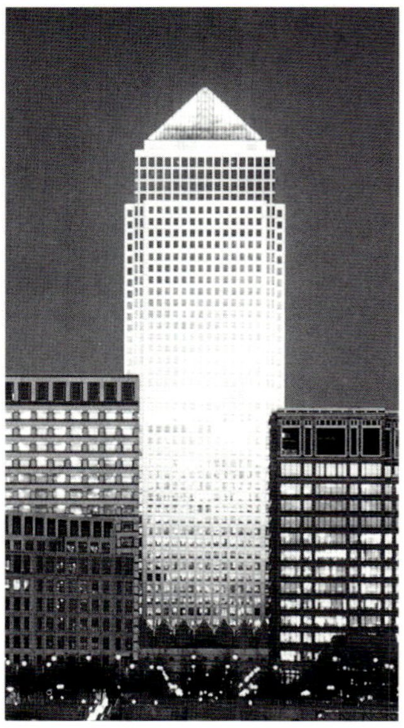

London, United Kingdom
50 stories
237 meters (777 feet)
1991

Architects: Cesar Pelli & Associates, with Frederick Gibberd Coombes and Partners, Adamson Associates and Atkins Sheppard Fidler & Associates.
Structural engineers: MS Yolles & Partner, Waterman Partnership.
Mechanical engineers: TMP & DSSR Consulting Engineers.
Electrical engineers: HM Angus & Associates.
Developer: Olympia & York.
Steel structure.
Office tower, 167,000 square meters (1.8 square feet).

In addition to the tower, The Canary Wharf project includes a shopping and cultural center and the Docklands Light Railway station. It is part of an overall project to revitalize Thames Dockland, launched by the Thatcher government in 1981. Very controversial, the project encountered major economic difficulties in 1992.
In 1989 the Prince of Wales said of the tallest tower in the United Kingdom that it was "a monument to the wrong thinking of the 1960's, but built in the 1980's."

The Press Office, Canary Wharf Ltd.

IDS CENTER

76

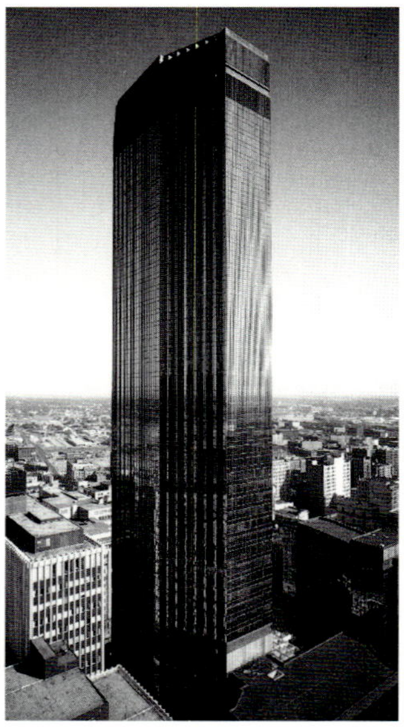

Minneapolis, United States
57 stories
236 meters (775 feet)
1972

Architects: Johnson / Burgee Architects, in association with Edward F. Baker Associates.
Structural engineers: Severud-Perrone-Sturm-Colin-Bandel.
Mechanical engineers: Cosentini Associates.
Developer: IDS Properties (Investors Diversified Services, Inc.).
Mixed steel and concrete structure.
Office tower, 120,000 square meters (1.3 million square feet).

The tower joins a complex including a hotel, a shopping center and other elements. The group of buildings enclose the Crystal Court, a large glazed-over public space.

© Richard Payne

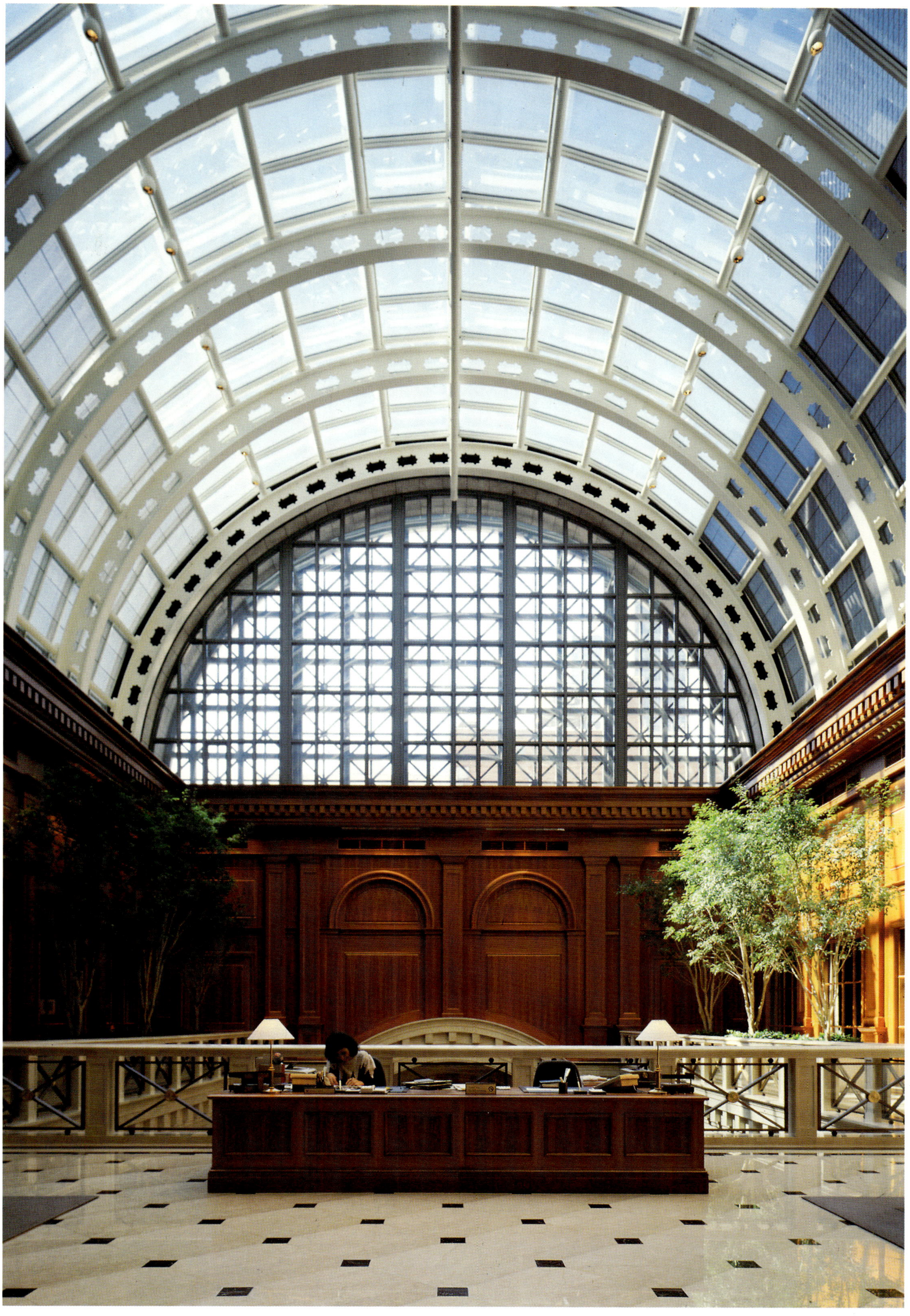

Bank One Center, Dallas, upper floor of the banking hall. John Burgee Architects, with Philip Johnson, 1987, in association with HKS Inc.

NORWEST CENTER

77

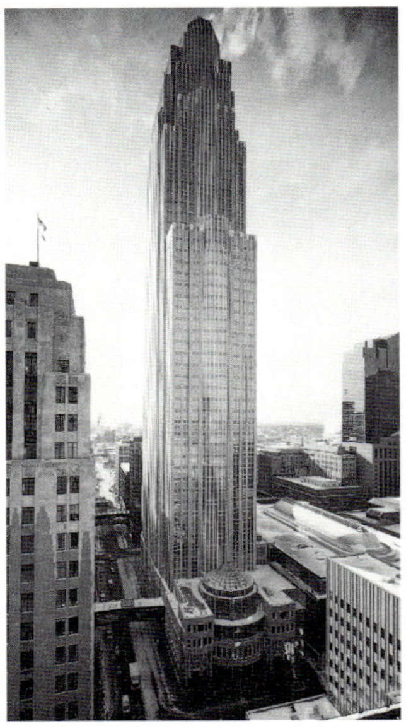

Minneapolis, United States
57 stories
236 meters (774 feet)
1988

Architects: Cesar Pelli & Associates, in association with Kendall / Heaton Associates.
Mechanical and electrical engineers: I. A. Naman + Associates.
Developer: Gerald D. Hines Interests.
Steel structure.
Office tower, 149,000 square meters (1.6 million square feet).

The tower stands on the site of the Northwestern Bank, destroyed by fire in 1982. Architectural salvage from the old bank has been incorporated in the rotunda and the lobbies of the tower. The walkway built over Marquette Street was designed by Cesar Pelli and the artist Siah Armajani.

© Balthazar and Christian Korab

FIRST BANK PLACE

78

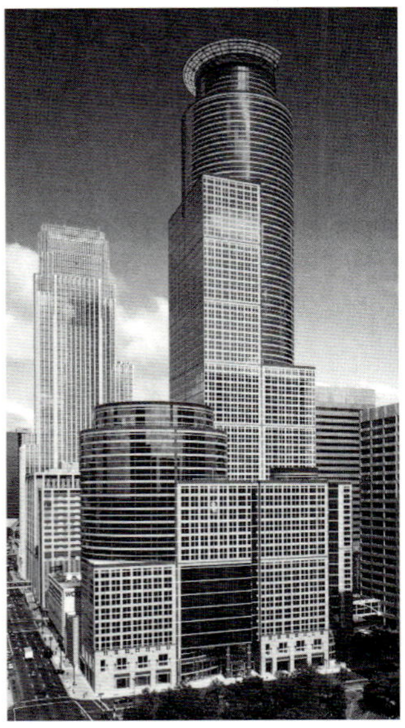

Minneapolis, United States
53 stories
236 meters (774 feet)
1992

Architects: Pei Cobb Freed & Partners (James I. Freed).
Structural engineers: CBM Engineers, Inc.
Mechanical engineers: Cosentini Associates.
Developer: IBM / Opus Corporation.
Steel structure.
Office tower.

The division of the tower into two distinct volumes meets the objective of identifying the two principal occupiers.

© Philip Prowse

SINGAPORE TREASURY BUILDING

79

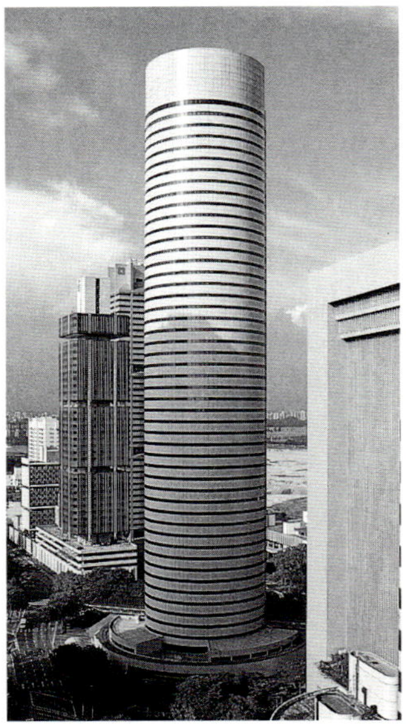

Singapore
52 stories
235 meters (771 feet)
1986

Architects: The Stubbins Associates; Architects 61, architects of record.
Structural engineers: Ove Arup and Partners and LeMessurier Consultants.
Mechanical engineers: Ewbanks Preece Partnership.
Developer: Singapore Treasury Building Ltd.
Mixed steel and concrete structure.
Office tower, 133,000 square meters (1.431 million square feet).

The base of the tower, linked to the subway system, is naturally ventilated.

Architects 61

SHINJUKU PARK TOWER

80

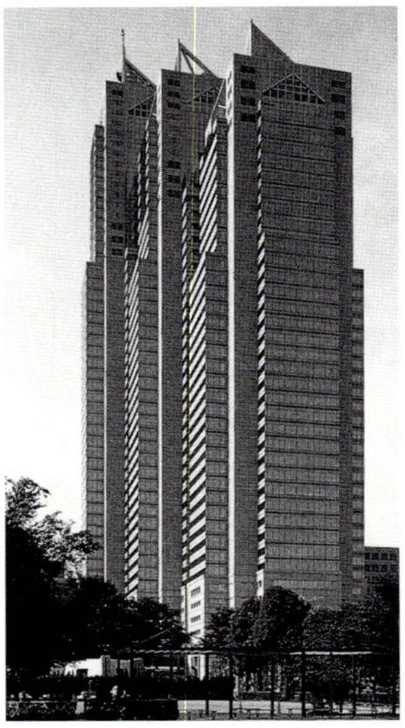

Tokyo, Japan
52 stories
233 meters (764 feet)
1994

Architects: Kenzo Tange Associates.
Structural engineers: Kobori Research Complex Inc.
Mechanical engineers: Inuzuka Engineering Consultants.
Developer: Tokyo Gas Urban Project.
Mixed steel and concrete structure.
Mixed-use building, 264,000 square meters (2.841 million square feet), containing, from top to bottom, a luxury hotel (178 rooms), 135,000 square meters (1.453 million square feet) of offices space on 30 levels, and showrooms.

The tower is situated near the new Tokyo City Hall Complex and is linked to a vast atrium backing on to the Shinjuku central heating station, also built by Kenzo Tange Associates.

Kenzo Tange Associates

HERITAGE PLAZA

81

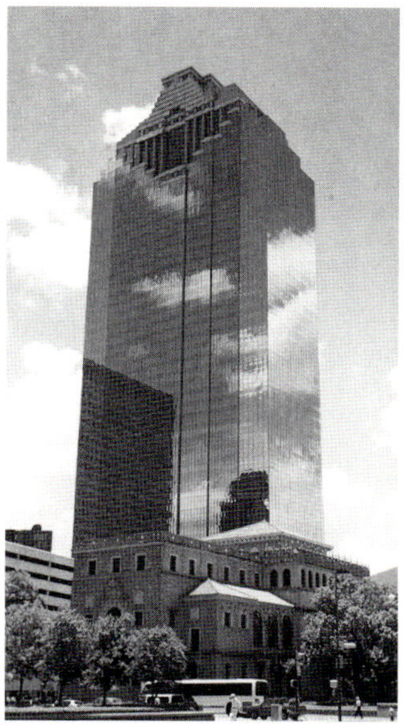

Houston, United States
53 stories
232 meters (762 feet)
1987

Architects: M. Nasr & Partners, P. C.
Structural engineers: CBM Engineers.
Mechanical and electrical engineers: EAM Engineers.
Developer: Wortham, Van Liew & Horn.
Mixed steel and concrete structure.
Office tower, 150,000 square meters (1.6 million square feet).

The last skyscraper of its size to be built in Houston prior to the recession.

PALACE OF CULTURE AND SCIENCE

82

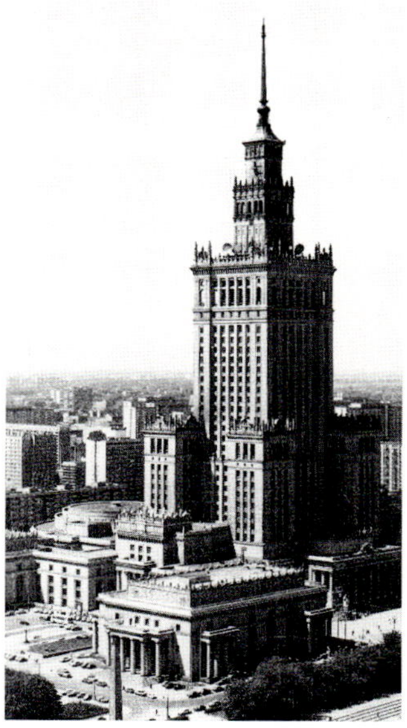

Warsaw, Poland
42 stories
231 meters (758 feet)
1955

Architect: L.W. Rudniew.
Mixed steel and concrete structure.
Mixed-use building: cultural and recreational facilities, exhibition rooms, museum and congress center on the lower floors, and offices on the upper floors.

"Gift of the Soviet Union to Poland," the Palace of Culture and Science of Warsaw is one of the most spectacular examples of Stalinist architecture promoted by Moscow in the countries of Eastern Europe after 1945. The building is surmounted by a 43-meter (140 feet) steeple.

CARNEGIE HALL TOWER

83

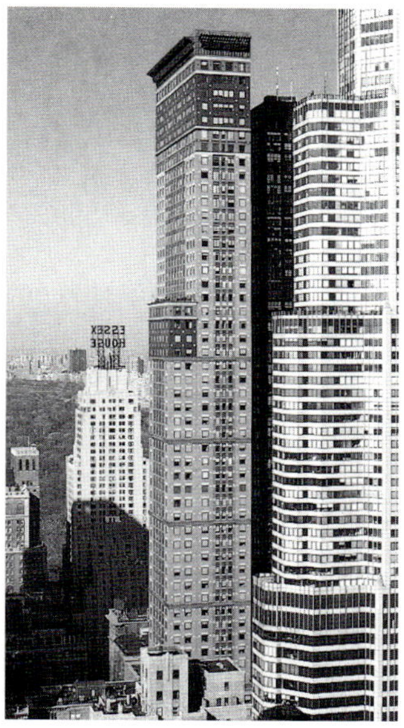

New York, United States
60 stories
231 meters (757 feet)
1991

Architects: Cesar Pelli & Associates; Brennan Beer Gorman, architects of record.
Structural engineers: Robert Rosenwasser Associates.
Mechanical and electrical engineers: Cosentini Associates.
Developer: Rockrose Development Corporation.
Concrete structure.
Office tower, 49,300 square meters (530,000 square feet).

The building uses the air rights of the historic Carnegie Hall and contains 2,300 square meters (25,000 square feet) of technical extensions to the concert hall.

THREE FIRST NATIONAL PLAZA

84

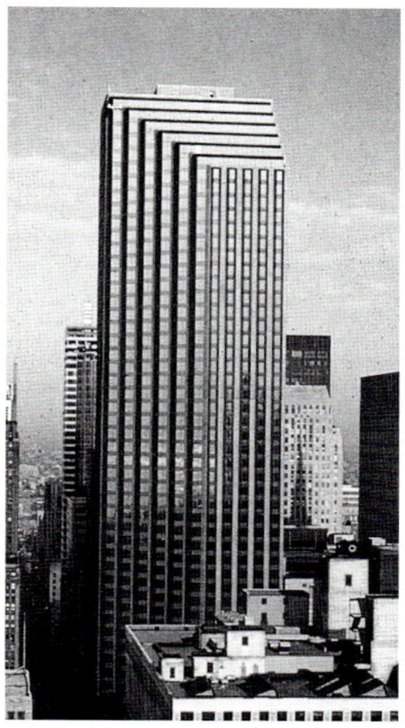

Chicago, United States
57 stories
230 meters (753 feet)
1981

Architects: Skidmore, Owings & Merrill, Chicago (Bruce Graham)
Structural engineers: Skidmore, Owings & Merrill (Srinivasa Iyengar et Stan Korista).
Mechanical engineers: I.A. Naman + Associates.
Developer: Gerald D. Hines Interests.
Mixed structure.
Office tower, 150,000 square meters (1.6 million square feet).

The building includes a nine-story glass-covered public lobby.

THE EQUITABLE TOWER

85

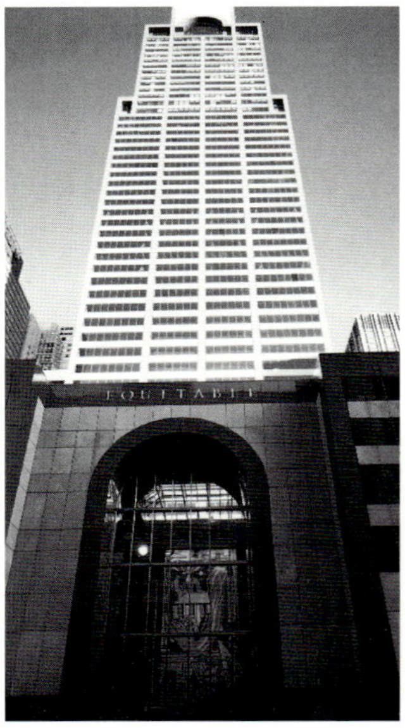

New York, United States
51 stories
229 meters (752 feet)
1985

Architects: Edward Larrabee Barnes and Associates.
Structural engineers: Weiskopf & Pickworth.
Mechanical and electrical engineers: Cosentini Associates.
Developer: The Equitable Life Assurance Society of the U.S.
Steel structure.
Office tower.

The 5-story atrium entrance is flanked by an impressive 10 by 20-meter (32 x 64 feet) mural by Roy Lichtenstein.

Buildings & Data

ONE PENN PLAZA

86

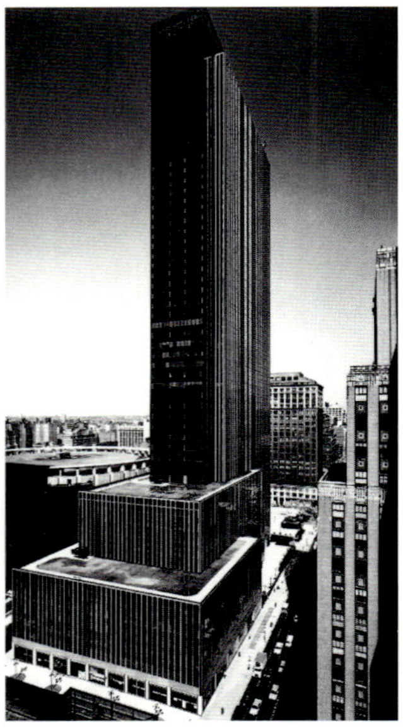

New York, United States
57 stories
229 meters (750 feet)
1972

Architects: Kahn & Jacobs.
Developer: Mid-City Associates (Harry Helmsley).
Steel structure.
Office tower, 165,000 square meters (1.776 million square feet).

The tower, built on the western edge of midtown Manhattan, revives the name of the old Pennsylvania Station (McKim, Mead and White, 1910), demolished in 1966 and replaced by a complex of buildings grouping a lower office tower (Two Penn Plaza, 31 stories), Madison Square Garden, the sports and exhibition hall, and a new underground railway station.
Conceived during the economic euphoria of the sixties, the tower was offered for rental in 1973 after the withdrawal of the main tenant. It just escaped the depression which then hit the New York real estate market.

Buildings & Data

1251 AVENUE OF THE AMERICAS

(Exxon)

87

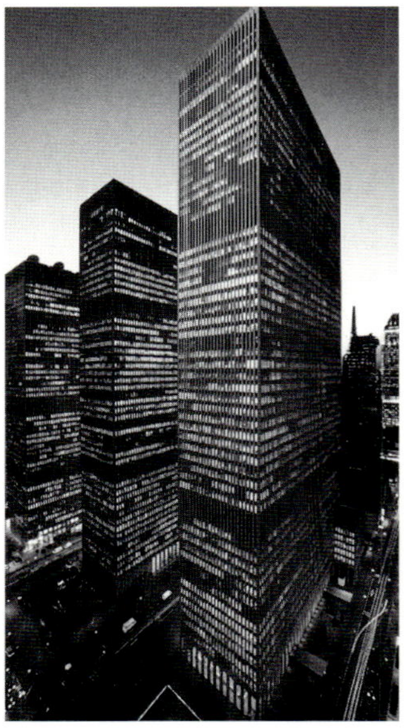

New York, United States
54 stories
229 meters (750 feet)
1972

Architects: Harrison & Abramovitz & Harris.
Developer: Rockefeller Center, Inc. and Standard Oil Company of New Jersey.
Steel structure.
Office tower.

The tallest of a series of three buildings designed on three adjoining blocks by the same architects and at the same period in the context of the extension to the Rockefeller Center on 6th Avenue.

Mitsui Fudosan

PRUDENTIAL CENTER

88

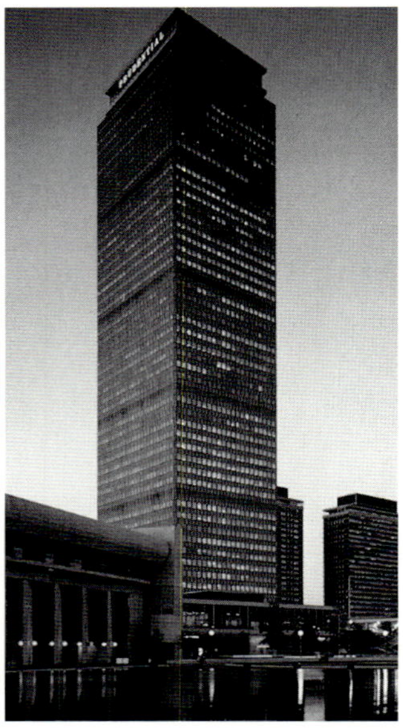

Boston, United States
52 stories
229 meters (750 feet)
1964

Architects: Charles Luckman Associates, in association with Hoyle, Doran & Berry.
Structural engineers: Edwards & Hjorth.
Mechanical and electrical engineers: Syska & Hennessy.
Developer: Prudential Insurance Company of America.
Steel structure.
Office tower.

The tower is the central feature of a larger complex including residential units, shops, and recreational facilities, all constructed on a podium raised above street level.

© Balthazar Korab

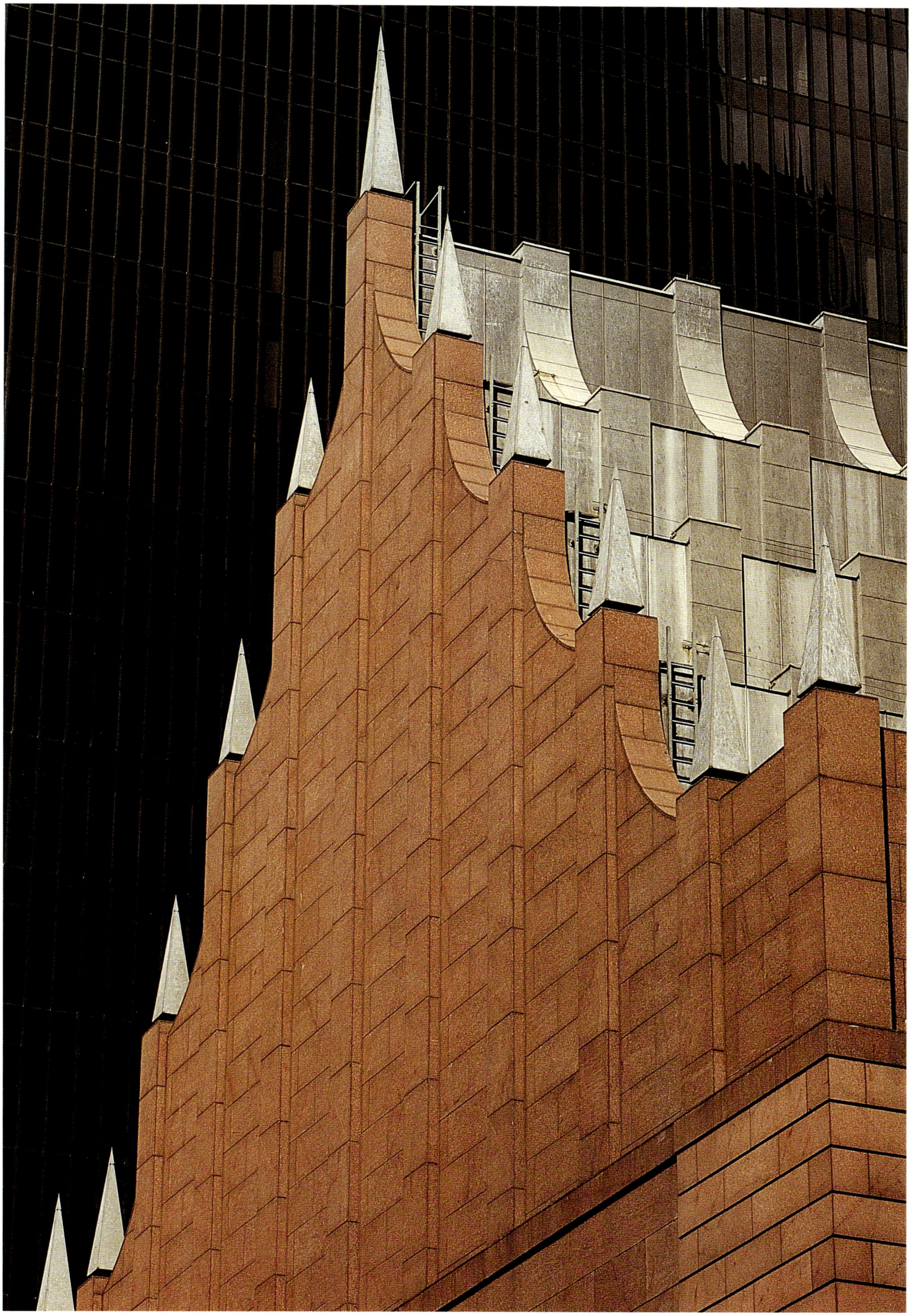

NationsBank Center, Houston, detail of the pinnacles. In the background, Pennzoil Place (1976). Johnson / Burgee, architects, 1984, in association with Kendall / Heaton Associates.

TWO CALIFORNIA PLAZA

89

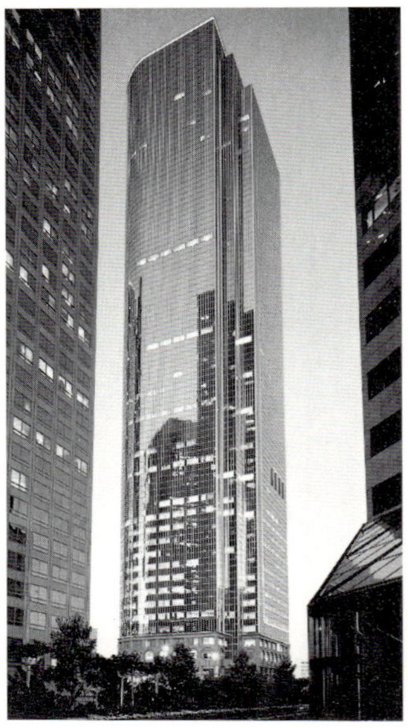

Los Angeles, United States
52 stories
229 meters (750 feet)
1992

Architects: Arthur Erickson Associates; Albert C. Martin & Associates, consultants. *Structural engineers:* John A. Martin & Associates. *Mechanical engineers:* Hayakawa & Associates. *Developers:* Bunker Hill Associates (Metropolitan Structures; Cadillac Fairview / California, Inc; Goldrich, Kest & Associates; Shapell Industries, Inc.). Steel structure. Office tower, 118,000 square meters (1.27 million square feet).

The tower is part of a project that includes One California Plaza, another lower tower built in a first phase.

MS Management Services

THE GAS COMPANY TOWER

90

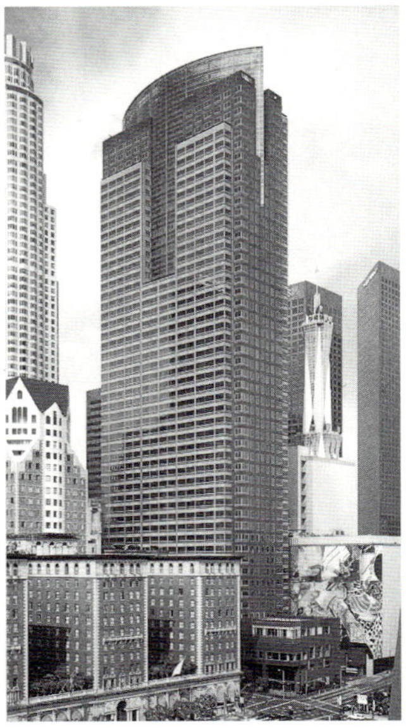

Los Angeles, United States
50 stories
228 meters (749 feet)
1991

Architects: Skidmore, Owings & Merrill, Los Angeles (Richard Keating). *Structural engineers:* CBM Engineers. *Mechanical engineers:* James A. Knowles & Associates. *Developer:* Maguire Thomas Partners. Steel structure. Office tower, 134,000 square meters (1.4 million square feet), including a restaurant, shops, and underground garage.

Built on a steep gradient—about 20 meters (60 feet) from one side of the site to the other—the tower has three entrance lobbies connected by a set of escalators, internal streets and hanging gardens. Its construction is part of a larger project to revitalize the center of Los Angeles that includes, under the aegis of the same developer, the restoration of the municipal library (with transfer of air rights), the construction of another skyscraper, First Interstate World Center (see No. 18), and the renovation of Pershing Square (architect Ricardo Legorreta).

© Erhard Pfeiffer

MLC CENTRE

91

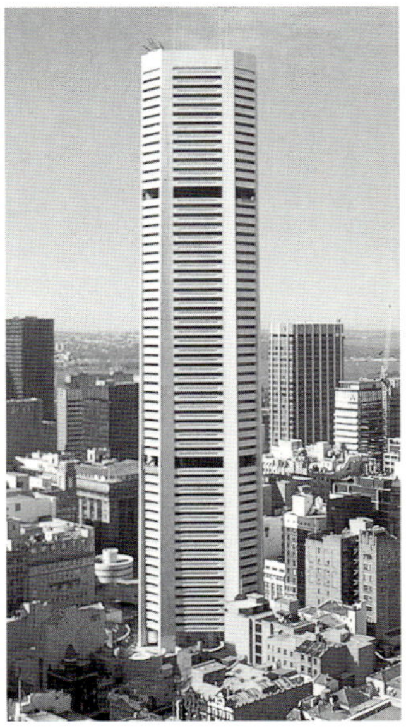

Sydney, Australia
65 stories
228 meters (748 feet)
1978

Architect: Harry Seidler & Associates. *Structural engineers:* Civil & Civic Pty, Lehmann & Talty Pty, DT Broughton & Associates. *Structural consultant:* Studio Nervi (Milan). *Mechanical engineers:* Environ Mechanical Services Pty. *Electrical engineers:* Civil & Civic Pty. *Developer:* The Mutual Life & Citizens Assurance Co. Concrete structure. Office tower, 1,650 square meters (17,760 square feet) per floor.

The base of the tower includes a theater (1,100 seats), two levels of shops, a movie theater, various cafés and restaurants articulated on a public pedestrian space linked to the existing road network. The engineer Pier Luigi Nervi was associated with the design of the ribbed ceiling of, among others, the theater and restaurant.

Harry Seidler & Associates

TWO PACIFIC PLACE / ISLAND SHANGRI-LA HOTEL

92

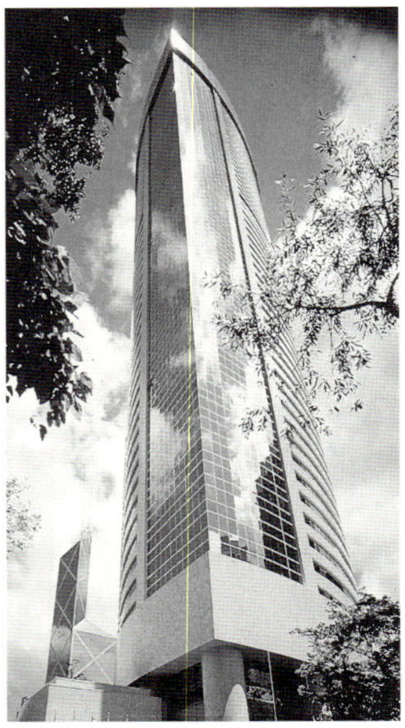

Hong Kong
56 stories
228 meters (748 feet)
1991

Architects: Wong & Ouyang (Hong Kong). *Engineers:* Wong & Ouyang (Hong Kong). *Developer:* Swire Properties. Concrete structure. Mixed use building containing 63,200 square meters (680,300 square feet) of offices and a 565-room hotel on the upper floors.

The tower is part of a complex situated beside Hong Kong Park, containing a shopping mall and three other office, hotel and residential towers. The Shangri-La Hotel is arranged around an 18-story-high atrium.

Island Shangri-La

1100 LOUISIANA BUILDING

(First International Plaza)

93

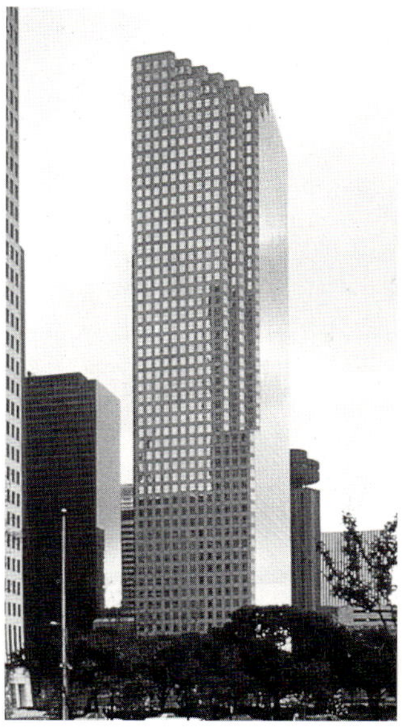

Houston, United States
55 stories
228 meters (748 feet)
1980

Architects: Skidmore, Owings & Merrill, San Francisco (Edward C. Bassett), in association with 3D / International.
Mechanical engineers: Colaco Engineers, Inc.
Mechanical engineers: I.A. Naman + Associates.
Developer: Gerald D. Hines Interests ; Prudential Insurance Company Realty (Houston).
Mixed steel and concrete structure.
Office tower, 148,000 square meters (1.6 million square feet).

At the foot of the tower there is a public plaza with the Monument au Fantôme *by Jean Dubuffet (1977).*

© R. Greg Hursley

KOREA WORLD TRADE CENTER

94

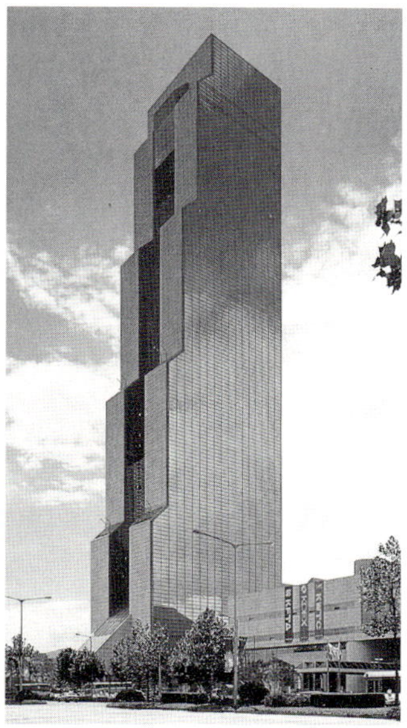

Seoul, South Korea
54 stories
228 meters (748 feet)
1988

Architects: Nikken Sekkei, in association with Wondosi Architects Group (Korea) and Junglim Architects & Engineers (Korea).
Engineers: Nikken Sekkei, in association with Wondosi Architects Group (Korea) and Junglim Architects & Engineers (Korea).
Developer: Korea Foreign Trade Association.
Mixed steel and concrete structure.
Office tower, 108,000 square meters (1.16 million square feet).

The tower is adjacent to the city's olympic stadium. It was built on the occasion of the Olympic Games, held in Seoul in 1988. It is part of a complex that includes a 800-room hotel, an exhibition center and the air terminal.

Nikken Sekkei

WING LOK STREET / QUEEN'S ROAD CENTRAL

95

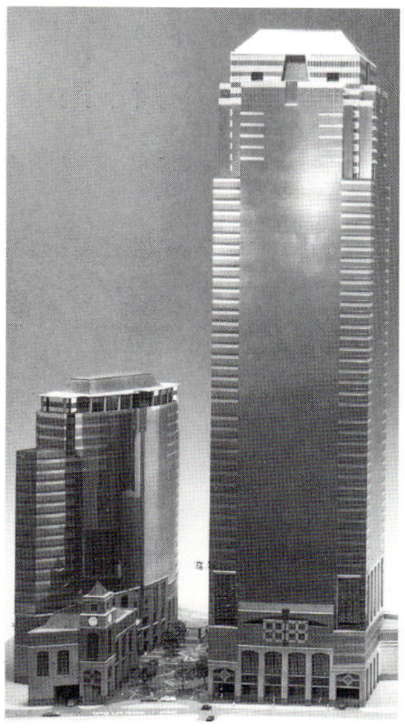

Hong Kong
54 stories
228 meters (748 feet)
1997, under construction

Architects: Hsin-Yieh Architects & Associates.
Engineers: Hsin-Yieh Architects & Associates.
Developer: Land Development Corporation.
Concrete structure.
Office tower and shops.

One of the two building projects recently engaged in by the same developer in the island's business center (see No. 25).

Land Development Corporation

GOVERNOR PHILLIP TOWER

96

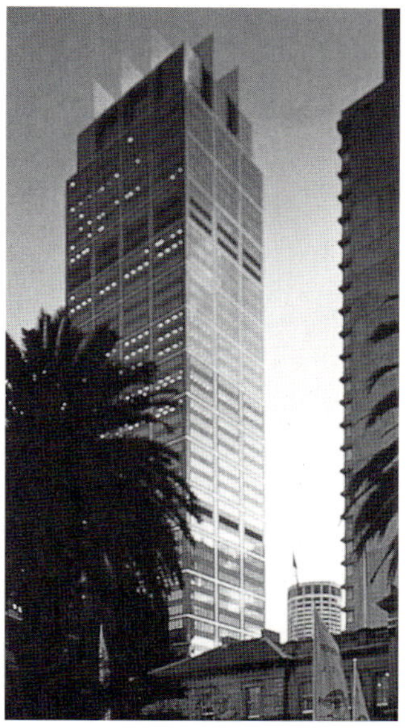

Sydney, Australia
54 stories
227 meters (745 feet)
1993

Architects: Denton Corker Marshall Pty.
Structural engineers: Ove Arup & Partners.
Mechanical engineers: TWA Consultants.
Developer: State Authorities Superannuation Board.
Concrete structure.
Office tower, 60,000 square meters (645,000 square feet).

The construction of this tower is part of a vast program of reconstruction of Sydney's business center promoted by the municipal authorities.

Denton Corker Marshall Pty.

J. P. MORGAN

(60 Wall Street)

97

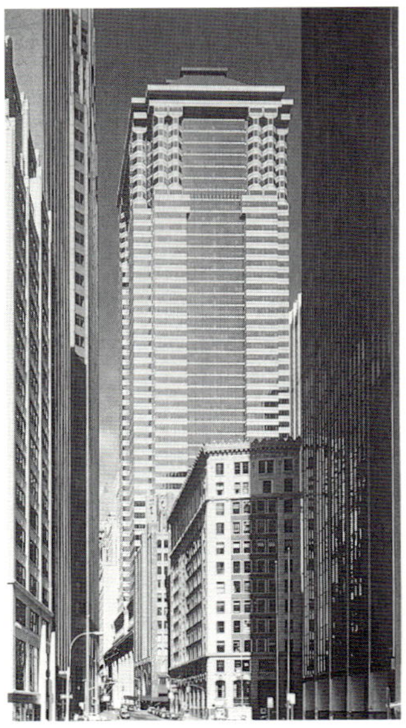

New York, United States
50 stories
227 meters (745 feet)
1989

Architects: Kevin Roche John Dinkeloo and Associates.
Structural engineers: The Office of Irwin G. Cantor.
Mechanical and electrical engineers: Syska & Hennessy.
Developer: Park Tower Group.
Steel structure.
Office tower, 149,000 square meters (1.6 million square feet).

At the foot of the building a large winter garden connected to the subway station is open to the public.

Kevin Roche John Dinkeloo and Associates

TWO UNION SQUARE

98

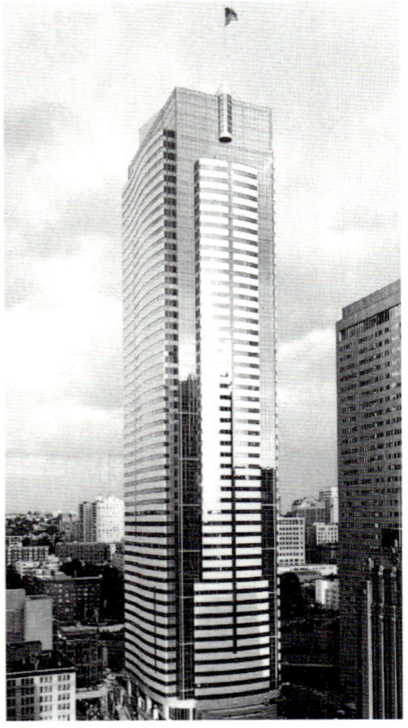

Seattle, United States
56 stories
226 meters (743 feet)
1989

Architects: NBBJ Group.
Structural engineers: SWMB.
Developer: Unico Properties, Inc.
Mixed steel and concrete structure.
Office tower, 98,000 square meters (1 million square feet).

Opposite the entrance a large public garden descends in successive levels of steps, waterfalls, and rock gardens towards a two-story commercial patio which can also be used for open air concerts or theater performances.

© Timothy Hursley

333 SO. HOPE BUILDING

(Security Pacific Plaza)

99

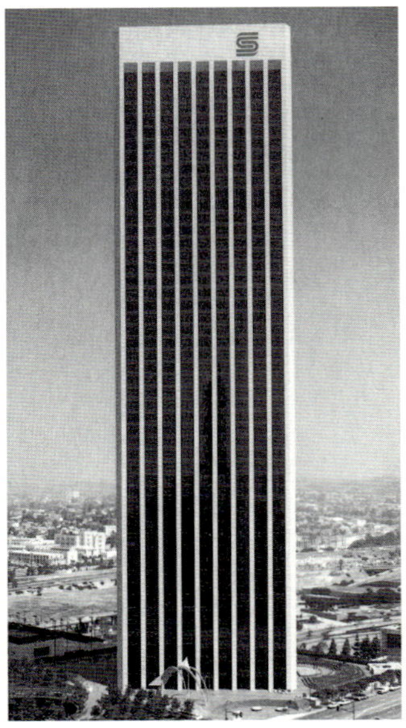

Los Angeles, United States
55 stories
226 meters (743 feet)
1975

Architects: Albert C. Martin and Associates.
Developer: Security Pacific National Bank.
Steel structure.
Office tower.

The tower is set at 45° angle to the alignment of the other buildings. There is a very large plaza at the foot of the building with a Calder sculpture.

Buildings & Data

ONE LIBERTY PLAZA

(U.S. Steel)

100

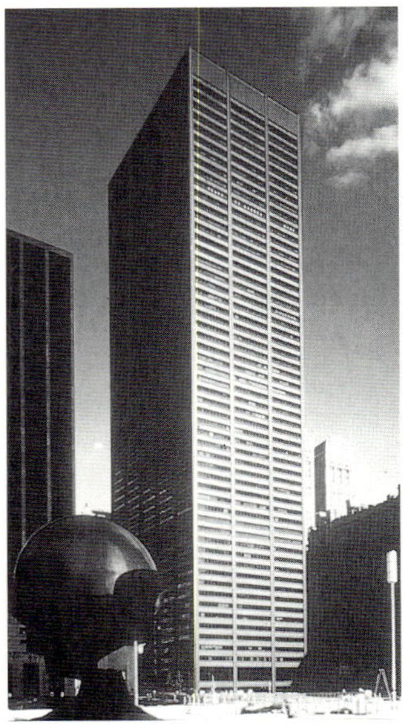

New York, United States
54 stories
226 meters (743 feet)
1973

Architects: Skidmore, Owings & Merrill, New York (Roy Allen).
Structural engineers: Weidlinger Associates, in association with Weiskopf & Pickworth.
Mechanical and electrical engineers: Syska & Hennessy.
Developers: Galbreath-Ruffin Corporation, in association with U.S. Steel.
Steel structure.
Office tower.

The exceptional density of the lot is compensated for by the installation by the developer of a garden square on an adjacent piece of land.

© Bo Parker

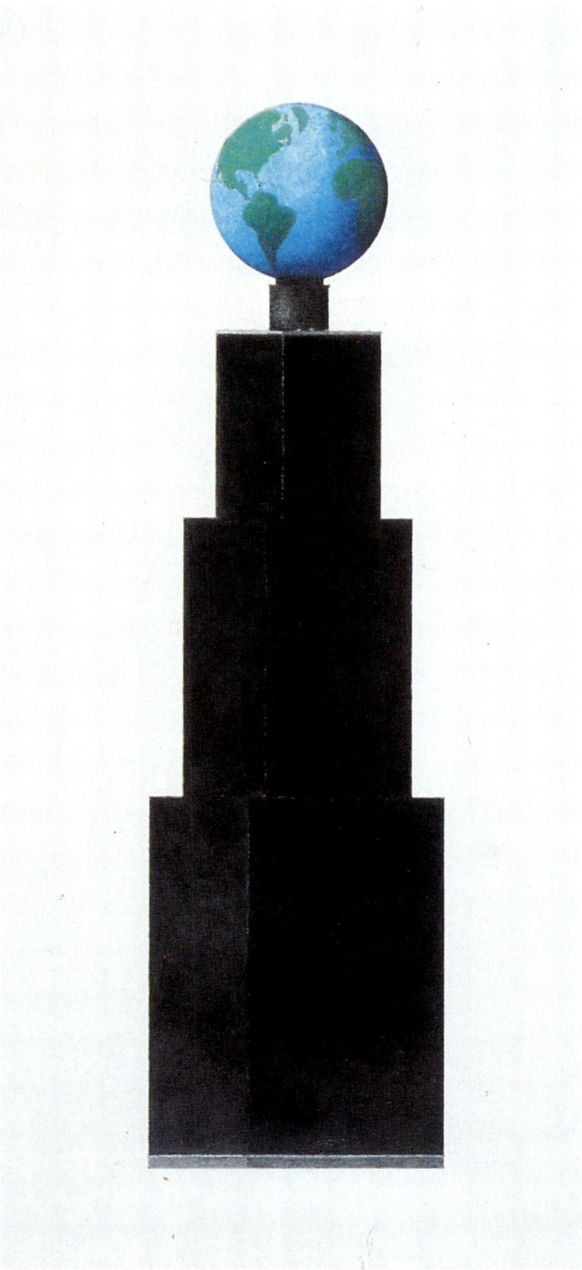

"The Smallest Skyscraper in the World,"
project for a monument for the Miami metro (48 feet).
Roberto M. Behar, architect, 1993,
in collaboration with C. Bancalari, J. Jaen and K. Storm.
Roberto M. Behar.

BIBLIOGRAPHY

This bibliography does not include works on individual architects, buildings, and cities.

Books and Catalogues

BIRKMIRE, William H., *Skeleton Construction in Buildings*, John Wiley & Sons, New York, 1893.

FREITAG, Joseph Kendall, *Architectural Engineering, with Special Reference to High Building Construction, Including many Examples of Chicago Office Buildings*, John Wiley & Sons, New York, 1895.

BIRKMIRE, William H., *The Planning and Construction of High Office-Buildings*, John Wiley & Sons, New York, 1898.

STARRETT, Col. W. A., *Skyscrapers and the Men who Built Them*, Charles Scribner's Sons, New York, London, 1928.

FERRISS, Hugh, *The Metropolis of Tomorrow*, Ives Washburn, Publisher, New York, 1929.
Reprint, Princeton Architectural Press, New York, 1986.

MUJICA, Francisco, *History of the Skyscraper*, Archaeology & Architecture Press, Paris, New York, 1929.
Reprint, by Da Capo Press, New York, 1977.

CLARK, William Clifford, *The Skyscraper: a Study in the Economic Height of Modern Office Buildings*, American Institute of Steel Construction, Inc., New York, 1930.

BOSSOM, Alfred C., *Building to the Skies, the Romance of the Skyscraper*, The Studio Ltd., London, The Studio Publications, Inc., 1934.

LE CORBUSIER, *Quand les cathédrales étaient blanches*, Librairie Plon, Paris, 1937.

CONDIT, Carl W., *The Rise of the Skyscraper*, University of Chicago Press, Chicago, 1952.

HAAG BLETTER, Rosemarie, ROBINSON, Cervin, *Skyscraper Style: Art Deco New York*, Oxford University Press, 1975.

HALPERN, Kenneth, *Downtown USA, Urban Design in Nine American Cities*, Whitney Library of Design, New York, 1978.

KOOLHAAS, Rem, *Delirious New York*, Chêne, Paris, 1978.

BARONI, Daniele, *Grattacieli, Architettura Americana tra Mito e Realtà, 1919-1939*, Electa, Milan, 1979.

JENCKS, Charles, *Skyscrapers-Skycities*, Academy Editions, Londres, 1980.
En français : *Gratte-Ciel*, éd. Academy Editions, Paris, 1980.

TIGERMAN, Stanley, *Chicago Tribune Competition & Late Entries*,Rizzoli, New York, 1980.

CROSS GIBLIN, James, *The Skyscraper Book*, Thomas Y. Crowell, New York, 1981.

GOLDBERGER, Paul, *The Skyscraper*, Alfred A. Knopf, New York, 1981.

GAVOIS, Jean, *Going up. An Informal History of the Elevator, From the Pyramids to the Present*, Otis Elevator Company, 1983.

HUXTABLE, A. Louise, *The Tall Building Artistically Reconsidered*, Pantheon Books, New York, 1984.

PYGMAN, James, KATELEY, Richard, *Tall Office Buildings in the United States*, The Urban Land Institute, Washington, 1985.

SCHLEIER, Merrill, *The Skyscraper in American Art, 1890-1931*, Da Capo Press, New York, 1986.

VAN LEEUWEN, Thomas A. P., *The Skyward Trend of Thought: Five Essays on the Metaphysics of the American Skyscraper*, AHA Books, The Hague, 1986.

PANIZZA, Mario, *Mister Grattacielo*, Laterza, Milan, 1987.

SABBAGH, Karl, *The Making of a Building*, Macmillan, London, 1989 (in association with Channel Four Television Company Ltd.).

SCURI, Piera, *Late-Twentieth-Century Skyscrapers*, Van Nostrand Reinhold Company, New York, 1990.

BERGER, Miles L., *They Built Chicago, Entrepreneurs Who Shaped A Great City's Architecture*, Bonus Books Inc., Chicago, 1992.

MARINO, Arnaldo, *Architettura del Grattacielo*, Gangeni, Rome, 1992.

YEANG, Ken, *Bioclimatic Skyscrapers*, Artemis, London, 1994.

NEUMANN, Dietrich, *«Die Wolkenkratzer Kommen !» Deutsche Hochhaüser der Zwanziger Jahre. Debatten. Projekte. Bauten*, Vieweg, Wiesbaden, 1995.

Collective Works

The International Competition for a New Administration Building for the Chicago Tribune MCMXXII, The Tribune Company, Chicago, 1923.

Office Buildings, F.W. Dodger Corporation / McGraw-Hill Company, New York, 1961.

Human Response to Tall Buildings, Dowden, Hutchinson & Ross, Inc., Stroudsburg PA, 1977 (edited by Donald J. CONWAY).

A Tower for Louisville. The Humana Competition, Rizzoli, New York, 1982.

Developments in Tall Buildings, Van Nostrand Reinhold Company, New York, 1983 (edited by Lynn S. BEEDLE, CTBUH).

Southwest Center. The Houston Competition, Rizzoli, New York, 1983.

Three New Skyscrapers, The Museum of Modern Art, New York, 1983 (exhibition catalogue).

Advances in Tall Buildings, Van Nostrand Reinhold Company, New York, 1986 (edited by Lynn S. BEEDLE, CTBUH).

Design for High-Intensity Development, Malaysian Institute of Architects PAM / The Aga Khan Program for Islamic Architecture at Harvard University and the Massachusetts Institute of Technology, Cambridge MA, 1986 (proceedings of the conference).

Tall Buildings of the World, Council on Tall Buildings and Urban Habitat, Bethlehem PA, 1986.

Second Century of the Skyscraper, Van Nostrand Reinhold Company, New York, 1988 (edited by Lynn S. BEEDLE, CTBUH).

Tours du monde entier, Livre Total, Lausanne, 1989.

Il Mondo delle torri da Babilonia a Manhattan, Mazzota, Milan, 1990 (exhibition catalogue).

Tall Buildings: 2000 and Beyond, Council on Tall Buildings and Urban Habitat, Bethlehem PA, 1990 (proceedings of the conference).

The Sky's the Limit, A Century of Chicago Skyscrapers, Rizzoli, New York, 1990.

Mythos Wolkenkratzer, A. M. Architekturmuseum in Basel, Bâle, 1992 (exhibition catalogue).

Hong Kong Architecture: The Aesthetics of Density, Prestel, Munich, New York, 1993 (edited by Vittorio M. LAMPUGNANI).

Habitat and the High-Rise. Tradition and Innovation, Council on Tall Buildings and Urban Habitat, Dutch Council on Tall Buildings, Bethlehem PA, 1995 (proceedings of the conference).

Architectural Periodicals

DESCAMPS, Henri, "Gratte-Ciel récents," *L'Architecture*, vol. XLIV, No. 1, Paris, 1931.

HABASQUE, Guy, "Evolution du gratte-ciel," *L'Œil*, No. 75, Paris, March 1961.

TAKAYAMA, Masami, "The Structural Architecture of Chicago," *Process: Architecture*, No. 102, Tokyo, April 1992.

"Le Gratte-Ciel américain," *Acier*, No. 3, Paris, 1931.

"Immeubles tours," *Techniques & Architecture*, 32e série, No. 2, Paris, May 1970.

"Vie et Mort des gratte-ciel," *L'Architecture d'Aujourd'hui*, No. 178, Paris, 1975.

"Retour aux tours," *Architecture Intérieure Créé*, No. 196, Paris, 3rd quarter 1983.

"On High-Rise Residences," *Process Architecture*, No. 64, Tokyo, January 1986.

"New York Art Deco Skyscrapers," *A + U*, Tokyo, April 1987.

"Vertical Design," *l'Arca*, No. 4, Milan, March 1987.

"American High-Rise Buildings," *A + U*, Tokyo, April 1988.

"The City's Thrusting Skyline," "Stability Towards the Top," "Elisha Graves Otis, Defeating Gravity," and other articles, *L'Arca*, No. 33, Milan, December 1989.

"Vertical Circulation Systems," "Mighty Office of Towers," "New Babylons," and other articles, *World Architecture*, No. 28, London, 1993.

Essays

WEISMAN, Winston, "A New View of Skyscraper History," *The Rise of an American Architecture*, Praeger Publishers, New York, 1970 (collective work).

PELLI, Cesar, "Skyscrapers," *Perspecta: The Yale Architectural Journal*, No. 18 / 1982, MIT Press, Cambridge MA, 1982.

TUCKER, Jonathan B., "Superskyscrapers, Aiming for 200 Stories," *High Technology*, Vol. 5, No. 1, New York, January 1985.

HAAG BLETTER, Rosemarie, "The Invention of the Skyscraper: Notes on its Diverse Histories," *Assemblage*, No. 2, MIT Press, Cambridge MA, February 1987.

LAINE, Christian K., "Ten Super Projects," *Metropolitan Review*, Vol. I, No. 1, Chicago, January / February 1988.

AGREST, Diana I., "Architectural Anagrams: The Symbolic Performance of Skyscrapers," in *Architecture From Without, Theoretical Framings for a Critical Practice*, MIT Press, Cambridge MA, 1991.
First publication in French: *A. A.*, No. 178, Paris, 1975.
First publication in English: *Oppositions*, No. 11, New York, 1977.

VAN LEEUWEN, Thomas A. P., "Le Gratte-Ciel synonyme de la ville," *Les Années 20 : l'âge des métropoles*, Musée des Beaux-Arts de Montréal, 1991 (exhibition catalogue, edited by Jean CLAIR).

WRIGHT, Gwendolyn, "Babel moderne et cité divine," in *Les Années 20 ...*, ibid.

VAN LEEUWEN, Thomas A. P., "Le Gratte-Ciel ou le Mythe de la croissance naturelle," in *Américanisme et modernité, l'idéal américain dans l'architecture*, EHESS / Flammarion, Paris, 1993 (collective work, edited by Jean-Louis COHEN and Hubert DAMISCH).

PASSANTI, Francesco, "Le Corbusier et le gratte-ciel, aux origines du Plan Voisin," in *Américanisme et modernité ...*, ibid.

DE POLI, Aldo, "Les Projets pour la métropole des années vingt," in *Américanisme et modernité ...*, ibid.

SOLOMONSON, Katherine, "Des gratte-ciel pour les journaux aux USA," in *Enquête sur les sièges de l'info*, Pavillon de l'Arsenal / Hazan, Paris, 1994 (exhibition catalogue; scientific concept Véronique PARENT).

INDEX

Plain numbers refer to the text, including footnotes.
Bold numbers refer to captions and illustrations.
References to footnotes appear in parentheses after the page number.

ARCHITECTS AND ENGINEERS

BUILDINGS

Names in italics refer to unexecuted projects.

MAIN ORGANIZATIONS PROVIDING INFORMATION ABOUT SKYSCRAPERS

COUNCIL ON TALL BUILDINGS AND URBAN HABITAT (CTBUH)

The Council is an international organization sponsored by engineering, architectural and planning professionals. Its mission is to study and report on all aspects of the planning, design, construction and operation of tall buildings.

A major focus of the Council is the publication of a comprehensive monograph on tall buildings as well as reports and proceedings of congresses, a data base on building heights and other statistics and the organization of international, regional and local meetings. It also publishes The Times, an information bulletin.

Lehigh University
13 East Packer Avenue
Bethlehem PA 18015-3191, USA.
Telephone (1.610) 758-3515.
Fax (1.610) 758-4522.
Dr. Lynn S. BEEDLE, director.

BUILDINGS & DATA s.a.

The Buildings & Data company specializes in collecting information on large buildings (mainly offices, hotel and mixed complexes, and skyscrapers), as well as their designers and owners.

It has more than 5,000 specialized books, magazines, commercial brochures, technical data sheets, and photographs that make up a unique documentation of its kind.

Buildings & Data advises architects and developers. The company also puts its documentation at the service of the press and takes part in various cultural and editorial activities in Europe.

Avenue de la Forêt 4
B - 1050 Brussels, BELGIUM.
Telephone (32.2) 673-0779.
Fax (32.2) 672-0957.
Georges BINDER, managing director.

WORLD FEDERATION OF GREAT TOWERS

The Federation was founded in Paris in 1989 on the occasion of the 100th anniversary of the Eiffel Tower.

It is an association of international monuments with the object of fostering universal awareness and developing promotional programs on an international scale.

The member towers must fulfill a certain number of conditions. Specifically, they must constitute a tourist attraction and have an observation deck accessible to the general public.

The Federation has 18 members, mainly telecommunication towers.

Parc Olympique de Montréal
4141, avenue Pierre-de-Coubertin
Montreal H1V 3N7, CANADA.
Telephone (1.514) 252-4618.
Fax (1.514) 252-8681.
L. Guy LEDUC, secretary-general.

REGIONAL ORGANIZATIONS AFFILIATED TO THE COUNCIL ON TALL BUILDINGS AND URBAN HABITAT

Chicago Committee on High-Rise Buildings

The Committee covers the full scope of tall building subject matter. It conducts symposia and advises on relevant codes and standards.

Schal Associates, Inc.
200 W. Hubbard Street
Chicago, IL 60610, USA.
Telephone (1.312) 245-2414.
Fax (1.312) 245-1379.
Contact: Jerry R. REICH.

Dutch Council on Tall Buildings

The Council promotes tall buildings in the appropriate context as a means of saving land. In May 1995 it organized the Fifth World Congress "Habitat and the High-Rise," in collaboration with the Council on Tall Buildings and Urban Habitat.

Corsmit Consulting Engineers
P.O. Box 208
2280 AE Rijswijk, HOLLAND.
Telephone (31.15) 785.488
Fax (31.15) 781.560
Contact: Jan Vambersky.

Los Angeles Tall Buildings Structural Design Council

The Council concentrates exclusively on structural aspects of high-rise building and in particular on the question of earthquakes.

It organizes an annual conference in May. Every three years this conference is twinned with that of the Council on Tall Buildings and Urban Habitat.

Nabih Youssef & Associates
800 Wilshire Boulevard, Suite 510,
Los Angeles, CA 90017, USA.
Telephone (1.213) 688-3014.
Fax (1.213) 688-3018.
Contact: Youssef NABIH.

Polish Group on Tall Buildings and Urban Habitat

The Group is concerned with the aspects covered by the Council on Tall Buildings and Urban Habitat in general and by regional questions in particular.

Warcent
UL. Okrzei, 35
03715 Warsaw,
POLAND.
Telephone (48.2) 621-7532.
Fax (48.2) 621-6653.
Contact: Jerzy SKRZYPCZAK.

Brazilian Group - CTBUH

The group seeks to encourage exchanges between Brazilian professionals and the Council of Tall Buildings and Urban Habitat. It also aims to better inform the Brazilians about opportunities abroad and vice-versa.

Av. Princesa Isabel, 323, 5° andar
Copacabana 22011-010
Rio de Janeiro, RJ, BRAZIL.
Telephone (55.21) 542-3344.
Fax (55.21) 275-3246.
Contact: Edison MUSA.

ACKNOWLEDGEMENTS

We sincerely thank all those who assisted in the creation of this book and, in particular:

Georges Binder (Buildings & Data S.A., Brussels), for his most valuable collaboration as well as the generosity and discernment with which he put his professional knowledge and documentation at our disposal;

Doctor Lynn S. Beedle, Engineer, Director of the Council on Tall Buildings and Urban Habitat (Lehigh University, Bethlehem), for his collaboration and that of the Council in Part Three of the book;

Paul Goldberger, Architectural Critic and Chief Cultural Correspondent of *The New York Times*, for his confidence in the project and his editorial contribution;

John J. Hellon for the English translation and Frances Faure for the copy editing;

Dominique Delaunay and Benoît Roland, photographers, for their research and their photographic surveys;

the many architects, engineers and developers, for the interviews that they gave, the visits they organized and the documentation they provided;

in Europe:

Tony Fitzpatrick, Engineer (Ove Arup & Partners, London), Francis Lhébrard and Jean-Pierre Bourbon (Otis International, Paris), René Provost, Architect (Lyons), René Ragheboom and Yves Arnaud, Engineers (Trouvin Ingéniérie, Paris) and Françoise Reynaud, Architect (Architectures Jean Nouvel, Paris);

in the United States:

James Anderson (Maguire Thomas Partners, Los Angeles), Roberto M. Behar, Architect (Miami), J. Paul Beitler and Mark L. Jarasek (Miglin-Beitler Inc., Chicago), Nancy Cheung and A. Eugene Kohn, Architect (Kohn Pedersen Fox, New York), Harlan Crow (Trammell Crow Company, Dallas), John Burgee, Architect (New York), Nan S. Easterlin (Cousins Properties Inc.), James I. Freed, Architect (Pei Cobb Freed & Partners, New York), Bruce S. Fowle and Thomas V. Czarnowski, Architects (Fox & Fowle Architects, New York), Richard Green and Joan E. Nelson, Architects (The Stubbins Associates, Cambridge, MA), John Harris (Hines Interests Limited Partnership, Houston), Helmut Jahn and Keith H. Palmer, Architects (Murphy/Jahn, Chicago), Philip Johnson, Architect (Philip Johnson, Ritchie & Fiore Architects, New York), Ralph E. Johnson and James C. Allen, Architects (Perkins & Will, Chicago), Richard Keating, Architect (DMJM Keating, Los Angeles), Beverly Keitz and George Klein (Park Tower Realty Corp., New York), Michael A. McCarthy, Mustafa K. Abadan, Architects, and Gretchen G. Bank (Skidmore, Owings & Merrill, New York), John Portman, Architect, and Danielle Martin (John Portman & Associates, Atlanta), Adrian D. Smith, Architect, and John D. Ravitch (Skidmore, Owings & Merrill, Chicago), R. Scott Johnson and Ralph M. Stanislaw, Architects (Johnson Fain and Pereira Associates, Los Angeles) and Robert Sobel, Architect (Emery Roth Group, New York);

in Asia:

Zurila Ahmad and Shalini Socklingam (Kuala Lumpur City Centre), Hiroshi Hara, Architect, and Hiroshi Yatsuo, Architect (Atelier Ø, Tokyo), Sumand Jumsai, Architect (Bangkok), Kisho Kurokawa, Architect (Tokyo), Paul Kosovsky (Dragages et Travaux Publics, Singapore), Dennis Lau Wing-kwong and Kenneth Wong, Architects (Dennis Lau & Ng Chun Man, Hong Kong), Zack McKown and Calvin Tsao, Architects (New York, Singapore), Keiichi Okamoto, Ikumi Nishimura, Satoshi Okuma and Yoshiaki Ogura, Architects (Nikken Sekkei, Tokyo), Edward G. Pryor, town planner (Planning Department, Hong Kong), Bruce Schlaitzer, Architect (Lehrer McGovern Malaysia), Winston Shu, Architect (Foster Asia, Hong Kong), Tay Kheng Soon, Architect (Singapore), Yoshinori Takahashi, David Rolland, Architects, and Tatsuya Matsui (Kenzo Tange Associates, Tokyo), Toshinori Teramoto, Hisashi Yosano, Mamoru Maeda and Satoshi Ezoe, Architects (Nikken Sekkei, Osaka), Lim Chow Weng, Architect (Architects 61, Singapore), Kenneth Yeang, Architect (T.R. Hamzah & Yeang, Kuala Lumpur), Rocco S.K. Yim, Architect (Rocco Design Ltd., Hong Kong) and Shigetsugu Yoshida, Architect (Takenaka Corporation, Osaka).

We also want to thank architectural and engineering firms, archives and documentation centers, photographers, teachers, specialists and embassy attachés for technical information and illustrative material that they kindly supplied, in particular:

Calatrava Valls EURL (Paris), Crone & Associates (Sydney), EPAD (Paris, La Défense), Sir Norman Foster and Partners (London, Frankfurt), Haines Lundberg Waehler (New York), Hentrich-Petschnigg & Partner KG (Dusseldorf), Hijjas Kasturi Associates (Kuala Lumpur), JPJ Architects (Dallas), Kajima Corporation (Tokyo), C.Y. Lee & Partners (Taiwan), Loebl Schlossman and Hackl (Chicago), Machado and Silvetti Associates (Boston), Marlin Land Ltd. (Hong Kong), MM21 Design Team, Mitsubishi Estate Co. (Yokohama), P & T Architects and Engineers (Hong Kong, Shanghai), Cesar Pelli & Associates (New Haven), Plan Architects (Bangkok), Pontiac Marina (Singapore), John Portman & Associates (Shanghai), The Richard E. Jacobs Group (Cleveland), Kevin Roche John Dinkeloo and Associates (Hamden), Paul Rudolph & Associates (New York), Harry Seidler & Associates (Sydney), David K. Specter & Associates (New York), Studio BBPR (Milan), Swanke Hayden Connell Architects (New York), Tao Ho Design (Hong Kong) and Wong & Ouyang (Hong Kong), Archives d'architecture moderne (Brussels), Art Institute of Chicago, Centre canadien d'architecture—Canadian Center of Architecture—(Montreal), Chicago Historical Society, Chicago Athenaeum, Fondation pour l'architecture (Brussels), Fondation Le Corbusier (Paris), The Frank Lloyd Wright Foundation (Taliesin West), Deutsches Architekturmuseum (Frankfurt);

and Silvia Arango, Frédéric Bereder, Pierre Chatauret, Jean-Paul Dany, Cultural Attaché at the French Embassy (Chicago), Philippe De Gobert, Agnieszka Drop, Cultural Attaché at the Polish Embassy (Brussels) Ehua Fang, Jean-Paul Ferrout, Daniel Gonzales Romero, Isabelle Gournay, Xavier Guillot, Gabriele Leuthäuser, Elie Levy, François Loyer, Dario Matteoni, Patrick Michel, Cultural Attaché at the French Embassy (Tokyo), Jean-Paul Midant, Jean-Pierre Porcher, Philippe Samyn, Linda Sansbury, member of the Hong Kong Economic & Trade Office (Brussels), Alberto Sato, Jean-Michel Six, Brian Taylor and Guy Van Beeck, among others.

ARUP

CAMPENON
BERNARD
SGE

CEP CONTRÔLE ET PRÉVENTION

COTEBA
MANAGEMENT

DUMEZ
GTM

Etablissement Public de la Région EPAD pour l'Aménagement de La Défense

OTH

OTIS

PERMASTEELISA

Schindler

SOGEA

TOURSANSFINS

TROUVIN INGENIERIE

Watson

Printed in November 1995
by MAME
in Tours, France

Photoengraving ROscan, Brussels